FAMILIES IN TRANSITION

HARRINGTON PARK PRESS

NEW YORK, NY • USA

FAMILIES IN TRANSITION

Parenting Gender Diverse Children, Adolescents, and Young Adults

EDITED BY

ARLENE I. LEV
ANDREW R. GOTTLIEB

Harrington Park Press
Box 331
9 East 8th Street
New York, NY 10003

http://harringtonparkpress.com

Library of Congress Cataloging-in-Publication Data

Names: Lev, Arlene Istar, editor. | Gottlieb, Andrew R., editor.
Title: Families in transition : parenting gender diverse children, adolescents, and young adults / edited by Arlene I. Lev and Andrew R. Gottlieb.
Description: New York, NY : Harrington Park Press, [2019] | Includes bibliographical references and index. Identifiers: LCCN 2018055863 (print) | LCCN 2018060291 (ebook) | ISBN 9781939594310 (ebook) | ISBN 9781939594297 (pbk. : alk. paper) | ISBN 9781939594303 (hardcover : alk. paper)
Subjects: LCSH: Gender-nonconforming youth—Family relations. | Parents of sexual minority youth. | Parent and child.
Classification: LCC HQ77.9 (ebook) | LCC HQ77.9 .F348 2019 (print) | DDC 306.76/8—dc23
LC record available at https://lccn.loc.gov/2018055863

To Andrew's aunt and godmother,
Elayne Bressler, for all of her love
and support over the years

To Ari's beautiful gender expansive
children, especially Shaiyah Ben Lev—
may his memory be a blessing.

CONTENTS

A NOTE ON THE EVOLUTION OF LANGUAGE

The field of transgender health is evolving at a rapid pace. As trans communities expand, language and self-definition have developed and continue to shift and transform. This is especially true among youth. In the past 25 years, words deemed offensive (transvestite, sex change) were replaced by more affirmative terms (cross-dresser, gender reassignment), and then evolved again (trans-feminine/trans-masculine, gender confirmation), and indeed, these words are now also under linguistic scrutiny.

In our clinical work, every few weeks new words are revealed, and identities are (re)defined; these represent emerging nomenclature and nuanced ways to define and express gender. As a cultural phenomenon, it is a glorious, inspirational, emergent process to witness. For us writers, it creates some anxiety, since language carefully chosen as we head to press can quickly devolve into restrictive, oppressive jargon, which dates our work and potentially dismisses our value, creating something that is not exactly the bee's knees[1]—more like moron sauce.[2]

Throughout this book, we have asked writers to use the phrase *gender nonconforming* as a descriptor of children and youth who express unconventional, atypical gender expression in behavior, mannerisms, clothing choices, and toys, and the terms *trans* and *transgender* for children and youth who live cross-gendered from the expectations of the sex they were assigned at birth. We recognize that referring to humans as *gender variant, gender atypical*, and *gender nonconforming* assumes that they are being compared to other humans who are assumed to be normal, average, typical, and usual, which too often can also imply natural, healthy, and acceptable. We also recognize that words like *cross, opposite*, and *other* (sex) assume a binary of gender and sex identities that we do not subscribe to. Stepping outside these linguistic boxes is challenging.

We have tried to highlight positive words, including *gender creative, gender diverse, gender expansive,* and *gender independent.* We encourage trans and nonbinary people to continue to critique language, discover and experiment with labels and words, and challenge the world to expand how we see and name genders. The editors and writers in this book have always intended respect, and we apologize if the language we have used becomes offensive or outdated between the time we go to press and when you read this.

May we all continue to listen with depth and care, until we hear our names and in our fullness say, "Yes, I am here."

Arlene I. Lev
Andrew R. Gottlieb

---

1. Something of excellent or very high quality.
2. When the word moron is simply insufficient to describe the level of idiocy that someone or something has achieved.

FOREWORD

Jean Malpas, LMHC, LMFT

From Transgression to Transition

I was raised in a middle-class family in French-speaking Belgium. Throughout my childhood, my parents were loving and gave me a sense of being valued and cared for. They were proud of me and my accomplishments. Well—mostly. I was a feminine boy, who loved wearing my mother's scarves, heels, and makeup. None of our family albums contains pictures of those moments of creativity, freedom, and delight. Sadly, those have been hidden away. As a young teen, I distinctly remember my mother saying: *It's okay if you're gay, just don't turn into one of those queens.* She meant: Don't be feminine! And I could extrapolate: Don't be transgender! Yet she was far from conventional herself. Early on, she left my father to partner with a butch woman, who loved me dearly, living a colorful life, full of art and late nights at the neighborhood lesbian bar.

What I've gleaned from my own childhood and from my years of experience as a therapist working with families of transgender and gender expansive youth, is that even the most loving, open-minded parents are challenged when their children transgress cultural gender norms. This is often referred to as *cisnormativity*—the assumption that we are all cisgender unless proven otherwise. Why do parents fear their child's gender diversity and/or transition? Why does any gender outside the binary box seem so ominous? And why do some parents end up rejecting the children they love? Is rejection ever an attempt—even if misguided—to protect? More broadly, how do we understand the ways in which families deal with a gender diverse child, a process one parent described to me as "initially mandated but ultimately welcomed allyship?"

A gender paradigm shift is truly a systemic change. As my colleague Randi Kaufman often reminds us, "When children transition, everyone transitions along." *Families in Transition* looks at the cultural, social, familial, and individual adjustments of parents, siblings, extended family vis-à-vis their social, medical, and educational communities. More precisely, this book uniquely explores all aspects of gender complexity from the perspective of cisgender caregivers—heterosexual and queer—describing their reactions, roles, internal and external resources, and processes as they uncover the pervasiveness and fallacy of the cisgender binary and prepare to accompany a child down the transformative road of gender affirmation.

The text stands on the shoulders of foundational writings that preceded it. To conceptualize what a family in transition might look like, different frameworks have been used to assist those clinicians, educators, and researchers who work with them. For example, Lev (2004) and later on with her colleague Alie (2012) describe the process of emergence through a systemic and developmental lens, illustrating how families of transgender children pass through—in the best-case scenarios—a series of nonlinear stages: Discovery and Disclosure, Turmoil, Negotiation, Finding Balance, ultimately arriving at a sense of Integration. Caitlin Ryan and her teams (2009, 2010) empirically anchored the lifesaving role of families by demonstrating the positive effect acceptance has on the physical, emotional, and social well-being of LGBT youth. Specifically, she highlighted that accepting parental attitudes and behaviors exert a strongly protective effect, resulting in significantly lower rates of suicide attempts and emotional distress and higher rates of overall satisfaction. Other researchers document how the difficulties parents and families have in adjusting to children's gender identities contribute directly or indirectly to the significant presence of suicide, self-harm, and homelessness (Allan & Ungar, 2014; Bauer, Scheim, Pyne, Travers, & Hammond, 2015; Durwood, McLaughlin, & Olson, 2017; Grossman, D'Augelli, & Frank, 2011; Olson, Durwood, DeMeules, & McLaughlin, 2016; Russell, Ryan, Toomey, Diaz, & Sanchez, 2011; Toomey, Ryan, Díaz, Card, & Russell, 2010).

As a theoretician and clinician, I conceptualize these dilemmas as a conflict in parental functions (Malpas, 2011; Malpas, 2016; Malpas & Glaeser, 2017; Malpas, Glaeser, & Giammattei, 2018). When cisgender parents raise cisgender children, gender is mostly a place of socially affirmed bonding. Nurturance, acceptance, multigenerational transmission, and socialization all align, sharing compatible versions of masculinity, femininity, and gender identities. I also describe how multidimensional support helps families move from rejection to an understanding that *acceptance is protection* (Malpas, 2011; Malpas, Glaeser, & Giammattei, 2018).

In *Far from the Tree,* Andrew Solomon (2012) captures another important aspect of the multigenerational dilemma by differentiating *vertical identities*—those features of nature or nurture shared by parents and their children—from *horizontal identities,* those features essential to children, shared by a select group, but *not* commonly shared by their parents. All these models emphasize core experiences of grief and loss, but with the potential for growth inherent in all conflict.

The Ingredients for Change

As our practices continue to expand, so do our frameworks. Eight years ago, I founded the Gender & Family Project (GFP) at the Ackerman Institute for the Family. Since then, the GFP has supported hundreds of families of transgender children. From this work we identified three changes families can potentially make as they begin to shift from cisnormativity to gender diversity: (1) a change of awareness; (2) a change of connection; and (3) a change of community—each of which involves psychological, relational, social, and cultural processes (Malpas, 2017). Together they constitute a nonlinear developmental line that will help expand family acceptance. Failure to change at any level manifests itself in particular forms of family rejection.

Change of Awareness

What is the usual question asked when someone is pregnant: *Is it a boy or is it a girl?* Why is knowing a child's gender so important? After he or she has been gender assigned, family and friends start imagining who the child could be: "Will he be handsome and athletic like his father? Will she be beautiful and creative like her mother?" Gender helps parents move from an abstract idea to the hopes and dreams about this person they are welcoming. In most Western traditions, gender seems to *humanize* life, taking the *it* and constructing a *he* or a *she*.

Parents of gender expansive and transgender youth face the challenge of relating to them through a lens other than the traditional gender binary, an antiquated construction as old as time itself. For example, the book of Genesis describes God as organizing energy and chaos through the creation of dichotomies: heaven and earth, light and darkness, man and woman. Dualistic thinking is endemic in many religious Eastern and Western traditions. When an individual challenges this construct, they challenge the ways in which we organize fathomable representations and, ultimately, how we recognize and relate to one another. When families struggle to change the normative expectations of their transgender child, a sense of dehumanization for that child can result. Experiencing children as fundamentally *other* can desensitize parents to their child's struggles, which can sometimes escalate to rejection, even violence. Parents can make this shift by *decentering* their cisnormative experience and humanizing life through the lens of gender diversity (Erhensaft, 2016). At a conscious level, it requires a change in their belief system and an openness to existential complexity; at an unconscious level, it requires dealing with discomfort, chaos, the unfamiliar, and the unknown, elements we all struggle with.

Change of Connection

As Solomon (2012) points out, while there are those who assume their children will share their core identities, "parenthood abruptly catapults us into a permanent relationship with a stranger" (p. 1). If parents experience their transgender child as "too different"—which varies from family to family—their empathy and desire to protect may be compromised. Damaged connections can result in emotional detachment, rejection, abusive enforcement of family rules, and neglect and culminate in total abandonment. Though most cisgender parents do not have a lived experience similar to that of growing up transgender, their ability to empathize with a transgender child is greatly enhanced by meaningful identification. By way of their own story of marginalization, difference, identity formation, empowerment, or pride, parents need to find an authentic point of connection with their child.

Change of Community

In addition to these internal and interpersonal changes, parents have to face where their own communities stand on gender diversity. It is to their benefit to facilitate tolerance inside those communities of belonging by trying to influence group norms or, if necessary, by leaving their original groups to join more welcoming communities. In many situations, family members, even though inexperienced themselves, can be powerful agents of change. But sometimes gender diversity and community norms are like oil and water. They don't mix. If a family lacks the privilege, resources, or ability to change its environment, its members might resolve the task by compartmentalizing their lives. For example, the trans youth may choose not to be "out" to the entire community, or parents in conflict might divorce. Each situation is unique, but acceptance should inherently be looked at as intersectional. Race, class, educational level, religion, and language—each carries great weight in the process of integrating a transgender child (Malpas, Davis, Colon-Otero, & Raad, 2016).

Acceptance Is Protection

Parental functions can be articulated as a combination of nurturance and protection, acceptance and socialization, "soft love" and "tough love" (Malpas, 2011). Although things are rapidly changing, cisgender parents often associate being transgender with a lifetime of hardship, increased exposure to violence, and discrimination. Indeed, in 2016 at least 23 trans men and women were murdered in the United States. In 2017 at least 28 transgender individuals lost their lives to horrific acts of violence in this country (Human Rights Campaign, 2018a, 2018b).

Faced with the dilemma of accepting their child's identity, which could endanger the child, or rejecting their child's identity as an attempt to protect them, parents sometimes choose the latter. This resolution often translates into situations in which parents may not necessarily resort to physical aggression or oust the child from the home, but instead prevent access to affirmative treatment, such as hormone blockers, or delay (or deny) a request to socially transition. Many of us will recognize those who hope "this is just a phase," or who say: "*At 18 years old, he will be able to do whatever he wants!*" Symptoms can appear as obstruction, ambivalence, delaying or postponing care, or enforcement of gender stereotypes.

The shift to a protective strategy is contingent on a parent's understanding of what is actually most dangerous versus most helpful for their child, garnering enough support for themselves to venture down a new path. Once we as clinicians comprehend the parents' intentions as positive, conveying the effect of acceptance and protection helps them understand the need for affirmative language and behaviors and being part of a supportive community. A fundamental aspect of this shift is a deep understanding that rejection does not work, but, rather, that acceptance is protection. Though that paradigm shift is necessary, it is not sufficient. Affirming family members will need every bit of emotional, behavioral, and social tools to take on the world as an ally. To borrow Gottlieb's (2000) concepts, families will, it is hoped, make the shift from *resigned acceptance* to *unconditional acceptance*.

Families in Transition takes the reader, professional and community member, further into the dynamics of this transformation. It presents affirmative material to support young people, taking into account the layers of complexity families inevitably face as they embark together on this journey, and what parents, clinicians, and educators should understand about it. Most sections are organized as a dialogue among professionals, many of whom are recognized leaders in the field, and parents (cisgender, both queer *and* straight), reflecting on their individual and collective experiences.

Combining developmental psychology, psychoeducation, and systemic therapy, the text highlights the importance of our own social locations and identities as clinicians. It puts the responsibility on us to challenge our own cisnormativity and blind spots, and evaluate the ways we can become "gender creative" (Erhensaft, 2016). Therapists working primarily with young children and adolescents and their families describe the range of emotional reactions of parents as well as outline psychoeducational tools and clinical strategies to support them in their quest toward acceptance.

While highlighting the need for a slow, insight-oriented process of reflection on the effect of gender diversity on the parent and the parent-child relationship, the transformative and potentiating aspects of having a gender diverse child are emphasized. Similarly, parents' own complex sexual and gender identities, expressions, and social locations are intertwined with the process of parenting. As Shelley Rio-Glick states in "Gender in Four Voices": "If anyone thinks that being gay makes it easier to navigate changes of gender identity within the family, they have never known the power of culture, parental fantasy, expectations, self-esteem, denial, and terror."

The book offers a contextual approach to the psychological and relational processes of families in transition. It takes into account the complexity, specific skills, and resources for advocacy required to deal with those medical, legal, and educational systems designed to administrate and discriminate against transgender children and their families, offering insight into cutting-edge best practices—medical, educational, and psychological. Ultimately, it confirms my own experience: if parents and caregivers are supported in coming to terms with survivalist fears, they can be among the fiercest protectors and most efficient agents of cultural change.

Though gender diversity has always existed, it has usually been repressed, subjugated, and silenced, at least in this culture. But today we have reached a tipping point. While still being murdered, criminalized, and pathologized, gender expansive voices, bodies, and communities are increasingly being heard and seen. No one can explain precisely why this shift has been possible or why it is happening now. It is likely that there is a conjunction of factors: the relentless fight for survival and equality of transgender communities around the world powered by the global connections and organizing capacities provided by the advent of the Internet. I believe the last bastion of cisnormativity was significantly breached when transgender children forced us to question everything the cisgender world assumed: *We do not know the gender of any child until they tell us who they are.* In the end, I hope this book is a step toward our accountability as allies and our empowerment as complexly gendered beings.

REFERENCES

Allan, R., & Ungar, M. (2014). Resilience-building interventions with children, adolescents, and their families. In S. Prince-Embury, D. H. Saklofske, S. Prince-Embury, & D. H. Saklofske (eds.), *Resilience interventions for youth in diverse populations* (pp. 447–462). New York: Springer Science + Business Media.

Bauer, G. R., Scheim, A. I., Pyne, J., Travers, R., & Hammond, R. (2015). Intervenable factors associated with suicide risk in transgender persons: A respondent driven sampling study in Ontario, Canada. *BMC Public Health, 15* (525), 1–15. doi:10.1186/s12889-015-1867-2.

Durwood, L., McLaughlin, K. A., & Olson, K. R. (2017). Mental health and self-worth in socially transitioned transgender youth. *Journal of the American Academy of Child and Adolescent Psychiatry, 56* (2), 116–123e2. doi:10.1016/j.jaac.2016.10.016.

Erhensaft, D. (2016). *The gender creative child: Pathways for nurturing and supporting children who live outside of gender boxes.* New York: Experiment.

Gottlieb, A. R. (2000). *Out of the twilight: Fathers of gay men speak.* Binghamton, N.Y.: Haworth Press.

Grossman, A. H., D'Augelli, A. R., & Frank, J. (2011). Aspects of psychological resilience among transgender youth. *Journal of LGBT Youth, 8,* 103–115. doi: 10.1080/19361653.2011. 541347.

Human Rights Campaign. (2018a). Violence against the transgender community in 2016. Retrieved from: https://www.hrc.org/resources/violence-against-the-transgender-community-in-2016.

Human Rights Campaign. (2018b). Violence against the transgender community in 2017. Retrieved from: https://www.hrc.org/resources/violence-against-the-transgender-community-in-2017.

Lev, A. I. (2004). *Transgender emergence: Therapeutic guidelines for working with gender-variant people and their families.* Binghamton, N.Y.: Haworth Press.

Lev, A. I., & Alie, I. (2012). Transgender and gender nonconforming children and youth: Developing culturally competent systems of care. In S. K. Fisher, J. M. Poirier, & G. M. Blau (eds.), *Improving emotional and behavioral outcomes for LGBT youth: A guide for professionals* (pp. 43–66). Baltimore: Brookes.

Malpas, J. (2011). Between pink and blue: A multi-dimensional family approach to gender nonconforming children and their families. *Family Process, 50* (4), 453–470.

Malpas, J. (2016). The transgender journey: What role should therapists play? *Psychotherapy Networker,* July/August 2016.

Malpas, J. (2017, August 1). *TEDx: The gift of gender authenticity* [video file]. Retrieved from www. youtube.com/watch?v=TCQEcR7pi_Q.

Malpas, J., Davis, B., Colon-Otero, S., & Raad, M. (2016, June). *The ethics of intersectionality and allyship in clinical work: Power analysis of racial and gender locations in mental health and community work with transgender clients.* Paper presented at the World Professional Association for Transgender Health, Amsterdam, Netherlands.

Malpas, J., & Glaeser, E. (2017). Transgender couples and families. In J. Lebow, A. Chambers, & D. C. Breunlin (eds.), *Encyclopedia of couple and family therapy* (pp. 1–6). New York: Springer International.

Malpas, J., Glaeser, E., & Giammattei, S. (2018). Building resilience in transgender and gender expansive children, families, and communities: A multidimensional family approach. In C. Meier and D. Ehrensaft (eds.), *The gender affirmative model: An interdisciplinary approach to supporting transgender and gender expansive children*. Washington, D.C.: American Psychological Association.

Olson, K. R., Durwood, L., DeMeules, M., & McLaughlin, K. A. (2016). Mental health of transgender children who are supported in their identities. *Pediatrics, 137* (3), 1–8. doi:10.1542/peds.2015–3223.

Russell, S. T., Ryan, C., Toomey, R. B., Diaz, R. M., & Sanchez, J. (2011). Lesbian, gay, bisexual, and transgender adolescent school victimization: Implications for young adult health and adjustment. *Journal of School Health, 8* (5), 223–230. doi:10.1111/j.1746-1561.2011.00583.x.

Ryan, C., Huebner, D., Diaz, R., & Sanchez, J. (2009). Family rejection as a predictor of negative outcomes in white and Latino lesbian, gay and bisexual young adults. *Pediatrics, 123* (1), 346–352.

Ryan, C., Russell, S. T., Huebner, D., Diaz, R., & Sanchez, J. (2010). Family acceptance in adolescence and the health of LGBT young adults. *Journal of Child and Adolescent Psychiatric Nursing, 23* (4), 205–213.

Solomon, A. (2012). *Far from the tree: Parents, children and the search for identity*. New York: Scribner.

Toomey, R. B., Ryan, C., Díaz, R. M., Card, N. A., & Russell, S. T. (2010). Gender-nonconforming lesbian, gay, bisexual, and transgender youth: School victimization and young adult psychosocial adjustment. *Developmental Psychology, 46* (6), 1580–1589.

FAMILIES IN TRANSITION

INTRODUCTION

Andrew R. Gottlieb

Transparent: Season 3, Episode 8 (Corey & Arnold, 2016) takes us into the private world of 12-year-old Morty Pfefferman. After being benched by his grandfather Haim, who coaches the Little League team, and who, after Morty misses the ball, in his exasperation screams, "I can't believe that fegela's my grandson," Morty returns home in shame. Upset, he dons his mother's nightgown, white pumps, and pearl ring and dances around the basement of his grandparents' Boyle Heights home to such 1958 pop standards as "If I Were a Bell." Morty lives for those brief moments. Only then does he feel totally free, totally himself, totally alive.

Those moments are rare, however. He has to grab them when he can. Others in the family — his grandmother Yetta and his mother, Rose — have become aware of his ritual. Though Rose is supportive, that support is tempered, as she fears that Haim will find out and dire consequences will result. Yetta pleads for Rose to "talk some sense into [Morty] before it's too late." But Rose can only muster, halfheartedly, "Can't anyone be happy?"

One afternoon, after the neighborhood sirens go off, signaling an air-raid drill, Haim quickly gathers his family together. Where is Morty? As everyone descends the ladder into the basement — which doubles as a shelter — Morty's little sister Bryna is the first to see Morty and quizzically wonders why he's wearing their mother's nightgown. In a panic, Rose tries to get him undressed and redressed before Haim comes down. It's too late. Haim goes ballistic: "What the fuck is wrong with you, Mort?" he asks as Rose and Morty freeze in sheer terror. "Mom said it was okay," insists Morty. "What? You let your little fegela wear a dress?" Haim wonders in disbelief. For Haim, history is repeating itself. His son Gershon, Rose's brother, was sent by the Nazis to the gas chamber for being a homosexual. Haim berates Rose, "This, this is all your fault! You want him to end up like Gershon?" Powerless, Haim first tries to reason with Morty, but his anger quickly escalates: "Do you want to know what happened to your uncle Gershon?. . . He burned to death in the oven. Do you want to know why? Because your mother and your grandmother let him run around in a skirt!" Rose tearfully tries to defend Morty, insisting that it "makes him happy." Haim explodes: "You make him stop this or you get out of my house!"

Later that night, while in bed, Morty observes his mother fully dressed, carrying a bag, getting ready to leave. In a panic, he calls out for her. Rose looks back with a mixture of fear and guilt, opens the door, and quickly closes it behind her.

Will she return?

Lev, Arlene I., Gottlieb, Andrew R., *Families in Transition*
dx.doi.org/10.17312/harringtonparkpress/2019.04.fit.00a

We live in a world of division — male/female, black/white, rich/poor, young/old, Democrat/Republican, gay/straight, cisgender/transgender — increasingly so under a president whose intrapsychic splits continually combust into a heightened sense of polarization on both the national and international stages. Culture and identity have now become battlefields on which we claim and sustain our place in this increasingly complex world. The political gains made by LGBTQ people over the last several years are starting to recede under the guise of the so-called religious freedom laws. Rescinding protections for transgender students to use the bathrooms of their choice and a proposed ban on future military service for transgender people are just two recent examples of this administration's blatant contempt for humanity. What easier way to regressively take us back to an idealized past, a time when, apparently, America was "great," than to scapegoat LGBTQ people. How catastrophic or how lasting the results will be remains to be seen. Sociopolitical divisions were obviously there already. Perhaps they just needed a match to ignite them. Now they burn uncontrollably.

In considering the ways we're different from one another, however, we must also consider the ways we're similar. While it's critical we recognize and honor our uniqueness, at the same time it's equally important to recognize and honor our commonalities.

In the articles and vignettes that follow, all our contributors highlight how critical it is that parents work toward achieving a level of acceptance of their child. But how can a parent offer that to a child who they may perceive as *too* different, almost unrecognizably different, a child who falls "far from the tree" (Solomon, 2012)? Certainly exposure can help. The more information that's available, the more times an issue makes headlines, the more the number of families who are directly affected, the more familiar an issue becomes. At this point, I can say with some certainty that most families, at least in this country, can identify a member—past or present—who is or was gay, lesbian, or bisexual. When I came out in the mid-1970s, I couldn't have said that. The closet was a crowded place. The message from my own parents at that time was: "You need help!" (Not exactly a history buff, my mother cited homosexuality as the reason the Roman Empire fell.) Their shame, which slowly diminished over the years, was never entirely extinguished.

Certainly we can point to other emotion-laden, poorly understood issues— suicide, trauma, drug abuse/alcoholism, eating disorders, domestic violence, incest, child sex abuse, and, most recently, sexual harassment, as well as mental illness in general—that remain secrets, even within the context of the family in which they occur. It may now be a bit easier to talk about them than it was ten or twenty years ago, but we still have a long way to go.

The first *Diagnostic and Statistical Manual (DSM)* I perused still listed homosexuality as a mental disorder. More recently, the change from *Gender Identity Disorder* (GID) in the *DSM-IV-TR* (American Psychiatric Association, 2000) to *Gender Dysphoria* in the *DSM-V* (American Psychiatric Association, 2013) represents a welcome cultural and conceptual shift. Though psychiatry and psychoanalysis have historically been proponents of the status quo, we have to acknowledge positive changes when they occur. So I have little doubt that, by the next generation, if history is any guide, the issue of gender nonconforming and transgender people will be less intimidating, less frightening, more familiar, and, perhaps, better understood. Progress, whether systemic or individual, is rarely, if ever, linear.

Given that cultivating a greater sense of openness takes work, how could parents of gender nonconforming and transgender people achieve and sustain a more accepting stance over time? Perhaps highlighting my own qualitative research (2000) on the ways in which fathers adapted to the reality of having a gay son might be relevant to the focus of our present volume. In her essay in this text, "But Doc, Is It Safe?" Irene Sills points out that looking at related medical research could generalize to and have application for other areas of inquiry. The same holds true for the psychological literature. That said, in my research, I uncovered three main adaptive strategies the fathers used, which I'll call the three Is: (1) Identification, (2) Internalization, and (3) Idealization (pp. 161–167).

Identification/Internalization: For the most part, Freud (1921/1971) discusses the concept of *identification* as a mechanism through which the child connects to the parent, for example, by way of the formation and resolution of the Oedipus complex: the son can't *be* the father so resigns instead to be *like* him. Identification, as defined in this context, represents both "an emotional tie" (p. 46) and a "common quality shared" with another (p. 49). Identification can also be built on common attitudes, feelings, values, and traits. In earlier writings, Freud (1914/1959) highlights the parent's identification with the child, who embodies both the parent's idealized past self as well as the hope for the future self—their self-to-be.

Among those fathers whom I interviewed, a central point of identification with their gay sons was their common experience of struggle. These older men came face to face with major obstacles over their many years, some enduring circumstances so treacherous in their early lives that their very survival was at stake. A few were first-generation immigrants, which necessitated the accommodation of a vastly different set of values; several struggled to find jobs or careers that were engaging, then had to work long hours to support their families; most were witnesses to the Crash of 1929 and its catastrophic financial and emotional effects; others were challenged by the reality of retirement; and the majority of them struggled with their guilt for not being present enough for their children early on, which resulted in a sense of their inadequacy as parents, dramatically illustrated by the distance they experienced mostly with their gay sons, with whom they had had difficulties connecting earlier in life.

Likewise, the fathers perceived their sons as struggling individuals as well—struggling with the option of going to and/or finishing college; struggling with finding a job or career that proved creatively satisfying; struggling with the desire to be financially independent; struggling with finding love; and struggling with ways to afford themselves a sense of safety as gay men in a homophobic society. A strong need to protect their sons was evident in the ways the fathers themselves were not protected by their *own* abusive, negligent, sometimes abandoning caretakers. That common link contributed to helping the fathers begin to forge a stronger connection with their sons—really for the first time. How might parents of gender nonconforming and transgender children and adolescents find common ground?

In discussing middle age, Jung (1933) highlights the notion that, like the sun at high noon, we start to reverse course. Some of our physical and psychological characteristics, so prided earlier in life, begin to shift into their opposite. The harder, sharper, shiny surfaces of the male torso begin to soften. Focus on career may diminish and be replaced with a greater interest in relationships with family and friends. In contrast, women may start to grow facial hair and their voices sometimes deepen into a richer, darker timbre. Earlier focus on the home and child rearing may be replaced with interest in the competitive, wider world. Cultural differences aside, men in late middle age start to take on (traditional) female characteristics; women in late middle age start to take on (traditional) male characteristics.

In my study, the fathers associated their gay sons with femininity on the basis of their sons' childhood histories of cross-dressing and doll play, their greater comfort with female peers, their resemblance to the mother both physically and temperamentally, and their closer relationship with the mother. I surmised that through the fathers' evolving acceptance, there was an *internalization* of that (female) part of their sons, making it the fathers' own, a part of them that, in the past, might have gone undeveloped and unrecognized, but a part that the fathers "needed" *developmentally* in order to feel whole, further concretizing an identification with their sons.

Thinking about my own life, listening to the experiences of my patients, and cataloguing the stories of biological families (2000, 2003, 2005, and, with Bigner, 2006) as well as what I term *families of choice* (2008), our lives seem to be characterized by a never- ending ebb and flow—periods of *transition* followed by periods of *consolidation*. Research confirms this as well (Levinson, Darrow, Klein, Levinson, & McKee, 1978). It is during those periods of transition in which vulnerability is heightened that the possibility of real change can occur.

In looking for points of identification with their gender nonconforming and transgender children, parents may not have to look that far. As the adult body transforms, and drives and interests change, in some sense parents themselves become gender nonconforming, successfully bringing together male *and* female, female *and* male, finally achieving a sense of wholeness. Transition, though used with specificity in this text, is a universal experience, all of us going through it in our own way, at our own time, thus a second point of identification.

Idealization: Another strategy or defense the fathers in my study employed was *idealization,* that is, they appeared to *overvalue* certain achievements, talents, physical and character traits of their sons, thus neutralizing their sexual orientation. When fathers perceived their sons as brilliant, creative, gifted, and handsome, their gayness became less central. And if the effect of the sexual orientation resulted in a narcissistic injury to the fathers, that wound then "healed" by way of the perception that, if their sons were special, then, by association, they *themselves* were special. What are the implications for parents of gender nonconforming and transgender people?

When a child comes out as LGBTQ, that part of them can become the central focus of "who they are" by the parent *as well as* the child—at least initially. Consolidation and integration evolve over time in the best-case scenarios. The parent is charged with the task of seeing their child both in a new(er) way as well as in ways already known, a challenge even for the most open parent. What is *already* known is the unique strengths their child possesses and how those can enrich themselves, their family, and their world. That knowledge may not exactly be sustainable during a crisis, but it can become clearer over time. The capacity to see their child in all their complexity—not just as gender nonconforming or transgender—is a challenge for most. It *can* happen. It *does* happen. The parents who told their stories in this book *made* it happen.

Most of the fathers in my study acknowledged that, over time, they were able to achieve a level of intimacy with their sons that they had never before known; this intimacy offered them a *second chance* to be the father they could *not* have been years earlier. The capacity to see more clearly who your child is—in those myriad ways—opens the door for a parent to see who they themselves are, creating the opportunity for a more expansive, real relationship, one that is deeper, richer, and more authentic.

Healthy aging entails challenging the earlier assumptions of youth and accommodating to a different reality, one in which the locus of evaluation gradually shifts from the external world to the internal one, the result being a greater sense of autonomy, which ideally culminates in a more expansive capacity to claim and proclaim oneself (Gould, 1978).

Despite the risks and the dangers inherent in being gender nonconforming and transgender in this society, those children, adolescents, and adults are heroically declaring who they genuinely are. At the same time, parents are on a similar path, exploring and defining who *they* are, moving toward what Erikson (1963) terms *ego integrity,* characterized by an adaptation to life's "triumphs and disappointments adherent to being . . . the acceptance of one's one and only life cycle as something that had to be and that, by necessity, permitted of no substitutions" (p. 168). Sheehy's (1998) term *coalescence* (p. 218) captures a similar sentiment—a shedding of all pretense and a final unapologetic declaration: "I am who I am." And so therein lies yet another point of identification: both parent and child, in their own ways, separately and together, are on the road to finding an authentic self, or as Winnicott (1960/1965) simply terms it, a *true self,* a self from which springs all that is creative, all that is spontaneous, all that is real.

A central task of parenthood is the capacity to relinquish oneself in favor of one's child. However cherished the goals, however well-meaning the expectations, however coveted the dreams, all must be held in abeyance: "Parental narcissism matures in the forging experience of expanding and deepening tolerance of differences and the ability to reconcile these where reconciliation and resolution are crucial" (Elson, 1984, pp. 301–302). Perhaps Kahlil Gibran (1923/2015) says it best:

> Your children are not your children.
> They are the sons and daughters of Life's longing for itself.
> They come through you but not from you,
> And though they are with you yet they belong not to you. (p. 18)

If we understand a crisis as characterized by a disruption in homeostasis, one in which the usual adaptive strategies may not work, one that sometimes calls for creative problem solving, one that reawakens conflicts of old, then parenthood presents a crisis on an operatic scale. Rossi (1968) points out the tension between the pressure to be a parent and the fundamental paucity in *preparing* for the role, an abruptness in *transitioning* to the role, and a lack of guidelines in *executing* the role. Further, as a child's needs change, the parents' attitudes and (re)actions should also change. But some parents cannot or will not accommodate those changes. And so the crisis continues—unabated.

The Chinese word for *crisis* is composed of two symbols—one signifying *danger,* the other signifying *opportunity.* It is my hope that parents seize on their child's difference as an opportunity not only to know their child better, but to know themselves better, and then to create a deeper, more meaningful relationship together.

In discussing his response to his son's sexual orientation, Walter, one of the fathers in my study, eloquently says it this way:

> I feel as if I've stepped though a door, and it's a brighter room than before. I could have gone through my whole life and not even been aware of the difficulties and the rewards and the joys of the lives of all those people [who] are now accessible to me. Whereas before, they were in that other room and I didn't go in. My son's in that other room. I want to be in the room with the light with him. I hope that he feels with my acceptance that I'm with him. He hasn't left me behind. (2000, p. 132)

REFERENCES

American Psychiatric Association. (2000). *Diagnostic and statistical manual of mental disorders (DSM-IV-TR)*. Washington, D.C.: American Psychiatric Association Publishing.

American Psychiatric Association. (2013). *Diagnostic and statistical manual of mental disorders (DSM-5)*. Washington, D.C.: American Psychiatric Association Publishing.

Corey, J. (producer), & Arnold, A. (director). (2016). *Transparent: Season 3, episode 8* (television series). Amazon Studios.

Elson, M. (1984). Parenthood and the transformation of narcissism. In R. S. Cohen, B. J. Cohler, and S. H. Weissman (eds.), *Parenthood: A psychodynamic perspective* (pp. 297–314). New York: Guilford Press.

Erikson, E. H. (1963). *Childhood and society* (2nd ed.). New York: W. W. Norton.

Freud, S. (1914/1959). On narcissism: An introduction. In *Collected papers*. Edited by E. Jones, translated by J. Riviere. (Vol. 4, pp. 30–59). New York: Basic Books.

Freud, S. (1921/1971). *Group psychology and the analysis of the ego.* Edited and translated by J. Strachey. New York: Bantam Books.

Gibran, K. (1923/2015). *The prophet.* New York: Vintage Books.

Gottlieb, A. R. (2000). *Out of the twilight: Fathers of gay men speak.* Binghamton, N.Y.: Harrington Park Press.

Gottlieb, A. R. (2003). *Sons talk about their gay fathers: Life curves.* Binghamton, N.Y.: Harrington Park Press.

Gottlieb, A. R. (ed.). (2005). *Side by side: On having a gay or lesbian sibling.* Binghamton, N.Y.: Harrington Park Press.

Gottlieb, A. R. (ed.). (2008). *On the meaning of friendship between gay men.* New York: Routledge.

Gottlieb, A. R., & Bigner, J. J. (eds.). (2006). *Interventions with families of gay, lesbian, bisexual, and transgender people: From the inside out.* Binghamton, N.Y.: Harrington Park Press.

Gould, R. L. (1978). *Transformations: Growth and change in adult life.* New York: Simon and Shuster.

Jung, C. G. (1933). *Modern man in search of a soul.* Translated by W. S. Dell and C. F. Baynes. New York: Harcourt, Brace, and World.

Levinson, D. J., Darrow, C. N., Klein, E. B., Levinson, M. H., & McKee, B. (1978). *The seasons of a man's life.* New York: Alfred A. Knopf.

Rossi, A. S. (1968). Transition to parenthood. *Journal of Marriage and the Family, 30,* 26–39.

Sheehy, G. (1998). *Understanding men's passages: Discovering the new map of men's lives.* New York: Random House.

Solomon, A. (2012). *Far from the tree: Parents, children, and the search for identity.* New York: Scribner.

Winnicott, D. W. (1960/1965). Ego distortion in terms of true and false self. In Winnicott, *The maturational processes and the facilitating environment* (pp. 140–152). New York: International Universities Press.

INTRODUCTION

Arlene I. Lev

My colleague and friend Dr. Carolyn Wolf-Gould reminds me that parenting is a heroic act. Parents *are* heroes. Being a parent requires round-the-clock care for years on end, managing the micro issues of diapers, food preferences and allergies, chauffeuring, and sex education, as well as the macro issues of maintaining shelter, providing health care, and negotiating educational institutions. The job description is clear: protect them, nurture them, guide them. Yet almost all parents find the job far more complex than they imagined and discover they are even less well prepared than they feared.

Undoubtedly some parents are more prepared, better resourced, perhaps even more highly skilled, possibly because they were well-parented themselves. It is also true that some children are simply more challenging than others. That may be because they require more attention (psychologically, physically, or psychically) because of mental health struggles, physical challenges, or just the sheer force of their emotional being. And there is, of course, the issue of "fit"—an energetic, extroverted child might not be as well suited for a taciturn, bookish, reclusive parent than one better matched to their own temperament. Regardless of skill, education level, financial resources, or knowledge of developmental psychology, parenting—let alone parenting *well*—is a challenge of the heart.

Our children are unique, every single one, and they test us in ways we could not have predicted. The more children we have, the more this truth resonates, for the skills we learn parenting one child may or may not be useful for the others. There are the expected challenges—and others that completely astonish, even stun. Parenting gender nonconforming children and transgender youth is simply not what most parents have expected. There is *no* chapter in the iconic parenting book, *What to Expect When You're Expecting* (Murkoff, Eisenberg, & Hathaway, 2002), titled "Gender Diverse, Transgender, and Intersex Children." And if there were, it would most likely be in the section under "Problems": infertility, birth defects, stillbirths—the tragedies, horrors, nightmares all parents dread.

The challenges for these children and youth are different from those of adult transgender people. Indeed, it is not simply the challenges that gender diversity bestows within a gender-rigid culture, or the complex decisions about transition one faces, or the consequences coming out can have on one's family and loved ones. For children and youth, it is the reality of being a powerless,

Lev, Arlene I., Gottlieb, Andrew R., *Families in Transition*
dx.doi.org/10.17312/harringtonparkpress/2019.04.fit.00b
© 2019 by Harrington Park Press

protected class of humans, who are dependent on parents and caregivers to understand and advocate for their needs. In the past decade, advocating for trans children and adolescents has become a rallying cry from many professionals, transgender activists, and some in the LGBTQ communities. And like all movements for social justice, a backlash movement has developed, in this instance by a disparate coalition (which I'm tempted to qualify with the adjective "odd" or "motley") made up of religious fundamentalists, conservative politicians, professional conversion therapy proponents, gender-essentialist feminists, and frightened, resistant parents of gender diverse children.

As transgender issues become part of the mainstream media, the families of gender diverse and transgender children are too often caught in the crosshairs. Parents are frequently isolated, frightened, and lacking both information and guidance; they may be confused about their child's gender expression, behavior, or stated identity. They are also tasked with protecting their child within a culture of rapidly changing mores regarding gender, and in which opposing positions flourish and dialogue is often vitriolic. Parents present in therapy offices embodying these extremes: some are resistant and even hostile to their children's gender expression, aggressively refusing an affirmative approach; others are supportive, fierce advocates of their child's expression, who sometimes becomes so caught up in their zeal for medical treatment that they cease listening to their child's goals and process. Although those extremes represent a minority of parents, all parents are caught in the middle, mediating their child's emerging identity while trying to assuage their own fears for their child's safety and well-being. Parents are charged with providing proper socialization for their children (and this typically means inculcating them with traditional gender roles), while they must also protect their children and nurture their uniquely emerging selves. These parents and caregivers need to negotiate complex societal institutions, familial and cultural expectations, their own confusion about what is "right," and their fears for their children's health and safety.

Parents have been forced to navigate complex social forces with minimal resources and support; they are blamed by some conservatives for "making" their child transgender, and by some liberals for reifying rigid gender norms rather than supporting broader gender expressions for both boys and girls; they are accused by activists on both sides of "child abuse" if they affirm their child's gender, or if they refuse to. These opposing opinions present a dilemma for parents and are a source of tension between those who share parenting; the process that ensues can cause a painful rift between parents and their children.

When families do seek help, they find few competent gender therapists available, even fewer who are also knowledgeable about child development, and still fewer trained in family therapy. They are vilified by some therapists for causing their children's gender "confusion" by not socializing their children correctly; they are vilified by other therapists for not immediately accepting their children and embracing them as transgender. They seek support from a burgeoning therapeutic community that lacks sufficient guidelines, has a paucity of training available, and has even less research on which to base clinical interventions.

As a family therapist who has worked with families of gender nonconforming and transgender children for decades, I find the stories told *about* them as well as the real stories told *by* them deeply compelling. The cultural narrative is slowly changing from one of tragedy to one of diversity and creativity. Research, clinical experience, and the lived lives of children and youth have proven that children do best when they are supported within their families and communities, and that is equally true for all children, regardless of their eventual identity. The stories of these children's lives are finally being told—often by the children and youth themselves, but also by parents, supportive therapists, and journalists. Brave families and youth have stepped forward to share their experiences on television and the Internet.

Parents' struggles are less well known. It is hard for parents to be fully revealing about their journey because their stories are intertwined with those of their children. So in order to tell their stories they are, to some extent, violating their children's right to author their own narratives. When parents do disclose, they are often criticized in the media for accepting the "transgender platform uncritically" or for "not setting proper limits for their child's behavior." None of these accusations could be further from the truth. Most of these families have accepted nothing "uncritically." They have spent many sleepless nights trying to be at peace with the consequences of their decisions; they have engaged deeply and thoughtfully with the nascent research, spent money they didn't have on consulting with professionals, and tried many different strategies to control, limit, explore, and understand their children. They have taken every decision seriously and tried to support their gender diverse children in every way possible—and still they are criticized by activists and often by therapists for "not moving fast enough," for "not being supportive," or for being "transphobic." Ultimately, many parents' views on what is best for their children have changed over time, and they have learned to trust their children's experiences, just as they trust their gender conforming and cisgender children's experiences.

I want this book to highlight the stories of parents and the collaborative work that therapists do with the families, to honor their journeys, to recognize the risks they take, and to celebrate the forging of new paths that trans children have unwittingly brought into our lives. Most of the stories in this book are success stories: children who are thriving, parents who are supporting them, and therapists who figured out how to help. All stories are not success stories, however, and I want to highlight here one very public story in which a transgender teen died, her parents were vilified, and the therapy provided was proven harmful.

In December 2014 a 17-year-old trans girl named Leelah Alcorn completed suicide by stepping in front of a truck. According to her blog on Tumblr, she felt unsupported by her family because she was transgender, and she stated her parents made denigrating comments about her gender. Leelah had come out at age 14 and asked her parents to help her transition when she was 16, but they refused, then forced her to attend a Christian-based reparative therapy. When she revealed she was attracted to boys, they pulled her out of school and cut her off from all social media and from all her friends. Feeling alone and desperate, Leelah posted on Reddit, asking if her parent's behavior could be considered abuse (Death of Leelah Alcorn, n.d.).

Two months later she completed suicide. Her suicide note read: "My death needs to mean something. My death needs to be counted in the number of transgender people who commit suicide this year. I want someone to look at that number and say 'that's fucked up' and fix it. Fix society. Please." The social media response in the trans community following her death was widespread, culminating in a petition demanding a ban on conversion therapy called "Leelah's Law," which was the fastest-growing change.org petition in 2014. In response to the public outcry, President Obama called for an end to conversion therapy (Death of Leelah Alcorn, n.d.). Numerous people and groups on social media began to raise the same question Leelah had asked: Are parents who send their kids to reparative therapy practicing child abuse? Fallon Fox, a transgender athlete and activist, clearly answered "yes" in a *Time* magazine article (Fox, 2015). Indeed, a petition was started to charge Leelah's parents with child abuse. One of its 28 cosigners said, "Take away all their other kids and put them in jail" (Huxter, 2015)! Dan Savage, an American LGBT activist and advice columnist, argued that her parents should be prosecuted and that their actions essentially "threw her in front of that truck" (Death of Leelah Alcorn, n.d). Following her death, Leelah's parents, despite repeatedly stating how much they loved their child, continued to refer to her as a boy and use a male name and male pronouns. This further infuriated many trans people and their allies, who felt this proved how abusive the parents were—even in her death they misgendered and mispronouned her; she died desperate to be seen as a girl, and in her parents' eyes she remained a boy.

In response to these accusations, her mother said she had actually never heard her child use the name Leelah and stated she had talked to her only once about being transgender (Fox, 2015). Could that be true? If it is true, how does it change the public narrative of Leelah's horrific death and her parents' alleged abuse?

I have thought about Leelah and her parents so many times over the intervening years. Many of the writers in this book wanted to use her story to illustrate what happens when trans youth are not supported. In some ways she is the perfect poster child for the effects on youth who are not respected for their authentic emerging identities. This narrative assumes, though, that Leelah was clearly articulating her identity to her parents as well as she was on social media and among her peers.

As a woman who has raised teens, and as a therapist who has worked with LGBTQ teens for decades, however, I know that often young people think they are saying things to their parents that are not being expressed in ways their parents can hear. They mumble, "I feel different" while watching a baseball game, and the parents think they are saying they have a bellyache, but the adolescent maintains they said, "I've always been gay." I have sat through so many therapy sessions over the years during which an angry child is telling the parents how they keep trying to communicate and feel they are not being listened to, and a confused parent responds, "Just tell me what you're feeling. I don't understand." Sometimes the child is not being clear; sometimes the parent is not listening well enough; sometimes we can miss each other very badly.

I know too well that the world is full of abusive parents, parents who do not or cannot listen to their children, parents who dismiss their children, reject their children, and beat their children. There are parents who will never accept a gender diverse child, a queer child, a nonbinary child, or a transgender child. The media report on fathers who beat and kill their sons because they "act gay" or are too feminine: children like 14-year-old Giovanni Melton, eight-year-old Gabriel Fernandez, and 17-month-old Roy Jones, whose mother's boyfriend said, "I was trying to make him act like a boy instead of a little girl" (Brammer, 2018; Einiger & Eyewitness News, 2010; Silva, 2017). There are too many parents who send their children to reparative therapy when the child deviates from expected gender expression and, if that fails, throw them out of the house. The streets are full of runaway and throwaway youth who are what a more affirming parent might call gender fabulous. Removing young people from these homes may be their only salvation; youth shelters and foster care may, sadly, be the best alternatives our broken society currently has to offer gender diverse and trans children and youth. Indeed, for the social worker who can facilitate the removal, this may be akin to releasing prisoners of war from their captors. For youth workers and advocates this is often experienced as a liberatory process, and when this is negotiated outside traditional legal and judicial processes, is can be a metaphorical underground railroad. We cannot minimize the actual danger for trans children and youth, and the essential role of adult advocates in their protection.

Abusive and murderous parents, however, remain a small minority of parents of gender creative and trans children. Parents are often resistant, angry, protective, even adamant, stubborn, and controlling. They are frequently confused, in emotional pain, and lack education about transgender identities. Sometimes they are in need of more support than their children, who can be very clear about their gender and how they want to live. As one six-year-old child, whose parents had been in therapy with me for a few months, said when we first met, *"The reason I brought my parents here is because they are having a very hard time with my gender. I am hoping you can help them."* This child understood that, although the child was the focus of therapy, they were not really the one most in need of help.

Children and adolescents often feel powerless to communicate their experience to their parents, even when their parents *are* willing to listen. They may not have the language; they may be in fear of the consequences. Unlike adults, they can't simply leave and get their own apartment if the relationship becomes difficult or abusive. They are dependent on their parents, not just financially, but emotionally—children and young teens cannot yet imagine a world outside their parents let alone negotiate for their own independence. For those who run away, the streets can be harsh, and their lives difficult; although many are able to successfully mature and thrive, far too many cannot. The consequences of disclosure are not just daunting; they are often terrifying.

Parental concerns can be grossly misunderstood by youth who can be nearly paralyzed because of this fear of the consequences of disclosure. Sometimes the most affirming parents can state blatantly and clearly, "Let's go see a therapist who specializes in gender, and if the therapist says that hormones are the right decision, we will go ahead, okay?" And the adolescent may still hear, "You will NEVER get hormones while living under my roof." I once worked with an adolescent whose parents were, by any objective standards, affirming. The teen kept repeating over and over again, "I am afraid they will reject me," offering numerous examples of the ways that might play out, including being thrown out of the house, being denied hormones, or being mispronouned. None of these was actually happening. The opposite was happening: their parents were driving them an hour back and forth to an alternative school to protect them from the bullying that went on at their local high school, providing them with access to hormone blockers, discussing the possibility of gender-affirming hormones, and always using their preferred pronoun. They had some awareness that their fears may have come from exposure to the Internet (YouTube and Tumblr)—reading accounts of horror stories about rejecting parents. I reminded them that people are often more compelled to tell horror stories publicly than to share positive stories (an awful meal will get a bad review on Yelp faster than a great meal); I reminded them of how loving and supportive their family was. I said, "Your parents allowed you to change schools, change your name, and start blockers." But they kept repeating, "I am afraid they will reject me," for weeks and months on end. They needed support to refocus their fears from stories of rejection and harm that they read online to the reality they were living that contradicted those fears—that their family was actively showing them love and support for who they were. The fear of rejection can be fierce for youth, even if there is little evidence of its likelihood.

Not all parents are able to be supportive, and some don't realize the seriousness of their child's attempts to communicate. One teen I worked with insisted, "I keep trying to tell them, but they keep dismissing me." I spoke with the mother, who said, "He changes his mind about everything every day. Last year he thought he had a terminal illness and we spent months seeing medical specialists; six months ago he wanted to be a Buddhist monk. He gets very serious about each of these things. I had no idea this was different, and I'm still not sure it is." Indeed, how could she be sure? How could anyone? It is easy to say that we should take all our children's needs seriously, but in the busyness of life—work, housework, the needs of other children and aging parents—parents may sometimes be less attentive than they should be, than they want to be, and may miss important cues, especially if a child is less than direct or has a history of having many intense, insistent, and diverse needs.

On the one hand, gender identity and expression are not the same as dress styles, musical interests, or career choices; they are part of a deeply embedded sense of self that emerges in the crucible of one's maturation. On the other hand, youthful experimentation with identity is developmentally appropriate, especially within a culture where gender norms are rapidly shifting and queer identities are proliferating. Even the most affirming, progressive parent might worry about introducing medical interventions when their adolescent affirms a gender identity different from the one they were assigned. After all, fluctuations in identity and experimentation with roles are a hallmark of youth. Gender therapists are trained to sort out the many issues influencing gender identity development, but parents are often just baffled.

Young people often feel threatened by parental attempts to understand. Questions are perceived as attacks. "They keep challenging my identity," insisted a 15-year-old, who, in the course of six months, changed their clothing style from nerdy collegiate to punk grunge, dyed their hair bright green, put gauges in their earlobes, dropped out of two school clubs they used to love, spent many solitary hours on the computer in their bedroom, and received failing grades in two high school classes. The parents witnessed these changes, saw their child becoming more and more sullen, and were rightly concerned. But all attempts to ask questions, to connect, were met with anger and resistance. Of course, the parents were worried. When gender was finally revealed to be the core issue, the parents did not immediately embrace gender transition as a solution. In their viewpoint, there was no apparent history of gender exploration or dysphoria, and their concern was that their child's obsession with gender was *the cause* of their deterioration. The more questions the parents asked, the more the child felt interrogated and policed. The more concerned the parents became, the more the child felt disbelieved, attacked, and alone. Sometimes young people do not know how to express what they are feeling; sometimes they simply do not want to try.

And sometimes it appears to explode out of the blue. One father once told me that he called his 15-year-old son downstairs and asked him to clean up the living room. The son looked at him, screamed at the top of his lungs, "I'm queer," and ran out the front door. From the parents' perspective, this disclosure came out of nowhere. They had no time to respond. Their son left, and it took them three days to find him. (He had taken a bus to the house of a friend he met online.) The parents were frantic. After reuniting with them, the teen was surly and indignant, and he kept repeating, "Just throw me out of the house. I know you hate me." The parents didn't hate him or have any intention of throwing him out of the house. They were confused and wanted to talk—they had almost no idea what "queer" meant. Every question they asked him was met with irritation and silence, and "You'll never understand." When I sat with him a few weeks later, he said, "They are old. They can't understand." I reminded him that I understood and I was about 20 years older than his parents. "Maybe we need to give them a bit more credit," I suggested, an idea that had never crossed his mind.

Adolescence is a rough time. To be genderqueer or trans complicates the challenges of adolescence even more. Communication with parents is almost always strained during this period. There are (at least) two sides to every family's experiences. *If we are not listening to both sides of the family story, we are missing important information.* I often think of all the runaway youth who tell "their side" of painful stories to youth workers about their rejecting and abusive parent, and I wonder about their parents: Are they the monsters they have been made out to be (they might be), or are they at home wringing their hands, worried about their child, who is out on the streets—alone and cold?

One story in my family that is now guaranteed to make us all laugh involves the time when my younger son yelled, phone in hand, "I'm going to call CVS and tell them about how abusive you are." He, of course, meant CPS (Child Protective Services), not CVS, the pharmacy. I said, "You go ahead and call them and tell them your abusive mother won't let you play a video game until you finish your homework." This may seem silly now, but he was totally serious at the time. He was angry, frustrated, and feeling trapped—and my parental attempts to keep him focused on a task *felt* abusive to him. He can laugh about it today, but it was not funny at all at the time. Teenagers often feel stuck, overprotected, and unheard—they push for autonomy and seek independence. They experience their emotions intensely. The path to maturity is often bumpy, sometimes tumultuous. Theirs is only one side of the story, however—not the only one. Parents are also struggling to let go, to support their child's growing independence, but parents also realize the world is so much more dangerous and complicated than most young people can even imagine. To understand the full story involves listening deeply to *both* sides. It is a tug-of-war and, in the end, youth (who survive) always win, but loving parents do not simply give up their end of the rope easily.

Conflicts between adolescents and their parents are exacerbated by the ways that sociocultural values can challenge religious values, especially fundamentalist ones (and it is not just Christianity that is to blame here, but all rigid and insular religious communities). If I believed there was a hell, I cannot imagine the pain it would cause me to think that my child was doing something that might cause them to go to hell. I cannot imagine any greater pain than believing that your child is on a path that will destroy them; I cannot imagine what it would take to step out of the beliefs of a religious system and challenge its basic tenets. I do not envy any parent faced with that.

Gene Robinson, former bishop of the Episcopal Church, wrote: "Leelah Alcorn's parents loved her. . . . But their control over her outlived its usefulness" (Robinson, 2015). I would agree with him, but I write this as the mother of a 17-year-old: I am not sure how to know when my "control" will have "outlived its usefulness." Is there some way to know when we have come too close to that edge? Or when our child is about to fall off a ledge? Remember the Alcorns' claim that they heard Leelah talk about being transgender only once, and that they were not aware she had a female name or identity? If that is true, their behavior seems less "controlling" and more benignly ignorant.

Their behavior was also consistent with the values within their Christian home. Andrew Solomon (2012) observes, "From the beginning, we tempt [our children] into imitation of us and long for what might be life's most profound compliment: their choosing to live according to our own system of values" (p. 2). Many of us reading this might find it horrific when we think that families with religious values that conflict with our own would impose those values on their children, but a moment of silent reflection may reveal that the process of inculcating our own values in our children is one of all parents' goals. Few Democrats want to raise Republicans; few scientists want to raise clergy; few vegetarians want to raise cattle farmers.

As parents we all realize at some point we will lose all control of how our children live and the value systems they will embrace. But it is a rare parent of a 17-year-old who is not still trying to direct them in ways they believe are healthier and will help them have a better future. The Alcorns cut Leelah off from social media because they thought those platforms posed a dangerous influence, not knowing they were, in all likelihood, her lifeline. Removing one's child from social media is a common consequence that parents impose when kids play too many video games, or spend too much time on Instagram, or don't do their homework. For that matter, we may be very critical of a family that didn't try to "control" influences that ended up causing harm: a child who wanted to drop out of school, was doing drugs, or was spending 15 hours a day in their room on social media. Indeed, the Internet is known for having a potentially dangerous influence on youth, and we are incredibly judgmental of parents who do not put controls in place. I know few parents who have not had to intervene in their child's online activities, and most of these involve their children joining "communities" perceived by the parents to be inappropriate or exploitive sexually or politically. For a religiously conservative Christian family like the Alcorns, I can well imagine online transgender communities fit that description.

Research shows that highly religious families are the most likely to use religious morals to reject their gay and trans children and the least likely to accept them (Ryan, Russell, Huebner, Diaz, & Sanchez, 2010). Religious families often respond to LGBTQ teens by isolating them, preventing access to others, sending them to carefully picked like-minded clergy and reparative therapy practitioners, and using theological arguments to condemn and change (fix) their LGBTQ identity. In other words, the Alcorns acted within the parameters that were common and expected in their social world. Their decision, within their religious framework, to send Leelah to reparative therapy came from the same loving place as my decision to send my child to drug and alcohol rehab. We try to inculcate our values to our children, with the best intentions, though not always the best outcomes.

Here's the rub: by the nature of living in a free society, we all get to raise our children within our own system of values—to be vegetarian or meat-eaters; to be Jewish, Muslim, Christian, or pagan; to embrace college education or to eschew higher education and work on the family farm. Of course, we may not succeed. Our children will become themselves—no matter what our goals or influence. At some point, we have to let go. But at what point? Solomon (2012) continues, "Though many of us take pride in how different we are from our parents, we are endlessly sad at how different our children are from us" (p. 2). Some of us reading this may flinch at the words *endlessly sad*, or we may believe that "we only want what is best for our children." But some children have a way of challenging us to reconsider our views on what is best for them. Many years ago I read an article about hippie parents who raised a child who became a pilot with the U.S. Air Force. They had spent their lives protesting war, and had a son who proudly wore a military uniform. It was hard for their son to become himself in that family, and the parents had to work to understand him and eventually share in his pride.

I believe that Leelah Alcorn's parents loved their child in the only way they knew how. There was much criticism that they "didn't love her," or "didn't love her enough," or "perhaps they loved her but they didn't support her," or "they didn't know what love is" (Death of Leelah Alcorn, n.d.; Robinson, 2015). I, however, don't doubt for a moment that they loved her. And as sad and outraged as our communities are about her death, I believe no one grieves her more every day than her parents, who must wonder what they could have done differently or how they could have listened more. I believe they are haunted daily by the cues they missed, what they could have done to keep their child alive. Leelah's life and death make for a rallying cry; she is prophetic poster child for a liberation movement, but for the Alcorns, there is an empty chair at their table and siblings who will mourn all their lives. The Alcorns acted within their worldview, in the only way they knew to save and protect their child. That was their way to prove their love. In the end, they lost their child, and whatever limitations they faced as parents of a trans child, they have paid the highest price imaginable.

There is an expression commonly iterated among parents of trans children: "When my child came out, I was faced with a decision: Do I want a happy daughter or a dead son?" The implication is that trans children who are not supported will become, like Leelah Acorn, more suicide statistics. It is a frightening thought.

The first time I heard a parent say that, my breath caught in my throat. It has now become a mantra, one I hear nearly daily in my office and online.

The suicide statistics are indeed terrifying; however, they are often distorted. As I was reading Facebook the other night, someone posted about the need to support trans youth because "41% of trans children will commit suicide." These statistics presumably refer to a 2011 study by the National Center for Transgender Equality that shows that 41% of transgender people have *attempted suicide* some time during their lives (Grant et al., 2011). Or perhaps it refers to their follow-up study in 2015, which showed a 40% rate of attempted suicide (James et al., 2016). Both studies included only people over 18 years old. To be clear, these are *not* completed suicides, but attempts—although still serious, a distortion of the research, which of course does not conclude that trans children *will* commit suicide. When Savin-Williams (2001) analyzed the data on suicidality among sexual-minority youth 17 years ago, he found that the research did not carefully distinguish suicidal *attempts* from suicidal *ideation*, a methodological problem that remains endemic. Sometimes people say they are suicidal—that is, they are thinking about suicide (fantasizing, wishing they were dead, but without a plan)—but don't actually go the next step by making an attempt. Although suicidal ideation is extremely concerning, elevating feelings to the same level as behaviors is simply inaccurate, and very few surveys (often conducted online) carefully control for these differences. Indeed, it may be hard to control for the difference, since the memory of *feeling* suicidal and *being* suicidal might be lost in retrospective reports.

Savin-Williams (2001) also documented that many suicide attempts were not life-threatening, were not real attempts to die, but were, rather, a way to communicate pain. Young people know that declaring they are suicidal, making suicidal gestures or attempts, and having visible signs of self-harm will garner adult attention. Indeed, it should! Young people often ask me: "Do you think if I tell my mom I'm going to kill myself that she'll let me start on hormones?" "The only reason I took those pills was because I knew that if I was admitted to the loony bin someone would see how serious I am." "A friend online told me that a good way to get my parents to change their mind is to threaten to kill myself." One young client said, "I knew I would not likely die, but I was playing at the edge; I was really in a lot of pain."

I am not attempting to minimize the actual feelings of depression and despair that underlie suicidal ideation, the reality of suicidal attempts, or the very real fear of suicidal completion. We may never know how many completed suicides were by people struggling with gender. The accurate statistics are bad enough without hyperbole and exaggeration. The Youth Suicide Prevention Program reported that over 30% of transgender youths attempt suicide at least once (Peterson, Matthews, Copps-Smith, & Conard, 2016). Caitlin Ryan (2015), a social worker and founder of the Family Acceptance Project, studied LGBT adolescents who were rejected by their families and found that they were eight times more likely to attempt suicide than other youth. There is, undoubtedly, an increase in suicidality—ideation, attempts, and perhaps completion—for sex- and gender-minority youth; it is, however, also important to note that suicide statistics for all youth—not just trans or LGBTQ youth—are very high. Suicide is the second-leading cause of death among *all* young people ages 10 to 24, according to the CDC (n.d.).

We need to recognize the pain and desperation that may compel a young person to use suicidality as a way to move mountains that they believe might not otherwise be easily moved. One young trans boy said, "Did you see that website where they memorialize dead trans people? If I killed myself my name would be there FOREVER." His eyes were dazed with joy. I reminded him he would be dead, unable to see his name in lights. "Yeah," he admitted, "that's the bad part." The "good" part, of course, was finally being visible to the world.

We must not let the threat of suicidality be used as a weapon against parents and therapists. It cannot be held up to young people as a way to immortalize their existence. I implore therapists to be careful not to feed this monster. Suicidality among our youth is already too high, the despair and pain that lead to it all too common; threats of suicidality should not be bargaining chips to determine the outcome of clinical assessments and control family processes. We must dissuade young people from seeing it as an option to get recognition here or in the hereafter. Suicidal feelings, threats, attempts, and, sadly, even completions require clinical attention and broad societal responses. Suicidality can open up a conversation between the youth and their family, not derail it.

Once I sat with a 16-year-old trans girl who was expressing suicidal hopelessness. When I was able to secure eye contact, I said: "No one likes being 16. There is a not a person in the world who would change where they are to be 16 again. Not an 18-year-old; not an 80-year-old. It is a really hard transit for almost everyone on the planet." I believe this is true, and it is exacerbated by being genderqueer in a less-than-accepting family. Her parents' ways of addressing her gender were not optimal; this family was highly dysfunctional and rejecting in many other ways also. We worked together to manage the struggles of being 16 within a chaotic home, and to assist her gaining her independence once she turned 18. I continued to work with her parents on both stabilizing their family life and supporting their trans daughter, who was finally able to fully embodying her identity. As she matured into her womanhood, she also began to address her traumatic upbringing. The more stable she became, the more supportive her family became, eventually paying for her gender-confirmation surgery. Our goal must be to assist youth in developing greater resilience, giving them a tool set that will serve them through all kinds of adversity.

I tell the youth I work with that if I were an adult in their lives who was resistant to their needs to transition, I would probably be swayed more by expressions of stability than by despairing threats of suicidality. I often talk with them about presenting with maturity and mental stability as a better negotiating tool than explosive threats. Our therapy together mirrors this process, as I am often the first adult who sees them and listens to them and validates them. I suggest they talk to their parents from the most solid and level-headed place they can find within. We work together to create and develop this place, where they are secure in their knowledge and identity. Parents need to witness (and ultimately reflect) their child's trans identity as healthy and genuine, a mature and well-adjusted part of their development. Interestingly enough, this often motivates parents to greater self-reflection. They are able to see their child more clearly, once the fighting and tension are lessened. For many families, the crisis of a child coming out is the first time that the youth has not only more information about their own identity, but also greater general knowledge about a topic (transgender, transition, medical treatment) than a parent does. It is an opportunity for older youth to face the parent as an emerging adult, and an opportunity for the parent to see their child as someone knowledgeable, capable of independence, and able to forge their own path—as all adults must do.

Research clearly shows that family rejection and lack of social supports increase suicidality and that family support significantly lowers it. Ryan and her colleagues (2010) found that LGBT youth who experience rejection from their families are at higher risk for suicide, depression, drug abuse, HIV, and other health-related concerns. Other research (Bauer, Scheim, Pyne, Travers, & Hammond, 2015) shows that parental support increases life satisfaction, positive mental health, and self-esteem and lowers suicidality. But even when parents *are* supportive, schools and communities may not be (Kuvalanka, Weiner, & Mahan, 2014), which can leave the child still at risk.

Sadly, even when parental and community acceptance abounds, suicide completion can still happen, just as it does in the general population. It's too easy to simply "blame the parents." Youth live in a complex social world, and parents are only one influence. We need comprehensive plans that address the depth of pain some trans youth are experiencing. We need to address the realities of suicidality, suicide attempts, and, sadly, suicide completions with compassion, advocacy, and understanding. We must remember that the parents of a child who completed suicide may need the most support.

Ryan (2015) did not recommend that Leelah Alcorn's parents be prosecuted for child abuse. She and her team at the San Francisco Family Acceptance Project suggested ways to support families like the Alcorns—first by starting where they are (the first tenet of all good social work)—and show them that "the behaviors they thought were helping their . . . child instead contribute to higher risks for health problems and family conflict." This means that providers and therapists must recognize that rejection is often an attempt—even if misguided—to protect. Ryan observes, "Parents who reject their LGBT children are typically motivated by trying to help, not hurt, them." Jean Malpas, director of the Gender Identity Project in New York City, substantiates the idea that we have to assist families in learning that what protects their child is acceptance—not rejection. Perhaps families like the Alcorns imagine that if they reject their child's emerging identity, the child will choose the safety of their family over their identity. They may be surprised to realize many will choose their identity over the family, though not without great pain and loss. Helping families understand that their rejection is causing many of their child's troubles and that acceptance could pave the way for a more successful future is a difficult task for many clinicians. But if we are to honor Leelah Alcorn's life by doing what she asked—"Fix society"—one of the places we can commit to fixing it is by working with parents who are rejecting of their gender creative and trans children.

As therapists, however, too often in our efforts to protect the children and youth we work with, we end up rejecting their families. I often consult with colleagues who are "burnt out," "exhausted by," and "frustrated with," the parents of the gender diverse children in their offices. They are angry at the parents for not supporting their children, and yet they are struggling with supporting the parents, not seeing that their own struggles mirror the families' struggles—it's hard to support someone who is behaving in ways you don't understand, whose actions are prompted by values that you do not share or actively oppose. When we support only the child, we are feeding the problems, not solving them. We often needlessly alienate youth from those who could potentially be their most important allies. Parents are viewed as the "bad guys" who are endlessly hurting their children and need to be "convinced" to see the world as the child and the therapist do. The parents' concerns are seen as "irrelevant," "damaging," and "abusive." Parents often do not feel listened to or heard or supported, because therapists are often not really witnessing and reflecting their fears and pain, concern and love for their children. Working compassionately with parents is one of the ways we can carry Leelah's memory forward—it is one way to "Fix society."

In *The Shelter of Each Other,* Mary Pipher (1996) suggests that, before a therapist encourages a client to cut off a member of their own family, to remember that the therapist "will not be there for clients when they cannot come up with rent or car payment, or when they are sick or need someplace to go for Thanksgiving dinner" (p. 129). While the clients in my office struggle with parents who are less than supportive, I carefully filter my words, thinking, "Am I going to make a chocolate cake for their birthday?" We need to look cautiously at the suggestions we make to our clients, especially youth, in helping them cope with their family members' anger, rejection, and ignorance. Unless we can replace all the ways that families nurture and support each other throughout the life cycle, we need to be vigilant not to encourage either side to see the other as dispensable. We enter into the lives of those we work with as a short chapter in a much larger story of their lives, no matter how influential or how powerful our interventions may be. Their relationships with their families—their parents and siblings—is (we hope) forever: the ground beneath their feet for the rest of their lives. Helping them get through what is often a crisis is best done by viewing the health of the family itself as being *as* important a goal as the authenticity of the child's gender—indeed, they are intricately entwined.

In 2004 I published *Transgender Emergence: Therapeutic Guidelines for Working with Gender-Variant People and Their Families.* This was the first clinical book to suggest that transgender people should not be pathologized for simply being trans. *And* it was the first clinical book to look at the family relationships of trans people. I saw these two foci as interconnected. When I began working with transgender people, my review of the existing literature revealed that families of trans people were perceived as extraneous. The assumption was that families would reject their transgender loved one, and the most affirmative therapies offered were to help the person transition, deal with the grief and move on, to establish a new life in their new gender. I challenged that view. I said, to mostly disbelieving colleagues at the time, including many transgender friends, that marriages could survive, and that trans people could remain integrated within their families as lovers/spouses/partners and parents. Although this viewpoint is far from universal, time has proven its veracity.

In the past two decades, increasing numbers of young children and teens have come out, marveled at by an adult trans community that could barely have imagined such a possibility when they were young. For so many adults these young people represent all they wish they could've had if the world had been more accepting when they were that age, as well as all they've lost living until adulthood in a gender that did not fit. Young gender nonconforming people represent a dream come true, civil rights long fought for, finally within reach.

Research shows that transgender youth who are supported by their families and make early gender transitions can have successful adult lives in terms of relationships, education, mental health, and overall stability (Cohen-Kettenis & van Goozen, 1997). Preliminary research on young social transitioners who have parental support for their affirmed gender show increased self-esteem and life satisfaction and no increase in depression when compared with non-trans children (Bauer et al., 2015; Olson, Durwood, DeMeules, & McLaughlin, 2016). Early transition means they would not need to develop a false self by assuming a gender identity and expression that feel inauthentic (Ehrensaft, 2012). Their socialization as boys or girls or nonbinary people would happen naturally during their pubescent years, so they would avoid the need to "unlearn" their original gender socialization, and then relearn a new one. This developmental process would ideally take place during the typical life-cycle stage for exploration of sexual and gender identity.

Parental authority and social mores are entwined in the minds of professionals as much as they are in young people themselves. Any resistance to complete autonomy is often challenged by adult activists who know the pain of living in oppressive homes as children. The desire to free children from their (perceived) oppressors reflects the memory of pain and the longing for freedom almost all of us remember who were also once young, yearning for independence and autonomy. All people who have experienced oppression identify, consciously or unconsciously, affirmatively or reactively, with the rallying cry of liberation.

Liberation cannot, however, become our only therapeutic tool. For adults, liberation does not solve the pain of losing custody of one's children, being unemployed, or separating from a spouse one adores. Living authentically can be a living hell when someone has lost everything. Sometimes there is no way to avoid this outcome. As clinicians supporting healthy transition processes, however, we can assist not just in the medical aspects of transition, but also in helping our clients prepare for and weather the social, familial, and work-related changes that may ensue. Our goal is to optimize the success of each person's gender-affirmation goals, which may involve advocacy, relationship counseling, using the weight of our professional licenses in the interests of policy changes, and enabling access to care.

Liberation as a therapeutic tool is even more precarious, dangerous even, when it is the only strategy for children and teens dependent on their parents for their food and shelter, not to mention their most intimate emotional needs. *Families are not extraneous.* They are integral to all of our well-being. The focus of our work should not be to save children and teens from oppressive parents, but, rather, to help families heal and integrate, to assist them in embracing their gender creative children, to move them from rejection as protection to acceptance as protection. I understand that not all parents can "come around," but I believe most can and will.

The research of the Family Acceptance Project (Ryan et al., 2010) highlighted that even small changes in parental support can make huge differences in the mental health and physical well-being of sex- and gender-minority youth. Most parents will do anything for their children; they just have to understand what their children really need. Validating the identities of young trans people is essential for their well-being, and we professionals must expand our tool set to also include validating their parents, who can potentially be their children's greatest allies.

Affirmative care for trans and gender nonconforming children and youth is still being defined, and it is important that part of the definition include family education and support as a foundation on which other supports and stability for youth can be based. Affirmation includes listening to and validating parental fears, as well as understanding that sometimes parents know their children in ways that therapists are not (yet) privy to.

Affirmative therapy recognizes that gender diverse children are having authentic experiences, and yet the outcome of those experiences—how they ultimately will come to see themselves—is not something that is yet knowable, not by professionals, parents, not even by the children and youth themselves. Adolescence is a time when young people should be exploring gender and sexuality. This process is dynamic and maturational and may continue to shift and change as they approach adulthood. Affirmative therapy asserts that whether a gender nonconforming child grows up to be gay, lesbian, or bisexual, socially transitions during prepuberty, transitions medically in adolescence, lives as nonbinary, transitions decades later, or identifies as heterosexual and cisgender as an adult, they deserve to be affirmed by their parents as being loved and valued. It is equally true that, regardless of the outcome for the child, the parent may need support in riding the waves of adolescent development and the process of evolution as gender identity emerges, sometimes changes, and then reemerges. Young people's identities in all areas often shift as they mature, and few parents are prepared to manage these changes, especially when gender is a major theme. This is when therapeutic work is most helpful—to assist parents in understanding why affirmation and acceptance *are* protective and to help them manage the intense storms that rearing a gender nonconforming or trans child may involve.

In closing, I want to discuss the emergence of three overlapping issues currently affecting the affirmative treatment of trans and gender nonconforming children and youth: the suggestion of social (peer) contagion, the proposal of a new diagnostic category, Rapid Onset Gender Dysphoria, and the emergence of detransitioners.

Affirmative care of gender diverse children is a relatively new sociocultural phenomenon and a burgeoning clinical specialty. It should not surprise us that there is cultural backlash. Anyone familiar with child and adolescent development, especially the maturational process of the frontal lobe, might be concerned about decisions young people make—especially when those involve permanent medical interventions. Of course, some parents express apprehension for their own child's future well-being. Opposition to trans people living their authentic lives is nothing new, and given the obvious vulnerability of children and youth in general, communities of concerned people have formed to challenge affirmative treatment of gender diverse children. I referred earlier to this coalition as "odd" and "motley," which many colleagues suggested was judgmental language that I should remove, but this coalition is an extremely incongruent group of citizens, having little in common except their resistance to affirming gender diversity in children and adolescents. Conservative religious extremists have partnered with proponents of conversion and reparative therapies, and they have joined a group of gender-essentialists, mostly self-identified radical feminist women who believe that biological sex is innate and immutable and therefore deny transgender identities in adults and children. The only goal of this disparate partnership is to oppose the rights of gender diverse children to live authentic lives with parental and community support.

Online communities of parents, often influenced by gender-essentialist feminists who are specifically concerned with their daughters identifying as transmasculine, have challenged the upsurge of young transitioners. Their concern is embedded in feminist ideals that girls should be able to be tomboys without being pressured into early medical treatment, an idea that no one disputes. They raise concern about hormone blockers that contradict current medical knowledge. They express concern for what they refer to as the "transgender trend," the idea that transgenderism is a damaging ideology and experiment, a fad; they resist the development of policies that make schools safer for trans and gender nonconforming children. Their vitriolic stance, which denies the authenticity of trans youth and attempts to block youth's access to medical care until they are adults, makes it difficult to hear the validity of any concerns they have without defensiveness.

A suggestion has recently emerged from this community for a new diagnosis called Rapid-Onset Gender Dysphoria (Littman, 2017), describing what appears to be the sudden formation of a transgender identity among teenagers. There is, of course, no such clinical entity; it is not recognized in any diagnostic manual used in psychology, social work, or medicine. Littman's published research has evoked much criticism from academics and researchers as illustrating a kind of junk science all too popular today. The study has numerous methodological flaws, including a biased sample: it presents the results of an online survey distributed on websites extremely critical of the concept of transgender children and includes only the parents' opinions of their children's experiences (Tannehill, 2018).

The study states that young people are identifying themselves as trans after becoming part of peer groups of other transgender teens (often online), suggesting (in their parents' view) a kind of contagion effect.

Marchiano (2017), a Jungian therapist, expresses concern that some young people will regret their transitions (and medical treatments). She describes Jung's theory of "psychic epidemics," suggesting that youth experiencing gender dysphoria are actually experiencing a social contagion, transmitted by peer interaction, particularly on the Internet. Indeed, the emergence of a vocal group of detransitioners, people who transitioned as teens and young adults who have now returned to living in their assigned gender (mostly those assigned female at birth), seems to bolster these concerns.

The increase of these critical voices is viewed by many trans activists and allies as a backlash to the gains of the transgender civil rights movement, and indeed they are. But I also think those of us who work with gender diverse children and trans teens need to take these concerns seriously and respond to them effectively.

Transgender adults often state that they were aware of their authentic gender identity from the time they were very young. This has been documented since Harry Benjamin began to assist people in transitioning in the 1960s. Young people today are maturing within a culture more open to discussing gender and gender dysphoria than at any other time in Western history. They are exposed to trans people on television living their authentic lives. They are able to explore their identities, including sexual orientation and gender expression, at younger ages, within communities of peers, online or otherwise. A little-known phenomenon a few years ago, trans youth are now a visible community. It may appear to be a "rapid-onset gender dysphoria," but perhaps it is only their coming-out to parents that is "rapid"; perhaps their evolution has been more internal. Some young people may have hidden their gender dysphoria. They may have had a difficult time naming or understanding what they were experiencing, and then read something or talked to someone and come to what appears to others to be a "rapid" realization. In actuality, it might have been a much longer process. It is certainly not new for parents to blame their children's behavior and experience (especially when it contradicts their own values) on "peer influence."

And it is possible it was a "rapid onset"; perhaps a young person who never knew the possibility of actualization existed, learned about it online, with friends, and "suddenly" understood something important and deep about who they really are. That is just one of the ways that some (including adults) arrive at their authentic identity. What many trans and nonbinary youth are experiencing is normal, healthy adolescent exploration, experimentation, and identity development. It is just taking place in a different cultural climate, where they are free to explore gender, and, yes, it is certainly influenced by social media. The onset is not so much "rapid" or "trending," as it is emerging among youths in communities of like-minded individuals; are we confusing social contagion with social support?

Of course, this can frighten parents who worry about whether their child's declarations about their identity are permanent or will ultimately be harmful for their child. When a teenager who never seems to have struggled with their gender suddenly discloses that they are trans or nonbinary, the parent may worry that this is peer influenced, that their teen wants to make a life-altering decision, one they may come to regret. It is normal for parents to be concerned, and grown-ups know that much will change for their children as they mature. The adolescent brain does not experience the world in the same way as the adult brain; young people "think" more with their amygdala than their frontal cortex—they experience their emotions intensely (Yurgelun-Todd, 2007). The adolescent years are often conflictual, and adding gender dysphoria (rapid or slow onset) to the picture can be destabilizing.

Young people often struggle with identity issues; they can change and shift as they sort through their potentialities. Not all influences, especially those online, seem healthy or in the youth's best interests. It's hard to navigate the vast changes that social media have brought to all our lives. Certainly support from peers may influence youth summoning the courage to come out. It is, however, unlikely that a young person would be drawn to these discourses online if they didn't find something compelling about them, something that has spoken to them. It is even more unlikely that peer influence would be enough to sustain their gender identity over time, and the vast majority of trans youth do not desist. Gender exploration is part of the social world of youth, and it is essential for parents to see not only the potential danger, but also the infinite possibilities. Youth, as we all know, are the harbingers of the future.

It is important to state that Rapid-Onset Gender Dysphoria is simply *not* a diagnosis. It is not recognized as a real clinical entity within any therapeutic system. It may describe a rare phenomenon by which some young people will be drawn to gender narratives and discussions online and see them as solutions to problems that may have little to do with gender—but that does not make it a diagnosis. Peer pressure can certainly be powerful. Gender exploration may, for some young people, seem like an answer to the complex challenges that all youth must navigate. This, of course, should be explored within families and by therapists as part of a comprehensive assessment before any medical interventions are provided.

In my own work, I help families and teens explore many aspects of identity and gender expression, talk about options for gender exploration, and, most important, help the family maintain stability and support through this sometimes challenging process. This includes exploring youth's online activities, their relationships with their peers, and the challenges they have sharing their lives with family members. It also includes listening to parents' honest concerns for their children and validating them as consultants on their child's journey. Encouraging supportive healthy dialogue between parent and child is essential to the clinical process. Social transitions are completely reversible, although potentially disruptive and confusing. Medical treatment for gender affirmation requires *consistent, insistent*, and *persistent* gender dysphoria, and, by definition, that assumes that time is a factor in the assessment process (i.e., it is not "rapid"). Of course, young people hate waiting. Patience is not a virtue of most maturing adolescents.

Will some people change their minds? Of course. There have always been adults who regret transition; they represent a small number of people who transition (1–4%). In the past few years, a group of young adults who transitioned during their teen years have transitioned back to their birth-assigned sex, the majority of them assigned female at birth. These detransitioners may represent not so much a newly emerging population as a younger cohort, those who transitioned as teens, and later came to transition back to their birth-assigned gender. To my knowledge, there are no detransitioners who socially transitioned as young children and received medical treatment as adolescents, who then detransitioned as mature adults. Mostly, those who transition young appear to have stable, affirmed identities through their teen and adult years.

Detransitioners have compelling stories. They often describe unremitting gender dysphoria that transition did not cure. They are in emotional pain about the effects hormones and surgeries have had on their bodies. They raise challenging and critical questions about therapeutic assessments that lacked depth, particularly regarding previous trauma histories. They are sometimes a vocal, angry minority challenging the clinical community, believing they were not adequately evaluated by their therapists or were seduced by peer pressure (or both). Clinicians (and, yes, parents) would be fools not to listen carefully to these voices. Indeed, it should challenge us to ensure careful, holistic assessments, especially relating to issues involving sexual trauma and peer (especially social media) influence.

Detransitioners should not be seen as threats to the trans community or to those of us working in affirmative care. They represent a small number people who are as deserving of our care as anyone else. It seems logical that as transgender people come out in larger numbers and as gender identities and expressions expand in possibilities, some people will find that decisions made earlier no longer relate to who they are. If people transition younger, they may come to realize this at younger ages than has previously been seen. Most admit to having had gender dysphoria, and many still do. Many found that transition did not fully address their gender dysphoria; that is, they remained uncomfortable with their bodies and their genders regardless of the gender affirmation treatments they accessed or how they modified their bodies and gender expressions. It does not necessarily mean they should have waited (waded) through their youth until they were "old enough" to know. How could they have known without the experiences that led to their current knowledge?

The presence of detransitioners reaffirms the reality that gender can be dynamic and fluid and that identities continue to evolve. Some regret having transitioned, and others view detransitioning more as an evolution, another step in their process of understanding themselves and how they can best live in the world. People who detransition also require support from family, friends, and professionals who serve the trans community. The last thing someone in pain needs is to feel judged and rejected by those who love them. People who are questioning their gender identity—including those who have transitioned—require the same respect and quality care as anyone else.

Young detransitioners raise important questions about the process of gender development, maturation of the adolescent brain, and identity exploration within a culture of shifting social mores. I think we are wise to listen as carefully to their stories as we listen to affirmed youth. As therapists, we need to embrace the reality that "our clients" are not just children and youth with affirmed identities, but also their resistant (or sometimes overzealous) parents, and detransitioners, who also need our support.

Young people today have the potential to live authentic lives in ways transgender people never have before. This should be celebrated. Anyone who has known trans people who lived for decades with "slow-onset gender dysphoria," a lifetime of hiding, shame, fear, and self-hatred, knows how important and exciting it is that another generation does not have to live that way. Affirmative therapists can facilitate this process and support all family members in successful transitions, as part of a healthy developmental trajectory. And this includes holding an open and compassionate heart to resistant parents, as well as those who find transition was not the right path for them.

We are witnessing a continuing emergence of gender identities and gender expressions and ways to live in the world that were not possible even a few decades ago. My nibling (both niece and nephew), AJ Rio-Glick, wrote a college thesis on butch identities and female masculinity. They asked: "If butch exists as a very real, yet socially constructed identity, can it exist without the society which constructed it? Or does it become reshaped as society changes over time?" Indeed, I speak with older butch women who say, "I might have transitioned if I were younger today, but the option didn't exist." And I speak with young nonbinary folk, whose description of their newly emerging neither/nor identities does not sound so different from the voices of nelly queens and stud bois of a generation before—although of course they are—different narratives and themes emerging in different times for a new generation.

Although I cannot know the outcome for any child or youth exploring their gender, I do believe that those who know the pain of gender dysphoria as well as the joy of gender euphoria are telling the truth about who they are to the best of their knowledge at a particular point in time. Young children who eschew established gender roles, four-year-olds who insist, "Stop saying I'm a boy, I'm a girl with a penis," nonbinary preteens, trans boys and girls, are not on this journey because of peer pressure, though they may be under the influence of peer support. Most will persist, some might desist, all will continue to evolve. If we listen deeply, they can teach us a lot about gender diversity and the endurance of family.

AndreAs Neumann Mascis in this book writes: "For cisgender parents, gender identity congruence is an aspect of experience that exists like the functions of the autonomic nervous system, so innate and so easily taken for granted that unless there is a problem, there is hardly reason to be made conscious of it." Having gender nonconforming and trans children can be a consciousness-raising experience for those parents willing to walk that journey with their child.

As a family therapist, I often work with families on and off over long periods. Parents often seek me out when they recognize a young gender creative child. Sometimes I do not even meet the child for many years. Often the children are blissfully happy if their parents are supportive, at least until they enter school, or as they are becoming preteens and adolescents, entering puberty, and becoming more conscious of gender, the outside world, and their place in it—a time when gender dysphoria often increases and social and medical transitions become the focus of the family. I see this as ongoing clinical work over the course of childhood and through maturity. Although gender nonconforming children and youth may have many challenges, the more their families are supportive, the easier their journey will be.

Many years ago I worked with a conventional, traditional father who struggled with his female child's decision to remove their breasts and have a male chest constructed. The dad was opposed to this for many reasons politically and religiously, but mostly he simply couldn't understand why his "beautiful daughter, who loved hand-making her own dresses" would want to "mutilate her body." Indeed, in the days before nonbinary identities were articulated, his child was a bit confusing clinically. Eschewing male *and* female pronouns, dressing very femininely, they were clear, "I have beautiful breasts; they just don't belong on my body." The father came into therapy with a copy of the book *GenderQueer: Voices from beyond the Sexual Binary* (Nestle, Howell, & Wilchins, 2002) under his arm, an odd juxtaposition with his conservative suit and tie. He struggled to understand his child: "How is she . . . I mean he . . . I mean they . . . going to have sex with her . . . his . . . their girlfriend? Their girlfriend is not a lesbian. I think she wants to be with a man. My daughter does not have that plumbing. I just don't know what to do . . ." He was forlorn and confused, head held in his hands, embarrassed to be having this conversation, a crumbled mess sitting on my couch. I said, "Dad, you know, your kid is 19 years old. However they work out their sexuality is not really something you have to fix. It has nothing to do with their gender or plumbing . . . sex is just kind of a private adult thing." He looked at me, with a glimmer of hope in his eyes, "You mean I don't have to fix this . . . I can let go." "Yes, Poppa, you can let go. They've got this." I had no doubt that they did.

REFERENCES

Bauer, G. R., Scheim. A. I., Pyne, J., Travers, R., & Hammond, R. (2015). Intervenable factors associated with suicide risk in transgender persons: A respondent driven sampling study in Ontario, Canada. *BMC Public Health, 15.* doi:10.1186/s12889-015-1867-2.

Brammer, J. P. (2018, February 16). Woman pleads guilty in murder of son, 8, thought to be gay. NBC News. Retrieved August 4, 2018 from https://www.nbcnews.com/feature/nbc-out/mom-pleads-guilty-murder-8-year-old-boy-thought-be-n848741.

CDC. (n.d.). *Web-based injury statistics query and reporting system* (WISQARS). Retrieved March 11, 2018, from http://www.cdc.gov/injury/wisqars/index.html.

Cohen-Kettenis, P., & van Goozen, S. (1997). Sex reassignment of adolescent transsexuals: A follow-up study. *Journal of American Academy of Child and Adolescent Psychiatry, 36* (2), 263–271.

Death of Leelah Alcorn. (n.d.) *Wikipedia.* Retrieved March 11, 2018, from https://en.wikipedia.org/wiki/Death_of_Leelah_Alcorn.

Edwards-Leeper, L., Leibowitz, S., & Sangganjanavanich, V. F. (2016). Affirmative practice with transgender and gender nonconforming youth: Expanding the model. *Psychology of Sexual Orientation and Gender Diversity, 3* (2), 165–172. http://dx.doi.org/10.1037/sgd0000167.

Ehrensaft, D. (2012). From gender identity disorder to gender identity creativity: True gender self child therapy. *Journal of Homosexuality, 59* (3), 337–356.

Einiger, J., & Eyewitness News (2010, August 3). Baby killed by mom's boyfriend, police say. ABC. Retrieved August 4, 2018, from http://abc7ny.com/archive/7588056/.

Fox, F. (2015, January 8). Leelah Alcorn's suicide: Conversion therapy is child abuse. *Time.* Retrieved March 11, 2018, from http://time.com/3655718/leelah-alcorn- suicide-transgender-therapy/.

Grant, J., Mottet, L., Tanis, J., Harrison, J., Herman, J., & Keisling, M. (2011). Injustice at every turn: A report of the National Transgender Discrimination Survey. National Center for Transgender Equality and National Gay and Lesbian Task Force.

Huxter, C. (2015). "Charge Leelah Alcorn's parents with child abuse." Change.org. Retrieved March 11, 2018, from https://www.change. org/p/transgender- charge-leelah-alcorn-s-parents-with-child-abuse.

James, S. E., Herman, J. L., Rankin, S., Keisling, M., Mottet, L., & Anafi, M. (2016). *The Report of the 2015 U.S. Transgender Survey.* Washington, DC: National Center for Transgender Equality.w

Kuvalanka, K. A., Weiner, J. L., & Mahan, D. (2014). Child, family, and community transformations: Findings from interviews with mothers of transgender girls. *Journal of GLBT Family Studies, 10* (4), 354–379. doi:10.1080/1550428X.2013.834529.

Lev, A. I. (2004). *Transgender emergence: Therapeutic guidelines for working with gender-variant people and their families.* Binghamton, N.Y.: Haworth Press.

Littman, L. L. (2017). Rapid onset of gender dysphoria in adolescents and young adults: A descriptive study. *Journal of Adolescent Health, 60* (2), Supp. 1, S95–S96. doi:https://doi.org/10.1016/j.jadohealth.2016.10.369.

Marchiano, M. (2017). Outbreak: On transgender teens and psychic epidemics. *Psychological Perspectives, 60* (3), 345–366. doi:10.1080/00332925.2017.1350804.

Murkoff, H., Eisenberg, A., & Hathaway, S. (2002). *What to expect when you're expecting.* 3rd edition. New York: Workman.

Nestle, J., Howell, C., & Wilchins, R. (eds.). (2002). *Genderqueer: Voices from beyond the sexual binary.* Los Angeles: Alyson Books.

Olson, K. R., Durwood, L., DeMeules, M., & McLaughlin, K. A. (2016). Mental health of transgender children who are supported in their identities. *Pediatrics, 137* (3), [e20153223]. doi:10.1542/peds.2015-3223.

Peterson, C. M., Matthews, A., Copps-Smith, E., & Conard, L. A. (2016). Suicidality, self-harm, and body dissatisfaction in transgender adolescents and emerging adults with gender dysphoria. *Suicide and Life-Threatening Behavior, 19.* doi:10.1111/sltb.12289.

Pipher, M. (1996). *The shelter of each other: Rebuilding our families.* New York: G. P. Putnam's Sons.

Robinson, G. (2015, January 18). *Letting go: Leelah Alcorn and the hardest part of being a parent. Daily Beast.* Retrieved March 11, 2018, from www.thedailybeast.com/articles/2015/01/18/leelah-alcorn-and-the-hardest-part-of-being-a-parent.html.

Ryan, C. (2015, January 7). Parents don't have to choose between their faith and their LGBT kids (commentary). *Washington Post.* Retrieved March 11, 2018, from https://www.washingtonpost.com/national/religion/parents-dont-have-to-choose-between-their-faith-and-their-lgbt-kids-commentary/2015/01/07/e3ec4a9c-96bc-11e4-8385-866293322c2f_story.html?utm_term=.4aedad7a1a1d.

Ryan, C., Russell, S. T., Huebner, D., Diaz, R., & Sanchez, J. (2010). Family acceptance in adolescence and the health of LGBT young adults. *Journal of Child and Adolescent Psychiatric Nursing, 23* (4), 205–213. doi:10.1111/j.1744-6171.2010.00246.x.

Savin-Williams, R. C. (2001). Suicide attempts among sexual-minority youths: Population and measurement issues. *Journal of Consulting and Clinical Psychology, 69* (6), 983–991.

Silva, C. (2017, November 6.). Father kills 14-year-old son: "He would rather have a dead son than a gay son." *Newsweek.* Retrieved August 4, 2018, from https://www.newsweek.com/father-kills-14-year-old-son-he-would-rather-have-dead-son-gay-son-703282.

Solomon, A. (2012). *Far from the tree: Parents, children, and the search for identity.* New York: Scribner.

Tannehill, B. (2018, February 20). Rapid onset gender dysphoria is biased junk science. *Advocate.* Retrieved March 11, 2018, from https://www.advocate.com/commentary/2018/2/20/rapid-onset-gender-dysphoria-biased-junk-science.

Yurgelun-Todd, D. (2007). Emotional and cognitive changes during adolescence. *Current Opinion in Neurobiology, 17* (2), 251–257.

PART 1

Gender Nonconforming Children and Trans Youth: What You Didn't Expect When Expecting

Diane Ehrensaft brings her warmth, sensitivity, and clinical acumen to the notion that "It Takes a Gender Creative Parent" to effectively raise what she terms a gender creative child, one who has the vision and the assertion to actively (re)shape the gender they intuitively know themselves to be. In our efforts to guide those parents to a more informed, more understanding place, it behooves us medical and mental health professionals to, in effect, become "gender creative" ourselves, that is, less rigid and more expansive in how we think about cultural norms and how those inform our work. As more people question the binary (gender) boxes, and as we see more clients who either are struggling with their gender identity or are affirmed and need a safe space to explore how this affects their lives, professionals need guidelines on how to proceed.

Challenging traditional developmental gender theory, Ehrensaft offers us the concept of the *gender web*, one built around three dimensions—nature, socialization, and culture. Each web is unique, and each can change over time, a model she feels more accurately reflects the kaleidoscopic breadth and range of gender possibilities. She then takes us into her consulting room, where she illustrates, step by step, through an array of case examples, practical intervention strategies, as she simultaneously juggles the child's perspective, the parents' perspectives, and the clinician's perspective.

She is child-centered in her approach, and her therapeutic efforts with parents are focused on what Ehrensaft calls *de-centering*, a gradual relinquishment of the parents' hopes and dreams for their child and a gradual replacement of those with the child's hopes and dreams for themselves, a task central to parenthood, but which has specific resonance in this context. Assisting the parent to understand what beliefs and attitudes they hold, ones they might not be aware of, and how those play out in relationship with their child are key. At the same time, this process reinforces the importance of clinicians being aware of our own beliefs and attitudes, both positive—our *gender angels*—and negative—our *gender ghosts*—and how those inform the work.

Ehrensaft's piece is aimed at a broad audience—from the less experienced clinician to the more experienced—and is solidly theoretical as well as clinically practical.

All identifying information has been changed to protect the confidentiality of clients and family members.

Irwin Krieger identifies a central conflict parents are confronted with: a desire for their child or adolescent to live authentically, alongside a desire to protect them. Posing nine key questions, which serve to organize the article, he aims to help parents "face their fears," offering us a how-to guide for ways to begin unpacking those concerns within the context of two extended, contrasting case examples. Highlighting the importance of the role parents play in shaping how children and adolescents feel about themselves, he stresses that parents' having accurate information is critical—a general knowledge about gender identity and a personal knowledge about who their child is—as well as maintaining an openness to explore their own attitudes and behaviors, both fundamental to facing and combating those fears. Notable is the delineation Krieger consciously makes between the younger child and the adolescent, and the developmentally informed, individualized ways parents can approach the subject of gender identity with the overall goal of moving them from a position characterized by fear to one more imbued with understanding.

Lisette Lahana takes us into the world of Dakila, a Filipina transgender teen whose parents, Julio and Talo, both from conservative, Catholic backgrounds and both having emigrated from the Philippines to the United States as teenagers, resigned themselves to having a feminine boy. "What they didn't expect when expecting" was Dakila, who, against all the odds, and with only the reluctant support of her mother, is determined to live her truth—no matter what.

1

It Takes a Gender Creative Parent

Diane Ehrensaft, PhD

"Mr. and Mrs. Little often discussed Stuart quietly between themselves when he wasn't around, for they had never quite recovered from the shock and surprise of having a mouse in the family" (White, 1945, p. 9). In Stuart's infancy, his doctor "was delighted with Stuart and said that it was very unusual for an American family to have a mouse" (p. 3). It was, however, not always so delightful for Stuart's parents, Mr. and Mrs. Little. Mr. Little banned references to mice in their conversations and ordered Stuart's mother to tear out the nursery rhyme page where "Three Blind Mice" appeared, saying, "I should feel badly to have my son grow up fearing that a farmer's wife was going to cut off his tail with a carving knife" (p. 9).

Many of us remember hearing the classic story of *Stuart Little* when we were children, or recall reading it to our own children. I am sure that when E. B. White wrote this archetypical tale for a mid-twentieth-century readership, he had no idea that it would someday serve as the perfect parable of the twenty-first-century true story of the parents who find out they have a gender expansive or transgender child. Unlike the Littles, who knew from the beginning that their child was different, millennium parents may not know until years later. But when families uncover that the child's gender is not the one matching the sex marker inscribed on their birth certificate, or that the child is not complying with the gender norms of their culture, it can be no less shocking than discovering your child is a mouse. Like Mr. Little, they may fear for their child's safety, not at the hand of a farmer's wife, but in the grip of an unaccepting, hostile world. Some parents and family members will learn to take it in stride, as the Littles did; others come ready to embrace their child no matter what their gender identity or expression; still others will struggle to recover from the assault on their sensibilities; and the rest, sadly, never recover.

For the mental health professional, the task will always be the same: joining with the family to facilitate creativity in raising what I have dubbed a *gender creative child*, one who does not abide by the binary gender norms, prescriptions,

Lev, Arlene I., Gottlieb, Andrew R., *Families in Transition*
dx.doi.org/10.17312/harringtonparkpress/2019.04.fit.001

or proscriptions that might exist in the child's culture, but who transcends and transgresses those norms to evolve independently, uniquely, and imaginatively into the gender that is "me" (Ehrensaft, 2011; 2014; 2016). This group of children seems to have grown exponentially in the most recent decade, as reported by gender programs throughout North America and beyond (Hidalgo et al., 2013; Zucker, Wood, & VanderLaan, 2014). They challenge the adults around them to find new ways to promote their health and well-being while both standing on and contributing to a major shake-up in our systemic organization of gender.

Always considered bedrock, gender has been transformed, metaphorically, into a terrain of moving boulders rolling and bouncing against each other — exciting, dynamic, bold. Youth and adults alike are protesting against confining their gender to one of the two boxes assigned to them — male or female. New paradigms are emerging that suggest gender is not a binary that neatly fits into boxes, but is actually an infinite array of identities and presentations (Brill & Pepper, 2008; Ehrensaft, 2011, 2016; Harris, 2005). In human development, we pay special attention to moments of expectable disequilibrium — when a child is transitioning from one developmental stage to another and demonstrates some dis-ease or dis-orientation in the process. If we apply this thinking to families who are living with a gender expansive or transgender child, we have just such systemic disequilibrium as parents attempt to (1) have a clear and accurate vision of the child who has come to them; (2) deal with their potential surprise or shock about their child, given their own experience, upbringing, and gender sensibilities; and (3) support their child in the way they see fit. How can mental health professionals provide anchors in this process, always keeping our eyes on the prize — the best interests of the child?

The Child's Tasks/The Parents' Tasks

The family and the clinician come together as a team to assist the child in discovering the gender that feels most authentic. In traditional developmental theory, the task of the child was threefold: (1) to learn their assigned sex on the basis of chromosomes and anatomy, that is, I am male or female (*core gender identity*); (2) to understand what it means to be male or female (*gender role socialization*); and (3) to establish a stable and permanent understanding of one's gender as always female or always male (*gender identity*). If all went well, these developmental milestones were fully reached by age six (Kohlberg, 1966).

A critical factor in achieving those milestones was the attitudes and behaviors of the parents and whether they performed their job "correctly." To do this, they were expected to (1) provide both a male and female parent; (2) teach the appropriate gender label ("I am boy," "I am girl"); (3) serve as both a role model and instructor in gender socialization, shaping the child's behaviors to conform to social expectations and their gender label; and (4) work out any of their own conflicts about masculinity and femininity, either within themselves or with each other. For healthy gender development, no room was left for ambiguity in the differentiation between boys and girls.

Now those gender boulders have begun to shift the earth itself. Science has offered us evidence that the determination of our gender identity is not necessarily dictated by our chromosomes and anatomy, but is located primarily in our brain and/or mind (Diamond, 2000; Dimen, 2003; Rosenthal, 2014), which may take precedence over both anatomy and X and Y chromosomes. Observations of gender expansive individuals have led us to the conclusion that gender exploration and discovery are not necessarily a task finished at age six, but can evolve over an entire lifetime. We have also learned that some people exchange one gender for another with positive rather than adverse effects, and also that gender can come in an infinite variety of identities and presentations, not just boy or girl. In other words, gender lies between our ears rather than between our legs, and it will also be influenced by the world around us.

Recent gender reformulations offer the concepts of a gender spectrum or a gender rainbow to expand our thinking to include gender as being multiple rather than binary. Cross-cultural and anthropological studies have further challenged our Western binary biases regarding the narrow normativity of boy/girl, male/female, masculinity/femininity, gender/sex identities. Other cultures have more complex, nondual gender identities, such as the Native American and First Nation Two-Spirit people, South Asian Indian *Hijra,* and Samoan *fa'afaline* (Besnier, 1994; Reddy & Nanda, 2009; Roscoe, 1993).

In that context, I have constructed the model of the gender web as an attempt to account for gender in all its infinite varieties and to acknowledge the components that go into children's construction of their unique gender selves (Ehrensaft, 2011, 2012, 2016). I developed this to substitute for the model of the gender spectrum that, at the time, was developed to replace the gender binary. Though I liked the concept of an infinite variety of gender hues between two poles, I mused that a gender spectrum is only two-dimensional and still tips toward the binary—male/female—at each end. So, just as a spider web in your window can stretch up, down, and sideways, the gender web is a three-dimensional model, threading together nature, nurture, and culture. If we break those down into all their individual components, we have (1) nature—chromosomes, hormones, hormone receptors, gonads/primary sex characteristics, secondary sex characteristics, brain, and mind; (2) socialization—family, school, and community; and (3) culture—values, ethics, laws, theories, and practices. So, for example, Stacey was born with XX chromosomes but received high doses of androgens in utero, and she was raised in a household that believed in letting children be self-defining but within a culture that does not look so kindly on children who go against the grain of that culture's strict codes for behavior, including gender presentations. How Stacey will weave together her desire to wear her brother's clothes, her parents' permissiveness to do so, and her culture's proscriptions about the same behaviors will be an unfolding process. At any cross section in time, we can capture Stacey's unique gender web as she spins together all the threads of nature, nurture, and culture. It is the task of every child to compose their own gender web. Like fingerprints, no two gender webs will look the same. But unlike fingerprints, the gender web is not indelible. It can change over the course of a lifetime; it is not fixed or permanent at age six, as many developmental theorists have suggested (Kohlberg, 1966; Maccoby & Jacklin, 1974; Tyson, 1982). Whereas nature, nurture, and culture will all play a part, for some nature will be the strongest set of threads; for others, nurture; and for yet others, culture—all interwoven in unique ways.

It is up to the child, not the parents, to spin their gender web. If the parents grab the threads, the gender self is at risk of getting all tangled up. This rubric is connected to a basic dictum for both family and professionals: if you want to know a child's gender, ask them. It is not for us to tell them, but for them to tell us. If the parents are able to be facilitators and supporters of the child's efforts, that child stands to grow up with a sturdy and confident sense of their gender self. Put another way: the task of the parents, along with any other family members, friends, or professionals, is to promote *gender health,* defined as the right to live in the gender that feels most real and/or comfortable along with the ability to express that gender with freedom from restriction, aspersion, or rejection. The challenge, never an easy one, is figuring out just how to accomplish that task.

First Step: The Art of Listening

Let us start at the very beginning: a family contacts a therapist for help. Formerly, the initial inquiry typically came through a phone call. Today, it is more likely to come through an e-mail, and if it's a query about their child's gender, that parent's e-mail may very well read something like one that came to me recently: "Hi Dr., I came across your information while I was researching for my son. He recently turned four and wants to be a girl and is only drawn to girl toys/clothes for the past two years. We have not spoken with a professional doctor. But wanted to reach out early and find ways we as parents can support him. Please let me know if you could help. Thank you!"

For a moment, let us dial back a generation. If this child's name was Kyle and the same query came to a mental health professional trained in the traditional model of gender development outlined above, the treatment recommended and implemented could very well have looked like this: "When he was five, Kyle entered a behavior modification program . . . in a laboratory setting and at home . . . [where] a token reinforcement program was instituted. Kyle received blue tokens for 'desirable' behaviors, such as play[ing] with boys' toys or with boys, and red ones for 'undesirable' behaviors, such as doll-play, 'feminine' gestures, or playing with girls. Blue tokens were redeemable for treats, such as ice cream. Red tokens resulted in loss of blue tokens, periods of isolation, or spanking by father. The treatment program lasted ten months" (Green, 1987, p. 295). This was the model implemented by mental health professionals at the program run by Dr. Richard Green at UCLA to help children accept the sex assigned to them at birth and comply with the culturally defined gender behaviors that would match that sex assignment.

This therapy model is now prohibited in nine states in the United States, and the province of Ontario in Canada, which all have statutes on the books identifying any mental health interventions attempting to alter the gender behaviors or expressions of a minor as unethical and reportable to licensing boards (e.g., see California Legistlature, 2012; New Jersey Assembly, 2013). So then what are we to do instead when a family comes to us concerned, puzzled, or alarmed by their child's gender expressions and behaviors?

The first step is no different from any other response to a request for help: find out exactly what brings the family in. As an explanation for why gender clinics are seeing a recent swell in their populations, Pasterski, Gilligan, and Curtis (2014) offer the possibility that "gender variant behavior has become more widely accepted and seeking social support for distress related to GD [gender dysphoria] may be less stigmatized than in the past" (see also de Vries & Cohen-Kettenis, 2012; Spack et al., 2012; Wood et al., 2013). This suggests that more parents are contacting mental health professionals because they recognize that their gender expansive children are in need of support, not necessarily because they have a gender disorder. If it is less stigmatized than in the past, that means that there is more opportunity to consider gender nonconformity as a normal variation, rather than a condition to be cured. The fact that there might also be psychological distress indicates that the social environment is not yet free of stigma or prejudices, attitudes that may seep into a child's psyche in the form of anxiety and/or depression. Additionally, in a culture that dictates boys have penises and girls have vaginas, children with penises who know they are female or children with vaginas who know they are male may suffer from *body dysphoria,* in which, by their culture's norms, they can never be the gender they know themselves to be because their body and their psyche are not in alignment. Either way, let us consider that the parents seek our help to find out how best to support their child in the context of a world that is bridging both the old and the new as it moves toward greater acceptance, or at least lessened stigmatization, of gender diversity. In this world we are developing a new lens on gender nonconformity as a variation of human development to be facilitated rather than repaired or extinguished with token reinforcement programs or gender prohibitions.

So what might a family coming to us want from a mental health professional? Do they want to try to get a better reading of who their child is—a child who might be different from them? Do they want affirmation that the way they are handling their child's gender situation is the "right" way? Do they want reassurance that they did not cause whatever is going on with their child? Do they want us to "fix" their child? Do they want to make sure that their child will be safe, will not suffer, and will be happy? Do they want a referee as they battle among themselves about the "right" path along which to lead their gender expansive child? Do they simply need someone to hold them as they try to get their bearings in this moving-boulder world of gender diversity that has rolled right into their own home?

At the Family Acceptance Project, Ryan, Russell, Huebner, Diaz, and Sanchez (2010) found that LGBT minors who receive support from their families demonstrate positive mental health outcomes; LGBT minors who do not receive support do not fare as well psychologically. For many mental health professionals, these findings have been mistakenly oversimplified into the following equation: supportive parents are good; nonsupportive parents are not. This is not in the spirit of Ryan's findings (2014), nor does it conform to them. The situation is that the vast majority of parents walking through our doors with questions about their gender expansive children do so not to punish but to support their children. Few come in with the intention of rejecting their child, even if their initial attitude is that gender nonconformity is either a violation or a sin. So it is better to start from the assumptions that (a) parents who come to us with a gender issue love their child and (b) parents who come to us with a gender issue have every intention of supporting their child. It is the form that support takes which will be our therapeutic concern. Although even some parents who are skeptical, perhaps actually condemning, at first will probably change their position over time, we must also remain open to the possibility that efforts in that direction might fail.

> Miranda and Samuel Watson have a four-year-old son, Maxwell. They are an African American family, very involved in their church, living in a small conservative city on the West Coast. Maxwell has taken to telling everyone in his nursery school that he wants to be a girl, grow his hair long, and wear flowing, sparkly dresses. Miranda is puzzled but is trying to support her son by reading up on gender nonconformity and giving him some room to explore. She is even wondering herself whether Maxwell might be transgender. To test the waters, she shared a toy catalogue with Maxwell and asked him to circle all the ones he liked best. Her intent was to explore which toys Maxwell would gravitate toward—"boy" toys, "girl" toys, or gender-neutral toys—hoping to understand his gender preferences. When Samuel heard about this, rather than seeing this as support, he minced no words in objecting to Miranda's actions. As the father of a young black boy in a racist society, he sees his responsibility as helping his son grow up with strength and pride, shepherding him toward becoming a credit to both his gender and his race. He is a very involved father and Maxwell is the apple of his eye. He told the therapist with deep emotion that he knows how many of the children in his community are missing a father to guide them, and he wants to ensure that will never be Maxwell's experience. With these hopes for Maxwell, there is no way that Samuel can envision letting his son prance through the neighborhood in sparkles and jewels: "I let my kid go out in the streets like that in our neighborhood, a skinny little black kid, and he's gonna get creamed. I mean creamed. Not a snowball's chance in hell am I going to let that happen to my boy. I want him to grow up. Period. And I want him to grow up proud to be a black man."

Who is the more supportive parent here, Miranda or Samuel? Actually, that is the wrong question. There is no contest. You could not find two parents more conscientious and concerned. So the first step, if Miranda and Samuel Watson were to come to us, is to listen to each of their narratives about their son and his gender development, guided by the following queries:

- Tell me what you see in Maxwell—his gender behaviors, feelings, sensibilities.

- How do you understand these behaviors, feelings, sensibilities — where do they came from, what do they mean?

- How do you respond to his gender behaviors, feelings, sensibilities?

- How does he respond to you once you respond to him?

- What are your own sensibilities about gender?

- How about in the culture you grew up in?

- How about in the community you are living in now?

- Do you feel satisfied with how you are handling Maxwell?

- Do you think your ways of handling Maxwell's gender are working?

Since gender can be such a loaded issue, it is never easy to ask one parent to answer all these questions while the other parent sits and listens. But in the context of a safe space provided by the therapist, taking turns helps parents suspend their own thoughts and feelings in order to better hear and understand their partner, particularly when there are tensions between them. The therapist does not sit by passively but, with empathy and curiosity, reflects back the gist of what one parent is expressing, inviting the other parent to be curious as well. Beyond invitation, through listening, the therapist sets the stage, models, and facilitates an interaction between the parents in which they can come to realize that they are both being supportive of their child, albeit with potentially very different content of support and perspective on what will best lead their child to a healthy gender life.

> When Samuel expressed angst about his son being thrown to the wolves if he is allowed full expression of his gender desires in public, the therapist noticed Miranda literally arching her back and, with great intensity, launching into an attack on Samuel's gender policing stance. The therapist acknowledged her agitation, but asked her to wait a bit so the therapist could ask Samuel a few questions: What was it like when he was growing up—did boys get bullied if they didn't follow the rules about how they were supposed to act? Did he ever actually see a boy being beaten up for breaking the gender rule? What does he think his responsibility toward his own son is? What would his own parents say if they witnessed him letting Maxwell dance around the house wrapped in his mother's sparkly scarves? Samuel is close to tears as he admits he would feel like a failed father and an ostracized son. And he couldn't get the image out of his head of Maxwell lying on the sidewalk—pummeled. Miranda was visibly moved by Samuel's

emotionality and his obvious love for his child. It also helped when she heard the therapist concur that they all had to put their heads together to figure out how to keep Maxwell safe in their community. At the same time, the biggest danger for Maxwell might not be the bullying, but the shame and despair he could feel if he got messages from his own parents that it "wasn't okay" to be the boy he was. This caught Samuel's attention, and he was then able to open up to what Miranda had been trying to tell him: the reason she was letting his hair grow long was because she witnessed how Maxwell sobbed each time she pulled out the clippers for his monthly haircut. And it was only getting worse. Samuel grew tearful again, imagining his boy in such pain. He looked over at Miranda, moved closer, and took her hand in his. Miranda's whole body relaxed.

Waiting a few moments for Miranda and Samuel to experience the rapprochement between them, the therapist took the opportunity to introduce the idea of acceptance as a form of protection: if Maxwell feels proud of the way he looks with his longer hair, backed by both his parents, that sensibility can bolster his confidence and resilience to live in his world happily. This in turn would allow him to develop the ability to push back when someone says, "Hey, how come you have long hair, that's for girls?" He could say, with confidence, "Well, that's the way I like it." Alternatively, if Maxwell feels caught in the crossfire of his parents' conflict, he will lose that protection and instead be at risk for anxiety. Neither Miranda nor Samuel would ever want that for Samuel, and this created the bridge for them to explore the best possible solution for balancing safety against freedom of self-expression. Their solution for the time being: create safe spaces where Samuel could feel free to fully express himself.

As you can see, the therapist's role is not that of a referee, but rather of a buffer between the parents so they can both agree to work on providing their child with consistent guidance in paving a path in the unfolding gender journey. To do otherwise would be to leave the child at risk and the parents destabilized in their relationship. In serving as that buffer, you are establishing a collaborative relationship with the family, not forgetting that, from beginning to end, your goal remains the same: ensuring that this child's gender health—discovering the gender that is "me"—is being facilitated by those around the child. As you listen, you are simultaneously filing away queries for future reference to be woven in only after you have developed a trustworthy alliance with the family:

- Does this family seem to be able to see their child for who they are?

- Will they need to "de-center" — that is, move away from their own gender sensibilities and pay attention to the child's — one whose gender sensibilities might be very different from theirs?

- Are there silent partners in the room — messages from grandparents, from religious institutions, from teachers, that are pressing against the parents' own sensibilities?

- Would you consider these parents facilitators of their child's gender health?

- Does their present strategy for handling their gender expansive child have any risk factors, including the potential for doing direct harm?

- Are they afraid for their child's safety?

- What else might they be afraid of?

- Are they having trouble balancing everyone's needs, especially if there are other children in the family?

Given all these considerations, it is generally advisable to conduct these initial sessions without the child in the room in order to give the parents a safety zone in which they can speak freely of their concerns and to protect the child from any statements that could be bruising, if not traumatic.

Honing in on Acceptance

Now comes the more challenging work: using your expertise to shed a different light on the child and inviting the family to do the same. As mentioned earlier, a parent's efforts to support their child do not necessarily translate into best practices. For example, drawing from another sphere of development, parents who want to support their children's independent thinking and confidence in their own strivings toward autonomy have sometimes translated that into giving them an equal voice in family affairs by saying, for example, that every person's vote counts, even when it comes to going to bed or brushing their teeth, and consequently avoiding, whenever possible, two words: *Stop* and *No*. This is rarely in children's best interests; it leaves them in a state of anxiety in which they desperately clamor for some leadership from benign authorities, as they are clearly not developmentally ready for that kind of responsibility themselves (Ehrensaft, 1997).

A father who tells his son, "You don't want that Barbie doll, it's only for girls," may feel he is helping him fit in and fare well in the community, but that will rarely be in the child's best interests if it sends a message that who he is is not worthy in his father's eyes. This may be shaming and also experienced as a *microaggression*—everyday verbal or nonverbal communication, not necessarily delivered with hostile intent, that insinuates to a person of a particular marginalized group (in this case, gender expansive children) that who they are is not acceptable (Sue, 2010). Even a seemingly more supportive comment, "Honey, you know boys can play with Barbies, too. You don't have to be a girl to play with Barbies," in response to a son who has just said, "Mommy, I want to be a girl who plays with Barbies," can be experienced as a microaggression. Her intent to support by offering a more expansive world of gender expression is there, but her actions can have just the opposite effect: deflating his positive sense of self by ignoring his plea and misattuning to his need to be recognized for the gender he is coming to know himself to be—a *girl* who likes Barbies. Instead of feeling held by his mother, he may slink away feeling frustrated, putting all his efforts into calming a bruised psyche all by himself.

Your work at this point is to offer the parents an opportunity to view their child through a different lens. Let us move from the parents of a Barbie-loving child to the single father of a 16-year-old high school boy whose strong wish is to wear dresses—at home, at the mall, at weekend social events. His father says, "When he's eighteen, he can do anything he wants. But as long as he lives in my house, that's never going to happen." By exploring the "for future reference" questions listed above, this father acknowledged he was not actually that worried about his son's safety. He just thought it was "plain wrong" and it therefore "wasn't going to occur on [his] watch." There would be no point in arguing with this father about whether it is right or wrong for high school boys to wear dresses. Instead, a more helpful intervention is to create a situation of *cognitive dissonance,* defined as a situation in which two competing thoughts, beliefs, or feelings are in contradiction with each other, the resolution of which involves relinquishing one set of beliefs in favor of the other, creating a disequilibrium where there previously was none.

In this case, the response to the father was as follows: "I certainly understand your position and, absolutely, until your son is eighteen, it is appropriate that he accepts the rules of your household. But I just wanted to share some other information with you. For a number of youth who are told they'll have to wait until later to express their gender the way they desire, they end up at risk for a lot of psychological turbulence—some get anxious and socially withdraw, some turn to drugs, some to alcohol, some become depressed, some stop doing their schoolwork, some start harming themselves, some even become suicidal.

I'm not saying this will happen to your son. I just think you should know the risk factors. You know your son best—do you think any of these could happen to him? Or maybe are already happening?" I say this not to be an alarmist, but to offer the parent information that we as mental health professionals know about gender expansive youth who are policed or monitored, in the same way we would expect a medical doctor to fully disclose the risks of withholding an intervention that could be beneficial to the child. With that information, the father is left with a dilemma: "My authority allows me to prohibit dress-wearing" versus "My prohibition of dress-wearing could put my son at risk. Maybe it already has."

Through ongoing family therapy, the hope is that the father will eventually understand the meaning that wearing dresses has for his son and begin to see life through his son's eyes. If the best interests of the child can be defined at its most minimal level—shielding the child from risk factors to better ensure well-being—this alone might be enough for the father to come to understand that prohibiting wearing dresses may be on the side of harm, not protection, thus exposing his son to the untoward psychological consequences of policing his gender. Instead, permission will be on the side of protection, sheltering his child from those very same consequences and even giving his son the opportunity to enhance his psychological well-being by being allowed to be the gender that is "me." If that can happen, the cognitive dissonance might be resolved and the form of parental support will shift from gender monitoring to gender acceptance.

Learning to De-center

A key factor in this therapeutic movement toward acceptance is developing the practice of de-centering, which is the act of suspending one's own wishes, needs, and desires and instead prioritizing the child's wishes, needs, and desires. In the vernacular, it means putting oneself in the other person's shoes to understand their experience. Parents often see their children through their own eyes, projecting their hopes and dreams onto them. When they have a child who is very different from them, they can feel off-kilter or disoriented or confused, not knowing how to secure a connection or make sense of this creature—this "mouse."

In *Far from the Tree,* Andrew Solomon (2012) explores in-depth the parental experience in these situations, including that of parents of transgender or gender expansive children. He first defines the concept of a *horizontal identity*—a child who will have much in common with others like themselves (e.g., a child who is deaf, a child who is a dwarf, a child who is transgender), but less in common with their own parents. In those situations he offers a guide: "To look deep into your child's eyes and see in him both yourself and something utterly strange, and then to develop a zealous attachment to every aspect of him, is to achieve parenthood's self-regarding, yet unselfish, abandon" (p. 6). That very abandon is the essence of de-centering, a gift to any child but a possible stretch for the parent who struggles to get beyond their own needs to attend to their child's.

Let us assume for a moment that a family is coming to you experiencing their own child as being profoundly, perhaps strangely, different from themselves in gender presentation. The parents themselves are *cisgender,* that is, they comfortably identify with the sex designated at birth, and have lived in accordance with that gender and its social guidelines. In other words, their gender is "on the same side" as their assigned sex, *cis* being the Latin term for "on the same side as" (Queer Dictionary, 2011). Then their child shows up, either challenging the social gender norms accompanying the sex they were designated at birth or protesting their mistaken gender identity because someone made an error and put the wrong label on their birth certificate. Maybe their child is transgender; maybe their child is simply *gender creative* or gender expansive. In either case, your therapeutic intervention is to invite the parent to de-center and instead step into their child's experience—learning to have a better understanding and ultimately embrace this child who may be so different from themselves in gender identity and/or expression, while allowing space for the difficult feelings that accompany that realization. As mentioned in the introduction, some parents, like the mother who sent me an e-mail about her four-year-old child, will be apprised of that difference very early on. Some may not bump up against this difference until much later, as was the case with the single father of the teenage son.

Learning to de-center may be complicated by unconsciously driven blind spots. Parents of young gender expansive children, working to grasp who their child is, will often say, "Truly, I don't know where this comes from. She's been saying she's a boy since she was eighteen months old, and will throw a tantrum any time the word *dress* is even mentioned in relation to her. She has stomped on every doll anyone ever gave her. We have three other children, and *none* of them are like that, and, honestly, we raised them all the same." In other words, their child "just comes to them"—they didn't create it, they didn't invite it, their child just showed up in their family that way, very early on. Yet other parents never see it coming. This can be because the child has so thoroughly masked their inner desires and sensibilities, even from their own consciousness, often as a result of implicit or explicit messages from the social environment. Alternatively or coincidentally, the parents, fearing the worst given their own gender stance, may operate from the tenet "Hear no evil, see no evil, speak no evil," which renders them unable to recognize the gender creative child standing before them.

Here is another example. A lesbian couple came to discuss their 16-year-old daughter, reporting that "all of a sudden, out of the blue," she was telling them she was confused about her gender and thought she might be a boy. The mothers were floored and deeply perplexed. In their eyes, and they were both in agreement, nothing about their child's history or recent experience in high school had given them any reason to suspect that gender was a point of confusion. I met with the parents alone first, and they both stated that their daughter was very willing to have an individual meeting with me, to which I agreed. When I went to the waiting room to greet this young woman, whom I had never met before, my eyes told me she wasn't there. Instead, *I* saw a high school boy waiting for an appointment, I presumed, with one of my suitemates. But there were no suitemates there that day. My own gender stereotypes had blinded me to the mothers' daughter who awaited her appointment with me, a daughter who in every way, by present cultural standards, presented as a male. Chastising myself for my own assumptions, I was even more struck by the mothers' obliviousness to the highly visible cross-gender presentation of their daughter, a presentation so extreme, not just in mode of dress and comportment, but in body presentation, that I went back to the parents to do a more thorough prenatal history to assess for in utero hormonal virilization and requested a hormonal screening. Fast-forward a year. With the parents' support, this young person is transitioning from female to male, which has been established over the course of a year's therapy, as his true and authentic gender self. Yet before the parents could offer that acceptance, they had to remove the blinders that initially prevented them from seeing a "she" who had been, for some time, in the process of becoming a "he."

To remove gender blinders so that we can actually see who this child is, both the families and the mental health professionals need to embark on the process of examining both our *gender ghosts* and our *gender angels*. I define gender ghosts as those internalized thoughts, attitudes, feelings, beliefs, and experiences that draw us toward culturally defined binary gender boxes and make us anxious when we or anyone else strays. Our gender ghosts may show themselves consciously or reside in our unconscious. Mine were evident when I doubted the youth in the waiting room was the person scheduled to see me because she did not fit my cultural stereotype of how a female should look. You could see the gender ghosts in her mothers when it took them by surprise that their daughter was thinking she might be a boy. Ironically, these two parents were freed from the stereotypes that girls must look "feminine" to identify as female, but they were trapped in their own belief system that, if freed from sexist stereotypes of "femininity," girls would always want to remain girls.

Then we have our gender angels, defined as the internalized thoughts, attitudes, feelings, beliefs, and experiences that allow us to be gender creative and live or accept others living outside the culturally defined binary gender boxes. Identical to our gender ghosts, our gender angels may show themselves consciously or reside in our unconscious (Ehrensaft, 2011). Relearning gender, challenging our own socialized beliefs about gender, and immersing ourselves in a new world where gender possibilities are expanded, accepted, and celebrated are the nutrients that feed our gender angels and allow them to come to the light of day. For some, this seems to happen rather seamlessly; for others, it is a struggle; and for still others, the process is nurtured by the presence of a gender creative child in their midst. So when Jenna, a mother of a six-year-old, sheds her own queasiness about boys in dresses and shifts her attitude to "people should get to wear whatever they want" after repeatedly witnessing her beloved son prancing with exuberance and delight each time he gets to wear his dress, we are witnessing the surfacing of Jenna's gender angels, a new gender expansive stance catalyzed by her love for her son.

When they do surface, we call on our gender angels to help us de-center from our own desires, hopes, and expectations and offer our child the freedom to weave their own gender web. We challenge our gender ghosts, who are whisperers, warning us to "stay put" in those binary boxes where gender is knowable, predictable, and acceptable. A good predictor of a child's gender health will be the ability of the adults in the child's life, both caretakers and professionals, to bring both the angels and ghosts into the light of day and allow the voices of the gender angels to triumph.

Acceptance = Protection

Every parent, no matter what their culture, will be assigned an identical set of child- rearing tasks: keeping their child safe and helping them grow into a thriving adult. The definitions of *safe* and *thriving* will indeed be subject to cultural variations. But if we home in on gender development as one of those areas where parents in any culture may find themselves balancing their child's safety, both physical and psychological, with their child's right to live an authentic gender life, parents now have another dilemma, not driven by competing thoughts, feelings, or beliefs, but by safety versus authenticity. It is not uncommon for a parent to express to a therapist in the course of the family work, "Look, it's okay for my daughter to wear her brother's clothes while we're here in Canada, but when we go back to India, where we are from, she'll be attacked in our village if she shows up looking like a boy."

If we use Maslow's (1943, 1968, 1970) hierarchy of need—from physiological to safety to love and belonging to esteem to self-actualization—physiological need and safety are indeed going to take precedence over self-actualization. That said, it would be reasonable for a parent to want to monitor their child's full gender creativity if its open expression is perceived as putting the child in danger. In those situations the work is to help the family communicate to the child that the reason for suppressing their gender creativity is not that there is anything wrong with *them,* but that the world we are living in has not yet learned to accept all the varieties of gender. So to the child we say, "Until that time we will keep your authentic gender protected from the people who still have to learn to accept you and who can sometimes say unkind things. But we will create a safe place where people do understand and where you can be your true self." I have written about this elsewhere as the consciously constructed *false gender self* (Ehrensaft, 2011), created by the child either to adapt to the environment or to keep the *true gender self*—that authentic sense of self as male, female, or other, dictated not by others, but by what the child knows from within—from harm. As long as the child has authorship over consciously constructing these false presentations of self rather than having them be unconsciously embedded and seemingly out of their control, and as long as they understand that the people who care for and love them are working to make that world more understanding, the child stands a better chance of preserving their self-confidence and positive gender self. So that little girl traveling to India may pack her boy clothes in her suitcase, to be worn freely in her hotel room, and go in "drag" in her girl clothes when visiting the relatives who don't know about such things. As long as *she* knows it's not because there is something wrong with her, but rather that the world hasn't changed enough yet, she can maintain her gender resilience. I have seen children as young as four years old begin to be able to maintain this differentiation and develop their own creative strategies to meet up with the "unfair" world while maintaining their positive sense of self. As those same children grow older, the parents will best put it in the youth's hands to make their own decisions about whether they want to conceal or express their gender authentic selves to the outside world, be it accepting or not.

There is, however, another consideration regarding the balance between safety and self-expression. Sometimes acceptance can be the strongest form of protection a family can offer (Malpas, 2011). Its protective function is in fortifying a child's gender resilience and ability to stand up to a world that may not be as accepting as the child might like. For example, Amy, a Japanese American single mom, explained to me that there was no way she was going to accept her daughter Lucy's insistent demand that she be allowed to change her name to

Luke and go to school as a "he." It was bad enough that Amy was criticized for raising her daughter without a father. Lucy attended a very conservative school where she would inevitably be rebuffed and spurned for being a "freak" if she returned after the summer as a boy. Amy had her own anticipatory grief about potentially losing the little girl whom she treasured so dearly. But she professed she herself could handle the transition; it was just that she would be "throwing her to the wolves" if she indulged Lucy's wishes. That is the moment to share with the parent the risk factors that go along with monitoring the child's gender to ensure their safety in the world—the potential for anxiety, depression, and self-harm when we ask a youth to suppress the expression of their gender. So we can ask: Will the suppression of Lucy's true gender self, if it is indeed male, actually protect her? Will it expose her to an unreality in which the person she knows herself to be is never mirrored back? Will she be forced to live in a fun house of distorted mirrors where every reflection is an affront to the personal gender web she has been spinning? Recall that Lucy is not just dipping her toe in the water of gender expansiveness. She is insistent that she is not Lucy but Luke.

Suppose Amy moved in another direction: working through her own issues about being a single mother, so that she could find pride rather than fear of aspersion from that, putting effort into her own and others' acceptance of the gender Lucy is discovering she is, rather than the gender others are telling her she has to be in order to feel safe? Those interventions may very well be the most protective ones Amy could introduce into Lucy's life, thus diminishing the possibilities of anxiety, depression, and/or self-harm (D'Augelli, Grossman, & Starks, 2006; Roberts, Rosario, Corliss, Koenen, & Austin, 2012), building gender resilience so that she can meet the challenges ahead, and promoting her own right to be the person she is.

To help hold the concept of acceptance as protection for families of a gender expansive child, I would like to offer the seven Ts gender formula. For the purposes of alliteration with a stream of Ts, I am using *transgender* in its broadest definition, which is any child who does not fit the traditional binary male-female gender model. You can think gender creative, gender expansive, gender nonconforming, or whatever term seems to best fit your understanding of the child who defies the cultural norms of gender and/or the sex assignment at birth. Here are the seven Ts:

- Transgender
- Transgression
- Transphobia

- Trauma
- Transcendence
- Transformation
- Transition

Strung together in an extraordinarily long sentence, the seven T's read like this: The *transgender* child who *transgresses* social gender norms may face *transphobia* and *trauma* within the family, helping the family's *transcendence* of that *transphobia* by providing parents and family members with *transformative* experiences as the child *transitions* from the gender connected to the sex designated at birth (and the expectations for that gender) to their authentic gender identity and/or expression.

If, on the one hand, transformation trumps transphobia, the child stands a good chance of emerging with a positive gender identity. If, on the other hand, transphobia and trauma run transformation into the ground, the child may be left with a bruised and battered psyche, a contorted self, and even a wish to self-destruct.

It Takes a Gender Creative Therapist

Parents have a child they were not expecting. It is not a mouse. It is one of Andrew Solomon's children with horizontal identities—different from the parents but like so many of the gender creative children who are popping up all across the globe. They turn to a mental health professional for guidance and support. The gender creative child fares best with a gender creative parent; the gender creative family fares best with a gender creative therapist. Coming full circle, our best teachers are the gender creative children themselves along with their parents.

I would like to finish with a true story of a father and son. Nils Pickert lives in Germany. He was relocating from Berlin to a small city, far more conservative in nature than Berlin. He had a five-year-old son who loved to wear dresses. What was he to do on the first day of school in his new community—let him wear the dress? Tell him to leave it at home? What he did was don a skirt himself and proudly walk his son to school, he in a red skirt, his son in a red dress. Nils's story went viral and he was hailed father of the year by Gawkers media. His son still gets teased about his skirts and dresses, but when that happens, he tells his classmates: "You don't dare to wear skirts and dresses because your dads don't dare to either" (Reynolds, 2012).

With acceptance as protection, Nils and his son teach us all what we need to know to promote our children's gender health: listen, reflect back what you see and hear, and let the gender angels reign.

REFERENCES

Besnier, N. (1994). Polynesian gender liminality through time and space. In G. Herdt (ed.), *Third sex, third gender: Beyond sexual dimorphism in culture and history* (pp. 285–328). New York: Zone.

Brill, S., & Pepper, R. (2008). *The transgender child.* San Francisco: Cleis Press.

California Legislature. (2012, September 30). California State Senate Bill no. 1172: Sexual orientation change efforts.

D'Augelli, A. R., Grossman, A. H., & Starks, M. T. (2006). Childhood gender atypicality, victimization, and PTSD among lesbian, gay, and bisexual youth. *Journal of Interpersonal Violence, 21*, 1462–1482.

de Vries, A. L., & Cohen-Kettenis, P. T. (2012). Clinical management of gender dysphoria in children and adolescents: The Dutch approach. *Journal of Homosexuality, 59* (3), 301–320.

Diamond, M. (2000). Sex and gender: Same or different? *Feminism & Psychology, 10,* 46–54.

Dimen, M. (2003). *Sexuality, intimacy, power.* Hillsdale, N.J.: Analytic Press.

Ehrensaft, D. (1997). *Spoiling childhood.* New York: Guilford Press.

Ehrensaft, D. (2011). *Gender born, gender made.* New York: Experiment.

Ehrensaft, D. (2012). From gender identity disorder to gender identity creativity: True gender self child therapy. *Journal of Homosexuality, 59* (3), 337–356.

Ehrensaft, D. (2014). From gender identity disorder to gender identity creativity: The liberation of gender-nonconforming children and youth. In E. J. Meyer & A. P. Sansfacon (eds.), *Supporting transgender & gender creative youth* (pp. 13–25). New York: Peter Lang.

Ehrensaft, D. (2016). *The gender creative child: Pathways for nurturing and supporting children who live outside gender boxes.* New York: Experiment.

Green, R. (1987). *The "sissy boy syndrome" and the development of homosexuality.* New Haven: Yale University Press.

Harris, A. (2005). *Gender as soft assembly.* Hillsdale, N.J.: Analytic Press.

Hidalgo, A., Ehrensaft, D., Tishelman, A. C., Clarke, L. F., Garofalo, R., Rosenthal, S. M., . . . & Olson, J. (2013). The gender affirmative model: What we know and what we aim to learn. *Human Development, 56,* 285–290.

Kohlberg, L. (1966). A cognitive-developmental analysis of children's sex-role concepts and attitudes. In E. E. Maccoby (ed.), *The development of sex differences* (pp. 82–173). Stanford: Stanford University Press.

Maccoby, E. E. & Jacklin, C. N. (1974). *The psychology of sex differences.* Stanford: Stanford University Press.

Malpas, J. (2011). Between pink and blue: A multi-dimensional family approach to gender nonconforming children and their families. *Family Process, 50* (4), 453–470.

Maslow, A. H. (1943). A theory of human motivation. *Psychological Review, 50* (4), 370–396.

Maslow, A. H. (1968). *Toward a psychology of being.* (2nd ed.). Princeton, N.J.: D. Van Nostrand.

Maslow, A. H. (1970). *Motivation and personality.* New York: Harper & Row.

New Jersey Assembly. (2013, August). Bill no. A3371. Protects minors by prohibiting attempts to change sexual orientation.

Pasterski, V., Gilligan, L., & Curtis, R. (2014). Traits of autism spectrum disorder in adults with gender dysphoria. *Archives of Sexual Behavior, 43* (2), 387–393. doi:1007/S10508-013-0154-5.

Queer Dictionary. (2011). S.v. "Cisgender" (adj.). http://queerdictionary.tumblr.com/post/92642 28131 /cisgender-adj.

Reddy, G., & Nanda, S. (2009). Hijras: An "alternative" sex/gender in India. In C. B. Brettell & C. F. Sargent (eds.), *Gender in cross-cultural perspective* (pp. 275–282). (5th ed.). Upper Saddle River, N.J.: Pearson/Prentice Hall.

Reynolds, E. (2012). German father wears women's clothing in show of solidarity with his cross-dressing five-year-old-son. *Daily Mail,* August 30, 2012. Retrieved from www. dailymail.co.uk/news/article-2195876/Nils-Pickert-German-father-wears-womens-clothing-solidarity-cross-dressing-year-old-son.html.

Roberts, A. L., Rosario, M., Corliss, H. L., Koenen, K. C., & Austin, S. B. (2012). Childhood gender nonconformity: A risk indicator for childhood abuse and posttraumatic stress in youth. *Pediatrics, 129* (3), 410–417.

Roscoe, W. (1993). *Changing ones: Third and fourth genders in native North America.* New York: St. Martin's Griffin.

Rosenthal, S. (2014). Approach to the patient: Transgender youth: Endocrine considerations. *Journal of Clinical Endocrinology Metabolism, 99* (12), 4379–4389. doi:10.1210/jc.2014 -1919.

Ryan, C. (2014, October 18). Personal communication.

Ryan, C., Russell, S. T., Huebner, D., Diaz, R., & Sanchez, J. (2010). Family acceptance in adolescence and the health of LGBT young adults. *Journal of Child and Adolescent Psychiatric Nursing, 23* (4), 205–213.

Solomon, A. (2012). *Far from the tree: Parents, children and the search for identity.* New York: Scribner.

Spack, N. P., Edwards-Leeper L., Feldman H. A., Leibowitz, S., Mandel, F., Diamond, D. A., & Vance, S. R. (2012). Children and adolescents with gender identity disorder referred to a pediatric medical center. *Pediatrics, 129* (3), 418–425.

Sue, D. W. (2010). *Microaggressions in everyday life: Race, gender, and sexual orientation.* New York: Wiley.

Tyson, P. (1982). A developmental line of gender identity, gender role, and choice of love object. *Journal of the American Psychoanalytic Association, 30,* 61–86.

White, E. B. (1945). *Stuart Little.* New York: Harper & Brothers.

Wood, H., Sasaki, S., Bradley, S. J., Singh, D., Fantus, S., Owen-Anderson, A., . . . & Zucker, K. J. (2013). Patterns of referral to a gender identity service for children and adolescents (1976–2011): Age, sex ratio, and sexual orientation. *Journal of Sex and Marital Therapy, 39* (1), 1–6.

Zucker, K. J., Wood, H., & VanderLaan, D. P. (2014). Models of psychopathology in children and adolescents with gender dysphoria. In B.P.C. Kreukels, T. D. Steensma, & A.L.C. de Vries (eds.), *Gender dysphoria and disorders of sex development: Progress in care and knowledge* (pp. 171–192). New York: Springer.

2

Helping Parents Face Their Fears

Irwin Krieger, LCSW

Parents base most of their child-rearing decisions on a mixture of personal experience, cultural norms, and common sense. But for those raising gender nonconforming children and transgender adolescents, these traditional sources do not provide much guidance. Most parents feel unprepared to help their child or teenager explore questions of gender identity.

Parents of prepubertal children who are strongly gender nonconforming or who verbally express a transgender identity have a wide range of responses (Coolhart, Baker, Farmer, Malaney, & Shipman, 2013; Riley, Sitharthan, Clemson, & Diamond, 2011). Many fear their child is confused and will be subject to harassment. Some worry that if they do not immediately go along with their child's wishes, they will risk harming their child. Similarly, parents of transgender adolescents may think their teen is misguided and fear a life fraught with danger. Others respond to their disclosure with a willingness to be helpful and become strong advocates. In rare cases, there are those who push more strongly for transition than their child does. Some of these parents are uncomfortable with their child's remaining in what they perceive to be a persistent state of uncertainty or having an androgynous presentation. Others may be worried about the kind of negative outcomes they have heard LGBT kids with rejecting families experience.

When parents grapple with a child's expression of transgender identity, a conflict may arise between the child's push for authentic self-expression and the parents' fears for their safety. Ideally, we want to help parents support their child's need for authenticity while also attending to their own valid parental concerns. As Diane Ehrensaft (2011) says, they "have to figure out how to balance the blossoming of their children's true gender self with the natural parental urge . . . to keep those children as safe as possible" (p. 102).

Lev, Arlene I., Gottlieb, Andrew R., *Families in Transition*
dx.doi.org/10.17312/harringtonparkpress/2019.04.fit.002
© 2019 by Harrington Park Press

Gender Nonconformance and Transgender Identity in the Family Context

How parents respond to a gender nonconforming child or a transgender adolescent has a profound effect on that young person's well-being, and the parents may need help adopting a more thoughtful, inquisitive, and compassionate stance. We know that LGBTQ (lesbian, gay, bisexual, transgender, questioning) children and adolescents who are rejected by their families have an elevated risk of low self-esteem, social isolation, depression, suicide, substance abuse, and HIV infection (D'Augelli, Grossman, & Starks, 2006; Roberts, Rosario, Corliss, Koenen, & Bryn Austin, 2012; Ryan, Huebner, Diaz, & Sanchez, 2009). Even incremental improvements in the family's response will increase the young person's self-esteem while decreasing the incidence and severity of these other problems (Ryan, Russell, Huebner, Diaz, & Sanchez, 2010; Travers et al., 2012). We must help parents examine their attitudes so they can potentially shift from a rejecting response to a supportive one. We can point out that, on the basis of the research, safety for their child requires a reduction in the negative messages they receive from parents, peers, school staff, and society at large. Efforts to change their overt and covert messages of rejection will have a tremendously positive influence on their child (Brill & Pepper, 2008; Ryan, 2009).

Parents need accurate information about gender identity to have a framework for understanding who their child is and what they may be disclosing. This includes understanding the concepts of *assigned sex, gender identity*, and *gender expression,* as well as the difference between gender identity and sexual orientation. They should also know that gender identity in children may change as they mature into adolescence (Crawford, 2003; de Vries et al., 2014; Drummond, Bradley, Peterson-Badali, & Zucker, 2008; Menvielle, Tuerk, & Perrin, 2005; Pleak, 2009; Steensma, Biemond, DeBoer, & Cohen-Kettenis, 2011; Steensma, McGuire, Kreukels, Beekman, & Cohen-Kettenis, 2013). Providing children with the greatest freedom of gender expression and the least amount of societal or familial disapproval allows them to develop an authentic sense of themselves, free from shame (Ehrensaft, 2012; Lev, 2004).

Gender identity is a child's inner sense of being male, female, neither, or both. Nonbinary gender terms such as *genderqueer* or *genderfluid* may be used by those who feel that neither "female" nor "male" accurately describes them. *Gender expression* encompasses how the child presents to others, on a spectrum of feminine to masculine, as these qualities are understood within a particular cultural context. This includes clothes, mannerisms, and grooming, as well as preferred toys, playmates, and activities. *Gender nonconforming children* are those whose gender identity and/or gender expression is not in accordance with societal and familial expectations that are based on the sex they were assigned at birth. They may or may not experience *gender dysphoria,* that is, discomfort, sadness, or distress because of this discordance. In gender-affirmative models, gender health is defined as "a child's opportunity to live in the gender that feels most real or comfortable to that child and to express that gender with freedom from restriction, aspersion, or rejection" (Hidalgo et al., 2013, p. 286).

For parents, it can be difficult to ascertain whether it is in the child's best interest to live freely in their affirmed gender, given that transgender identities are stigmatized in most communities (Riley et al., 2011). Parents can be guided by their child's insistence on making a *social transition*—living in the gender they identify with—and their continual distress about conforming to their assigned gender. In a survey of parents of gender variant children, the most important needs they identified were for correct information about gender identity, strategies for raising a gender variant child, and support from professionals and from other parents (Riley et al., 2011).

Adolescence is a time of identity exploration and integration (Erikson, 1968). For those who recognize that their gender identities and bodies don't match, being authentically themselves becomes of paramount importance. Their distress about the discordance between who they feel they are inside and who they appear to be on the outside increases. They struggle with disclosure, perhaps hinting about it at first. They may feel attracted to those of their same natal sex and disclose this to others. They may wonder if they are lesbian, gay, or bisexual, and publicly try out one of those identities first. Their parents' reactions to all of this will help them guess how well they will respond to disclosure of a transgender identity.

It is helpful to distinguish between adolescents who feel a strong discordance between gender identity and assigned sex and are therefore more likely to seek medical interventions, and those with nonbinary transgender identities, such as *genderqueer* and *genderfluid*. Not all transgender teens seek medical intervention. They have varied histories, self-concepts, and future intentions, which may also continue to evolve as they mature. A social transition can be an extremely useful step in gaining certainty about who they are. The individual finds out how they feel when they are viewed, addressed, and socially included in their affirmed gender, getting a lived sense of whether this is right for them. They discover the extent to which they may receive negative responses from others and whether they are prepared to handle these responses at this time. Parents often see that their child is more at ease, more confident, and happier during the social transition. This reassures them about moving ahead with a fuller gender transition. If there are significant negative responses from others, parents and educators have a responsibility to improve or change the social environment. If a social transition feels wrong to the teen (other than the problem of negative responses from others), further counseling and self-examination are needed.

A teenager who has begun to come out as transgender may be extremely impatient about making a transition. They may feel they have been suffering for years, forced to live in the wrong gender, and cannot fathom how difficult it may be for a parent to view a daughter as a son or a son as a daughter. We can help adolescents better understand that even the most loving, open-minded parent is likely to experience some discomfort and reluctance in accepting this. Even when parents express legitimate fears, teenagers may still feel rejected. Transgender teenagers often feel completely certain about their identity and have little or no fear of taking hormones or having surgery, while parents have tremendous anxieties and concerns. Most often, teens advocate for immediacy, whereas parents advocate for caution, which puts the two parties at odds. If both parent and child see you, the clinician, as an ally, they are more likely to accept your efforts to find common ground.

How Do I Know If My Child Is Really Transgender?

Parents may believe that their child's disclosure is a sign of confusion or a symptom of a psychiatric disorder. They may wonder if their child is just trying to get attention or upset them. With younger children, it is less certain that this budding sense of themselves will persist. But generally, teens who say they are transgender know who they are (Steensma et al., 2011). So it is important that parents learn as much as they can about transgender identities.

Once parents have a basic understanding, they can talk to their child about how their sense of gender developed over time, and how it continues to develop, keeping in mind that this can change as they move toward adolescence. Good questions to ask younger children: How long have you felt this way? How do you feel about your body? How do you feel about being grouped with the boys or the girls? Which group do you fit in with best? Who do you want to be when you grow up? Additional questions to ask adolescents: How did you fit in with girls and boys when you were younger? How do you feel about the changes in your body that come with puberty? How do you feel when people view you as male or female? Who have you talked to about this so far? How certain do you feel about your gender identity? (For a more extensive list of questions, see Coolhart et al., 2013.)

Parents whose teenager was gender nonconforming in childhood may find it easier to grasp that they identify as transgender in adolescence. On the basis of stereotypes that gay men are more feminine appearing than heterosexual men and that lesbians are more masculine appearing than heterosexual women, they may have wondered in the past if their child would turn out to be gay or lesbian because of their gender nonconforming behavior. Having considered that possibility, they may be more prepared for this new disclosure. But when a child fits in easily with peers of the same assigned sex and shows no sign of gender atypical behaviors or interests, they are more likely to think their child's disclosure is misguided. In the media and in memoirs (Andrews, 2014; Herthel & Jennings, 2014; Mock, 2014), early awareness and expression are usually part of the transgender narrative. Parents who are trying to educate themselves may therefore believe that gender discordance is always expressed in early childhood. This can lead them to doubt the veracity of their child's experience.

There are a number of approaches that may be helpful in this instance. One is to encourage the child to tell their parents about earlier times when they had a sense of not being in accordance with their assigned sex, or if they suppressed gender variant interests and behaviors in order to fit in, or engaged in them secretly. One trans female youth explained that she suppressed her female interests to get the approval of her older brother. Other children wished to be transformed into the other gender overnight, or imagined themselves becoming adults of the other gender. As the idea that transgender identity is an aspect of human diversity becomes more widely understood, fewer children may feel the need to hide these thoughts and feelings.

In some instances, teenagers do not have these earlier experiences to report. They may have gone through childhood unfazed about gender. One youth told me, "It was a little bit of a surprise when I first figured it out [at age 16], but there was always something that didn't feel right." Others have said they felt neither boy nor girl growing up, or they felt "genderless," but never really thought about it. For many, their dysphoria arose with the onset of puberty, coinciding with the strong emphasis on gendered social groups typical of middle school. This is when the tomboy, for example, is expected to give up her "masculine" interests and become just like other girls. It is helpful to explain to parents that puberty is a common time to become more consciously aware of identity in general, including gender identity (Grossman & D'Augelli, 2006). I let them know that in my practice, about 40% of the transgender adolescents I evaluated were gender conforming in their manner, behaviors, and expressed interests before puberty. By giving their child the benefit of the doubt and honoring the wish for a social transition, we can find out whether the child thrives in the new gender presentation, which will allow them to confirm, adjust, or reject it entirely.

Monique and Donald

Monique and Donald came to see me about their 13-year-old eighth grader, Daniel.[1] He had become depressed over the previous six months, moping around and not doing his homework or chores. Previously good-natured and cooperative, he was now irritable and sullen. His parents took him to a therapist, but he refused to speak. One night just before bedtime he told his parents, "I'm a girl." He would not elaborate at the time, nor would he in the days that followed. Daniel began dressing and acting more feminine at home and at school. Soon he was getting harassed at school and, as a result, began skipping some days. His parents contacted his former therapist, who referred them to me. When I met with Monique and Donald, they told me they had tried to be accepting of Daniel's feminine expression, saying it was "fine at home" but suggested he "tone it down" at school. Daniel told them he did not want to try to fit in as a boy. He asked to attend an arts high school that would probably be more accepting.

After meeting once with the parents, I met for a few sessions with Daniel alone. He was upset that they wanted him to be less feminine at school and felt misunderstood, even though he knew they were trying to be supportive. He had been feeling depressed ever since his voice started to change six months earlier. And despite having a male body, he felt female "inside." Becoming a man felt entirely wrong. After viewing YouTube videos about transgender teens, he wanted puberty blockers.

When I met alone with Daniel's parents, they expressed a great deal of skepticism. Though it was true he was less boyish than his two brothers and not interested in sports, he had not previously displayed any feminine attributes or interests. He was shy and had only a few friends, mostly boys who, like him, were not particularly interested in sports, either. He shared other pursuits with these friends, such as playing video games.

It seemed implausible to Donald and Monique that Daniel could be female,

---

1. I begin each family case using the child's birth name, pronouns, and accordingly gendered words, such as son. I change over to the child's affirmed name and pronouns toward the end of each story, somewhat in keeping with the timing of the social transition. This is often done earlier in telling a trans person's story to reflect that they were of their affirmed gender before they asserted it publicly. For these case presentations, I chose to use language that more closely tracks the parents' perspective on their child's transition.

as there were no earlier indications. It seemed "sudden" and therefore unreal. They wondered if he was confused about his gender because he was socially awkward and did not fit in with the more popular boys. Was he coping with his social difficulties by imagining he was a girl? Perhaps he believed that being female was an answer to his problems. They thought his sadness was caused by loneliness, not gender discordance.

I met again with the parents to talk about the components of transgender identity so they would have a framework for understanding what Daniel would be discussing when we met together. These included one's sense of self as male, female, neither, or both; feelings of belonging with boys or girls; discomfort with gendered aspects of one's anatomy; and a preference for being viewed as a gender other than the one that coincides with assigned sex. I informed them that many transgender individuals realize their gender discordance at the onset of puberty, so Daniel's recent awareness of this was not unusual.

I explained the importance of honoring their child's request for a different gender expression, name, and pronoun. This would help Daniel feel supported and allow him to see if living in the affirmed gender identity felt right. We talked about the hurtful aspect of suggesting he "tone it down" at school. We discussed their appropriate concern for his safety with a focus on minimizing the dangers at his current school or finding a more accepting academic environment, rather than expecting him to continue to suppress himself in order to avoid harassment. I spoke about the psychological risks to any child who is forced to alter their authentic self-expression.

The next step was for all of us to meet together so Daniel could more fully explain his feelings. For some families, these discussions can happen at home. More often there has been a breakdown in communication. Children may refuse to speak about this further for a number of reasons: they may be embarrassed; they may have great difficulty tolerating their parents' discomfort; or they may be offended by a parent's dismissive response and not be willing to give them another chance. Since parents of children who were previously gender conforming are not expecting to hear this news, their first reaction is often one of shock or doubt. Children may interpret this as hostile. In recent years, I have been moved when hearing about some parents initially offering, "How can I help?" Even when parents and kids get off to such an affirming start, it can be helpful to have one or more family sessions to provide parents with a deeper understanding of their child's gender identity, strategize about specific transition steps such as disclosure to other family members, and address any unexpected challenges that arise.

I usually structure the first of these by interviewing the child in the presence of the parents to elicit the child's thoughts and feelings. This includes any recollection of earlier experiences of gender awareness or expression. I base my questioning on the information I have already gleaned from our previous individual sessions. When necessary, I clarify any language that is imprecise or may be unfamiliar to the parents. Once I think they have a good understanding of their child's experience, we move on to discussing the parents' fears, doubts, and other concerns. I am careful to address statements or questions that contain dismissive or derogatory language, and to help them reframe their questions to convey curiosity rather than judgment. Family sessions are generally interspersed with separate meetings for reflection on what was discussed and preparation for what will be discussed. This is a point at which parents may raise issues such as sullenness, school refusal, social withdrawal, or academic downturns. As they respond with more understanding and respect, the child is more likely to take these concerns seriously. These topics then become a part of our ongoing dialogue. In most cases, when children feel more validated, some or all of these other symptoms improve spontaneously.

Daniel's parents were willing to listen with an open mind, continuing to ask questions at home in a spirit that Daniel recognized as curious, respectful, and supportive. Given this shift in their attitude, he was, in turn, respectful of their doubts. Adamant about trying out a female identity, and with the school unable to provide a safe enough environment, they agreed to enroll him in the arts school, where Daniel could finally be Danielle. They agreed to meet with an endocrinologist to learn more about puberty blockers and the effect those would have at this stage.

Danielle's parents were comforted that social transition and puberty blockers were both reversible. They were pleased to see how happy and engaged she was at her new school and at home. She maintained some of her friendships from her old school and made new friends at the arts academy. Her parents told me they could see that Danielle was happier as a girl and more at ease socially. While they continued to feel challenged, the benefits of the social transition confirmed for them that Danielle was, in fact, transgender.

Will My Child Be the Target of Bullying and Violence?

Gender nonconforming children are often bullied by peers and sometimes by adults. By the time teenagers come out to their parents, many, if not most, have already experienced some harassment (Menvielle & Hill, 2010; Toomey, Ryan, Diaz, Card, & Russell, 2010). Parents expect it will worsen if their child discloses at school that he is now a girl or she is now a boy. Refusing to allow a child or teen to live authentically, however, can be extremely harmful to their mental health, self-esteem, and social functioning (Brill & Pepper, 2008; Kuvalanka, Weiner, & Mahan, 2014; Ryan, 2009). Parents have to carefully weigh the consequences of *not* allowing their child to make a transition. Ultimately it is the responsibility of the school to create a safe environment and the responsibility of parents to ensure that one is available.

Remarkably, many children and adolescents are quite accepting of those who make a transition. I have worked with a large number of transgender teens, most of whom attend public and private high schools in Connecticut. They report that whatever harassment they experienced, if any, came from a small number of peers and diminished over time. Those whose nonconformance had previously elicited harassment were generally more accepted by peers *after* the social transition. My impression is that students exude more confidence once they begin transitioning and, in turn, most of their peers respond positively. This is especially the case in schools that have already addressed diversity and developed antibullying practices and policies.

On the basis of my experience, I am able to reassure parents that their child's school environment is likely to be more accepting than they imagine. Young children will take their cues from how the classroom teacher responds. Parents must advocate in advance to ensure that staff members are adequately trained. This includes being able to respond appropriately to other parents who have questions and concerns about the effect a classmate's transition might have on their own child.

Most adolescents have already come out to at least a few friends, with a positive response, before telling their parents. If they do not feel safe coming out at school, or if they experience conflict that the school is unable to mediate, home schooling or a small alternative setting is usually the best option. One of the reasons to get parents "on board" before their child socially transitions is so they can advocate for a safe academic environment.

Tragic incidents in which transgender adolescents are attacked unfortunately do occur (Minter, 2012). But "withholding puberty suppression and subsequent feminizing or masculinizing hormone therapy is not a nèutral option" (Coleman et al., 2012, p. 178). As has been shown, teenagers who are *not* allowed to transition are at increased risk of depression, substance abuse, self-harm, or suicide ideation (Andrews, 2014; Hidalgo et al., 2013; Lev, 2004; Riley et al., 2011; Ryan et al., 2010). We must establish as much safety as possible without resorting to repression of the teen's identity or delays that are unmanageable.

Will My Child Have an Unhappy Life?

Parents may fear that their child will have a bleak future: no friends, no job, no love relationships. It is helpful for them to hear personal narratives about those who have thrived, to read memoirs, and to connect with others through support groups. It is also important to point out that repression of one's gender identity in order to gain access to jobs or relationships can have dire emotional consequences.

Invite parents to think about times in their own lives when they faced a struggle between authenticity and safety. Was there a moment when they chose to honor and disclose something about themselves that they believed others would criticize or condemn? Did they ever feel they had to keep an important part of themselves secret to gain approval from peers or family? On reflection, most parents will agree that it is better to be true to oneself and worry less about the opinions of others. In the words of Eleanor Roosevelt (1960), "Courage is more exhilarating than fear and in the long run it is easier" (p. 41).

Parents know that fitting in is an especially tough challenge for adolescents. It is important for parents to be supportive while their teens grapple with issues of authenticity, integrity, and societal disapproval. This is true even when they themselves are struggling with feelings of shame because of who their child is. Once parents address their own discomfort, they are better able to focus on helping their family move through this challenging time, paying attention to both authenticity and safety.

Jen and Martin

Since Becky had always been a tomboy, her parents, Jen and Martin, thought she might turn out to be gay. Though she dated a boy in middle school, she came out as a lesbian in ninth grade, and Martin and Jen were supportive. When she was 17 and a junior in high school, she told her parents she was transgender and wanted to start taking male hormones. Martin and Jen panicked. Becky could see they were upset and was angry about that, expecting them to respond the same way they had to her news about dating girls. Things were tense at home from the time of her disclosure until they came to meet with me. During the first session, they were frustrated and angry with each other.

When I met alone with Becky, she told me she never fit in with girls. As a child she preferred to play with her older brother and his friends, daydreaming about growing up to be a man and marrying a woman. In middle school, she tried dressing a little more feminine to see what that was like. Over the past two years she had been increasingly uncomfortable with having a female body and presenting as female. Identifying as a lesbian was the closest fit she could find at the time to understand her identity. She started dating a girl and joined the Gay Straight Alliance at school, hoping to feel more at ease in that group. It was there that she first heard the word *transgender*. Becky started dressing more androgynously and asked some friends to call her "Ron" instead of Becky. Friends were quietly supportive. It did not seem like a big deal to any of them, which was why she was so surprised when her parents were upset.

Martin and Jen told me Becky's disclosure was overwhelming. It was confusing to try to think of her as a boy. They wondered, "Why would *she* would want to be a *he*?" Did their attention to her brother's achievements cause Becky to lack confidence as a girl? Had she been influenced by a senior at her high school who had transitioned earlier that year? Was she trying to claim a unique identity and feel special? Meeting with them alone, I shared information about the ways kids arrive at an understanding of gender identity. For most children, this starts with a feeling that something is different, followed by an exploration of gender identity or gender expression. This can include searching for information online, watching YouTube videos of young people in transition, talking to friends, or trying out differently gendered clothing or grooming. For younger children, it may begin with playing dress-up, trying out gender roles in fantasy play, or affiliating strongly with girls or boys. In each instance, they get a greater sense of clarity about whether their birth-assigned gender is right for them. Most teens have a strong sense of certainty before telling their parents. Reviewing Becky's history together, I felt I could assure them that this was neither a response to something they had done nor an effort to feel special or act out.

When we all met together, Martin and Jen were angry at Becky for "forcing this on us." They worried aloud about how neighbors, extended family, and other parents would react. Becky felt hurt that they seemed most concerned about how this news affected them.

When parents react with extreme anger, or when they dwell on how they might be judged by others, or when they harshly and vindictively express certainty that their child will have a bleak life if this persists, it's apparent that shame is playing a strong part in their response. These parents may be the hardest to reach, and because of my acceptance of gender diversity, they tend to see me as taking sides. As a result, some have terminated treatment. Others have refused to allow a full social transition or any medical interventions, but they have continued the therapy to help protect their child from despair and self-harm.

But when parents are amenable to talking about their shame, they can often find a way to free themselves of it and focus instead on their child's needs: "Pointing out that the child is not hurting anyone and that the parents' discomfort comes from conscious or unconscious prejudice can be very important" (Menvielle, Tuerk, & Perrin, 2005, p. 45). Examining societal, cultural, and religious beliefs that underlie the feeling that the child's identity or expression is wrong, sick, or sinful may help alleviate some of the shame and guilt. Recalling how they felt if they were ever shamed by others when they were younger and what that was like encourages parents to treat their child more empathically. Asking parents what they cherish, value, and admire about their child reminds them that gender is only small part of who their child is. Most of the attributes they love are independent of gender identity. Sharing the view that gender variance is a natural part of human diversity helps parents become more accepting. I encourage them to face significant others who they think will disparage them for having a transgender child. Doing this externalizes the source of the shame and helps parents tap into their protective parental instincts, should they receive a hurtful response. Some who are initially angry and ashamed eventually become advocates and celebrate uniqueness, especially after they see their child is happier once they are free to be themselves.

At the next session, when I met only with Jen and Martin, they were able to express their anger, guilt, and shame. They could see that these feelings were rooted in prejudice and remembered how they felt when *they* had been criticized harshly by others. In thinking about what their child was going through, they affirmed the importance of being true to oneself, even if others don't approve. They admired Ron for his determination and courage, even though his intent to transition made them uncomfortable; they remembered how proud they had been in the past that he was self-confident and did not "follow the crowd." Thinking about those qualities placed his transition in a new light.

They agreed to continue discussing their feelings at home, as a couple. During the next session, we explored their fears for their child's safety, as well as the harm that could come from "not allowing Ron to be Ron." They shared their concern that, in the future, Ron might regret his decision to transition, a concern that even the most supportive parents have. In the next family session, I asked questions to help Ron describe his gender identity development for his parents and express his feelings about the possibility of continuing life as female. Jen and Martin were able to see that Ron's feelings were genuine and had persisted over time. They could sense his distress and his need for their help and support to feel fully himself. They saw clearly that Ron was not trying to hurt or embarrass *them*.

Will Our Child Be Sorry Later On If We Let Them Transition Now?

There are many important questions for parents and clinicians to consider when contemplating a social transition for a prepubescent child. Disagreement among the experts only complicates the issue (Drescher & Pula, 2014). Pertinent questions remain: Can we determine which children will persist in their affirmed gender identity? How important is a social transition to a child's emotional well-being? How harmful will negative responses be to a child who makes a social transition? Will reverting to birth-assigned gender be harmful for those who choose to do so? Parents may feel caught between "the fear of being too accepting and therefore exposing their child to danger . . . and the fear of damaging their child's personality by not allowing them full liberty to express themselves" (Malpas, 2011, p. 466). The child's certainty about their gender identity and their distress about not being able to transition are important factors that guide parents and clinicians in these decisions (Ehrensaft, 2012).

For adolescents, more data are available. Research shows that 16-year-olds who have felt certain for a number of years that they are transgender will sustain this into adulthood (Reed, Cohen-Kettinis, Reed, & Spack, 2008). There is also a very low rate of regret among adults who have made a full medical transition (DeCuypere & Vercruysse, 2009). For teenagers under 16, the only intervention recommended by the Endocrine Society Guidelines is the administration of puberty-blocking hormones (Hembree et al., 2017). Teens on puberty blockers experience no further masculinization or feminization of their bodies. They retain the option of subsequently going through puberty in accordance with their innate biology if they discover that puberty congruent with their birth-assigned sex is right for them. If the treatment is terminated, a delayed but otherwise normal puberty will occur. For those who continue to identify as transgender, a recent study shows that puberty blockers followed by cross-sex hormone treatment leads to improved psychological functioning (de Vries et al., 2014).

Medical professionals with extensive experience treating transgender youth are now endorsing cross-sex hormone treatment for adolescents younger than 16 who have persisted in their affirmed gender identity (Olson, Forbes, & Belzer, 2011). Earlier treatment with cross-sex hormones allows the teen to experience puberty at an age more congruent with that of their peers.

Parents will rely in part on a gender identity evaluation by an experienced mental health clinician to help determine the appropriateness of treatment with puberty blockers and/or cross-sex hormones. A central part of the evaluation is to assess how long gender variant feelings have persisted, including the time before they were openly expressed. Other areas of the assessment include past and present comfort with masculine and/or feminine gender expression; feelings about primary sex characteristics and existing or impending secondary sex characteristics; and preferences in being regarded by others as male, female, neither, or both. A social transition will give the young person, parents, and clinician much more information about their gender identity as well as their readiness for hormone treatment. Initiation of the social transition can be stressful, especially if there is obvious hostility from others. But over time, parents can expect to see an increase in emotional well-being if the social transition is right for their child (Ehrensaft, 2012).

Does the Therapist Have a Preset Agenda?

Parents may fear that the clinician is starting out with the assumption that the best outcome will be a gender transition. It is essential to let parents know that you understand their fears and to assure them that the goal is to find out what is best for their child. This may help them move past their mistrust and toward a more collaborative relationship. Let parents know that you do not have an agenda, and that the goal of an evaluation is to make recommendations that are based on their child's individual needs. Tell them if there have been cases in your practice when an evaluation led to an outcome that did not include social transition or medical intervention. These may include realization of a nonbinary gender identity, such as *genderqueer* or *genderfluid*, or a non–transgender identity, also referred to as being *cisgender*. This clarifies for parents that your goals are (1) to gain a full understanding of their child, and (2) to help them move forward in the child's best interest.

Do Kids Who Feel Different Really Need to Transition?

Parents may wonder why their child would feel a need to transition at all. Many say, "In this day and age, girls and boys have the same opportunities." But being transgender is not a way to gain access to certain activities or jobs or relationships. Rather, there are three core issues at stake for those seeking transition: (1) the sex they were assigned at birth feels wrong; (2) they have a strong need to be viewed by others in accordance with the gender they feel inside; and (3) they are deeply uncomfortable with the gendered aspects of their bodies. These ideas may be difficult for parents to grasp when the concepts are foreign to them.

I am now treating more adolescents and young adults who identify with nonbinary identities, such as *genderqueer*. Parents may have a hard time understanding their teen's comfort with or need for an androgynous presentation, their rejection of the idea that everyone is either male or female, their choice of a gender-neutral name and/or pronouns, and their consideration of medical interventions *without* first making a full social transition.

For those whose child would like to initiate a social and/or medical transition, the role of the clinician is to (1) gain a full understanding of the child's gender identity and their related needs; (2) help parents understand transgender identities in general and their child's in particular; (3) discuss the pros and cons of the desired transition steps; and (4) outline and follow through on a process that may include disclosures to significant others, meeting other gender variant children and their parents, trying out comfortable gender presentations on a limited or a full-time basis, and eventually considering any medical interventions requested by the child.

Is It My Fault?

Many parents worry that they caused their child to be transgender (Menvielle, Tuerk, & Perrin, 2005). If they had kept their son from playing with dolls and encouraged more rough-and-tumble activities, would things have turned out differently? If they had been less enthusiastic about their daughter being such a tomboy and had steered her toward more stereotypically feminine activities, would she have grown up feeling more like a girl? Did they influence her subconsciously because they had wanted a son after already having two daughters? Did this happen because a single mom didn't make sure there were adult men in her son's life after his father left?

It is helpful to let parents know it is unlikely they did anything to cause their child to be transgender. Most experts postulate that transgender identities have multifactorial causes (Diamond, 2006; Hidalgo et al., 2013). Research exploring a genetic basis, or hypothesizing that prenatal hormonal changes lead to discordance between assigned sex and gender identity, has been inconclusive (Erickson-Schroth, 2013). For Zucker, Wood, Singh, and Bradley (2012), biological determinants "are conceptualized as possible predisposing factors for the expression of a particular gender identity phenotype," while "psychosocial factors, social cognition, associated psychopathology, and psychodynamic mechanisms . . . can be conceptualized as predisposing, precipitating or perpetuating factors" (p. 375). Hidalgo and colleagues (2013) suggest that the child's gender identity is "informed by a complex interplay of cultural, social, geographic, and interpersonal factors. . . . Those whose behaviors (and/or dysphoria) 'persist' do so even while vulnerable to facing considerable isolation and disdain from family, peers and others. . . . This suggests a strong constitutional component for gender nonconforming children, albeit one never exempt from environmental forces" (p. 288). Since there is no evidence that any one thing leads to a transgender identity, it is unreasonable and unhelpful for parents to hold themselves responsible for this outcome.

Parents do, however, have a strong effect on their children's self-esteem, social adjustment, and emotional well-being (Malpas, 2011). It is important to love and accept children as they are (Menvielle et al., 2005). Many realize that in the past they criticized or shamed their child for behaviors they personally found embarrassing. Generally this was done out of fear, ignorance, or both. Equipped with new understanding, parents have a chance to offer a corrective emotional experience, even though the child's intentions and behaviors may still make them uncomfortable (Crawford, 2003). Research shows that strong parental support leads to higher self-esteem and improved mental health. Anything less may have a deleterious effect (Travers et al., 2012).

What If This Is Too Difficult for Me?

One of the tasks in counseling parents is to help them identify and address the sources of their discomfort. In addition to fears and concerns they have for their child, they may experience a range of highly charged emotions. Most parents do not know anyone else who is transgender, and they may view being transgender as sick, immoral, or perverted. Offering information about gender diversity is an important part of the clinician's role. It is helpful to have this discussion without the child present so parents can speak more freely than they might otherwise. Once they have established a degree of comfort with the notion of transgender identity and acquired some insight about their reactions, they might want to disclose to their child their understanding of their own internal struggles (Coolhart et al., 2013). Since most parents ultimately want what is best for their children, the role of the therapist is to help parents put aside feelings that are based on ignorance and prejudice and focus on the more important questions of authenticity and safety.

Parents also worry about what friends, colleagues, neighbors, and extended family members might think. How will others react? Will they blame them? Menvielle and Tuerk (2002) found that parents "experience secondary stigmatization that can result in isolation and feelings of shame" (p. 1010). Sharing their feelings with a few open-minded family members or friends or with other parents of gender diverse children can help diminish their isolation and shame over time.

I advise them to inform only a few close friends or family members initially. Once a decision has been made for a social transition, parents can consider various options for informing others, presenting this new information in a positive, affirming light. It is best to say that their child has come to understand something essential about their identity and request that others respond respectfully. Parents may want to acknowledge their own initial discomfort and say how they have come to be supportive, especially since seeing their child is much happier now. When a child makes a social transition, it can be a life-changing journey for the parents as well.

How Can I Cope with Losing My Son or Daughter?

When parents face the possibility that a child is transgender, many experience a sense of loss. Ideas about the differences between the sexes deeply affect our views. Parent-child relationships incorporate notions of what it means to have a son or a daughter. When finding out that a child will be changing in outward appearance to conform to who they feel they are inside, it may seem that someone they know is being replaced by someone they don't.

It is important to help parents understand that this feeling is common (Menvielle et al., 2005; Vanderburgh, 2009). They will need time to accept the loss. For those who are immersed in sadness, it is helpful to provide time for them to speak at length. Grieving with others who share or at least understand what they are feeling can help the healing process. Support groups (Malpas, 2011; Menvielle & Tuerk, 2002), regional conferences, and online listservs can all be helpful.

Some may feel it is important to disclose to their child how difficult this transition has been for them. This must be done thoughtfully and sensitively and not in a way that is burdensome. In response to expressions of loss, children generally assure their parents that they are simply becoming more of who they really are—inside and out—not a different person altogether. This is usually helpful to hear and may be easier to grasp if their child has been gender nonconforming all along. If the child is happier as a result, most parents will feel their sadness diminish. As social transition advances, they create a new gendered understanding of their child to replace the one they feel they have lost, simultaneously creating a broader understanding of gender and, in best case scenarios, a more in-depth understanding of themselves.

The Importance of Additional Supports

Just as children and adolescents need support from their peers, parents benefit from speaking to other parents. Group meetings held in their area or online and conferences in various parts of the country can be tremendously helpful. Parents can encourage their children to keep in touch with transgender peers and provide opportunities for them to spend time together, even if this makes the parents a little uneasy. Seeing their child happily engaged may help them feel more comfortable, just as seeing that their child is happier after coming out helps them acknowledge that their identity is authentic. Meeting the parents of transgender friends can be an additional support.

Most families begin this process in conflict: children and adolescents desire a speedy transition to a life of full authenticity, whereas parents worry about safety and need time to adjust. By offering support to the parents as well as the child, you can help the family shift over time to a collaborative approach (Malpas, 2011) that takes into account all their needs and concerns. Clear information and improved communication lead to a shared understanding of who the child is and how best to move forward.

REFERENCES

Andrews, A. (2014). *Some assembly required: The not-so-secret life of a transgender teen.* New York: Simon & Schuster.

Brill, S., & Pepper, R. (2008). *The transgender child.* San Francisco: Cleis Press.

Coleman, E., Bockting, W., Botzer, M., Cohen-Kettenis, P., DeCuypere, G., Feldman, J., . . . & Zucker, K. (2012). Standards of Care for the health of transsexual, transgender, and gender-non-conforming people, Version 7. *International Journal of Transgenderism, 13* (4), 165–232.

Coolhart, D., Baker, A., Farmer, S., Malaney, M., & Shipman, D. (2013). Therapy with transsexual youth and their families: A clinical tool for assessing youth's readiness for gender transition. *Journal of Marital and Family Therapy, 39* (2), 223–243.

Crawford, N. (2003). Understanding children's atypical gender behavior: A model support group helps parents learn to accept and affirm their gender-variant children. *Monitor on Psychology, 34* (8), 40–42.

D'Augelli, A. R., Grossman, A. H., & Starks, M. T. (2006). Childhood gender atypicality, victimization, and PTSD among lesbian, gay, and bisexual youth. *Journal of Interpersonal Violence, 21,* 1462–1482.

DeCuypere, G., & Vercruysse, H., Jr. (2009). Eligibility and readiness for sex reassignment surgery: Recommendations for revision of the WPATH standards of care. *International Journal of Transgenderism, 11* (3), 194–205.

de Vries, A.L.C., McGuire, J. K., Steensma, T. D., Wagenaar, E.C.F., Doreleijers, T.A.H., & Cohen-Kettenis, P. T. (2014). Young adult psychological outcome after puberty suppression and gender reassignment. *Pediatrics, 134* (4), 696–704.

Diamond, M. (2006). Biased-interaction theory of psychosexual development: "How does one know if one is male or female?" *Sex Roles, 55* (9–10), 589–600.

Drescher, J., & Pula, J. (2014). Ethical issues raised by the treatment of gender-variant prepu-bescent children. *Hastings Center Report, 44* (s4), s17–s22.

Drummond, K. D., Bradley, S. J., Peterson-Badali, M., & Zucker, K. J. (2008). A follow-up study of girls with gender identity disorder. *Developmental Psychology, 44* (1), 34–45.

Ehrensaft, D. (2011). *Gender born, gender made: Raising healthy gender-nonconforming children.* New York: Experiment.

Ehrensaft, D. (2012). From gender identity disorder to gender identity creativity: True gender self child therapy. *Journal of Homosexuality, 59* (3), 337–356.

Erickson-Schroth, L. (2013). Update on the biology of transgender identity. *Journal of Gay & Lesbian Mental Health, 17* (2), 150–174.

Erikson, E. (1968). *Identity, youth and crisis.* New York: W. W. Norton.

Grossman, A. H., & D'Augelli, A. R. (2006). Transgender youth: Invisible and vulnerable. *Journal of Homosexuality, 51* (1), 111–128.

Hembree, W. C., Cohen-Kettenis, P. T., Gooren, L. J., Hannema, S. E., Meyer, W. J., III, Hassan Murad, M., . . . & T'Sjoen, G. G. (2017). Endocrine treatment of gender-dysphoric/gender-incongruent persons: An endocrine society clinical practice guideline. *Journal of Clinical Endocrinology & Metabolism, 102* (11), 3869–3903.

Herthel, J., & Jennings, J. (2014). *I am Jazz.* New York: Dial Books for Young Readers.

Hidalgo, M., Ehrensaft, D., Tishelman, A., Clark, L. F., Garofalo, R., Rosenthal, S. M., & Olson, J. (2013). The gender affirmative model: What we know and what we aim to learn. *Human Development, 56* (5), 285–290.

Kuvalanka, K. A., Weiner, J. L., & Mahan, D. (2014). Child, family and community transformations: Findings from interviews with mothers of transgender girls. *Journal of GLBT Family Studies, 10* (4), 354–379.

Lev, A. I. (2004). *Transgender emergence: Therapeutic guidelines for working with gender-variant people and their families.* Binghamton, N.Y.: Haworth Press.

Malpas, J. (2011). Between pink and blue: A multi-dimensional family approach to gender non-conforming children and their families. *Family Process, 50* (4), 453–470.

Menvielle, E. J., & Hill, D. B. (2010). An affirmative intervention for families with gender-variant children: A process evaluation. *Journal of Gay & Lesbian Mental Health, 15* (1), 94–123.

Menvielle, E. J., & Tuerk, C. (2002). A support group for parents of gender-nonconforming boys. *Journal of the American Academy of Child & Adolescent Psychiatry, 41* (8), 1010–1013.

Menvielle, E. J., Tuerk, C., & Perrin, E. C. (2005). To the beat of a different drummer: The gender-variant child. *Contemporary Pediatrics, 22* (12), 38–46.

Minter, S. P. (2012). Supporting transgender children: New legal, social, and medical approaches. *Journal of Homosexuality, 59* (3), 422–433.

Mock, J. (2014). *Redefining realness: My path to womanhood, identity, love & so much more.* New York: Atria Books.

Olson, J., Forbes, C., & Belzer, M. (2011). Management of the transgender adolescent. *Archives of Pediatric Adolescent Medicine, 165* (2), 171–176.

Pleak, R. (2009). Hormones, identities, and cultures: Clinical issues in transgender youth; Formation of transgender identities in adolescence. *Journal of Gay and Lesbian Mental Health, 13* (4), 282–291.

Reed, B. W., Cohen-Kettinis, P. T., Reed, T., & Spack, N. (2008). Medical care for gender variant young people: Dealing with the practical problems. *Sexologies, 17* (4), 258–264.

Riley, E. A., Sitharthan, G., Clemson, L., & Diamond, M. (2011). The needs of gender-variant children and their parents: A parent survey. *International Journal of Sexual Health, 23* (3), 181–195.

Roberts, A. L., Rosario, M., Corliss, H. L., Koenen, K. C., & Bryn Austin, S. (2012). Childhood gender nonconformity: A risk indicator for childhood abuse and posttraumatic stress in youth. *Pediatrics, 129* (3), 410–417.

Roosevelt, E. (1960). *You learn by living.* Philadelphia: Westminster Press.

Ryan, C. (2009). *Supportive families, healthy children: Helping families with lesbian, gay, bisexual and transgender children.* San Francisco: Family Acceptance Project.

Ryan, C., Huebner, D., Diaz, R., & Sanchez, J. (2009). Family rejection as a predictor of negative outcomes in white and Latino lesbian, gay and bisexual young adults. *Pediatrics, 123* (1), 346–352.

Ryan, C., Russell, S. T., Huebner, D., Diaz, R., & Sanchez, J. (2010). Family acceptance in adolescence and the health of LGBT young adults. *Journal of Child and Adolescent Psychiatric Nursing, 23* (4), 205–213.

Steensma, T. D., Biemond, R., DeBoer, F., & Cohen-Kettenis, P. T. (2011). Desisting and persisting gender dysphoria after childhood: A qualitative follow-up study. *Clinical Child Psychology and Psychiatry, 16* (4), 499–516.

Steensma, T. D., McGuire, J. K., Kreukels, B. P. C., Beekman, A. J., & Cohen-Kettenis, P. T. (2013). Factors associated with desistence and persistence of childhood gender dysphoria: A quantitative follow-up study. *Journal of the American Academy of Child and Adolescent Psychiatry, 52* (6), 582–590.

Toomey, R. B., Ryan, C., Diaz, R. M., Card, N. A., & Russell, S. T. (2010). Gender-nonconforming lesbian, gay, bisexual, and transgender youth: School victimization and young adult psychosocial adjustment. *Developmental Psychology, 46* (6), 1580–1589.

Travers, R., Bauer, G., Pyne, J., Bradley, K., Gale, L., & Papadimitriou, M. (2012). *Impacts of strong parental support for trans youth: A report prepared for Children's Aid Society of Toronto and Delisle Youth Services.* Retrieved on April 25, 2014, from http://transpulseproject.ca/wp-content/uploads/2012/10/Impacts-of-Strong-Parental-Support-for-Trans-Youth-vFINAL.pdf.

Vanderburgh, R. (2009). Appropriate therapeutic care for families with pre-pubescent transgender/gender-dissonant children. *Child and Adolescent Social Work, 26* (2), 135–154.

Zucker, K., Wood, H., Singh, D., & Bradley, S. (2012). A developmental, biopsychosocial model for the treatment of children with gender identity disorder. *Journal of Homosexuality, 59* (3), 369–397.

3

On the (L)edge of Transition: The Reyes Family

Lisette Lahana, LCSW

"Don't jump!" the security guard yelled from the other side of the school rooftop. Dakila Reyes, a slim, 14-year-old Filipina teen, was teetering on the ledge, mascara tears gathering at the corners of her eyes, her long hair slick with sweat. She was sick of the teacher who gave her nasty looks and blamed her for a fight she didn't start; she was tired of feeling guilty for what she was putting her parents through. Eventually, the school principal and a few of her more sensitive teachers talked her off the ledge. Shortly afterward she was taken to a hospital where she was evaluated in the emergency room and then admitted for suicidality.

This event was a turning point. Assigned male at birth, Dakila had been wearing feminine clothing at school for over a year. Everyone was acting like she was gay, but she really didn't think so. She now felt ready to talk.

The Reyes family lives in a home owned by Dakila's paternal grandparents, Mary and Angelo, situated in a small farming town in Northern California. Her mother, Tala, and father, Julio, had immigrated from the Philippines to California in their early teens. Tala has a warm smile and bobbed hair and works as a bookkeeper for a local supermarket. Julio is a loving father who takes great pride in his family. A few years ago, he sustained an injury in a factory that left him struggling with depression and chronic back pain. In addition to the grandparents, who also live in the home, is the mother's younger sister, Gizelle, age 28. Tagalog is their primary language, though Dakila, her sister, Angela, age 12, and both parents speak English.

Dakila had felt like a girl her entire life. As a young child, she loved women's fashion and frequently draped towels across her head, pretending she had long, lustrous hair. At an early age, Dakila spoke with a more feminine inflection, and once she was old enough to voice a preference, she begged to wear more androgynous clothing. As Filipinos from conservative, Catholic backgrounds, her parents did not expect this behavior from their first and only son and were confused. Dakila felt accepted by them as a feminine boy—until she hit puberty.

Lev, Arlene I., Gottlieb, Andrew R., *Families in Transition*
dx.doi.org/10.17312/harringtonparkpress/2019.04.fit.003
© 2019 by Harrington Park Press

At age 13, a year before her suicide attempt, Dakila began treatment with one of my colleagues, Dr. Gold. Initially, no one, including Dakila herself, understood whether her conflicts were related to sexual orientation or gender. A few months into treatment, however, her confusion began to lift. But, Grandma Mary warned her, "You need to be the way God made you." After that conversation, Dakila began to reconsider a gender transition, and she told Dr. Gold, "Maybe I'm too young to be thinking about this."

During this phase of therapy, Dr. Gold encouraged the parents to accept Dakila's gender expression by supporting her clothing choices, which could potentially be in conflict with the more traditional Catholic/Filipino norms. Although her parents tried to accept Dakila as an emerging gay teen, explicit conversations about her gender identity or potential use of medical treatments to stall physical changes through the use of puberty blockers never occured with them.

Having been taken out of therapy and caught between cultural and religious expectations and her own desire to express herself, Dakila continued to present in a feminine way. However, she did not talk about herself having a nonbinary gender, being transgender, or being gay. She continued to go to school wearing extremely feminine clothing, grew her hair, and wore makeup while her parents watched from the sidelines, not talking openly with her about what was going on. While at school Dakila expressed her gender courageously, but she still found herself feeling hurt by occasional verbal jabs, stares, and laughter she heard behind her back. She felt targeted and misunderstood by others, which in her school system could have been prompted by transphobia or homophobia.

The accumulated stress of her parents' unhappiness, her social transition at school, her teacher's harsh comments, and the harassment by her peers all built up to the suicide attempt. During her hospital stay, the family had a few therapy sessions, during which Dakila expressed a desire to go further with her transition, that is, to be on hormones and have bottom surgery. Though her parents were distressed about this, the suicide attempt was sobering. They both began to understand the seriousness of the gender concerns for their child.

After her hospitalization, Dakila reengaged in treatment with Dr. Gold. Julio and Tala met with Dr. Gold alone and shared the struggle to accept their child. Julio said, "I wish he [Dakila] would be struck by lightning and wake up and just go back to who he is supposed to be." Tala, wishing for more support, spoke to her mother in the Philippines. In response, Julio got angry, feeling ashamed of what they were going through, saying, "Gossip will only make things worse." Dakila felt guilty and responsible for an increase in her mother's drinking and her parents' conflicts. After a number of family therapy sessions, Tala finally acknowledged that the stress related to both her husband's depression and Dakila's gender issues was more than she could handle, and she agreed to see a therapist on her own. Though this seemed promising, the family then dropped out of treatment with Dr. Gold.

At 17, Dakila was referred to me by her primary care doctor at a busy out-patient mental health clinic. She came to our first session dressed in stylish feminine clothing, poised, with a confident air about her that said, "I know who I am." Dakila reported that since eighth grade, most people closest to her used female pronouns. When I met her, she had essentially made a social transition, and had been living as a girl since age 14. When Tagalog was spoken at home, it caused less conflict, as there are no pronouns like *he* or *she* in that language. When English was spoken, however, her father refused to use female pronouns and her female name, but "out of respect for him," she didn't insist. Overall, in most areas of her life, including the school environment, she was integrated as a female—everything except her body.

Though Tala accompanied her to the session, she looked uncomfortable when I asked if she wanted to join us, replying, "We just want her to be happy." I understood that Dakila had, in effect, taken the reins. She showed no signs of depression, felt a consistent gender identity over time, and was clear about her desire for hormone treatment. She maintained that her mother was making supportive efforts by having taken her shopping for female clothing. While Tala worried about the road ahead, she remembered how frightening the suicide attempt had been. Julio was struggling, and he continued looking for signs of masculinity or any desire in Dakila to live as a male. Dakila still sought his approval. Seeing his frowns when she applied makeup in the morning before school saddened her.

To move forward with the transition, I felt it was important to speak to the whole family. Dakila and her mother didn't think it was necessary. Earlier Dakila had insisted, "They're all fine with it." I explained that the pediatric endocrinologist may want to prescribe a puberty blocker before the feminizing hormone (estrogen). (The pediatric endocrinologist typically does this as a way to block testosterone's effects in teens rather than using an anti-androgen.) I also wanted to have a discussion with Dakila, then together with her parents, about fertility and the option of sperm banking. This can be an uncomfortable conversation to have jointly, but it's one that's important so everyone knows what is happening. Parents can later discuss the issue with their teens and weigh the costs and benefits. Dakila emphatically stated she had no desire to bank sperm, though she might consider adopting. Early on I phoned Julio and started to ask him to come in for a family session. He interrupted, deferred to Dakila's mother, then hung up. While it can be culturally typical that child rearing is left to mothers, he had been extensively involved in previous therapy exchanges with Dr. Gold, so this confused me. Dakila tried to prepare me for the phone call, saying, "He can seem angry, but he's not."

Since Julio refused to come in, I decided to move forward with only the mother and daughter, though I shared with Tala that I wished he were present since Dakila could use the support of both parents. In this case, as Dakila was nearly 18, and I had the consent of her mother, I decided I would not try to engage Julio further. I gave priority to Dakila's need for hormone treatment over having both parents present. As much as I would've liked to help them change this well-established communication pattern, I did not want to put Dakila's transition on hold. It did not seem fair to her. Because of the limits of their managed care insurance, time was of the essence. Given that I had only a few sessions each month to work with Dakila and her family, I wanted to expedite a referral to the endocrinologist.

Over the course of two months with Tala and Dakila, we explored Dakila's readiness for physical transition and the general effect of puberty blockers and feminizing hormones. Tala also was now clear how important a gender transition was to her daughter. "This is what she wants to do," she said with a resigned shrug. We discussed Dakila's desire for vaginoplasty and reviewed the World Professional Association for Transgender Health (WPATH) standards of care. My hope was that Tala would communicate some of this to her husband. However, I did not say this to her directly. My sense was that while he didn't want to stand in the way, at the same time he didn't feel ready to let go of his son. Tala told me, "He's fine with it."

I'll admit that I found myself feeling angry at both parents. I wanted her mother and father to be more passionately involved, to show they cared more about this critical phase of her life. As I read her previous therapist's notes, it looked as if they *had* been more actively involved when they thought she might be gay or suicidal. Now both seemed detached in a way that concerned me. Perhaps Tala didn't feel comfortable saying how she truly felt and just defaulted to "We just want her to be happy"; perhaps there was a sense of resigned acceptance in giving precedence to her daughter's needs over her own; perhaps what I perceived as detachment was, in fact, grief. Whatever the case, I saw Dakila as a young girl yearning for more affection and acceptance than she appeared to receive.

Shortly after starting hormones, she ended therapy, having achieved her main goal: greater comfort with her body, knowing breasts and other bodily changes were soon to develop. A few times a year, Dakila would call to set an appointment, then not show, schedule again, and cancel again, until she would finally make it, apologetically saying, "I was so busy, I'm so sorry!" I was sometimes confused and frustrated. Was our relationship really that important if she kept canceling? When we did talk, however, she stressed how important it was just to *have* the appointment, to know I was there for her, even if she didn't always take advantage of the opportunity.

At 19, Dakila was starting community college and was comfortable living at home. She reported that her parents were feeling better about her transition and she was less worried about their mental health. Julio, though still loving, continued to keep his distance, which was painful for Dakila. Her Auntie Gizelle was a source of consistent support and fashion advice. Though Tala was involved in her daughter's life, she was concerned about what the future would be like for a transgender woman. Dakila's fears echoed her mother's, anxious also about being a trans person of color, and therefore at greater risk for violence, discrimination, and sexism.

During our last session, Dakila, now 20, was preparing for a rare visit to her family in the Philippines, intending to spend time with her younger cousins, who never knew she had been assigned male at birth. She felt the tension between her family's more traditional culture and her own pride as a transgender woman. Her parents asked her not to disclose to her cousins, but she felt torn, wanting to respect their wishes but also wanting to respect herself. I heard myself saying, "Good for you!" when she talked about not being ashamed of who she was, but I realized the difficult position she was in, straddling two cultures. My support felt genuine, rooted as it was in the portion of my own culture that values individualism and self-determination; I also wanted to offset her experience of being told by others to camouflage parts of herself, much the same way I was treated during my own coming out.

Perhaps Dakila will return to treatment. Perhaps she won't. No doubt, Tala and Julio will continue to love their daughter while they process the meaning all this has had for them. And that frightened little girl on the ledge will, I hope, one day step fully into her family's loving embrace.

Kelley Winters confronts the research community head-on, challenging the oft-quoted 80% desistance rate, or the claim that 80% of those who identify as trans in childhood will "desist" and identify as cisgender in adolescence. In her thorough analysis of four key research studies, Winters cites a misrepresentation of missing research results, sample bias, conflations of gender expression with gender identity and gender dysphoria in the diagnostic manual, poorly substantiated outcome measures in relation to treatment, lack of reliable long-term follow-up criteria, and employment of an ad hoc or "sticky flypaper" hypothesis, that is, one supported by unsubstantiated evidence. Although there is still much that is unknown, the extant research does *not* support the notion that most gender creative children will evolve into gay or lesbian adults or desist from a cross-gender identity.

Drawing our attention to a sorely neglected, underinvestigated area of inquiry is Katherine Kuvalanka, Molly Gardner, and Cat Munroe's paper, "All in the Family," based on the Trans*Kids longitudinal study, which explores the attitudes and behaviors of extended relatives—grandparents, aunts, uncles, cousins—vis-à-vis the gender nonconforming or transgender child and their parents or caretakers. Informed by a social ecological perspective and resilience theory, their study—a mix of qualitative and quantitative data—highlights the bi-directionality of both negative and positive influences extended family and primary caretakers can reciprocally exert on each other, underlining how critical support can be in a world that remains largely intolerant of difference.

AndreAs Neumann Mascis imagines what it would be like for gender variant children and adolescents, their parents, and their families to live in a world in which clinically, culturally competent, affirming care was not the exception but the rule. In "More Than the Sum of Your Parts," he observes that we are at a point in our history when that could become a reality, a time in which repeated trauma resulting from abuse and neglect could be short-circuited. Through the lens of self psychology, Neumann Mascis sensitively and eloquently examines the effect on a parent—both intrapsychically and interpersonally—of having a gender diverse child, and how that, in turn, affects the marital dyad and the family system. He argues that we, as clinicians, have to go beyond the focus on mere behavioral change on the part of the parents, that the crisis of gender identity presents an opportunity to explore how family roles, power alliances, and internal and external boundaries are affected, and that this ideally results in a deeper attachment between parent and child. Neumann Mascis then broadens his argument to include a complementary discussion of the brain, demonstrating that what we intuitively know psychologically can also be understood neurobiologically: that an attuned, relational environment is critical to healing.

4

The "80% Desistance" Dictum:
Is It Science?

Kelley Winters, PhD

> **The burden of proof in science rests invariably on the individuals making a claim, not on the critic.**
>
> — LILIENFELD, LYNN &, LORH, 2003, P. 3

The most pervasive and damaging stereotype about transgender children that is used to frighten parents, therapists, and medical professionals is that the vast majority of them are "going through a phase." The "80% desistance" dictum alleges that *gender dysphoria,* defined as distress with their physical sex characteristics or associated social roles, and identification as trans will remit for approximately 80% of young trans children. It predicts that most young trans boys will spontaneously revert to identifying as girls by puberty and develop into cisgender lesbian women, and that most young trans girls will spontaneously revert to identifying as boys by puberty and develop into cisgender gay men. This adage has become ubiquitous in medical policy, research literature, and political discourse and is quoted as a principle of science. But is the 80% desistance stereotype actually supported by evidence and reason?

A Pervasive Perception

The seventh version of the Standards of Care (SOC7), published by the World Professional Association for Transgender Health (WPATH), repeats the 80% desistance claim uncritically: "[Gender] dysphoria persisted into adulthood for only 6–23% of children" (Coleman et al., 2012, p. 11). It also appears in the current *Diagnostic and Statistical Manual of Mental Disorders,* fifth edition: "Rates of persistence of gender dysphoria from childhood into adolescence or adulthood vary. In natal males, persistence has ranged from 2.2% to 30%. In natal females, persistence has ranged from 12% to 50%" (APA, 2013, p. 455). The 80% figure is cited in medical policies that discourage authentic social transition and public policies that deny education and even restroom access for trans children and

Lev, Arlene I., Gottlieb, Andrew R., *Families in Transition*
dx.doi.org/10.17312/harringtonparkpress/2019.04.fit.004
© 2019 by Harrington Park Press

youth. Its overall effect on their lives, as well as specific access to education and public accommodation in socially authentic gender roles, cannot be overstated. For example, Roger Severino, director of the Office of Civil Rights at the U.S. Department of Health and Human Services and former executive for the conservative think tank Heritage Foundation, attacked Title IX protections for trans school children in 2016, stating, "Not only must government employees play along with a gender confused child's subjective wishes, so must every other student, even though the large majority of children with gender identity issues grow out of them."

Desistance Research

The claim that gender dysphoria and non–birth assigned gender identities will spontaneously or otherwise desist by puberty or early adulthood stems from four primary studies in Canada and the Netherlands. The first, a 2008 study conducted by Drummond, Bradley, Peterson-Badali, and Zucker at the Centre for Addiction and Mental Health in Toronto (CAMH), identified a cohort of 37 birth-assigned girls who had been referred to their Gender Identity Clinic. It is important to note that this CAMH clinic practiced behavior modification treatments for children that attempted to reinforce birth-assigned gender identification. These are no longer accepted as ethical treatment practices (Coleman et al., 2012). The subjects were between the ages of three and 12 at referral and were at least 17 years of age at follow-up. In childhood, 60% of subjects met childhood criteria for gender identity disorder (GIDC) in three versions of the DSM (APA, 1980; APA, 1987; APA, 1994). The remaining 40% were described as "subthreshold" for GIDC diagnosis and were included as study subjects, even though they did not meet the GIDC diagnostic criteria. Of 37 subjects, 25 were contacted and agreed to participate at follow-up. The authors found that 22 of 37 subjects, or 59% of the original cohort, showed desistance, defined as identification with their birth-assigned female gender at follow-up. Three were found "persistent" in "GID or gender dysphoria," and the status of 12 nonparticipants at follow-up was unknown. The authors, however, retroactively redefined the sample size from the original 37 to just the 25 who participated at follow-up. This bumped the reported desistance ratio from 59% of the study cohort to 88% of the final participants: "The present study found that the vast majority of the girls showed desistance: 88% of the girls did not report distress about their gender identity at follow-up" (p. 42). This inflated ratio has since been widely cited in medical and academic journals

In the second paper, also published in 2008, Wallien and Cohen-Kettenis at the Vrije Universiteit (VU) University Medical Center in Amsterdam studied a cohort of 77 children who had been referred to their clinic between the ages of five and 12 and reevaluated at age 16 or older: 75% of subjects met childhood criteria for GIDC in the *DSM-IV* (APA, 1994) and *DSM-IV-TR* (APA, 2000), and the remainder were subthreshold for diagnosis. At follow-up, they found that just 23 of 77 subjects, or 30%, "were no longer gender dysphoric" by first-person examination and were classified as desistant; an additional 10 subjects, or 13%, were not examined at follow-up but were reported as desistant by parents or third parties; 21 subjects, or 27%, "were still gender dysphoric" (p. 1413) and labeled persistent; and 23 subjects, a full 30%, did not participate at follow-up and their status was unknown. Notably, the authors found half of the birth-assigned female subjects in the cohort, nine of 18, to be persistent (four of 19 did not participate at follow-up). This is far greater than the 12% rate reported at CAMH by Drummond and colleagues (2008) and does not include possible persistent subjects from the nonresponder group. Nevertheless, the authors substantially inflated their reported rate of desistance from 30% (based on first-person follow-up) to 73% by adding nonresponding subjects and third-party reports as "desistant." They concluded, "Most children with gender dysphoria will not remain gender dysphoric after puberty," adding that "the most likely outcome of childhood GID is homosexuality or bisexuality" (Wallien & Cohen-Kettenis, 2008, p. 1413).

In addition, while the authors acknowledged subjects who did not respond or participate in the follow-up assessment, they speculated that all these nonparticipants were "desisters." They reasoned that, because VU University Medical Center was the only clinic for youth trans services under the Dutch health system, all nonparticipants must have lost interest in transition care and desisted to identify with their birth sex. This assumption ignored the growing Stop Trans Pathology movement among young trans people in Europe and a willingness for teens to seek out alternative resources that meet their care needs on their own terms. Researchers also potentially discounted trans youth driven into the closet by societal prejudice, who would return for transition services later in life.

Overlapping studies at the Dutch VU University Medical Center were published as a qualitative paper in 2011 and a quantitative paper in 2013. The first of these, by Steensma, Biemond, de Boer, and Cohen-Kettenis, examined a cohort of 53 Dutch-speaking children referred to their clinic at age 12 or younger. Subjects met the diagnostic criteria for GIDC in the *DSM-IV* (APA, 1994) or *DSM-*

IV-TR (APA, 2000) and were at least 14 years old at follow-up. None of the subjects had socially transitioned to non—birth assigned gender roles with name change and corresponding pronouns. Researchers found that more than half, 29 of 53 subjects, or 55%, persisted in gender dysphoria and reapplied for medical transition treatment at the clinic. Ten subjects, 19%, were found desistant, identifying with their birth-assigned sex. One subject identified as "50% male and 50% female." Once again, the results for participants who desisted were far lower than the "vast majority" figure from the 2008 CAMH study. The gender identities and status of the remaining 13 nonrespondents, a full 25%, were unknown at follow-up. Unlike the previous paper by Wallien and Cohen-Kettenis (2008), this study combined all 24 subjects who did not reapply for medical transition treatment at their clinic with subjects they had classified as desistant. This set an unfortunate historic precedent of misrepresenting null results by speculating that nonparticipants at follow-up, as well as the nonbinary-identified subject, had reverted to identify with their birth-assigned sex: "The other 24 adolescents (45.3%) did not reapply for treatment at the Gender Identity Clinic during adolescence. As the Amsterdam Gender Identity Clinic for children and adolescents is the only one in the country, we assumed that their gender dysphoric feelings had desisted, and that they no longer had a desire for sex reassignment" (Steensma et al., 2011, p. 501).

Finally, a quantitative analysis was authored by Steensma, McGuire, Kreukels, Beekman, and Cohen-Kettenis (2013) at VU University Medical Center in Amsterdam. They examined a larger sample of 127 subjects who had been referred to the Gender Identity Clinic when younger than 12 and were at least 15 years old at follow-up. Nearly two-thirds, 80 of 127, met the childhood GIDC criteria in the *DSM-IV* (APA, 1994) or *DSM-IV-TR* (APA, 2000), and the remaining 47 were deemed "subthreshold." At follow-up, 47 subjects, or 37%, persisted in gender dysphoria and reapplied for medical transition treatment at the clinic. Only 46 of 127, or 36%, were confirmed as desistant, based on reassessment at follow-up. An additional six, or 5%, were reported by parents, secondhand, as desisters. The remaining 28 subjects, or 22% of the cohort, did not respond at follow-up, and their gender identities and gender dysphoria status were unknown (19%), or "indicated" as desistant by third parties but not confirmed by reassessment (3%). Yet again, the Dutch researchers attributed nonresponding subjects as if "their GD had desisted" (p. 583). This inflated their reported desistance rate from 36% (based on direct, first-person follow-up) to 63%, or 80 of 127 subjects (including nonrespondents and secondhand parental reports of desistance).

Methodological Concerns

The 80% desistance adage for prepubertal trans youth is widely promoted as "a solid scientific consensus" (Singal, 2016, para. 10) and continues to be canonized in medical policy (APA, 2013; Byne et al., 2012; Coleman et al., 2012; Hembree et al., 2017). New, unprecedented longitudinal studies of transgender youth, such as a current study by Fast and Olson (2017) at the University of Washington, are under way to address unanswered questions from this dated Canadian and Dutch research. The validity of the 80% claim, however, remains largely unquestioned, independent of new research.

A fundamental tenet of science is that those who state a claim that is based on prior research bear the burden of evidence and reason to support that claim (Lilienfeld, Lynn, & Lohr, 2003). Questions of validity and methodology have been raised about the 80% desistance adage and its supporting research (Ehrensaft, 2016; Olson, 2016; Temple-Newhook et al., 2018; Winters, 2014). The first concern is attribution of missing data as desister data in the two Steensma et al. (2011; 2013) papers. Subjects who had dropped out or had not participated in follow-up studies were presumed by researchers to have become cisgender and to no longer be gender dysphoric. This is a misrepresentation of null results (Ehrensaft, 2016; Winters, 2014). The authors have offered an explanation that VU University Medical Center is the only clinic for trans youth in the Netherlands under the state health-care system. It is common, however, for transgender teens to seek new providers of hormonal and other services for a variety of reasons, including their needs not being met. Others may be driven into closets of birth-assigned roles by societal intolerance in their youth, only to reemerge and seek transition care later in life.

Furthermore, sample bias due to invalid selection criteria is a concern for all four of these studies. In other words, children who participated had been selected on the basis of criteria that skewed the results of the study to a particular out-come. Researchers relied on diagnostic criteria for gender identity disorder of childhood (GIDC) in the *DSM-IV* (APA, 1994) and earlier editions to select study cohorts. Criterion A in the GIDC diagnosis in the *DSM-IV* (APA, 1994) and *DSM-IV-TR* (APA, 2000) had required that any four or more of the following sub-criteria were met:

1. repeatedly stated desire to be, or insistence that he or she is, the other sex
2. in boys, preference for cross-dressing or simulating female attire; in girls, insistence on wearing only stereotypical masculine clothing

3. strong and persistent preferences for cross-sex roles in make-believe play or persistent fantasies of being the other sex

4. intense desire to participate in the stereotypical games and pastimes of the other sex

5. strong preferences for playmates of the other sex (APA, 2000, p. 581)

Only subcriterion 1 indicated non–birth assigned gender identity and was relevant to the distress of gender dysphoria. The other four described only gender nonconforming expression, such as clothing, interests, and play not stereotypical of the assigned birth sex. Since subcriterion 1 was not required to meet Criterion A, gender expansive or gender nonconforming children with no indication of gender dysphoria could easily receive a false-positive diagnosis of gender identity disorder. The criteria could include boys with feminine interests and expressions and girls with masculine interests and expressions who were content with their birth-assigned sex.

In fact, conflating gender expression with gender identity was a deliberate decision of the *DSM-IV* (APA, 1994) subcommittee on gender identity disorders: "It was the recommendation of the subcommittee that the explicit wish to be of the opposite sex be combined with other behavioral markers of gender identity disorder into one criterion. This would eliminate the pivotal role that the verbalized wish to change sex plays in the *DSM-III-R* criteria" (Bradley et al., 1991, p. 337).

Half of the members of this subcommittee, including the chair, were affiliated with the Clarke Institute of Psychiatry, now the Centre for Addiction and Mental Health (CAMH), where the Drummond study was conducted. Its authors acknowledged this false-positive selection bias in their study: "It is conceivable that the childhood criteria for *GIDC* may 'scoop in' girls who are at relatively low risk for adolescent/adult gender dysphoria that revolves so much around somatic indicators" (Drummond et al., 2008, p. 42).

Critics of this research and its perpetuation of the 80% desistance adage have been more blunt: "Close inspection of these studies suggests that most children in these studies were not transgender to begin with" (Olson, 2016, p. 156). To paraphrase a fruitful metaphor from Diane Ehrensaft (2016): *they studied oranges and publicized conclusions about apples.*

All four research papers used the terms *gender dysphoria* and *childhood gender identity disorder* (GIDC) very nearly synonymously, in which gender dysphoria referred to distress with one's biological sex characteristics or associated social role (Fisk, 1973), and GIDC was the overly broad *DSM-IV* (APA, 1994) diagnosis used to select the study samples. This conflation was explicit in the Drummond paper. Gender dysphoria appeared in the titles of the three Dutch studies, even though the childhood GIDC criteria were used for sample selection and did not actually require evidence of distress of gender dysphoria. These terms are not interchangeable.

The most parsimonious interpretation of the Toronto and Dutch desistance studies is that children who experience distress of gender dysphoria are a subset, probably a small subset (Hidalgo et al., 2013), of gender expansive or gender nonconforming youth who meet the childhood GIDC criteria in the *DSM-IV* (APA, 1994) and *DSM-IV-TR* (APA, 2000). It follows that most gender expansive children identify with their birth-assigned sex and have no gender dysphoria to desist. Conflating gender dysphoric children with the far greater superset of gender nonconforming children is like conflating zebras with the entire *Equus* genus and insisting to the world that the vast majority of zebra colts will grow up without stripes.

All four studies reported that a majority of the gender expansive or gender nonconforming children in their samples were found to be both cisgender (termed "desisters," by these researchers) and attracted to the same sex at follow-up. The language used to describe the sexual orientations of subjects with trans outcomes offers insight into the researchers' attitudes toward gender diversity. For example, Drummond and colleagues stated, "Girlhood cross-gender identification is associated with a relatively high rate of bisexual/homosexual sexual orientation in adolescence and adulthood" (2008, p. 42). These terms misgender and erase the heterosexual orientation of the subjects who identified as straight, trans men. Steensma and colleagues placed sneer quotes around the sexual orientations described by subjects with trans outcomes but not around those of subjects with cisgender outcomes (2011, p. 513). Such language is misleading with respect to the broad sexual diversity of trans people. For example, the current WPATH Standards of Care cite prior persistence studies to describe gay and transgender populations as mutually exclusive: "Boys in these studies were more likely to identify as gay in adulthood than as transgender" (Coleman et al., 2012, p. 11). By casting LGB versus trans outcomes as dichotomous, such statements marginalize the existence of lesbian transgender women and gay transgender men.

The Drummond study was conducted within a clinical practice at the Gender Identity Clinic at CAMH, where behavioral interventions for children attempted to reinforce birth-assigned gender identification and expression and suppress gender nonconformity. Such treatments, often called gender conversion therapies, have been prohibited for minors in nine U.S. states, Washington D.C., and the Canadian province of Ontario (Frankel, 2017). The SOC7 states that such treatments are "no longer considered ethical" (Colemen et al., 2012, p. 32). CAMH gender identity services for children were shut down in 2015, following investigations into these practices (Ubelacker, 2015), which aimed at forcing desistance: "I would argue, therefore, that it is as legitimate to want to make youngsters comfortable with their gender identity (to make it correspond to the physical reality of their biological sex) as it is to make youngsters comfortable with their ethnic identity (to make it correspond to the physical reality of the color of their skin)" (Zucker, 2008, p. 359).

In science, external factors that interfere with both those factors being studied (called independent variables) and the observed results of a study (called dependent variables) are known as confounding factors. Researchers ignore confounding factors at the peril of reaching invalid results and false conclusions. In the Drummond study, behavioral treatments attempting to force desistance potentially altered the results by pressuring young subjects into the closet before follow-up or to drop out of the study entirely. Furthermore, such treatments potentially altered the study sample itself, by attracting parents who were more intolerant of their gender nonconforming children and more likely to take them to a mental health clinic without actual distress of gender dysphoria. Yet CAMH researchers refused to discuss the effect of their gender conversion treatments: "It is beyond the scope of this report to describe the types of therapies . . . received between the assessment in childhood and follow-up" (Drummond et al., 2008, p. 39). They neglected a first-order confounding factor that very probably affected the results.

A related concern is that none of these studies has adequately acknowledged the societal intolerance and violence that transgender youth and young adults experience with minority stress (James, Herman, Rankin, Keisling, Mottet, & Anafi, 2016), which undermines them in their affirmed gender roles and relentlessly pressures them to surrender to the closets of their birth-assigned genders. None of these studies has attempted to differentiate desistant outcomes from closeted outcomes at follow-up or even to discuss the difference. Doing so would necessitate much longer-term longitudinal studies, taking into account that, even in the twenty-first century, most transgender people do not find it safe to reveal their authentic gender identities until middle age: "The median age at which trans people first visited their GP to discuss their gender dysphoria has been rising and is currently 42" (Reed, Rhodes, Schofield, & Wylie, 2009, p. 15). At the least, appropriate prospective studies should extend past the median age of coming out.

Dismissing Inconvenient Data

A corollary to the 80% desistance hypothesis asserts: "It is currently not possible to differentiate between preadolescent children in whom *GIDC* will persist and those in whom it will not" (Byne et al., 2012, p. 4). All four papers, however, noted contrary evidence, suggesting the possibility of identifying which children would remain gender dysphoric through adolescence and which would identify with their birth-assigned sex:

> There was some evidence of a "dosage" effect, with girls who were more cross-sex typed in their childhood behavior more likely to be gender dysphoric at follow-up and more likely to have been classified as bisexual/homosexual in behavior. (Drummond et al., 2008, p. 34)

> We replicated the earlier findings on the link between the intensity of GD in childhood and persistence of GD. . . . In addition to this, we found that formerly nonsignificant (age at childhood assessment) and unstudied factors (cognitive and/or affective gender identity responses on the GIIC and a social role transition) were associated with the persistence of GD. (Steensma et al., 2013, p. 587)

Although the Dutch approach practiced at VU University Medical Center has long discouraged early childhood social transition (de Vries & Cohen-Kettenis, 2012), nearly 30%, or 37 of 127 subjects, of the Steensma et al. (2013) study cohort had social transitions that were either "complete" or "partial" (p. 585), in defiance of clinic policies. Researchers found that "social role transition accounted for the largest portion of unique variability (12%), whereas each of the other significant predictors accounted for 6–7% of unique variability in persistence of GD" (p. 586). In other words, they found that social transition in childhood was a strong predictor of persistence of gender dysphoria and non–birth assigned gender identities, especially for trans girls assigned male at birth. This contradicted the assumption within the 80% desistance stereotype that it was not possible to predict which children would be persisters and which would be desisters.

Presented with evidence that contradicts a hypothesis, scientists are obligated to question the validity of the hypothesis. For young trans children with supportive families and providers who overcome enormous societal barriers and socially transition to authentic non–birth assigned gender roles, the 80% desistance hypothesis is frequently contradicted.

In the Steensma and colleagues (2013) study, four of 127 subjects socially transitioned completely, including gender expression, names, and pronouns, and all were persistent at follow-up; 33 subjects socially transitioned partially, by gender expression only. Of those, 21 were persistent at follow-up, nine self-reported as desistant, one was reported as desistant by parents, and three were nonparticipants with unknown status. Rather than question the 80% desistance premise, however, the researchers proffered a second hypothesis without explanation or citation, suggesting that childhood social transition itself is somehow a cause of gender dysphoria rather than a relief; that it reinforces non–birth assigned gender identities rather than socially affirms them: "Social transitions . . . have never been independently studied regarding the possible impact of the social transition itself on cognitive representation of gender identity or persistence. . . . [Increasing prevalence of transitioned children] may, with the hypothesized link between social transitioning and the cognitive representation of the self, influence the future rates of persistence" (2013, pp. 588–589).

Moreover, Dutch researchers added yet another hypothesis to explain away observed persistence in socially transitioned children, speculating that those who socially transition to non–birth assigned gender roles could be prevented from retransitioning back to birth-assigned roles by overwhelming social forces: "[Parents and care providers] may help the child to handle their gender variance in a supportive way, but without taking social steps long before puberty, which are hard to reverse. This attitude may guide them through uncertain years without the risk of creating the difficulties that would occur if a transitioned child wants to revert to living in his/her original gender role" (Steensma et al., 2011, p. 514).

This frightening warning against childhood social transition was based on a small number of birth-assigned girls in the first study by Steensma and colleagues (2011), who had never fully transitioned socially and never changed names or pronouns. Yet the authors extrapolated dire conclusions about gender dysphoric children who fully transition socially at early ages. These influenced medical policy and practice far beyond academia, including very recent treatment guidelines from the Endocrine Society: "If children have completely socially transitioned, they may have great difficulty in returning to the original gender role upon entering puberty" (Hembree et al., 2017).

These two additional theories, one claiming that social transition causes gender dysphoria and the other claiming that reversing social transition is very difficult, are examples of "ad hoc hypotheses" (Gould, 1979, p. 163), invented after the fact to attempt to explain away data that contradict the original hypothesis of the research. They are not supported by evidence for young gender dysphoric children who have fully transitioned into congruent gender roles. Both are suspect on the merits of reason as they presume that cisgender identities in youth are so fragile that they can be toppled by any number of social factors, whereas non–birth assigned identities and social roles somehow stick like flypaper in spite of the strong social pressures that punish them (Winters, 2014). If these were the case, it would be hard to imagine how the species has sustained itself this long.

Conclusion

When it is not clear under which law of nature an effect or class of effect belongs, we try to fill this gap by means of a guess. Such guesses have been given the name conjectures or hypotheses.

—ØRSTED, 1811/1998, P. 297

At its core, science is the iterative formulation of hypotheses based on observation and testing of their validity. Not every guess, however, is a valid hypothesis. Scientific hypotheses must be crafted so that it is possible to devise tests to prove them false. In other words, hypotheses must be falsifiable. When a hypothesis, such as the 80% desistance theory, is contradicted by data, such as socially transitioned children who do not remit before adolescence, the validity of the hypothesis is called into question. Instead, desistance researchers chose to invent additional ad hoc, "sticky flypaper" hypotheses that attempted to explain away inconvenient evidence posed by socially transitioned children and rendered the 80% desistance hypothesis unfalsifiable. This is not scientific method. Hypotheses that are unfalsifiable do not create science. They create dicta.

A growing body of research is focused on transgender children with supportive families and care providers and is refuting the stereotype that most trans or gender dysphoric children are "confused" and will become cisgender gay or lesbian adults. For example, trans children have been found to exhibit cogent social cognition of their expressed gender equal to that of cisgender peers of the same gender identity (Olson, Key, & Nicholas, 2015). Socially transitioned trans children supported by their families exhibit far less psychopathology than previously reported among closeted and unsupported youth (Olson, Durwood, DeMeules, & McLaughlin, 2016). Prospective studies in progress will no doubt shed much more light on the outcomes of trans children who are supported in socially authentic gender roles.

In the meantime, the prevalent 80% desistance stereotype should be viewed skeptically. Research cited to support the 80% adage is problematic with respect to (1) a misrepresentation of missing results as desistant results for nonparticipating subjects at follow-up; (2) a sample bias in the selection of gender nonconforming children who were never necessarily gender dysphoric or trans; (3) a conflation of gender identity with gender expression; (4) a conflation of gender dysphoria with the childhood Gender Identity Disorder diagnosis in the *DSM-IV*, which did not require evidence of gender dysphoria; (5) a neglect of confounding factors of gender conversion therapies practiced at CAMH and their effect on results; (6) a lack of long-term follow-up to distinguish desisted outcomes from closeted outcomes at the ages when trans people typically come out of the closet; and (7) a resort to unsubstantiated ad hoc hypotheses about socially transitioned children to render the 80% desistance hypothesis unfalsifiable. On each of these concerns, the 80% desistance claim has fallen short of its burden of proof.

REFERENCES

American Psychiatric Association. (1980). *Diagnostic and Statistical Manual of Mental Disorders* (3rd ed.). Washington, D.C.: American Psychiatric Association Publishing.

American Psychiatric Association. (1987). *Diagnostic and Statistical Manual of Mental Disorders* (3rd ed., revised). Washington, D.C.: American Psychiatric Association Publishing.

American Psychiatric Association. (1994). *Diagnostic and Statistical Manual of Mental Disorders* (4th ed.). Washington, D.C.: American Psychiatric Association Publishing.

American Psychiatric Association. (2000). *Diagnostic and Statistical Manual of Mental Disorders* (4th ed., text revision). Washington, D.C.: American Psychiatric Association Publishing.

American Psychiatric Association. (2013). *Diagnostic and Statistical Manual of Mental Disorders* (5th ed.). Washington, D.C.: American Psychiatric Association Publishing.

Bradley, S., Blanchard, R., Coates, S., Green, R., Levine, S., Meyer-Bahlburg, H., Pauly, I., & Zucker, K. (1991). Interim report of the *DSM-IV* subcommittee on gender identity disorders. *Archives of Sexual Behavior, 20* (4), pp. 333–343.

Byne, W., Bradley, S. J., Coleman, E., Eyler, A. E., Green, R., Menvielle, E. J., Pleak, R., & Tompkins, D. A. (2012). Report of the American Psychiatric Association Task Force on Treatment of Gender Identity Disorder. *American Journal of Psychiatry, 169* (8), 1–35.

Coleman, E., Bockting, W., Botzer, M., Cohen-Kettenis, P., DeCuypere, G., Feldman, J., . . . & Zucker, K. (2012). Standards of Care for the health of transsexual, transgender, and gender-nonconforming people, Version 7. Available at https://www.wpath.org/media/cms/Documents/Web%20Transfer/SOC/Standards%20of%20Care%20V7%20-%202011%20WPATH.pdf.

de Vries, A., & Cohen-Kettenis, P. (2012). Clinical management of gender dysphoria in children and adolescents: The Dutch approach. *Journal of Homosexuality, 59* (3), 301–320. Retrieved from https://www.researchgate.net/publication/223135170_Clinical_Management_of_Gender_Dysphoria_in_Children_and_Adolescents_The_Dutch_Approach.

Drummond, K. D., Bradley, S. J., Peterson-Badali, M., & Zucker, K. J. (2008). A follow-up study of girls with gender identity disorder. *Developmental Psychology, 44* (1), 34–45.

Ehrensaft, D. (2016, September). Apples, oranges, and fruit salad: Sorting out transgender, gender non-conforming, & non-binary children and youth. Paper presented at the Gender Infinity conference, Houston. https://gidreform.wordpress.com/2016/09/23/apples-oranges-and-fruit-salad-sorting-out-transgender-gender-non-conforming-non-binary-children-and-youth/.

Fast, A., & Olson, K. (2017). Gender development in transgender preschool children. *Child Development, 89* (2), 620–637.

Fisk, N. (1973). Gender dysphoria syndrome. (The how, what, and why of a disease). In D. Laub & P. Gandy (eds.), *Proceedings of the second interdisciplinary symposium on gender dysphoria syndrome* (pp. 7–14). Stanford: Stanford University Medical Center.

Frankel, J. (2017, July 10). More and more states are outlawing gay-conversion therapy. *Atlantic.* https://www.theatlantic.com/health/archive/2017/07/states-outlawing-conversion-therapy/ 533121/.

Gould, S. (1979). *Ever since Darwin: Reflections in natural history.* New York: W. W. Norton.

Hembree, W., Cohen-Kettenis, P., Gooren, L., Hannema, S., Meyer, W., Murad, H., . . . & T'Sjoen, G. (2017). Endocrine treatment of gender-dysphoric/gender-incongruent persons: An Endocrine Society clinical practice guideline. *Journal of Clinical Endocrinology and Metabolism, 102* (11), 1–35. Retrieved from https://academic.oup.com/jcem/article/doi/10.1210/jc.2017-01658/4157558/Endocrine-Treatment-of-Gender-Dysphoric-Gender.

Hidalgo, M., Ehrensaft, D., Tishelman, A., Clark, L., Garofalo, R., Rosenthal, S., Spack, N., & Olson, J. (2013). The gender affirmative model: What we know and what we aim to learn. *Human Development, 56,* 285–290. Retrieved from https://www.karger.com/Article/FullText/355235.

James, S., Herman, J., Rankin, S., Keisling, M., Mottet, L., & Anafi, M. (2016). *2015 U.S. Transgender Survey.* www.ustranssurvey.org/.

Lilienfeld, S., Lynn, S., & Lohr, J. (2003). *Science and pseudoscience in clinical psychology.* New York: Guilford Press.

Olson, K. (2016). Prepubescent transgender children: What we do and do not know. *Journal of the American Academy of Child & Adolescent Psychiatry, 55* (3), 155–156. Retrieved from www.jaacap.com/article/S0890-8567%2815%2900794-7/abstract.

Olson, K., Durwood, L., DeMeules, M., & McLaughlin, K. (2016). Mental health of transgender children who are supported in their identities. *Pediatrics, 137* (3). Retrieved from http://pediatrics.aappublications.org/content/early/2016/02/24/peds.2015-3223.

Olson, K., Key, A., & Nicholas, E. (2015). Gender cognition in transgender children. *Psychological Science 26* (4), 467–474, http://journals.sagepub.com/doi/abs/10.1177/0956797614568156.

Ørsted, H. (1811/1998). *First introduction to general physics.* In K. Jelved, A. Jackson, and O. Knudsen (eds.), *Selected scientific works of Hans Christian Ørsted* (pp. 282–309). Princeton: Princeton University Press.

Reed, B., Rhodes, S., Schofield, P., & Wylie, K. (2009). Gender variance in the UK: Prevalence, incidence, growth and geographic distribution. Gender Identity Research and Education Society. www.gires.org.uk/wp-content/uploads/2014/10/GenderVarianceUK-report.pdf.

Severino, R. (2016, May 6). New Chicago schools bathroom policy courts controversy. *Daily Signal.* http://dailysignal.com/2016/05/06/new-chicago-schools-bathroom-policy-proves-liberals-extreme-agenda/.

Singal, J. (2016, July 25). Gender dysphoria: What's missing from the conversation about transgender kids. *New York Magazine.* http://nymag.com/scienceofus/2016/07/whats-missing-from-the-conversation-about-transgender-kids.html.

Steensma, T. D., Biemond, R., DeBoer, F., & Cohen-Kettenis, P. T. (2011). Desisting and persisting gender dysphoria after childhood: A qualitative follow-up study. *Clinical Child Psychology and Psychiatry, 16* (4), 499–516.

Steensma, T. D., McGuire, J. K., Kreukels, B.P.C., Beekman, A. J., & Cohen-Kettenis, P. T. (2013). Factors associated with desistence and persistence of childhood gender dysphoria: A quantitative follow-up study. *Journal of the American Academy of Child and Adolescent Psychiatry, 52* (6), 582–590.

Temple-Newhook, J., Winters, K., Pyne, J., Jamieson, A., Holmes, C., Feder, S., Pickett, S., & Sinnott, M. (2018). Teach your parents and providers well: Call for refocus on the health of trans and gender-diverse children. *Canadian Family Physician, 64* (5), 332–335. Retrieved from www.cfp.ca/content/64/5/332.long.

Ubelacker, S. (2015, December 15). CAMH to "wind down" controversial gender identity clinic services. *Globe and Mail.* https://beta.theglobeandmail.com/news/toronto/camh-to-wind-down-controversial-gender-identity-clinic-services/article27766580/.

Wallien, M. S. C., & Cohen-Kettenis, P. T. (2008). Psychosexual outcome of gender-dysphoric children. *Journal of American Academy Child & Adolescent Psychiatry, 47,* 1413–1423.

Winters, K. (2014, February 16). Methodological questions in childhood gender identity "desistence" research. Paper presented at the 23rd WPATH Biennial Symposium, Bangkok, Thailand, from Loveland, Colo. https://gidreform.wordpress.com/2014/02/25/methodological-questions-in-childhood-gender-identity-desistence-research/.

Zucker, K. (2008). Children with gender identity disorder: Is there a best practice? Enfants avec troubles de l'identité sexuée: Y-a-t-il une pratique la meilleure? *Neuropsychiatrie de l'Enfance et de l'Adolescence, 56,* 358–364.

5

All in the Family: How Extended Family Relationships Are Influenced by Children's Gender Diverse and Transgender Identities

Katherine A. Kuvalanka, PhD, Molly Gardner, MA, Cat Munroe, PhD

Researchers have begun to build on the observational work of clinicians (Coolhart, 2012; Lev, 2004) to further investigate how children's transgender identities and gender nonconformity influence families (Hill & Menvielle, 2009; Kuvalanka, Weiner, & Mahan, 2014; Rahilly, 2015; Sansfaçon, Robichaud, & Dumais-Michaud, 2015). Parents of transgender and gender diverse youth often struggle, at least initially, to understand their children's gender identities and expressions while simultaneously facing blame from family members, friends, neighbors, even health-care professionals for causing gender "confusion" in their children (Johnson & Benson, 2014; Sansfaçon et al., 2015). While parents may undergo a profound transition—from uneducated novices to ardent advocates (Brill & Pepper, 2008; Rahilly, 2015; Sansfacon et al., 2015)—siblings of these children, especially those who are school-age, may face secondary social stigma from peers (Menvielle, 2012). Like their parents, they, too, may grow into allies who have greater appreciation for transgender issues in particular and diversity in general (Kuvalanka et al., 2014; Norwood, 2013b). Although there is still much to learn about how parents and siblings are influenced by and respond to children's transgender identities and gender nonconformity, even less is known about how other family members are affected, such as grandparents, aunts, uncles, and cousins, who may play significant roles in the lives of these youth.

Family researchers and clinicians increasingly understand that *family acceptance*—often thought of as parental acceptance—has important implications for the well-being of sexual- and gender-minority (i.e., LGBTQ) youth. Studies coming out of the Family Acceptance Project report that both acceptance and rejection have a strong influence on their emotional and behavioral health, affecting the possibility of substance use, the presence of suicidality, and their capacity for self-esteem regulation (Ryan, Huebner, Diaz, & Sanchez, 2009; Ryan, Russell, Huebner, Diaz, & Sanchez, 2010). These findings were underscored by

Lev, Arlene I., Gottlieb, Andrew R., *Families in Transition*
dx.doi.org/10.17312/harringtonparkpress/2019.04.fit.005
© 2019 by Harrington Park Press

the 2014 suicide of a transgender teen, Leelah Alcorn, age 14, which brought media attention to the negative effect that actual or perceived familial and societal rejection can have. In her suicide note, Leelah wrote:

> After 10 years of confusion I finally understood who I was. I immediately told my mom, and she reacted extremely negatively, telling me that it was a phase, that I would never truly be a girl, that God doesn't make mistakes, that I am wrong. If you are reading this, parents, please don't tell this to your kids. Even if you are Christian or are against transgender people don't ever say that to someone, especially your kid. That won't do anything but make them hate them self. That's exactly what it did to me. (Fantz, 2015)

More recently, a pioneering community-based study of 73 prepubescent transgender children who had socially transitioned (i.e., changed their names, pronouns, hairstyles, and clothing to align with their gender identities) with the support of their parents revealed no significant differences in depressive symptoms compared to population and control group averages (Olson, Durwood, DeMeules, & McLaughlin, 2016).

Those in the immediate family (i.e., parents, other primary caretakers, siblings) obviously have a critical role to play when it comes to providing support, and clinicians have rightly focused their attention on them when aiming to increase familial acceptance for these children. But what roles can and do other family members play? How can aunts, uncles, cousins, and grandparents help each other overcome the transphobic messages encountered in society and, perhaps, within their own families? How can these family members assist parents as they try to make sense of the children's binary (e.g., *trans girl*, *trans boy*) and nonbinary (e.g., *genderfluid*, *genderqueer*) gender identities and expressions, and figure out how to respond to a child's desire to socially transition? How can they themselves assist the child directly? In addition to worrying about threats to a child's physical safety and social estrangement, parents and other caregivers often have to navigate their own anxieties and apprehensions (Coolhart, 2012; Sansfaçon et al., 2015). Clinicians working with these parents and caregivers will probably find it useful to look beyond the immediate family and consider extended family when identifying other sources of support (Norwood, 2013b).

Our analysis of Trans*Kids Project data—interviews with more than 40 primary caregivers of transgender and gender diverse children ages six to 12 years old—explored the reactions of extended family members, including grandparents, aunts, uncles, and cousins. We will describe what we learned about how family relationships are influenced by a child's gender identity and expression, positing the role others can play in their well-being. We begin by sharing our theoretical perspective and a brief research review.

A Social-Ecological and Resilience Perspective When Considering Extended Family

According to a social ecology perspective, development occurs within multiple interacting contexts, ranging from the proximal (e.g., immediate and extended family) to the distal (e.g., media, community laws, and policies). The exploration of both personal and contextual variables is therefore of critical importance (Bronfenbrenner, 1988; McLeroy, Bibeau, Steckler, & Glanz, 1988). With this in mind, we are interested in understanding the range of responses extended family members have to a transgender or gender diverse child's gender identity and expression, all of which can have direct and indirect influences on the child's development. We are clear that children are directly affected by positive and negative interactions with family members. But if the child is personally *unaware* of an extended family member's response, though the parent is aware, then the child may still be indirectly affected by that influence (Brown-Smith, 1998). For example, parents who affirm their transgender child's gender identity but receive no support for that decision from extended family may experience self-doubt (Kuvalanka et al., 2014; Sansfaçon et al., 2015), which could possibly lead to anxiety or less affirming behaviors. Alternatively, if parents struggle to accept their children's gender identities, extended family members may serve as critical sources of support for those children (Devor, 1997; Koken, Bimbi, & Parsons, 2009). An extended family member may encourage parents to be accepting of the gender variance, or may themselves create a close, nurturing bond with the child, which may be enough to help a developing child overcome adversity (Koken et al., 2009; Werner, 2005).

Also informing our perspective are theories of resilience, which help conceptualize how marginalized and stigmatized families may strengthen their relational ties. Oswald (2002) identified two primary processes—*intentionality* and *redefinition*—through which families with lesbians and gay men sustain and affirm their relationships and sense of family in the context of societal heterosexism. For example, before nationwide access to civil marriage for same-sex couples in the United States, an *intentionality* strategy of "legalizing" (Oswald, 2002, p. 379) was pursued by some same-sex couples when they entered into domestic partnerships or filed power-of-attorney documents with the aim of being legally interdependent with one another. "Politicizing" (Oswald, 2002, p. 380) is identified as a *redefinition* strategy that occurs when sexual-minority individuals and their family members come to realize how they are influenced by heterosexism and become politically active in an effort to effect change for their own and other LGB families.

We have applied aspects of Oswald's (2002) resilience framework to families with transgender and gender diverse children who live amid cisnormativity (McGuire, Kuvalanka, Catalpa, & Toomey, 2016). For example, parents of a transgender child may use an *intentionality* strategy of "managing disclosure" (Oswald, 2002, p. 377). By disclosing a child's gender identity to extended family members and their intent to support the child, parents may be "inviting in" (Moore, 2012) those who are or will be affirming, while signaling to others that lack of acceptance is not welcome. Further, families may engage in *redefinition* processes, such as "naming" and "envisioning" (Oswald, 2002, p. 380), in which they affirm the existence of their transgender and gender diverse family members and their relationships. For example, extended family members can show their support of a social transition and their shift in thinking by using the correct pronouns and relational terms, such as changing from "granddaughter" to "grandson." Actions such as these can foster resilience (Ryan et al., 2010).

In line with a social-ecological theory of resilience (Ungar, Ghazinor, & Richter, 2013), factors such as emotional and geographical proximity as well as cultural and religious beliefs are expected to influence the reactions of extended family members and the significance of those reactions for both parent and child (Norwood, 2013b; Zamboni, 2006). Given that influences in a social-ecological model are thought to be bidirectional, attitudes are expected to move toward greater acceptance over time, especially if family members see children's well-being improve as these children are increasingly able to express their true selves (Ehrensaft, 2012; Kuvalanka et al., 2014).

Extended Family in the Lives of Transgender Individuals

Although parents are most often the "major players" (Devor, 1997, p. 89) in terms of who is most influential in a child's life, certainly siblings and extended family members can also play significant parts. Most obviously, when families experience transitions and challenges, such as separations, divorces, deaths, drug and/or alcohol abuse, physical abuse, or illness, others may step in and take on primary caregiving roles (Devor, 1997; Werner, 2005). This was the case for two grandmothers in our study who became primary caregivers to their transgender grandchildren. But even in the absence of such challenge and tragedy, extended family members may wield significant influence, both positive and negative. For example, in Devor's 1997 study, more than a third of the 45 adult female-to-male transgender individuals, upon reflecting on their childhood and adolescence, described grandmothers, grandfathers, aunts, and uncles as influential. Although some recalled negative interactions, most had positive, warm childhood memories, even finding "refuge" (p. 109) and "safe havens" (p. 144) with them when parents were more rejecting. Although these ties mostly dissipated during adolescence, some remained strong. One participant spoke of an uncle who contributed money for gender-affirmation surgery—a gesture of love that had profound significance. In a study of 20 trans women, half reported experiencing warmth and affection from close family members, especially female relatives, both extended and immediate, who demonstrated acceptance to them in addition to or in lieu of parental acceptance (Koken et al., 2009).

Discovery or disclosure of transgender and gender diverse identities can be a stressor, necessitating a change in family systems (Hines, 2006; Lev, 2004; Zamboni, 2006), the worst-case scenarios being overt rejection and ostracization. Norwood (2013b) contends that the meanings assigned to transgender identities relate to how supportive or rejecting those family members might be. Those meanings are influenced by competing cultural discourses relating to the origins of transgenderism, as well as to moral and religious beliefs. For example, many of Norwood's 37 participants, who were mostly mothers but who also included fathers, siblings, adult children, and former and current spouses or partners, were supportive of their transgender family member and conceived causation as biological, thus nobody's "fault." Three other participants, also supportive, did not view being transgender as a disorder, rejected the cultural notion of gender as binary, and defined it as a natural part of the gender spectrum. The two who were rejecting perceived being transgender as a "selfish, and even sinful, choice" (p. 165). Feelings and reactions can change over time as family members move through one or more of the four stages of Lev's (2004) Family Emergence Model. The first two stages are characterized by shock, confusion, stress, and conflict; the second two by negotiation, balance, and, in best-case scenarios, acceptance.

Norwood (2013b) also found that her participants, all of whom were immediate family of transgender individuals, had considered the religious, social, and political beliefs of their extended family in making decisions about disclosure. Some participants avoided it or reluctantly disclosed in anticipation of negative responses. Others felt it was important to disclose and to model ways to respond. A few were happily surprised by positive reactions, having expected more negative ones. A mother of an adult transgender individual stated, "I have one Evangelical, nutcase sister . . . and her son, . . . they were absolutely lovely" (p. 169).

More studies are needed to shed light on the reactions of extended family during a social transition, given that these are times when extended family may be particularly influential and when the family as a whole may be most vulnerable. The Trans*Kids Project—the focus of our work—is one such study that aims to provide a better understanding of the experiences of these families.

The Trans*Kids Project

The Trans*Kids Project is a longitudinal study of families with transgender and gender diverse children, ages six to 12 years old at the time of wave 1 data collection, which spanned 2011–2012. During that phase, complete demographic information was collected on 46 caregivers of 46 transgender and gender diverse children (29 natal males and 17 natal females). One-on-one, semistructured telephone interviews were conducted with participants in order to gather qualitative data about their experiences raising a transgender or gender diverse child. Quantitative survey data about children's and caregivers' well-being were also collected through follow-up questionnaires. The participants (42 mothers, two fathers, and two grandmothers) and their families were primarily from the United States; one family was from Canada. Almost all ($n = 44$) identified as white, and most (more than 75%) had earned a bachelor's degree or higher. The children's average age was 8.5 years old. Most (78%) of the children were identified as white by their caregivers, five were identified as both Latina and white or both Mexican and white, two were described as Native American and white, one as African American, one as white/Dutch Antillean, and one as white/Greek.

Most of our participants had heard about the Trans*Kids study through online or in-person groups for caregivers and were relatively supportive of their children's gender identities and expressions, though a handful were still struggling. More than 70% of the children had socially transitioned at wave 1: 20 of the 29 natal males were living as affirmed girls, and 14 of the 17 natal females were living as affirmed boys.

The family members of the caregivers—their partners or co-parents, other children in the family, the caregivers' own parents, siblings, cousins—were also relatively accepting, though acceptance took more time and was not always equal to that of the participants. About 10% of participants reported that they had immediate and extended family members who were all just as accepting as they were, almost 78% said they had family members who were mostly as accepting as they were, whereas the remaining 12% reportedly had only some or very few who were as accepting. Preliminary analyses indicate that these measures of acceptance were negatively correlated with the children's behavior problems, that is, the greater the acceptance from family members, the fewer the behavior problems. This concurs with the work of the Family Acceptance Project (Ryan et al., 2009; 2010).

Acceptance and rejection can be conceptualized as distinct but on an overlapping continuum (i.e., low, medium, or high levels) rather than binaries (i.e., accepting or not; rejecting or not) (Koken et al., 2009; McConnell, Birkett, & Mustanski, 2015). Individuals—in this case, extended family members—can (1) be both accepting and rejecting; (2) be in different places along an acceptance–rejection continuum; (3) become more accepting or rejecting over time; (4) demonstrate their acceptance or rejection in different ways; and (5) wield differing degrees of influence on a caregiver, and ultimately, on the child. Further, two primary types of acceptance—resigned and unconditional—have been identified by Gottlieb (2000) in studying those strategies fathers use to adapt to having a gay son.

On the basis of our qualitative interview data, we created a general, four-point measure of family acceptance—(1) completely accepting, (2) mostly accepting, (3) somewhat accepting, and (4) not at all accepting—with the aim of delineating the range of responses. Reports of outright rejection were interpreted as evidence of less accepting attitudes, and changes over time were noted. We assigned each of our participant families to one of the four categories, citing excerpts from each transcript as justification.

Nonaffirming Behaviors: From "Don't Ask, Don't Tell" to Outright Rejection

Most participants reported at least some negative, nonaffirming attitudes and behaviors toward the children on the part of their extended family. It could have been a lack of acceptance at first that gradually evolved into a greater openness; or attitudes and behaviors that had been consistently rejecting, necessitating a decision to break off the relationship; or a persistent lack of explicit communication about the children—a kind of "don't ask, don't tell." A mother of a nine-year-old affirmed girl described how this worked: "I can't say that they really understand. But they kind of 'don't ask, don't tell.' . . . They really don't get it, but they don't say anything about it, either. So, I mean, that works for us." Other participants took pains to be very explicit with extended family, often by writing letters to explain a child's social transition. This process would traditionally be considered "coming out," but could also be conceptualized as "inviting in"

(Moore, 2012). Some worked hard to educate and be patient. Another mother expressed that it was a concerted effort to help her extended family understand and be more accepting: "It took a lot of work and energy to kind of bring our families . . . around to . . . our way of thinking."

Lack of acceptance did not always look the same, nor did it always have the same effect. Some used more passive forms of rejection (e.g., silence), whereas others actively rejected the child's gender identity or gender-related preferences (e.g., buying toys and clothing that stereotypically aligned with the child's assigned sex at birth as opposed to their affirmed gender). Other extended family members vocalized opposition to the caregiver's approach. Still others showed a degree of sensitivity, but they still questioned whether the participant was doing the right thing. For example, the mother of a six-year-old affirmed girl explained how both sets of her child's grandparents "don't necessarily agree that it's the best thing to do at her age," though they continue to use female pronouns and buy her dresses rather than pants.

Factors that appeared to contribute to a lack of acceptance included strong religious and cultural beliefs—similar to reports by Norwood (2013b) and Potocz-niak, Crosbie-Burnett, and Saltzburg (2009)—and geographical proximity. One parent of an eight-year-old noted that she was offended by her own mother sug-gesting she take her child to a Christian psychologist to get a "different perspec-tive." Geographical distance and amount of time spent with the child also seemed to play a role. If family were not close enough to witness the child's persistence and insistence or the positive transformation when allowed to express their authentic selves, some family members had a harder time than perhaps they might have had, had they been more present in the child's day-to-day life. Another participant explained it this way: "So my parents live in the same town as us, and so they came along much faster because they had . . . been close to her more. . . . David's [husband's] family took a little bit longer because . . . they're . . . about a half hour or 45 minutes away. But because it was enough distance away, they didn't have as much exposure to her early on."

Although proximity may facilitate acceptance, distance may provide pro-tection (Oswald, 2002). Overtly rejecting attitudes and behaviors on the part of extended family members led to some participants distancing themselves and their children from them. One mother explained: "And my mother-in-law, it's the same thing: We're going to 'burn in fiery pits in Hell,' and if we'd just 'take him down to Brother so-and-so, he could lay hands on him and heal him.' You know? So we just excised those cancers from our lives. We don't need that." Another mother described her reaction to the maternal grandfather leaving his grandchild out of the family tree because she was transgender: "Yeah, so he had done this book of the family tree and he basically just left her out completely, so there was an empty, blank spot where she should have been. We were both quite alarmed by that, so we haven't talked to him since then." The grandfather's "removal" of the child from the family, in turn, led to the mother and child "removing" *him* from their lives. Similarly, a parent reported that her aunt called her to tell her she was ruining her child's life. The family has intentionally not seen the aunt since in order to protect the child from negativity and rejection.

Affirming Behaviors:
Effect on Parent, Child, and Family Relationships

Extended family members can and do play a vital part in the lives of transgender and gender diverse children. Two participants, both grandmothers, were, by definition, extended family members themselves who assumed a primary caregiving role and who remained guardians thereafter. Some extended family members initially reacted to the child's gender identity and expression with shock, though this often gave way to acceptance. Although reactions were often mixed and more likely to be negative immediately following disclosure, those who exhibited acceptance often became a consistent, reliable, and positive presence for both the children and the parents. Perhaps not surprisingly, given that participants who volunteer for a study such as ours are likely to be supportive of their children's gender variance and may also have extended family who are accepting, primary caregivers were the recipients of many more positive, affirming experiences than negative ones.

Affirmation was not only expressed verbally, but also communicated in other ways, including the use of correct pronouns, provision of material goods, such as clothing and toys consistent with the children's desires and tastes, and validation of the parents' approach. One participant stated about her *own* siblings: "They don't question what I'm doing, or they say, 'I don't know what I would do, you know, if I were in your shoes, but I respect that you're the parent and you're making the decision that you think is right.' So I feel support coming from them. . . . This summer we were visiting back there, and they all were . . . working really hard to get the name change thing straight, and . . . if they didn't get it, they apologized, and they were really, really making a great effort."

Other extended family members communicated their support by intervening with those who partially or wholly resisted affirming the child's gender, which at times proved effective, particularly when it was done with the caregiver. According to participants, this served to increase family cohesion, improve family functioning, and provide better psychological and physical outcomes for the children. One participant, a mother of a 10-year-old affirmed girl, described early conflict with her husband about his refusal to use their child's desired pronoun. Her own sister then intervened:

> His position was that he would start calling her Brittany when she fully transitioned. And then at one point we had, and I remember we'd had a discussion about it, when I told him that I thought this is something she really needed from him as her dad. . . .That night my sister texted about a documentary about a transgender kid, and there was a maternal aunt that was interviewed that kept calling the child by her natal name and using, you know, natal pronouns and all of that. And he [the child in the documentary] was so upset at how this aunt that said she was supportive was using the wrong name. And from that point forward, he called her Brittany and that was the end of it.

Just as signs of rejection included the intentional provision of items that were incongruent with the child's affirmed gender and/or preferences, communication of acceptance included giving gifts, clothes, and toys that aligned with the child's personal desires and tastes. One participant, a mother of a 10-year-old gender diverse boy, explained how extended family members respected the wishes of her child: "Grandparents on both sides . . . buy him things that are pink. So he's got a lot of family members that do respect his choices." A mom of a six-year-old affirmed girl said, "Some of our more open-minded relatives started giving her Barbie dolls." By offering gender-stereotypical toys and clothing that align with the child's identified gender, these relatives are trying their best to demonstrate acceptance. Other ways support was demonstrated included volunteering at gender conferences and furthering their own knowledge about gender issues. The father of a participant and grandparent of an eight-year-old gender diverse child wrote a letter to the family in which he said: "I'm going into therapy because I want to understand this. . . . I don't have to say this to you, but I support you guys 100%."

The encouragement our participants received from their extended family members made a difference in many of their lives—and even proved inspirational. When asked about the biggest source of support, one mother responded: "Family, number one. I don't know that I could've done this if I were completely just single, by myself. I'm not sure that I would've been able to do all of this. I mean, I'm lucky that [my child] has [a] personal support system. You know, she has all of these moms and these grandparents."

As reported in the literature (Kuvalanka et al., 2014; Lev, 2004), exposure to a transgender or gender diverse child and bearing witness to their insistence and persistence often played a role in moving family members toward greater acceptance. Another mother described the gradual change in her own parents: "And my parents are, you know, in their 80s and they . . . [now] get it. I mean at first they were sort of like, 'I don't know. This is going to be a hard life. You know, are you sure you want to encourage this?' But you can't be around this kid for very long without realizing that it's not put on. You know it's not pretend. It's not something that comes and goes. It's just that completely consistent presentation and . . . so gradually they've just sort of gone with it."

Many extended family members of our participants began to be more accepting as a result of seeing the positive changes in the children's dispositions after transition. As one mother attested: "Basically, all it took was one dinner with Becca presenting as . . . female, and they said, 'Oh, my god.' They were just shocked that she was talking like that, 'This child's talking to us!' You know? . . . I mean, they were just confused by it, and once they started seeing her as female, they really quickly caught up."

Many participants reflected on the positive influence that their transgender or gender diverse sons and daughters had on both their immediate and extended families just by being themselves. One parent spoke about how the changes her family went through strengthened their relationships: "I think it's a very enlightening experience, and it brought my family closer together, very much closer together. And people that I thought that would not be accepting have been the most accepting, which is very odd." As similarly reported by Norwood's (2013b) participants, several of the parents in our study were happily surprised by the positive reactions of family members who they had assumed would react negatively. Thus, the process of coming to understand and accept their children allowed for a more intimate knowledge of each other and a closer and more resilient relationship as they collectively broadened and transformed their conceptualizations of gender and family.

Implications for Clinicians

The clinical implications of these findings are numerous. Taken together, they underscore the importance of social support for family resilience as well as the complexity of familial support systems. A number of families may have "nontraditional" structures that include the presence of grandparents, aunts, and uncles as caregivers. Rather than this signifying dysfunction, it may indicate flexibility and resilience and promote positive outcomes. There is empirical evidence that adults who report gender dysphoria have less social support, which is associated with decreased quality of life and a lessening of personal well-being, particularly for trans women (Davey, Bouman, Arcelus, & Meyer, 2014). Because limited social support is shown to impede a sense of comfort, contentment, and satisfaction (Davey et al., 2014), clinicians should pay particular attention to assessment of clients' social networks so that sources of support can be identified and maximized, given the crucial role it plays in health and adjustment.

Individuals who are close to a child who is transgender or gender diverse may be going through their own processes of loss and transition as the dyad renegotiates their understanding of each other and their relationship (McGuire, Catalpa, Lacey, & Kuvalanka, 2016; Norwood, 2013a; Zamboni, 2006). According to Norwood (2013a), these processes tend to fall within one of four domains: (1) *replacement,* in which the individual describes the transgender person as being a substitute for the original; (2) *revision,* in which the individual describes a change in their gendered perception only in physical terms; (3) *evolution,* which describes an individual who conceptualizes the transgender person as progressively changing or "updating"; and (4) *removal,* in which sex/gender is reconceptualized as irrelevant to essential selfhood. These four categories, each of which we found evidence for in our participants' stories, may be differentially construed as affirming or rejecting, and they may render extended family members relatively unavailable to respond to the child's emotional and physical needs or to provide support to the caregivers. Understanding the grief and relational processes is central to understanding the level of family cohesion, current family functioning, and availability of social support for the child (Zamboni, 2006).

Although disclosure can lead to a wide range of reactions, immediate and extended family members may be best positioned to provide consistent support to both children and their primary caregivers (Devor, 1997; Israel, 2005; Koken et al., 2009). For these reasons, it is essential to stay mindful of the unique experiences of the parents of transgender and gender diverse children (Hines, 2006), the wide variability of responses to disclosure within families of origin (Norwood, 2012), known stages of family adjustment (Emerson, 1996; Lev, 2004), and the stigma facing gender minority kids (Lev, 2013; Mayer, Garofalo, & Makadon, 2014). Just as social support is essential for the adjustment of these children, it is equally important for their caregivers.

Also central is an understanding of and participation in family rituals (Oswald, 2002; Zamboni, 2006), which have been found to provide families with structure and stability over time (Imber-Black & Roberts, 1992). Indeed, rituals such as birthdays, family reunions, and holidays, as well as specific rites of passage—first haircut or first dress purchase—are opportunities for families to demonstrate acceptance or rejection of the child and the caretaker as well as presenting key moments for clinical intervention. Family members with strong religious beliefs might benefit from reading about, hearing about, and meeting religious individuals who embrace transgender identities and gender noncon- formity. Clinicians could facilitate an understanding of how these family mem- bers might reconcile their religious beliefs in the context of their relationships with their transgender or gender diverse family member.

Finally, politicizing and awareness raising may become a source of family meaning making (Oswald, 2002). For example, family members may become ardent supporters of and advocates for their children by attending, speaking at, and organizing gender conferences, PFLAG groups, or Pride marches (Brill & Pepper, 2008; Kuvalanka et al., 2014; Sansfaçon et al., 2015). These may also serve as opportunities to connect with other families—relationships that could be mutually beneficial. Thus, clinicians should be aware of local LGBTQ resources and events and selectively share this information with clients.

Conclusion

Extended family members are an underinvestigated source of potential support for transgender and gender diverse children and their caregivers. Notions of fam- ily acceptance should be expanded beyond parent acceptance, given the critical role that grandparents, aunts, uncles, and cousins can and do play in the well- being of these families. As illustrated through the experiences of participants in the Trans*Kids Project, aspects of Oswald's (2002) framework of resilience can be applied to families with gender minority members as they undergo change after the disclosure and navigate a cisnormative and transphobic society. Extended family members' involvement in processes that transform conceptualizations of gender and familial relationships to reflect acceptance can promote the health of individual family members and overall resilience. On the one hand, some who actively reject their transgender and gender diverse relatives and their caregivers may be intentionally cut off in an effort to protect the child. On the other hand, those more affirming may help guide primary caregivers and other family mem- bers toward greater acceptance. All these scenarios were illustrated in our sam- ple of those who were prone to be highly accepting of their children, given the nature of our study and recruitment methods.

The bidirectional nature of familial relationships as described by a social- ecological perspective (Bronfenbrenner, 1988; McLeroy et al., 1988) allows for a reciprocity of influence among transgender and gender diverse children, their parents, and their extended families. After witnessing the authenticity of children's expression of their "true gender selves" (Ehrensaft, 2012), some of those who were reluctant moved quickly toward acceptance. This change can have both direct and indirect effects—direct when acceptance is expressed to the child, indirect when acceptance is expressed to the parents and other family members who support the child. This can be especially critical in situations where families are living in intolerant communities that stigmatize gender differences.

More research is needed to better understand how extended family members are influenced by the presence of transgender and gender diverse relatives and the role extended family can play in well-being and resilience, and to better represent a wider range of racial, ethnic, and socioeconomic familial makeups. Cultural notions of gender and family intersect in different ways and must be considered by clinicians and researchers as they aim to better understand and assist. Although increased exposure to LGBTQ issues has resulted in rapid and positive attitudinal change in Western societies, high rates of suicide attempts and harassment are still experienced (Haas, Rodgers, & Herman, 2014). Thus, finding ways to strengthen and broaden support from both immediate and extended family members continues to be of vital importance.

REFERENCES

Brill, S., & Pepper, R. (2008). *The transgender child: A handbook for families and professionals.* San Francisco: Cleis Press.

Bronfenbrenner, U. (1988). Interacting systems in human development: Research paradigms: Present and future. In N. Bolger, A. Caspi, G. Downey, & M. Moorehouse (eds.), *Persons in context: Developmental processes* (pp. 25–49). Cambridge: Cambridge University Press.

Brown-Smith, N. (1998). Family secrets. *Journal of Family Issues, 19,* 20–42.

Coolhart, D. (2012). Supporting transgender youth and their families in therapy: Facing challenges and harnessing strengths. In J. J. Bigner & J. L. Wetchler (eds.), *Handbook of LGBT-affirmative couple and family therapy* (pp. 199–213). New York: Routledge.

Davey, A., Bouman, W. P., Arcelus, J., & Meyer, C. (2014). Social support and psychological well-being in gender dysphoria: A comparison of patients with matched controls. *Journal of Sexual Medicine, 11* (12), 2976–2985. http://doi.org/10.1111/jsm.12681.

Devor, H. (1997). *FTM: Female-to-male transsexuals in society.* Bloomington: Indiana University Press.

Ehrensaft, D. (2012). From gender identity disorder to gender identity creativity: True gender self child therapy. *Journal of Homosexuality, 59* (3), 337–356. doi:10.1080/00918369.2012.653303.

Emerson, S. (1996). Stages of family adjustment in family members of transgender individuals. *Journal of Family Psychotherapy, 7,* 1–12.

Fantz, Ashley. (2015, January 4). An Ohio transgender teen's suicide, a mother's anguish. CNN. www.cnn.com/2014/12/31/us/ohio-transgender-teen-suicide/.

Gottlieb, A. R. (2000). *Out of the twilight: Fathers of gay men speak*. Binghamton, N.Y.: Haworth Press.

Haas, A. P., Rodgers, P. L., & Herman, J. L. (2014). *Suicide attempts among transgender and gender-nonconforming adults: Findings of the National Transgender Discrimination Survey*. Los Angeles: Williams Institute at the UCLA School of Law. Retrieved from http://williams institute.law.ucla.edu/wp-content/uploads/AFSP-Williams-Suicide-Report-Final.pdf.

Hill, D. B., & Menvielle, E. (2009). "You have to give them a place where they feel protected and safe and loved": The views of parents who have gender variant children and adolescents. *Journal of LGBT Youth, 6*, 243–271.

Hines, S. (2006). What's the difference? Bringing particularity to queer studies of transgender. *Journal of Gender Studies, 15* (1), 49–66. doi.org/10.1080/09589230500486918.

Imber-Black, E., & Roberts, J. (1992). *Rituals for our times*. New York: HarperCollins.

Israel, G. E. (2005). Translove: Transgender persons and their families. *Journal of GLBT Family Studies, 1* (1), 53. http://doi.org/10.1300/J461v01n01•05.

Johnson, S., & Benson, K. E. (2014). "It's always the mother's fault": Secondary stigma of mothering a transgender child. *Journal of GLBT Family Studies, 10* (1/2), 124–144.

Koken, J. A., Bimbi, D. S., & Parsons, J. T. (2009). Experiences of familial acceptance-rejection among transwomen of color. *Journal of Family Psychology, 23*, 853–860.

Kuvalanka, K. A., Weiner, J. L., & Mahan, D. (2014). Child, family, and community transformations: Findings from interviews with mothers of transgender girls. *Journal of GLBT Family Studies, 10* (4), 354–379. doi:10.1080/1550428X.2013.834529.

Lev, A. I. (2004). *Transgender emergence: Therapeutic guidelines for working with gender-variant people and their families*. Binghamton, N.Y.: Haworth Press.

Lev, A. I. (2013). Gender dysphoria: Two steps forward, one step back. *Clinical Social Work Journal, 41* (3), 288–296. http://doi.org/10.1007/s10615-013-0447-0.

Mayer, K. H., Garofalo, R., & Makadon, H. J. (2014). Promoting the successful development of sexual and gender minority youths. *American Journal of Public Health, 104*, 976–981.

McConnell, E. A., Birkett, M. A., & Mustanski, B. (2015). Typologies of social support and associations with mental health outcomes among LGBT youth. *LGBT Health, 2*, 55–61. doi:10.1089/lgbt.2014.0051.

McGuire, J. K., Catalpa, J., Lacey, V., & Kuvalanka, K. A. (2016). Ambiguous loss as a framework for interpreting gender transitions in families. *Journal of Family Theory and Review, 8*, 373–385. doi:10.1111/jftr.12159.

McGuire, J. K., Kuvalanka, K. A., Catalpa, J., & Toomey, R. (2016). Transfamily theory: How the presence of trans* family members informs gender development in families. *Journal of Family Theory and Review, 8*, 60–73. doi:10.1111/jftr.12125.

McLeroy, K. R., Bibeau, D., Steckler, A., & Glanz, K. (1988). An ecological perspective on health promotion programs. *Health Education Quarterly, 15* (4), 351–377.

Menvielle, E. (2012). A comprehensive program for children with gender variant behaviors and

gender identity disorders. *Journal of Homosexuality, 59* (3), 357–368. doi:10.1080/00918
369.2012.653305.

Moore, D. L. (2012, July 12). Coming out or inviting in? Part 1. Retrieved from http://thefeministwire
.com/2012/07/coming-out-or-inviting-in-reframing-disclosure-paradigms-part-i/.

Norwood, K. (2012). Transitioning meanings? Family members' communicative struggles surrounding transgender identity. *Journal of Family Communication, 12* (1), 75–92. doi:10.1
080/15267431.2010.509283.

Norwood, K. (2013a). Grieving gender: Trans-identities, transition, and ambiguous loss. *Communication Monographs, 80* (1), 24–45. doi.org/10.1080/03637751.2012.739705.

Norwood, K. (2013b). Meaning matters: Framing trans identity in the context of family relationships. *Journal of GLBT Family Studies, 9*, 152–178. doi:10.1080/1550428X.2013.765262.

Olson, K. R., Durwood, L., DeMeules, M., & McLaughlin, K. A. (2016). Mental health of transgender children who are supported in their identities. *Pediatrics, 137* (3), 1–8. doi:10.1542/
peds.2015-3223.

Oswald, R. F. (2002). Resilience within the family networks of lesbians and gay men: Intentionality and redefinition. *Journal of Marriage and Family, 64*, 374–383.

Potoczniak, D., Crosbie-Burnett, M., & Saltzburg, N. (2009). Experiences regarding coming out
to parents among African American, Hispanic, and white gay, lesbian, bisexual,
transgender, and questioning adolescents. *Journal of Gay & Lesbian Social Services, 21*
(2/3), 189–205. doi:10.1080/10538720902772063.

Rahilly, E. P. (2015). The gender binary meets the gender-variant child: Parents' negotiations
with childhood gender variance. *Gender & Society, 29*, 338–361.

Ryan, C., Huebner, D., Diaz, R. M., & Sanchez, J. (2009). Family rejection as a predictor of negative health outcomes in white and Latino lesbian, gay, and bisexual young adults.
Pediatrics, 3 (1), 346–352. doi:10.1542/peds.2007-3524.

Ryan, C., Russell, S. T., Huebner, D., Diaz, R., & Sanchez, J. (2010). Family acceptance in adolescence and the health of LGBT young adults. *Journal of Child and Adolescent Psychiatric
Nursing, 23* (4), 205–213. doi:10.1111/j.1744-6171.2010.00246.x.

Sansfaçon, A. P., Robichaud, M., & Dumais-Michaud, A. (2015). The experience of parents who
support their children's gender variance. *Journal of LGBT Youth, 12*, 39–63. doi:10.1080
/19361653.2014.935555.

Ungar, M., Ghazinor, M., & Richter, J. (2013). Annual research review: What is resilience within
the social ecology of human development? *Journal of Child Psychology and Psychiatry,
54*, 348–366.

Werner, E. (2005). Resilience and recovery: Findings from the Kauai Longitudinal Study. *Focal
Point: Research, Policy, and Practice in Children's Mental Health, 19* (1), 11–14. Retrieved
from https://www.pathwaysrtc.pdx.edu/pdf/fpS0504.pdf.

Zamboni, B. D. (2006). Therapeutic considerations in working with the family, friends, and
partners of transgendered individuals. *Family Journal: Counseling and Therapy for Couples and Families, 14* (2), 174–179. doi:10.1177 /1066480705285251.

6

More Than the Sum of Your Parts: A Theoretical Perspective

AndreAs Neumann Mascis, PhD

Gender Affirmation and the Journey of the Self

"You don't understand. I'm not going to deal with this!" So begins my phone call with the parent of an adolescent who had come to see me to discuss gender transition. "You have no idea what it has meant to raise this child," the parent continues. "I am a single parent. My child has had a lot of needs and a lot of services. There have been learning issues, social issues, and behavioral issues. We have seen doctors, psychiatrists, psychologists, behavioral specialists, learning coaches. We have tried individual therapy, group therapy, inpatient therapy, outpatient therapy, and group homes. Last week there was something about transgender on TV and now you're calling me to tell me there's a whole 'nother problem that I have never heard about at all, and I am telling you I am not going to deal with this! I am not!"

As I listened to this overwhelmed, exhausted, but loving parent, I found myself longing for access to the support that includes her wants and desires as well as the support that gender affirmation needs and deserves. There was a time in legitimizing and defending the importance of gender affirmative care when a popular colloquialism was "Even if this person was on an island by themselves, they would need this care." But we are, none of us, on that island. We are parents and children and loved ones and friends — all relational beings — depending on each other for survival. Finding intervention strategies and treatment plans that meet the needs of gender variant children and their parents is not a simple task since everyone, including clinicians, may have different, potentially competing, agendas. Identifying strategies that support the well-being of children, parents, and their families requires attention to the identities and self structures of the whole system (Israel & Tarver, 1997; Lev, 2004).

We are at a place in our history in which gender identity is more legitimized and medical intervention is more available than ever (Bryant, 2006; Coolhart,

Lev, Arlene I., Gottlieb, Andrew R., *Families in Transition*
dx.doi.org/10.17312/harringtonparkpress/2019.04.fit.006
© 2019 by Harrington Park Press

Baker, Farmer, Malaney, & Shipman, 2013; Israel & Tarver, 1997; Kane, 2006; Lev, 2004). As a result, health practitioners are seeing an unprecedented number of gender nonconforming children and transgender youth (Case & Meier, 2014; de Vries, Doreleijers, Steensma, & Cohen-Kettenis, 2011). The effect of this cultural shift is complex.

From the perspective of the clinical community, it is powerful to consider an emerging generation of transgender people who have potentially avoided the chronic trauma inherent in the experiences of many trans people unable to access care until adulthood. Postponing care *creates* trauma. The effect of gender incongruence can be a kind of social and emotional neglect in which vital intrapsychic experiences of feeling fully and accurately seen, understood, and valued are inhibited. In the language of self psychology, when the assigned gender identity does not reflect the felt sense of self, the richness of the relational connection is compromised. Inadequate experiences of *mirroring* (feeling seen and validated), *idealization* (feeling safe and aspirational), and *twinship* (feeling a sense of alikeness and belonging) limit the resource of *transmuting internalization,* or the process of integrating affective connections into the structure and function of the self (Kohut, 1971). Those social and emotional resources influence the core of psychological functioning, including affect regulation and resiliency (Wolf, 2002). Those resources not only shape the long-term ramifications of a traumatic event, but may also shape the relational environments that the self can access.

We know that people who have experienced a trauma have an increased likelihood of experiencing another trauma (Van der Kolk, 2000). The reasons for this are complex. A contributing factor in the increased likelihood of trauma, however, is a compromised relational environment and its concurrent effect on the neurobiological and psychological resources that facilitate connection (Van der Kolk, 2000). Gender variant children, vulnerable to being targeted by peers and adults, are then made further vulnerable by the compromise in intrapsychic resources that not only shape their capacity to respond to ordinary and extraordinary stressors, but further affect the ability to elicit or even recognize nourishing, nontraumatic connection. This level of neglect, facilitated by the constraints of gender socialization, which conceivably begins even before birth, has the potential to create a lifelong pattern of neglect and injury. This complex neuropsychosocial experience is reflected in disproportionate experiences of violence, sexual and physical abuse, substance use, and suicidality as a defining aspect of their life experiences, and reflected in the work that must be addressed clinically (House, Van Horn, Coppeans, & Stepleman, 2011).

The social and emotional trauma and neglect that are expressed in the profound emotional and psychological deprivation of an identity may never meaningfully be reflected or affirmed (Ryan & Rivers, 2003; Siegel & Hartzell, 2004). As clinicians we see, even more chronically, the damage that is evident in a self that is not seen or responded to, one in which incongruence between perceived identity and felt identity fundamentally influences attachment, affect regulation, resiliency of a self not seen—and worse, of a self shamed (Cozolino, 2013; Mills, 2005). Chronic failure of attunement from the earliest age is reflected in transgender adults who seek care and manifested in a history of relationship and professional disruptions, trauma histories, dysregulated affect, eating disorders, and substance use concerns (Israel & Tarver, 1997; Lev, 2004; Ryan & Rivers, 2003). What was once considered clinical contraindications for access to transgender-related care, including dysregulated emotions, relational or resource instability, or limitations in compliance, are now understood as the adaptive consequences of fundamental attachment failures, the healing of which is dependent on access to culturally competent treatment (Lev, 2004).

In that way, it is a profound shift in clinical possibility to imagine that children might avoid decades of injury and instead have access to the ordinary and challenging business of growing up. The aspiration of early intervention includes the hope of restoring access to an ordinary developmental history. Parents certainly share that aspiration. As therapists, it is our enthusiasm for that possibility that can, at times, inhibit our ability to respond meaningfully to the needs of parents and families beyond a kind of behavioral push for acceptance. What is also sometimes lost is an awareness that parents have come into a challenge to their own identity, their sense of self, and their relationships interpersonally and institutionally (Lev, 2004). Parenting a gender variant child requires renegotiating and advocating for the needs of their child with each other, with the child's siblings, with immediate and extended family members. It further demands advocacy with educators, medical providers, and sometimes social services. Parenting a gender variant child includes having unwittingly come into a role of helping the child navigate systems with a stigmatized identity—an identity that the parents themselves do not share, may be ill-equipped to advocate for, and may feel, at best, ambivalent about (Diamond & Glenn, 2006; Lev, 2004; Solomon, 2013).

"We Don't Care If It's a Boy or a Girl — as Long as the Baby Is Healthy"

This anthem of expecting parents is a deceptively simple assertion that belies a complexity of ideas, images, beliefs, and hopes for a child that reflect the developmental experiences of the parents. Coming into an awareness of having a gender variant child is intrapsychically and relationally significant for them. Parents are invariably confronted with their own fears related to its etiology: "What did I do wrong?" "How did this happen?" "How do we fix this?" These questions not only confound treatment choices, but also directly shape a parent's identity. One whose sense of self includes having been a good-enough parent, who has had a sense of knowing and feeling known by one's child, and has enjoyed positive reflections on one's parenting abilities from others may face the fear that these perceptions have been false or will now be withdrawn (Lev, 2004; Vanderburgh, 2009).

A parent who believes that gender variance emerges as a consequence of their family or parenting may not only fear failure, but also question aspects of their child's experience that they had taken for granted. This can include the (often) erroneous fear that their child may have experienced a trauma that could account for "their condition." For those who have chronically feared or experienced parental shortcomings, or have had their limitations as parents reflected back to them, gender variance in their child may seem to validate deeply held fears. Shame has a particularly toxic effect on the self, the brain, and the capacity for attachment (Siegel & Hartzell, 2004), and it can be at the core of ways in which parents become galvanized in limiting the treatment options available to their children.

Parenting a gender variant child requires a significant and consistent level of attunement at the same time that confidence in their ability to attune has been strained. Identity is further informed by the projected narrative of what it means to be a parent and of the life they have imagined for their child (Siegel & Hartzell, 2004). The feelings invoked in the face of gender variance are informed by their own experience of gender identity or role expectations, both of which, as measures of mental health, have deep roots in psychodynamic theory. Those who share the gender identity that the child was assigned at birth are vulnerable to that legacy and feelings of rejection. Intrapsychically, that rejection may challenge the parent's own identity, sense of self, or self-efficacy. In a culture where masculinity ("manhood") can be won or lost and femininity ("womanhood") has no inherent value and remains the metaphor for weakness or failure, the perceived rejection of either gender identity can threaten the self-concept of either parent. At times, those feelings emerge as fears of having inadequately modeled gender identity and role expectations for the child. For the parent who shares the gender that the child is moving toward, there can be complex feelings associated with the ways in which the emerging identity is performed by child and parent (Vanderburgh, 2009).

These intrapsychic conflicts meaningfully affect functioning in the family system. Roles and boundaries are underscored in parental responses to gender variance. This can be vividly expressed in the parental dyad, particularly if the parents take very different positions in their understanding and desire for intervention on behalf of the child. These dynamics, while significant, often remain largely unconscious, and their expressions can be challenging to recognize. Both the clinician and the child are at times preoccupied with the perceived strength of the more accepting parent. This can easily mask a preexisting rupture in the marital dyad that more accurately accounts for expressions of acceptance. From a family systems perspective, choices that are made as a reflection of dyadic instability will result in instability in other parts of the system and make changes unsustainable. A clinician's role must be informed by the stability of the system over the content of the conflict while also advocating for the needs of the individual.

Acceptance and advocacy for care that is a reflection of marital conflict can destabilize the family system in such a way that short-term progress may be met with unanticipated regression. This can be a regression in parental support or an increase in comorbid symptoms of the child or siblings as an outgrowth of the conflict between the parents (Lev, 2004; Pattison, Defrancisco, Wood, Frazier, & Crowder, 1975). Gender variant children and adolescents can exhibit a heightened sense of fear that they are causing harm to their parents in how their identity is emerging (Baker & Baker, 1987; Coolhart et al., 2013). That heightened awareness is neurologically reflected in the significant increase in neuronal connectivity in adolescence (Siegel & Hartzell, 2004). Neurological development across gender identity demonstrates a heightened integration of regions of the brain that are thought to be reflected both in an increased complexity of affect states and in a craving for affective stimulation and risk (Siegel, 2012). For the gender variant adolescent, these ordinary developments are compounded by the demands of a stigmatized identity. Gender variant children may evidence anxiety and shame that is informed not only by a fear of abandonment, but by an acute awareness of the transphobia parents are unwittingly forced to confront in every aspect of their own psychosocial environment (Coolhart et al., 2013).

Understanding a parent's position relative to the treatment of their child and the narrative that shapes that position both informs the relationships and affects the parent's sense of self, which is central to integrated treatment (Coolhart et al., 2013; Lev, 2004). It can be the complexity of the emotional experience of the parents that sometimes fuels the clinician's and client's desires to focus on simple behavioral change. Treatment and intervention strategies that are limited to determining the "truth" of the child's gender identity and then facilitating its implementation in the psychosocial environment may achieve behavioral success, even relief, but may miss the opportunity to respond to the intrapsychic and attachment injuries that have inevitably affected every aspect of the family system. It can be a time of tremendous parental confusion, feelings of helplessness, or blame (Diamond & Glenn, 2006).

For some parents there can also be a profound sense of loss. The way that it is most simply expressed is a sense of loss of the offspring's assumed gender (Lev, 2004). The actual loss experienced may be more nuanced, and it has more to do with a loss of emotional intimacy with one's child. A parent's sense that they and their child are known to one another is sometimes challenged in the disclosure of gender identity incongruence. This challenge echoes the experience of anyone parenting an adolescent, but gender identity is experienced in this culture as core to the very structure of identity. Perceived loss experienced by parents can be profound. They may also be alienated from their own relational resources as their parenting challenges now significantly diverge from those of their cohort, who had been available to provide significant and reciprocal mirroring, idealization and twinship, and who may now distance themselves or actively reject the parent of a transgender youth. Within the parent-child relationship, though gender identity needs might coincide with a sense of loss of emotional intimacy, or a change in emotional boundaries between parent and child, they may also, in fact, be developmentally appropriate, although expressed through gender variance. Patterns of differentiation that challenge even the most unremarkable development can take on meaning for parents with gender variant children. Increased systems involvement can also foster some regression on the part of parents and children. Intergenerationally, unresolved patterns of connection and differentiation may be reignited between parents and their families of origin (McGoldrick & Hardy, 2008).

The identity needs that parents have and the ways in which their choices are reflected back to them will directly affect the emotional flexibility and resilience they can bring to parenting. From a family systems perspective, we understand that as part of the transmission of internal and external boundaries. Neurologically, emotional attunement has a fundamental influence on the ability to process affects, deepen attachments, and make use of new information, all of which is fundamental to resiliency. A parent who is experiencing attunement and relationship safety will have an increased capacity to have and manage feelings and make use of those feelings to further the relationship. The neuro-physiological effect of attunement between parent and child is increasing the acuity of attunement to further emotional resources of attachment. This social and emotional resource can make a profound difference, as both parent and child can emerge together into a potentially transphobic relational world. That attunement can create the relational foundation for both parent and child in their abilities to navigate systems, develop coping strategies, and increase social supports. Even a parent who is new to understanding gender variance can be a vital emotional resource in mitigating the consequences of chronic microaggressions or empathic failures in other parts of the child's world—the inverse of mirroring.

The emotional complexity of these dynamics can create a situation in which clients and providers alike are eager for behavioral simplification. The work becomes supporting the parents to do the "right thing," that is, use the right pronoun, use the right name, and be generally accepting (Vanderburgh, 2009). With acceptance comes a new set of demands on parents and child to develop a plan to move forward. Here enter all the demands and difficult choices regarding social transition, medical intervention, and timing. Parents, children, and clinicians can find themselves organizing complex familial and institutional systems dynamics into questions of timing. Identifying with families when and how disclosure of the emerging identity will happen inherently illustrates issues related to communication, boundaries, and power. As with all family systems work, the question of gender identity transition becomes a magnification of systemic functioning that crosses generational lines. As the family engages with the outside world—medical, educational, therapeutic—family roles, power alliances, and internal and external boundaries are challenged (Brown, 2010). Recognizing this, providers may be able to support change in a context that feels congruent with the existing structure rather than ignoring that structure or absenting the needs of various members in favor of the gender variant child, thereby further destabilizing the system.

An additional demand can be inadvertently placed on parents and children in that there can be a growing expectation that they, by virtue of their own needs, be "experts." As an increasing number of social systems become engaged with the child and the family, those systems will also look to parents and children to identify what those needs are and how they should "best" be met. With all these pressures, what can get lost is the opportunity for otherwise good-enough parents to parent, and for their children to experience themselves as more than just their gender identity. Meeting the needs of gender variant children and their parents involves successfully responding to the effects of gender variance on the identities and relationships in the family, and restoring for parents a sense of confidence and commitment to their child's well-being and development within and beyond gender. The shattering consequence that gender incongruence can have on the core of identity and attachment is also the site of some of our most powerful opportunities for healing. Engaging that healing requires a context that acknowledges the identity needs of both the parent and the child and cultivates a relational environment through which a transgender child and a skilled, fortified parent of a transgender child can emerge into a changed and ultimately enriched attachment.

The following is an effort to conceptualize healing and growth for parents and children using the science of interpersonal neurobiology as understood through a psychodynamic framework. With this foundation we will explore the active nature of healing and develop strategies to support the identity and needs of the child and the parent.

The Brain and the Self

Offering a comprehensive understanding of the needs of gender variant children and their parents starts with a basic understanding of the brain and the self. We have entered a time in which we know more about the brain and brain development than ever before (Blakemore, 2010; Siegel & Hartzell, 2004). Brain imaging technology has allowed us to examine both structural changes and changes in activity of regions of the brain across a life span (Burnett, Sebastian, Cohen-Kadosh, & Blakemore, 2010). This ever-growing body of knowledge supports what psychodynamic theory strives to articulate and explore: we are created and re-created in the context of our relationships and our experiences. The effect of social interaction and relationships on the brain is dynamic. Relationships shape brain activity; brain activity changes brain structures; changes in brain structure affect changes in brain function; changes in brain function influence the capacity for relationships; relationships affect the self. A parent who is able to empathically mirror their child's felt identity is not simply asserting a perspective on gender, but also cultivating the capacity to attune, and attunement is elemental to developing the ability for affect regulation and resiliency.

The neurological consequence of attunement is expressed through the limbic system. It begins with felt safety, which leads to a capacity for attachment and for affect regulation (Siegel, 2014; Vicario & Hudgins-Mitchell, 2017). This process was expressed through Marcia Linehan's (1993) work, one of the early recognitions that mindfulness and affect regulation have to be structurally achieved to make attachment possible (Cullen, Westlund, LaRiviere, & Klimes-Dougan, 2013). Self psychology describes this process as *transmuting internalization* or the ability to internalize the felt experience of relationships in order to construct the self. Feeling safe, feeling seen, and feeling a sense of belonging are the foundation of a rich relational environment that regulates the nervous system and constructs the self. For gender variant children, feeling seen and safe and feeling a sense of belonging can be painfully difficult to access. Social transition, or the opportunity for the child to live in their affirmed gender identity through nonmedical interventions, including name and pronoun change, change in gendered clothing, and change in school, can offer the opportunity to live fully in an affirmed relational environment. These interventions can have a profound effect on healing (Siegel, 2012; Vicario & Hudgins-Mitchell, 2017).

The brain generates neuronal growth and increased connectivity with stimulation, and it prunes neurons that are not engaged. An increasing body of research provides a physiological template for connection (Cozolino, 2013; Siegel, 2011). These advances demonstrate structurally what we have understood psychodynamically: we are fundamentally relational beings (Banai, Mikulincer, & Shaver, 2005). Our physical and psychological health and functioning depend almost entirely on the social and emotional connections we make with our primary caregivers and throughout our life span. Those connections change the structure and function of the brain and the (re)structure of the self.

Self psychology offers a useful framework for understanding the self and attachment (Banai et al., 2005; Kohut, 1971; Rowe & Isaac, 2000). It first identifies *self objects,* or the significant relationships and experiences that serve an affective function, which are then internalized to shape and reshape the self. This occurs in three key ways. The first is through *mirroring*—the accurate, realistic reflection of the emotional state or experience of the self by another, or *attunement.* The second is *idealization,* defined as having two essential aspects: the experience of safety and the experience of aspiration. Idealization can be as simple as having an adult to turn to with a dilemma or as complex as finding a cultural reflection of an adult that represents what could be possible in an imagined adulthood. The third is *twinship,* which is the experience of alikeness and belonging. Twinship is reflexively sought and cultivated. Fashion, haircuts, and music are all social cues that signal not only gender identity but interests, desires, and beliefs. Finding "people like us" is not just a social reflex but a fundamental psychological need (Banai et al., 2005; Kohut, 1971; Rowe & Isaac, 2000).

Self psychology describes what is neurologically evident. In a relational environment, the experiences of being seen, feeling safe, and belonging become internalized. That internalization both constructs and heals the self. Because our survival depends on it, we are neurobiologically driven to attach. We are driven to attune and resonate emotional experience as well as meet the needs of others (Banks, 2006; Cozolino, 2013; Siegel, 2001). Attachment creates neuroplasticity. The activity of emotional attunement fortifies neuronal connection and determines the pattern of pruning. Neurologically, connection engages the limbic system. The limbic system comprises the structures of the brain that navigate emotion and memory. We are neurophysiologically dependent on social and emotional connection to facilitate learning, affect regulation, and resiliency (Banks, 2006).

Understanding that attunement, or failures in attunement, shapes neurological capacity articulates the significance of gender-identity affirmation. Gender variant children experience disruption in social and emotional connection. They experience higher levels of physical, sexual, and emotional abuse than do many of their cisgender peers (Russell & Fish, 2016; Ryan & Rivers, 2003). Neurologically, overt traumatic events have a profound effect. The polyvagal theory (Porges, 2009; 2011), illustrating the magnitude of that effect, refers to the growing body of knowledge that links cranial nerves, which become active in response to social and environmental stimuli, to the autonomic nervous system. Porges (2009) found that chronic traumatic events alter the functioning of the nervous system. Having a gender identity that is different from how you are perceived inherently creates disruptions in experiences of mirroring, attunement, belonging, twinship, safety, and idealization. Deficits in attention, concentration, and memory that characterize cognitive symptoms of trauma impede attachment and affect regulation.

Disruptions in attachment and connection are no less significant. Social rejection has been shown to activate the same centers of the brain as physical pain (Cozolino, 2013), whereas positive connection activates the same centers of the brain as physical warmth (Eisenberger, Lieberman, & Williams, 2003). In addition to the effect of connection, the brain evidences critical periods of significant structural changes in adolescence. With a decrease in gray matter (neuronal volume) comes an increase in white matter (connectivity). There is evidence of increasing connectivity in the areas that facilitate emotions and sense of self. Brain imaging studies comparing adolescents and adults demonstrate differences in connectivity and activity (Burnett et al., 2010; NIMH, 2011). What we psychodynamically might think of as mirroring begins neurologically with facial recognition, which cues the presence of interaction and provides interpersonal information about that interaction, thereby engaging the polyvagal system (Siegel, 2012). The experience of mirroring (attunement) and twinship (belonging) activates serotonin, dopamine, and norepinephrine, which generate a sense of safety (idealization) and well-being, which in turn optimizes neuroplasticity and creates the capacity for learning and relationship (Cozolino, 2013; Porges, 2011).

When we compare neural activity between adolescents and adults, imaging suggests that adolescents increase their acuity of recognition across time and show a greater intensity of response to emotionally loaded material. Adolescents also reflect differences in the ability to accurately interpret affect states and are, for example, better able to read anger than fear (Burnett et al., 2010). Structural changes, including a shift in activity from the medial prefrontal cortex (MPFC) to posterior temporal structures as adolescents move into early adulthood, are thought to account for a heightened awareness or self-consciousness and attention to the appraisal of others. There is also a significant increase in white matter or cortical connectivity in the hippocampal and temporal regions. These structural changes reflect an increase in cognitive and affective processing, language, memory, and attachment activity (Burnett et al., 2010).

Gender variant children emerging into adolescence can experience a devastating level of crisis associated with the development of secondary sex characteristics (Alegria, 2016; Israel & Tarver, 1997; Lev, 2004). We understand that clinically as a part of the difference between biological sex and felt gender identity. Beyond that, the development of secondary sex characteristics that highlight assigned gender identity can inflame barriers to relationship and access to attunement. The effects of those barriers are deterioration of the developing self. Social isolation and alienation influence affect regulation and attachment, generating physical and emotional pain as well as immunological suppression. For gender variant children and adolescents, the ordinary stressors of development are made more stressful in the absence of calming or re-regulating social connections (Siegel, 2001).

Parenting the Brain

For cisgender parents, gender identity congruence is an aspect of experience that exists like the functions of the autonomic nervous system, so innate and so easily taken for granted that unless there is a problem, there is hardly reason to be made conscious of it. For cisgender parents, then, it is easy to perceive gender nonconformity as a socialization failure and a behavior problem. Working with parents of gender variant children, as we have seen, cannot be limited to developing parental knowledge regarding gender. Parents' experiences and beliefs about the identity of the family can also be a source of distress. For parents who have a biological, genetic connection to their child, the meanings attributed to that genetic connection can be potent. A parent's experience of confusion regarding what they have understood about their child's identity in that context of meaning can be experienced as a deeper rejection. The meaning of genetic traits is so much more dynamic and so much more relational than simple heredity would suggest. The ways in which brain, body, and self are shaped by relationship are more fully demonstrated in an understanding of genetic potentials. Genes provide a template for potentials, but the activation of those potentials occurs in relationship. Experience and connection facilitate changes in the biochemistry of the cell and genetic activation potentials (Cozolino, 2013). The meaning of this adds to the critical effect of attunement and gender identity. Chronic alienation affects well-being and capacity on a cellular level. The value of gender affirmation is fundamentally the opportunity to strengthen neurological connectivity and regulate the central nervous system. With affect regulation and resiliency comes increased relational richness (Siegel, 2012).

Providing care for gender variant youth, then, means maximizing the wisdom of interpersonal neurobiology. The most essential element of psychological health is relationships. Feeling safe affects, neurologically, the ability to perceive and process information (Banks, 2006; Vicario & Hudgins-Mitchell, 2017).

Restoring the path between parent and child facilitates access to attachment, mirroring, or limbic regulation. What we know is that attuned reflection of an infant's experiences creates a pattern of attachment that persists and influences affect regulation and resiliency (Cozolino, 2013). Those attachment patterns persist unless they are reshaped by novel relationship experiences *and* a narrative that explains the previous attachment pattern or emotional resources. A child who experiences the parent as generally available and responsive will not lose that internalization with a single or even a series of failures unless those failures are accompanied by a change in meaning about the relationship (Belsky & de Haan, 2011). As we have seen, there are tangible neurological expressions of relationship patterns and the available narratives about those patterns. The neurological effect of attachments includes increased neuronal connectivity, cranial nerve interaction with the central nervous system (brain and spinal cord) and the peripheral nervous system (nerves and ganglia outside the brain and spinal cord), and engagement of the limbic system. This engagement generates further attachment and facilitates affect management, information processing, and resilience. What interpersonal neurobiology teaches us is what psychodynamic theory has been striving to articulate. It is attachment that shapes the structure, function, and activity of the brain, and it is attachment that builds and heals the structure of the self. Parenting a gender variant child at its core is less a question of gender and more a question of cultivating and healing attachment relationships for the health of the brain and the self (Ehrensaft, 2011).

Where to Begin?

Finding healing for cisgender parents of gender variant children is a process that is constructed by and transcends the infrastructure of medical and mental health treatment decisions. It is a process that elicits and challenges the identity and the self of parent and child, illuminating the functioning of the entire family system. It is also an opportunity to restore functioning, cultivate empowered parenting, and enrich connection for the brain and the self.

Cisgender parents and families who attempt to redirect or avoid gender incongruity can be supported by highlighting the psychic damage that can be inflicted, however unintentionally. That damage can ignite or increase alienation between parents and children and/or between families and other systems of support. Understanding the relational needs of the brain and the self creates different opportunities for healing. The goal of treatment for gender variant children must fundamentally be defined as facilitating access to the kind of rich relational environment that heals and facilitates neurological connectivity and a self that is adept at processing and integrating stimuli, affect regulation, and further connection. An affirmed gender identity that is seen and responded to is the backdrop through which attunement and failures in attunement are vividly expressed. The beginning of that treatment is less about determining gender identity than it is about facilitating attunement. A decision to see and validate a child's experience of self is inherently healing. Parents and children can be supported in exploring a dynamic expression of self and relationship; gender identity and expression become a side effect of attunement. An attuned relational environment facilitates the emotional agility to manage stressors, seek connection, and find nourishing relationships. That foundation generates a baseline of psychological health across the life span.

REFERENCES

Alegria, C. A. (2016). Gender nonconforming and transgender children/youth: Family, community, and implications for practice. *Journal of the American Association of Nurse Practitioners, 28* (10), 521–527. doi:10.1002/2327-6924.12363.

Baker, H. S., & Baker, M. N. (1987). Heinz Kohut's self psychology: An overview. *American Journal of Psychiatry, 144* (1), 1–9.

Banai, E., Mikulincer, M., & Shaver, P. R. (2005). "Selfobject" needs in Kohut's self psychology: Links with attachment, self-cohesion, affect regulation, and adjustment. *Psychoanalytic Psychology, 22* (2), 224–260. doi:10.1037/0736-9735.22.2.224.

Banks, A. (2006). Relational therapy for trauma. *Journal of Trauma Practice, 5* (1), 25–47. doi:10.1300/J189v05n01_03.

Belsky, J., & de Haan, M. (2011). Annual research review: Parenting and children's brain development: The end of the beginning. *Journal of Child Psychology and Psychiatry, 52* (4), 409–428. doi:10.1111/j.1469-7610.2010.02281.x.

Blakemore, S. J. (2010). The developing social brain: Implications for education. *Neuron, 65* (6), 744–747. doi:10.1016/j.neuron.2010.03.004.

Brown, J. (2010). Psychotherapy integration: Systems theory and self-psychology. *Journal of Marital and Family Therapy, 36,* 472–485. doi:10.1111/j.1752-0606.2010.00196.x.

Bryant, K. (2006). Making gender identity disorder of childhood: Historical lessons for contemporary debates. *Sexuality Research & Social Policy, 3* (3), 23–39.

Burnett, S., Sebastian, C., Cohen-Kadosh, K., & Blakemore, S. J. (2010). The social brain in adolescence: Evidence from functional magnetic resonance imaging and behavioural studies. *Neuroscience and Biobehavioral Reviews, 35* (8), 1654–1664. doi:10.1016/j.neubiorev.2010.10.011.

Case, K., & Meier, S. C. (2014). Developing allies to transgender and gender non-conforming youth: Training for counselors and educators. *Journal of LGBT Youth, 11* (1), 62–82. doi:10.1080/193653.2014.840764.

Coolhart, D., Baker, A., Farmer, S., Malaney, M., & Shipman, D. (2013). Therapy with transsexual youth and their families: A clinical tool for assessing youth's readiness for gender transition. *Journal of Marital and Family Therapy, 39* (2), 223–243. doi:10.1111/j.1752-0606.2011.00283.x.

Cozolino, L. (2013). *The social neuroscience of education: Optimizing attachment and learning in the classroom.* New York: W. W. Norton.

Cullen, K. R., Westlund, M. K., LaRiviere, L. L., & Klimes-Dougan, B. (2013). An adolescent with nonsuicidal self-injury: A case and discussion of neurobiological research on emotion regulation. *American Journal of Psychiatry, 170* (8), 828–831. doi:10.1176/appi.ajp.2013.12121598.

de Vries, A. L. C., Doreleijers, T. A. H., Steensma, T. D., & Cohen-Kettenis, P. T. (2011). Psychiatric comorbidity in gender dysphoric adolescents. *Journal of Child Psychology and Psychiatry, 52* (11), 1195–1202. doi:10.1111/j.1469-7610.2011.02426.x.

Diamond, M., & Glenn, H. (2006). The right to be wrong: Sex and gender decisions. In S. E. Sytsma (ed.), *Ethics and intersex* (pp. 103–113). Dordrecht, Netherlands: Springer. www.hawaii.edu/PCSS/biblio/articles/2005to2009/2005-right-to-be-wrong.html.

Ehrensaft, D. (2011). *Gender born, gender made: Raising healthy gender-nonconforming children.* New York: Experiment.

Eisenberger, N. I., Lieberman, M. D., & Williams, K. D. (2003). Does rejection hurt? An fMRI study of social exclusion. *Science, 302* (5643), 290–292. doi:10.1126/science.1089134.

House, A. S., Van Horn, E., Coppeans, C., & Stepleman, L. M. (2011). Interpersonal trauma and discriminatory events as predictors of suicidal and nonsuicidal self-injury in gay, lesbian, bisexual, and transgender persons. *Traumatology, 17* (2), 75–85.

Israel, G. E., & Tarver, D. E. (1997). *Transgender care: Recommended guidelines, practical information, and personal accounts.* Philadelphia: Temple University Press.

Kane, E. (2006). "No way my boys are going to be like that!" Parents' responses to children's gender nonconformity. *Gender & Society, 20* (2), 149–176. doi:10.1177/0891243205284276.

Kohut, H. (1971). *The analysis of the self.* New York: International Universities Press.

Lev, A. I. (2004). *Transgender emergence: Therapeutic guidelines for working with gender-variant people and their families.* Binghamton, N.Y.: Haworth Press.

Linehan, M. M. (1993). *Skills training manual for treating borderline personality disorder.* New York: Guilford Press.

McGoldrick, M., & Hardy, K. V. (eds.). (2008). *Re-visioning family therapy: Race, culture, and gender in clinical practice* (2nd ed.). New York: Guilford Press.

Mills, R. S. L. (2005). Taking stock of the developmental literature on shame. *Developmental Review, 25* (1), 26–63. doi.org/10.1016/j.dr.2004.08.001.

National Institute of Mental Health. (2011). *The teen brain: Still under construction* (brochure). Retrieved from https://infocenter.nimh.nih.gov/pubstatic/NIH%2011-4929/NIH%2011-4929.pdf.

Pattison, E. M., Defrancisco, D., Wood, P., Frazier, H., & Crowder, J. (1975). A psychosocial kinship model for family therapy. *American Journal of Psychiatry, 132* (12), 1246–1251. doi:10.1176ajp.132.12.1246.

Porges, S. W. (2009). The polyvagal theory: New insights into adaptive reactions of the autonomic nervous system. *Cleveland Clinic Journal of Medicine, 76* (S2), S86–S90. doi:10.3949/ccjm.76.s2.17.

Porges, S. W. (2011). *The polyvagal theory: Neurophysiological foundations of emotions, attachment, communication, and self-regulation.* New York: W. W. Norton.

Rowe, C. E., Jr., & Isaac, D. S. M. (2000). *Empathic attunement: The "technique" of psychoanalytic self psychology.* Northvale, N.J.: Jason Aronson.

Russell, S. T., & Fish, J. N. (2016). Mental health in lesbian, gay, bisexual, and transgender (LGBT) youth. *Annual Review of Clinical Psychology, 12,* 465–487. doi:10.1146/annurev-clinpsy-021815-093153.

Ryan, C., & Rivers, I. (2003). Lesbian, gay, bisexual, and transgender youth: Victimization and its correlates in the USA and UK. *Culture, Health & Sexuality, 5,* 103–119.

Siegel, D. J. (2001). Toward an interpersonal neurobiology of the developing mind: Attachment relationships, "mindsight," and neural integration. *Infant Mental Health Journal, 22* (1–2), 67–94.

Siegel, D. J. (2011). *Mindsight: The new science of personal transformation*. New York: Bantam Books.

Siegel, D. J. (2012). *The developing mind: How relationships and the brain interact to shape who we are* (2nd ed.). New York: Guilford Press.

Siegel, D. J. (2014). *Brainstorm: The power and purpose of the teenage brain*. New York: Penguin.

Siegel, D. J., & Hartzell, M. (2004). *Parenting from the inside out*. New York: Penguin.

Solomon, A. (2013). *Far from the tree: Parents, children and the search for identity*. New York: Scribner.

Vanderburgh, R. (2009). Appropriate therapeutic care for families with pre-pubescent transgender/gender-dissonant children. *Child and Adolescent Social Work Journal, 26* (2), 135–154.

Van der Kolk, B. (2000). Posttraumatic stress disorder and the nature of trauma. *Dialogues of Clinical Neuroscience, 2* (1), 7–22.

Vicario, M., & Hudgins-Mitchell, C. (2017). Attachment, trauma, and repair from infant to adolescent development: Counseling implications from neurobiology. In S. Smith-Adcock and C. Tucker (eds.), *Counseling children and adolescents: Connecting theory, development, and diversity* (pp. 59–97). Thousand Oaks, Calif.: Sage.

Wolf, E. S. (2002). *Treating the self: Elements of clinical psychology*. New York: Guilford Press.

PART 3

Clinical Issues: What Are the Parents' Concerns and Challenges Regarding Cultural Diversity, Clinical Models, and Psychiatric Treatment?

Scott Leibowitz sometimes feels as though he is "walking a tightrope." With the dearth of literature to uniformly guide clinical practice, there are wide-ranging viewpoints on what constitutes effective care. Since the long-term ramifications of those decisions are not yet known, and as the field itself continues to evolve, the lives of gender nonconforming and transgender children and adolescents hang in the balance. Dr. Leibowitz rightly points out that child and adolescent psychiatrists, by virtue of their training and knowledge, are uniquely positioned to play key roles in the treatment of these young patients, given that the centrality of focus is the mind-body connection. But since psychiatry has, until more recently, historically pathologized LGBT people, there is much work to be done in regard to building relationships between those two communities.

But relationship building is what Dr. Leibowitz is all about, not only with his young patients, but with their parents and the members of his treatment team — in whatever setting he finds himself. He models a psychiatric approach that is holistic; that is, he views his patients as multifaceted, complex human beings, not just a collection of symptoms requiring a "cure." He treats parents and caretakers as collaborative partners, offering vital information, modeling affirming behaviors, and addressing their anxieties. With both patient and family, he favors a methodical, thorough, yet flexible assessment, one that considers as many factors as possible in an effort to reach an informed decision with the family and other treatment team members, a process Dr. Leibowitz terms *collaborative path-paving*. While working within institutional parameters, he believes that being both creative and comprehensive does not have to come at the cost of patients having less access to care. Similarly, among members of his treatment team, effective relationship building takes place when consistent communication, and an openness to alternative viewpoints are shared. This helps coordinate professional efforts and minimize confusion for the family.

Perhaps one day soon, Dr. Leibowitz won't be walking that tightrope any longer.

Nena Wang and Wallace Wong highlight issues specific to Chinese Canadian families with transgender youth. How the collectivist perspective, the one-child policy, acculturation, and the divide between first- and second-generation immigrants powerfully affect the entire system—parents and youth alike—s all theoretically articulated, then dramatically illustrated by their case "Marshall, Lucy, and John," which emphasizes that the success or failure of treatment depends on a firm grasp *of*, a profound respect *for*, and a deep sensitivity *to* cultural and ethnic experiences.

Arlene I. Lev presents us with an in-depth, historical overview, contrasting the *reparative* and the *affirmative models* of treatment. More philosophical perspectives than therapeutic regimens, their unique approaches are implicit in the names. The former emphasizes repair, that is, aligning the child or youth with their assigned gender; the latter emphasizes affirmation, that is, supporting the child or youth in the gender they know themselves to be. Between these polar opposites lies a middle ground, the protective response, or "wait-and-see," a more conservative stance, a suspension that allows time for gender exploration to proceed cautiously without any real parental validation or therapeutic support.

The reparative model, which, over the course of decades, destroyed countless lives, has now been replaced by an affirmative model, one that offers gender nonconforming and trans people a chance to live more freely and more authentically. Understanding the history of treatment strategies is necessary for practitioners as well as families as we embark on a new era for gender creative children.

Lisette Lahana illustrates how difficult treatment can be when an adolescent is reticent to address their gender identity directly with their parents, and when parents either have little information or, worse yet, are in denial. This is the situation in which she finds herself when working with "Micah," a 17-year-old, multiracial, trans male, son of Corrine, a white mother, and Greg, an African American father, now divorced from each other, and stepson of Nick, an Asian American male. Lisette's work clearly demonstrates the fact that it is possible to be thorough and effective and move parents and the extended family to another level of understanding, *despite* the treatment's being short-term.

7

Walking a Tightrope: A Child and Adolescent Psychiatry Perspective on the Spectrum of Affirmation and Pathologization with Gender Diverse Youth

Scott Leibowitz, MD

Introduction

As awareness of gender diversity becomes more woven into the fabric of society, providers across health disciplines are frequently encountering children and adolescents with gender-related concerns. There is a relative dearth of literature guiding clinical practice, and the medical field is at a point at which individual practitioners find themselves addressing treatment options by adhering to general ethical principles versus relying on specific clinical guidelines that are based on strong scientific evidence. Many questions exist regarding best practices, and the care for those with gender dysphoria often requires being open to a range of perspectives across multiple disciplines (Edwards-Leeper, Leibowitz, & Sangganjanavanich, 2016). There is a wide variation in viewpoints about how best to approach clinical care, and the lives of gender diverse children and adolescents are at stake. The long-term ramifications of significant decisions made at these crucial points are often unknown. Providers are striving to offer the most efficacious treatments in a sometimes murky climate rife with complexity as the field shifts from conceptualizing gender categories dichotomously (binary male/female genders) to dimensionally (along the male–female spectrum).

For the child and adolescent psychiatrist, additional dynamic layers often present in the clinical relationships among the doctor, our patients, and their families. We often find ourselves walking a tightrope. Only very recently has our discipline moved away from pathologizing transgender individuals through nomenclature that classified this normal variant of human identity as "disordered." More broadly, the field of psychiatry often arouses negative connotations of pathology that are reinforced by the idea that psychiatrists are used

Lev, Arlene I., Gottlieb, Andrew R., *Families in Transition*
dx.doi.org/10.17312/harringtonparkpress/2019.04.fit.007
© 2019 by Harrington Park Press

only to provide care for individuals suffering from the most severe mental health conditions. Although we are trained to work with challenging psychiatric cases, we are also trained to understand and provide therapy modalities, assess the psychological functioning of those who are not necessarily suffering from significant psychopathology, while applying our more extensive knowledge of biological processes that affect the brain, mental cognition, and the relationship between the brain and physical body.

Additionally, among licensed mental health clinicians, psychiatrists and psychiatric nurse practitioners are the only ones licensed to prescribe medications when they are indicated for treatment of mental health disorders, including psychopathology that can sometimes be rather severe. On the one hand, our nonprescribing mental health colleagues sometimes relegate us to the role of *prescriber;* on the other hand, our non–mental health physician colleagues sometimes relegate us to the role of *therapist.* A common denominator is that our colleagues across all disciplines ask us to consult and treat those individuals who are the most at risk. Even among ourselves, many psychiatrists and the systems within which we practice reinforce the notion of pathology-centered care. It is true that some psychiatrists do view their patients more in terms of their symptoms, but an increasing number of psychiatrists — in particular, child and adolescent psychiatrists — are interested in practicing more holistic care with a focus on family dynamic issues. Considering the need for health systems to offset the costs of treating patients with psychiatric issues, we are, sadly, often required to see a large number of individuals with only enough time and space to provide psychotropic medication rather than the broader range of therapeutic services for which we are trained.

As I've had the unique opportunity to specialize in caring for gender diverse and transgender young people both before and after completing my psychiatry training (Leibowitz & Spack, 2011), I feel that I can speak to the trends that my generational cohort experiences when serving this population. Though some senior, experienced child psychiatrists have appropriately evolved to approach gender identity in children and adolescents without any preconceived notion or overt bias, many of my contemporaries — those who have completed training within the last ten to fifteen years — have a different view regarding the role we play in improving young peoples' lives from that of those in the field for a long time.

Child and adolescent psychiatrists have a vital role in promoting *positive* behavioral health outcomes because of our wide scope of training as clinicians, physicians, healers, therapists, and developmentalists who understand identity processes from childhood through young adulthood. Trained as physicians with an understanding of both the physiological aspects of the maturing body as well as the psychological components of the developing mind, we are poised to approach aspects of the human experience in which a mind-body connection is most salient. Given the mind-body disjunction that exists for individuals with gender dysphoria, transgender and gender diverse children and adolescents are precisely those whom child and adolescent psychiatrists *should* be prepared to assist. Further, we can also play a central role as a conduit between or among providers, many of whom are trained exclusively in either the physical or the psychological aspects of the human experience.

The mistrust of psychiatry by the transgender community, however, must not go unnoticed. It can often be an additional hurdle within the treatment relationship. Many hear the word *psychiatrist,* and their gut instinct is to say, "I'm not crazy." Nevertheless, the importance of the role we can play in the lives of these youth cannot be overstated. Once (and if) the societal hurdles that reinforce the stigma of mental health are overcome, life may be easier for everyone, not just psychiatrists. Because of the culture and attitude within psychiatry that have led to significant suffering on the part of gender diverse and transgender individuals, on the bases of historical definitions and nomenclature alone, we are at a crossroads regarding how our role can be reconceptualized and how the relationship with the community can be healed.

There is a spectrum of complexity within which individuals can present, and transgender and gender diverse adolescents are no exception. Acknowledging the presence of potential complexity should not inherently imply pathology; however, in a culture of doctor-patient mistrust, it sometimes can. Rather, complexity might mean different family systems exist with different generational beliefs about what gender roles should be; it might mean that different ethnic and/or racial groups may approach gender from different vantage points; it might mean that one parent is fully on board and another one needs more education. Complexity itself is a spectrum. It can wax and wane in the way a particular family or child presents. Embracing the complexity—and acknowledging that we, both doctors and patients, all have flaws—is the direction that allows for growth of the physician and healing for the patient.

For those families that are seeking care for a gender-related concern (often identified as a concern by the parents themselves), an affirming, balanced, and comprehensive assessment—however that is defined on a detailed level—and the determination that ongoing behavioral health treatment may be indicated are extremely useful. It can be helpful for those seeking medical interventions to transition as well as assist in identifying potential challenges that can support gender diverse people in an oppressive culture.

Working with parents is a crucial element when treating minors. The child and adolescent psychiatrist must be keenly aware of the parents' unique set of beliefs and behaviors—which also fall on a spectrum—but these become clearer only over time, as the therapeutic relationship evolves. First, we can provide a sense of relief that *someone* on the team—a physician (which often carries significant weight for parents)—is approaching their child in a way that can distinguish mental health pathology from gender diversity, and their potential interplay, if any. Second, we can offer psychoeducation about the fact that transgender individuals can lead productive, emotionally healthy lives, but may also have concurrent psychiatric concerns, such as depression and anxiety, that need to be addressed. Third, we can identify potential "red flags" that may negatively affect the course of a gender transition, discuss those with parents, and move toward addressing them.

A parent who at first appears to be supportive, perhaps using the youth's desired name and pronouns, may ultimately turn out to be more resistant to learning about how other behaviors might be considered unaffirming, for example, by referring to the youth by their birth-assigned name when referring to the past, insisting that this is reasonable despite the youth's objections. The combination of a rigid parent and a highly reactive adolescent can perpetuate negative interactions that result in the parent's questioning their adolescent's authenticity; the combination of a highly reactive parent and a reticent child can also perpetuate anxiety and limit the degree to which a child's authentic self is expressed. Parents may not understand the developmental considerations that go into addressing complex aspects of gender identity and expression, nor would they be expected to. The child and adolescent psychiatrist can most certainly play a role by assisting families in better understanding identity development and by making recommendations that are designed to reduce parental anxiety, thus improving the child's or adolescent's ability to freely express themselves.

An assessment does not need to be viewed as a barrier to care, as I believe many individuals, including both our medical colleagues and the youth and families themselves, often perceive it to be. The clinical dilemmas that exist for children and teens at different points in their development are necessary to acknowledge and treat. Transgender people are not immune to the same mental health challenges that cisgender people experience. If anything, the added stigma and oppression that trans youth face can exacerbate a co-occurring mental health concern that may have manifested itself regardless of the person's trans identity. Therefore, a psychiatrist brings the ability to assess what might be, for example, a reactive depression in response to societal oppression versus a biologically based major depression. Both situations benefit from treatment so that patients can move forward and live productive lives.

Being affirming of gender identity does not have to be synonymous with avoiding being comprehensive. An assessment with a psychiatrist can, in fact, be both comprehensive *and* affirming. It can at the same time focus on positive psychological well-being and assess for underlying psychopathology, either as a consequence of or as distinct from gender dysphoria—or both. To do anything different risks conforming to the stigma that mental health problems carry within our society. To avoid addressing mental health issues in the lives of trans people is neither clinically sound nor affirmative. This chapter will provide an overview of my experience as a child and adolescent psychiatrist serving these children and adolescents in different multidisciplinary settings and institutions.

Affirming Treatment and the Child and Adolescent Psychiatrist

The term *affirming* has become increasingly common in describing clinical care in relation to LGBTQ youth. It is an important term to use because when their identity is affirmed by a professional, years of feeling invalidated and marginalized by an oppressive society can be countered. But I also believe that the term *affirming* has been hijacked to some extent in the context of describing a treatment model. To say, "This is the affirmative treatment model," implies that if you do anything other than what the patient and family perceive as affirming, then you, as a clinician, are not adhering to the model. An interaction is affirming. A model of care that describes hundreds of interactions, including how to approach decision making on complex issues, cannot inherently be *affirming* or *not affirming* exclusively on the basis of the perception or satisfaction of the child or adolescent.

Having assessed and treated youth in three different multidisciplinary programs, each with different systems and protocols, I can say that one constant remains: *gender diversity is not inherently pathological.* Individuals who are gender diverse present in different ways, and one's felt or lived experience as male, female, or gender nonbinary is only *one aspect* of who one is. Having witnessed a complex galaxy of such experiences, I have found that the power of validating my patients' experience as transgender, particularly when they expect a different response because I am a psychiatrist, has been palpable. To miss and not address a potential source of pathology, however, does not do justice to our patients, and so I have found that it is important to recognize and intervene when certain trends of pathology are present in the clinical relationship. In reference to the use of the word *pathology* as a term itself, I would like to clarify that I personally use it as a broad umbrella term to describe concerns or challenges in a psychiatric treatment frame, and not necessarily something that should imply stigma. I am cognizant of the fact that others often associate the term with a far more negative connotation than I do.

First, pathology may lie in the environment. And while the idealist in me wishes this were not the case, the realist in me has an obligation to serve them in a way that appreciates gender transition as a potentially complex task in a sometimes harsh world. Second, pathology may also be reflected in their different capacities to reconcile an internal sense of self with that of discrepant societal expectations and/or their anatomy. Third, pathology can manifest itself in the inability of patients and their family members to acknowledge and appreciate the other unique, evolving, complex aspects of themselves, remaining paralyzed by their gender discordance. I can say that of those children and adolescents I've treated, however, many are simultaneously able to successfully navigate transition and appreciate how gender identity affects their lives. For those who cannot do this, who remain "stuck" seeing through only one lens, I believe I have an obligation as a healer to help them expand their self-perception of the many *other* aspects of identity that contribute to their entire being, especially if the patient has the capacity to grow and benefit psychologically from that. For example, when I ask about their hobbies, their future desires and aspirations, their families, or their political philosophies, there is almost a universal response of surprise, since they had not expected to have to think or talk about anything other than their gender and the problems *they* think they have as a result.

I have been witness to those initially stuck in a cycle of depression and anxiety who are then be able to build on their capacity to be flexible and learn how to deal with the challenges of living in the world as transgender, often as a by-product of psychological affirming interventions alone, ones that may or may not precede medical intervention. Sometimes this capacity to be flexible can go only so far without addressing their gender dysphoria through medical interventions. Without initially working through the totality of these possible elements of psychological distress, however, the notion that they are defined exclusively by their gender dysphoria may be inadvertently reinforced. I feel that a lack of affirmative exploration reduces them to their transness and doesn't appreciate their wholeness. Parents are also reassured when a provider takes a holistic view of their child, alleviating the anxiety of a parent who may feel that gender has become the central part of their child's being.

Fourth, I believe that pathology may exist in the inability of young people and their families to appreciate the dynamic identity changes that take place from childhood, through adolescence, and into adulthood. Though Lady Gaga's 2011 song *Born This Way* may help many feel as though they are who they are and nothing will change that, I would expand on that notion by saying it is impossible to predict that they definitively won't evolve in some other ways in the future. This is not to say that suggesting someone who has always identified as transgender might have an epiphany and realize that they are truly cisgender. Rather, this is about recognizing (1) that children's minds may be more malleable than is understood; (2) that adolescents are evolving and sorting out many complex tasks as they physically and psychologically mature; and (3) that adults are confronted with new ideas and perspectives. The changes one might experience over the life span are more a function of "the how" than "the what." How a person integrates their trans or cisgender identity into their overall sense of self might change over time, and there is absolutely nothing morally wrong with pausing to explore the possibilities that may exist, especially when they seek an intervention that would have irreversible ramifications, particularly on their reproductive systems. This is not *gate-keeping*. This is *collaborative path-paving* that involves the physician, the youth, and their parents, the last often having an intuitive knowledge of their children and adolescents as developmental, growing, changing beings, which might lead them to resist any formal labeling.

In a climate that has evolved from the historic *gatekeeper model* to an *informed-consent model* for transgender adults, the field has reached a juncture for these youth as we inch our way toward defining best practices. At the root of the conflict lies the discrepancy between the single moment in time that the word *affirm* connotes and the unknown future that a developing adolescent will grow into. Does affirming the here and now automatically affirm the future? Or is that simply presumptuous? For example, if a child insists that theirs is an identity they will have for life, then by affirming the child's statement, is the provider reinforcing an idea that may or may not be true in the future, despite that child's belief that things will never change? Balancing the affirmation of a child's existing belief with the knowledge of dynamic and complex changes and factors that can shape a maturing child or adolescent is an important task of the provider, as well as the family. Reconciling this difference can be difficult and often leads me to reflect: How can I best affirm this individual where they are right now while, at the same time, I sensitively explore the unknown possibilities? To master this skill is not always easy, but I believe it is integral to being able to form a positive therapeutic alliance with young people and their families while maintaining a healthy, evidence-based, developmentally informed approach to determining effective treatment strategies.

A Psychiatrist in a Multidisciplinary Setting

Given the etiological and clinical complexities often associated with treating those presenting with gender-related concerns, considering a range of perspectives from differing disciplines is often necessary to provide optimal care. In 2007 the first formal pediatric multidisciplinary gender identity clinic of its kind, at Boston Children's Hospital, was conceived (Edwards-Leeper & Spack, 2012). By 2014 over 30 similar clinics had been developed (Hsieh & Leininger, 2014), and the number continues to grow. The degree to which multidisciplinary services are offered varies, however. For example, some clinics may be based in a medical department (Edwards-Leeper & Spack, 2012); others may be based in a psychiatry or behavioral health division (Menvielle, 2012). For clinics housed in medical-based departments, such as Endocrinology or Adolescent Medicine, behavioral health clinicians may or may not be an integrated component of service delivery. Similarly, those based in psychiatric or behavioral health divisions may not have in-house access to those able to offer puberty suppression and hormonal and/or surgical treatments. The importance of a multidisciplinary approach is supported by clinical practice guidelines from several major professional organizations, including the World Professional Association of Transgender Health (Coleman et al., 2012), the American Academy of Child and Adolescent Psychiatry (Adelson et al., 2012), the American Psychological Association (APA, 2015), and the Endocrine Society (Hembree et al., 2017).

The importance of developing a collaborative care model has been described (Lev & Wolf-Gould, 2018); others have highlighted various multidisciplinary models (Chen et al., 2016; Edwards-Leeper & Spack, 2012). But, to date, there is no literature on evidence-based treatment interventions specific to this population. The six C's have been highlighted in the literature with respect to how multidisciplinary teams can provide optimal treatment: care, compassion, competence, communication, courage, and commitment (Ndoro, 2014). The one that stands out for me is *communication,* which can be challenging in today's busy world of productivity demands and differing schedules.

Child psychiatrists sometimes take an unpopular *wait-and-see* approach when it comes to treating emotional and behavior-related issues in *all* children and adolescents. This dynamic, which sometimes contrasts with the perspectives that our pediatric colleagues may offer, is not uncommon and exists in other situations besides gender dysphoria. Our recommendations may differ from the desire of the youth and/or the family, who often seek concrete, immediate assistance. On the one hand, delaying a desired treatment intervention may be considered cruel and unusual punishment; on the other hand, as providers, we may sometimes feel that factors other than gender may be at the root of a presenting issue. Correcting the mind-body misalignment through physical means *could* be the answer. But once a holistic picture emerges, there may be more to the story that could lead to other effective interventions and improved outcomes.

Grounded in knowledge of development over the life cycle, we child and adolescent psychiatrists may be more inclined to believe that slowing down a process could potentially lead to better long-term life satisfaction. We often recommend small steps and methodically determine what effect those have had—if any. "Start low, go slow" is our mantra when, for example, we initiate a regimen of psychotropic medication. When working with a well-intentioned parent, one who is struggling with the notion that their child may be transgender, it is vital to help them understand the effect their mis-gendering might have. Or in the treatment of a mature transgender youth whose gender dysphoria has never wavered, who has been suffering immensely from the incongruence, who would probably benefit from hormonal intervention, and who has extremely ambivalent parents with legitimate fears about giving consent, we might want to spend extra time helping them navigate their thoughts and feelings about what gender transition means for them. For the adolescent, experiencing a clinician as an ally, one who validates their experience, can be extremely powerful. Even more critical is creating a positive shift in the family dynamic that moves the rejecting parent to an ambivalent one, or an ambivalent parent to a more affirming one. My desire is for family members to look back in ten, twenty, or even thirty years and be confident that those key decisions made (e.g., starting hormones) were the best decisions at that time. If waiting can help serve that end, then we will create the possibility of a *successful transition,* and one not likely to be perceived as impulsive by *any* family member.

Parents who may be misguided in their belief that this is a "passing phase" are sometimes able to evolve in their perspective and benefit from experiencing their child's relief after feeling affirmed through supportive social interactions. This can serve as a feedback loop and be an indicator to those parents that this "phase" is not "passing" any time soon. I have found that when we reframe and model supporting behaviors, such as the use of the correct pronoun, to the parents as an experiment, skeptical parents often make the necessary shift that allows them to grieve the loss of what they expected their child would be.

The ideal multidisciplinary team is one in which all perspectives are heard and consistent messages about the treatment recommendations are sent. Without open communication, it's obviously difficult to create a coordinated effort. And when this is not in place, care can be compromised. For example, when one practitioner describes time lines for interventions that differ from those described by another practitioner working with the same family, confusion and mistrust can develop between the team and the family. Additionally, these differences can further tension between family members who share differing viewpoints. The presence of diverse perspectives among providers is to be expected. However, managing those perspectives and demonstrating a unified treatment plan to the family minimizes disruptions in the treatment by any one specific provider. This prevents the focus from becoming about the differences in clinical viewpoints, which only delays the main priority at hand: helping the child or teen to live an authentic, healthy life.

The Assessment: Gatekeeping or Collaborative Path-Paving?

A biopsychosocial assessment by a mental health provider is an invaluable tool when it comes to delivering evidence-based, affirming care. It presents an opportunity for the child or adolescent and the family to offer a contextualized, complete description of their distress and ways to ameliorate it. Obtaining a full, comprehensive psychological picture of the child or adolescent is not simply a mechanism to examine them under a microscope and procure diagnostic clarity. It is also a means to assist in *planning* and *optimizing* outcomes should they choose to embark on some form of a gender transition socially, medically, surgically, or some combination thereof. Adolescents "want what they want," and they typically want it yesterday. Their need for immediate gratification is universally characteristic of this developmental stage. The families I've worked with will tell you that I typically tell them, "It's not just about transitioning, it's about *successfully* transitioning."

Every individual brings with them a unique constellation of experiences, temperaments, personality attributes, and values. Their racial, ethnic, and social identities are simultaneously developing as they evolve into young adults. Of course, to compartmentalize each part of themselves negates the fact that all parts are intertwined. Therefore, optimizing one's ability to live authentically—which for a transgender individual depends on the alignment between their gender identity or expression and their physical self—enhances the likelihood that other aspects of them will flourish. To reduce an individual to a body that needs hormonal and/or surgical correction in the absence of a comprehensive understanding of who that individual is, however, does them a disservice. To assume that one's depression, anxiety, self-injury, suicidal ideation, or risk-taking behavior is rooted in one's gender dysphoria may or may not be accurate.

We are all complex beings, and the society in which we live is generally not a welcoming place for those who are gender diverse. Additionally, the ways in which people identify their gender—for example, *genderfluid, genderqueer, demigender*—are markedly different from the ways they did so even a few years ago. We are also seeing these young people present with complex, co-occurring psychiatric conditions. This includes young people on the autism spectrum, which can affect how they perceive the social world. It also includes those with emotional and behavioral conditions, such as anxiety, depression, mania, PTSD, and eating disorders, which can influence their relationships with others as well as their relationship with their bodies. Sometimes these issues are obvious to a medical professional; other times they are not.

A biopsychosocial, developmentally informed assessment administered by a trained psychiatrist or other mental heath clinician yields insights that contextualize emotional, psychological, behavioral, and cognitive capacities. For me, these are the six most important questions:

1. How do people understand the complex interrelationships between their gender identity, gender expression, and/or sexual orientation?

2. Is there the presence of any psychiatric diagnoses that might affect their understanding of gender identity and/or gender transition?

3. Does interpersonal functioning help or hinder negotiating interactions that can be inherently challenging as one undergoes transition?

4. How accurate is their understanding of the expectations about the future of their body and the changes it may/will experience?

5. In what ways does the adolescent understand and experience intimacy and sexuality in the present, and what are the expectations of how that might or might not change in the future?

6. What are the actual and hypothetical risks and benefits that gender transition interventions might have, including prepubertal social transition and pubertal suppression?

A comprehensive, biopsychosocial assessment need *not* present a barrier to receiving gender-affirming care. In fact, the opposite is true. I believe that providing effective care is dependent on having as complete a picture as possible. To suggest that a thorough assessment and subsequent recommendations for treatment are pathologizing merely reinforces the notion that availing oneself of therapy is a stigma. As much as I wish that gender diverse and/or transgender youth were immune to psychological or psychiatric difficulties, the reality is that they are not. Prioritizing the treatment of these co-occurring challenges in a systematic way—one intervention at a time—allows the team to better grasp cause and effect. For this reason, in some situations it is worthwhile to proceed with caution; in other situations, that might not be necessary. Without a comprehensive assessment, however, how would a treatment team know about some of the challenges that wouldn't necessarily present themselves in a brief mental health screening? I repeat: when talking about decisions with lifelong ramifications, a holistic understanding of one's emotional, psychological, and social functioning need not be considered *gatekeeping*, but rather *collaborative path-paving*. To those who disagree with me, I respond in part by saying that this is a "glass half-full, half-empty" debate. If framed as a hurdle, the family will see it as a hurdle. If framed as the proverbial yellow-brick road, the family will view this as a path toward the Emerald City.

A Vision of the Future

I am not oblivious to the fact that many in my profession are unaware of the nuances involved in approaching assessment and treatment of gender diverse populations. Some feel less well-prepared and fear that they will "make a mistake" or "do the wrong thing." As I stated earlier, many child psychiatrists view a person as a set of symptoms that need treatment. It is this attitude that fosters the belief that we pathologize those we serve.

I am also optimistic that the landscape is changing, however. Now more than ever, regional organizations want to make this issue a priority. Clinicians are more receptive to trainings, such as those offered by the World Professional Association of Transgender Health; medical schools are integrating gender identity competencies throughout their curricula; allied health professionals are joining medical professionals in didactics and multidisciplinary clinics to enhance their competencies; mainstream child psychiatry textbooks now have chapters that address correct pronoun usage for gender diverse youth. So, as the covers of magazines such as *National Geographic* proudly increase the visibility of transgender youth, a parallel process is occurring among clinicians. Education and training on these issues are now becoming the rule—not the exception.

Underneath layer on layer of potential complexity within the dynamics that can exist for child psychiatrists treating gender diverse youth lies a grounding thought that defines the core of my own professional identity: my patients, including those who are gender diverse or transgender, eventually have the opportunity to discover and live their most authentic sense of self. And, in turn, this optimizes their potential to overcome the psychological and psychosocial challenges that they initially presented with. In many other situations, we spend so much time trying to lower families' expectations regarding the quality of life that their schizophrenic or bipolar child might have. But when it comes to helping individuals for whom the main goal is to be able to successfully live in the most authentic way possible, my job becomes a whole lot more rewarding. It's what keeps me walking the tightrope every day, even with a wobble or two here and there..

REFERENCES

Adelson, S. L., Walter, H. J., Bukstein, O. G., Bellonci, C., Benson, R. S., Chrisman, A., . . . & Medicus, J. (2012). Practice parameter on gay, lesbian, or bisexual sexual orientation, gender nonconformity, and gender discordance in children and adolescents. *Journal of the American Academy of Child and Adolescent Psychiatry, 51* (9), 957–974.

American Psychological Association. (2015). Guidelines for psychological practice with transgender and gender nonconforming people. *American Psychologist, 70,* 832–864. http://dx.doi.org/10.1037/a0039906.

Chen, D., Hidalgo, M. A., Leibowitz, S., Leininger, J., Simons, L., Finlayson, C., & Garofalo, R. (2016). Multidisciplinary care for gender-diverse youth: A narrative review and unique model of gender-affirming care. *Transgender Health* 1 (1), 117–123. doi:10.1089/ trgh.2016.0009.

Coleman, E., Bockting, W., Botzer, M., Cohen-Kettenis, P., DeCuypere, G., Feldman, J., . . . & Zucker, K. (2012). Standards of Care for the health of transsexual, transgender, and gender-nonconforming people, Version 7. *International Journal of Transgenderism, 13* (4), 165–232.

Edwards-Leeper, L., Leibowitz, S., & Sangganjanavanich, F. (2016). Psychology of sexual orientation and gender diversity. *American Psychological Association, 3* (2), 165–172. http://dx.doi.org/10.1037/sgd0000167.

Edwards-Leeper, L., & Spack, N. P. (2012). Psychological evaluation and medical treatment of transgender youth in an interdisciplinary "Gender Management Service" (GeMS) in a major pediatric center. *Journal of Homosexuality, 59* (3), 321–336.

Gaga, L. (2011). *Born this way.* London: Abbey Road Studios.

Hembree, W., Cohen-Kettenis. P. T., Gooren, L. J., Hannema, S. E., Meyer, W. J., Murad, M. H., . . . & T'Sjoen, G. G. (2017). Endocrine treatment of gender-dysphoric/gender-incongruent persons: An Endocrine Society clinical practice guideline. *Journal of Clinical Endocrinology & Metabolism, 102* (11), 1–35.

Hsieh, S., & Leininger, J. (2014). Resource list: Clinical care programs for gender-nonconforming children and adolescents. *Pediatric Annals, 43*, 238–244.

Leibowitz, S., & Spack, N. P. (2011). The development of a gender identity psychosocial clinic: Treatment issues, logistical considerations, interdisciplinary cooperation, and future initiatives. *Child & Adolescent Psychiatric Clinics of North America, 20* (4), 701–724.

Lev, A., & Wolf-Gould, C. (2018). Collaborative treatment across disciplines: Physician and mental health counselor coordinating competent care. In C. Keo-Meier & D. Ehrensaft (eds.), *The gender affirmative model: An interdisciplinary approach to supporting transgender and gender expansive children.* Washington, D.C.: American Psychological Association.

Menvielle. E. A. (2012). Comprehensive program for children with gender variant behaviors and gender identity disorders. *Journal of Homosexuality, 59* (3), 357–368.

Ndoro, S. (2014). Effective multidisciplinary working: The key to high-quality care. *British Journal of Nursing, 23* (13), 724–727.

8

Chinese Canadian Families with Transgender Youth

Nena Wang, MA, Wallace Wong, PsyD, R Psych

Transgender clients from non-Western backgrounds face unique challenges in the process of transitioning into their affirmed gender, requiring specialized care that takes into account the influence of their cultural/ethnic background. Though this subject presents an infinite range of possibilities, we will focus on the experience of Chinese Canadian families with transgender children and youth. While the topics we highlight are specific to the Chinese population, they may apply to other Asian groups, cultural communities, racial minorities, and immigrant families as well. The makeup of both the Canadian and U.S. populations is quite ethnically and culturally diverse, and the discussions presented in this paper apply to racial minorities and immigrant families that are facing similar issues in both countries. The unique difficulties that affect non-Western transgender clients, including individualistic versus collectivistic worldviews, the one-child policy, acculturation frameworks, and the divide between first- and second-generation immigrants, have received little attention. A clinical vignette will illustrate these issues and provide guidance for professionals working with this population.

Collectivism versus Individualism

Transgender persons are estimated to make up approximately .5% of the Canadian population (Bauer, Zong, Scheim, Hammond, & Thind, 2015), or about 180,000 people. In contrast, there are an estimated 9.5 million transgender persons living in the Asia-Pacific region (Asia Catalyst, 2015). The Chinese are the second-largest foreign-born group living in Canada: 545,535 Chinese persons immigrated there in 2011 alone (Statistics Canada, 2016). Despite these numbers, transgender clients from China and other non-Western backgrounds are rarely seen in clinical practice. Though our office served over 150 transgender children and youth during 2016, only 1 percent were ethnic minorities, even though we are the only publicly funded gender clinic for children and youth in British Columbia.

Lev, Arlene I., Gottlieb, Andrew R., *Families in Transition*
dx.doi.org/10.17312/harringtonparkpress/2019.04.fit.008
© 2019 by Harrington Park Press

There are several reasons that transgender youth from minority, non-Western backgrounds do not typically present themselves to mental health or medical professionals. First, Eastern cultures tend to emphasize a collectivist perspective, in contrast to Western culture, which is more individualistic. Collectivist worldviews are characterized by an interdependence on others within the family or group. These cultures view the stability of the whole system as extremely important and perceive the individual as a potential threat to the homeostasis of that system. People from Chinese cultures are apt to be (1) apprehensive about their self presentation; (2) concerned about how their actions will affect others; (3) more likely to follow group norms; and (4) more focused on maintaining the group's reputation (Hui & Triandis, 1986; Triandis, 1995).

In contrast, persons raised in an individualistic culture are more likely to give precedence to personal goals and achievements than those raised in collectivist cultures. Asserting one's independence is highly respected and an indicator of success. In Chinese families, however, deference to the system is emphasized while the needs of the individual are minimized.

It is easy to understand how transgender children and youth from collectivist cultures are prone to feeling distressed, given that the directive is that they should give more weight to the feelings and desires of others. The family is seen as *the* main social unit, and the actions of those in it play an enormous role in the construction of its identity (Ohnishi, Ibrahim, & Grzegorek, 2007). A transgender youth who attempts to separate themselves from the system and instead pursues their personal goals is more likely to be perceived as rejecting their social roles. By openly asserting their authentic self, the child is viewed as behaving contrary to the expectation that they remain in their natal sex and carry out their responsibilities relative to their gender. Typically, parents we see ask us: "Why is my child being so selfish? Don't they think about our family at all?"

The One-Child Policy and Its Effects on Transgender People

In a real-world example of collectivist interests versus individual freedoms, China's 1979 one-child policy carries severe and lasting social consequences for Chinese transgender children and youth. Most of the Chinese Canadian parents seen in our office are middle-aged and typically have only one child, even after they immigrate to North America. For many, immigrating to Canada is a lengthy process that requires them to spend years in school and develop successful livelihoods in China in order to meet the strict qualifications for residency. Upon arrival, many parents face challenges in conceiving because of their age or because they have already had surgery to decrease or eliminate the likelihood of having children. The psychological effect of the one-child policy is that the parents' hopes and desires are projected onto that child. The sense of loss, disappointment, and frustration experienced when their son or daughter discloses their gender identity can generate a crisis, as all of their expectations for the child's future—and their own—may be shattered.

The policy created a situation in which parents, and often grandparents, rely on that child for financial support and physical care later in life (Settles, Sheng, Zang, & Zhao, 2013). Having a son or daughter who is transgender (or gender nonbinary) may raise concerns about how they will make a living, whether they will have a family of their own, and whether they will be able to support aging parents. Further, Asian culture has historically dictated that sons have the duty of carrying on the family lineage. If their son becomes their daughter, that lineage is perceived as broken. Bearing the burden of all their parents' expectations makes it much more treacherous to come out, as their shame about having failed their family may be crushing, at times necessitating going "back in the closet."

Considering the Effect of Acculturation on Transgender People

Mental health professionals must also take into account the family's level of acculturation or the degree to which foreign-born persons adapt to the language, values, beliefs, and behaviors of their new environment. An understanding of Berry's (1997) acculturation model is critical to providing care for ethnic minority clients and their families. In brief, there are four strategies of adaptation, depending on their relationship with their home culture and their interaction with and perceptions of the host culture: (1) *assimilation* is embracing the host culture but holding negative attitudes or losing contact with the original culture; (2) *marginalization* is withdrawing from the original *and* host cultures and/or holding negative views of both; (3) *separation* is espousing positive attitudes toward one's original culture but not participating in the host culture; and (4) *integration* is holding positive views of both cultures, retaining contact with the home culture while simultaneously becoming immersed in the host culture.

Chinese Canadian transgender youth can be seen as a *double minority,* both ethnic and sexual. For clients, learning to integrate these two identities can be very challenging. Several writers present frameworks that are based on an acculturation strategy model that prompts clinicians to consider cultural attitudes and attitudes toward gender identity simultaneously (Chung & Szymanski, 2007; Ohnishi et al., 2007). These models were originally designed to better understand sexual orientation, but we have found them applicable to familial attitudes toward the home culture and the transgender community. As figure 8.1 shows, an *assimilationist* harbors negative attitudes toward the home culture but embraces their affirmed gender identity and the transgender community; a *marginalist* feels isolated from their home culture and may be ambivalent about their gender identity as well as the transgender community; a *separationist* is strongly attached to their home culture and rejects or dismisses personal feelings of gender incongruity as well as the transgender community; an *integrationist,* the most psychologically healthy, maintains connections with their original culture and embraces their gender identity as well as develops connections with the transgender community.

FIGURE 8.1 Potential acculturation strategies of ethnic minority transgender persons

| | | ATTITUDES TOWARD GENDER IDENTITY | |
		Positive	*Negative*
ATTITUDES TOWARD HOME CULTURE	*Positive*	Integrationist	Separationist
	Negative	Assimilationist	Marginalist

Attitudes toward Gender Identity

It is important for clinicians to determine where children and their parents intersect, since this information is crucial for developing appropriate treatment plans and to the success of the client's transition. Western-trained clinicians who have worked mainly with Western clients may have a strong individualistic bias and may unknowingly impose those views, encouraging more independence than the client is psychologically prepared for, thus creating further disruptions in the family and greater distress for the client. It is helpful to consider cultural background when matching a client to a therapist on the basis of where the client is on the continuum, particularly if the client or parents are in the separation or marginalization stage and are more suspicious of Western ideas.

Families in these two stages are also at risk of turning to biased sources within the home culture that may reinforce negative feelings toward their child. They may feel uncomfortable, unable, or unwilling to seek out others going through similar circumstances and further isolate themselves from information and those community programs that offer help.

First- and Second-Generation Families

First- and second-generation immigrant families may also respond differently to their child's gender identity. First-generation families, or those who were born in one country and then relocated to another along with their children, are naturally more strongly attached to their home culture and are more comfortable turning to their cultural/ethnic community for support in times of stress. The length of time living in the new society, however, does not necessarily predict how acculturated the family is. Those who have resided in the West for years may still feel a real sense of belonging to their home culture, particularly if they continue to socialize primarily with those from the home culture and engage in those activities associated with the place they know best. Second-generation families, which consist of children of first-generation immigrants, are generally much more acculturated. Typically, they attend school here, become exposed to all things Western, and are better positioned to create meaningful social connections. Unfortunately, this process is often viewed by the family as contradicting collectivist values. Parents view the child as disowning or abandoning their culture of origin. In turn, the child may internalize their process of individualizing as an act of selfishness. This may be especially true for children struggling with gender identity issues and trying to manage their socialization and who may already feel guilty for ways that they have individualized.

Many immigrate to North American countries because they value democratic ideals. Simultaneously, they may also be threatened by new cultural values, feeling those are being imposed on them, and fear losing their own values. Individualism, in particular, is often seen as a direct threat to Chinese culture. For example, education systems may be considered too liberal and progressive—the teaching of sex education in grade school and the presence of the Gay-Straight Alliance in high schools attesting to that charge. Sexual health awareness campaigns and LGBT community events broadcast in the media are often seen as contradictory to and challenging of more traditional cultural values in newly immigrated families, who view this as "propaganda." A common concern raised by parents we treat is that after immigrating to North America, their children become "exposed" to information in the media and on the Internet, and they fear this exposure has a negative influence on the child's sense of their gender identity and/or sexual orientation. In this context, parents often experience a loss of control, and they sense that their cultural values are being undermined.

To better understand these principles, we present a clinical vignette, highlighting some of the key issues.

Marshall, Lucy, and John

Marshall, age 14, an only child, and his mother, Lucy, emigrated from China to Canada when he was eight years old. As is typical of many immigrant families, Marshall's father, John, lives and works in China, financially supporting his family here. Lucy's command of the English language is very limited, and she has had difficulties acculturating. Her main responsibilities are maintaining the home and overseeing Marshall's studies. Primary social support comes from members of the Chinese Evangelical church. Marshall has a better grasp of English. He attends high school and associates mainly with other Chinese-speaking students, as it is easier to relate to them, though he has a few white friends and is interested in some aspects of popular Western culture.

Lucy initiated individual treatment for Marshall because of concerns about his OCD symptoms—sitting in the bathroom for hours, repeatedly folding towels—and self-harming behaviors—cutting both forearms with a razor blade. During intake, he privately disclosed that his affirmed gender identity was female, and that he had experienced gender dysphoria since childhood, reporting that he "never felt like a male inside" and had been confused about those feelings when he was younger. When Marshall was 12, he found a book about transgender people, which helped clarify his experience, but which also created a conflict about whether to come out. At the time of intake, he had not directly disclosed to his mother. All this left him socially isolated and fearing he would be stigmatized and rejected by the Chinese community; he anticipated, as a foreigner, not feeling a sense of belonging to the local, predominantly white, transgender community.

Lucy did not understand why he was increasingly depressed, short-tempered, and often in conflict with others. While she had positive views of her home culture and was closely connected with the local Chinese community, she harbored stereotypical ideas about gender, encouraging Marshall to wear more "masculine" clothing and "build muscle," and she was openly derogatory about sexual minorities. In terms of the acculturation framework, Marshall's profile was that of a marginalist, Lucy, a separationist. It seemed that Marshall needed help building supports in both communities, whereas Lucy was skeptical of any guidance we offered. She reported that before attending our clinic, they had seen a Western-trained therapist who, she complained, was "buying into" Marshall's distress over his dysphoria. As the interview progressed, it became clearer that Lucy was probably in denial that her child could be transgender and was angry that the therapist was "pushing his personal liberal values" and had not consulted with her before speaking to Marshall, actions she considered "disrespectful" and "crossing the line," terminating with him after two sessions.

After intake, we conducted a thorough mental health assessment using structured clinical interviews and several evidence-based measures to assess Marshall's anxiety, depression, and self-harming behavior. We then presented our findings, which concurred with Marshall's own ideas, to Lucy: that the severe and persistent anxiety and depression was related to his gender dysphoria. Research has shown that Chinese families accord physicians and health professionals a great deal of authority, and Chinese clients typically do not appreciate ambiguity but, rather, prefer concrete advice (Leong, 1986; Ng & James, 2013). Therefore, we explained that it would be impossible to treat Marshall without addressing his central conflict. After that, we asked Lucy for permission to talk to him about these issues. We then asked her to consider what we presented and make an informed decision about whether she wanted to move forward. By including her in this process, we minimized the imbalance of power.

Though we stressed it would be beneficial for Marshall to become more comfortable with his identity in order to decrease his symptoms and improve his functioning, we did not have any personal investment in what he should do in the future, emphasizing that our role would be supportive, not directive. Exposure to other families with transgender children, we thought, might help her better understand the issues and cope more effectively as well as help Marshall make sense of his own thoughts and emotions. Being sensitive to and respectful of the family system, we acknowledged that information about transgender persons in their native language was very limited and offered her a few psychoeducational sessions. Following this conversation, Lucy was noticeably distressed and withdrew for a few weeks. Our attempts to contact the family were ignored.

In the early fall, Lucy and Marshall returned to the clinic. She reported at the time that since no one in her community had ever gone through anything like this, she turned to her church for support. The consensus was to send Marshall back to China for the entire summer in order to saturate him with core cultural values in the hopes that this experience would "man him up" and reverse his desire to live as a female. In China, Marshall resided with his father, John, and his grandparents. Because John was at work most of the time, his grandparents were the ones overseeing his care. The strategy was to try to convince Marshall to "give up" the notion of being transgender, insisting he speak and act in a way that was more stereotypically masculine.

Since that time, Marshall had become increasingly anxious and depressed, and he had recently made a suicide attempt by overdosing on medications he found at home. As a result, Marshall's father flew in from China to monitor his son and support his wife. Lucy and Marshall both reported that, until that time, he and his father had a more distant relationship. Though skeptical at first, John was actually more open than Lucy had been. He also played a supportive role in consoling his wife about her confusion and grief. The fact that John was more receptive than the mother helped forge a greater sense of connection between father and son.

We conducted a reassessment and determined that Marshall's symptoms has significantly worsened; we maintained that gender dysphoria was the root cause of the acting out and reiterated our supportive/educational approach. We requested that Lucy and John consent and sign the treatment plan, that they be available for collateral meetings, and that they communicate with us about Marshall's adjustment. A few sessions were offered to the parents to give them space to process their feelings and to explore what all this meant for them as individuals, as a couple, and as members of their church and community. We also suggested that Lucy and John pair up with another Chinese family with a transgender youth, whom we had previously assessed, to decrease both the stigma and their isolation.

As we began to explore these issues with Marshall while encouraging Lucy and John to allow him more freedom to express himself in the home, his symptoms began to remit, and his daily functioning and school attendance showed improvement. We encouraged Marshall to attend a support group for transgender youth, despite his ambivalence, and to his surprise, he found himself making friends.

When transgenderism strongly goes against cultural values, it's not uncommon that once the child is able to live freely, the parents go into hiding. After Marshall began his social transition at home and at school, Lucy stopped attending church, knowing that if she continued to go, she would eventually have to disclose Marshall's transition. Though she is looking for other sources of support and facing potential stigmatization and isolation within the Chinese community, she is relieved that Marshall's symptoms have largely remitted and does not regret the choice to go forward with the assessment, which spanned two months.

After that, we continued to work with Marshall and monitor his adjustment. John stayed in Canada for a month and returned to China once Marshall's mental health improved. As is common in many Chinese Canadian families, his transition largely remains a secret to their relatives. Concurrently, Lucy sought individual therapy of her own with a clinician we recommended. In addition, her relationship with the Chinese family with whom we paired them helped Lucy evolve into a more accepting person.

Clinical Guidelines

1. Clinicians working with gender variant children and youth should begin with a comprehensive assessment of the presenting problems, which are typically issues such as depression, anxiety, suicidality, daily functioning, and school avoidance. These problems should be assessed in a valid and reliable manner, using multiple measures and across multiple time points in order to provide an abundance of evidence-based findings. If the child or youth presents with or is suspected of having a developmental disorder, we also encourage the client to obtain a psychoeducational assessment and/or an autism assessment with a specialist.

2. Clinicians should use the acculturation framework in their practice in order to take into consideration any divergence in attitudes between the youth and the parents. The clinician should empathize with the parents' more collectivist views, demonstrating an understanding of and respect for cultural values, while also engaging in a supportive relationship with the child. Clinicians should be mindful of how their words and actions may be interpreted and remain close to the family's lived experience. For example, encouraging clients to move out of the home so that they can have greater control over their transition could disrupt the family system and leave the child too vulnerable.

3. Clinicians must recognize how culture influences a family's life and educate themselves on what is similar to or different from their own backgrounds. Parents will probably be skeptical early on and will try to determine if the therapist's value system is compatible with theirs. Neutrality is key on issues such as gender dysphoria, particularly at the beginning of a relationship with the parents. They may feel threatened and prematurely terminate if they perceive the clinician as too liberal-minded or too preachy.

4. Following the comprehensive mental health assessment, clinicians should review the findings from validated assessment measures with the family. As parents are often concerned about these more overt symptoms, they may be more receptive to the idea that the root cause lies in the child's gender dysphoria. At this point, clinicians may ask the parents for their permission to discuss issues of gender variance and gender dysphoria with their child. Remember that if the clinician prematurely engages with the child about these issues without speaking to the parents, this will probably alienate and heighten distrust in the parents.

5. Clinicians may proceed to a gender-specific assessment. This typically will consist of assessing gender identity, gender expression, body image, and gender dysphoria. Following this assessment, the clinician should reconvene with the client

and the family to review these findings, provide further education about gender variance, make appropriate recommendations, and help develop a care plan for the child or youth. Including parents in decision making and treatment planning gives them a greater sense of control as well as more of a grasp of their child's situation, making it likely that they will ultimately be accepting of who their child is.

6. Clinicians should provide psychoeducation on gender variance, gender dysphoria, and the distinctions between natal sex, gender identity, gender expression, and sexual orientation. Emotional work should be incorporated as trust builds between the primary clinician and the family. This process is a good opportunity to build rapport, minimize the power imbalance between health professionals and the parents, demonstrate that we value their input and welcome their feedback, and work toward forming a team or co-partnership with the parents in order to implement the best ways of supporting the child.

REFERENCES

Asia Catalyst. (2015). *"My life is too dark to see the light": A survey of the living conditions of transgender female sex workers in Beijing and Shanghai.* Retrieved from http://asiacatalyst.org/wp-content/uploads/2014/09/Asia-Catalyst-TG-SW-Report.pdf.

Bauer, G. R., Zong, X., Scheim, A. I., Hammond, R., & Thind, A. (2015). Factors impacting transgender patients' discomfort with their family physicians: A respondent-driven sampling survey. *PLoS ONE 10* (12), e0145046.

Berry, J. W. (1997). Immigration, acculturation, and adaptation. *Applied Psychology: An International Review, 46* (1), 5–68.

Chung, Y. B., & Szymanski, D. M. (2007). Racial and sexual identities of Asian American gay men. *Journal of LGBT Issues in Counseling, 1* (2), 67–93.

Hui, H. C., & Triandis, H. (1986). Individualism-collectivism: A study of cross-cultural researchers. *Journal of Cross-Cultural Psychology, 17* (2), 225–248.

Leong, F. T. L. (1986). Counseling and psychotherapy with Asian-Americans: Review of the literature. *Journal of Counseling Psychology, 33,* 196–206.

Ng, C. T. C., & James, S. (2013). "Directive Approach" for Chinese clients receiving psychotherapy: Is that really a priority? *Frontiers in Psychology, 4* (49), 1–13. doi:10.3389/fpsyg.2013.00049.

Ohnishi, H., Ibrahim, F. A., & Grzegorek, J. L. (2007). Intersections of identities: Counseling lesbian, gay, bisexual and transgender Asian-Americans. *Journal of LGBT Issues in Counseling, 1* (3), 77–94.

Settles, B. H., Sheng, X., Zang, Y., & Zhao, J. (2013). The one-child policy and its impact on Chinese families. In C. Kwok-Bun (ed.), *International handbook of Chinese families* (pp. 627–646). New York: Springer.

Statistics Canada. (2016). *Immigration and ethnocultural diversity in Canada.* Retrieved from https://www12.statcan.gc.ca/nhs-enm/2011/as-sa/99-010-x/99-010-x2011001-eng.cfm.

Triandis, H. C. (1995). *Individualism and collectivism.* Boulder, Colo.: Westview Press.

9

Approaches to the Treatment of Gender Diverse Children and Transgender Youth

Arlene Lev, LCSW-R, CASAC, CST

Historically, there has been limited psychological or medical treatment available for gender nonconforming, gender diverse, and transgender children and youth. The assumption has been that being transgender was a "rare phenomenon" (Meyer-Bahlburg, 1985), and although it has long been known that transgender people often identify gender discomfort very early in life, the clinical treatment has been based on the perspective that transition could take place only in adulthood. The dearth of research on gender diverse children and transgender youth (Olson, Durwood, DeMeules, & McLaughlin, 2016) has been referred to as "a large empirical black hole in the treatment literature" (Zucker, 2008a, p. 359).

The American Psychiatric Association Task Force on the Treatment of Gender Identity Disorders (Byne et al., 2012) states that because of the lack of any randomized controlled treatment outcome studies, treatment recommendations can be made only with a low level of evidence that "can best be characterized as expert opinion" (p. 762), which varies greatly. It might be most accurate to say that much of the research to date has assumed that gender dysphoria in childhood and youth is evidence of pathology, and the focus has been on ameliorating atypical gender expression. Although this reflects some of the clinical work currently being practiced, it does not represent the newer models that have developed, which view gender diversity as a normative developmental process for some children. Corbett (2009) writes: "A social or developmental lag has opened between the formal empirically based discourse and the day-to-day clinical work" (p. 355). In other words, accumulated research data do not often reflect the treatment approaches actually used in clinical practice by many contemporary therapists.

The two most common models for treating gender diversity in children and adolescents are the *reparative* and the *affirmative models*. Most models of treatment

Lev, Arlene I., Gottlieb, Andrew R., *Families in Transition*
dx.doi.org/10.17312/harringtonparkpress/2019.04.fit.009

were reparative in nature until the 1990s, when more affirmative approaches began to develop (Tishelman et al., 2015). The *reparative model* is based on the assumption that being transgender is pathological; thus, the aim is to try to fix (repair) the child by encouraging them to conform to socioculturally prescribed gender norms; this is sometimes referred to as conversion therapy. This term was historically used to describe interventions aimed at changing sexual orientation, *not* gender expression, but these categories have been conflated throughout most of the treatment literature. Researchers and clinicians who subscribe to this model rarely embrace this term, probably because of the negative media ramifications and the fact that major professional organizations have deemed reparative therapies unethical (Hill, Menvielle, Sica, & Johnson, 2010).

In contrast, the *affirmative model* is based on supporting children and youth in an authentic exploration of gender expression and identity, as they themselves define and communicate it, recognizing that gender diversity is part of healthy human experience. This model also acknowledges the ways that gender is rigidly socioculturally prescribed, and it recognizes that these prescriptions inevitably lead to stigmatization and pathologization of diverse gender expressions. This necessitates that adults play a role in advocating for, supporting, and assisting in the empowerment of vulnerable children and youth. Although psychological and/or medical treatment may play its part, the model is not so much a treatment administered *by* professionals as it is a perspective or a philosophy of affirmation within the family and community (see Appendix: Best Practices for the Care of Transgender Youth).

Both models are broad, overarching frameworks that have been conceptualized differently by various theorists, and practitioners who use them do so in different ways. Perhaps it is best not to view such models as binary concepts—reparative versus affirmative—but rather as a theoretical continuum, where the outside edges represent diametrically divergent perspectives, as they relate not only to treatment, but also to theoretical understandings of identity development, sexed bodies, the acquisition of gender identity, and the value of gender diversity expression within the larger society. Between these opposite poles, the middle ground is not so discrete, since treatment perspectives vary by the ideological views of the clinicians, the needs of the children and the families, parents, and communities in which they live, and diverse views on how best to affirm and support children and youth who experience varying levels of distress, dysphoria, and gender expansiveness.

Reparative Models

Treatment aimed at trying to change a person's gender identity and expression to become more congruent with sex assigned at birth has been attempted in the past without success. . . . Such treatment is no longer considered ethical.

— WORLD PROFESSIONAL ASSOCIATION OF TRANSGENDER HEALTH
(COLEMAN ET AL., 2012, P. 16)

The reparative model, referred to by some as the "pathology response" (Gale & Syr-ja-McNally, 2014), is a treatment philosophy based on the belief that gender identity and expression should emanate naturally from one's assigned sex, the goal of intervention being to assist children and adolescents in accepting that their natal sex is unchangeable (Green & Schiavi, 1995). Clinical intervention is focused on fixing or repairing the child's gender atypical expression. Within this treatment philosophy, it is often believed that gender diversity in children is linked to gender dysphoria, as well as homosexuality and transsexualism in adulthood, which are often conflated, and should all be ameliorated. (The terms *homosexuality* and *transsexualism* were, and are often still, used in the research and clinical literature. Despite the many difficulties in operationalizing their meaning, and the bias implied in their use, these words are retained here, the goal being to remain as accurate as possible regarding the intentions and contexts of the professionals who used them. To simply insert the terms *gay* or *trans* to replace them dilutes the social and historical context of these studies and ideologies). Additionally, gender atypical behavior is etiologically believed to be related to pathological parenting, so that the earlier the intervention is introduced in childhood, the greater the likelihood of "success," defined as adult heterosexuality and gender-normative expression.

The theoretical ideas that form the framework of the pathologizing modalities for treating gender diverse children developed in the 1960s and 1970s (Williams, 2017). Ansara and Hegarty (2011) examine how these approaches to treating gender atypical children are theoretically interconnected through the collegial relationships of what they refer to as the "invisible college"—professional networks of researchers, clinicians, and academic publishers. Housed in a few clinics in major cities in the United States and Canada, a small handful of clinicians developed theories that became the hallmark treatment strategies directed toward gender atypical children, mostly those assigned male. It is important to understand the history and theory underlying reparative treatment strategies in order to understand the emergence of, and resistance to, more affirmative models.

The Invisible College

The theories of reparative and pathologizing approaches to treating gender atypical children were established by a small cadre of professional psychiatrists and psychologists, most notably John Money, Robert Stoller, Richard Green, George Rekers, Susan Coates, and Ken Zucker. Their theories, research, ideologies, and treatment strategies were developed in different clinics and through professional affiliation and shared research.

John Money, a professor of pediatrics and medical psychology at Johns Hopkins University, helped establish one of the first gender identity clinics for adults in the United States in 1965. He was a prolific writer and the first sexologist to distinguish natal sex from gender identity and gender role. He believed that gender rearing was more important than anatomical sex, and that babies were born psychosexually neutral. This became the foundational theory in the development of behavioral protocols for treating both intersex and gender atypical children.

At the same time John Money was advancing his theories, the UCLA Gender Identity Research Clinic began studying feminine boys and the etiology of adult and adolescent homosexuality and transsexualism. The psychiatrist Robert Stoller (1968) coined the term *gender identity disorder,* which later became the nomenclature used in the *Diagnostic and Statistical Manual of Mental Disorders* (DSM). He theorized that femininity in males was caused by mothers who are excessively close to their sons, which he referred to as *blissful symbiosis.* Susan Coates (1990), a psychiatrist and the director of the Childhood Gender Identity Service at St. Luke's–Roosevelt Hospital Center in New York City from 1980 to 1997, identified the mothers of gender nonconforming boys as controlling, anxious, and intrusive. The research showing that mothers caused femininity and homosexuality in their sons (Bieber et al., 1962) had serious methodological flaws and has long since been debunked (Friedman, 1988; Gottlieb, 2000; Lewes, 1989).

Richard Green, a student and close collaborator of Money's, worked at the UCLA clinic with Stoller. He is the founder of the *Archives of Sexual Behavior,* which has published copious research on the topic of gender identity development. Green designed a comprehensive longitudinal study on "effeminate" behavior in boys, which was funded by the National Institute of Mental Health (NIMH) from 1972 to 1986. The Feminine Boy Project, also known as the "sissy boy study," posed this question: Do cross-gender behaviors in childhood correlate with later adult homosexuality and transsexuality (see Burroway, 2011)? At UCLA, Green and Stoller worked closely with their colleague the psychologist

George Rekers, who provided behaviorally based therapies to feminine boys (Kohli, 2012). Williams (2017) cites letters between Drs. Green, Money, and Stoller that predate Green's research. Stoller was treating "transsexual boys and their families" with *reeducation therapy;* he clarified his clinical focus this way: "In contrast to adolescent and adult male transsexuals, whom we have so far found untreatable by psychotherapeutic means (if the goal is to make gender identity compatible with sex), the situation is more hopeful in children."

In 1975 the Clarke Institute/Centre for Addiction and Mental Health (CAMH) in Toronto, Canada, established a gender program for youth led by the psychiatrist Susan Bradley, who was later joined by the psychologist Ken Zucker. Informed by Green's emerging research, the Child, Youth, and Family Gender Identity Clinic (GIC) in Toronto studied gender "disorders" in children and adolescents and advanced treatment methods also based on the idea that gender atypical behaviors led to adult homosexuality and transsexualism. Zucker became the editor in chief of the *Archives of Sexual Behavior* and was also active in the development of the Gender Disorders section in the *DSM,* assuring their enduring pathologization. Zucker's clinic based its treatment strategies on the psychoanalytic theories that gender nonconformity is rooted in codependent mother-child relationships and specifically affects boys who are emotionally fragile.

These researchers and clinicians developed etiological theories about the development of gender identity, specifically in feminine boys, but they "often slid easily from their data on gender variant boys to discussions of gender variant *children*" (Bryant, 2006, p. 25, emphasis added) and formulated treatment strategies that pathologized gender nonconforming boys *and* girls for decades.

The Pathologization of Boyhood Effeminacy

Richard von Krafft-Ebing was an Austro-German psychiatrist who authored a foundational study of human sexuality, *Psychopathia sexualis,* in 1886. One of his theories was that there exists a "hierarchy of pathology" that assumes childhood feminine behavior in boys is a precursor to homosexuality and, in its more severe forms, transsexualism (Kuhl & Martino, 2018). Homosexuality and transsexualism were postulated to be etiologically related, and same-sex attraction was seen as a milder pathology than cross-dressing and transsexuality.

Those studying gender atypical behavior in boys viewed femininity itself as a symptom (Corbett, 2009), a pathological precursor to the development of adult homosexuality, transsexuality, and transvestism (Bryant, 2006). Corbett (2009) writes, "A discourse has accumulated around feminine boys, constructing them as nonconforming, extreme, and disordered" (p. 353). Their goal was to reduce the boy's "sissy" behaviors (e.g., dressing in female attire, playing with dolls, voicing a preference to be a female) and mannerisms, and to inculcate masculinity. Initially, the study's goals were the treatment of what was called *prehomosexuality*. The removal of homosexuality from the *DSM* and the rise of the gay liberation movement, however, made the continued pathologization of homosexuality politically complex, so it became problematic to have (pre) homosexuality labeled as the focus of treatment. Although their research goals and treatment strategies remained basically the same, the language used in their publications was changed from treating homosexuality to treating faulty gender-identity development (Green, 1987; Kuhl & Martino, 2018), especially the intense "rigidness" of feminine expression in boys (Bryant, 2006, p. 30), which, they believed if it was not treated, would lead to transsexuality, the most severe form of pathology linked to effeminacy (Green, 1987).

What these theorists all have in common is the promulgation of a story about the pathology of being a sissy boy and the outcomes for adult development. Zucker conceded that treating homosexuality was no longer ethical in 1985, but he said, "It would seem that preventing transsexualism is a goal that will never gather systematic opposition" (Zucker, cited in Pyne, 2014, p. 3). From the earlier treatments developed by Rekers to the later treatments of Zucker and his colleagues, Ansara and Hegarty (2011) maintain that "both approaches share a focus on preventing transsexual adulthoods" (p. 3).

Sissy Boys and Their Pathogenic Mothers

Zucker and Bradley (1995) outline four reasons that feminine boys need to be treated. In addition to the two I've already highlighted—preventing homosexuality and transsexualism in adulthood—a third reason was to treat what they saw as the underlying psychopathology in the families, including anxiety, depression, primitive object relations, and borderline traits found in the mothers of extremely feminine boys (see Lev, 2004).

Mother blaming is endemic in psychoanalytic thinking, affecting virtually all therapeutic modalities since Philip Wylie (1942) coined the term *momism* to label mothers' toxic influence on their innocent offspring. Feminists have long critiqued theories that indict mothers for all their children's problems, paradoxically for either being too close, that is, "smothering," *or* being like "refrigerators," that is, coldly distant. Since mothers were thought of as the root cause of a range of pathologies, including autism, schizophrenia, and delinquency, it's no surprise that they were held accountable as *the* destructive element in the lives of their "sissy boys."

These mothers were believed to be deficient and insecure, temperamentally vulnerable, anxious, and depressed, which then increased the male child's anxiety. On the basis of psychoanalytic theories, Stoller (1968) postulated that difficulties in relationships were caused by dominant, overprotective mothers who smothered their sons and who were usually married to ineffective, distant, passive men. He actually suggested that mothers of gender atypical boys had gender-identity conflicts and *themselves* evolved into masculine and bisexual women who, in turn, were responsible for shaping their sons' femininity.

Coates (1990) hypothesizes that these mothers have difficulty separating from their sons, which results in conflicts regarding attachment: separation anxiety is a primary manifestation. She also theorizes that the loss or absence of mothers, possibly through illness or death, or maternal psychopathologies or traumas that devalue men, contribute to the development of femininity in boys.

Zucker and Bradley (1995) observe that mothers of gender dysphoric boys are intimidated by male aggression and encourage femininity to ensure intimacy with their sons. Indeed, Zucker often speaks of the maternal ambivalence toward, encouragement of, or tolerance of feminine behaviors in boys, and how these interfere with treatment (Zucker, 2008b). Green (1987) was even more direct: "You've got to get these mothers out of the way. Feminine kids don't need their mothers around" (p. 275).

Fathers were, of course, also to blame for not being masculine enough, allowing their wives to control the home, and not spending enough time with their children. The literature on the etiology of homosexuality is rife with images of hypermasculine wives, and weak, passive fathers (Bieber et al., 1962). Similarly, Green (1987) highlights "feminine boy"–father alienation, hypothetically a result of the boy's identification with the mother, which drives the father further away. As Gill-Peterson (2014) writes, "The misogynist blaming of the mother was complemented by the archetypal, pathologically distant, uninterested father, who failed to intervene in the closeness of child to mother to create a stable superego that would pre-empt feminine identification."

Given the cultural context of the times—homosexuality being both illegal *and* a clinical diagnosis—Burroway (2011) notes that "it would have been an exceedingly rare mother who wouldn't be worried about what may be in store for her effeminate son—and to feel personally responsible for it." These theories led to the development of treatments to intervene in the child's atypical gender issues that were believed to be induced by pathological family environments, particularly the encouragement of cross-gender behavior by mothers or the absence of strong father figures—or both—in the daily life of the family.

Treatment Strategies

Treatment strategies have been aimed at coercing the child to adapt to the societal expectations of proper male or female behavior and punishing deviations from stereotypical male and female sex roles in young children, which were viewed as signs of pathology (Rekers, 1995; Zucker & Bradley, 1995). Although these treatment strategies are based in psychoanalytic thinking that postulates that cross-gender identity is caused by pathological parenting, behavioral interventions are endorsed that focus primarily on the child, not the assumed pathogenic parent. Treatment was generally provided in outpatient settings using behavioral modification and psychodynamic interventions, as well as individual and family therapy—although some children have been forcibly removed from their homes and subjected to inpatient treatment (Burke, 1996).

Most of these programs employ behavior-modification techniques developed to socially reinforce "appropriate" behaviors and extinguish those deemed "inappropriate" or cross-gendered. The clinicians at the UCLA Gender Identity Research Clinic who pioneered this work would target cross-gender behaviors using rewards and punishments. Bryant (2006) describes a token economy system in which the boy being treated was given "blue tokens for positive reinforcement (e.g., for masculine play with his brother) and red tokens for negative reinforcement (e.g., for feminine play with his sister)" (p. 28). The goal was to extinguish specific feminine behaviors, such as playing with Barbie dolls, and rewarding masculine behaviors. Rekers (1995) believed that "skill deficits in athletic games in gender-disturbed [sic] boys can be remediated" (p. 283). The children in the study were "diagnosed" by measuring how they walked or sat or moved compared to normative expectations. They were then treated through selective reinforcement and taught to play with toys believed to be gender appropriate. Treatment continued in the absence of the therapist as children were expected to wear a special wrist counter to self-monitor when they played with gender-inappropriate toys.

Zucker and Bradley (1995) outline a treatment plan used by CAMH's Child, Youth, and Family Gender Identity Clinic, including the following guidelines for requesting that parents "not allow cross-dressing, discourage cross-gender role play and fantasy play, restrict play with cross-sex toys, tell the child that they value *him as a boy or her as a girl*, encourage same-sex peer relations, and help the child engage in more sex-appropriate or neutral activities" (p. 280, emphasis added). These recommendations are all based on the belief that by praising masculine behaviors and ignoring or punishing feminine behaviors, clinicians would be able not only to modify the cross-gender behaviors and gender dysphoria, but also to avert future cross-gender identity.

Challenges to Reparative Therapy

In the past two decades, these theories and treatment strategies have come under intense scrutiny, as has the work of the professionals who championed them. John Money's claim that children were psychosexually neutral until the age of three has proved to be much more complex than he envisioned—or admitted. In 1966 he suggested that David Reimer, whose penis was severed in a botched circumcision, be reared as a girl. Because the child was one of a set of identical twin boys, this was the perfect case for Money to "prove" his theory: that the gender of rearing is more important than the genetic sex. For decades Money published journal articles boasting the success of his theory and how "Joan" (David's pseudonym in the literature) was flourishing as a girl and later as a woman. His research was exposed as flawed by Milton Diamond (2002), however, after a decades-long feud. Indeed, Joan was not flourishing but had suffered living as a girl. Money had purposely concealed the truth that David's sex reassignment to female was unsuccessful. David was not only failing at living as a girl, but when he learned what had happened to him, relieved to know the truth, he immediately chose to live his life as a man (Colapinto, 2000). Money never admitted this publicly or recanted his theories, and he administered clinical treatment to both David and his brother that would now be considered ethically questionable. David spoke extensively about the negative effects of these experiments, and he tragically completed suicide in 2004.

Money's research was used for decades as evidence that socialization always trumps biology, and he supervised the medical treatments of both intersex children and gender atypical children. It is now known that the relationship between biology and society is far more complex. Ostensibly, Money's theories appeared to dovetail nicely with early feminist criticisms of societally conditioned gender-role limitations: biology is *not* destiny. Surely rigid gender-role expectations constrict the potentialities of children. Diamond (2002), however, suggests that Money's theory of psychosexual neutrality ignored the interaction of biological underpinnings and the way that they are mediated and modified by complex transactional processes within society. Money was correct in assuming that sociocultural mores influence gender development; yet it seems he was incorrect in concluding that such forces are the only influence on individual psychosocial development. He was also misguided in believing that gender is completely malleable by upbringing and expectations on the part of parents and society.

The UCLA program also revealed the limitations and dangers of trying to change gender expression and sexual orientation. Green's research revealed that nearly 75% of the subjects in the study identified as homosexual or bisexual as adults. Other studies showed similar results (Bailey & Zucker, 1995; Zuger, 1984), confirming that a majority of feminine boys grow up to be homosexual, and a small number identify as heterosexual or transsexual, which led one researcher to mistakenly conclude that "all male homosexuality begins with early effeminate behavior" (Zuger, 1984, p. 96).

Green's research clearly shows the limits of treating feminine boys, since a majority grew up to identify as gay despite intervention. Moreover, years after these studies were concluded, information about the interventions themselves and the harmful effects they had on the children and their families came to light.

In 2010 it became public that one of the boys in this program, Kirk Murphy, had completed suicide as an adult. Kirk was known in the treatment literature as "Kyle" by Green and as "Kraig" by Rekers, but they both proudly shared his story as a successful case for reparative therapy:

> There is no doubt that our treatment intervention produced a profound change in Kraig. When we first saw him, the extent of his feminine identification was so profound (his mannerisms, gestures, fantasies, flirtations, etc., as shown in his "swishing" around the home and clinic, fully dressed as a woman with long dress, wig, nail polish, high screechy voice, slovenly seductive eyes) that it *suggested irreversible neurological and biochemical determinants*. At the 26-month follow-up he looked and acted *like any other boy*. People who view the videotaped recordings of him before and after treatment talk of him as "two different boys." (Rekers & Lovaas, 1974, p. 187, emphasis added)

The family members, however, remember this time in a very different way, and they believe that these treatments led to a suicide attempt at age 17 and a completed suicide at age 38. His mother believes that reparative therapy ruined her son's life (Hughes, 2011). Like the parents of all the boys enrolled in treatment, Kirk's parents were expected to monitor their child's program (Burke, 1996). Bryant (2006) explains that "these treatment approaches resulted in a host of new adults intervening in their lives. A small army of researchers and research assistants descended upon the boy and his family—in the clinic of course, but also in the home and the school where they observed periodically (sometimes several visits per week) and trained others to take over as therapist in their absence" (p. 28). Parents and teachers took on these new roles, monitoring and attempting to modify the child's behavior. There was no discussion about how this might negatively influence family relationships or their home and school life.

The family described the treatment protocol as "severe" (Hughes, 2011), and the father was instructed to "spank" Kirk (sometimes with a belt) if he played with girl's toys (Burroway, 2011). His siblings believe these treatments changed Kirk's personality. His sister says, "It left Kirk just totally stricken with the belief that he was broken, that he was different from everybody else" (Hughes, 2011).

The fourth rationale Zucker and Bradley (1995) offer for why feminine boys need to be treated was to eliminate "peer ostracism," or the belief that being a sissy was so damaging to a boy's social life that it must be obliterated at all costs. Green (1987) predates Zucker, coining the phrase *male-affect starvation*, that is, what the "sissy" didn't emotionally receive from other boys he later tries to compensate for by searching for love from other men. It does not seem that these researchers recognized that ostracism and bullying are not the fault of the child but the responsibility of adults to eliminate in social and educational environments. Nor do they seem to realize that peer socialization can take place within gay communities that is both healthy and potentially healing.

The homophobia underlying these treatments is obvious to all today; additionally, the costs of these treatments are not benign and need to be tallied. Bryant (2006) outlines the damage caused to these boys by referring to what Kuhl and Martino (2018) term a "legacy of harm." Rekers (1995) insists that therapy was intended to produce a heterosexual adult. Green (1987), however, laments the "apparent powerlessness of treatment to interrupt the progression from 'feminine' boy to homosexual or bisexual man" (p. 318). The program not only was a failure in eliminating future homosexuality, but also caused irreparable psychological harm to the boys and their families. Like Money's research, it was falsely reported as "successful," and the researchers and clinicians never acknowledged or took responsibility for the problems they created.

Rekers, who is a Baptist minister in addition to being a psychologist, built his career on treating homosexuality, Kirk being one of his index cases. He was a founding member of the Family Research Council in 1983, an anti-gay Christian organization, and was on the Scientific Advisory Committee and the Board of Directors of NARTH—the National Association for Research and Therapy of Homosexuality, an organization founded in 1992 by a small group of psychologists who thought homosexuality should not have been removed from the *DSM* and who practice and advocate for reparative therapies. On April 12, 2010, a story broke in the alternative newsweekly *Miami New Times* showing a photograph of Rekers at Miami International Airport returning from a European vacation in the company of a 20-year-old male escort. Rekers employed the man through rent boy.com, although he claimed he hired him only to carry his luggage and provide massages. The profile on rentboy, according to one report, showed "a shirtless young man with delicate features, guileless eyes, and sun-kissed, hairless skin"; it touted his "smooth, sweet, tight ass" and "perfectly built 8 inch cock (uncut)" and claimed that he is "sensual," "wild," and "up for anything" (Bullock & Thorp, 2010). This exposé destroyed Rekers's reputation, and he resigned from his work treating "unwanted homosexuality," a phrase promoted by NARTH.

It is perhaps easy to dismiss Rekers, in part because of the religious fervor of his writing and his own embarrassing fall from grace. It is harder to dismiss the decades of work of Zucker and his colleagues at CAMH. Zucker is an accomplished researcher and a prolific writer who has not shied away from the conflict that has emerged in recent years regarding the treatment of gender atypical children. As recently as 2008 (2008a), he wrote about the "best practices" he developed at CAMH's clinic, and his belief that it is not only possible, but ethically warranted, to assist children in having their gender identity match their biological sex. He was quoted in the *Canadian National Post* in 2015 as saying, "You are lowering the odds that as such a kid gets older, he or she will move into adolescence feeling so uncomfortable about their gender identity that they think that it would be better to live as the other gender and require treatment with hormones and sex-reassignment surgery" (cited in Williams, 2017).

Concerns about the CAMH clinic have persisted for many years and have been debated on the Internet and at professional conferences. In many ways, CAMH and Zucker have become the focal point of activism to change the ways gender nonconforming children and transgender youth are treated. After years of criticism from Canadian gender-affirmative professionals who worked in the shadows of CAMH's power, Zucker's Gender Identity Clinic (GIC) became the focus of an independent review led by Drs. Zinck and Pignatiello. In November 2015 their findings were released; it was announced that Dr. Zucker was no longer with the clinic, that the program was "insular" and "out of step with ethical clinical practices" (Williams, 2017), and that it was being restructured. One of the many suggestions made was to "consider adding Social Work or other professionals with expertise in family therapy to the GIC team" (*Summary of the External Review*, 2016). Zucker's removal was viewed as cause for celebration by providers and activists committed to more affirmative treatments. It heralds a hopeful end to "sissy boy" treatments, despite the ongoing backlash by Zucker's supporters, who believe he should not have been removed (Ubelacker, 2016).

Of course, ending clinical practices is not as simple as closing one clinic—regardless of its prominence. Protests against reparative therapies started as early as 1975 (Bryant, 2006), and yet numerous clinicians still practice under various reparative therapy models, some with blatantly religious-based philosophies, and others use behavioral or psychodynamic techniques to treat cross-gender behaviors, with the goal of redirecting homosexuality and transgenderism. Most are probably in smaller private practices and not necessarily publishing their results, so they remain under the radar of criticism.

Contextualizing the "Sissy Boy" Research

As stated, the research on feminine boys revealed that 75% of them identified as gay and/or bisexual in adulthood. Retrospective studies (see Bailey and Zucker, 1995) and anecdotal reports (Rottnek, 1999) confirm gender nonconforming behavior to be common in children who eventually identify as lesbian, gay, or bisexual. Clearly, many LGB people transgress societal gender rules in childhood, and, indeed, the gay liberation movement was one of the first modern communities that supported gender diverse expression.

The use of this research must be contextualized, however. At the time it all began, homosexuality was still a *DSM* diagnosis and illegal in most jurisdictions. The hope was to discourage or redirect homosexuality through psychological treatment. At the time the research ended, when Green interviewed his adult subjects, the United States was experiencing the burgeoning gay liberation movement. It is not surprising that so many men identified as gay during this era, and only a very few identified as trans. The emergence of a transgender liberation movement would not occur for another two decades.

Now that homosexuality is far more socially acceptable, that is, it has been removed from the *DSM,* is now legal in all states, and is supported through major mainstream institutions like marriage and family building, Green's research is currently being used to deter young people from social transitioning. The concern is that children who are transitioning may *not* be transgender but, in actuality, may be gay, lesbian, or bisexual. In an odd Kafkaesque move, the same research that attempted (and failed) at eliminating homosexuality is now being (mis)used to suggest that homosexuality is the natural outcome for *all* cross-gender children, and that allowing them to socially transition is, in essence, oppressing or repressing their "true" future gay identities.

The true meaning of cross-gender behavior for any individual child can not be known until they mature and label themselves. The outcome possibilities for "sissy boys" today, however, would probably reveal a far more diverse set of identities, including many who are gay identified, and also a higher number of self-identified trans women and nonbinary people, simply because it is now possible to affirm these identities. *The conflation of sexual orientation and gender identity in science continues to muddle outcome studies.*

Affirmative Therapies

A large proportion of parents accept gender-variance, while being mainly concerned for their child's welfare and unsure about the adequate ways to handle the challenge.

— MALPAS, 2011, P. 454

Affirmative therapies with gender nonconforming children and transgender youth were practiced long before they surfaced in the literature in the 1990s. Only recently have affirmative therapists published their clinical practices, and have researchers begun studying the results. Affirmation therapy is based on the belief that all expressions of gender by children and youth should be celebrated as authentic, and that gender nonconforming behavior, identity, or expression should not be viewed as pathological (Ehrensaft et al., 2018; Hidalgo et al., 2013; Vanderburgh, 2009), but as the emergence of the child's true gender self (Ehrensaft, 2012). Labels such as *gender deviant* and *sissy boys* have now been replaced with terms like *gender creative* (Ehrensaft, 2012) and *gender independent* (Pyne, 2014). There is no attempt to fix or repair gender identity or expression since their gender is not viewed as broken. Rather, this approach aims to provide space for young people to explore their gender, affirm their identity, and be supported in living healthy lives.

Wallace and Russell (2013) state that the work for gender affirmative therapists "shifts away from a focus on fixing the child to fixing the system that pathologizes them and on developing strategies to mitigate the injuries of that system" (p. 114). The "outcome" of the child's maturation—whether it is heterosexual, gay, lesbian, bisexual, transgender, nonbinary, genderqueer, or cisgender—is not viewed as the focus of treatment. All gender identities and expressions as well as all sexual orientations are viewed as successful outcomes. The goal is *gender health,* which Hildago and colleagues (2013) define as "a child's opportunity to live in the gender that feels most real or comfortable to that child and to express that gender with freedom from restriction, aspersion, or rejection" (p. 286). The clinical focus is always on supporting the child's gender health through advocacy, compassion, and fostering an environment of familial love and safety (Ehrensaft et al., 2018).

Gay-Affirmative Therapy

The concept of affirmative therapy for LGBTQ people was originally developed during the early days of the gay liberation movement. Its earliest appearance in print was in Alan Maylon's 1982 article, "Psychotherapeutic Implications of Internalized Homophobia," part of a seminal issue of the *Journal of Homosexuality* titled "Homosexuality and Psychotherapy: A Handbook of Affirmative Models," published by the pioneering Haworth Press. Gay-affirmative therapy expanded the concept that homosexuality was not a mental illness, but, rather, a normal variation in human sexuality. It suggested that gay and lesbian people internalized societal bias and judgment and proposed that psychotherapists become sensitized to the role of homophobia in the psyches of gay men and lesbians, ideas that were introduced by George Weinberg, a heterosexual psychologist and psychotherapist, in his 1973 classic, *Society and the Healthy Homosexual*. As I've stated elsewhere:

> Historically, its great significance is that it was the first therapeutic movement that acknowledged the harm done to [LGBTQ] people through heterosexist socialization and institutional homophobia. The unconditional affirmation of homosexual relationships by psychotherapists was intended to serve as a counterbalance for the negative sociocultural and familial environments within which most [LGB] people mature and live. Thus, gay affirmative psychotherapy was supposed to ameliorate the negative impact of growing up gay in an oppressive society, as well as to assist the gay or lesbian client in a coming out process that actualized a healthy homosexual identity. Central to gay affirmative therapy is the attempt to enhance the dignity and self-respect of clients by establishing a supportive and accepting atmosphere. (Lev, 2005)

During the decades that followed, gay-affirmative therapy expanded to include lesbian and bisexual people, then transgender people, and it has eventually influenced the evolving treatment of LGBTQ youth and gender nonconforming children. Interestingly, gay-affirmative therapy explicitly states that therapists who espouse negative views toward homosexuality cannot be effective clinicians with gay or lesbian clients, an idea that can now be expanded to reparative therapists treating gender nonconforming children and transgender youth. Affirmative therapies represent the first therapeutic movement to acknowledge the harm done to LGBTQ people through heterosexist socialization and institutional homophobia, including their treatment within therapeutic systems of care.

The role of affirmative therapies in the lives of LGBTQ people was intrinsically linked to the depathologization of homosexuality. Would LGB people have the broad civil rights they have today, including marriage equality, if homosexuality were still in the DSM? "Throwing off the yoke and stigma of 'pathology' allowed not only for the coming out of gay, lesbian, and bisexual people, but also allowed for legal, political, and clinical transformations that could never have been granted a 'mentally ill' population" (Lev, 2013, p. 289). Reparative therapies are based on the belief that growing up to be gay, lesbian, bisexual, gender nonconforming, transgender, transsexual, and/or queer is less optimal that being heterosexual and cisgender. The development of affirmative therapies challenges the idea that there is nothing disordered, dysfunctional, problematic, or "treatable" for sissy boys and tomboy or masculine girls. Affirming practices support the potential emergence of both LGB sexualities and transgender identities with the same joy that they view the development of heterosexual and cisgender identities.

One important distinction, however, is that transgender identities often involve medical interventions, which potentially require supportive relationships with institutions and professionals in a way that LGB identities do not. The first affirmative treatment model for transgender youth began in the Netherlands in 1987 at what is now the VU University Medical Center in Amsterdam (de Vries & Cohen-Kettenis, 2012). They pioneered early medical transitions for adolescents, and these Dutch protocols were adapted by Dr. Norman Spack in the United States at what is now the Gender Management Service (GeMS) in Boston (Edwards-Leeper & Spack, 2012).

The Children's Gender and Sexual Advocacy and Education Program, based in Washington, D.C., under the leadership of Dr. Edgardo Menvielle, began the first program for prepubescent children in the 1990s (Menvielle & Hill, 2011). When Hsieh and Leininger published a resource list of gender-affirming clinics in North America in 2014, there were over 30 clinics included. It did not cite individual therapists in private practice or collaborative efforts by interdisciplinary teams located outside hospital settings (Lev & Wolf-Gould, 2018). There has clearly been an explosion of affirmative modalities, a "paradigm shift" in treatment strategies (Pyne, 2014).

Defining Affirmative Therapy

Although there is not one standard way to practice, affirmative therapy starts with the conviction, regardless of the child's anatomy, that no expression of gender is pathologized and that the goal is to support and validate gender diversity. Affirmative therapy states that "gender identity and related experiences asserted by a child, an adolescent, and/or family members are true, and that the clinician's role in providing affirming care to that family is to empathetically support such assertions" (Edwards-Leeper, Leibowitz & Sangganjanavanich, 2016, p. 165). It is assumed that a child or adolescent knows or understands their own gender better than anyone. The clinician's role then is to help the client know that there is a range of "viable and valid options among which the patient can choose, and that the patient should make the best decision for themselves, free from external pressures to conform to gender ideals" (Menvielle, 2012, p. 365).

Research shows that it is in the best interest of all children expressing gender nonconformity to have their authentic selves supported by peers, parents, teachers, and other adults in their lives (Riley, Sitharthan, Clemson, & Diamond, 2011; Ryan, Russell, Huebner, Diaz, & Sanchez, 2010) as well as the institutions in which they are engaged, such as school and religious communities. Recent studies suggest that children whose emerging gender identity is affirmed have better mental health outcomes than those who are pressured to live as their assigned sex (Durwood, McLaughlin, & Olson, 2017; Olson, Durwood, DeMeules, & McLaughlin, 2016; Travers et al., 2012). The WPATH Standards of Care state: "Acceptance and removal of secrecy can bring considerable relief to gender dysphoric children/adolescents and their families" (Coleman et al., 2012, p. 15).

Affirmative therapies have never represented one school or modality, but, rather, they have used diverse theories and techniques available across the psychotherapeutic spectrum. To date, there is not one definitive description of affirmative therapies. Salient positions from prominent theorists are presented below.

The Multi-Dimensional Family Approach (MDFA), developed by Jean Malpas (2011), incorporates many of the key theoretical underpinnings, including: (1) parental engagement and education; (2) individual assessment and child therapy; (3) parental coaching; (4) systemic family therapy, and (5) parent support groups. Malpas observes, "Parents are the pillars of this therapeutic model" (p. 457), so parent coaching is integral, the goal being to move them from helplessness to empowerment. Menvielle and Hill (2011) also focus on parent education, encouraging parents to advocate for their children and educate other adults in their lives, thus creating a safe space for the child. They insist it is necessary for parents to lessen their own shame, which may also help the child lessen theirs. If shame remains undiluted and is allowed to contaminate the parent-child bond, it "can function as an organizing emotion in the process of identity formation" (Wallace & Russell, 2013, p. 117).

Hildalgo and her colleagues (2013) outline five major premises that inform affirmative-therapy models. The first is: "Gender variations are not disorders" (p. 285). The WPATH Standards of Care (Coleman et al., 2012) are clear: "Being transsexual, transgender, or gender nonconforming is a matter of diversity, not pathology" (p. 4). This premise alone challenges reparative therapies. If there is no pathology, then there is nothing to repair, fix, ameliorate, or change.

The second premise is: "Gender presentations are diverse and varied across cultures, therefore requiring our cultural sensitivity" (Hidalgo et al., 2013, p. 285). Research in history, anthropology, as well as the biological sciences shows that gender diversity is ubiquitous across culture, nation, class, and epoch (Bullough & Bullough, 1993; Lev, 2004; Roscoe, 1998; Roughgarden, 2004), and that newer ways of describing and understanding gender identities and expressions continue to emerge and expand. The ways that the psychiatric community has understood and classified trans people historically (Benjamin, 1966; Lev, 2004) are of limited value in today's world. It is essential that affirmative therapists respect and remain open to culturally diverse ways of defining and exploring gender, especially when working with clients from different cultural, religious, ethnic/racial, and class backgrounds from their own.

The third premise is: "Gender involves an interweaving of biology, development and socialization, and culture and context, with all three bearing on any individual's gender self" (Hildago et al., 2013, p. 285). Reparative therapies are obsessed with causation, endlessly searching for the etiology of gender differences, with an obvious focus on curing and fixing. Affirmative models accept that there are influences that may be biological as well as those that are environmental—ideas that Freud repeatedly affirms in his discussion of the origins of male homosexuality (1905a/1965; 1905b/1977, 1910/1964, 1920/1968)—and that each human being—trans or cis—is influenced by individual developmental processes as well as those unique to their cultural influence, both the dominant and "minority" cultures.

The authors also extend an important clause to this third premise: "to the best of our knowledge at present" (p. 285). This is an especially important concept and one that reparative therapists neglect to acknowledge: the sciences of both biology and sociology are continually expanding. As knowledge about the etiology and evolution of gender continues to grow, so will the understanding of human development and diversity. Humanity is probably much closer to the beginning of this field of study than to the end of it.

The fourth premise is: "Gender may be fluid, and is not binary, both at a particular time and if and when it changes within an individual across time" (p. 285). A number of important ideas are embedded in this phrase. It states that "gender *may* be fluid" (emphasis added), which recognizes that this will vary from child to child. For some, gender identity or expression will shift over their life span, perhaps being especially malleable in childhood and adolescence; for others, it will remain stable or unchanging. Neither is better, and both are normal and healthy. They also state that "gender . . . is not binary." For affirmative therapists, neither gender nor sex is viewed as a pairing of opposites—male/female, boy/girl, man/woman—since increasing numbers of people identify as nonbinary or genderfluid. This is consistent with the new nomenclature of the *DSM*-5 diagnosis for gender dysphoria, which it clearly states is a "strong desire to be of the other gender," but adds, "*or some alternative gender different from one's assigned gender*" (APA, 2013, p. 452, emphasis added). Affirmative therapy recognizes many paths to the actualization of gender expression and a broad array of gender identities as normal and healthy human variations.

The fifth and final premise is: "If there is pathology, it more often stems from cultural reactions (e.g., transphobia, homophobia, sexism) rather than from within the child" (Hildago et al., 2013, p. 285). They correctly assume that most gender creative and trans children do not exhibit signs of mental illness. It is equally true that children and youth who are gender expansive, like all "minorities," face significant sociocultural biases and are at higher risk for many psychological stressors that can manifest themselves as bona fide mental health problems, such as anxiety or depression (Institute of Medicine, 2011; Meyer, 2003).

It must also be acknowledged, however, that some gender nonconforming children and youth can exhibit signs of pathology, which may or may not be related to their gender, and which warrant further investigation because it can be "difficult to separate gender as symptom from gender as journey toward an authentic self" (Ehrensaft, 2012, p. 347). Ehrensaft reports that she has seen children in whom "gender dysphoria was the manifestation of internal psychological disturbances," and although "these are the exceptions rather than the rule" (p. 347), a thorough clinical assessment that sorts out these differences is certainly one of the more necessary and challenging aspects of working with young people. Regardless of their etiology, or the ultimate expression of gender, it is important that mental health issues be addressed to assist in the optimal functioning of the child.

Research shows that adolescents with gender dysphoria can exhibit internalizing disorders, such as anxiety and depression, and/or externalizing disorders, such as oppositional defiant disorder (de Vries, Doreleijers, Steensma, & Cohen-Kettenis, 2011; Grossman & D'Augelli, 2006; Olson et al., 2016; Wallien & Cohen-Kettenis, 2008). Gender dysphoria has an unusually high overlap with the autism spectrum (de Vries, Noens, Cohen-Kettenis, van Berckelaer-Onnes, & Doreleijers, 2010; Janssen, Huang, & Duncan, 2016; Kuvalanka, Mahan, McGuire, & Hoffman, 2017). Therefore, a broad assessment for potential mental health complications is supported by many affirmative therapists (Coolhart, Baker, Farmer, Malaney, & Shipman, 2013; Menvielle, 2012). Edwards-Leeper and colleagues (2016) suggest that "youth who present with co-occurring mental health problems, including autism spectrum disorders, suicidality, self-injury, severe eating disorders, and/or trauma histories require additional assessment and consideration of how and whether these factors might be related to gender identity" (p. 170). They refer to this as "expanding the model" (pp. 169–170) and state that affirmation can include nuanced assessment, especially when there are complex mental health conditions that can potentially coexist with gender dysphoria. Affirmative therapists should not be *just* cheerleaders for gender diversity, but clinicians skilled in mental health assessment and knowledgeable about developmental processes. The struggles of being gender nonconforming or trans in a cisnormative culture, and the challenges of living with mental illness, even one of lesser severity, require additional support from family and professionals.

A Note about Protective Responses

In addition to reparative and affirmative models, some scholars list "protective responses" as a third perspective (Gale & Syrja-McNally, 2014), sometimes referred to as "watchfully waiting" (de Vries & Cohen-Kettenis, 2012; Zucker, 2008b). For many, watchful waiting is seen as a less severe form of reparative therapy, one in which the child is not punished for gender nonconformity but is offered little or no active validation. Some refer to this as a "wait-and-see (-and hope) response" (Gale & Syrja-McNally, 2014, p. 192), sarcastically drawing attention to the projected fantasy that this is only a phase that the child will—somehow—pass through. Cautionary responses are based on desistance research that suggested most children exhibiting gender dysphoria would grow out of it. These theories are based on research that is currently being challenged on methodological grounds (Newhook et al., 2018); desistance and regret rates actually appear to be quite low.

Wait-and-see might be a healthy attitude toward a child who is gender nonconforming, is not experiencing distress or dysphoria, and is living in a supportive environment. In such a case, "waiting" is not a passive act, nor are parents restricting or denying the child's expression. "Waiting" simple means not making any active decisions about social or medical transitions, but, rather, allowing the child a chance to creatively explore all options as their identity emerges. This is not a long-term plan but a time for the child to begin coalescing their gender. For those children who are confidently *insistent, consistent,* and *persistent* in their understanding of their gender, wait-and-see would not be recom-mended.

Clinical approaches that are protective are certainly more conservative than most affirming ones. For example, watchful waiting emphasizes caution when it comes to the social transitioning of prepubescent children (Ehrensaft et al., 2018; Zucker & Cohen-Kettenis, 2008). Even within protective approaches, however, there are differences. Whereas some clinicians, such as Zucker and Bradley (1995), strongly discourage cross-gender play, others, like de Vries and Cohen-Kettenis (2012), take a more flexible approach. But there is a vast difference between parents who withhold necessary treatments, including social and/or medical transitions, because they are rejecting the possibility that their child may be transgender and those who are moving ahead cautiously, supporting their child and allowing the child's self to emerge. Distinguishing this difference should be part of an ongoing assessment.

It is part of the work of parenting to reject things that feel potentially dangerous, such as skateboards, wild parties, and premature sexuality, and do all they can to protect their children. When children begin to take risks, especially those that may feel morally challenging or life-threatening, parents are expected to be firm in their protective position. For most parents, gender diversity is an unknown world—and a frightening one. A transgender child feels like a stranger, and they cannot imagine a successful future. Parenting theories rarely start with: "If your child deviates from what is expected, support them in that, because ultimately we all know ourselves best."

Malpas (2011) says that "acceptance *is* protection" (emphasis added), but when children defy societally prescribed gender rules, parents' first response is rarely "Oh, I should protect my child by accepting them"—especially if theirs is a rebellious teen who wants to take medications that will permanently alter their body and potentially make them infertile and who may also be exhibiting labile moods. They are likely to see the emerging gender expression as the "cause" of the child's problem, in much the same way they might view adolescent drug experimentation. Indeed, a parent who expresses no caution at all, who does not have any protective concerns about their child's experiences and future, might be as concerning as ones who are overly cautious and overly protective.

The journey toward acceptance is sometimes a difficult one, taking families through dangerous and complex terrain. Protective responses are best seen as part of a continuum, a halfway point between reparative and affirmative, giving the family time to catch up emotionally to their child's needs.

Depending on the family, it may be necessary to start with more cautious, protective strategies, while working toward creating an accepting, affirming environment. Affirmative approaches require the support of parents and caregivers and, to some degree, the extended family, communities, and educational and religious institutions in which family life is embedded. If these supports are not (yet) available, moving slowly and cautiously may be the most affirming decision. Families should not be pushed too quickly toward that end. Clinicians need to carefully weigh how to manage parental rejection, especially if that would mean treatment would be prematurely terminated and the child could end up being seen by a clinician working within a corrective religious or reparative model. Affirmative therapy approaches must include strategies to assist the more "protective" parent into increasingly supportive positions without harsh judgment. To accomplish that, their concerns, fears, judgments, rigid gender views, and/or cultural and religious biases must be respected and viewed as attempts to protect the children they love. Assisting children and youth in practicing patience in the face of adult caution, can also be incorporated into a larger affirmative approach.

In Conclusion

There are rich, complex, and often contentious accounts of the development and advancement of treatment approaches for young people who are gender nonconforming. The philosophies of these approaches range from a pathologizing view of sexuality and gender identity to an affirmation of sexual and gender diversity as natural, healthy, and requiring treatment only as a result of sociopolitical stigma and oppression. This chapter has offered a brief summary of reparative approaches (and their legacy) and the emergence of more affirming ones.

The assumptions underlying reparative, affirmative, and protective approaches have been outlined, offering clinicians who work with youth and families an opportunity to review their own thinking. Clinicians' assumptions are inextricably linked and informed by these philosophies and the unique needs and experiences seen in daily practice with clients. An awareness of the various treatment approaches provides the clinician with a contextual framework to understand the assumptions and perspectives that may be informing not only their own practice but the families who seek their care.

REFERENCES

American Psychiatric Association. (2013). *Diagnostic and statistical manual of mental disorders (DSM-5)*. Washington, D.C.: American Psychiatric Association Publishing.

Ansara, Y. G., & Hegarty, P. (2011). Cisgenderism in psychology: Pathologizing and misgendering children from 1999 to 2008. *Psychology & Sexuality*, iFirst, 1–24. doi:10.1080/19419899.2011.576696.

Bailey, J. M., & Zucker, K. J. (1995). Childhood sex-typed behavior and sexual orientation: A conceptual analysis and quantitative review. *Developmental Psychology, 31* (1), 43–55.

Benjamin, H. (1966). *The transsexual phenomenon*. New York: Julian Press.

Bieber, I., Dain, H. J., Dince, P. R., Drellich, M. G., Grand, H. G., Gundlach, R. H., . . . & Bieber, T. B. (1962). *Homosexuality: A psychoanalytic study of male homosexuals*. New York: Basic Books.

Bryant, K. (2006). Making gender identity disorder of childhood: Historical lessons for contemporary debates. *Sexuality Research & Social Policy, 3* (3), 23–39.

Bullock, P., and Thorp, B. K. (2010, May 6). Christian right leader George Rekers takes vacation with "rent boy." *Miami New Times*. Retrieved December 2, 2017, from www.miaminewtimes.com/newschristian-right-leader-george-rekers-takes-vacation-with-rent-boy-6377933.

Bullough, B., & Bullough, V. (1993). *Crossdressing, sex, and gender*. Philadelphia: University of Pennsylvania Press.

Burke, P. (1996). *Gender shock: Exploding the myths of male and female*. New York: Anchor Books/Doubleday.

Burroway, J. (2011, June 7). What are little boys made of? An original Box Turtle Bulletin investigation. *Box Turtle Bulletin*. Retrieved December 17, 2017, from www.boxturtlebulletin.com/what-are-little-boys-made-of-main.

Byne, W., Bradley, S. J., Coleman, E., Eyler, A. E., Green, R., Menvielle, E., . . . & Tompkins, D. A. (2012). Treatment of gender identity disorder. *American Journal of Psychiatry, 169* (8), 759–796.

Coates, S. (1990). Ontogenesis of boyhood gender identity disorder. *Journal of the American Academy of Psychoanalysis, 18* (3), 414–438.

Colapinto, J. (2000). *As nature made him: The boy who was raised as a girl*. New York: HarperCollins.

Coleman, E., Bockting, W., Botzer, M., Cohen-Kettenis, P., DeCuypere, G., Feldman, J., . . . & Zucker, K. (2012). Standards of Care for the health of transsexual, transgender, and gender nonconforming people, Version 7. Retrieved December 17, 2017, from https://s3.amazonaws.com/amo_hub_content/Association140/files/Standards%20of%20Care%20V7%20-%202011%20WPATH%20(2)(1).pdf.

Coolhart, D., Baker, A., Farmer, S., Malaney, M., & Shipman, D. (2013). Therapy with transsexual youth and their families: A clinical tool for assessing youth's readiness for gender transition. *Journal of Marital and Family Therapy, 39,* 223–243. http://dx.doi.org/10.1111/j.1752-0606.2011.00283.x.

Corbett, K. (2009). Boyhood femininity, gender identity disorder, masculine presuppositions, and the anxiety of regulation. *Psychoanalytic Dialogues, 19,* 353–370.

de Vries, A. L., & Cohen-Kettenis, P. T. (2012). Clinical management of gender dysphoria in children and adolescents: The Dutch approach. *Journal of Homosexuality* 59 (3), 301–320.

de Vries A. L., Doreleijers, T. A., Steensma, T. D., & Cohen-Kettenis, P. T. (2011). Psychiatric comorbidity in gender dysphoric adolescents. *Journal of Child Psychology and Psychiatry, 52,* 1195–1202.

de Vries, A. L., Noens, I. L., Cohen-Kettenis, P. T., van Berckelaer-Onnes, I. A., & Doreleijers, T. A. (2010). Autism spectrum disorders in gender dysphoric children and adolescents. *Journal of Autism and Developmental Disorders, 40,* 930–936.

Diamond, M. (2002). Sex and gender are different: Sexual identity and gender identity are different. *Clinical Child Psychology & Psychiatry, 7* (3), 320–334.

Durwood, L., McLaughlin, K. A., & Olson, K. R. (2017). Mental health and self-worth in socially-transitioned transgender children. *Journal of American Academy of Child and Adolescent Psychiatry, 56* (2), 101–102.

Edwards-Leeper, L., Leibowitz, S., & Sangganjanavanich, V. F. (2016). Affirmative practice with transgender and gender nonconforming youth: Expanding the model. *Psychology of Sexual Orientation and Gender Diversity, 3* (2), 165–172. http://dx.doi.org/10.1037/sgd0000167.

Edwards-Leeper, L., & Spack, N. P. (2012). Psychological evaluation and medical treatment of transgender youth in an interdisciplinary "gender management service" (GeMS) in a major pediatric center. *Journal of Homosexuality, 59,* 321–336.

Ehrensaft, D. (2012). From gender identity disorder to gender identity creativity: True gender self child therapy. *Journal of Homosexuality, 59* (3), 337–356.

Ehrensaft, D., Giammattei, S. V., Storck, K., Tishelman, A. C., & Keo-Meier, C. (2018). Prepubertal social gender transitions: What we know; what we can learn—A view from a gender affirmative lens. *International Journal of Transgenderism, 19* (2), 251–268.

Freud, S. (1905a/1965). *Three essays on the theory of sexuality.* J. Strachey (ed. and trans.). New York: Avon Books.

Freud, S. (1905b/1977). *Case histories I: Fragment of an analysis of a case of hysteria.* A. Richards (ed.), A. Strachey & J. Strachey (trans.) (pp. 29–164). New York: Penguin.

Freud, S. (1910/1964). *Leonardo da Vinci and a memory of his childhood.* J. Strachey (ed.), A. Tyson (trans.). New York: W. W. Norton.

Freud, S. (1920/1968). The psychogenesis of a case of homosexuality in a woman. In A. Strachey (ed. and trans.), *The standard edition of the complete psychological works of Sigmund Freud* (vol. 18, pp. 145–172). London: Hogarth Press.

Friedman, R. C. (1988). *Male homosexuality: A contemporary psychoanalytic perspective.* New Haven: Yale University Press.

Gale, L., & Syrja-McNally, H. (2014). Expanding the circle: Serving children, youth, and families by integrating gender diversity and affirming gender-independent children. In E. J. Meyer & A. Pullen Sansfaçon (eds.), *Supporting transgender & gender creative youth: Schools, Families, and Communities in Action* (pp. 190–206). New York: Peter Lang.

Gill-Peterson, J. (2014). Core gender identity: The transgender child and the inversion of Freud. Retrieved from https://juliangillpeterson.wordpress.com/2014/03/07/core-gender-identity-the-transgender-child-and-the-inversion-of-freud/.

Gottlieb, A. R. (2000). *Out of the twilight: Fathers of gay men speak.* New York: Routledge.

Green, R. (1987). *The "sissy boy syndrome" and the development of homosexuality.* New Haven: Yale University Press.

Green, R., & Schiavi, R. C. (1995). Sexual and gender identity disorders. In G. O. Gabbard (ed.), *Treatments of psychiatric disorders* (2nd ed.), (pp. 1837–2079). Washington, D.C.: American Psychiatric Press.

Grossman, A. H., & D'Augelli, A. R. (2006). Transgender youth: Invisible and vulnerable. *Journal of Homosexuality, 51* (1), 111–128.

Hidalgo, M. A., Ehrensaft, D., Tishelman, A. C., Clark, L. F., Garofalo, R., Rosenthal, S. M., Spack, N. P., & Olson, J. (2013). The gender affirmative model: What we know and what we aim to learn. *Human Development, 56,* 285–290.

Hill, D. B., Menvielle, E., Sica, K. M., & Johnson, A. (2010). An affirmative intervention for families with gender variant children: Parental ratings of child mental health and gender. *Journal of Sex & Marital Therapy, 36* (1), 6–23. doi:10.1080/00926230903375560.

Hsieh, S., & Leininger, J. (2014). Resource list: Clinical care programs for gender-nonconforming children and adolescents. *Pediatric Annals, 43* (6), 238–244.

Hughes, S. A. (2011, June 10). Family of Kirk Murphy says "sissy boy" experiment led to his suicide. *Washington Post.* Retrieved December 16, 2017, from https://www.washingtonpost.com/blogs/blogpost/post/family-of-kirk-murphy-says-sissyboy-experiment-led-to-his-suicide/2011/06/10/AGYfgvOH_blog.html.

Institute of Medicine. (2011). *The health of lesbian, gay, bisexual, and transgender people: Building a foundation for better understanding.* Washington, D.C.: National Academies Press.

Janssen, A., Huang, H., & Duncan, C. (2016). Gender variance among youth with autism spectrum disorders: A retrospective chart review. *Transgender Health, 1* (1), 63–68. https://doi.org/10.1089/trgh.2015.0007.

Kohli, S. (2012, November 15). Gender behavior therapy and gay conversion: UCLA's past, California's future. *Daily Bruin.* Retrieved December 2, 2017, from http://dailybruin.com/features/conversion-therapy/.

Kuhl, D., & Martino, W. (2018) "Sissy" boys and the pathologization of gender non-conformity. In S. Talburt (ed.), *Youth sexualities: Public feelings and contemporary cultural politics.* Santa Barbara: Praeger.

Kuvalanka, K. A., Mahan, D. J., McGuire, J. K., & Hoffman, T. K. (2017): Perspectives of mothers of transgender and gender-nonconforming children with autism spectrum disorder. *Journal of Homosexuality, 64,* 1–23. doi:10.1080/00918369.2017.1406221.

Lev, A. (2004). *Transgender emergence: Therapeutic guidelines for working with gender-variant people and their families.* Binghamton, N.Y.: Haworth Press.

Lev, A. I. (2005). *Psychotherapy.* GLBTQ Encyclopedia. Retrieved December 24, 2017, from http://www.glbtqarchive.com/ssh/psychotherapy_S.pdf.

Lev, A. I. (2013). Gender dysphoria: Two steps forward, one step back. *Clinical Social Work Journal, 41* (3), 288–296. doi.org/10.1007/s10615-013-0447-0.

Lev, A. I., & Wolf-Gould, C. (2018). Collaborative treatment across disciplines: Physician and mental health counselor coordinating competent care. In C. Keo-Meier & D. Ehrensaft (eds.), *The gender affirmative model: An interdisciplinary approach to supporting transgender and gender expansive children*. Washington, D.C.: American Psychological Association.

Lewes, K. (1989). *The psychoanalytic theory of male homosexuality*. New York: New American Library.

Malpas, J. (2011). Between pink and blue: A multi-dimensional family approach to gender non-conforming children and their families. *Family Process, 50*, 453–470.

Malyon, A. (1982). Psychotherapeutic implications of internalized homophobia. In J. C. Gonsiorek (ed.), *Homosexuality and psychotherapy: A handbook of affirmative models* (pp. 59–69). New York: Haworth Press.

Menvielle, E. (2012). A comprehensive program for children with gender-variant behaviors and gender identity disorders. *Journal of Homosexuality, 59* (3), 357–368.

Menvielle, E., & Hill, D. (2011). An affirmative intervention for families with gender-variant children: A process evaluation. *Journal of Gay and Lesbian Mental Health, 15*, 94–123. doi :10.1080/19359705.2011.530576.

Meyer, I. H. (2003). Prejudice as stress: Conceptual and measurement problems. *American Journal of Public Health, 93* (2), 262–265.

Meyer-Bahlburg, H. (1985). Gender identity disorder of childhood: Introduction. *Journal of the American Academy of Child Psychiatry, 24*, 681–683.

Newhook, J. T., Pyne, J., Winters, K., Feder, S., Holmes, C., Tosh, J., Sinnott, M.-L., Jamieson, A., & Pickett, S. (2018). A critical commentary on follow-up studies and "desistance" theories about transgender and gender-nonconforming children. *International Journal of Transgenderism, 19* (2), 212–224.

Olson, K. R., Durwood, L., DeMeules, M., & McLaughlin, K. A. (2016). Mental health of transgender children who are supported in their identities. *Pediatrics 137* (3). Retrieved from http:// pediatrics.aappublications:org/content/early/2016/02/24/peds.2015-3223.

Pyne, J. (2014). Gender independent kids: A paradigm shift in approaches to gender non-conforming children. *Canadian Journal of Human Sexuality, 23* (1), 1–8. doi:10.3138/cjhs .23.1.CO1.

Rekers, G. A. (ed.) (1995). *Handbook of child and adolescent sexual problems*. New York: Lexington Books.

Rekers, G. A., & Lovaas, O. I. (1974). Behavioral treatment of deviant sex-role behaviors in a male child. *Journal of Applied Behavior Analysis, 7* (2), 173–190.

Riley, E. A., Sitharthan, G., Clemson, L., & Diamond, M. (2011). The needs of gender-variant children and their parents: A parent survey. *International Journal of Sexual Health, 23*, 181–195. doi:10.1080/19317611.2011.593932.

Roscoe, W. (1998). *Changing ones: Third and fourth genders in native North America*. New York: St. Martin's Press.

Rottnek, M. (ed.). (1999). *Sissies & tomboys: Gender nonconformity and homosexual childhood*. New York: New York University Press.

Roughgarden, J. (2004). *Evolution's rainbow: Diversity, gender, and sexuality in nature and people.* Berkeley: University of California Press.

Ryan, C., Russell, S. T., Huebner, D., Diaz, R., & Sanchez, J. (2010). Family acceptance in adolescence and the health of LGBT young adults. *Journal of Child and Adolescent Psychiatric Nursing, 23* (4), 205–213. doi:10.1111/j.1744-6171.2010.00246.x.

Stoller, R. J. (1968). Male childhood transsexualism. *Journal of the American Academy of Child Psychiatry, 7,* 193–209.

Summary of the external review of the CAMH Gender Identity Clinic of the Child, Youth & Family Services. (2016, January). CAMH. Retrieved December 25, 2017, from http://2017.camh.ca/en /hos pital/about_camh/newsroom/news_releases_media_advisories_and_backgrounders/ current_year/Documents/ExecutiveSummary-GIC_ExternalReview.pdf.

Tishelman, A. C., Kaufman, R., Edwards-Leeper, L., Mandel, F. H., Shumer, D. E., & Spack, N. P. (2015). Serving transgender youth: Challenges, dilemmas, and clinical examples. *Professional Psychology: Research and Practice, 46* (1), 37–45.

Travers, R., Bauer, G., Pyne, J., Bradley, K., Gale, L., & Papadimitriou, M. (2012, October 2). Impacts of strong parental support for trans youth: A report prepared for Children's Aid Society of Toronto and Delisle Youth Services. Retrieved from http://transpulse project.ca/wp-content/uploads/2012/10/Impacts-of-Strong-Parental-Support-for-Trans -Youth-vFINAL.pdf.

Ubelacker, S. (2016, January 23). CAMH gender identity clinic closure sparks protest. *Huffington Post.* Retrieved December 16, 2017, from www.huffingtonpost.ca/2016/01/23/group-protests-closure-of-youth-genderidentity-clinic-at-camh-director-s-removal_n_ 9061480.html.

Vanderburgh, R. (2009). Appropriate therapeutic care for families with pre-pubescent transgender/gender-dissonant children. *Child and Adolescent Social Work, 26* (2), 135–154.

Wallace, R., & Russell, H. (2013). Attachment and shame in gender non-conforming children and their families: Toward a theoretical framework for evaluating clinical interventions. *International Journal of Transgenderism, 14,* 113–126. doi:10.1080/15532739.2013.824845.

Wallien, M. S. C., & Cohen-Kettenis, P. T. (2008). Psychosexual outcome of gender-dysphoric children. *Journal of the American Academy Child & Adolescent Psychiatry, 47,* 1413–1423.

Weinberg, G. (1973). *Society and the healthy homosexual.* Garden City, N.Y.: Anchor Books.

Williams, C. (2017, January 20). Disco sexology, part two, the history. TransAdvocate. Retrieved December 2, 2017, from http://transadvocate.com/part-ii-the-history-the-rise-and-fall-of-discosexology-dr-zucker-camh-conversion-therapy_n_19630.htm.

Wylie, P. (1942). *Generation of vipers.* New York: Rinehart.

Zucker, K. J. (2008a). Children with gender identity disorder: Is there a best practice? *Neuropsychiatrie de l'Enfance et de l'Adolescence, 56,* 358–364.

Zucker, K. J. (2008b). On the "natural history" of gender identity disorder in children. *Journal of the American Academy of Child and Adolescent Psychiatry, 47,* 1361–1363.

Zucker, K., & Bradley, S. (1995). *Gender identity disorder and psychosexual problems in children and adolescents.* New York: Guilford Press.

Zucker, K. J., & Cohen-Kettenis, P. T. (2008). Gender identity disorders in children and adolescents. In D. L. Rowland & L. Incrocci (eds.), *Handbook of sexual and gender identity disorders* (pp. 376–422). Hoboken, N.J.: John Wiley & Sons.

Zuger, B. (1984). Early effeminate behaviors in boys: Outcome and significance for homosexuality. *Journal of Nervous and Mental Disease, 172* (2), 90–97.

10

Micah and His Protectors

Lisette Lahana, LCSW

Seven months before the start of college, Micah and his mother, Corinne, drove two hours to begin working with me. Early on, he made it clear he wanted me to use the name Micah—along with male pronouns—instead of his assigned name, Mia. Assigned female at birth, he was 17, tall, lanky, sweet-faced, with short, curly hair, soft facial features, a bright smile, and a high-pitched voice. He identified as multiracial—"half white and half black"—and as trans. Although intelligent, he was not particularly talkative. The clinical work was a challenge because of competing goals. Micah began socially transitioning two years earlier and just wanted to start hormones as well as get both of his parents, especially his stepdad, Nick, on board. Corinne, deeply connected to her child, was supportive, but was at the early stages of understanding what it meant to be transgender. Until that point, Nick had showed no real interest in furthering his knowledge about the transgender experience, so neither Corinne nor Micah knew what to expect from him. Beyond this insular unit was Micah's biological dad, Greg, who had been mostly exempt from his parenting role, and his older sister, Jessica, who lived far away. Acceptance from both of them was still important to Micah. Given the distance from their home to my office, our work was a combination of in-person visits and video sessions.

Micah's biological parents, Corinne and Greg, had been together a total of eight years. Corinne was of mixed European heritage and Greg was African American. Micah was born seven years after his sister, Jessica. Once Corinne and Greg divorced, Greg had some early visitation, but contact became very sporadic once Corinne married Nick, who was Asian American. Micah was two years old at the time. Greg, Nick, and Corinne had all served in the military, so Micah and Jessica had grown up moving from city to city, which limited Micah's opportunity to develop long-term friendships. Corinne and Nick had relocated to Northern California four years earlier in order to be closer to Corinne's beloved elderly parents. She had grown up in a Catholic home; however, as an adult, she had raised her children outside the church. Nick had little family to speak of but was embraced by Corinne's parents. Corrine began to teach kindergarten after

Lev, Arlene I., Gottlieb, Andrew R., *Families in Transition*
dx.doi.org/10.17312/harringtonparkpress/2019.04.fit.010
© 2019 by Harrington Park Press

she left the military and Nick, recently retired, was in graduate school. Sunday afternoons usually involved a family drive to Corinne's parents, who had always considered Micah their "little doll."

Micah showed no significant signs of gender dysphoria until age 12, when he more actively avoided using public bathrooms, a pattern that had begun in fifth grade. His dysphoria was exacerbated during puberty: he camouflaged his growing breasts by layering his clothing, experienced shame and anxiety during menstruation, and envied other boys' bodies. Though he dated one guy during his freshman year of high school, Micah viewed sex and romance as issues to avoid. A turning point came in his sophomore year, when he met someone who was transgender. Searching online for answers, Micah found the missing piece: he himself was trans. He recalled a pivotal moment when he looked at himself in the mirror dressed in masculine clothing and thought, "This feels right," relieved about having located the source of his problem: "I knew then that I wanted to transition and live as a man."

Over the next two years, Micah moved forward, transitioning on his own. He adopted a short haircut, began binding his chest, and socially changed his name to Micah, all of which helped him feel more comfortable. He talked to his friends and teachers about wanting them to use his new name, but he did not talk to his parents about his formal attempts to make a social gender transition. At home, Micah still used the name Mia. The school, having no experience with transgender students, did not recognize what was taking place—a teen in transition. Tensions arose between Micah and his physical education teacher, who didn't permit him to use a single-stall bathroom to change his clothes. After that, he started to stay home from school for long periods because of severe anxiety. But neither parent understood what the problem was. I believe they were in denial about what was going on with Micah but, like many parents, had no exposure to gender diversity. They saw their daughter as simply dressing in a more masculine way—nothing more. After one last failed attempt to get Micah to return to school, Corrine enrolled him in a virtual high school. He soon lost the few friends he had, which resulted in increased isolation and depression. Six months before seeing me, he had finally disclosed his male gender identity to his mother. The one local therapist who Corinne found knew nothing about transitioning, and Micah didn't feel it was the right fit.

I met with Micah over the course of a month to do a gender assessment, which included gathering information about his mental health, his gender history, and his relationship with his body over time. I also met with his mom to (1) help her understand the purpose of the assessment; (2) gather developmental history, including information about gender identity and expression; and (3) discuss the role of family collaboration, which would probably include meeting with her husband and the family unit. Micah, Corinne, and I discussed their goals for an upcoming family meeting with Nick. My goals would be to discuss the results of my assessment, to learn about the parents' feelings about Micah's gender, and to help Micah express his feelings to his parents about his experience. Corinne encouraged Nick to be a part of our discussions. Though he agreed to attend, which was a relief to Corinne, Micah, and me, we didn't know what his reaction would be.

During our first family session, it was clear that Nick and Corrine still misgendered Micah as a girl, which was evidenced by their calling him Mia. Earlier, when I asked the reasons for that, given all the work Micah had put into a social transition, Micah simply said, "I hate confrontation." Earlier I had offered him the option of having his parents meet with me alone to offer them some psychoeducation. Sometimes this is helpful because parents can be offensive, hurtful, or unwittingly transphobic. These negative behaviors can become lodged in a teen's mind and endure—painfully—into adulthood. Micah, however, wanted to be present for all our meetings. I prepared him for comments from his parents that might be uncomfortable for him, given their lack of information and exposure.

During that first family session, Corinne explained that, even though she had been learning more about being transgender, she still had many questions. As a teenager, she had not liked being a girl with curves and breasts. She wondered if it was possible that Micah would "grow out of this"—as she had. We talked about the differences in their experiences. I clarified that Micah's identity as a boy, including a desire to have male sex characteristics, was different from her own discomfort with bodily changes and the social expectations of becoming a woman. We discussed the results of the assessment, the meaning of gender dysphoria, and the likelihood that his anxiety and distress would improve significantly with gender-related changes that would affirm Micah's male identity. It probably helped that the parents observed me, a cisgender woman, being an ally to Micah. In general, I often use my position of gender privilege to make supportive statements about gender diversity as a positive part of human diversity, rather than emphasizing diagnosis, which could be perceived as a mental illness to be treated.

Early on, Corrine and Nick expressed anxiety and fear that transition would be a mistake. They pointed out that, from an early age, Micah had a strong desire to be pregnant and to parent, which continued into early adolescence, and they wondered if his intention to transition was somehow contradictory.

First, I clarified that wanting to be a parent was a human desire and didn't mean Micah was ambivalent about transition or "not really transgender." Feelings about gender and the body are often complex and difficult to put into words. This was the case for Micah: he shared the fact that he still thought about having children, but now he wasn't so sure about being pregnant. I explained that while it was important to consult with an ob/gyn who specializes in trans health, current research suggests Micah could *still* bear a child through pregnancy even after having been on testosterone, or he could use reproductive technologies to harvest his eggs. This was new information for both parents and they needed to think about it further.

Initially, working with Nick was challenging. He said outright that transition was like a "runaway train" that was going to "crash and burn." He spent months refusing to read the educational material that Corinne offered. I worried Nick would prohibit Micah from returning to therapy. As we explored further, however, Nick opened up and expressed fears that Micah would be a victim of harassment, bullying, or, worse yet, violence. As a man of color himself, he understood that Micah was transitioning into a world that was not kind to black men, let alone black trans men. *Not* transitioning, in his mind, meant his child remained "protected." I was convinced after meeting Micah, hearing his history, and learning about his increased comfort living as a male that transitioning was an imperative. Early on, however, I suggested the family consider a social transition, which was a compromise to help his parents become more used to the idea of gender change. Sometimes moving more slowly can help ease the family into transition, building a foundation of support for the teen and giving the family time to move through early stages of grief. I recommended a more formalized social transition, including a name change and working with a speech therapist to help Micah alter his voice.

At almost 18, however, Micah was resolute about the need to masculinize through hormones before college began in five months. Though Micah wanted his parents to support his physical transition, he and his parents understood that at age 18, far from home, he could procure hormones on his own. I shared with Nick and Corinne the benefits of beginning the process before he left for college. He would have his mom's support during doctor's visits as well as more time to help his parents and extended family get used to gender changes. It can be difficult for families to have their adolescents immediately transition in the first year of college. They return home looking and sounding different, which can be disorienting to their families.

In a later session, Micah came out as a gay male to his parents and was emphatic that this was not going to change. It seemed Nick had been holding on to the idea that his child was heterosexual—that is, until we began to talk about the implications of transition. Confused, Nick responded, "This is too much! First you tell me he is transgender and now you are telling me he's gay, too? Are you serious?" We talked about the difference between gender and sexuality. And while those can be fluid, for Micah both had been consolidated. Looking back, Micah interpreted that, when he was a child, playing with dolls and applying nail polish were expressions of his "inner gay male." Nick's fears about Micah's possible victimization resurfaced. I emphasized that those were normal fears for any parent to have as their child transitions. We explored what it would mean to focus on acceptance as opposed to fighting Micah's reality, and helping him prepare for and respond to whatever forms of injustice he might encounter. Again, I believe it helped for me to act as an ally here, to be perceived as heterosexual, that is, more like them, owing to my appearance, and to say, "I accept and support your child as a gay trans male." At home, Corinne helped Nick deal with his fears and discussed feelings that had come up in our sessions.

Some of our clinical work involved discussing Micah's coming out to his extended family. What about Corrine's religious parents, Micah's grandparents? We discussed many possible reactions from different family members. If Mom were to disclose, what might she say, and what could possible reactions be? Corinne felt torn between the love for her child and the love for her parents. I emphasized that any initial negative reactions can change positively over time.

A few months before Micah left for college, Corinne told her parents and extended family and found them more open than she'd expected, her parents being the most accepting. Though they had seen Micah's hairstyle change during those Sunday visits, it had not occurred to them that there was a gender change in progress. With that information, Corinne's own father researched whether the college had Micah picked had protective policies in place for transgender students. Grandpa's biggest question was: Why had Micah avoided telling them for so long?

Though there had been occasional contact over the years between Micah and Greg, there was still some anxiety about telling him about the transition. I encouraged Micah to talk to his father and sister early on. I suggested a video session to help answer their questions or facilitate dialogue. Micah continued to say "No" and wanted to begin his transition without their involvement. Micah expected Greg would have a hard time with a gender transition. Micah knew that Greg had once cut off communication with a stepson when he came out as gay. As fearful as Micah was about disclosing to his biological father, he was even more concerned about possible rejection from his sister, Jessica. We explored ways to talk to them when he felt ready. It wasn't clear whether his sister and dad would support him, but the secret appeared to be a burden. When he learned that Greg had viewed his current male Facebook profile, Micah did not want to talk to him about it. Our work together ended after three months; Micah chose to not disclose to his father.

I could see how Micah's fear of confrontation and related anxiety might affect him in the future. Being a first-year student at an out-of-state college while going through a physical transition would be challenging. Though these could have been central issues to address, Micah chose to end therapy. Now that Nick and Corinne were calling him Micah and using male pronouns, he was happier. I recommended he involve himself in a peer transgender group to break down his isolation and talk about the coming-out process. However, they lived over an hour away from any support groups. Micah didn't want the challenge of cultivating new connections and preferred a "fresh start" at college. Now on hormones, he felt he was doing well enough and said he would get help on campus if needed.

I met with his parents in late May to get an update and learn how they were doing with the beginning of Micah's physical transition. Micah had given his mom permission to disclose to his dad, whose reaction was "indifference." This reaction was actually better than the one he and Corinne had expected. Jessica was coming to terms with the transition but from a distance. The family was waiting to see how the December holidays would be when she visited.

Nick and Corinne were still mourning the loss of their daughter, trying hard to acknowledge the reality of having a trans son. Both parents reflected on how helpful a workshop for parents of trans youth had been and felt a desire to help other parents. Corinne was still somewhat conflicted, however, wondering whether her child was "really transgender" and whether his dysphoria was the result of social pressures on girls. I tried to reassure her that her questions were a normal part of the ways in which the parents "transition," and that those would probably come up less in the future as she saw him progress over time.

Despite her doubts, both Corrine and Nick were beginning to let go of their hopes and dreams about who they wanted their child to be and replacing those with a greater acceptance of who their child actually is, concerned yet hopeful as they watch their son move out into the world. For his part, Micah was excited about starting a new life and making friends, ones who would come to know him as he comes to know himself.

PART 4

Identity Transformation: How do Children's Gender Identity/Non-conforming Behaviors Shift Parents' Perceptions of Their Child and of Themselves as Parents?

In "Transforming the Identity of Parents of Transgender and Gender Nonconforming Children," Margaret Nichols and Stephanie Sasso argue that while the need for parental support is key for gender expansive children and teenagers, that road may be blocked at multiple intersections, notably by the parents' ignorance and fear when they are called on by their child to make important decisions before they are psychologically prepared to do so. The stigma once felt only by their child alone has now become a shared reality. The authors offer a conceptualization of the stages parents may go through to get to the other side: (1) Disclosure and Disbelief are marked by confusion, guilt, and fear; (2) Deconstructing and Distancing are characterized by an internal split between the pull to grieve for the child they thought they had and their (imagined) future, and the need to mobilize to advocate for their child's needs, simultaneously developing greater knowledge and empathy; (3) Reconstruction/Reconciliation occurs when the coexistence of positive and negative feelings about the reality of their child's identity may be most evident, as parents seek to reconceptualize the ways they've previously thought about gender, which ideally results in granting the child greater autonomy; and (4) Recovery, which is a time of a reintegration of the child into the family and the acquisition of enhanced coping capacities on the part of the parents, who are now able to perceive themselves in new ways. A range of case examples as well as a section on identifying those factors that help or hinder parents to develop a fuller understanding of themselves conclude this important piece.

Elena Moser offers a moving account of her own transition, not only one focused on coming to terms with her trans son, Robbie, age 20, when he came out, but one centered on her reawakened fears and anxieties. Despite the fact that Moser has been out as a lesbian since the mid-1970s, has had an extensive history of professional experience with LGBT people, has lived all her life in cosmopolitan, liberal cities, and seen much evidence of gender dysphoria in Robbie's childhood, his disclosure sent her into a crisis, feeling as though she had "fallen into an abyss." Surprised by some of the beliefs she held but was not fully cognizant of, Moser offers a painfully honest self-examination of the process parents can go through in order to forge a deeper, richer connection with their child and a fuller, more complex understanding of themselves.

11

Transforming the Identity of Parents of Transgender and Gender Nonconforming Children

Margaret Nichols, PhD, Stephanie Sasso, PsyD

Introduction

Researchers and clinicians who work with same-sex-oriented people have long observed that gay people, who usually have heterosexual parents, do not enjoy the same kind of family support and protection offered to members of some other stigmatized minorities. For example, children who are African American or Muslim usually grow up in families and communities where they are culturally like their parents, siblings, relatives, even neighbors. Although they may be ostracized or mistreated by "outsiders" and the larger society, they can count on belonging to a network of others who will try to protect, validate, and educate them about how to survive in a hostile environment. The importance of this cannot be overstated. Research has shown that lesbian and gay children who enjoy family support do better, suffer less from the rejection of peers, are less suicidal and depressed, and practice safer sex more frequently than those whose parents reject them (Grossman & D'Augelli, 2007; Haas & Drescher, 2014; Lasser, Tharinger, & Cloth, 2006).

In many ways, parenting a child who is transgender or gender nonconforming is similar to having a gay child (LaSala, 2010). In both cases, the child is different, not only from most peers, but from the sexual orientation and/or gender identity of most of their family members. The child needs protection from the very people who have the potential to do the most harm—the child's identity representing something the parent fears, dislikes, or believes sinful. If parental support is critical for gay and lesbian youth, it's even more so for gender diverse and transgender youth. On the one hand, most gay children don't come out—to themselves or others—until adolescence, and until that happens, their sexual orientation can be masked. Gender identity, on the other hand, is often obvious as young as toddlerhood, which forces parents to deal with gender nonconformity early on. Gender diverse children get bullied and harassed more than oth-

Lev, Arlene I., Gottlieb, Andrew R., *Families in Transition*
dx.doi.org/10.17312/harringtonparkpress/2019.04.fit.011
© 2019 by Harrington Park Press

ers (Roberts, Rosario, Corliss, Koenen, & Austin, 2012), so they are even more in need of parental advocacy with, for example, the school system than are gay youth. Additionally, the treatment needs of a transgender teenager may include medical care, which must be authorized, procured, and paid for by their parents. Given this, it is not surprising that Erich, Tittsworth, Dykes, and Cabuses (2008) find that adult transgender people who enjoyed support from their parents report greater life satisfaction, or that Krieger (2011) describes the greater well-being of teens who have parental acceptance and validation. Ryan, Russell, Hueber, Diaz, and Sanchez (2010) show that family support versus rejection predicts the mental and physical health of adult LGBT people. Unfortunately, many gender diverse children and transgender teens do not get the love they need and may, in fact, be abused and/or thrown out of their homes. Other researchers (Grossman, D'Augelli, Howell, & Hubbard, 2005) report that 59% of transgender youth faced negative initial reactions from parents, and that the more gender nonconforming a child is, the more likely they are to suffer parental verbal or physical violence. Just as the goal of family therapy with a gay or lesbian teen is to facilitate parental acknowledgment, understanding, and acceptance, so too is this the goal of a gender-affirmative therapist.

But not all therapists working with these families have this goal. Although the World Professional Association for Transgender Health (WPATH) Standards of Care (Coleman et al., 2012) considers therapy aimed at coercing children into traditional gender roles unethical, in the United States and Canada this therapeutic approach is still sometimes espoused (Zucker, Wood, Singh, & Bradley, 2012). The goal of reparative approaches is for parents to discourage or attempt to extinguish gender nonconforming behaviors, in effect a form of conversion therapy. In contrast, gender-affirming therapists (1) view gender diverse children as psychologically normal, although statistically unusual; (2) believe that gender identity, for some, evolves in spite of, not because of, parental socialization; (3) consider encouraging gender conformity tantamount to encouraging inauthenticity; and (4) emphasize the significance of parental support in the development of children's self-esteem as critical for healthy development. Therefore, gender-affirmative therapists help parents learn to nurture, encourage, and protect their gender variant children (Ehrensaft, 2011a, 2011b; Lev & Alie, 2012; Malpas, 2011; Menvielle & Hill, 2011; Vanderburgh, 2009).

To do this, it is helpful to have an appreciation of how difficult this task may be. Andrew Solomon's (2012) *Far from the Tree* is an examination of families in which the children are dramatically different from their parents, either by way of a disability, such as deafness, dwarfism, Down syndrome, or chronic mental illness, or through a perceived societal strength, such as being a prodigy. Solomon explains that we all have multiple identities—ethnic, racial, gender, religious, sexual orientation, physical abilities—and that most of the socially significant ones are what he terms *vertical identities,* or those passed down from one generation to the next. What he terms *horizontal identities* are based on traits held by a child but not by the parents, which necessitate that the child seek out and derive support from peers or from another community, not primarily from their family of origin. This is true whether the horizontal identity is prized or marginalized, but it is particularly difficult for the latter group. Horizontal identities that are stigmatized present difficulties that can precipitate family crises, which is often the case for LGBTQ children. The parents of a child with a stigmatized horizontal identity face very real, concrete challenges as well as psychological ones. Most eventually face the fact that they, too, by virtue of who their children are, are likely to be stigmatized, perhaps suffering rejection from their own families, peers, and communities, a phenomenon known as a *courtesy stigma* (Goffman, 1986). LaSala's (2010) sample of parents of gay and lesbian children report that this was the most difficult aspect of coming to terms with their child's identity. Their children demand skills and emotional resources from them that they have probably not acquired. The parents must confront personal beliefs that devalue or pathologize their child, such as religious convictions or biases against effeminate boys. Similarly, Reed (2005) describes a ripple effect of stigma that affects an entire family when a child comes out as transgender. Major shifts in the parents' attitudes must develop before they can advocate effectively for their children and which then prepare them for newfound ways to view themselves.

Solomon (2012) explores the process and dynamics of those parents who were able to accept their children's difference. Looking at research with parents of disabled children, he notes they overwhelmingly report that their child brought them closer to their spouse, other family members, and friends, taught them what was important, and increased their empathy and compassion. He reports that the process of acceptance transformed and strengthened their identities as parents. Similarly, Ehrensaft (2007, 2011a, 2011b), Gottlieb (2000), and Kuvalanka, Weiner, and Mahan (2014) all concur that parents who accept their children were themselves transformed in the process: "Children with horizontal identities alter your self painfully; they also illuminate it" (Solomon, 2012, p. 46).

Therapists working with transgender and gender diverse youth often interpret a parent's difficulties as trans/homophobia, especially if they see themselves as aligned with the child as opposed to aligned with the entire family. Teenagers, often impatient to make changes, interpret the parent's reticence as resistance. Sometimes, of course, the parents are battling their own biases and prejudices. But often they are reacting to what they perceive as a frightening situation. Parents may feel blindsided when their adolescent comes out, even if their gender identity has been evident from early on. Though the child may experience some relief, for the parent it may be like having a bomb suddenly detonate. Parents of very young children frequently have a different experience, gradually recognizing that a child who is different has "shown up" in their household (Ehrensaft, 2007) and, for an extended period, may deny who their child is or hope it's "just a phase." In either case, even parents who might be prepared for and able to cope with a gay or lesbian child are usually surprised, even shocked, by a transgender one. The parents of adolescent trans men interviewed by Hegedus (2009) report that their four most common thoughts immediately after disclosure include: "I want to be supportive"; "I don't know my kid as well as I thought"; "I never heard of transgender"; and "I was ok with my kid being lesbian" (p. 45). And the parents of transgender children highlighted information as their greatest need (Riley, Sitharthan, Clemson, & Diamond, 2011). What is striking here is the desire to be supportive and accepting combined with a level of ignorance. Gays and lesbians are so much a part of popular culture that most people have some familiarity with them. But no transgender person, not even Caitlyn Jenner or Laverne Cox, is yet the equivalent of an Ellen DeGeneres or an Anderson Cooper. Moreover, there are no culturally familiar guidelines for coping with children who eschew their assigned gender or are gender unconventional.

Even the parent who becomes educated will not necessarily have their fears allayed. As Solomon (2012) says, "Parents are right to fear for their transgender children. The level of prejudice against them is unimaginable" (p. 650). Turning to mental health professionals, the parent may become more confused when some suggest that gender variance is an illness while others view it as a normal variation. Other therapists may tell them they can prevent later hormone treatments and surgery by discouraging cross-gender behavior. Still others feel the child needs support and a place to express their nonconformity to avoid serious mental health consequences.

Parents of transgender and gender diverse children may experience a conflict between their need to protect their child and their need to accept them, particularly if the child is a gender nonconforming natal male, since boys are held to higher gender standards (Malpas, 2011). The parents of prepubertal children may be faced with a choice between socially transitioning their child—

allowing them to live full-time in their affirmed gender, which carries with it the possibility that they may change their mind later—and attempting the sometimes difficult task of supporting a child whose gender identity may be fluid or whose behavior is extremely divergent from gender expectations. Parents of children who are at or beyond puberty face decisions about medical procedures, such as the use of cross-sex hormones, which may be irreversible. Often parents are called on to make these decisions before they have psychologically adapted to the new reality, as they face pressure exerted by their child.

As stated, parents are thrust into a horizontal identity of their own; that is, they become stigmatized on the basis of the mere fact of being parents of a transgender or gender diverse child. For some, this may be their first experience of stigma. Moreover, if the child is obviously transgender, they are forced to be public about their status. It may be possible to hide having a gay child, but gender changes are obvious. Thus, parents of gender diverse kids or those who have transitioned may be harshly judged by their own families, friends, and community, or fear they will be. Just as LaSala's (2010) research finds that stigma was the hardest obstacle for parents, Malpas (2011) and Menvielle and Hill (2011) report social exclusion and isolation as primary difficulties for parents.

Given these challenges, it is in some ways remarkable that so many parents *are* able to accept their gender diverse children. Even if 59% of parents are initially rejecting (Grossman et al., 2005), a significant percentage are positive from the beginning. Many others change their attitudes and behaviors over time. In this paper, we describe the journeys of parents who *do* come to accept their children and outline factors that, in our experience, help or hinder the process. We discuss how parents' own identities are transformed, which makes them better able to accept their children. LaSala (2010) talks about the "gift of the gay child," referring to how some families became closer after dealing with a teenager who comes out. The parents (and families) we describe benefited from having a child who is different in ways they would never have anticipated.

We focus primarily on those who were able to evolve into proud parents of a transgender or gender diverse child. When we refer to transgender and gender diverse children, we are referring to those who transition male to female, female to male, and a wide variety of other gender presentations, including a range of nonbinary identities. Clearly, these parents are not representative of all parents. Those we encountered—more mothers than fathers—are self-selected, as our agency website is quite clear about our affirmative stance. Most of the families we see are white, middle-class, and college-educated. We are describing a process of identity transformation that takes place in those who already have liberal attitudes, who generally lead advantaged lives with access to resources, and who have a belief in the value of science, medicine, and mental health treatment. Those we describe are not necessarily typical. But, with any luck, they are a harbinger of the future.

Parental Identity Transition

Being a parent is a major aspect of one's identity, heavily informed by one's child's identity. When a family includes a gender nonconforming or transgender child—an unexpected, unfamiliar, and, for most families, frightening reality—the parents' identities inevitably change. Those who ultimately come to accept their child's identity follow a typical trajectory as they deconstruct and reconstruct their own identities in order to integrate and accept their child's. At the heart of this trajectory is a process of grief: letting go of the image the parent had of their child, including the future they imagined, and accepting a new reality. For example, Hegedus (2009) delineates *Disclosure, Mourning, Adjustment,* and *Acceptance* as stages many families follow. Similarly, Lev and Alie (2012) label these *Discovery and Disclosure, Turmoil, Negotiation,* and *Finding Balance.* In both models, after the family receives the information, there is an evitable period of turmoil. Hegedus (2009) focuses on the mourning process during the second stage, whereas Lev and Alie (2012) describe critical parental concerns, such as safety—that is, "trying to manage their child's emerging needs with the expectations of the social world in which they reside" (p. 58). We conceptualize our phases as (1) *Disclosure and Disbelief;* (2) *Deconstruction and Distancing;* (3) *Reconstruction and Reconciliation;* and (4) *Recovery;* we discuss each of them below.

LaSala (2010), in his work on disclosure of gay identity in families, describes a *Sensitization Period* that may occur before actual *Disclosure.* During this time, a family may be grappling with a vague recognition of difference in the child that remains unspoken. The difference often involves gender nonconformity or, for children closer to or at puberty, a same-sex attraction, sometimes including a period when the child first identifies as gay, lesbian, or bisexual. Lev and Alie (2012) state, "Parents may begin to suspect that their child has a gay or lesbian sexual orientation, or wonder about transgender expression, especially as more information is available in the media" (p. 58).

Adriana, the mother of a child transitioning from female to male, described not relating to the grieving others were expressing. Her affirmed male son, Riley, had been so gender atypical from an early age that "she was always more like a son," which had, in fact, sensitized Adriana, who had become accustomed to her child being read as male by strangers and presenting as masculine over a number of years. Further, Riley had initially come out as a lesbian before identifying as transgender. Like many parents, Adriana processed some of the experience of a horizontal identity—stigma, minority stress—after this disclosure, which prepared her somewhat for what was to come. For the vast majority of parents, however, no matter what precedes it, transgender identity disclosure is experienced as negative, traumatic, and radical. Even those who appear overtly supportive may be experiencing a *reaction formation,* a defense in which strongly negative, pre/unconscious feelings may be masked by expressing strongly positive feelings.

Disclosure and Disbelief

Our clinical observation is that most parents of gender diverse youth seek alternative explanations for their child's disclosure before accepting that it reflects an authentic and stable identity for their child. We label this period *Disbelief* because transgender identity is still such an unknown in our gender-binary culture. Rather than actively denying reality, most parents, in our experience, are simply rejecting what is too far afield from their own gender schemas. Common explanations that parents consider to understand their child's gender include mental illness and childhood trauma (e.g., "Perhaps she was abused and being male makes her feel safe"), identity confusion (e.g., "There's no such thing as bigender, so she must just be confused"), family dynamics (e.g., "Dad always wanted a girl, now his son is trying to be one"), attention seeking (e.g., "Everyone in town is talking about her, maybe she likes that"), and peer and social media influences (e.g., "He's just copying kids he's met online"). Hegedus (2009) describes "dismissal" during the disclosure phase, depicting a mother who initially believed "this transgender thing was something that she had found on the computer and kind of latched onto" (p. 63). Coolhart, Baker, Farmer, Malaney, and Shipman (2013) state that some families hope therapy will attest that their child is not trans.

Self-blame is apparent in virtually all the parents we work with. Many of them—and many professionals less experienced with transgender youth—believe that being transgender must be the result of trauma, neglect, or inappropriate parenting. Some point to family dynamics, such as exercising extreme permissiveness of gender nonconforming behavior, conforming to the gender the parent fantasized about, and rejecting or identifying with an abusive or absent parent. Whether purported by clinicians or popular culture, these theories reinforce guilt. But parents who believe that being transgender is a matter of nature do not necessarily feel less guilty. They may chastise themselves for not picking up on cues earlier, feeling their child could have felt less alone and more supported if they had known sooner. In her interviews with mothers of transgender youth, Hegedus (2009) finds that self-blame lengthens the grieving process.

Parental guilt is often reinforced by the judgments of others. The belief that ineffective parenting causes transgender identity is so pervasive that many are blamed by those around them—strangers, family, neighbors, and friends. If parents find their own sense of peace in their parental identity, however, they can reject these judgments rather than internalize them. The mother of a trans-feminine child spoke of being in Toys "R" Us with her affirmed son in the girls' aisle when another parent passed her hissing, "Shame on you." Without missing a beat, she retorted, "No, shame on you!"

The *Disclosure* stage is one that involves information seeking. For many parents this begins with the most basic questions, ones that force them to deconstruct their own unarticulated assumptions about gender. It may never have occurred to them that one's identity could be incongruent with the one assigned at birth and that gender is more than just genitals. Understanding what for many are unfamiliar concepts, including *gender identity* (one's internal sense of gender), *gender role* (social expectations assigned to gender), and *gender presentation* (the signals about gender in one's appearance and body language), requires learning a new, less binary model. This process of education and reworking is more difficult the more rigid one's existing gender schemas.

In addition to confusion and self-blame, parents almost invariably experience some degree of fear: fear of the unknown, fear for their child's future. Kuvalanka, Weiner, and Mahan (2014) discuss these fears as stemming from a difficulty in picturing a successful transgender adult. Commonly, parents express concerns that their child will never have a good job or find a partner. Education is helpful, as is exposure to transgender adults. At the Institute for Personal Growth, we have invited transgender adults into our parent groups, something they experience as very reassuring. Additionally, and crucially, parents fear loss of connection. They fear losing their child if they can't accept or relate to him/her/them or losing relationships with extended family and community—or both.

For many privileged families, having a transgender child means facing significant loss of status and sense of entitlement, examples of *minority stress,* which is caused by a variety of social realities, including discrimination and bias, health and mental health disparities, violence and the threat of violence, and microaggressions (Sue, 2010). For other families, the disclosure of transgender identity means managing the intersectionality of more than one stigmatized identity and, thus, multiple sources of minority stress. Joanne, the mother of a child with special educational and health needs, bemoaned having to repeatedly come out to providers, neighbors, acquaintances, and church members, in addition to her entire extended family, as the parent of a transgender child, on top of explaining her child's other struggles. She had experienced some stigma because of those other challenges, but she had never experienced this level of judgment. Her ordinarily quiet, people-pleasing nature was jolted by the disapproval that, though by no means universal, was real. Ultimately Joanne became a more assertive person through negotiating these repeated encounters. Whatever other identities a family holds, the minority stress stemming from transgender identity is experienced not only by the trans person, but by the family as well. The more those stigmatized or misunderstood identities are present, the greater the potential stress on the family.

Deconstruction and Distancing

When parents ultimately accept that their child is transgender, the degree of family turmoil can reach a crescendo. Lev and Alie (2012) describe a *Negotiation* stage, "noted by the realization that the gender issue will not simply 'go away'" (p. 58). We see parents negotiating not only how the child will present, identify, and pursue medical or social transition, but also their own very strong feelings and whatever challenges to their identities and cognitive frameworks the reality of their child's gender presents. Their grief may become overwhelming. Yet the child, in addition to wanting support and acceptance, is often impatient for change. Reed (2005) discusses how adult transgender people often desire to move quickly, no longer feeling a need to suppress their authentic selves. This need to move forward may be even more intense for children and youth. Parents often have to make critical decisions during this period—for example, whether to socially transition a young child, medically delay puberty in preteens, or consent to cross-sex hormones for older teens. Coolhart and her colleagues (2013) stress that gender transformation heightens reactions, such as grief, shame, self-blame, and confusion. We have found it critical in working with families to validate both the needs of the youth, desperate to stop hiding and to lessen dysphoria, and the needs of parents for time to educate themselves and grieve their loss. If different therapists are working with parents and child, they must collaborate and cooperate.

Once they are no longer seeking alternative explanations for who their child is, parents often find themselves in the position of explaining their child to others and advocating for them in settings outside the family, while simultaneously experiencing their deepest grief. Some researchers talk about parents having to negotiate this internal split (Kuvalanka et al., 2014). The same parent who is mourning for her son in the therapy room may demand that the school refer to "him" by a female name. This advocacy role, while challenging, can assist the parent in gaining knowledge and developing more empathy for their child. Joanne, for example, found herself combing through resources on transgender identity in order to be able to explain her son's dysphoria and his need for transition. She experienced the coming-out process described above as invasive and anxiety-provoking. While a part of Joanne felt angry at her son for putting her and the family through this, another part was amazed by his strength: she now had some sense of what he faced every day.

Typically, with more empathy and knowledge comes a willingness to engage in the difficult process of not only using a child's preferred name and pronouns, but also altering their mental image of that child—and of themselves. Parents usually have a harder time with pronouns than anyone else since they have used the archaic ones more than anyone else. These mental shifts are especially hard for those who must use different pronouns in different settings. Myra talked about responding to questions about her "son," an affirmed female, at a very religious workplace, saying she felt like she was talking about a stranger. As Myra navigated this confusing, disorienting task, she understood better what her daughter had been facing during her transition when she had to continue to present as a male at religious functions.

As a child presents their affirmed gender outside the home, parents must themselves come out as parents of a gender diverse youth. This can lead to further empathy for the child's situation, as it did for Myra and Joanne, but it can also raise the level of fear if parents receive negative reactions. The process of coming out to others is strikingly similar for parents and children, except that the child often feels ready to begin coming out before the parent does, so parents are more often trying to "catch up." Myra's daughter came out to her extended family and friends through a post on Facebook, leaving Myra scrambling to answer phone calls and e-mails from confused relatives. Within his Multi-Dimensional Family Approach, Malpas (2011) discusses assisting parents to "control their fears and reactivity" so they "can differentiate their child's needs from their own" (p. 457). Because of generational differences, parents' perceptions of stigma among their own peers may be dramatically different from the child's. For millennials and younger youth, at least in some geographical areas, negative reactions to transgender identity may be virtually nonexistent.

It is important to validate that the realities of parents and youth may be dramatically different, and still appropriate and understandable given their respective contexts, experiences, and emotional states. One mother found her friends to be quite judgmental and critical of her permissiveness in "allowing" her child to transition, while her transmasculine child, who became head of the GSA, was popular and widely respected by peers. Owing to these different realities, as well as the fact that most young transgender people have been processing their identity longer than their parents have, the two may temporarily feel at odds.

Separation and individuation are normal processes during adolescence regardless of gender identity, but in some families this distancing may create either a temporary or permanent rupture, one that goes beyond what would be developmentally expected. This distancing usually results from the parents' and child's vastly different experiences during this phase. For example, a parent may not yet be able to use the chosen name or may misspeak pronouns. Particularly when this is intentional, it can significantly exacerbate the child's dysphoria, causing them to avoid interactions with the parent. At this point, the child is desperate for a path forward where they can live authentically and be accepted. Waiting feels excruciating. Meanwhile, changes in the child's gender presentation may trigger a profound sense of loss in the parents, who may feel their child has become someone they don't recognize. Many need space to process internal conflicts in order to accommodate the child's trans identity and their own deep sense of grief. Because of the gravity of these feelings, which for many parents are akin to losing the child to death, they often struggle to maintain their attachment to the child during this time and may physically or emotionally withdraw. Lev and Alie (2012) point out that "youth need to examine what their bottom lines are: what they can and cannot compromise about" (p. 58). Depending on what they conclude, some youth may feel a need to distance themselves emotionally from their parents or, if they are older teens, even leave home. We believe these ruptures often escalate beyond normal separation and individuation because transgender identity is so stigmatized.

Physical and emotional threats to trans persons are very real and, for most parents, elicit substantiated fears. The majority experience safety concerns, profound grief and confusion, as well as a genuine desire to nurture and accept. During the distancing stage, however, many parents' own grief and terror at the sense they are losing their child may overwhelm their capacity to provide support and validation. Most often, we see parents maintain a lower level of fear as they experience their child living authentically. The benefits to a child whose mental health has improved and who is thriving in their identity often trump a sense of loss and worries about safety over time. In addition, as the child's identity becomes more solidified and parents' feelings more stabilized, the aspects of their child that are constant become more apparent, and that sense of loss is diminished.

Initially, however, many parents of youth who are puberty age and older experience a choice between medical interventions, which are invasive, and living with a depressed child. Quite often, we hear them vocalize their many misgivings about hormones and then say, "But I'd rather have a living child than a dead one." Concerns often stem from medical realities, such as potential loss of reproductive capacity and side effects of hormones. Almost all worry that their child will regret their decision to transition upon realizing they are not, in fact, transgender. While research (Spack et al., 2012) suggests it is extremely rare for youth who have reached puberty to regret medical transition, trusting a child in the throes of adolescence to make life-altering decisions affecting their health and reproductive capacity is a confusing, anxiety-ridden, and challenging prospect—one with no roadmap. However, a depressed child who does not want to continue living, or is simply failing to thrive, is heartbreaking as well. Among pre-pubescent children, the likelihood of some shifting back or shifting their gender identity again over time is higher, and because more and more young children are socially transitioning, we don't yet know the true likelihood of such shifts.

While parents are processing fear and grief, they are also forced to rethink a deeply ingrained construct of gender. For most parents, a major deconstruction of the concept of gender itself and the formation of a new language and mental model of gender are required. Questions about the meaning of gender characterize some of the most profound moments in our support groups when parents struggle together to understand how and why gender matters. The question of who their child is *aside* from gender is critical because they so often feel as if the child they know is gone. Often they can understand rationally why gender should not encompass so much of their child's identity, but on a more visceral, emotional level, gender feels like it's tied up with every aspect of their child. It requires significant cognitive reworking to disentangle, at least in part, gender from personality, temperament, and other aspects of identity. The reworking of one's gender schema is perhaps the most profound in parents of youth who espouse a nonbinary identity in that their gender may be something a parent has never conceptualized. Regardless, the deconstruction usually results in parents developing a less binary mental model. It often leads to a reassessment of the parent's own identity as well. Most are able to draw on ways in which their own gender identity, role, and presentation don't exactly culturally align, even when the parents are cisgender. One heterosexual couple came to recognize quite consciously that they had always had an unconventional relationship, as each of them took on a less traditional gender role. Rather than something unspoken and unacknowledged, this became a source of pride and a way to relate to their male-affirmed adolescent. Many parents also deconstruct beliefs about sexual orientation, coming to understand it as a concept separate from gender identity.

Interestingly, because of the possibility of a genetic component to gender and sexually diverse identities, parents of gender diverse youth may be more likely to be gender nonconforming or queer themselves. But because of generational gaps, they may experience those identities very differently from the way their child does. In our experience, some gay and lesbian parents have quite a difficult time accepting transgender identity. Some are more aware of minority stress and want to protect their child, whereas others have made sacrifices to their own authenticity to survive. A sense of jealousy, envy, anger, or fear—or some combination of these—may be evident. One pair of lesbian moms was stunned when their transgender daughter began doing public interviews when the parents themselves didn't feel safe being out at work. They were still struggling to accept themselves as well as feel safe in the world as lesbian women, experiencing confusion, envy, anger, and fear while their affirmed-female child seemed to achieve in a few months what they hadn't in their lifetimes. Another lesbian mother shockingly admitted to relating completely to her affirmed son's desire to transition during a family session, but wondered aloud why he "couldn't just accept being born in the wrong body," as she had had to do. She had difficulty recognizing that what she had internalized as a normal part of lesbian identity (the strong desire to be male, especially during adolescence) her child viewed as the very essence of *transgender* identity. This mother's ongoing conflict about her own unresolved gender identity triggered a whole array of feelings that affected her ability to accept her son's. Though she acknowledged herself as trans by her son's definition, she had come to view the desire to be male as a normal part of lesbian adolescence, and she thus concluded her child must be a lesbian as well.

Malpas (2011) concurs that gay and lesbian parents often need to address their own transphobia and/or homophobia when raising a transgender child. Other lesbian parents we have worked with found it more difficult to relate to their children than many heterosexual parents because they themselves were gender nonconforming but felt no desire to transition. For example, butch lesbians and more feminine gay men are not traditionally gendered, but, unlike the mother described above, they may have no experience with thoughts about or desire for transition. Because gender expansiveness—but not transition—feels quite understandable and comfortable for them, they may find it extra hard to relate to a need to transition. Or they may view their child's desire to transition and take on a more traditional gender expression than their own as a betrayal or rejection of more visible gender expansiveness.

In part because of the emphasis our culture places on gender, as a youth changes, their relationship to the parent changes. For a variety of reasons, the parent may feel they will lose the bond they have with the child. There is a common stereotype that same-sex parent-child dyads—mother-daughter, father-son—are closer than opposite sex dyads, and this belief may pervade the sense of loss for some parents. Other researchers describe parental "loss around the child they imagined" (Coolhart et al., 2013, p. 230). Some grieve the loss of future events about which they had fantasized, such as weddings and the birth of grandchildren. Eleven of the 12 parents of FTM children Hegedus (2009) interviewed said that in order to accept their child as a son, they were going to have to first mourn the loss of a daughter. Though the grieving process varies dramatically in intensity and length, the "lose a daughter, gain a son/genderqueer child" (or vice versa) idea seems to resonate. Parents often experience the grief as if the child they knew is gone, but there are other losses being processed as well. These can include the loss of status and loss of control, as transgender youth are often in a position to make adult-like decisions at young ages.

Finally, turmoil is often exacerbated because transgender youth may need much more in the way of medical and mental health attention than most other children. Kennedy and Hellen (2010) discuss the "internalization of self-hatred, guilt, self-doubt and low self-esteem" (p. 41), and we know that rates of depression, suicidality, and self-harming behaviors are higher as well, especially after youth come out (James et al., 2016; Peterson, Matthews, Copps-Smith, & Conard, 2016). Menvielle and Hill (2011) state, "For many children whose parents participated in the study, being cross-gendered was the least of their worries" (p. 104). For many parents a child's other challenges, such as a diagnosis of autism, self-harming behaviors, or hostility and aggression, are much more stressful and pressing than the child's gender dysphoria, whether or not these other challenges are related.

Reconstruction/Reconciliation

This phase is characterized by the tenuous reconstruction of the new parental identity and the reintegration of the gender diverse youth into the family. In addition to all the feelings associated with loss, many parents now begin to experience empowerment, joy, pride, and/or relief as their child comes out more publicly or makes steps toward transition. During the phase of Reconstruction, parents may alternate between feeling that they genuinely accept the change and employing a "fake it 'til you make it" attitude. Overall, they believe they *will* come to accept their child, even if they have not fully done so at that point. This belief usually results from a deeper level of understanding or empathy for the child's dysphoria. Often, this is accompanied by the recognition that their child is experiencing a level of pain that does indeed go beyond more normal adolescent concerns about identity confusion or body image.

The vast majority of parents we work with have critical moments when they begin to let go of the alternative explanations they had been holding on to and consider that transgender identity may be real. These feelings are often spurred by a visceral experience of the child's pain, as well as by the observed positive aftereffects on the child of authentic gender expression and/or affirming medical or mental health interventions. Spack and colleagues (2012) identify major mental health gains in youth given puberty blockers, especially those who were suicidal or self-harming at baseline. Shifts in attitudes become self-generating: when parents allow more outside help, they tend to see more improvement. One mother, who at first could not imagine her child socially transitioning or using puberty blockers, saw a dramatic shift after her transmasculine 14-year-old attempted suicide. Hospital staff—both inpatient and out—accepted the teen and used the preferred name and pronoun, thereby alleviating his depression. Once this mother witnessed the change, she allowed him to socially transition upon returning to high school. It is important to note that levels of training and cultural competency in medical settings vary dramatically. In a less gender-affirming setting, the outcome for this child could have been catastrophic.

Parents' groups can play an invaluable role in helping gain perspective on a child's internal experience. One mother tearfully described misunderstanding the depth of her autistic son's dysphoria. She said that despite his becoming extremely anxious, lethargic, and socially isolated, his difficulty in expressing emotion prevented the depth of his dysphoria from being visible to those around him. Hearing other parents' stories helped her gain perspective about the relationship between her son's gender dysphoria and his other symptoms.

As part of the Reconstruction phase, parents begin to rebuild their conceptions of gender and reconcile these alongside existing religious beliefs and values, thus opening up a more expansive environment in which to truly see their child as a full person again. Kuvalanka and her colleagues (2014) emphasize "expressing externally who they always were on the inside" (p. 12) as key. Parents come to view their child more as the same person, but with a different gender presentation, rather than as some stranger. Others use transitions in their own lives to relate to and identify with a child. After one mother had bariatric surgery, the family saw a parallel between parent and child, both striving externally toward the self that they experienced internally. Often family narratives relating to the genesis of the gender nonconformity shift from a focus on blame or external influences to an essential or genetic aspect of the child, whether pre- or post-puberty. Hegedus (2009) writes, "Parents began to use stories and signs from the child's early life to create a through-and-through narrative of the child's identity" (p. 81). Often the product of this phase is a full narrative that is nonpathological and a more innate aspect of who the child is rather than something that occurred because of outside forces, such as peer pressure.

In addition to increased empathy for the transition process, a key to reconciliation and reconnection is a parent's ability to grant their child psychological autonomy. Hedegus (2009) discusses parents who "felt their child mirrored their own best attributes, and when the child rejected their assigned sex and gender, it felt like a rejection of the parents' bodies and values" (p. 95). The extent to which a parent is capable of seeing their child as separate from them greatly influences the extent to which reconciliation is possible, just as it would affect the normal process of healthy separation and individuation. Hedegus refers to an "autonomy-granting process," and Ehrensaft (2011b) similarly describes parents who are able to accept a transgender child as having "the capacity to de-center and recognize their child as a separate person" (p. 539). The journey to acceptance of a transgender child is often tied to and intertwined with parents' general challenges to let go of the hope or belief that their children will live out or emulate certain aspects of their own selves. These challenges can occur with children of any age but are often exacerbated during adolescence, when youth are already in the midst of a developmentally normal separation and individuation process, which can be difficult for parents under any circumstances.

Recovery

When parent and child are "in sync"—that is, when the parent has become accepting of a transgender child, and transgender identity is integrated as part of the family identity—the family has fully recovered. Though parents may state their child's coming out was a net positive, they may still experience grief for the lost son or daughter and the future they imagined for them and for themselves. They may miss aspects of their "former" relationship while simultaneously appreciating and enjoying their "new" relationship. Though they may relate differently at this point, the essential attachment is intact. The family has successfully navigated a major crisis, developed an understanding of each other and themselves, and strengthened their capacity to cope. Often, the key is mutual empathy. Parents understand how alone their child felt before they were able to accept them, and youth understand that their parents' journey began later and was complicated in many ways, as was theirs. The family in the recovery stage typically has created a narrative about the child's identity and the process each member and the family as a whole engaged in to reintegrate the child in a positive way, regardless of age.

In the best circumstances, a child's transition becomes a parent's transition as well. Solomon (2012) highlights the fact that many parents not only ultimately respond positively to children who are different, but also view that difference as life-enhancing. Parents often uncover new aspects of self, locate abilities to cope, and/or develop new capacities to adapt. The obvious growth in those we've worked with is astounding and quite moving. Many become leaders who assist others in making their communities more welcoming. One single father of an affirmed son continued attending parent groups, conferences, and workshops for several years, long after he needed the support himself, in order to lovingly guide others in their process. The mother who braved a lawsuit against her former husband so that she could legally obtain medical treatment for their transgender child experienced a huge surge in self-confidence and pride that forever changed her.

Factors That Facilitate or Hinder Parental Identity Transformation

There are many ways that the gender-affirmative therapist can facilitate the transformation of parents of unconventionally gendered children. The first is through psychoeducation. Parents benefit from understanding that their children aren't mentally ill and that they are not the cause of their child's gender nonconformity. Menvielle and Hill (2011) point out that it is helpful for parents to learn to locate the source of the problem in the culture, not in their child or themselves. To make informed choices, they need to know about the research on young children and adolescents as well as the controversy surrounding that research. They need to hear how critical it is that they support their child and provide space for authentic expression.

Second, parents need space of their own to voice the powerfully negative feelings they may have, at least initially. Many will protect their children from their own darkest thoughts and feelings, quite appropriately in most cases. But these parents still need a forum in which to process. Third, they need to understand that although they have no control over their child's gender identity or expression, parents have an important role to play in protecting and advocating, understanding that protection is not in conflict with acceptance (Malpas, 2011). In addition, parents should be directed to sources of peer support, such as PFLAG (Parents and Friends of Lesbians and Gays) or other online groups (Reed, 2005). Just as transgender children need support to develop their identities, parents need support to evolve *their* new identities as parents of trans children. Clinicians who work with these parents need to be able to fully empathize with their point of view. This may require that separate therapists counsel parent and child. It is easy to become impatient with a parent who is just beginning to grasp the significance of having a child who is different when you are counseling the hurting young person desperate for full acceptance.

Therapists working with parents of children of various ages across the transgender spectrum need to assess what is most likely to help or impede progress toward the goal of acceptance. Using a systemic approach, it is possible to identify factors in the child, in the parent or couple, in the extended family, and in the community. We have already touched on many of these variables and summarize them here.

Child variables: In our experience, the age of the child and the severity of the dysphoria are major factors affecting a parent's process. In large part this is because during prepuberty it is nearly impossible to assert that the child is definitively transgender and should socially transition. Early-outcome research suggests that many prepubertal children diagnosed with gender dysphoria do not persist in the desire to be the opposite sex once they become adolescents (Drummond, Bradley, Badali-Peterson, & Zucker, 2008; Wallien & Cohen-Kettenis, 2008), but instead develop into gay, lesbian, or bisexual adults. Although this research is methodologically flawed and outdated (Winters, 2014), even those critical of it would agree that not every child who expresses discomfort with their assigned gender will become a transgender adult. There are some indications that those who assert that they *are* a different gender may continue a trans identification more than children who merely express a wish or desire to be (Steensma, McGuire, Kreukels, Beekman, & Cohen-Kettenis, 2013). But this finding needs more confirmation before a clinician can act on it with confidence. While at first this might seem counterintuitive, children identified as gender nonconforming at a young age seem to be less likely to become transgender adults than those whose gender dysphoria does not become evident until they are teenagers (Spack et al., 2012). For these reasons, many gender-affirmative therapists approach the issue of early social transition with great caution. It may be preferable to create an environment where the child can express their gender safely without a full social transition, whenever possible.

And yet it is in some ways much harder to create an environment that supports a gender nonconforming child than one that supports a transitioned child. Those who transition at age five or six typically become integrated into their schools, peer groups, and communities as the opposite sex of their natal birth, even if initial acceptance is rocky. But gender nonconforming children are likely to seem more odd or unconventional as they get older, making bullying and social rejection more likely as well. And many parents, ironically, will find less support from peers for a nonconforming child and less public understanding in general. The uncertain outcome for many gender diverse children puts parents in limbo as well. It can be easier to cope with a child you know will eventually undergo medical treatment and full transition than to handle one whose gender falls somewhere "in between."

Parent reactions to a gender expansive child may hinge on what other concomitant problems the child has. Since gender nonconforming children are bullied and victimized more than other children, they are also more likely to suffer from depression, suicidality, and posttraumatic stress disorder (Mustanski, Garofalo, & Emerson, 2010; Roberts, Rosario, Corliss, Koenen, & Austin, 2012; Toomey, Ryan, & Diaz, 2010). In addition, there may be a correlation between autism spectrum disorders and being transgender (Jacobs, Rachlin, Erickson-Schroth, & Janssen, 2014). Gender diverse kids with mental health problems or those "on the spectrum" may present so many other challenges that their gender nonconformity seems less pressing than it otherwise would. A family dealing with their child's self-harming behavior and the possible need for hospitalization and intensive aftercare programs may have no resources at the moment to deal with gender issues. Parents who have been taking their children for therapy for years may have little energy or enthusiasm for one more problem, although the earlier experience dealing with their child's difficulties may make other parents feel more prepared. To the extent that the child's mental health issues are a direct or indirect result of their gender expansiveness, gender-affirmative treatment and appropriate medical care may produce dramatic results (Spack et al., 2012). Parents who see a marked improvement in their child that has come with support and validation may be powerfully influenced to become more accepting.

Factors in the parent or couple: Parental acceptance is greatly influenced by variables such as their religiosity and conventionality, their views and attitudes on gender and sexual orientation, and their own minority status in the culture. Clearly, the mental health of the parents and the stability of the family unit influence the degree of support. One of the most accepting pairs of parents we've encountered was a white, upper-middle-class couple with liberal beliefs, many gay and lesbian friends, and a child, Alex, who was gender nonconforming from an early age. Though these parents assumed they were raising a gay child, and were a bit surprised when the child disclosed being transgender at age 13, they were quickly and easily able to progress toward total acceptance within a period of months. By the time Alex was three, he preferred to play with Barbies and everything pink, and he used scarves and towels to fashion dresses or skirts to wear whenever he was at home. Alex's parents were convinced not only that he was gay, but that his gender nonconformity was a sign of his gayness and needed to be supported. They explained to him that life would be difficult for him if he chose to wear dresses to school, but outside school he had free rein to express himself. They advocated for him at school and in their community, and Alex, who was blessed with a charming and likable personality, generally avoided bullying. These parents were not only sensitized; they had already accepted their child's gayness years before he came out to them, were proud of their unconventional child, and had become strong, respectful allies of LGBT causes. When Alex disclosed her true identity, it was not because she had been hiding it; rather, at 13 she had just figured it out. The shift in identity that her parents needed to make was minor compared to that of parents who have not been sensitized and are taken completely by surprise.

Extended family and community: The extended family, schools, religious institutions, neighbors, and community all exert influence in both direct and indirect ways. The family unit is influenced to the degree that the parents are prepared or unprepared for social rejection. In other words, families that are thoroughly integrated into and dependent on their larger social networks are more strongly affected by social approval and disapproval than those less dependent. One Orthodox Jewish couple was prepared to accept their gender nonconforming son. They had a less rigid interpretation of religious doctrine but lived in a highly traditional and gender-segregated religious community. They moved elsewhere so their adolescent could get support, acknowledging both their need for such a community and their need to protect him. In general, a more conservative community not only creates realistic difficulties for the family, but it also subtly reinforces the parents' denial and their reluctance to get help.

Summary and Conclusions

Parenting a child with a *horizontal identity*—one different from that of their parents—usually presents challenges. Parents of children who are transgender and gender expansive encounter obstacles that are both psychological—accepting a child who contradicts their image of who the child is or should be—and based on hard reality—learning how to support a child about whose condition they may be ignorant, and who faces many real-life dangers. Cognizant of the crucial importance that parental support plays, the gender-affirmative therapist models for them what acceptance and protection of the child should ideally look like.

Parental rejection and its negative effect cannot be minimized. But we have experienced parents who, though initially skeptical or overtly rejecting, transform not only their attitudes, but also their own identities for the better. Many of the parents with whom we have worked feel that their lives have benefited from having a transgender child, and that the experience has made them healthier and happier.

We have described the processes parents typically experience, normal phases, and what helps or hinders transformation. We have suggested that the difficulties they experience in adjusting to and accepting their children are often more reflective of realistic dangers their children face and integrating challenges to their own identities than evidence of genuine transphobia. Gender-affirmative therapists must be careful not to pathologize parental responses in addition to validating the experiences of gender diverse youth. The difficulty parents experience coming to terms with having a transgender child is the result of having to face problems most have never encountered and for which they do not have the tools to cope—at least initially. Given these major obstacles, it is perhaps extraordinary that so many do so well.

When parents have fully "transitioned" along with their child, they often arrive at a place they could never have imagined when the journey began. Many come to feel that having a transgender child, something that at first seemed like an unmitigated disaster, has turned out to be beneficial to the entire family. Some become allies, even advocates, working with PFLAG or speaking publicly about their experiences. Others transform more quietly but no less deeply. Rhonda, the parent of a 14-year-old, transmasculine child, had her life shaken to the core. Although a liberal, accepting person, she defined herself by approval from others, and so the courtesy stigma was particularly difficult to manage. Her family and friends thought of her as easygoing because she avoided conflict in interpersonal relationships at all costs. After her teen's social transition, Rhonda was frequently placed in situations in which she needed to deal with negative reactions to her or her son. She became stronger and more assertive, initially in order to defend her child, but eventually in her own behalf. Rhonda learned she could tolerate others' disapproval and felt proud of her newfound ability to stand up for herself. In addition, although happily married to a man, she had suppressed strong romantic and sexual attractions to women her whole life. Her son's disclosure encouraged Rhonda to confront her own unexplored sexuality as well as her fears of social disapproval. Rhonda disclosed her bisexuality to her therapist, the first person she had ever told, as she was overwhelmed by an eruption of thoughts, feelings, "what ifs," grief for the life she might have had, and guilt because she felt hers had been the genes that "made" her child transgender. But ultimately Rhonda processed her grief, guilt, and pain. She disclosed her bisexuality to a small circle of people, including her husband, and she came to feel that she was no longer a fraud, but was, rather, living her life authentically. And, as so often happens when one lives authentically, Rhonda became invigorated with new energy. Ultimately, she declared having a transgender child had been one of the best things that had ever happened to her.

Finally, the challenges parents of transgender and gender expansive children face are constantly shifting as the culture becomes more accepting. This strong cohort effect must be acknowledged. By the time you read these words, if the current trend continues, parents and children will find slightly more acceptance than when we wrote them. We experience many of the parents of our gender diverse young clients as heroes. But one shouldn't have to be a hero to parent a child. We hope that the task will get easier with time.

REFERENCES

Coleman, E., Bockting, W., Botzer, M., Cohen-Kettenis, P., DeCuypere, G., Feldman, J., . . . & Zucker, K. (2012). Standards of Care for the health of transsexual, transgender, and gender nonconforming people, Version 7. *International Journal of Transgenderism, 13* (4), 165–232.

Coolhart, D., Baker, A., Farmer, S., Malaney, M., & Shipman, D. (2013). Therapy with transsexual youth and their families: A clinical tool for assessing youth's readiness for gender transition. *Journal of Marital and Family Therapy, 39* (2), 223–243.

Drummond, K., Bradley, S., Badali-Peterson, M., & Zucker, K. (2008) A follow-up study of girls with gender identity disorder. *Developmental Psychology, 44,* 34–45.

Ehrensaft, D. (2007). Raising girlyboys: A parent's perspective. *Studies in Gender and Sexuality, 8* (3), 269–302.

Ehrensaft, D. (2011a). *Gender born, gender made: Raising healthy gender-nonconforming children.* New York: Experiment.

Ehrensaft, D. (2011b). Boys will be girls, girls will be boys. *Psychoanalytic Psychology, 28* (4), 528–548.

Erich, S., Tittsworth, J., Dykes, J., & Cabuses, C. (2008). Family relationships and their correlations with transsexual well-being. *Journal of GLBT Family Studies, 4* (4), 419–432.

Goffman, E. (1986). *Stigma: Notes on the management of spoiled identity.* New York: Simon & Schuster.

Gottlieb, A. (2000). *Out of the twilight: Fathers of gay men speak*. Binghamton, N.Y.: Haworth Press.

Grossman, A., & D'Augelli, A. (2007). Transgender youth and life-threatening behaviors. *Suicide and Life-Threatening Behavior, 37,* 527–537.

Grossman, A., D'Augelli, A., Howell, T. J., & Hubbard, S. (2005). Parents' reactions to transgender youths' gender nonconforming expression and identity. *Journal of Gay and Lesbian Social Services,* 18 (1), 3–16.

Haas, A. P., & Drescher, J. (2014). Impact of sexual orientation and gender identity on suicide risk: Implications for assessment and treatment. *Psychiatric Times, 30* (12), 24–25.

Hegedus, J. K. (2009). When a daughter becomes a son: Parents' acceptance of their transgender children. PhD diss., Alliant International University.

Jacobs, L. A., Rachlin, K., Erickson-Schroth, L., & Janssen, A. (2014). Gender dysphoria and co-occurring autism spectrum disorders: Review, case examples, and treatment considerations. *LGBT Health,* 1 (4), 277–282.

James, S. E., Herman, J. L., Rankin, S., Keisling, M., Mottet, L., & Anafi, M. (2016). *The report of the 2015 U.S. Transgender Survey.* Washington, D.C.: National Center for Transgender Equality.

Kennedy, N., & Hellen, M. (2010). Transgender children: More than a theoretical challenge. *Graduate Journal of Social Science, 7* (2), 25–43.

Krieger, I. (2011). *Helping your transgender teen: A guide for parents.* New Haven, Conn.: Genderwise Press.

Kuvalanka, K., Weiner, J., & Mahan, D. (2014). Child, family, and community transformations: Findings from interviews with mothers of transgender girls. *Journal of GLBT Family Studies,* 10 (4), 1–26.

LaSala, M. (2010). *Coming out, coming home: Helping families adjust to a gay or lesbian child.* New York: Columbia University Press.

Lasser, J., Tharinger, D., & Cloth, A. (2006). Gay, lesbian, and bisexual youth. In G. G. Bear & K. M. Minke (eds.), *Children's needs III* (pp. 419–430). Bethesda: National Association of School Psychologists.

Lev, A. I., & Alie, I. (2012). Transgender and gender nonconforming children and youth: Developing culturally competent systems of care. In S. K. Fisher, J. M. Poirier, & G. M. Blau (eds.), *Improving emotional and behavioral outcomes for LGBT youth: A guide for professionals* (pp. 43–66). Baltimore: Brookes.

Malpas, J. (2011). Between pink and blue: A multi-dimensional family approach to gender nonconforming children and their families. *Family Process, 50* (4), 453–470.

Menvielle, E., & Hill, D. (2011). An affirmative intervention for families with gender-variant children: A process evaluation. *Journal of Gay & Lesbian Mental Health,* 15 (1), 94–123.

Mustanski, B. S., Garofalo, R., & Emerson, E. M. (2010). Mental health disorders, psychological distress, and suicidality in a diverse sample of lesbian, gay, bisexual, and transgender youths. *American Journal of Public Health,* 100 (12), 2426–2432.

Peterson, C. M., Matthews, A., Copps-Smith, E., & Conard, L. A. (2016). Suicidality, self-harm, and body dissatisfaction in transgender adolescents and emerging adults with gender dysphoria. *Suicide and Life-Threatening Behavior, 47* (4), 475–482. doi:10.1111/sltb.12289.

Reed, T. (2005). Families and transsexualism: A better understanding. *Gender Research and Education Society (GIRES),* 1–18.

Riley, E., Sitharthan, G., Clemson, L., & Diamond, M. (2011). Recognizing the needs of gender-variant children and their parents. *Sex Education, 23* (3), 644–659.

Roberts, A., Rosario, M., Corliss, H., Koenen, K., & Austin, S. (2012). Childhood gender nonconformity: A risk indicator for childhood abuse and posttraumatic stress in youth. *Pediatrics, 129* (3), 410–417.

Ryan, C., Russell, S., Hueber, D., Diaz, R., & Sanchez, J. (2010). Family acceptance in adolescence and the health of LGBT young adults. *Journal of Child and Adolescent Psychiatric Nursing, 23* (4), 205–213.

Solomon, A. (2012). *Far from the tree: Parents, children and the search for identity.* New York: Scribner.

Spack, N. P., Edwards-Leeper, L., Feldman, H. A., Leibowitz, S., Mandel, F., & Diamond, D. A. (2012). Children and adolescents with gender identity disorder referred to a pediatric medical center. *Pediatrics, 129* (3), 418–425.

Steensma, T. D., McGuire, J. K., Kreukels, B. P., Beekman, A. J., & Cohen-Kettenis, P. T. (2013). Factors associated with desistence and persistence of childhood gender dysphoria: A quantitative follow-up study. *Journal of the American Academy of Child & Adolescent Psychiatry, 52* (6), 582–590.

Sue, D. (2010). *Microaggressions in everyday life: Race, gender and sexual orientation.* Hoboken, N.J.: John Wiley & Sons.

Toomey, R., Ryan, C., & Diaz, R. M. (2010). Gender-nonconforming lesbian, gay, bisexual, and transgender youth: School victimization and young psychosocial adjustment. *Developmental Psychology, 46* (6), 1580–1589.

Vanderburgh, R. (2009). Appropriate therapeutic care for families with pre-pubescent transgender/gender-dissonant children. *Child and Adolescent Social Work Journal, 26,* 135–154.

Wallien, M. S. C., & Cohen-Kettenis, P. T. (2008). Psychosexual outcome of gender-dysphoric children. *Journal of American Academy of Child & Adolescent Psychiatry, 47* (12), 1413–1423.

Winters, K. (2014, February 16). Methodological questions in childhood gender identity "desistence" research. Paper presented at the 23rd WPATH Biennial Symposium, Bangkok, Thailand.

Zucker, K., Wood, H., Singh, D., & Bradley, S. (2012). A developmental, biopsychosocial model for the treatment of children with gender identity disorder. *Journal of Homosexuality, 59* (3), 369–397.

12

My Own Transition

Elena Moser, LCSW

In 2008 my 20-year-old son, who at the time I believed to be my daughter, told me that he was transgender, planned to begin taking testosterone, and wanted to have top surgery as soon as possible. I was shocked, but not really surprised. As he spoke these words, my ears were filled with a wooshing sound, as if I were being engulfed by a huge windstorm. I think my expression remained neutral, but inside I felt as though I had fallen into an abyss. I was flooded with half-formulated thoughts and memories.

R. had been unconventionally gendered since the time he had any control over expressing himself. When he was three, he would change his clothes several times a day, as though he couldn't quite get it right. By the time he was four and in preschool, he was adamant about wearing only clothing that was dark blue and dark green: boys' underwear, boys' bathing suits, and boys' T-shirts. He had come to see something about the gendering of T-shirts I had never noticed before—that girls' T-shirts have slightly lower necklines and slightly shorter sleeves. He wanted to have a blue pickup truck when he was older, and he was interested in what the *DSM-IV* diagnosis of Gender Identity Disorder (GID) referred to as "rough-and-tumble play." We had to stop playing the board game Life because of his agitation about having to choose to represent himself with either a blue peg or a pink peg in the car that players "drive" through the game.

I recalled an image of R. in a dress at age five that I convinced him to wear to a family wedding in which he was hiding under the table because he felt so uncomfortable. Soon after that, he said to me, "Mama, why do you want me to wear girls' clothes when I feel like killing myself when I wear them?" This was my dilemma: as a feminist mother, I wanted both my children to have expansive ideas about gender; as a lesbian mother, I worried that people might think I was "making" him dress like a boy. In the late 1980s, it was still a relatively new phenomenon to be an intentional lesbian family, and I felt an internal pressure to be a model.

I had a visceral memory of the times in R.'s early childhood when I thought he might grow up to be transgender, which would fill me with anguish, and I quickly made myself think about something else. I was relieved when he went through

Lev, Arlene I., Gottlieb, Andrew R., *Families in Transition*
dx.doi.org/10.17312/harringtonparkpress/2019.04.fit.012
© 2019 by Harrington Park Press

puberty and came out as a lesbian when he was 12, not because I had any investment in his being a lesbian, but because I hoped he could find some comfort with his gender expression in the lesbian community, where there is a wider range of what is acceptable. Although he didn't talk about being unhappy living in a female body, it was obvious that he was uncomfortable having breasts. How he struggled to find clothes that fit him as his body became more and more overtly female!

When R. disclosed that he was transgender, I looked into his face, one that I had loved since the moment he was born. I knew I had to respond. He was waiting expectantly, his vulnerability covered over with bravado. I heard later that my other son, R.'s cisgender twin, responded beautifully, saying, "I always wanted a brother." I wish I had been able to say something so gracious and affirming and welcoming, but I did not. Instead, I asked whether he had thought fully about this decision and whether he had considered living as a very masculine woman. Later on in the conversation I also told him I was glad he was telling me, that I wanted him to be happy, that I would always love him, but that it was going to take me some time to get used to this. We talked for quite a while, and I could see he was more relaxed as I communicated my desire to support him, but internally I was struggling with my own feelings. When I came out as lesbian to my family in the mid-1970s as a young adult, I had not understood what the big deal was for my family members. I had always imagined that I would react with enthusiasm if my child ever came to me with an identity that was outside the norm.

When I was in my early twenties, I read an anthology called *Nice Jewish Girls* (1982), edited by Evelyn Torton Beck, a collection of short, autobiographical stories about the experience of being both Jewish and lesbian. Harriet Malinowitz has a piece in the book in which she wrote about her experience attempting to share her joy in having come out as lesbian to her brother, which, while not a disaster, was unsatisfying. She had grown up hearing repeatedly that her beloved grandmother looked forward to dancing at her wedding. She realized that this was what she had been hoping for—that her brother would be so overjoyed in her becoming more of herself that he would want to dance. I know that there are many parents who would have responded less enthusiastically to R.'s coming out as transgender than I had, but still I was humbled to have not been able to live up to my ideal of how I wished my parents had responded to my disclosure.

I spent the next six months thinking about (or avoiding thinking about) R.'s transition. Some days it just felt too overwhelming, and I would pretend R. had never told me. Compartmentalization was my main defense, as I went about my life not talking about it except with very close friends, most of whom had known R. for all of his life. It was a great source of comfort that they were supportive and mirroring of my struggle to digest his transition, forming what felt like a protective web around me as I took my time working up to "coming out" to my wider communities. I am not proud to say this, but even at age 52, I was dreading what other people would think of me for having a trans son. And the people I dreaded telling most were my parents. But it wasn't only them. It was also my professional community. Looking back, I can see that I was experiencing the social stigma of being a mother of a transgender child.

I have been a licensed clinical social worker since 1985. From that time, I have maintained a private psychotherapy and consultation practice and been the clinical and training director at two local nonprofits, one of which focused on serving the LGBTQ communities, while the other served women and, to a lesser extent, transgender and genderqueer people. In both my psychotherapy and my training and teaching work, I have been interested in the intersection of sociocultural norms and hierarchies with individual experience, and how that intersection shapes who we become. I believe that cultural forces surround and permeate families and that they are then internalized, interpreted, and transmitted in universal and unique ways. It is in our families that we learn about values and norms, and this teaching and learning is happening on conscious and unconscious levels. Being gender nonconforming is to exist outside these values and norms and results in distress for the person as well as for the family members, each of whom has to come to terms with having a member whose gendered existence is marginalized. The part I want to focus on is how the cultural stigma of living outside the gender binary affects the family. The stigma of being *transgender* (and I'm using this term broadly to include anyone who exists outside the gender binary, whether or not they want to transition or live in one gender or another) radiates out from the individual toward their family and friends. I believe that the management of this stigma is affected by how past stigmas and cultural traumas have been navigated. To be able to find acceptance and stability, there must be a working through of the shame as well as the grief over the loss of the son or daughter, brother or sister they thought they had.

About my background: I am a white, Ashkenazi-Jewish lesbian, raised in the middle to upper middle class in the New York City metropolitan area in an intact family comprising my mother, father, younger sister, and brother. I came out in 1974 while in high school. Being a lesbian is what prompted me to move to the Bay Area in 1980. Although at the time my family sort of tolerated my sexual orientation, I couldn't see a way to integrate my lesbian world with my family world. My ex-partner and I had a commitment ceremony in 1986, which a number of my family members attended, including my parents, an aunt and uncle, a cousin, and my beloved grandmother who, along with my sister, came a full week before to help in spite of her not understanding why we felt a need to be so public about our relationship. My ex-partner and I began an alternative insemination process, and I became the nonbiological mother of twins in 1988. After initially being resistant and confused about the nonbiological nature of parenting, my whole family, including my parents, embraced my children.

After R. came out to me, he went back to school on the East Coast. I had hoped he would keep this private while I was working through my feelings. But he posted his transition on Facebook, so word spread. I was fortunate because my oldest niece had a trans friend from college who had come home with her during a spring break. So those in my family sitting at the Passover Seder now had some experience with a trans person who everyone agreed seemed wonderful.

Coming out to "friends" on Facebook in one fell swoop is different from talking more intimately, and R. asked me to tell Grandma and Grandpa so that he wouldn't have to be the one to break the news himself. I agreed because, although I believed they would want to be supportive (after all, I had broken them in decades ago), I wasn't sure how they would react in the moment, and I wanted them to be able to process and digest the information with me before speaking with R. Ever since my siblings and I had our children, we gathered for a week in December at my parents' home. R. and my siblings wanted me to disclose to my parents before our next time together, which I also wanted to do, but I was still anxious about it. I gave myself until the week before Thanksgiving. So one afternoon, sobbing on the phone, I told them. It was a relief. My mother immediately recalled the wedding where R. had hidden under the table because he so hated wearing a dress. My father wondered whether a doctor had made a definitive diagnosis. Overall, they were actually loving and supportive and wanted to talk with R. to communicate their support.

Even with their support, I continued my grieving process for the daughter I thought I had, which was severely complicated by my shame and my fears for his future. Whom would he find to create a life with? What kind of career would he have? Ironically, when I had told my grandmother about my partner being pregnant with twins, her number one concern focused on who would ever want to marry someone who had been born into a lesbian family. I felt a new empathy for my parents' struggle to embrace me when I came out as lesbian, not having a picture at the time of how I could live life fully as a gay person and anxious as they were about other people knowing. It was all so very humbling. I knew I wanted to get through these fears and anxieties and trust that my son would find his way to create a full life, but I couldn't yet see a path for either of us.

As a therapist quite familiar with the role psychotherapy has played in reinforcing gender norms as well as the tendency our field has to hold mothers responsible, I was worried that my peers would pathologize my child and place the "blame" on me. The field of mental health, psychoanalytic thinking in particular, has historically viewed mothers as the source of all problems, autism and schizophrenia among them. As Dr. Peggy Drexler (2009) said about her training: "In case conference after case conference, it was always the mother who was held at fault for her child's problems. She was too close or too distant, too strict or too permissive, hadn't set clear enough boundaries, or was found wanting in the empathy, love, or affection departments. Whatever the issue, it always pointed back to the mother." I remember hearing a little mantra many years ago that went like this, "If it's not one thing, it's your mother." I imagined, in my slightly paranoid anxiety, that as the news of R.'s transition spread like wildfire through my professional community, I would be scrutinized and overexposed. I began avoiding social situations and tried to change the topic when the subject of my children came up. And in my circle of psychotherapists, whom I have been in community with for many years, it was astonishing to see how many people were loosely tracking my kids, remembering to ask where they were, how they were doing in college, or what they were doing for the summer. I guess it had been going on all the time, but during that period it often felt jarring to have a discussion of R. (whom they only knew as my daughter) when I was working so hard to compartmentalize.

During this time, even in my despair and shame and grief, I had a strong sense of knowing that I was going to work this out, that I would be able to talk about R.'s transition and ultimately be a strong ally. But I also knew I needed to have the privacy to just be with my own feelings. I was glad R. was on the East Coast in college during much of this time, and I had the space to be with myself, only rarely having to move into "mother" mode. Although I was trying, I was having a hard time with the use of pronouns, especially in the past tense. I needed to sort out my grief about the daughter I was losing, even if she had only been in my mind. I loved having a daughter. It was a big loss to come to terms with. I found myself looking at old photographs and trying to decide at what point R. stopped being a girl.

I don't exactly know what all of that means to me—"mourning the loss of being a mother to my daughter"—but I do know it has many meanings—some conscious, some unconscious; I have been part of women's communities for many years; I came of age during the feminist movement of the 1970s; I am fairly well read in the contemporary psychoanalytic literature, and I believe in gender being fluid and existing on a continuum; I support the idea that culture makes gender, although I will say that I had stopped being a purist many years ago; I also had a wide definition of what male and female could look like; I knew that if society could likewise expand what was permissible behavior for men and women, the world would be a better place for everyone.

Several years before R. came out to me, I had engaged in many conversations about the internalized misogyny that was resulting in butch women's transitioning to being men. At that time there were multiple conversations going on in the lesbian communities about the loss of butches, especially young ones, conversations that continue today in some circles. Then it hit me: many of those butch women, or butches — the word being a noun, not an adjective — saw themselves as a gender unto themselves, and they had really been trans, or would have been if the medical technology had been readily available. And I knew some of them were transitioning in their fifties and sixties.

A few months into my own transition, I had a new thought that moved me into a deeper despair. I began to grapple with the fact that, through no fault of my own, I had not quite seen R.'s true self. Because his outer body was female, I assumed his inner self was also female. I had had fears that he might be transgender, but I could never let myself think about it, let alone ask him about it. I began to imagine how alone he had been with this terrible dilemma of feeling unseen by everyone in his life, even the people who loved him. I remembered the times when he would be mistaken for a boy and how angry he would get when I would correct the person. I felt, and still feel, so sad when I think that it was only at these moments with strangers that he had the pleasure of having his gendered self accurately reflected back. And I felt such shame and regret in needing to take that away from him.

As painful as they were, and they were unbearably so, these thoughts and feelings were constructive. They became the pathway for me to find my empathy for him in a way that ultimately allowed me to locate his experience at the center, and also helped me understand that the daughter I was grieving had never really existed inside R. At that point in my process, I was fluidly using the pronoun *he* in the present tense, but I was still struggling with using it to describe R. in the past. When I realized that R. had always been a *he* to himself, even if he hadn't had the words to articulate it, was when I began to consistently use the pronoun *he* for him both present *and* past.

Over the next few years, R. began taking testosterone, then had "top" surgery. He was privileged to have family support, both emotional and financial, because most health insurance policies at that time did not cover either. One of the highlights of this experience for me was meeting Dr. Michael Brownstein, a plastic surgeon, who began performing bilateral mastectomies for female-to-male trans people in the late 1970s. Dr. Brownstein told me that after his first one, patients began referring other people to him. After a couple of dozen surgeries over the next year or two, his practice solely consisted of performing top surgery on trans men. His professionalism and respect toward R. were normalizing and comforting to me.

My mother came to California to be present for R.'s surgery. This was no small feat, as she had a lifelong fear of flying and had never flown by herself before. My father's health didn't allow him to travel at the time, but he sent along a dopp kit, a leather travel bag for men's toiletries and shaving supplies, for R. as a sort of "welcome to the world of men" present.

Because of the hormone treatment, R. became more muscular and grew hair on his face and body. He also began to talk more, which was amazing because he had always been a person of few words. His voice, in addition to a deepening in timbre, evidenced a greater self-confidence. It seemed to me that the way R. held his masculinity after transition was more fluid and complex. Pretransition, he had stayed with darker colors in clothing styles, ones associated with conventional masculinity. As he transitioned and began consistently passing in the world, he discovered pink, delighting in adding touches of it to his wardrobe. He got more serious about school and was able to move ahead on his professional goals. But it was his increasing capacity for connection that was most astonishing. He was able to use what had always been a keen understanding of people to engage more deeply. He put more energy into family and friendships, became more empowered, and trusted that others would value him for who he was. Our own relationship has gotten deeper and more complex, with more conflict, but with more intimacy. Surprisingly, it is more satisfying to be in relationship with him now because he is so much more embodied as a person.

Contrary to my earlier fears, my professional community has been nothing but supportive. I think had R. come out five years earlier than he did, there would have been more raised eyebrows; had it been even two years later, I might have had fewer worries. Trans acceptance has changed much over the last few years.

So this has been my process. Each parent's and each family member's transition will be unique. For some, the disclosure will come as a complete shock; others, like me, will have seen the signs but be shocked nevertheless. My process was complicated by extremely high expectations I had of myself as a mother to be all-accepting as well as the internalization of the idea that everything in a child's life is somehow the "fault" of the mother. Although I did not rationally believe these things, I was surprised how powerfully they existed in my unconscious. Furthermore, what made this process so tumultuous was that I didn't yet understand that although on the surface I was grappling with R.'s transition, it was *my* transition from being the mother of a daughter to being the mother of another son that was so powerful.

There are a couple of models of family adjustment. Emerson and Rosenfeld (1996) propose one based on Kübler-Ross's (1969) five-stage model—denial, anger, bargaining, depression, and acceptance. In her seminal book, *Transgender Emergence*, Lev (2004) developed a four-stage model: the first—*Discovery and Disclosure*—is often marked by shock, a feeling of betrayal, and confusion upon the realization that a family member is gender variant; the second—*Turmoil*—may be a period of emotional volatility as family members begin to come to terms with the reality; the third—*Negotiation*—is a time of adjustment and compromise; and the fourth—*Finding Balance*—is characterized by a lessening of the turmoil, a recognition of differences, and a fuller integration of the transgender person into the family. These are not linear and can be experienced in unique and different ways. As clinicians, it's important for us to keep in mind that the specifics of these models are less important than being cognizant that family members and trans people alike go through their own processes. For me, Lev's second stage, *Turmoil,* aptly describes my own experience of feeling as though my world had just changed overnight and that I had not had any say in the matter. There were times I worried I would feel raw and vulnerable for the rest of my life.

In working with a family of a trans person, it is important to be attentive to the ways that a person's social location intersects with the stigma of having a trans family member. The gender binary operates in most cultures, but different groups have different relationships to how gender is performed. People from marginalized ethnic groups have additional burdens in accepting yet another stigmatized identity. When R. first started taking testosterone shots, we went to the youth services at the Dimensions Clinic in San Francisco, which is located in the neighborhood between the Castro and the Mission. We were two of the few European-American people in the waiting room. The others were mostly Latina mothers with trans daughters. And the mothers appeared to be interested in helping them "pass" as females by encouraging a highly gender conforming performance of femininity. LaSala and Frierson (2012) suggest that one reason African American mothers are less accepting of their sons' homosexuality is because of the concern about the burden of a dual stigma. I imagine that these Latina mothers were doing what they could to support their trans daughters out of love as well as out of fear of what might happen to them if they were recognized as genetic males dressed as girls.

The adaptive style of each family and how they've dealt with previous stressors and crises will probably be used to grapple with having a trans member. Families that have multiple unprocessed interpersonal conflicts are likely to experience relational distress and disruptions; families that tend to abuse substances are more at risk for increased drinking and using; families that are less differentiated have trouble tolerating individual members different from the norm; and families, like mine, that are particularly sensitive to how they are perceived by others are extremely prone to isolation, secrecy, and shame.

Additionally, it is very expensive to transition. Those with fewer economic resources are going to experience all the concerns and difficulties of middle- and upper-class families, along with an increase in financial stress. Although it is true that money can't buy happiness, it is also true that money can provide a trans person the ability to purchase medical and cosmetic services that enhance their capacity to walk through the world in such a way that they will be recognized as being the gender they experience themselves to be.

In closing, I'd like to leave you with one final thought. It takes time to acknowledge, accept, and embrace change. Terrible things are happening to trans people—at the hands of strangers and, many times, at the hands of their own families. You probably know that trans kids are disproportionally represented among the homeless. When I was young, places like San Francisco and New York City were flocked to by gays and lesbians, some because they were rejected by their families, others because they had heard those cities offered the possibility of leading an authentic life. I knew people in college and in my twenties who had little or no contact with their parents because of the rejection they felt about being gay or lesbian. But many of those families, unless they had a very limited capacity to tolerate difference of any kind, worked it out enough for the gay or lesbian member to be reintegrated.

I hope it will be like that for families of trans people; I hope that professionals in the fields of mental health will be taking the lead in helping these families make room for gender diversity; and I hope we get to the point when, as my son R. predicts, we'll create birth certificates that read, "Gender Assigned at Birth," affirming that we don't always know what—or who—lies ahead.

REFERENCES

Drexler, P. (2011, November 17). Mother blaming has to stop. *Huffington Post*. https://www.huff
ingtonpost.com/entry/mother-blamimg-has-to-sto_b_359622.

Emerson, S., & Rosenfeld, C. (1996). Stages of adjustment of family members of transgender
individuals. *Journal of Family Psychotherapy, 7,* 1–12.

Kübler-Ross, E. (1969). *On death and dying.* New York: Macmillan.

LaSala, M., & Frierson, D. (2012). African-American gay youth and their families: Redefining
masculinity, coping with racism and homophobia. *Journal of GLBT Family Studies, 8* (5),
428–445.

Lev, A. I. (2004). *Transgender emergence: Therapeutic guidelines for working with gender-variant people
and their families.* Binghamton, N.Y.: Haworth Press.

Malinowitz, H. (1982). Coffee and cake. In E. T. Beck (ed.), *Nice Jewish girls: A lesbian anthology*
(pp. 179–189). Watertown, Mass.: Persephone Press.

PART 5

Medical Concerns: How Do Puberty Suppression and/or Hormonal Considerations Affect Parents?

Irene Sills reiterates the question routinely asked of her, "But Doc, is it safe?" — a central anxiety that parents justifiably have when considering puberty-suppressing medications and cross-gender hormone therapy for their adolescents. Although there is no body of longitudinal research relating to their use specifically with trans youth, we *do* have conclusive evidence of their efficacy in treating other conditions. Despite safety concerns, there are clear arguments for their being prescribed.

Adolescence is, itself, a period of transition that, even for those relatively well-adjusted, challenges both the teenager *and* their family. For young people who are gender dysphoric, the suppression of puberty allows time for exploration of gender identity and consideration of the feasibility of gender reassignment while minimizing the possibility of short- or long-term psychological damage. Cross-gender hormone therapy, which promotes the growth of secondary sex characteristics in the desired gender, allows the adolescent to mature in a way that is developmentally in line with their peers.

After extensively detailing the possible risks in the use of these medications to treat other conditions, Sills states that, with consent, parents have to be willing to live with uncertainty, though they can perhaps be comforted in the belief that the immediate and future mental health benefits may outweigh any longer-term negative health consequences.

As a physician, her commitment to "relieve pain and suffering" is a guiding medical principle that she aptly applies to all aspects of her practice, including her work with transgender youth.

Damien Riggs brings a breadth of knowledge and experience as a clinician, a researcher, and an academician to "Discussing Aspects of Medical Transition with the Parents of Young Transgender People." His is foremost a child-centered orientation, subtly shifting the balance of power between parent and child in order to ensure a protected space for his young patients, simultaneously reaching for a more open, collaborative relationship among child, parents, and himself. While clearly delineating the more concrete dimensions of his role vis-à-vis the medical system — exploring the family's expectations and helping them readjust those if necessary, clarifying the physician's function and purpose, teaching them ways to interact with the medical establishment, encouraging the gathering of information, making referrals, advocating, and being a conduit between the doctor and the family — he expands relevant clinical discussion to include the psychomedical aspects of the body, all while being mindful of and placing the work squarely *in* the current sociopolitical climate. Though he encourages parents to probe and understand their feelings, thoughts, and attitudes, those efforts must always be *in the service of* supporting the child and facilitating the transition.

Carolyn Wolf-Gould builds a compelling argument for the expansion of clinical practice beyond the typical illness-driven or preventative models of care, given the complexities of treating gender nonconforming and transgender youth and their families. Her "fresh paradigm" requires, at the very least, a three-pronged approach: (1) an in-depth knowledge of puberty suppression and gender-affirming hormone therapy; (2) an awareness of the ripple effects these treatments have on the family, the school, and the community; and (3) a willingness and a capacity to work collaboratively with professionals from other disciplines who are concurrently treating the adolescent and their family. Her article "Family-Oriented Medical Care for Gender Nonconforming Children, Adolescents, and Their Families" is a formidable mix of theory and practice, clearly articulating — step by step — the breadth and scope of her vision, the passion for her work shining through on every page. Why so many of her patients come from miles away to access care at the Gender Wellness Center in rural upstate New York is obvious.

C.V.R. could not have anticipated how the next few years of her life would unfold when she was invited to her (then) son Daniel's therapy session where he disclosed he was transgender. Her response that day captures the place many parents find themselves: a desire to be a loving, nurturing presence, but limited by their lack of knowledge and experience, which is further complicated by a fear for their child's safety and future.

Having successfully navigated Daniel's coming out as a gay man three years earlier *might have* prepared the mother in some way for this new reality. Experiencing the trials and tribulations of her (now) daughter Annie's transition, including outrage at the ways Annie was treated in public spaces after beginning hormone treatment, her suicidal threat, disclosure that she had been raped, and the necessity for a second surgery after complications developed from the first one, *might have* strengthened the mother's capacity to confront the next reality: Annie's drug addiction.

"When My Son Became My Daughter" is a story of unconditional love of a parent for her child. Out of a series of major crises, both mother and daughter grew separately as individuals and grew together as family, preparing the way for the next set of challenges life inevitably has in store.

13

But Doc, Is It Safe?
Effects of Pubertal Suppression and
Trans Hormone Therapy for Youth

Irene N. Sills, MD

Reports of medical and psychological interventions that support transition of gender dysphoric children and transgender adolescents are being published, the results of which show clear benefits to mental health. Providing cross-gender hormones to youth in later adolescence who have been carefully evaluated is likewise proving to be optimal for future adult life.

Despite overwhelmingly positive outcomes, parents and guardians remain concerned about the potential ill effects of stopping puberty in their young adolescents and/or giving older adolescents gender-affirming hormone therapy.

Positive Effects of Medical Interventions

There are two kinds of medical interventions I will discuss: (1) treating gender dysphoric adolescents in early puberty with puberty suppression, and (2) treating older adolescents with cross-gender hormone therapy. Note that no medical interventions are provided for children before the onset of puberty.

The positive effects of early puberty suppression include buying time for youth to explore their evolving gender identity and to assess whether eventual gender reassignment is appropriate. Research has shown that the development of puberty in the direction of their natal body often causes great emotional distress and potential long-term psychological harm that can frequently be alleviated by the suppression of biological puberty (de Vries, Steensma, Doreleijers, & Cohen-Kettenis, 2011). Additionally, for those adolescents who do transition, delay in the growth of secondary sex characteristics will assist them in passing better in their chosen gender expression (deVries & Cohen-Kettenis, 2012). Beginning

Medical knowledge is continuously growing in this field and readers should be certain to seek out the most recent studies.

Lev, Arlene I., Gottlieb, Andrew R., *Families in Transition*
dx.doi.org/10.17312/harringtonparkpress/2019.04.fit.013
© 2019 by Harrington Park Press

cross-gender hormones will allow their socialization, including dating, to occur naturally during adolescence, that life-cycle stage suitable for the exploration of sexuality and gender (Lev, 2004).

Gooren and Delemarre-van de Waal noted as early as 1996 that many adult transsexuals remember puberty as a very painful time when their maturing bodies were at odds with their gender identity. Gender-related violence resulting in high levels of depression has been noted in transgender youth (Nuttbrock et al., 2010). Puberty-blocking treatments followed by cross-sex hormones may lower the psychosocial stresses and ameliorate many consequent mental health problems: "Despite the understandable concern about potential harm that could be done by early physical medical interventions, it seems currently that withholding intervention is even more harmful for the adolescents' wellbeing during adolescence and in adulthood" (de Vries & Cohen-Kettenis, 2012, p. 315).

Potential Concerns of Medical Interventions

The concern in providing medical interventions for children and teens with gender dysphoria is the lack of evidence supporting the lifelong safety of these treatments. Few long-term studies have been done to evaluate the physical health consequences. These therapies are relatively new and are only now being offered in numbers that allow data collection and analysis. The first published report of the outcome of a patient 22 years after receiving pubertal-suppression medication and trans hormone therapy reveals a lack of any long-term harm (Cohen-Kettenis, Schagen, Steensma, de Vries, & Delemarre-van de Waal, 2011). Without the benefit of more longitudinal data, there remains some degree of risk in taking these medications.

In an attempt to ensure safety, screening for potential side effects of puberty-suppression medication is based on the known risks of patients who need puberty suppression for other medical conditions. These concerns may or may not apply to this population, but progress in medicine always starts with what is already known. Knowledge about the side effects of hormone therapy in adolescents and young adults who have needed sex steroids for other conditions guides screening for physical harm in adolescents who are taking cross-sex hormones. Although health-care providers harbor concerns about long-term safety, an increasing number are proceeding with prescribing the medications because we understand the mental health distress that remains if we do nothing.

An excellent review of the current knowledge of the risks of hormone therapy is available (Coleman et al., 2012). My article will highlight some of the concerns that I, as a pediatric endocrinologist, bring to this field seeking to answer parents' questions.

Pubertal Suppression

Ms. K. brings her 11-year-old daughter, Lisa, to see me with concerns about the child's recent behavior. Lisa has always been a happy child, who routinely engages in sports with the neighborhood kids and with her brothers. She is now sullen and has lost her "spark." After a complete history is taken and a physical examination performed, I tell her mom that she has started puberty because I can palpate breast buds. This news makes her mom proud but her daughter angry and sad; the daughter insists, "I wants to cut off my breasts," and believes she is not really a girl but a boy. She and her mother were referred to a mental health therapist for evaluation for pubertal suppression.

As this case illustrates, children with gender dysphoria often sense their greatest unease when puberty begins, which is possibly indicative of the veracity of their gender incongruence. As stated, medical treatment that suppresses puberty can help the child avoid experiencing the physical signs and symptoms of puberty in the undesired gender, which allows time for them to mature and explore their options for gender expression. Mental health therapists can monitor the persistence of their gender dysphoria as they age and assess their suitability for long-term cross-gender hormone therapy.

Pediatric endocrinologists have been prescribing medication to suppress puberty since the 1960s in children of both genders who begin puberty significantly earlier than their peers. In the 1980s a more efficacious group of medications, gonadotropin-releasing hormone (GnRH) analogs, were developed and continue to be used; these block the receptors of cells that release pituitary hormones that stimulate gonads (ovaries and testes) to make pubertal hormones (estrogen and testosterone). By administering this medication as a periodic injection, a nasal inhalant, or a skin-embedded implant, precocious puberty may be "turned off" until the age at which a child is deemed old enough to reenter it. Since the early part of the twenty-first century, experience has been accumulating with the use of this class of medications to treat gender dysphoria and validating its psychological benefits (Cohen-Kettenis, Delemarre-van de Waal, & Gooren, 2008).

Pubertal suppression for those with precocious puberty has been generally found to be safe and effective and is usually well tolerated in children and adolescents (Carel, Eugster, Rogol, Ghizzoni, & Palmert, 2009). Pubertal suppression at a "normal" pubertal age, or for conditions other than precocious puberty, however, has not been widely studied. In 2009 the Lawson Wilkins Pediatric Endocrine Society and the European Society for Paediatric Endocrinology convened a consensus conference to review the clinical use of puberty suppression for children and adolescents and concluded that further investigation is needed before these treatments are routinely suggested for conditions other than precocious puberty (Carel et al., 2009).

Puberty suppression presents some concerns about long-term physical health, including (a) the effect on the pubertal growth spurt; (b) the effect on bone health when children do not make the sex steroids at the usual ages that lead to the final phase of bone mineral accrual; and (c) the effect on a developing brain that typically matures in a hormonal milieu of sex steroids. Last, this category of medication is quite expensive and insurance companies are not routinely covering it. The hopeful news is that more health care insurers are being successfully petitioned to underwrite the costs. Each of these concerns is discussed below.

Growth: One medical concern of taking a blocker is the inhibition of the growth spurt that occurs in puberty that may affect eventual adult stature. Pubertal growth accounts for 15% of the total final adult height and occurs mostly as a result of the pubertal growth spurt. Estrogen from the ovaries in natal females and by biochemical conversion of testosterone from the testes in natal males is a crucial factor for the accelerated growth during this period and eventual growth-plate fusion when adult height is attained. The growth spurt is an early pubertal event in female development coinciding clinically with the onset of breast development. In boys it occurs an average of two years after girls and is a late pubertal event coinciding with attainment of midpuberty-sized testicular volume.

In the first 21 patients who were treated at the Amsterdam Gender Identity Clinic with GnRH analogs, a decrease in height velocity was found (Delemarre-van de Waal & Cohen-Kettenis, 2006). Body proportions as measured by sitting height and sitting-height/height ratio remained in the normal range. The presumption is that there will be "catch-up" growth when the pubertal suppression is stopped or when the appropriate sex steroid is added for cross-hormone treatment; however, that remains to be validated in studies with adequate numbers of patients. For many male-to-female patients, a shortened adult height may be viewed as a benefit.

Bone health: Another concern of puberty suppression has been its effect on bone mass, which increases dramatically during childhood and adolescence and peaks in young adulthood. Bone mass is accrued during adolescence and is enhanced by sex steroids. Research shows that adolescent girls treated with intramuscular progesterone for contraception have decreased serum estrogen levels and decreased bone mineral density when compared to their peers (Kaunitz, Arias, & McClung, 2008). In 2004 this led to a federally mandated label warning about the risk of bone demineralization in those taking only progesterone-containing contraception. Follow-up studies have shown, however, that bone mineral density increases and reverts to normal when the progesterone is stopped (Kaunitz, Arias, & McClung, 2008). The data from a Dutch cohort of adolescents who had been treated with GnRH analogs suggest that, after an initial slowing down, bone accretion significantly catches up after cross-sex steroid hormone treatment is begun (Delemarre-van de Waal & Cohen-Kettenis, 2006). These are reassuring data, but they await further confirmation in other studies.

Brain development: The period of puberty has been long known to be associated with dramatic changes in psychological development. Anatomical changes in brains have been seen through noninvasive brain imaging, especially magnetic resonance imaging (MRI). A recently published review discusses the potential role of sex steroids in promoting or facilitating these changes, pointing out that the effects of sex steroids on brain structures have been best studied in animal models (Blakemore, Burnett, & Dahl, 2010). It is not clear at this point what stopping puberty in pubertal-aged children may or may not do to brain structures and what that may mean for a child's development.

Recommendations for the timing to begin pubertal suppression have varied. Although some have advocated for waiting until an adolescent has gone through natal puberty for at least a year, others have proposed pubertal cessation at the onset of puberty. The medication can be continued until gonadectomy is performed when the youth becomes a young adult, but often it is discontinued when an adolescent begins trans hormone therapy. The age to begin trans hormone therapy has been 16 years. This recommendation, however, is being challenged by many medical providers and parents who feel that starting pubertal hormones at earlier ages allows pubertal development to proceed more closely parallel to that of the child's peers.

Feminizing Hormone Therapy

Tony, a 16-year-old boy, was brought to see me because his parents were concerned that he may have a "hormone imbalance." His mother remembered that, as a young child, he played with dolls with the neighborhood girls. His favorite movies were about princesses. She thought he might be gay because, during early adolescence, he was more interested in designing sets for his school play than trying out for the sports teams. In the previous six months, however, Tony had read an article about transgender people, and his response to this was, "I really want to live my life as a woman." His parents wondered if his chromosomes or his hormones were "off." An evaluation yielded no hormonal or genetic findings that indicated an endocrine or genetic disorder. He was then assessed by a mental health clinician, who concluded that he was an excellent candidate for cross-gender hormone therapy.

The male hormone testosterone is a powerful virilizing steroid. That makes it difficult to overcome its physical effects with feminizing estrogen therapy in those adolescents who have not received pubertal suppression. The doses of estrogen required are four to six times higher than the doses given to a natal girl adolescent who does not have ovarian function (Hembree et al., 2009). Estrogen may be prescribed as a pill, a patch, or an intramuscular injection. The progression is to start with low dosing and increase according to the measured blood level of estradiol. For example, if a 16-year-old starts estrogen, they will be prescribed a lower dose and increase quickly. If the patient is 14 years old, I might increase more slowly. Natal women have cyclic levels of estrogen that vary every four weeks in a recurring pattern. Trans women receive a single dose of estrogen that maintains it at a constant level.

Spironolactone is also part of feminizing therapy. It is an antihypertensive agent that was recognized to perhaps decrease testosterone production and have blocking effects at the receptor for testosterone. It is the only "testosterone blocker" that is available in the United States, although there are other options in other countries.

The addition of progestin in trans feminizing therapy is controversial. Some providers advocate its use for improved breast development. A report of the comparison of feminizing regimens with and without progestin found that its addition did not enhance breast growth (Meyer et al., 1986). There are concerns about the potential side effects of progestin use, including weak androgen receptor stimulation; depression, weight gain, and lipid changes (Tangpricha, Ducharme, Barber, & Chipkin, 2003). In a large-scale study of postmenopausal hormone use in women, the combination of estrogen and progestin seemed to be associated with a higher incidence of breast cancer (Chlebowski et al., 2003). Data on the effects of hormone treatment of the postmenopausal population are not strictly applicable to trans women because they differ in many respects, such as their pretransitioning exposure to years of testosterone production. Warnings gleaned from this population may serve as possible alerts for the trans women community, however.

Tony's parents recognized his interest in traditionally female pursuits and assumed those were related to his sexuality. When Tony first began to talk about living as a woman, his parents thought there was something "off" about his hormones. As an endocrinologist, I was able to reassure them that their child's natal male body was functioning fine. They were eventually able to accept that Tony, now identifying as Donna, was actually transgender. I prescribed this now-19-year-old increasing doses of estrogen and spironolactone and, after three years, she reports decreased facial hair, more hip fat than abdominal fat, increasing breast size, and softer skin. She was satisfied with the physical changes to her body.

But Doc, Is It Safe?

As stated earlier, there are no longitudinal studies of youth starting cross-sex hormones and maintaining them for decades. The only research we have is on those who began treatment as adults. It is important to note that as this research has expanded in recent decades, many treatment protocols have changed, including dosages and methods of administration, which has lowered some of the risks.

The main safety concerns of feminizing therapy with estrogen are the risk of a blood clot or embolus from high-dose estrogen, worsening cardiovascular disease, a rise in serum prolactin, liver damage, premature closure of epiphyses in adolescents with growth stunting, and future prostate and breast malignancies. Each of these is reviewed. Prescribers should be aware of potential clinically significant interactions between estrogen and other medications: anticonvulsants (decreased estrogen effect), rifampin (decreased estrogen effect), and corticosteroids (increased corticosteroid effect).

Blood clotting: The use of estrogen for contraception and other medical problems in otherwise healthy adolescent girls includes a risk of blood clotting. Most providers advocate the use of estrogen for appropriate indications, however, because the benefit of its use outweighs the risks. The risks of blood clots causing stroke, pulmonary embolus, and venous thrombosis may be mitigated by not smoking tobacco and the type of estrogen used. Anyone taking estrogen of any type is advised to cease smoking cigarettes, although there is no way for a physician to completely monitor whether patients are complying with this advice. It has been established that of the choices for estrogen therapy, oral ethinyl estradiol increases the possibility of blood clots (Toorians et al., 2003), so this form of estrogen is no longer recommended for trans women. The most commonly prescribed estrogen is oral estradiol. A study reported good news: only 1% of adults developed venous clots of 1,076 subjects followed for 5.4 years

(Asscheman et al., 2014). The recommendations were to avoid oral ethinyl estradiol, stop all estrogen treatment at least two weeks before any elective surgery, and resume estrogen only after complete mobility has been established.

Cardiovascular disease: Risk for cardiovascular disease multiplies with unhealthy lipid levels, increased weight, decreased insulin sensitivity, and diabetes mellitus. In a well-constructed table, Gooren, Giltay, and Bunck (2008) summarize the changes in cardiovascular risk reported in six studies of trans women who were treated with feminizing hormone therapy. Weight, body mass index, total body fat, and visceral fat increased during treatment. These physical findings led to increased risk for the metabolic syndrome that a group of clinical findings associated with a greater likelihood for developing cardiovascular disease in any population. Fasting insulin levels increased—a future risk factor for type 2 diabetes—while insulin sensitivity decreased (Elbers et al., 2003). LDL cholesterol levels decreased (Elbers et al., 2003), and lower LDL cholesterol levels are cardio protective. One study showed slight elevation in blood pressure among trans women (Giltay et al., 1999). Another study reports that the incidence of myocardial infarction in 214 trans women who were treated with estrogen for 7.4 years matched that of natal males but exceeded that of natal females (Wierckx et al., 2013). There are not sufficient studies looking at youth who begin estrogen therapy in their teens that address the odds for developing cardiovascular disease in later life. It therefore is important that patients are encouraged to adopt lifestyles at all ages that promote healthy weight and fitness to lower any as-yet-undetermined risk from trans hormone therapy.

Elevated prolactin levels: Prolactin is a hormone from the pituitary gland that is important for establishing lactation in cisgender women who have delivered newborns and will be nourishing them with breast milk. Its secretion from pituitary cells is promoted by high levels of serum estrogen circulating during gestation and in the postpartum period. There have been reports of the development of elevated prolactin levels (Nota et al., 2017) and benign prolactin-secreting adenomas in the pituitary gland (prolactinomas) after high-dose estrogen administration in trans patients with normal serum prolactin concentrations before therapy (Gooren, Assies, Asscheman, de Slegte, & van Kessel, 1988; Serri, Noiseux, Robert, & Hardy, 1996). These small pituitary tumors are usually treated in males and females with years of oral medication intended to shrink their size and decrease the level of serum prolactin. Elevated prolactin levels in usual circumstances will inhibit sex steroid production. In trans patients with elevated prolactin levels, estrogen doses must be lowered since the prolactin-induced tumors can grow to large sizes and, although not malignant, can cause impingement on the optic nerves and affect sight.

Liver damage: Estrogen therapy is associated with several liver-related complications, including cholestasis (bile duct disease) and gallstones. These side effects are more common with higher doses of estrogens, which were used in the early high-dose estrogen formulation of oral contraceptives, but they have also been described with the use of birth control pills with low-dose estrogen. Liver function test results may be mildly abnormal in patients receiving estrogen therapy (American Society of Health System Pharmacists, 2014) and this has been reported transiently in trans women (Wierckx et al., 2014). Since the change is only transient, it is not a worrisome side effect.

Premature closure of epiphyses: Estrogen is key in growth-plate fusion, and an excess will cause fusion earlier than would have occurred naturally. Estrogen therapy started at 16 years (beyond the average male adolescent growth spurt at 13–14 years in natal boys) is likely to have minimal effects on height. Some adult shortening of height might be viewed as a benefit since natal women are on average shorter that natal men.

Future risks of malignancies: A concern regarding long-term administration of cross-gender hormones is the possibility of an increased risk of hormone-dependent cancers later in life. There are reports of breast cancer occurring in trans women (Ganly & Taylor, 1995; Gooren, Bowers, Lips, & Konigs, 2015; Pritchard, Pankowsky, Crowe, & Abdul-Karim, 1988) and reports of prostate cancer in trans women taking estrogen (Dorff, Shazer, Nepomuceno, & Tucker, 2007; Turo, Jallad, Prescott, & Cross, 2013; Van Haarst, Newling, Gooren, Asscheman, & Prenger, 1998). Three of the patients were over 50 years of age when they started trans hormone therapy. Experience has shown that estrogen therapy with androgen deprivation usually does not increase the risk of prostate cancer (Van Kesteren et al., 1996), and the prostate cancer may not have been caused at all by the estrogen therapy initiated after 50 years of age. One report, however, describes a trans woman who had sex-reassignment surgery, which included bilateral orchiectomy at age 45 years, and was diagnosed with metastatic prostate cancer after thirty years of cross-hormone therapy (Turo et al., 2013).

Rare cases of hormone-dependent tumors in organs other than the reproductive organs—for example, lung, colon, and brain (meningioma)—have also been reported in transsexuals who have undergone estrogen treatment (Knight & McDonald, 2013). Mueller and Gooren (2008) conclude that although there is little evidence that trans hormonal treatment increases cancer risk, the available data are from studies that looked at relatively short-term exposure. As subjects age and the duration of hormone exposure increases, the risks may increase.

Spironolactone adverse effects: Possible adverse effects of spironolactone include high serum potassium levels, particularly when the medication is given with other medications that tend to promote high potassium, in which case, adjustments in dose may need to be made. There are no long-term risks known in trans patients who take this medication.

Overall mortality: In a report published by Asscheman and colleagues in 2011, the total mortality rate in 966 trans women who had started trans hormone therapy before July 1997 was "51% higher than in the general population, mainly due to suicide, acquired immunodeficiency syndrome, cardiovascular disease, drug abuse, and unknown cause[s]. No increase was observed in total cancer mortality, but lung and hematological cancer mortality rates were elevated. Current, but not past ethinyl estradiol use was associated with an independent threefold increased risk of cardiovascular death" (p. 635). Although these rates are concerning, there is some comfort in learning that the hormone therapy did not appear to be directly linked.

Monitoring for safety: To assist in monitoring for adverse effects, baseline values should be recorded for lipid profile, fasting blood glucose (and hemoglobin A1c if diabetes or glucose intolerance is suspected), liver enzymes, prolactin, electrolytes, urea, and creatinine. Ongoing monitoring once therapy has begun should include follow-up of these same parameters. A 2009 publication of the Endocrine Society provides practice guidelines for endocrine treatment of trans adolescents and adults and includes detailed monitoring protocols (Hembree et al., 2009). Ongoing surveillance will lead to "fine-tuning" of the optimal monitoring regimens. Monitoring for breast malignancy in trans women with no increased risk for breast cancer includes following the guidelines for natal women and for prostate cancer using screening guidelines in natal men (Hembree et al., 2009).

Donna returns for medical follow-up every six months and reports that she has become a vegetarian, does not smoke cigarettes, is an occasional cannabis user, and is exercising a few times a week. In monitoring Donna's medical care, particularly the side effects of estrogen and spironolactone, there have been no worrisome laboratory findings. She is planning to have genital reconstruction surgery when she can accumulate sufficient funds.

Masculinizing Hormone Therapy

Nancy, a 16-year-old girl with type 1 diabetes since age 10, who was my patient for diabetes treatment, was admitted to the hospital after she tried to commit suicide by standing in front of a moving truck. She was bruised but had no crush injuries. A medi-

ocre student who made only minimal efforts to care for her diabetes, Nancy was trans-
ferred to the psychiatry unit after stabilization of her diabetes, where she received a
thorough psychological assessment, including questions about sexual and gender iden-
tity. The assessment revealed considerable gender dysphoria, and Nancy began outpa-
tient therapy to address these concerns. She was then referred back to me for masculinizing
therapy as well as continued treatment of her diabetes. Nancy changed his name to
Adam, began receiving testosterone injections regularly, and is happy about transitioning.
But he continues to struggle with managing both his diabetes and his ongoing feelings of
depression, for which he receives mental health treatment.

Testosterone is such a powerful masculinizing agent that natal women can be virilized without using doses any higher than one would for a natal adolescent male who has poor or no testicular function. Testosterone therapy may be given as an injection either intramuscularly or subcutaneously, as a gel, as a patch, and most recently as implanted beads. Androgen preparations that are administered intramuscularly and transdermally with patches or gel instead of oral pills minimize risk of liver damage. Because intramuscular androgen preparations are administered intermittently, some people may notice cyclic variation in effects—for example, fatigue and irritability at the end of the injection cycle or aggression or expansive mood at the beginning of the injection cycle. This may be mitigated by using a more frequent dosage schedule—weekly rather than every two weeks—or by using a transdermal preparation.

Low doses of testosterone are started and increased according to the serum testosterone level that is well characterized for pubertal males and adult men. The main short-term adverse physical concern is the development of acne, which can be managed as it is with any adolescent. Eventually the monthly uterine bleeding ceases, though it may distressingly reappear after a time before it ceases completely. Since testosterone therapy rarely begins before menarche in a natal girl, the potential for premature fusion of the epiphyses and growth stunting is negligible; the growth plates are usually fused by the time the testosterone is started. With increasing availability of GnRH analogs, there could be an argument made to continue pubertal suppression longer and start testosterone therapy later in the hope of increasing stature. Testosterone increases serum levels of anticoagulants and sulfonylureas (blood sugar–lowering drugs for diabetes), and drug interactions should always be checked as one would for any pharmaceutical prescribed.

Progestins are not typically included in trans male endocrine therapy, but they can be used for a short period to assist with menstrual cessation. Depo-Provera, an intramuscular progestin used as a birth control, can be given by intramuscular injection (150 mg every three months) to stop menses either before or concurrent with starting testosterone. These injections are usually stopped after three to six months on testosterone.

Adam, now 17 years old, has had increasing facial hair growth and more muscle mass, but his depression and anxiety have not abated. He has no regrets about hormone therapy and feels certain that this was the correct decision to treat his gender dysphoria. However, he still struggles with suicidal feelings, specifically the urge to overdose on his insulin, but fortunately he continues to receive counseling.

But Doc, Is It Safe?

The main concerns for safety in treating FTM patients are increased chances for cardiovascular disease, liver damage, the increase in hemoglobin level, and future risks in breast, uterine, and ovarian malignancies. The increase in hemoglobin level will occur soon after starting testosterone, but the other concerns are lifelong and may begin in the young adult years.

Cardiovascular disease: The likelihood of cardiovascular disease is increased in those with elevated lipid levels, hypertension, and diabetes mellitus. Since the risk is higher in natal men than natal women, the thought was that testosterone therapy would increase the chance for disease in trans men. An excellent review of six studies is detailed by Gooren and Giltay (2008) and shows no increase in rates of cardiovascular disease for trans men as compared to age-matched subjects, despite the fact that testosterone therapy is associated with an increase in weight, BMI, and visceral fat. Androgen use may decrease the "good" HDL cholesterol and thereby increase risk. There has been shown, however, to only be a slight decrease in insulin sensitivity and increased cardiovascular disease risk and no change in blood pressure. More recently, Wierckx and colleagues (2013) found no increased chance of cardiovascular disease compared to male controls. Encouraging trans men to adopt lifestyles that promote healthy weight and fitness is key.

Liver damage: Intramuscular, subcutaneous, and cutaneous testosterone will minimize the liver's exposure to the hormone and decrease the risk of any serious adverse hepatic effects. It has been reported, however, that trans males will have transient elevation in liver enzymes (Van Kesteren, Asscheman, Megens, & Gooren, 1997; Wierckx et al., 2014), which is not concerning if the elevation is only transient. Sustained elevations in liver enzymes may indicate liver dysfunction.

Hemoglobin level: There are case reports of polycythemia (elevated red blood cells) in non–trans men treated with androgens (Viallard et al., 2000). Wierckx et al. (2014) reported two trans men who had nonworrisome elevated red-cell levels out of a population of 53 subjects. It is important that a trans man who may already have elevated hemoglobin levels due to, for instance, respiratory disease, be identified before beginning testosterone therapy.

Risk of future malignancies: A concern regarding long-term administration of cross-sex hormones is the heightened possibility of cancers in breasts, ovaries, and uterus that might be increased because of testosterone exposure. There have been rare reports of ovarian, breast, and vaginal cancers in trans males. The biochemical conversion of testosterone to estrogen in many organs in the body may increase the chance of malignancy in patients with a strong family history of cancers that grow faster in the presence of estrogen. Breast cancer has been reported in a 33-year-old trans male after bilateral mastectomy while receiving treatment with testosterone (Burcombe, Makris, Pittam, & Finer, 2003). This occurred in residual mammary tissue after 10 years of treatment with testosterone. An additional two trans males have also been reported to have breast cancer (Gooren et al., 2015).

There is concern about the possibility of uterine cancer in trans men who do not have a hysterectomy (Futterweit & Deligdisch, 1986); this concern is based on the known risk of uterine cancer in women with polycystic ovarian syndrome who do not have regular menses. Polycystic ovarian syndrome is characterized by infrequent menses, excessive weight, and vulnerability to type 2 diabetes. Women with polycystic ovarian syndrome may have excessive virilizing hormones and do not have the usual fluctuating estrogen levels during a 28-day cycle. The constant estrogen elevation causes the uterine lining to become hyperplastic and predisposes to uterine cancer. The uterus in a trans man is exposed to highly virilizing hormones that may be metabolized to estrogen but not to directly elevated estrogen levels, so the analogy may not apply.

Ovarian cancer has been reported in trans men (Dizon, Tejada-Berges, Koelliker, Steinhoff, & Granai, 2006; Hage, Dekker, Karim, Verheijen, & Bloemena, 2000). Ovaries exposed to higher-than-typical female levels of testosterone may develop polycystic features that are sometimes seen in polycystic ovarian syndrome. Ovaries in trans men have shown polycystic features (Gooren & Giltay, 2008), but there is no documented evidence of this leading to ovarian cancer.

At this time the evidence indicates that shorter-term testosterone exposure is not associated with significant increase in risk of malignancy. Beginning testosterone therapy during adolescence and the early twenties, however, may or may not change this outcome. This generation of young people starting cross-gender hormone therapy will be the first to take it for a lifetime, which may alter the long-term outcomes that have been reported only in adults starting hormone therapy as adults.

Overall mortality: In the report cited earlier (Asscheman et al., 2011), in which 365 trans men started trans hormone therapy before July 1997, total mortality was not significantly different from that in the general population.

Monitoring for safety: To assist in monitoring adverse effects, baseline values should be recorded for lipid profile, fasting glucose (and hemoglobin A1c if there is a high risk for diabetes and glucose intolerance), complete blood count, and liver enzymes. Ongoing monitoring once therapy has begun should include follow-up of these same parameters. A 2009 publication of the Endocrine Society provides practice guidelines for endocrine treatment of trans adolescents and adults and includes detailed monitoring protocols (Hembree et al., 2009). Since a portion of administered testosterone is metabolized by many organs in the body to estradiol, female-to-male transsexuals who have not had breast removal and oophorectomy/hysterectomy should be monitored for estrogen-sensitive cancers of the breast, endometrium, and ovaries (Hembree et al., 2009). With ongoing surveillance, the optimal monitoring regimens will be refined.

Adam, now 18 years old, has been monitored for the side effects of testosterone and has not developed any worrisome laboratory tests. His diabetes, however, remains poorly regulated, and he has had three additional in-patient psychiatric admissions.

Suppression of Future Reproduction Capability

There have been no studies that offer guidance on the effects of long-term trans hormone therapy on the ability to reproduce with one's own genetic material after the trans hormones are stopped for a period. Natal boys who have progressed to mid-male puberty and are able to ejaculate are encouraged to bank sperm for potential future use. Natal girls who have reached menarche are encouraged to bank eggs or ovarian tissue to be saved for future use. The latter recommendation, however, is often not practical because of the expense of the procedure, the potential discomfort to the adolescent, and the relative lack of encouraging results when ova or ovarian tissue is banked, as opposed to fertilized embryos. This is an ongoing area of research, as there are many adolescent girls who are treated for cancer and lose ovarian function but wish to reproduce later with their own ova.

Parents, physicians, and mental health providers understand how little adolescents can anticipate how they will feel about the importance of biologically producing a child in later years, although this must be discussed before initiating hormone therapy. The termination of reproductive rights is a serious and complex bioethical issue, and the question of whether adolescents are capable of fully informed consent remains a controversial subject. Nonetheless, this is a necessary conversation to have with youth and their parents by both the therapist and the physician. The options to become a parent by adoption or partnering with an adult who is already a parent, or who is willing to become one, must be accepted as a possible outcome of trans hormone therapy.

So Why Does a Doctor Advise Parents to Take These Risks?

Medical professionals have always practiced the dictum "Physician do no harm" with the added instruction to "Relieve pain and suffering." These are the two ends of the risk-to-benefit ratio that physicians are constantly evaluating when they prescribe any drug or treatment program. Caring for children needing pubertal suppression and trans hormone therapy is another situation in which physicians believe that the benefit to a child's mental health and future adult functioning will outweigh any risks involved in prescribing these drugs. Recommendations for monitoring possible medical complications are comprehensive and are being provided with utmost care and attention by medical providers trained in trans health care. Parents must understand the mental health benefit and be willing to accept the unknown. Pubertal suppression allows a child to avoid developing physical features in the unwanted gender, and hormone therapy supports full feminization or masculinization, both enormous benefits to children who suffer from gender dysphoria.

Future generations will benefit from what we now learn about treating this generation of youth. I am confident that, on the basis of current studies that show mental health benefits, what we are doing is right for these children. That is how I answer parents who want to know: "But Doc, is it safe?"

REFERENCES

American Society of Health System Pharmacists. (2014). *AHFS drug information.*

Asscheman, H., Giltay, E. J., Megens, J. A. J., de Ronde W., van Trotsenburg, M. A. A., & Gooren, L. J. G. (2011). A long-term follow-up study of mortality in transsexuals receiving treatment with cross-sex hormones. *European Journal of Endocrinology, 164,* 635–642.

Asscheman, H., T'Sjoen, G., Lemaire, A., Mas, M., Meriggiola, M. C., Mueller, A., Kuhn, A., . . . & Gooren, L. J. (2014). Venous thrombo-embolism as a complication of cross-sex hormone treatment of male-to-female transsexual subjects: A review. *Andrologia, 46,* 791–795.

Blakemore, S., Burnett, S., & Dahl, R. E. (2010). The role of puberty in the developing adolescent brain. *Human Brain Mapping, 31,* 926–933.

Burcombe, R. J., Makris, A., Pittam, M., & Finer, N. (2003). Breast cancer after bilateral subcutaneous mastectomy in a female-to-male trans-sexual. *Breast, 12,* 290–293.

Carel, J. C., Eugster, E., Rogol, A., Ghizzoni, L., & Palmert, M. (2009). Consensus statement on the use of gonadotropin-releasing hormone analogs in children. *Pediatrics, 123* (4), e752–762.

Chlebowski, R. T., Hendrix, S. L., Langer, R. D., Stefanick, M. L., Gass, M., Lane, D., . . . & McTiernan, A. (2003). Influence of estrogen plus progestin on breast cancer and mammography in healthy postmenopausal women: The Women's Health Initiative randomized trial. *Journal of the American Medical Association, 289,* 3243–3253.

Cohen-Kettenis, P. T., Delemarre-van de Waal, H. A., & Gooren, L. J. G. (2008). The treatment of adolescent transsexuals: Changing insights. *Journal of Sexual Medicine, 5,* 1892–1897.

Cohen-Kettenis, P. T., Schagen, S. E. E., Steensma, T. D., de Vries, A. L. C., & Delemarre-van de Waal, H. A. (2011). Puberty suppression in a gender-dysphoric adolescent: A 22-year follow-up. *Archives of Sexual Behavior, 40,* 843–847.

Coleman, E., Bockting, W., Botzem, M., Cohen-Kettenis, P., DeCuypere, G., Feldman, J., . . . & Zucker, K. (2012). Standards of Care for the health of transsexual, transgender, and gender-nonconforming people, Version 7. *International Journal of Transgenderism, 13* (4), 165–232.

Delemarre-van de Waal, H. A., & Cohen-Kettenis, P. T. (2006). Clinical management of gender identity disorder in adolescents: A protocol on psychological and paediatric endocrinology aspects. *European Journal of Endocrinology, 155,* S131–S137.

de Vries, A. L. C., & Cohen-Kettenis, P. T. (2012). Clinical management of gender dysphoria in children and adolescents: The Dutch approach. *Journal of Homosexuality, 59,* 301–320.

de Vries, A. L., Steensma, T. D., Doreleijers, T. A., & Cohen-Kettenis, P. T. (2011). Puberty suppression in adolescents with gender identity disorder: A prospective follow-up study. *Journal of Sexual Medicine, 8,* 2276–2283.

Dizon, D. S., Tejada-Berges, T., Koelliker, S., Steinhoff, M., & Granai, C. O. (2006). Ovarian cancer associated with testosterone supplementation in a female-to-male transsexual patient. *Gynecologic and Obstetric Investigation, 62* (4), 226–228.

Dorff, T. B., Shazer, R. L., Nepomuceno, E. M., & Tucker, S. J. (2007). Successful treatment of metastatic androgen-independent prostate carcinoma in a transsexual patient. *Clinical Genitourinary Cancer, 5,* 344–346.

Elbers, J. M., Giltay, E. J., Teerlink, T., Scheffer, P. G., Asscheman, H., Seidell, J. C., & Gooren, L. J. (2003). Effects of sex steroids on components of the insulin resistance syndrome in transsexual subjects. *Clinical Endocrinology* (Oxf), *58*, 562–571.

Futterweit, W., & Deligdisch, L. (1986). Histopathological effects of exogenously administered testosterone in 19 female to male transsexuals. *Journal of Clinical Endocrinology and Metabolism, 62*, 16–21.

Ganly, I., & Taylor, E. W. (1995). Breast cancer in a trans-sexual man receiving hormone replacement therapy. *British Journal of Surgery, 82*, 341.

Giltay, E. J., Lambert, J., Gooren, L. J., Elbers, J. M., Steyn, M., & Stehouwer, C. D. (1999). Sex steroids, insulin, and arterial stiffness in women and men. *Hypertension, 34*, 590–597.

Gooren, L. J., Assies, J., Asscheman, H., de Slegte, R., & van Kessel, H. (1988). Estrogen-induced prolactinoma in a man. *Journal of Clinical Endocrinology and Metabolism, 66*, 444–446.

Gooren, L. J., Bowers, M., Lips, P., & Konigs, I. R. (2015). Five new cases of breast cancer in transsexual persons. *Andrologia, 47*, 1202–1205.

Gooren, L., & Delemarre-van de Waal, H. (1996). The feasibility of endocrine interventions in juvenile transsexuals. *Journal of Psychology & Human Sexuality, 8*, 69–74.

Gooren, L. J. G., & Giltay, E. J. (2008). Review of studies of androgen treatment of female-to-male transsexuals: Effects and risks of administration of androgens to females. *Journal of Sexual Medicine, 5*, 765–776.

Gooren L. J., Giltay, E. J., & Bunck, M. C. (2008). Long-term treatment of transsexuals with cross-sex hormones: Extensive personal experience. *Journal of Clinical Endocrinology and Metabolism, 93*, 19–25.

Hage, J. J., Dekker, J. J., Karim, R. B., Verheijen, R. H., & Bloemena, E. (2000). Ovarian cancer in female-to-male transsexuals: Report of two cases. *Gynecologic Oncology, 76*, 413–415.

Hembree, W. C., Cohen-Kettenis, P., Delemare-van de Waal, H. A., Gooren, L. J., Meyer, W. J., Spack, N. P., Tangpricha, V., & Montori, V. M. (2009). Endocrine treatment of transsexual persons: An Endocrine Society clinical practice guideline. *Journal of Clinical Endocrinology and Metabolism, 94*, 3132–3154.

Kaunitz, A. M., Arias, R., & McClung, M. (2008). Bone density recovery after depot medroxyprogesterone acetate injectable contraception use. *Contraception, 77*, 67–76.

Knight, E. J., & McDonald, M. J. (2013). Recurrence and progression of meningioma in male-to-female transgender individuals during exogenous hormone use. *International Journal of Transgenderism, 14*, 18–23.

Lev, A. I. (2004). *Transgender emergence: Therapeutic guidelines for working with gender-variant people and their families.* Binghamton, N.Y.: Haworth Press.

Meyer, W. J., Webb, A., Stuart, C. A., Finkelstein, J. W., Lawrence, B., & Walker, P. A. (1986). Physical and hormonal evaluation of transsexual patients: A longitudinal study. *Archives of Sexual Behavior, 15*, 121–138.

Mueller, A., & Gooren, L. (2008). Hormone-related tumors in transsexuals receiving treatment with cross-sex hormones. *European Journal of Endocrinology, 159*, 197–202.

Nota, N. M., Dekker, M. J. H. J., Klaver, M., Wiepjes, C. M., van Trotsenburg, M. A., Heijboer, A. C., & den Heijer, M. (2017). Prolactin levels during short- and long-term cross-sex hormone treatment: An observational study in transgender persons. *Andrologia, 49* (6).

Nuttbrock, L., Hwahng, S., Bockting, W., Rosenblum, A., Mason, M., Macri, M., & Becker, J. (2010). Psychiatric impact of gender-related abuse across the life course of male-to-female transgender persons. *Journal of Sex Research, 41* (1), 12–23.

Pritchard, T. J., Pankowsky, D. A., Crowe, J. P., & Abdul-Karim, F. W. (1988). Breast cancer in a male-to-female transsexual. A case report. *Journal of the American Medical Association, 259,* 2278–2280.

Serri, O., Noiseux, D., Robert, F., & Hardy, J. (1996). Lactotroph hyperplasia in an estrogen treated male-to-female transsexual patient. *Journal of Clinical Endocrinology and Metabolism, 81,* 3177–3179.

Tangpricha, V., Ducharme, S. H., Barber, T. W., & Chipkin, S. R. (2003). Endocrinologic treatment of gender identity disorders. *Endocrine Practice, 9,* 12–21.

Toorians, A. W., Thomassen, M. C., Zweegman, S., Magdeleyns, E. J., Tans, G., Gooren, L. J. G., & Rosing, J. (2003). Venous thrombosis and changes of hemostatic variables during cross-sex hormone treatment in transsexual people. *Journal of Clinical Endocrinology & Metabolism, 88,* 5723–5729.

Turo, R., Jallad S., Prescott S., & Cross, W. R. (2013). Metastatic prostate cancer in transsexual diagnosed after three decades of estrogen therapy. *Canadian Urological Association Journal, 7,* e544–546.

Van Haarst, E. P., Newling, D. W., Gooren, L. J., Asscheman, H., & Prenger, D. M. (1998). Metastatic prostatic carcinoma in a male-to-female transsexual. *British Journal of Urology, 81,* 776.

Van Kesteren, P. J. M., Asscheman, H., Megens, J. A., & Gooren, L. J. G. (1997). Mortality and morbidity in transsexual subjects treated with cross-sex hormones. *Clinical Endocrinology* (Oxf), *47,* 337–342.

Van Kesteren, P. J. M., Meinhardt, W., van der Valk, P., Geldof, A., Megens, J. A., & Gooren, L. J. G. (1996). Effects of estrogens only on the prostates of aging men. *Journal of Urology, 156,* 1349–1353.

Viallard, J. F., Marit, G., Mercié, P., Leng, B., Reiffers, J., & Pellegrin, J. L. (2000). Polycythaemia as a complication of transdermal testosterone therapy. *British Journal of Haematology, 110,* 237–238.

Wierckx, K., Elaut, E., Declercq, E., Heylens, G., De Cuypere, G., Taes, Y., Kaufman, J., & T'Sjoen, G. (2013). Prevalence of cardiovascular disease and cancer during cross-sex hormone therapy in a large cohort of trans persons: A case-control study. *European Journal of Endocrinology, 169,* 471–478.

Wierckx, K., van Caenegem, E., Schreiner, T., Haraldsen, I., Fisher, A., Toye, K., Kaufman, J. M., & T'Sjoen, G. (2014). Cross-sex hormone therapy in trans persons is safe and effective at short-time follow-up: Results from the European Network for the Investigation of Gender Incongruence. *Journal of Sexual Medicine, 11,* 1999–2011.

14

Discussing Aspects of Medical Transition with the Parents of Young Transgender People: A Psychotherapist's Perspective

Damien W. Riggs, PhD, FAPS

Introduction

The day before beginning this chapter, I met jointly with a mother and her transgender son. In previous appointments the mother had presented as highly supportive—a strong advocate for her child, willing to challenge those around her. During this appointment, I made some time to speak with her alone. Much of our previous joint discussions had centered on her son's desire to commence hormone therapy. Being under 18 years of age, he legally had to have his parents' consent, and at the time they in turn had to petition the Family Court of Australia for permission. Because the two psychiatrists who had evaluated him did not support treatment, the mother decided that maybe it would be best to wait until after her son's 18th birthday.

With the young person's desire for hormone therapy in mind, I suggested that a way to sort through the mother's ambivalence might be to have an open discussion about what *dysphoria* meant for her son, since he had expressed to me he felt his parents "didn't understand" the extent of the problem. Surprisingly, the mother rejected my idea, seemingly contradicting her stance as supportive and affirming. What became clearer as we spoke was that while she was fine with her child's being transgender, she wasn't satisfied with her own lack of understanding of his sense of dysphoria, repeatedly stating that she wanted to be more competent—to understand more and to do more. Thus, the problem was not the mother's degree of acceptance of her son; rather, the problem was that she felt inadequate as a parent.

I open with this example because it clearly illustrates the challenges mental health clinicians face in working with parents of transgender young people in regard to the medical aspects of transition. What we witness is, in many cases, their conflicting emotional responses: they want to support their child but are unsure about what's best, particularly when they are at odds with the "experts."

Lev, Arlene I., Gottlieb, Andrew R., *Families in Transition*
dx.doi.org/10.17312/harringtonparkpress/2019.04.fit.014
© 2019 by Harrington Park Press

In this chapter I explore a number of key issues that I experience in my own clinical practice as a psychotherapist. Specifically, I outline how I work directly with transgender young people—mostly between the ages of six and 20—and their parents and describe my focus on decision making and the right to bodily self-determination. At times my approach counters the presumed right of parents to control all aspects of their child's life, instead encouraging parents to consider ways of working in collaboration with their child to achieve the best outcomes for both. This can involve (1) encouraging parents to explore their own values and viewpoints; (2) helping young people understand why their parents might not support certain aspects of their transition; and (3) negotiating ways in which they might work collaboratively.

I also focus on fertility, future bodily changes, and the broader social context that shapes the experiences of being transgender. While the emphasis of this text is primarily on the experiences of parents, talking from a parent's perspective does not necessarily exclude talking from a child's perspective. Instead, I suggest that it is possible to explore how parents and children influence each other, how parents can understand the challenges their child faces, and how they may cultivate greater empathy for their child.

Conceptually, I liken my role as a clinician to the role of a midwife (Lev, 2004). As clinicians, we bring into being new ways of thinking about bodies, relationships, and the future. Though I am, in many ways, often directive, I am always open to what families bring to the therapeutic encounter.

Approaches to Working with Parents

Working with parents involves three approaches. The first is that I am affirmative, meaning that the young person's account of their gender and embodiment is what I take as the truth, which includes accepting that some young people experience a very real sense of dysphoria. Being affirming always means using preferred names and pronouns, politely correcting misgendering, and not engaging in conversations with parents that in any way undermine their child's sense of their gender.

The second approach involves clarifying to parents that though my role is to listen to and validate their feelings, their struggles, and their need to be informed about their child, this must always coexist with, and at times be preceded by, the needs of the child. I frame my explanation in terms of power differentials; that is, in most contexts, adult rights are privileged over those of young people. I highlight the importance of creating spaces where children are offered the opportunity to make their needs known and, when appropriate, for those needs to be met. Drawing attention to power imbalances can be useful, even when working with parents who are struggling the most and who may be tempted to simply withdraw support for their child, including terminating treatment.

The third approach is acknowledging explicitly that this work sits in a broader context in which a diagnosis of *gender dysphoria* is at times required, the pathologization of transgender people continues, and not all clinicians adopt affirming approaches. I state my appreciation for parents' own values and viewpoints and acknowledge that our appointments are often shaped by systemic demands (e.g., the need for assessment), but my primary focus is on affirming young people and helping parents do the same.

Of course, an affirmative approach must include directly responding to the concerns of parents. To support their children, it is important for parents to have open and honest conversations that hold the potential to shift their understanding of who their children are. To achieve this, my work is implicitly and, at times, explicitly framed with reference to the broader context of what Ansara and Hegarty (2014) refer to as *cisgenderism*, the ideology that delegitimizes people's own understandings of their bodies and genders. Conceptualizing in this way allows me to acknowledge the concerns of parents while respectfully positioning them as the products of *cisgenderism*. Centrally, this involves affirming that an individual's experience of their gender is what is most important, rather than their assigned sex at birth.

A set of questions I routinely ask parents includes: "Who do you want your child to be in the future?" "How does this differ from your child's hopes for their own future?" and "What would it mean if your child had to live a life that was not authentic?" This encourages parents to recognize that sometimes the values they hold, which may be faith-based or culturally or socially determined, will differ from those held by their child. To a large extent, this is counterintuitive for many parents, who feel that they must establish clear limits and enforce those limits, and that those limits should be premised on the family's belief system. An affirming approach requires that, at times, the balance of power shifts to the young person, encouraging them to voice their needs. This can involve drawing on research documenting poor mental health outcomes among transgender people who experience family rejection (Koken, Bimbi, & Parsons, 2009), as well as inviting discussions about what it would mean for their child to feel alienated from them, or even to leave home

Often parents elaborate very clear reasons why supporting a transgender child does not reflect their belief systems. But after breaking down the fundamentals, we frequently find that those beliefs primarily emphasize respect, support, and caring. I am then able to discuss how those core values can be best affirmed by supporting their child's transition and acknowledging the primary value they place on their relationship with their child.

Another part of my role is to advise parents about what to expect when they consult with medical professionals. In Western nations we place considerable trust in doctors. Our very lives depend on them. This can result in having unrealistic expectations and exercising blind faith. When speaking with parents, I often find it necessary to first outline the doctor's role, making it very clear that the doctor's job is to diagnose and treat—not to be their friend.

In so doing, I prepare parents for the types of responses they are likely to receive. Many parents say that doctors are "too clinical"—that is, they are cold and distant. In response, I suggest that what we primarily want from medical professionals is assessment and treatment. Understanding the role of doctors in this way helps parents maintain a focus on what's most important. This is also useful in helping them understand the different roles other professionals play. For example, a social worker or psychologist might be actively involved in diagnosis, counseling, and referral, whereas a psychiatrist might be more focused on prescribing.

I also highlight the importance of parents' educating themselves about their child's transition. Medical intervention continues to rapidly evolve, and it is likely that some professionals may not be aware of the latest research. As part of my role, I spend considerable time assuring them that I *am* cognizant of the current trends worldwide and can share this information, as well as suggesting how they might go about finding that information themselves.

Simultaneously, I emphasize the importance of having faith in medical practitioners. Though some are unfamiliar with the needs of transgender people, those who specialize in this area are knowledgeable and skilled. Part of my work, then, involves knowing which specialists are available and making appropriate referrals. My role can also involve playing mediator, interpreting the reasoning behind decisions made by their doctor. In contrast, I often consult with the psychiatrist or surgeon by providing insights into family dynamics, so that they better understand the factors that influence a parent's response.

Approaches for Working Jointly with Parents and Children

All the young people I work with display a keen desire to know as much as possible about what lies ahead. Most come to see me with a real understanding of themselves. This, however, is often framed by narratives gleaned from the media, from websites, and from their parents, which typically center on "being in the wrong body." Some report a strong sense of dysphoria; others do not. Though affirming their sense of self is key, concurrently I introduce conversations, often based on academic research, about the diversity of all bodies, exploring the experiences of transgender adults relating to intimacy and embodiment. This research indicates that, for many transgender people, intimate interactions with cisgender others help them see that bodily discomfort and bodily dissatisfaction are common experiences for many people (Doorduin & Van Berlo, 2014). This is not to discount the unique experiences of transgender people living in a context of *cisgenderism,* which presumes that natally assigned sex determines gender. Rather, it is to open up a range of ways of thinking about embodiment and gender.

Further, it is important for parents to understand that their child's sense of dysphoria can increase with age. Waiting to access medical treatment can feel like an eternity and lead to anxieties that in some instances become generalized. To address this, I use terms that are degendered or regendered. Again, academic research suggests that many transgender adults renegotiate the normative meanings ascribed to particular body parts. Some transgender men will be comfortable with receptive vaginal intercourse when they understand their vagina as a *bonus hole* or as a term other than *vagina* (Schleifer, 2006). Similarly, other transgender men refer to the clitoris as *a little guy, penis,* or *dickclit* (Edelman & Zimman, 2014). Research suggests that some transgender women who have not had vaginoplasty regender the penis so that it signifies femininity (Bolin, 1988). Talking about bodies in ways that open them up to reinscription is an important counter to some of the fears and anxieties that young people have and can be useful for parents to talk about as well.

Helpful, too, is talking about bodies and genders in ways that locate them in a wider social context. Sometimes this means addressing unrealistic norms and stereotypes, making reference to my own body or their parents' bodies to discuss the expectations and the differences between us. For example, I might comment on how gaining weight or aging has changed the shape of my body, and that while this is challenging, it doesn't change my gender. Parents will often share similar stories to further demonstrate the effect of body norms on them. We might also discuss the sources of our knowledge about bodies and gender, and what beliefs and assumptions inform that knowledge. All this is not to discount experiences of dysphoria, or to promote a liberal narrative that "we are all the same." Instead, the intention is to highlight the broader social forces that shape how we understand our bodies and ourselves. It can be empowering for young people to appreciate other ways of thinking about their lives and experiences, and parents can play a pivotal role in affirming that diversity.

An example of the *bodies as diverse* idea comes from my work with a young transgender girl. When we first met, she reported a significant fear that she would grow up to be hairy like her father and habitually pulled out the hair on her legs. Her perception was that her mother had hairless legs and that this was a key signifier (along with breasts) of what it meant to be female. Over the course of our work, her parents and I were able to discuss the expectations that are placed on women in our society, which involved her mother disclosing that she shaves her legs, but that not all women do, nor are all men hirsute. Her mother also addressed the challenges of having large breasts, and while she could appreciate their importance in terms of identifying as female, she could also cite examples of family members who were not similarly endowed but who, nevertheless, strongly identified as female.

These conversations were not intended to discount the child's sense of dysphoria or to delegitimize her desires. Rather, they were intended to facilitate a broader understanding of diversity, that the expectations we have of bodies marked as female or male are normative, and that to a degree she can have ultimate control over the outcome. This involved frank discussions among the parents, the young person, and myself about the effects of puberty blockers and hormone therapy. Speaking honestly about what hormones do—primarily in nongendered ways (e.g., testosterone can produce or inhibit hair growth, estrogen can change the growth of breasts, but without discussing these hormones as male or female)—assisted her to understand that hormones have different effects, and the possibilities that lie ahead.

Much of the work I do with young people takes the form of coaching them on how to interact with their doctors, which is most often done in conjunction with their parents. Importantly, my intention is not to "train" them in how to get what they want. Again, drawing from the research (Speer & Parsons, 2006), it is important to acknowledge that there are certain expectations that the medical community has, that is, that there is a system patients must negotiate, that different rules drive the system, and that those rules are determined by social norms and beliefs. Understanding all this can assist young people and their parents in developing the critical thinking skills that can result in negotiating the outcomes they want. Speaking honestly about the diagnosis of *gender dysphoria*, for example, is something I have found to be a vital step.

Another important topic is fertility. Understandably, for most transgender young people, the idea of having children may be one they haven't fully considered. For others it is a source of significant distress. For some transgender boys, the idea of a pregnancy is a normative gendered expectation that further arouses feelings of dysphoria. Conversely, for some transgender girls, the idea of not being able to carry a child is a source of anxiety. Still others have developed a very clear idea of how they might have children, including preserving their own genetic materials (through sperm or ovum storage) or adopting or fostering children. Of course, the question of fertility and children is very much shaped by the information that young people are exposed to in their families, at school, and in their communities. Often I find that parents avoid the topic of fertility in the presence of their children. Some fear triggering their child's experience of dysphoria; others may consider it socially inappropriate to talk to a young person about their body and future reproductive aims.

To open up a space for potentially difficult conversations and, at the same time, manage the potential discomfort of parents, sometimes I engage in *ventriloquizing,* that is, voicing the thoughts and concerns parents are struggling to express. Before doing this I always check in first with them about what they think and feel about a specific topic. Often parents will request that I speak with their child on their behalf. The conversations are typically led by me with the parents present. Sometimes the parents will join in the conversation, and often the young person will look to the parents to see how they are responding. Typically these are very productive and can be both serious and lighthearted. Often their legacy is felt long-term: parents report feeling satisfied knowing that the topic has been broached, and young people often want to return to the topic. And, of course, this opens up the possibility for parents themselves to talk to their child about issues that concern them, rather than requiring me to do so on their behalf.

Conclusions

To return to the example that opened this chapter, it is important to acknowledge that, at different points, most parents will struggle. Some may feel they are not doing enough—as was the case for the mother described; others may view being transgender as an illness or a phase; still others get the message that supporting their child is wrong, that message sometimes coming from the medical community. In those cases, while parents may be very supportive of their child, they may also need support themselves in weighing the range of options. They may need mental health clinicians to play an advocacy or mediator role to open up conversations with medical professionals about the best course of action. Regardless of any individual parent's experience, if our starting place as clinicians is an affirming response to young people, then it is possible to negotiate modes of engagement that both allow parents to wrestle with their emotional responses and support their needs, while centering on the importance of affirming children in their transition.

As I have emphasized throughout, engaging with parents and young people requires openness and honesty, which are ideally framed within an awareness of the broader context of *cisgenderism*. For me, preparing transgender people and their parents for both the challenges and joys ahead is critical. To do otherwise would be disingenuous. While my aim is never to provide a "script," I am convinced of the importance of priming families with information about what to expect, how to negotiate the expectations placed on them, and how to respond when they feel marginalized by the demands of the medical system.

At times, I acknowledge to parents that it might be easier if we lived in a world where gender binaries were not dominant. I always make this statement with caution, however. My purpose is never to deny the experiences of transgender people, nor is it to set them up as dupes of a gender binary. Rather, my goal is always to shift the focus away from transgender people as the source of difference, and instead help parents reflect on how difference is engineered by rigid modes of classification. Though this does not bring an end to their struggles or to their child's dysphoria, it can help them develop a broader perspective that, I believe, will be an asset to both parents and their children as they negotiate the future.

REFERENCES

Ansara, Y. G., & Hegarty, P. (2014). Methodologies of misgendering: Recommendations for reducing cisgenderism in psychological research. *Feminism and Psychology,* 24, 259–270.

Bolin, A. (1988). *In search of Eve: Transsexual rites of passage.* London: Bergin & Garvey.

Doorduin, T., & Van Berlo, W. (2014). Trans people's experience of sexuality in the Netherlands: A pilot study. Journal of Homosexuality, 61 (5), 654–672.

Edelman, E. A., & Zimman, L. (2014). Boycunts and bonus holes: Trans men's bodies, neoliberalism, and the sexual productivity of genitals. *Journal of Homosexuality,* 61 (5), 673–690.

Koken, J. A., Bimbi, D. S., & Parsons, J. T. (2009). Experiences of familial acceptance-rejection among transwomen of color. *Journal of Family Psychology,* 23 (6), 853.

Lev, A. I. (2004). *Transgender emergence: Therapeutic guidelines for working with gender-variant people and their families.* Binghamton, N.Y.: Haworth Press.

Schleifer, D. (2006). Make me feel mighty real: Gay female-to-male transgenderists negotiating sex, gender, and sexuality. *Sexualities,* 9 (1), 57–75.

Speer, S. A., & Parsons, C. (2006). Gatekeeping gender: Some features of the use of hypothetical questions in the psychiatric assessment of transsexual patients. *Discourse & Society,* 17 (6), 785–812.

15

Family-Oriented Medical Care for Gender Nonconforming Children, Adolescents, and Their Families

Carolyn Wolf-Gould, MD

Medical providers for gender nonconforming (GNC) and transgender youth can and should play an important role in the process of gender exploration and transition. These children require a unique model for health care as well as a skill set that is not typically part of traditional medical education. Illness-driven or preventive models are inadequate to the task of assisting patients and families through the complex and transformational process of supporting children and youth as they develop an authentic gender expression. A fresh paradigm is required, one that acknowledges not only biomedical knowledge about pubertal suppression and gender-affirming hormone therapy, but also an understanding of the ripple effect these interventions create for the patient's family, school, and community. As medical providers attending to the health of a GNC child during gender exploration or transition, we must oversee an intricate endocrinologic process, as well as the psychological, educational, social, and legal changes that result. To rise to this task, we must also forge collaborative relationships with a myriad of helping individuals who are also assisting the patient and family. Medical providers are rarely taught collaborative skills and must develop proficiency by immersing themselves in the transformative process along with the patient, the family, and the therapeutic team.

In this chapter I propose an approach to medical care for GNC and transgender youth and their families that is based on the Family-Oriented Primary Care model outlined by McDaniel, Campbell, and Seaburn (1990) and describe techniques for its implementation.

Family-Oriented Medical Care

A biomedical model of health care, with its narrow focus on illness and pharmaceutical cure, fails to meet the complex needs of gender diverse youth. It behooves

Lev, Arlene I., Gottlieb, Andrew R., *Families in Transition*
dx.doi.org/10.17312/harringtonparkpress/2019.04.fit.015
© 2019 by Harrington Park Press

us to develop a broad biopsychosocial approach, one in which prescribing pubertal blockers or gender-affirming hormones (Olson & Garofalo, 2014; Steever, 2014) is just a part of a larger treatment plan (Svetaz, Garcia-Huidobro, & Allen, 2014; Zucker, Wood, Singh, & Bradley, 2012). The term *biopsychosocial,* first coined by George Engel (1980), stresses the need for attention to all the usual biomedical concerns *within* the context of the clinician-patient relationship, the family, the community, the culture, and the society. To help a patient attain a healthy gender identity, we must attend to the immediate consequences of medical interventions on a child's body *and* mind, while continually assessing the effect of these changes on the family, school, and community.

The Family-Oriented Primary Care model described by McDaniel and her colleagues (1990) encourages the development of a profound awareness of how the health of individuals is influenced by their families and communities, and it uses this knowledge to explore medical problems and organize care. I have adapted McDaniel's premises as a method to meet the medical needs of GNC youth. The paradigm presented is based on the conviction that gender variance is a normal phenomenon and that, as medical providers, our task is to address the crippling effects of gender *dysphoria,* the discomfort or discrepancy between a person's gender and sex assigned at birth (Coleman et al., 2012).

Figure 15.1 offers a schematic representation of the model, which identifies a core therapeutic team composed of the child, the parents, the therapist, and the medical professional. For our purposes, *family* is defined as any group of people related either biologically, emotionally, or legally (McDaniel et al., 1990). The definition of *parents* includes both biological parents and nonbiological caretakers. The larger therapeutic team includes individuals from a wide range of disciplines, who play a secondary but important role in supporting all team members.

Basic Premises of Family-Oriented Medical Care for GNC Youth

Premise 1: Family-oriented health care for GNC children is based on a biopsychosocial systems approach.

A biopsychosocial model stresses the importance of evaluating the medical and psychological aspects of gender dysphoria within the context of the patient's family and social system. Biomedical treatments for GNC youth must be incorporated into a comprehensive plan to assess and address physical and emotional needs, while developing support within the family, school, community, and society (Svetaz et al., 2014; Zucker et al., 2012).

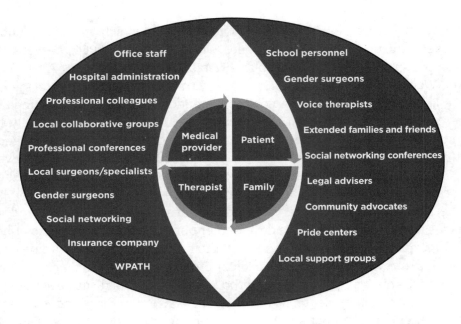

FIGURE 15.1 A model for family-centered medical care for gender nonconforming patients and families

Premise 2: *The primary focus of medical care is the patient in the context of the family.*

The complex and layered nature of medical and social transition requires intensive family involvement to ensure successful treatment for gender diverse children and youth. Family connections and communication styles may be dramatically altered by a child's gender exploration or transition, and family members may pass through stages of development that can mirror the child's transition. Medical providers must develop skills in family interviewing (Campbell, McDaniel, Cole-Kelly, Hepworth, & Lorenz, 2002), decision making, and problem solving and involve family members as an integral part of the therapeutic team.

The family is the primary source of many health beliefs and behaviors. Families that initiate treatment for a GNC child often present with a host of fears, worries, and misconceptions about their child's condition (Grossman, D'Augelli, Howell, & Hubbard, 2005; Wisnowski, 2011). The first task is to interact with family members in ways that reveal their understanding of the child's gender expression and how they believe this affects their family system. The behaviors of the child and parents are driven by these convictions, and exploring both the gender-affirming and nonaffirming beliefs and behaviors in a nonjudgmental manner can help normalize distress and set the tone for healthy discussion, education, and treatment (Coolhart, Baker, Farmer, Malaney, & Shipman, 2013). Providers who meet family members "where they are" and expect that people are at different points of relative health and function will be better able to facilitate education and support. As the family begins to appreciate their child's transition as a movement toward health and wellness, a more gender-affirming belief system will often emerge (Ehrensaft, 2012; Grossman et al., 2005).

The stress that a family experiences while passing through developmental stages with a GNC child can become manifest in emotional and physical symptoms and can cause family dysfunction. Symptoms of gender dysphoria may manifest themselves in myriad ways, including depression, anxiety, headaches, abdominal pain, substance use or abuse, nonsuicidal self-harm, or school failure (Lombardi, Wilchins, Priesing, & Malouf, 2002; Roberts, Rosario, Slopen, Calzo, & Austin, 2013; Savin-Williams, 1994; Toomey, Ryan, Diaz, Card, & Russell, 2010; Wyss, 2004), all driving families to seek care. During the initial visit, families often focus on a child's symptoms, which not only are a manifestation of distress but may also be the reported cause and expression of intense family disruption. The task of sorting through physical and psychological symptoms as well as other symptoms of family conflict can be daunting and may require frequent office visits as well as collaboration with mental health clinicians. One of the first tasks of the therapeutic team is to identify and address causes of a child's distress or family dysfunction that are not related to gender exploration, but which may be contributing to symptoms. For example, parental discord or substance abuse can profoundly affect the capacity of a family to meet a child's needs. We must also determine which symptoms are related to physical processes unrelated to gender exploration (e.g., abdominal pain from early appendicitis) and reflect on how symptoms of dysphoria may exacerbate underlying medical conditions (e.g., migraine headaches). Though all individuals and families respond differently to stress, family members often pass through predictable stages as they adapt to the needs of a GNC family member (Lev, 2004). We must be attentive to the symptoms that occur at critical points of development, appreciate how these symptoms contribute to family dysfunction, and work to identify and address the concerns that emerge over time.

These somatic and emotional symptoms can also serve an adaptive function within the family. Providers can frame somatic and emotional symptoms in a manner that educates all family members and normalizes gender exploration. When a parent who is traumatized by atypical behaviors begins to think of their child as normal, everything changes. One way to frame this might be: "It's common for gender non-conforming children, like Lena, to want to wear dresses. It soothes her discomfort with her gender." We can also encourage parents to use symptoms as a way to evaluate responses to their own changing attitudes, asking, "Have you noticed a difference in Lena's mood and behavior when you allow her to wear dresses?" For helping professionals, symptoms serve as a barometer for the pressure felt within families and as a gauge for measuring treatment response (McDaniel et al., 1990).

Families are a valuable resource and source of support for the management of gender dysphoria. The process of accompanying a child through a medical and/or social transition often triggers a similarly transformative period of personal growth and change for others. As parents confront the immediate and ever-changing needs of their GNC child over time, they often become experts on the child's medical, social, educational, and legal concerns. This kind of persistent work and focus may drive family members to become powerful advocates and push for changes within the child's social environment—from the family to school policy, even to state legislation (Cook & Cook, 2013). We assist family members in learning how to function as advocates and affirm that this work is important to the health of their child.

Premise 3: The patient, family, mental health clinician, and medical provider are partners in health care.

The process of gender exploration and transition can be challenging, even perilous, and the collaborative efforts of the therapeutic team are of paramount importance. The core therapeutic team—child, parents, therapist, medical provider—must work closely together to assess and monitor all stages of treatment, assist with problem solving, and create a safety net during difficult times. As medical professionals, we can stress the expectation that both youth and families will work consistently with mental health clinicians while we too commit to forming collaborative relationships with these professionals and develop ways to communicate quickly, easily, and reciprocally about care over time (Doherty, 1995; Feierabend & Bartee, 2004).

Premise 4: The physician and mental health providers are seen as "a part of" rather than "apart from" the treatment system.

Because of the complex, intense, and lengthy nature of this work, the quality of the provider-family relationship is inextricably linked to the clinical process and outcome (Epstein, 2014). Patients and families are profoundly affected by the ways they are cared for, and we are similarly moved, changed, and even personally transformed by the process of caring for gender diverse patients and families. The needs of these patients and families can be enormous, and they may require a large time commitment and extraordinary levels of resourcefulness and compassion on our part. A healthy collaborative relationship between medical and mental health clinicians creates a safe space to process the emotional effect of this work, and it reflects on how our own beliefs and behaviors influence treatment and contribute to change within a family system.

Premise 5: *The therapeutic team can be expanded to include helping professionals across many disciplines when appropriate to the family's care.*

As we assist patients and families in negotiating paths toward a healthy gender expression in their schools and communities, the core therapeutic team can be expanded to include school personnel (Caitlyn, Patraw, & Bednar, 2013; Greytak, Kosciw, & Boesen, 2013; Slesaransky-Poe, Ruzzi, Dimedio, & Stanley, 2013), community advocates, and legal advisers. The *health* of these children and families must continually be assessed within the health of the community setting, and treatment may necessitate intervention with these other professionals in the child's world. For example, we may be called to educate school staff or assist administrators in formulating policies to accommodate the needs of GNC students (Orr & Baum, 2015). When students face discrimination, we can attest to the psychological or medical consequences and assist with finding legal representation from an advocacy group (Lambda Legal, 2014). We may need to locate LGBT outreach programs, support groups, or institutionalized living programs to coordinate services (Greytak et al., 2013).

Similarly, as medical providers, we benefit from collaborative relationships with many different kinds of groups and individuals, who can inform us about or help us process issues faced by our patients. Those with personal ties to the transgender community have a distinct advantage in understanding the concerns of these patients and families. Those who lack these connections can develop them by attending networking and educational events. Professional associations, such as the World Professional Association for Transgender Health (WPATH), offer educational, networking, and mentoring opportunities that can be tremendously valuable. Professional listservs offer forums for those who wish to discuss patient care with others in the field. Medical professionals who serve this population may be stigmatized by the same societal prejudice that affects our patients and be viewed by colleagues as suspect or quacks. Legitimizing our work and the lives of our transgender patients requires attention to the process of educating our colleagues and networks, forging relationships with advocacy and legal organizations and insurance companies, and creating local professional associations for case review and coordination of care.

Premise 6: Work with GNC youth requires high levels of provider involvement with families.

Doherty and Baird (1986) reflect on the stages medical professionals pass through as they develop competency in family-centered care and describe the five levels of physician involvement—a hierarchy—learned over time. Level One emphasizes solely the biomedical aspects of care; Level Two highlights communicating with family members to explain medical findings and offer advice; Level Three focuses on soliciting information about the family's feelings concerning the medical process and identifying areas of dysfunction or stress; Level Four addresses the provision of systematic assessment of family functioning, engaging reluctant family members, and planning interventions to reframe difficulties and work toward collaborative efforts; and Level Five suggests either implementing or being a part of a family treatment experience.

To offer thoughtful and comprehensive care, we need to consistently operate between Levels Three and Four and participate in Level Five as part of a therapeutic team when necessary. Those who are cognizant of the need for higher levels of care can take steps to develop skills in family interviewing and primary care family counseling techniques. Collaborating mental health clinicians can be enormously helpful to medical providers by teaching these skills.

Case Study: Lena, Part 1

Lena, a 14-year-old self-identified girl who was assigned male at birth, comes to the office with her mother, Brenda. Lena presents as a boy, with a short, masculine haircut and wearing jeans and a Red Sox T-shirt. When asked how she'd like to be addressed, she whispers that she'd like me to call her Lena and prefers feminine pronouns. She says she's here today because she "wants to be a girl," but she otherwise answers questions in monosyllables, huddles against her chair, and refuses to make eye contact. Brenda says that Lena has been depressed for years, and six weeks ago she told Brenda that she "feels like a girl inside." Brenda says that since hearing this she cannot sleep and doesn't know what this means or what to do. She wonders if her acrimonious divorce from Lena's father, Matt, many years ago is the "cause" of Lena's "disorder." She asked the school nurse about it, who told her she "hadn't noticed anything odd but she'd better nip this thing in the bud before it gets out of control." Despite the claim that she isn't coping well, Brenda found a therapist with expertise in GNC youth and Lena has started counseling. Brenda went once too and says it was helpful. Brenda has been reading everything she can find, including information about pubertal blockers, and asked the therapist for a medical referral immediately so they "don't miss the boat." Brenda and Matt share custody of Lena. They often disagree about parenting styles. Brenda states that Matt is angry and upset about Lena's disclosure and refuses to let Lena wear girl's clothes in his home. He has accused Brenda of encouraging Lena and has threatened to sue for sole custody because of her "crazy influence." Lena is afraid to be in her dad's home and has told Brenda that she doesn't want to go there this weekend. During the interview Brenda frequently refers to Lena as Scott and uses mixed pronouns. Brenda appears worried and distracted but appropriately concerned, and her love for Lena is apparent. An examination shows that Lena is advanced in puberty by Tanner staging (Bordini & Rosenfield, 2011) but still has a slight build and her face has not masculinized, which indicates it's not too late for pubertal blocking.

PART 1   TOOLS FOR THE INTAKE ASSESSMENT

Recognize the Path to the Medical Provider

For some parents, the first health professional they speak to about their child's gender nonconformity is their primary care provider. Therefore, it is incumbent on all medical professionals to develop basic skills for assisting these patients and families. Sadly, most health-care professional training programs do not include the evaluation or treatment of gender dysphoria in their curricula. Many parents are misled by uninformed medical professionals, like Lena's school nurse, who dismiss the child's behaviors as something they'll grow out of and neglect to make appropriate referrals. The medical system is slowly becoming more aware of gender dysphoria in youth as a condition requiring treatment, as evidenced by the surge in literature in the popular press and pediatric journals (Garofalo, 2014). We can help allay parental fears by describing the usual trajectory for GNC children, acknowledging that we have experience treating this condition, and explaining the treatment protocols: "Yes, this is something we see, and your child's behavior is normal. These are the ways this condition can be disruptive to children and their families. This is how we treat it."

Cultural Sensitivity Training for Providers and Office Staff

The office staff sets the tone for each visit, and those who are trained in cultural sensitivity can help create a professional and compassionate environment (Coren, Coren, Pagliaro, & Weiss, 2011; Lev, 2004; Polly & Nicole, 2011; Robinson, 2010). Staff should be educated on basic gender terminology, as well as the importance of asking patients how they wish to be addressed and which pronouns they prefer. All personnel should have an understanding of the gender-transition process, be fluent with the limitations of insurance companies and binary-driven electronic medical records, and show a willingness to work with families to find creative solutions for working within these systems. They should be trained to offer explanations and advice to testing centers or specialists who will be involved in the care of their patients. This attention to detail may help put patients and families at ease and models what patients have a right to expect from the larger world.

Part of cultural sensitivity is attention to language. There is ongoing discussion (Lev, 2013) about how we refer to the condition now defined in the *DSM-V* as gender dysphoria (American Psychiatric Association, 2013). Over time, the diagnostic terminology has changed to reflect the growing understanding that gender variance is a matter of diversity, not pathology (Coleman et al., 2012). Options for coding in the ICD-10, however, still include the antiquated and pathologizing term *gender identity disorder* (American Psychiatric Association, 2000). It's important to remember that when we choose pathologizing language when communicating with patients and families, whether by mistake, for insurance purposes, or because of our own ignorance, this will shape how individuals feel about diagnosis and treatment.

Family Interview and Medical Genogram

A family-centered medical interview (Campbell et al., 2002), rather than a patient-centered one, will enable the clinician to quickly recognize important details about the child's medical, family, and social history and family dynamics, as well as to explore belief systems about the child's gender issues. The family interview also allows everyone, especially those who may be struggling, to feel heard and appreciated. The first step is to invite all the individuals who accompany the child to attend the first part of the intake, have each person introduce themself, and explain their relationship to the child. I then ask the child or adolescent, "How can I help you?" This is followed by more focused questions to elicit their understanding of their own gender history as well as their medical and social histories. I then ask parents and others accompanying the child why they are here and to describe their specific concerns.

A medical genogram is a simple and efficient way to document family dynamics and structure as well as family medical history (McDaniel et al., 1990; McGoldrick, Gerson, & Petry, 2008). Belous, Timm, Chee, and Whitehead (2012) approach the genogram with queer-critical theory, including information about gender, sexual orientation, non-heterosexist relationship structures, and sexual communication and environments, all of which is helpful in understanding how a family reacts to their GNC child.

In the case presented in this essay, I started by asking Lena, "Whom do you live with?" sketching her genogram as she described her family constellation. I asked Brenda to contribute as I expanded the genogram to include both extended and "chosen" family. I documented the health and social/psychiatric issues of individuals on the chart, and I included occupations and identifying information or phrases used by contributors to describe family members: "Bat-shit crazy," "Supportive," "Black sheep," "Guardian angel," "Crack addict." I included information the mother offered about the sexual environment by identifying family members with homophobic tendencies. It's also important to take note of those who are absent (in this case, Lena's father, Matt), perhaps a sign of their outrage, their fear, their desperation, or their apathy. We may need to actively reach out to these individuals to assist with education and support.

Figure 15.2 depicts the genogram for Lena.

Acknowledging Medical Uncertainty: "Why is my child like this?"

Medical professionals learn early in our careers that living and working with uncertainty is the rule rather than the exception. But patients and families come to us for answers, direction, and guidance. We must recognize the anxiety uncertainty provokes and address it early in treatment to help families cope better with their fears. By adopting a "not knowing" stance, and joining with the uncertainty, we can help reduce anxiety about outcome and create a healthier environment for gender exploration.

The first question parents ask is usually "Why is my child like this?" There are many theories that suggest a biomedical etiology for gender dysphoria, including exposure to intrauterine hormones, differences in brain structure, or inherited tendencies (Erickson-Schroth, 2013), but no conclusive cause has been identified. Most parents aren't aware of the research. They have their own set of theories, secretly wondering if this is somehow *their* fault. They acknowledge that they didn't provide appropriate role models, used substances during pregnancy, or had a bout of severe depression when the child was an infant. Many parents are reassured by an explanation of what is known and not known about etiology.

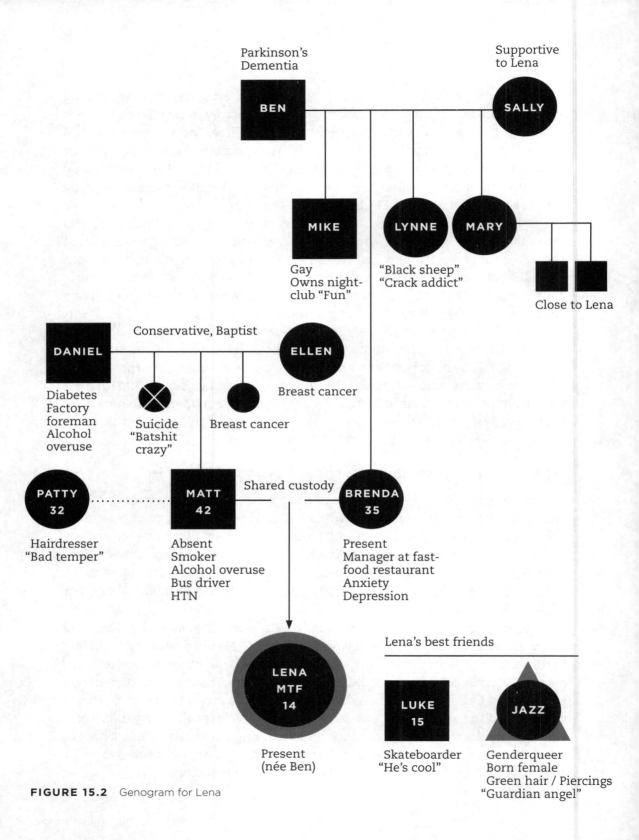

FIGURE 15.2 Genogram for Lena

Another concern is that something is physically wrong with their child. Some ask for genetic testing, or a karyotype (chromosomal analysis). If there are no physical findings suggestive of genetic conditions, these tests are unlikely to provide useful information (Goedhart et al., 2015).

It's important to remember that parents are searching for "how, what, and why." We don't always have the answers, but we can explain what is known and not known in a way that may ease anxiety—for example, by saying, "We don't understand the etiology of gender diversity but we do know that, like other human conditions, it's present in all racial, ethnic, and socioeconomic groups. It's unlikely that something *you* did is the cause. We do know quite a bit about treatments, however, and after I get a sense of your child's situation, I'll make recommendations for care."

Establish Expectation of Collaborative Care

Most children come to my office with a referral letter from a mental health clinician who has already started to work with them, outlining the child's psychosocial history and specific treatment concerns. Parents are reassured to know that I have read the referral letter and intend to develop a collaborative relationship with their therapist. It's also helpful to state the expectation that ongoing mental health care is a vital part of their family's treatment plan.

Identify the Developmental Stage of the Family in Regard to Its Understanding of Gender Dysphoria

Arlene Lev (2004) describes the developmental process families go through in her Family Emergence Model. Stage One, *Discovery and Disclosure,* is often characterized by feelings of shock, betrayal, and confusion. Family members may present with panic, somatic complaints, behavioral issues, and outrage. Stage Two, *Turmoil,* is often a time of intense stress and conflict as family members struggle to accept the new reality. We may see parental discord or displaced rage toward caregivers, and youth with depression and self-harming behaviors. Stage Three, *Negotiation,* occurs when family members begin to adjust to their situation. As parents seek information and engage in conversations with their child, systemic symptoms start to abate. Stage Four, *Finding Balance,* signals that the family is now ready to reintegrate the transgender member and discuss medical options for care. By identifying these stages early in the treatment, we become less reactive to the process and are better able to understand and meet the needs of these families.

The Physical Exam

We need to be aware that many GNC youth have profound *anatomic dysphoria,* painful distress with their primary sex characteristics, and that the process of submitting to a physical exam can be difficult. We should routinely ask patients what we can do to make them more comfortable (e.g., inquiring about the presence or absence of a chaperone or parent, asking what words they prefer when referring to body parts), be attentive to the use of gowns and drapes to ensure privacy, and adopt a kind yet professional demeanor when touching patients. We can use a child's discomfort as a gauge for discussing sensitive topics about bodily functions or sexuality, saying things like, "I see how uncomfortable you are when I examine your vagina [or use the word the patient prefers for this body part]. How do you manage your periods?" Or, "I know you don't like touching your testicles, but checking them regularly is an important way to screen for testicular cancer." Parents may be baffled by a child's inability to accept their own body parts, and normalizing this experience is helpful for everyone.

Case Study: Lena, Part 2

Shortly after the last visit, Lena was hospitalized for a suicide attempt. She ingested a bottle of ibuprofen while at her father's house and immediately reported to him what she'd done. During her hospitalization, she was again diagnosed with gender dysphoria as well as depression and started on antidepressants. Matt was initially furious with the hospital team for "encouraging Brenda's crazy parenting," but after several sessions with Lena's psychiatrist, he began to describe his fears for Lena and his grief about "losing [his] son." Upon Lena's discharge, the parents were advised to continue to see the therapist with expertise in this area. Matt and Brenda first met alone with Lena's therapist and discussed their concern about Lena and how their ongoing anger with each other made it difficult to negotiate this trying time. Matt read literature about gender dysphoria provided to him by the therapist and began to talk to Lena about her gender issues. Lena and Matt attended therapy sessions together, and Lena started to talk more freely about her pain and confusion. Eventually, Lena, Matt, and Brenda all agreed that treating Lena with pubertal blockers was the next step. When they came back to the office, Lena's hair had grown out and she was wearing feminine clothing. When I examined her, I saw mild progression of puberty, and Lena, with tears in her eyes, told me, "We waited too long. I look too much like a guy now. This won't work."

Family Conferences: Which Treatment Path Is Right for This Child?

A family conference can be an effective tool for formulating a treatment plan. The act of calling family members to meet is powerful, offering the patient, family, and professional time and space to discuss individual concerns and ask for input and assistance with problem solving. Sometimes the plan for a child is clear, but more often, family members need time to discuss options and timing for various treatments, to process how physical changes will affect the child in the larger world, and to review the risks and benefits of pharmaceutical interventions. We can also provide anticipatory guidance by assembling a packet of educational handouts, as well as other resources for families, including lists of books, films, websites, conferences, camps, and local support organizations. Family meetings often serve as a vehicle to help move from anxiety and distress toward hope and resolve.

Discussions about Fertility

A family meeting also provides an opportunity to counsel patients and families about the loss of fertility that results from treatment with pubertal blockers and gender-affirming hormones. Young children may not understand reproductive biology and may believe that they will be able to cause or carry a pregnancy in their experienced gender after transition. Others may understand the implications of loss of fertility and will need time to discuss gamete-banking options or to process their feelings of grief. Adolescents tend to underestimate the psychological effect that loss of fertility may have. Many youth are dismissive of concerns and say, "I'll just adopt." Parents may be painfully aware of how this decision could affect their child later in life and suffer distress about making this decision for or with their child when the child's understanding of the costs and challenges of adoption is limited. Most youth press for immediate treatment with blockers or hormones, but it's important to insist on time to process these concerns and make appropriate referrals to fertility-preservation specialists before prescribing medications that cause permanent loss of fertility (De Roo, Tilleman, T'Sjoen, & De Sutter, 2016).

Informed Consent

The WPATH Standards of Care (Coleman et al., 2012) outline the need for informed consent before initiating treatment with pubertal blockers or gender-affirming hormones. The consent process provides a final opportunity to systematically review the known risks and benefits before starting treatment. The provider must ascertain who is legally able to provide consent for a child, though it is good practice to obtain consent from all parental figures involved in the child's care, if possible, so that all parents, particularly those with more doubts, are included in this process. Although children are not legally able to consent for themselves in the United States until age 18, we can involve minors by requesting their informed *assent*. Consent forms can be downloaded from the web (UCSF, 2016).

Payment for Treatments: Insurance and Beyond

Many insurance companies do not cover the cost of pubertal blockers (GnRH agonists), which, at the time of this writing, can amount to $30,000 per year. To assist with obtaining these medications, it's helpful to know which insurance companies cover pubertal blockers and how to petition for treatment authorization. During visits for prepubertal surveillance, we should advise parents which insurance carriers to choose so that these drugs are a covered benefit when their child reaches the appropriate stage of puberty. To assist families without coverage, we can prescribe the less costly Vantas (histrelin) implant, apply for compassionate medications from drug companies (AbbVie, n.d.), or counsel families on the risks and benefits of using medroxyprogesterone as a pubertal blocking agent (Lynch, Khandheria, & Meyer, 2015).

Working with Medical Uncertainty:
"What are the long-term risks of these treatments?"

Families usually ask about the long-term risks of medical interventions, and they are understandably concerned about the paucity of reassuring data. By the time providers and families decide to initiate treatment with pubertal blocking medications, most parents understand the importance of preventing irreversible pubertal changes in the undesired natal gender. There are numerous studies that outline the risks of depression, suicide, and substance abuse in transgender youth without treatment (Burgess, 2000; Grossman & D'Augelli, 2006; Grossman & D'Augelli, 2007; Haldeman, 2000; Mallon & DeCrescenzo, 2006; Mathy, 2003). Conversely, research shows that the use of pubertal blocking medications has a beneficial effect on mental health and well-being in the short term, but data on the long-term safety of these treatments are limited (Cohen-Kettenis, Schagen, Steensma, de Vries, & Delemarre-van de Waal, 2011). By reviewing what is known and not known about the risks and benefits, and by acknowledging the discomfort of medical uncertainty, we can usually help parents decide which treatment option is best.

Ongoing Collaborative Care: Tasks for the Second Stage of Treatment

The families of children starting pubertal blockers have usually passed through Lev's (2004) first two stages — (1) *Discovery and Disclosure* and (2) *Turmoil* — and have decided that medical intervention is important for the health of their child. Pubertal blockers are prescribed so that the family and team have time to process the child's unique situation and consider transition without the added burden of the child's suffering through puberty in their natal gender. Psychotherapy during this period is essential. Therapeutic tasks include exploration and assessment of the child's gender identity, coming out, social transitions, and family adjustment. Medical providers and therapists should discuss and agree on an appropriate schedule for mental health visits, depending on how the child and family are coping. Group therapy for both GNC youth and their parents can also be helpful during this time, and all professionals working with this population should be aware of community resources in their area. Most families struggle with decisions about how and when children should socially transition in school. Details of this process are usually worked out with mental health clinicians, but medical professionals may also be called on to assist schools with establishing policies to support gender nonconforming students.

Case Study: Lena, Part 3

Lena presents for a routine follow-up with her father. Brenda had to work, but Matt says he will contact her after we meet to give her an update. Lena has now been on hormone blockers for a year. She is 15 and doing well. Her mood is improved. She has shoulder-length hair and wears feminine clothing to this appointment. She still presents as Scott in school but is always Lena at home. She's considering a social transition at school but says she's scared she will be bullied. Her dad is worried that he won't be able to control his rage if this happens. Lena reports that her mom met with the school principal, who said he'd never had a transgender student before but was willing to learn what to do. He's worried about bathrooms and locker rooms and suggested Lena could use the bathroom in the nurse's office. Lena doesn't like this suggestion and wants to be able to use the girls' room, which is also a social hub. Lena came out to a few close girlfriends, who were supportive. She "likes" one of these girls "more than a friend," and thinks this friend "might like [her] back." Matt is confused by this and says he had assumed Lena would want to date men. Lena and Matt are uncertain about how to approach her paternal grandparents, who are conservative Christians. She came out to her Uncle Mike, who is gay, and he was "awesome." Lena has developed severe seasonal allergies and sees an allergist for shots several times a month. She's worried about presenting as female in the allergist's office since they've known her only as male. Lena would like to begin gender-affirming hormone treatment so that her puberty is more congruent with that of her peers. Her parents are supportive. "It's time," says Matt. "Her Mom thinks so, too." Lena has been reading about surgical options and asks, "How old do I have to be for surgery?"

PART 3   FOLLOW-UP CARE

Family Interviews: Assessing Response to Treatment and Moving Forward

By the time most families arrive at our office for this kind of follow-up care, they are immersed in the biomedical treatment process and have a better understanding of gender transition; many parents have become fierce advocates for their children. At this stage, family interviews are useful for gauging response to treatment, making decisions about how and when to move on to partially reversible gender-affirming hormones (Steever, 2014), and processing ongoing social concerns related to transition.

The discussion about when to begin gender-affirming hormones needs to take place with both the medical and mental health clinicians, and the therapeutic team must reach agreement before proceeding. The Standards of Care recommend waiting until a child reaches age 16, but is clear that these are flexible guidelines and that each child's care needs to be handled individually (Coleman et al., 2012). Many teens and families are certain before age 16 that gender-affirming hormones are a necessary part of treatment, and they feel disadvantaged by a delay in puberty that is noticeable by their peers. Youth with supportive families who have been adequately assessed by a knowledgeable team may begin gender-affirming hormones before age 16.

Ongoing Collaboration with Mental Health Practitioners

Professionals and families face a new set of tasks as they begin gender-affirming hormones or contemplate gender-affirming surgeries. By this time, most families are in Lev's (2004) Stage Four, *Finding Balance,* and have a good understanding of the needs of the child, both present and future. Now the team must assist both child and family through puberty in the experienced gender. Puberty is a wild ride under ordinary circumstances, and the added task of working with gender incongruence can make this time even more difficult. We need to educate patients and families on what to expect physically and emotionally as a result of hormone therapy and assist them as they navigate adolescence.

Assistance with Document Changes

Medical providers play an important role in helping patients obtain documents that affirm their gender identity. Most federal and state organizations require a letter from us that attests to a change in gender. The requirements for some of these letters vary geographically. I suggest learning what is required for gender change on documents for (1) Social Security (Social Security Administration, n.d.); (2) the Department of Motor Vehicles (requirements differ by state); (3) passports (U.S. Dept. of State, n.d.); and (4) birth certificates (requirements differ by state). We keep templates for letters in our office and can quickly supply them when needed.

Assistance in Negotiating Large Health-Care Systems

The Report of the National Transgender Discrimination Survey indicates that transgender individuals often face severe discrimination in the medical setting (Grant et al., 2011). Of those surveyed, 19% reported they were refused medical care because of their transgender or GNC status; 50% reported having to teach their medical providers about transgender care; 28% reported delaying medical care because of discrimination; and 48% couldn't afford care at all.

Professionals can assist patients by developing a list of transgender-affirmative consultants to help with nontransition-related medical care, and by educating those consultants at the time of referral. I find most consultants will rise to the task if I call to educate or encourage them to develop the skills for working with this population, and many are grateful for the opportunity to learn. I avoid referring patients to specialists who express skepticism or hostility during these calls.

Coming of Age: Discussions about Sexuality and Safe Sex with GNC Youth

Those of us who care for GNC youth need to have an understanding of the challenges they face in terms of their emerging sexuality during years of treatment. Adolescent patients not only are exploring their own gender identity and expression while negotiating puberty, but may also be working through issues regarding intimacy and sexual orientation. To create a safe space for discussion, we need to include a sexual history as part of intake, understand that knowing about gender may not give us any information about sexuality or sexual orientation, and regularly check in about sexual concerns. Anticipatory guidance about contraception and safe sex should also be a routine part of health care for GNC youth. For example, a boy with a vagina may need contraception to avoid pregnancy. If youth and their families are instructed about packers, breast forms, stand-to-pee devices, and safe techniques for tucking and binding in the doctor's office, this normalizes the process of purchasing devices and practicing techniques that alleviate gender dysphoria.

Many adolescents struggle with how to find intimacy and express their sexuality with body parts that are not congruent with their gender identity. Transgender youth who are dysphoric about their genitalia may wish for intimacy but be disgusted by their erections or the idea of anyone touching their incongruent parts. Teens need coaching about how to safely disclose their status to partners and how to protect themselves around drugs and alcohol. We can introduce these subjects as part of an office conversation for age-appropriate patients. Paramount is the need to develop a working knowledge of how gender transition influences sexuality and ask questions that suggest a willingness to discuss intimacy and sexual health.

Gender-Affirming Surgical Options, and Inclusion of a Gender Surgeon in the Therapeutic Team

Though most surgeons prefer to wait until age 18 before proceeding with gender-affirming surgeries, many patients and families will want to discuss surgical options during earlier stages of treatment. Primary-care and endocrine providers should develop knowledge about the different surgical procedures, familiarity with the surgeons who offer them, and an understanding of insurance coverage and out-of-pocket costs. Physicians must learn to incorporate the surgeon as a member of the therapeutic team and often need to manage postoperative care for patients who travel for surgery (Schechter, 2009).

The process of choosing between various surgical options and picking a surgeon can be overwhelming. There are no official fellowship programs in the United States or an accreditation process for the various surgical techniques. There are no data available that compare the rates of complications for different surgeons. The better-known gender surgeons are scattered around the country, and many families have to travel a long distance at great expense for a consultation. Parents and GNC youth need help formulating the questions to ask, as well as finding the answers to their questions.

Many of the gender surgeons travel to social networking conferences to speak and provide consultations. Some of these conferences also host talks or discussions at which patients discuss their experiences with the surgical process and their particular surgeon. There are forums on the Internet in which people share photographs of their surgical outcomes and reflect on their experiences. Some of the surgeons have very detailed websites, which explain their training and approach to surgical care and offer photographs of their work. We can also assist by keeping lists of patients who are willing to speak to others about their surgical experience.

Conclusion

Medical providers routinely develop skill sets that enable us to care for the different conditions we encounter in our clinical practices. Those who are aware of the need to approach GNC youth and families with a comprehensive biopsychosocial and family-oriented model can deliberately and systematically develop the necessary skills to care for this population. It is my hope that eventually these skills will be taught as a part of traditional medical education. As both witnesses and guides through the transformative process of gender exploration and transition, we also have the opportunity for the kinds of personal growth and reflection that give meaning to our work and our lives. The process of developing collaborative relationships with the core and larger therapeutic team can be deeply rewarding. We who have immersed ourselves in learning to care for GNC youth and their families often experience a personally transformative process of growth and change that mirrors the transformative path of our patients, bringing home the reasons we have sought to be caretakers in the first place.

REFERENCES

AbbVie. (n.d.). Patient support. Retrieved March 29, 2016, from www.abbvie.com/responsibility/improve-health-outcomes/patient-support.html.

American Psychiatric Association. (2000). *Diagnostic and statistical manual of mental disorders (DSM-IV-TR)*. Washington, D.C.: American Psychiatric Association Publishing. Retrieved from http://dsm.psychiatryonline.org/doi/abs/10.1176/appi.books.9780890420249.dsm-iv-tr.

American Psychiatric Association. (2013). *Diagnostic and statistical manual of mental disorders (DSM-V)*. Washington, D.C.: American Psychiatric Association Publishing. Retrieved from http://psychiatryonline.org/doi/book/10.1176/appi.books.9780890425596.

Belous, C. K., Timm, T. M., Chee, G., & Whitehead, M. R. (2012). Revisiting the sexual genogram. *American Journal of Family Therapy, 40* (4), 281–296. http://doi.org/10.1080/01926187.2011.627317.

Bordini, B., & Rosenfield, R. L. (2011). Normal pubertal development. Part II: Clinical aspects of puberty. *Pediatrics in Review, 32* (7), 281–292. http://doi.org/10.1542/pir.32-7-281.

Burgess, C. (2000). Internal and external stress factors associated with the identity development of transgendered youth. *Journal of Gay & Lesbian Social Services, 10* (3–4), 35–47.

Caitlyn, R., Patraw, J., & Bednar, M. (2013). Discussing princess boys and pregnant men: Teaching about gender diversity and transgender experiences within an elementary school curriculum. *Journal of LGBT Youth, 10,* 83–105.

Campbell, T. L., McDaniel, S. H., Cole-Kelly, K., Hepworth, J., & Lorenz, A. (2002). Family interviewing: A review of the literature in primary care. *Family Medicine, 34* (5), 312–318.

Cohen-Kettenis, P. T., Schagen, S. E., Steensma, T. D., de Vries, A. L., & Delemarre-van de Waal, H. A. (2011). Puberty suppression in a gender-dysphoric adolescent: A 22-year follow-up. *Archives of Sexual Behavior, 40* (4), 843–847.

Coleman, E., Bockting, W., Botzer, M., Cohen-Kettenis, P., DeCuypere, G., Feldman, J., . . . & Zucker, K. (2012). Standards of Care for the health of transsexual, transgender, and gender-nonconforming people, Version 7. *International Journal of Transgenderism, 13* (4), 165–232.

Cook, T., & Cook, V. (2013). *Allies & angels: A memoir of our family's transition*. Marcellus, N.Y.: Hallowed Birch Publishing.

Coolhart, D., Baker, A., Farmer, S., Malaney, M., & Shipman, D. (2013). Therapy with transsexual youth and their families: A clinical tool for assessing youth's readiness for gender transition. *Journal of Marital and Family Therapy, 39* (2), 223–243. http://doi.org/10.1111/j.1752-0606.2011.00283.x.

Coren, J. S., Coren, C. M., Pagliaro, S. N., & Weiss, L. B. (2011). Assessing your office for care of lesbian, gay, bisexual, and transgender patients. *Health Care Manager, 30* (1), 66–70.

De Roo, C., Tilleman, K., T'Sjoen, G., & De Sutter, P. (2016). Fertility options in transgender people. *International Review of Psychiatry, 28* (1), 112–119. http://doi.org/10.3109/09540261.2015.1084275.

Doherty, W. J. (1995). The why's and levels of collaborative family health care. *Family Systems Medicine, 13* (3–4), 275–281. http://doi.org/10.1037/h0089174.

Doherty, W. J., & Baird, M. A. (1986). Developmental levels in family-centered medical care. *Family Medicine, 18* (3), 153–156.

Ehrensaft, D. (2012). From gender identity disorder to gender identity creativity: True gender self child therapy. *Journal of Homosexuality, 59* (3), 337–356.

Engel, G. L. (1980). The clinical application of the biopsychosocial model. *American Journal of Psychiatry, 137* (5), 535–544. http://doi.org/10.1176/ajp.137.5.535.

Epstein, R. M. (2014). Realizing Engel's biopsychosocial vision: Resilience, compassion, and quality of care. *International Journal of Psychiatry in Medicine, 47* (4), 275–287. http://doi.org/10.2190/PM.47.4.b.

Erickson-Schroth, L. (2013). Update on the biology of transgender identity. *Journal of Gay & Lesbian Mental Health, 17* (2), 150–174.

Feierabend, R. H., & Bartee, Z. L. (2004). A collaborative relationship between a community mental health center and family practice residency program. *Families, Systems, & Health, 22* (2), 231–237. http://doi.org/10.1037/1091-7527.22.2.231.

Garofalo, R. (2014). Tipping points in caring for the gender-nonconforming child and adolescent. *Pediatric Annals, 43* (6), 227–229. http://doi.org/10.3928/00904481-20140522-06.

Goedhart, C., Brain, C., Viner, R. M., Alvi, S., Mushtaq, T., Walker, J., Carmichael, P., & Butler, G. (2015). Chromosomal variations in children and adolescents with gender dysphoria: Is routine karyotyping indicated? *European Society for Paediatric Endocrinology Abstracts, 84.* Retrieved from http://abstracts.eurospe.org/hrp/0084/hrp0084P2-323.htm.

Grant, J., Mottet, L., Tanis, J., Harrison, J., Herman, J., & Keisling, M. (2011). *Injustice at every turn: A report of the National Transgender Discrimination Survey.* Washington, D.C.: National Gay and Lesbian Task Force and the National Center for Transgender Equality. Retrieved from www.thetaskforce.org/static_html/downloads/reports/reports/ntds_summary.pdf.

Greytak, E. A., Kosciw, J. G., & Boesen, M. J. (2013). Putting the "T" in "resource": The benefits of LGBT-related school resources for transgender youth. *Journal of LGBT Youth, 10* (1–2), 45–63.

Grossman, A. H., & D'Augelli, A. R. (2006). Transgender youth: Invisible and vulnerable. *Journal of Homosexuality, 51* (1), 111–128.

Grossman, A. H., & D'Augelli, A. R. (2007). Transgender youth and life-threatening behaviors. *Suicide and Life-Threatening Behavior, 37* (5), 527–537.

Grossman, A. H., D'Augelli, A. R., Howell, T. J., & Hubbard, S. (2005). Parent's reactions to transgender youth's gender nonconforming expression and identity. *Journal of Gay & Lesbian Social Services, 18* (1), 3–16. http://doi.org/10.1300/J041v18n01_02.

Haldeman, D. C. (2000). Gender atypical youth: Clinical and social issues. *School Psychology Review, 29* (2), 192.

Lambda Legal. (2014). A transgender advocate's guide to updating and amending school records. Retrieved March 19, 2016, from www.lambdalegal.org/know-your-rights/transgender/ferpa-faq.

Lev, A. I. (2004). *Transgender emergence: Therapeutic guidelines for working with gender-variant people and their families.* Binghamton. N.Y.: Haworth Press.

Lev, A. I. (2013). Gender dysphoria: Two steps forward, one step back. *Clinical Social Work Journal, 41* (3), 288–296.

Lombardi, E. L., Wilchins, R. A., Priesing, D. P., & Malouf, D. (2002). Gender violence: Transgender experiences with violence and discrimination. *Journal of Homosexuality, 42* (1), 89–101. http://doi.org/10.1300/J082v42n01_05.

Lynch, M. M., Khandheria, M. M., & Meyer, W. J. (2015). Retrospective study of the management of childhood and adolescent gender identity disorder using medroxyprogesterone acetate. *International Journal of Transgenderism, 16* (4), 201–208.

Mallon, G. P., & DeCrescenzo, T. (2006). Transgender children and youth: A child welfare practice perspective. *Child Welfare, 85* (2), 215–241.

Mathy, R. M. (2003). Transgender identity and suicidality in a nonclinical sample: Sexual orientation, psychiatric history, and compulsive behaviors. *Journal of Psychology & Human Sexuality, 14* (4), 47–65.

McDaniel, S. H., Campbell, T. L., & Seaburn, D. B. (1990). *Family-oriented primary care.* New York: Springer. Retrieved from http://link.springer.com/10.1007/978-1-4757-2096-9.

McGoldrick, M., Gerson, R., & Petry, S. S. (2008). *Genograms: Assessment and intervention.* (3rd ed.). New York: W. W. Norton. Retrieved from https://books.google.com/books?hl =en&l-r=&id=OMQ31lyXKPkC&oi=fnd&pg=PR13&dq=monica+mcgoldrick+genograms &ots=bJGzTY0_wo&sig=XL-7Ys_BugQZK3JyWdMLuK_Xtio.

Olson, J., & Garofalo, R. (2014). The peripubertal gender-dysphoric child: Puberty suppression and treatment paradigms. *Pediatric Annals, 43* (6), e132–137. http://doi.org/10.3928 /00904481-20140522-08.

Orr, A., & Baum, J. (2015). *Schools in transition: A guide for supporting transgender students in K–12 schools.* Retrieved from https://www.nea.org/assets/docs/Schools_in_Transition _2015.pdf.

Polly, R., & Nicole, J. (2011). Understanding the transsexual patient: Culturally sensitive care in emergency nursing practice. *Advanced Emergency Nursing Journal, 33* (1), 55–64. http:// doi.org/10.1097/TME.0b013e3182080ef4.

Roberts, A. L., Rosario, M., Slopen, N., Calzo, J. P., & Austin, S. B. (2013). Childhood gender non-conformity, bullying, victimization, and depressive symptoms across adolescence and early adulthood: An 11-year longitudinal study. *Journal of the American Academy of Child & Adolescent Psychiatry, 52* (2), 143–152. http://doi.org/10.1016/j.jaac.2012.11.006.

Robinson, A. (2010). The transgender patient and your practice: What physicians and staff need to know. *Journal of Medical Practice Management: MPM, 25* (6), 364.

Savin-Williams, R. C. (1994). Verbal and physical abuse as stressors in the lives of lesbian, gay male, and bisexual youths: Associations with school problems, running away, substance abuse, prostitution, and suicide. *Journal of Consulting and Clinical Psychology, 62* (2), 261–269. http://doi.org/10.1037/0022-006X.62.2.261.

Schechter, L. S. (2009). The surgeon's relationship with the physician prescribing hormones and the mental health professional: Review for version 7 of the World Professional Association for Transgender Health's Standards of Care. *International Journal of Transgenderism,* 11 (4), 222–225.

Slesaransky-Poe, G., Ruzzi, L., Dimedio, C., & Stanley, J. (2013). Is this the right elementary school for my gender nonconforming child? *Journal of LGBT Youth,* 10 (1–2), 29–44. http://doi.org/10.1080/19361653.2012.718521.

Social Security Administration. (n.d.). RM 10212.200 Changing numident data for reasons other than name change. Retrieved March 23, 2016, from https://secure.ssa.gov/poms.nsf/lnx/0110212200.

Steever, J. (2014). Cross-gender hormone therapy in adolescents. *Pediatric Annals,* 43 (6), e138–144. http://doi.org/10.3928/00904481-20140522-09.

Svetaz, M. V., Garcia-Huidobro, D., & Allen, M. (2014). Parents and family matter: Strategies for developing family-centered adolescent care within primary care practices. *Primary Care,* 41 (3), 489–506. http://doi.org/10.1016/j.pop.2014.05.004.

Toomey, R. B., Ryan, C., Diaz, R. M., Card, N. A., & Russell, S. T. (2010). Gender-nonconforming lesbian, gay, bisexual, and transgender youth: School victimization and young adult psychosocial adjustment. *Developmental Psychology,* 46 (6), 1580.

University of California, San Francisco, Center of Excellence for Transgender Health. (2016, June 16). Guidelines for the primary and gender-affirming care of transgender and gender nonbinary people: Initiating hormone therapy. Retrieved June 14, 2018, from http://transhealth.ucsf.edu/trans?page=protocol-hormone-ready.

U.S. Dept. of State. (n.d.). Gender designation change. Retrieved March 23, 2016, from https://travel.state.gov/content/passports/en/passports/information/gender.html.

Wisnowski, D. L. (2011). Raising a gender non-conforming child. *Child and Adolescent Psychiatric Clinics of North America,* 20 (4), 757–766. http://doi.org/10.1016/j.chc.2011.08.003.

Wyss, S. E. (2004). "This was my hell": The violence experienced by gender non-conforming youth in US high schools. *International Journal of Qualitative Studies in Education,* 17 (5), 709–730.

Zucker, K. J., Wood, H., Singh, D., & Bradley, S. J. (2012). A developmental, biopsychosocial model for the treatment of children with gender identity disorder. *Journal of Homosexuality,* 59 (3), 369–397. http://doi.org/10.1080/00918369.2012.653309.

16

When My Son Became My Daughter

C.V.R., PhD

I knew there must have been something important Daniel wanted to share when he invited me into his therapy session. I was asked to sit next to the therapist and across from Daniel, who was visibly nervous. As soon as he started to talk, he burst into tears, so I joined him on the couch and we both cried as we embraced. I was scared and couldn't fathom the magnitude of something that seemed well beyond my comprehension. My first impulse was to soothe him and make him feel comfortable. I thought it would be the perfect time to tell him that his father and I had always wanted to have two children, a boy and a girl, and that it was a great gift to have a daughter now. Though I must confess, I couldn't even begin to think of Daniel as anyone but my son. It was an emotional day, but just the beginning of a much longer, more arduous journey. When I think of that moment, I still wonder if I did the right thing, if I said enough to make him feel understood and loved. I wish I had told him then how much I recognized his suffering before his coming out and having had the courage to do so.

Three years earlier, Daniel had disclosed he was a gay boy. At the time, his father and I were used to the idea and to his unusual way of dressing. When he was a junior in high school, we admired his decision to invite another boy to his prom, to the surprise of most of the other parents. Daniel and his date were the first to break the school's tradition when he attended that event with a partner of the same sex.

As a child, we never noticed anything obvious that would have indicated Daniel was gay *or* transgender. He played with cars, dinosaurs, and monsters—like other boys—though he also had other, more stereotypically feminine items, among them a Snow White mask and dress, a Ken doll, and a dollhouse that he played with only at home—never around friends. He asked me to keep his secret, and I did, but without giving it too much weight. I recall his elementary school teacher's impressions that he was "too gentle" and lacked the necessary aggression when dealing with tougher classmates during competitive games like soccer. In retrospect, his difference earlier in life makes more sense now.

Shortly after coming out, Daniel started college at a very liberal institution, one in which LGBT students were highly visible and well integrated into campus

Lev, Arlene I., Gottlieb, Andrew R., *Families in Transition*
dx.doi.org/10.17312/harringtonparkpress/2019.04.fit.016
© 2019 by Harrington Park Press

life. We felt good about leaving him in a safe and inclusive community. But, at the same time, we were sad knowing that we had just become empty nesters. On top of these emotions, a difficult moment was about to occur. Daniel had made me promise not to tell his father before that day. So when we were in the car and driving away from the campus, I informed my husband that our son was transgender. His immediate reaction was to call Daniel and leave a long voicemail, saying how much he accepted and supported him, and that, no matter what, he would always have our unconditional love.

As modern, liberal, educated people, we thought we were ready to accept the new reality of having a transgender daughter. Little did we know that the journey ahead would be long, complicated, and painful, especially for Daniel. We were not prepared to understand the complexity of the situation: the stigma for transgender people and their struggle in a society organized around a binary system.

Daniel, however, knew all about transitioning: hormone treatments, GRS, available support groups. Through him I learned the concept of *gender dysphoria,* or the discomfort between one's assigned gender and one's felt gender. He encouraged us to read books and attend lectures, started seeing a therapist, began hormone treatment a few months later, became very active in the LGBT community, and changed his name from Daniel to Annie, dressing in a more feminine fashion, wearing skirts, dresses, and makeup, all two years before surgery. Transition was under way.

But all didn't go smoothly. She looked more like an effeminate boy and definitely attracted attention everywhere with her bizarre haircut and clothing choices. I still feel pain when I remember how people would curiously stare. One time when we were on vacation, one woman had the nerve to ask me if Annie was a boy or a girl. Another time, at the airport, waiting to board, someone kept staring at Annie while making comments to her friend. My husband became upset and screamed angrily at the woman.

Besides these hurtful episodes, I was terrified at the thought of somebody assaulting my daughter. The more aware I was of the terrible stigma surrounding transgender people, the more afraid I became. I learned that a high percentage of transgender individuals are sexually abused or assaulted and that many killed in violent hate crimes are transgender women. Shockingly, we later found out that Annie had been raped, something she disclosed over the phone and something she refused ever to talk about again. My heart still aches when I think of her suffering. She became a statistic. After that, not one day would go by without my worrying about Annie's safety. My fears escalated when I found out that many transgender people have histories of suicidal behavior and that rates of drug addiction and alcohol use are higher than in the general population. Though Annie told us she had a drug history, we were under the impression she was sober at that point. Our naïveté (or denial) made us think that her use had been an isolated episode. Little did we know.

We kept hoping there was a small chance Annie was just "going through a phase," and that she was gay—not transgender. But her firm conviction of being a female never wavered. Tired of waiting, she wanted some response from us. She was ready for real change.

One night when her father and I were watching TV, she came downstairs completely naked, pointed to her penis, and said: "If you don't pay for my surgery, I'll cut it off with a knife." We looked at each other in shock but understood her desperation. It was time to stop postponing and start planning.

We relied completely on Annie's knowledge and expertise in these matters because she had already researched every detail: who the best surgeon would be, what the costs and recovery time would be. We were concerned about money since our insurance would not cover any of it. What money we did have went toward paying her college tuition, which meant that we needed to take out a loan. Although finances were certainly a big worry, they were not nearly as terrifying as the thought of making a mistake. What if Annie changed her mind? What if she wanted to be male? We kept asking, "Are you sure you won't regret this decision?" But she was never doubtful. Not for one second.

At the same time that we were trying our best to understand all these issues, we had to ensure our family members, who are largely conservative, would get some basic information as well. It wasn't going to be easy to explain this to them. I didn't know how to approach it and struggled with the idea for years. The day before Annie's gender-reassignment surgery, I decided to write a general e-mail to all of them, explaining that Annie had not chosen this path, had been born in the wrong body, had tried hard to live as a male, but ultimately could not. She had to live her truth. To my surprise, most family members understood, especially my younger nieces and nephews. Two of my own sisters called me when I needed their support the most: on the day of Annie's surgery. My older sisters still have a problem using her new name and referring to Annie as *she,* but they love her dearly and pray for her daily. Unfortunately, both my mother and my father-in-law died without knowing Annie.

My husband and I had been very anxious in the weeks leading up to the surgery, although we felt confident Annie was in good hands but still needed our support. Before the surgery, Annie had had two years of psychotherapy, during which her identification as female persisted, which was substantiated by her therapist in a letter to the surgeon. As it turned out, the surgery went well and Annie was in good spirits. One day later, however, she started to bleed internally, was in terrible pain, and had to return to the operating room. Since my husband had to go back to his job, I stayed alone with her. Both of us were quite scared. I prayed and prayed. After a dreadful week, we returned home and Annie started a slow, steady recovery, content to finally have the body she wanted. From this point on, we made a concerted effort to use feminine pronouns and her chosen name, although we still occasionally slip up.

A year later, she completed her transition by getting her Adam's apple shaved and getting breast implants. This time around, the surgery went very well. But there was something the surgeon told us, something that changed our lives forever: Annie was addicted to cocaine *and* heroin. We were devastated. Petrified. We could not believe she had been using and that we had missed what we would now consider obvious signs. My husband and I were both in a state of disbelief. How could this happen? Was it something we did? Was the stress of being transgender a factor? Again, my daughter was a statistic.

Once more, we felt totally unprepared. From that moment on, Annie's recovery from surgery was our priority. We thought we had done the right thing by taking care of her at home. But, unbeknown to us, not only did she continue using cocaine and heroin, but she was also abusing the prescribed painkillers. After Annie started talking more about how "good" she felt when she was high, several weeks after surgery, we disclosed the discussion we had had with her surgeon. Going into rehab seemed like the best option. She resisted. My fear was that I would come home from work and find her on the floor unconscious—or dead.

One weekend, Annie decided to go to New York, something we thought would be a good idea after being cooped up in the house for so long. That Sunday, however, we got a call from her. She told us she had overdosed, had to go to the ER, and was now in detox. Our hearts dropped. We felt so scared and helpless. We were not allowed to visit or call her. After a week, her father picked her up and brought her home. She looked terrible! She was pale and her eyes looked lifeless and hollow. It is a somber picture we'll never forget.

At our insistence, she went into rehab for a month. After that, the road to sobriety was painful, dangerous, and filled with relapses. Although she lived in recovery houses, found work, attended Narcotics Anonymous meetings, and worked the 12-step program, she had dangerous overdoses, broke the rules, and lied to us about it. As we later learned, all the "ups and downs" are part of recovery. Reportedly, Annie got along well with her housemates, who at one point totaled 14 other women, many of whom she remains close with.

During this year and a half, we lived in constant fear that she would overdose and that we would lose our one and only child. My anxiety and depression became so extreme that I had to take medication to function. But through it all, the three of us persevered and found support in our families, friends, and colleagues. As a devout Catholic, I turned to prayer. Through the parents' support group, Nar-Anon, I learned that we needed to let our daughter run her own life, make her own mistakes, learn from them, and put her fate in the hands of a higher power.

We can only imagine how hard life has been for Annie. We have suffered only a fraction of what she has been through in her battles as a trans woman and as an addict. She has endured disdain and injustice and fallen into the deepest, darkest despair, but she managed to valiantly pull herself out—not once, but several times. Annie has seen many of her friends succumb to addiction, but she somehow manages to keep going. She has been sober for over two years now, and we couldn't be prouder.

No matter how the shadow of addiction and the stigma of being transgender sometimes come back to haunt her, Annie has built a new life for herself, far away from us; a new life in which she has learned a new language, experienced a new culture, developed new friendships, and become quite religious. We asked Annie to forgive us for not being "perfect." Because we love her so much, we made mistakes, but we tried to do our best. We learned a great deal through this journey and are so happy to see her transition into the beautiful, independent, and, most important, sober woman she has become.

PART 6

Family Functioning: What Is the Effect of Gender Atypical Behavior on Parental Relationships, Extended Family, and Siblings?

"Lighting rods" is how Shannon L. Sennott and Davis Chandler describe the vital role siblings can play in deepening a family's understanding of itself. A gender nonconforming or transgender child who requires a greater amount of support from their parents may leave the other children feeling abandoned. Reconceptualizing and reconfiguring the ways in which clinicians can assist parents to be inclusive of *all* their children is the central focus of their piece, "Supporting Siblings through Transition."

Their Child-Centered Transfeminist Therapeutic (CCTFT) approach comprises three separate building blocks: the Transfeminist Approach to Clinical Competency, the Family Emergence Model, and the Dialogic Practice Model, all based on the notions of authenticity, recognition of difference, and equality. The *tenets* and *best practices* that flow from these building blocks reflect a commitment to the same ideals, many of which are illustrated by fascinating case vignettes woven into their narrative, highlighting a unique blend of theory and practice. Referring to the families with whom they work as "pioneers," Sennott and Chandler must be considered pioneers in their own right for highlighting this neglected aspect of family work.

Elizabeth Anne Riley issues a call to arms: families, teachers, medical and mental health professionals, and community members must all band together in the service of supporting both the growing number of children and adolescents identifying as gender nonconforming or transgender and their parents, who are sometimes "hoping it would be a phase." Boldly arguing that the coercion to conform to gender stereotypes constitutes *gender abuse*, Riley offers a succinct overview of the challenges parents face in navigating gender nonconformity, all of which are complicated by the fact that the very people who are supposed to assist them, such as school staff, therapists, and physicians, may not be any better equipped, sometimes less so, than the parents themselves.

While struggling to sort out their own reactions and educate themselves—sometimes feeling quite alone in the process—parents may be trying to salvage, sustain, or disengage from relationships with family members and friends, whose hostility and blame could exacerbate the parents' own guilt and shame; they may be worried about their child's safety and what the future holds; they may be unsure of how and when to set limits in public and private spaces; and they may be confused about how to reconcile the child's past with the present. As professionals, we sometimes expect parents to accomplish tasks that require Herculean efforts, forgetting that they may need as much support, maybe even more, than the child. The very behaviors and attitudes we encourage parents to exhibit toward their children are the same ones we have to model toward those parents we serve in our practices.

Contrasting the experiences of the parents of those who transition during midlife (or later) with the parents of those who begin transitioning during childhood, adolescence, and young adulthood, Katherine Rachlin highlights a number of pertinent issues: (1) the increased awareness of transgender and gender nonconforming people in the media and how that affects disclosure and reactions to disclosure; (2) the difficulties of reconciling a history of who they thought their child *was* with the reality of who they actually *are*; (3) the challenges of a parent's disclosure and ways they navigate the reactions of friends and family; (4) the potential risks to the stability of the family as a result of a later-life transition; (5) the timing of the transition and how that intersects with the parent's own trajectory; (6) the ways in which the transition challenges a parent's capacities to cope; (7) the shifts in the roles played by both the parent and child; (8) the history and quality of the parent-child relationship as a gauge for how a parent might respond to disclosure and subsequent events; and (9) the importance of locating support for parents.

Though our text is primarily organized around the periods of childhood, adolescence, and young adulthood, Rachlin generously expands our focus for just a moment, offering a glimpse into the challenges a later-life transition can bring, not only for the patient but for the entire family.

River, Shelley, Sonya, and AJ Rio-Glick fittingly conclude this section with "Transition in Four Voices," a full-throated, polyphonic rendering of their separate experiences of AJ's coming out as a trans man. His moms, River and Shelley, actively defended against the assertion that AJ was male, which, early on, took the form of a request for a binder. But coming out at the all-girls' school AJ attended, then getting expelled for it, created a crisis. And, as we know, a crisis can be a turning point, an opportunity for change. This act of injustice served as a rallying cry, eventually helping shift the perspectives of River and Shelley, not only in the ways they approached AJ's gender identity, but also in the healthier, more open ways they connected as a family and related to the world. As for her part, AJ's sister (and identical twin), Sonya, has steadfastly stood by AJ, modeling for the rest of us what unconditional love looks like.

17

Supporting Siblings through Transition: A Child-Centered, Transfeminist Therapeutic Approach

Shannon L. Sennott, LICSW, AASECT-certified, Davis Chandler, LICSW

Radical and transformative models for guiding families through a child's gender transition are emerging (Coolhart, Baker, Farmer, Malaney, & Shipman, 2013; Ehrensaft, 2012; Malpas, 2011; Menvielle & Hill, 2010), but those models do not explicitly include how parents can effectively assist other children in their family. As Kuvalanka, Gardner, and Munroe (2019) describe, the availability of a wide network of support for gender nonconforming and transgender children is key to their self-image, health, and adjustment. But sometimes overlooked is the fact that parents of these children need support themselves. How can we, as clinicians, aid parents in helping those siblings of gender nonconforming and transgender kids?

In these families, as in many others, siblings are often lightning rods for what may be latent. Eliciting their voices can add richness to the family's understanding. When one child experiences a greater need or requires more family resources, the other children often suffer. Individuals who have a brother or sister who is gay or lesbian have a wide range of experiences: sometimes they become a primary ally; other times they themselves are bullied; many times they become more aware of their own sexuality; and most times, they evolve into people who experience a greater awareness of and appreciation for difference (Gottlieb, 2005). Similarly, siblings of gender diverse and transgender children may feel ignored, even abandoned, by their parents, may be victimized by peers, or may become strong allies (Menvielle & Hill, 2010; Norwood 2013).

This chapter will introduce Child-Centered Transfeminist Therapy (CCTFT)—an approach previously designed for clinicians and parents—which we adapted for working with siblings of gender nonconforming and transgender children.

CCTFT was developed by Shannon Sennott and the Translate Gender Family Group. In this chapter, we will (1) define specific language used in the CCTFT approach; (2) provide an overview of its theories and influences; (3) outline the tenets

Lev, Arlene I., Gottlieb, Andrew R., *Families in Transition*
dx.doi.org/10.17312/harringtonparkpress/2019.04.fit.017
© 2019 by Harrington Park Press

of CCTFT through the use of a clinical vignette; (4) illustrate an application of CCTFT; (5) offer clinicians best practices; and (6) conclude with two case examples.

Definitions

Trans families. Looking back over the years of our LGBTQ family therapy practice, we have seen a significant shift in the coping mechanisms and strategies that parents and extended family members use when it comes to supporting a gender diverse or transgender child.[1] There appears to be less fear about societal dangers that could stymie a child's social transition and greater commitment to the use of affirming language and communications. Families, parents in particular, are beginning to consider themselves as *LGBTQ families,* rather than as families with an *LGBTQ child.* Understanding this distinction is critical for parents to be able to support *all* their children, not just the one who is gender nonconforming or transgender. Working toward redefinition is the key to inclusion of siblings in the process of socially transitioning a gender nonconforming or transgender youth. This shift toward a full identification as a trans family seems crucial, especially when it is likened to the notion of white parents adopting a child of color, thereby becoming, in effect, an interracial family, thus reflecting the reality that the whole system has changed to support both the adoptee and the other family members (Trenka, Oparah, & Shin, 2006). Similarly, the entire family system changes identity when a gender nonconforming or transgender child comes out. With the families we see, identification by all members of the system as a trans family allows for the gender diverse or transgender young person to be protected by not explicitly naming them. This redefinition also includes their siblings in celebrating their family member's identity and creates space for them to know that it is not only possible but unconditionally acceptable for them to be their authentic selves.

Foundations of CCTFT

The three theoretical underpinnings of CCTFT are the Transfeminist Approach to Clinical Competency, the Family Emergence Model, and the Dialogic Practice Model. We offer a brief summary of each, highlight the tenets most central to working with gender nonconforming and transgender young people, their parents, and siblings, and demonstrate their application to CCTFT and our practice.

[1] It is important to note that the Translate Gender Family Group is situated in Northampton, Mass., a town known for being liberal and open-minded, in a state that is fairly progressive in its political leanings. Additionally, Shannon is known as a trans specialist in the area, and families come from all over New England to get support. Though her private practice and the family group consist largely of liberal-minded families, there is a wide range of racial, socioeconomic, educational, and cultural diversity among them.

The Transfeminist Approach to Clinical Competency relies on the concept of creating a commitment to self-reflection and community accountability within the context of the therapeutic relationship, acknowledging the matrix of intersecting oppressions that shape the lived experience of all individuals designated female at birth and all people who identify and live as women (Sennott & Smith, 2011). The transfeminist approach is "an alternative re-conceptualization of feminist theory based on the weaving of feminist thought, social justice frameworks, and principles of allyship" (Sennott, 2011, p. 102).

The transfeminist therapeutic approach assumes that we construct our own gender identity on the basis of what feels authentic (that is, ego-syntonic) to us as we live and relate to others within given social and cultural constraints. A clinician who adopts the transfeminist approach works to "disassemble the essentialist assumption of the normativity of the sex/gender congruence and acknowledges that those who do not fit neatly into one sex/gender/gender expression category or another can still feel as though they belong inside a gender identity and expression continuum that is not confined [by] the binary" (Sennott, 2011, p. 103). The transfeminist approach couples an awareness of the designated sex, gender identity, gender expression, and sexual orientation continuums with consideration of the matrix of intersecting marginalized and privileged identities. Special attention is paid to these intersecting identities because they inform the ways in which a person experiences and actualizes gender identity.

The foundational principles of the transfeminist approach are that a hierarchy of authentic, lived experience for women does not exist; that to privilege one *type* of womanhood or femaleness over another is inherently antifeminist; that no one individual, group, or type of woman can define what it means to be a woman or to identify as female; that most trans, nonbinary, gender nonconforming, genderqueer, and genderfluid individuals have had lived experiences as a girl or a woman and have suffered the direct repercussions of socially condoned misogyny and systemic gender-based oppression.

The transfeminist approach imbues all the work we do as clinicians, the practices of Translate Gender, an advocacy, education, and therapy nonprofit located in western Massachusetts that runs the Translate Gender Family Group, and how we work with children, siblings, parents, and family systems. This approach is used overtly, obliquely, and subtly. Educating and assisting parents and sisters and brothers of gender nonconforming and transgender children to understand how the gender binary oppresses everyone, not just those who are differently gendered, encourages the family to challenge their own biases and be more effective allies.

The Family Emergence Model (Lev, 2004; Lev and Alie, 2012) was developed as a guide for clinicians to understand the process that families go through as they become aware that they have a member who is trans identified. This model is critical to the CCTFT approach because it gives the therapist a trajectory of the coming-out process they can share with clients. Clear and simple to explain, it gives the treatment a tether to *stages of awareness*, which allows for individual differences of recognition and acceptance within the same family. The four stages are *Discovery and Disclosure, Turmoil, Negotiation,* and *Finding Balance.*

The elements of fidelity to the Dialogic Practice Model are another cornerstone of CCTFT. These elements were developed by a revolutionary family therapist, Mary Olson, who introduced them to the United States after over a decade of working with clinicians in Finland. She states: "Dialogic Practice is based on a special kind of interaction, in which the basic feature is that each participant feels heard and responded to. With an emphasis on listening and responding, Open Dialogue fosters the co-existence of multiple, separate, and equally valid 'voices,' or points of view, within a family meeting. This multiplicity of voices within the network is what Bakhtin calls 'polyphony.' In the context of a tense and severe crisis, this process can be complex, requiring sensitivity in bringing forth the voices of those who are silent, less vocal, hesitant, bewildered, or difficult to understand" (Olson, Seikkula, & Ziedonis, 2014, p. 5). Within a "polyphonic conversation," there is space for each voice, and the collaborative exchange among all the different voices weaves new, shared understandings to which everyone contributes an important thread.

The elements most central to our work include coleading the team/group meeting by two or more therapists; using open-ended questions; eliciting multiple viewpoints; cultivating transparency; and tolerating uncertainty. The CCTFT approach uses these key elements of Dialogic Practice as the structural guide for both family therapy sessions and the Translate Gender Family Group meetings. These structural elements allow the therapists and the trans families to co-create meanings and understanding of gender identities, roles, and behaviors.

Supporting Siblings Using the CCTFT Model

The CCTFT model integrates the components of these three frameworks and follows seven basic tenets while staying open to shifts and changes within the family systems. It has been developed for working with all children and families, but it will be illustrated here through a focus on working with siblings of gender nonconforming and transgender children. The first tenet is: *Educate parents, sib-*

lings, and gender nonconforming or transgender children about the concept of inclusion within a trans family identity. It is the clinician's job to introduce and celebrate the conceptual shift in identity as a trans family instead of a family with a trans child. This process potentially allows everyone to experience a cohesive and unifying identity while protecting the individual identities of its members. Identifying as a trans family without outing any one child to the larger community allows for family privacy and mutual respect. Sisters or brothers will often feel that their gender nonconforming or transgender sibling has been receiving a disproportional amount of attention and concern through the coming-out and transition process unless they are given some decision-making power.

Eliza came out at age eight to her mother, Maggie, father, Paul, and older brother, Kenny, age 12, after seeing an article in the local newspaper about a camp for children who are transgender and gender nonconforming. She stood over her mother's shoulder and read the article aloud as Maggie read it to herself. Kenny was sitting across the table from them as Eliza read, and the family recounted that it was he who said that Eliza might enjoy a camp like that because she "seemed to be a boy who was a girl on the inside." A month or so later, the family began therapy. Kenny was frustrated that he was forced to come to the session saying, "All this stuff with Eliza is taking up my ENTIRE LIFE!" I told Kenny that I understood, and I asked if he had brought something else to do in case he wanted to leave and sit in the waiting room. He looked at Maggie and Paul with pleading eyes and they both started to shake their heads "no," but I said that if he joined us at the beginning for 10 minutes, then he could spend the other 40 minutes reading outside. In a dialogical meeting, we frequently begin by asking the family whose idea it was to come for therapy, then inquire who least wants to be there. It is often siblings who are the least interested. We then ask the least interested what they hope to get from the meeting, allowing for the most dissenting voice to be heard first so the therapist can remain attuned to that person's needs. Obviously Kenny was the least interested, expressing annoyance at all the clamor about Eliza's "getting to pick a new name," but he worried about how other kids were going to treat Eliza if she started wearing girl's clothes, not wanting any attention paid to him if that happened. I validated that this was understandable and was a common feeling for older siblings when their brother or sister transitions. Kenny's feelings of both fear for Eliza's safety and embarrassment about potential attention being drawn were easy for him to chart when I diagramed Lev's (2004) stages. My assessment was that he seemed to be in Turmoil and Negotiation, and that it was completely normal to be in both. When I asked Kenny what he thought the plan should be if Eliza got harassed on the school bus, he paused for a second and then suggested, if that happened, their parents should drive them both to school. At that point, everyone in the family was relieved to hear this solution, and Kenny visibly relaxed.

This dialogue between the therapist and Kenny is an example of the second tenet of CCTFT: *Respect the voices and agency of all the children and adolescents in the family.* When we develop and encourage a language for the narrative of transition, *all* the children have their voices heard, which thus increases the strength of the system. Often brothers and sisters are either the first or the last to find out about their sibling's gender identity. At whatever point that occurs and why it unfolds that way are important for the clinician to explore. If the sister or brother is the first to know, it's likely they're perceived as a possible ally; if they are the last to know, it's likely they're perceived as potentially rejecting and may need extra support from parents and the clinician.

The third and fourth tenets of CCTFT are the best place to start when a sibling is struggling to understand or accept. The third tenet is: *Facilitate the development of each family member's identity as an ally.* Helping each family member, especially brothers and sisters and extended family (aunts, uncles, grandparents, cousins) articulate their own concerns and the ways that they feel they can be supportive of their relative is vital to the development of family pride and cohesion. Additionally, supporting all family members to be allies will encourage them to help one another along if they are at different points in the process. Through a dialogic lens, this is possible only if the fourth tenet is honored: *In family therapy and group family therapy, invite and value all members equally, no matter where each person is in the development of their identity as an ally.* To ensure that all voices are heard, it is helpful to have multiple therapists or facilitators for larger family and group meetings, a principal foundation of the Dialogic Process. This allows for the acknowledgment of a polyphony of understandings from all members. Even when a brother or sister is having difficulty being supportive, we have found that there is usually some voice inside them that wants their sibling to "be themselves." Often the unwillingness to be acknowledging and accepting is linked to the shame, fear, and anxiety about what others will think and not knowing exactly what to tell people. It is important for clinicians to help them find ways to talk about their worries, then interpret those concerns to their family.

In the next section, we see how multiple perspectives were useful in modeling how Kenny could be supportive to Eliza and how he could *get* support from his parents and the therapist.

I worked with Kenny and his parents to help him decide if and how he wanted to disclose to his close friends and to other important people, such as coaches and teachers, about Eliza. After her transition, Kenny chose to lessen his attendance at family therapy sessions. Everyone thought that the reason for this was that he had come to terms with his sister's situation and no longer needed support. The summer before Kenny was to start high school, however, about two years after Eliza had fully transitioned, Maggie phoned to set up a session. Because we had already established a close connection, Kenny was more inclined to be open. I asked him if he had a sense of why his folks wanted him to see me. He smiled sheepishly and said that his father had overheard him talking to a female friend on the phone about how embarrassed he was to have to tell people at school about Eliza being a trans girl. Kenny said that, a few days later, his parents asked him if he wanted to talk about it, and he lied, insisting that the phone conversation had not happened and that he was not worried about telling people about Eliza at all. It was then that Paul said he had overheard Kenny, and so he felt he was in "double trouble"—first for having lied to them and second for feeling embarrassed about Eliza. In response, I said it was common for a sibling not to feel "up" to going through the process of coming out to new people, and that does not need to be seen as negative or as nonsupportive. In fact, it could be seen as a sign that he is nervous about starting high school and the way his parents and Eliza could support him was to allow him to tell people when it felt right. When Kenny and his parents reconvened, we discussed the anxiety that Kenny and his parents felt about his starting at a new school. Two years before, when Eliza was coming out and Kenny was learning how to talk about his feelings, the focus was on helping him find the best way for him to tell those friends he already had. Now we needed to help him discern when, how, and with whom he would share his experience, and remind him that he should listen to his "gut" about these matters, as his instincts were good. Kenny was relieved to better understand that his desire to keep Eliza's identity a "secret" was a way to protect himself and his family. Paul and Maggie were also relieved, and they acknowledged that they had not thought about the differences between telling friends and family at the beginning and deciding when to tell new people in their lives.

The fifth tenet of the CCTFT model is: *Build community and networks outside the therapeutic context.* A true child-centered model will extend its reach to include organizing non-therapeutic gatherings, such as potlucks, in order to (1) encourage *mirroring,* as families are able to witness the full lives of other trans families outside the therapeutic group context; (2) provide opportunities for *mastery* through learning how other families are navigating social and community concerns related to their children; and (3) facilitate *imagination* through play as the kids are allowed to engage freely without the structure of the playgroup, developing rich relationships in the process. It has been our experience that non-therapeutic community building has been the single most effective way to keep siblings engaged. When we encounter those kids not willing to attend family therapy, their parents often require them to go to these gatherings. We observe that some, though skeptical at first, begin to connect with others. Not knowing who is trans identified and who is cisgender serves to normalize the experience.

The sixth tenet is: *Tolerate uncertainty.* It is critical to model for patients the acceptance of many unknowns. For example, when a son or daughter refuses to participate in any family-oriented activity, it is crucial that parents hold open the possibility that, over time, their child could develop a more positive attitude, sustaining the uncertainty of not knowing if they will ever feel comfortable identifying as part of a trans family.

The degree to which other people's perceptions can affect our own attitudes can shift over time. During adolescence, self-image is determined largely by how our peers judge us, which can weigh heavily on a teen struggling with having a gender diverse or transgender sibling or who may be struggling themselves with sexuality and/or gender. It is the therapist's job to contain and honor the polyphony of voices—accepting and nonaccepting alike.

This brings us to the seventh, and final, tenet of CCTFT: *Create networks of therapists who practice together and who value nourishing their connection to one another.* This is one of the most rewarding experiences in working with trans families, as it helps therapists shape and concretize their own dialogic and transfeminist perspectives as well as hone their clinical skills. Including multiple clinicians, especially in the context of large meetings with extended family, is work that CCTFT encourages to best accommodate multiple voices. With a network-based approach, we often get referrals for siblings or other family members. Having a consortium of therapists who are all working within the same model makes for a seamless continuity of care.

Application of CCTFT and How It Supports Siblings of Gender Nonconforming and Transgender Children

The Translate Gender Family Group was formed as a response to the overwhelming need for support of families who have transgender, gender diverse, gender creative, genderfluid, or gender nonconforming children. It is the only one of its kind that we know of that includes sisters and brothers from the first contact, the goal being to support the entire family. The group is two hours long and meets every other month. In the off months, different families host an informal potluck. This idea of building community and network support outside the therapeutic group meetings is the tether to the sustainability of community welfare, part of a true dialogic approach (Olson et al., 2014).

Currently, we have 22 families participating; there are three therapists and two child-adolescent educators who facilitate. The group begins with a 45-minute introduction, during which we go around the circle; everyone gives their names and pronouns and then is asked about what, if any, important experiences have taken place since the last meeting. After a short break, we divide into subgroups: children, tweens and teens, and parents. The facilitators of the parents' group are trained through the Institute for Dialogic Practice, and the three other facilitators for the children's groups have all worked with kids and adolescents and self-identify as queer or gender nonconforming (or both). These subgroups meet for about an hour and a half in separate spaces. The parents' group discusses issues related to supporting all their children. The kids' groups are divided only by age, so that everyone feels included, and are centered on making art or creating work that explores one's self. Gender and sexuality will often become topics, but the facilitators work only with the material presented and are careful not to introduce their own agenda.

Best Practices in Supporting Siblings of Gender Nonconforming and Transgender Children

The following areas of focus can aid clinicians in knowing how to help parents support the siblings of their gender nonconforming and transgender children. Two vignettes follow, which illuminate the practical application of these tenets and the ways brothers and sisters can be helpful as well as be helped by their parents and larger extended families and networks.

1. Practice responsive listening: Parents must try to listen openly in order to create a sense of safety for their children. Siblings may have a tendency to minimize their feelings in comparison to what they perceive their gender nonconforming or transgender brother or sister may be going through. It might be hard for them to repeat some of the things they hear from those outside the family, and parents should not pressure them to do so. Exploring things others might ask or say is a helpful way to practice what kids can do in a situation when a family member is not present.

2. Empower siblings: As stated, the sisters and brothers of gender nonconforming or transgender children are often asked questions about transitioning. Parents need to be careful not to get too upset when they hear what some of those questions are and try to focus on solutions. One way to empower their children is to include them in the decision about whether to disclose, helping them articulate their own feelings before the family decides to tell outsiders.

3. Honor all forms of alliance: Allyship can take different forms. All are invaluable. Some kids might be interested in actively educating others; others might be more reserved. Becoming an ally cannot be forced. The best are those who do it naturally and freely. Often there is a need for additional understanding from their parents and extended family before they can feel comfortable in that role.

4. Offer alliance engagement options: Parents can help their children understand that they always have the option to engage *with* or disengage *from* any conversation. If they choose engagement, however, this is a way of potentially cultivating awareness. Brainstorming different responses they feel comfortable with that indicate they either are ready or are not ready to have conversations is a useful exercise. Examples are:

a. *The story belongs to siblings, too.* Brothers and sisters of gender nonconforming and transgender children need to know that their family's transition story belongs to them, too. They have a right to privacy and should be asked permission by other family members before their story is shared.

b. *It's private.* When encountering outsiders, they themselves can choose to say they do not want to share information or that the information is private, or they can change the topic.

c. *Share, educate:* They can choose to share those pieces of information agreed on by the entire family, thereby educating others to better understand gender identity.

5. Help siblings find their own allies: Brothers and sisters are part of a family that is now vulnerable. For them to be allies, they must also have their own allies, such as a therapist, a teacher, or a close adult friend—a trustworthy person who can offer themselves as a confidant to help the sibling make sense of their experience.

The Lanne Family

Natasha and William Lanne are both in their mid-thirties and have been married for 16 years. William's parents were born and raised in Portugal and immigrated to the United States in their late twenties. William identifies as a first-generation Portuguese, cisgender, heterosexual male. Natasha's parents are an interracial couple—her mother was first-generation Puerto Rican American, and her father is of Italian decent. Natasha self-identifies as queer and genderfluid and as a person of color. Natasha and William have three children: Star, five years old, Meadow, seven years old, and Quinn (chosen name), 11 years old. The family joined the Translate Gender Family Group when Quinn came out as gender nonconforming, requesting a change of pronouns from she/her to they/them/theirs, and a change from a female-gendered birth name to the gender expansive Quinn. Natasha and William home-school their children. As part of that education, they talk openly with their kids about their multiple racial and ethnic identities and about Natasha's gender fluidity. When Quinn came out as nonbinary, both parents were understanding and immediately encouraged Quinn to talk with Star and Meadow. Quinn chose to tell them together with their parents present. Both sisters were excited and wanted to know what they could do to be supportive. Natasha and William began the process of educating both themselves and their extended families with guidance from friends and the Translate Gender family therapists.

Even though all of them were affirming, we needed to give the extended family, especially William's and Natasha's parents, more assistance. The therapists offered the grandparents two Skype sessions to talk about what it meant to be nonbinary and to normalize the stages of the Family Emergence Model (Lev, 2004). It was clear that William's parents were in Stage Two, Turmoil, insisting they could not understand or accept Quinn. Their reaction was very distressing for Meadow, and she felt angry with them for "mean-talking" about Quinn's new name. The therapists met with Star and Meadow for two sessions to help them come up with ways to talk to their grandparents. We also offered each sister her own therapist with whom she could meet.

After the first Translate Gender Family Group, all the siblings were thrilled to have met others like themselves. At their second group, during the family check-in, Meadow stated she wanted to be called "Bob" and used they/them pronouns merely as an act of solidarity with Quinn.

When William's mother and father came from New Jersey to visit, he explicitly asked both his parents to use the name Quinn along with they/them pronouns when addressing their eldest child. William's parents were deeply confused by this, and their confusion was complicated by the fact that English was not their native language; William often had to translate what Natasha and the children were saying into Portuguese. Natasha and William explained that it did not need to be understood—just respected. William's parents agreed that, though it was impossible to imagine why Quinn would ever want to change their birth name, they would nevertheless not question that choice. The next day, it was clear they were not going along with the plan: the grandmother repeatedly used Quinn's birth name. Meadow assertively stated that Quinn was no longer using that name. Everyone got very quiet, as though "time stopped," Natasha recounted. William's mother insisted that, until the name on the birth certificate was changed, she was not prepared to do anything different. Quinn was deeply wounded. Meadow turned to her grandmother and told her, "No, that's not right! Quinn's name is Quinn and you need to call Quinn Quinn." Natasha and William froze. Quinn told everyone, "Drop it." Natasha told her mother-in-law that Meadow was right, that they all respected Quinn's decision, and that she would have to leave if she could not do the same.

Meadow's act of allyship, and her desire to speak up when her parents were not willing to, was the beginning of Quinn's asserting the right to be called whatever name they chose. It was Meadow who was able to protect Quinn and even be a model for her parents. Since that time, William has followed in Meadow's footsteps, continuing to call attention to his parents' uncompromising behavior.

The Burne-Goldberg Family

River and Ellis are queer-identified parents of four-year-old fraternal twins, Lucy and Anna. River self-identifies as white and cisgender, is from the Southwest, and has no specific religious or cultural origin. Ellis self-identifies as a white trans man, grew up in New England, and is Jewish. River and Ellis first came for an evaluation of Lucy, who very early on identified as a girl, though a designated male at birth.

By the time Lucy and Anna turned three years old, they were both most comfortable dressing and behaving in ways traditionally feminine girls might.

And when Lucy was given a chance to engage in make-believe and dress-up play, she would explore her identity both as a little girl and as a princess. During the consultation, they were deeply concerned with her dysphoria. Lucy's distress was also becoming more confusing for her sister, who was beginning to understand that though Lucy was living as a girl when at home, she had not yet started living as a girl out in the world. It was clear that Anna saw herself in Lucy and Lucy saw herself in Anna, especially when they would play dress-up. It was likely that Lucy would not have been able to articulate her femaleness as clearly (or as early) had she not had Anna to mirror as well as the acceptance of her parents. It is also likely that Anna's allyship would not have felt so deeply protective if they were not twins.

Soon after we all began meeting, River and Ellis decided they wanted to help Lucy socially transition. They asked Lucy if that was what she wanted; she agreed, and she was elated to be given permission to wear dresses and girl's clothing all the time, as well as change her name. Anna was quick to make the switch. River and Ellis were concerned about how Lucy's social transition could affect Anna, even though it seemed she felt happy about it. I prepared them for the possibility that Anna could have many reactions to Lucy's transition: she could feel her unique position as "daughter" might now be threatened; or she might feel overshadowed when the family offered Lucy more attention. We discussed the need for Anna to be encouraged to talk about all the feelings she might have. River and Ellis both committed to frequent check-ins with her.

It was shortly after Lucy transitioned that the Translate Gender Family Group officially began. All four of them attended regularly, and the girls met other children close in age. Simultaneously, Lucy experienced and Anna witnessed a few significant incidents of bullying at summer camp, ones that were not immediately brought to their parents' attention. Most significantly, while the kids were unattended by adults, other campers told Lucy that "only boys have penises" and teased her for being "a girl with a penis." It was clear that Lucy started feeling more anxious about going there, an experience she normally enjoyed. Not until her parents began to question her did it become clear what was happening. River and Ellis immediately pulled both children out, and asserted to the staff that whatever occurred was completely unacceptable. Understandably, those memories lingered, ones that Lucy frequently revisits. What also lingered was that Anna stood up for her.

A moment that will always stay with us occurred when Lucy shared the incident with the group. The other children became very quiet and the adults froze in disbelief while her soft, strong voice detailed what had happened. Silently, Anna climbed down from the couch, walked over to Lucy, kneeled behind her, and placed a hand on her shoulder, saying that she, too, had told those bullies "they were wrong," stating, "Lucy is my sister." Lucy nodded and looked back at Anna, and then they both scanned our faces, our eyes full of tears as we witnessed the strong bond between them.

Conclusion

Siblings are often overlooked when another child comes out. We have found that with careful attention and thoughtful inclusion, not only can siblings be allies, but they can also be critical and integral voices, thereby strengthening the entire family system. Wider application of CCTFT as well as expanded implementation of the Translate Gender Family Group concept could be indispensable resources.

The parents of gender nonconforming and transgender children with whom we work are pioneers. A family that embraces a range of gender expressions and commits to their children no matter where they fall on the continuum is performing nothing less than an act of gender justice. We are creating a new language to capture the strengths and successes, the challenges and fears, and the hopes and dreams that parents hold for *all* their children. This radical act of alliance within families must extend to communities and schools, thus casting a wider net of support. When we all work together, we disengage from the oppression of the gender binary and allow everyone to move more freely on the gender continuum.

Resources

The Transfeminist Qualitative Assessment Tool (TQAT) (Appendix A) was created for use in the beginning stages of therapeutic consultations with trans families to aid therapists in shifting their theoretical lens to a transfeminist approach. The purpose of the TQAT is to explore individual and family emotional structures and to examine definitions of behaviors and feelings within a family system (Sennott, 2011). In conjunction with the TQAT, the Allyship Practice Model (APM) (Appendix B) was created for clinicians to follow when practicing the principles of the transfeminist approach. The APM provides detailed guidelines when working with gender nonconforming children and adolescents and their families (Sennott, 2011).

Appendix A: Transfeminist Qualitative Assessment Tool (TQAT)

Norms and Perceptions of Masculinity and Femininity

The first category of questions in the face-to-face interview examines the norms that gender nonconforming persons aspire to and the possible relational consequences of changing or shifting perceptions.

1. What are your ideas about masculinity? About femininity? As a gender nonconforming individual, how do you believe you should behave toward men and women? How do you expect them to behave toward you?

2. Do you believe that men should feel sad? Afraid? Worried? Unsure? In need of approval? Dependent on their partners for comfort?

3. Do you believe women should feel angry? Assertive? Entitled to put themselves first? Competitive?

Relational Consequences of Differences in Norms

This section asks participants about their personal experiences and emotional understandings of how they, as gender nonconforming individuals, learned to process and express emotions in light of their perceptions of masculinity and femininity.

4. If you were to show anger, how do you think those close to you would feel or react?

5. If you were to show a need or desire for protection, how do you think those close to you would feel or react?

6. If you feel frightened or need comfort or reassurance, could you freely show that to those close to you without risking a loss of self-esteem? What would that look like?

7. If you show feelings to others that you normally conceal, how might others think of you?

Parental Norms and the Effects of Family System Functions on Gender Nonconforming Members

This section is aimed at identifying the norms to which parents aspire and how those norms affect both the individual and the parents.

8. Did either one of your parents have a hard time meeting their own parents' expectations about masculinity or femininity?

9. If your parents had different ideas about male or female behavior, how might it have changed their relationship?

10. What effects did your parents' norms and values have on your ideas of masculinity or femininity?

11. Did your parents disapprove of the manner in which you expressed your gender nonconformity? How did you know that?

12. What is your earliest memory of being acknowledged by your parent(s) as gender nonconforming?

Establishing New Norms for Future Integration

Once the different possibilities of gender behaviors have been explored, the potential for establishing new norms, as well as altering how problems might continue, remains. This section asks participants to project into the future and imagine how they might influence their own children, as well as how their parents might perceive and interpret these influences.

13. If you have a child, would you like that child to feel differently from you about their masculinity or femininity?

14. Would your parents disapprove if you raised your children with different ideas from theirs about being a man or a woman?

15. Were (are) there any people who affirmed your gender identification growing up?

Appendix B: The Allyship Practice Model (APM) for the Transfeminist Therapeutic Approach

Transfeminist therapists DO

- Understand that everyone, regardless of their gender identity or expression, can be an activist and ally in the movement resisting gender oppression;

- Recognize the intersections of transgender justice with reproductive justice, the women's movement, and other justice movements;

- Identify the intersections of gender with other systems of oppression (including, but not limited to, racism, classism, sexism, ageism, ableism, heterosexism, misogyny, homophobia, transphobia);

- Acknowledge how gender privilege and oppression continue to operate;

- Assert that trans and/or gender nonconforming people need allies, just as all oppressed and marginalized people need allies;

- Provide space for people to identify their gender;

- Use gender-neutral language until preferred pronouns are established. This sometimes means asking what pronoun(s) and/or name a person goes by;

- Preserve confidentiality;

- Mirror language, especially self-identification;

- Expect to make some mistakes, but never use this as an excuse;

- Apologize for having made a mistake (e.g., mispronouning someone), correct it, and move on;

- Create inclusive nondiscrimination policies in schools, institutions, organizations, and communities;

- Maintain accountable spaces (e.g., encourage transparent communication, obtain consent, take ownership of personal actions);

- Challenge oppressive language and behaviors;

- Avoid and challenge gender assumptions and stereotyping;

- Ask questions respectfully.

Transfeminist therapists DON'T

- Believe that resisting oppression benefits only targets of oppression;

- Accept the status quo (e.g., the gender binary);

- Consider themselves experts on any person's identity other than their own;

- Assume an individual's sex, sexuality, or gender on the basis of that individual's appearance and/or presentation;

- "Out" a trans and/or gender nonconforming (or lesbian, gay, bisexual, queer, intersex, or questioning) person without their explicit consent;

- Place the name, pronouns, or self-identification of a trans and/or gender nonconforming person in quotation marks;

- Ask people about their bodies, genitalia, or sex lives;

- Assume that there are no trans and/or gender nonconforming people present;

- Purport that anyone knows what a trans and/or gender nonconforming person "looks like";

- Question a trans or gender nonconforming person's assessment of their identity or experience;

- Evaluate anyone's assessment of whether an incident was transphobic;

- Deny their own privilege;

- Assert that everyone has equal rights;

- Ignore acts of discrimination and oppression without taking action;

- Show pity for targets of oppression;

- Use guilt for one's personal and/or group actions as a reason not to act.

REFERENCES

Coolhart, D., Baker, A., Farmer, S., Malaney, M., & Shipman, D. (2013). Therapy with transsexual youth and their families: A clinical tool for assessing youth's readiness for gender transition. *Journal of Marital and Family Therapy, 39* (2), 223–243.

Ehrensaft, D. (2012). From gender identity disorder to gender identity creativity: True gender self child therapy. *Journal of Homosexuality, 59* (3), 337–356.

Gottlieb, A. R. (ed.). (2005). *Side by side: On having a gay or lesbian sibling.* New York: Routledge.

Kuvalanka, K., Gardner, M., & Munroe, C. (2019). All in the family: How extended family relationships are influenced by children's gender-diverse and transgender identities. In A. Lev and A. Gottlieb (eds.), *Families in Transition: Parenting Gender-Diverse Children, Adolescents, and Young Adults.* New York: Harrington Park Press.

Lev, A. I. (2004). *Transgender emergence: Therapeutic guidelines for working with gender-variant people and their families.* Binghamton, N.Y.: Haworth Press.

Lev, A. I., & Alie, I. (2012). Transgender and gender nonconforming children and youth: Developing culturally competent systems of care. In S. K. Fisher, J. M. Poirier, & G. M. Blau (eds.), *Improving emotional and behavioral outcomes for LGBT youth: A guide for professionals* (pp. 43–66). Baltimore: Brookes.

Malpas, J. (2011). Between pink and blue: A multi-dimensional family approach to gender nonconforming children and their families. *Family Process, 50* (4), 453–470.

Menvielle, E., & Hill, D. B. (2010). An affirmative intervention for families with gender-variant children: A process evaluation. *Journal of Gay & Lesbian Mental Health, 15* (1), 94–123. doi:10.1080/19359705.2011.530576.

Norwood, K. (2013). Meaning matters: Framing trans identity in the context of family relationships. *Journal of GLBT Family Studies, 9,* 152–178. doi:10.1080/1550428X.2013.765262.

Olson, M., Seikkula, J., & Ziedonis, D. (2014) *The key elements of dialogic practice in open dialogue.* Worcester, Mass.: University of Massachusetts Medical School.

Sennott, S. L. (2011). Gender disorder as gender oppression: A transfeminist approach to rethinking the pathologization of gender non-conformity. *Women & Therapy, 34,* 93–113.

Sennott, S., & Smith, T. (2011). Translating the sex and gender continuums in mental health: A transfeminist approach to client and clinician fears. *Journal of Gay and Lesbian Mental Health, 15,* 218–234.

Trenka, J. J., Oparah, J. C., & Shin, S. Y. (eds.). (2006). *Outsiders within: Writing on transracial adoption.* Cambridge, Mass.: South End Press.

18

"I Was Hoping It Would Be a Phase": The Challenges Parents Face Raising a Gender Nonconforming Child

Elizabeth Anne Riley, PhD

Parents expecting a child these days may already know the physical sex of their infant-to-be. This knowledge grants them the opportunity to make preparations for the much-anticipated birth, plans that will vary depending on whether the child is identified as a boy or as a girl. Research shows that girls are presumed to be "warm, neat and clean, helpful, and gentle," whereas boys are expected to engage "in rough play and [be] active" (Martin, 1995, p. 739). In short, parents apply a gendered perspective to many aspects of a child without any awareness of the child's internally experienced gender. The cultural and social prediction that gender corresponds to sex amounts to an infiltration of pressure intending to cement the expected gender roles, preferences, and future pathways (Blumer, Ansara, & Watson, 2013). Research on the prevalence of gender nonconformity in high school students indicates that many more families than previously thought are raising children with differences in gender identity and gender nonconforming behavior (Clark et al., 2014). This chapter addresses the challenges parents face when they realize that their understanding of their child's gender is different from their child's reality.

In the last ten years there has been a significant increase in the numbers of families recognizing gender identity concerns in their children (de Vries & Cohen-Kettenis, 2012; Wood et al., 2013). More professionals than ever before are now being faced with the fact that a child's physical sex and biology do not always match their internal gender identity or expression (Meyer, 2012; Telfer, Tollit, & Feldman, 2015). Terms like *gender creativity* (Erhensaft, 2011) and *gender independence* (Pyne, 2014) have entered the lexicon. Every school needs to take seriously the fact that it may have more than a few transgender children in its cohort. Clark and colleagues (2014) sampled over 8,000 New Zealand high school students and showed that 1.2% reported being transgender and another 2.5% reported being unsure about their gender. These statistics highlight the

Lev, Arlene I., Gottlieb, Andrew R., *Families in Transition*
dx.doi.org/10.17312/harringtonparkpress/2019.04.fit.018
© 2019 by Harrington Park Press

importance of teachers, medical and mental health professionals, families, and community members recognizing that there are a significant number of children with needs regarding gender expression and identity differences.

For children whose gender identity and preferences do not match the expected gender expressions and behaviors, the pathways available to them are often limited. The intensity with which pressure is applied to coerce conformity to gender stereotypes amounts to a form of *gender abuse,* which could result in the child's developing severe fear and anxiety after being rejected, punished, or harmed. Furthermore, young children may be unable to comprehend why they are being reprimanded (Hartley, 1959). Other researchers have described these attitudes toward and treatment of children (Alanko et al., 2008; Burke, 1996; Costa & Matzner, 2007; Gagne & Tewksbury, 1998; Grossman & D'Augelli, 2007; Landolt, Bartholomew, Saffrey, Oram, & Perlman, 2004; Riley, Clemson, Sitharthan, & Diamond, 2013). By way of these experiences, many children learn that gender nonconforming behavior is not approved of and, feeling shamed, may aim to please people by "performing" behaviors and roles while keeping their feelings about their gender a secret (Riley et al., 2013). Further, the more gender nonconforming a young person is, the more likely they are to be subject to harassment and bullying—both verbal and physical (Grossman, D'Augelli, & Frank, 2011; Riley, 2018). Therefore, undermining the child's experience is the overriding message that their beliefs about themselves are "wrong." Psychiatrically diagnosing a child for their gender expression or identity pathologizes and perpetuates stigma rather than considering the culturally induced bias that plays a part in the diagnostic process (Lev, 2004; Wallace & Russell, 2013). A diagnosis also ignores the fact that approaches to gender identity and expression not only vary across borders, countries, time, and cultures (Bullough & Bullough 1998; Herdt, 1993; Lev, 2004), but also are affected by attitudes toward "race, class, sexuality, age, ability, body type, health status, [and] ethnicity" (Sycamore, 2006). It is acknowledged, however, that the level of distress generated by the treatment of others or by the child's view of themselves as not acceptable may substantiate a clinical diagnosis of depression, anxiety, or other condition that may require intervention.

There are also differences in the *types* of gender experiences that an individual may recognize. Although it may be seen as desirable to remove gendered language, it is notable that gender labels are often applied to many aspects of personal experience, including identity, expression, role, appearance, emotions, play, performance, pronouns, sports, or a variety of other behaviors. For example, a child may "perform" the gender expected of them and feel that it is only when they are alone or with certain individuals that they can genuinely be themselves. Another example is a child's belief that knitting is a "girl's activity" or that soccer is a "boy's sport," where that belief influences their judgment about what is suitable behavior for them. These terms are defined in Table 18.1.

TABLE 18.1 Definitions of Gendered Attributes

- *Gender identity* is one's understanding of one's internal sense of self as male, female, somewhere in between, or having *no identification* with any gender.

- *Gender expression* is how we demonstrate who we are through speech, behavior, or dress, which may or may not align with gender identity.

- *Gender role* is an enactment of a culturally or societally sanctioned portrayal, stereotypically characterized as *feminine* or *masculine*.

- *Gender appearance* is the way we present ourselves through dress, hairstyles, and accessories to communicate personal gender preferences.

- *Gendering emotions* is the labeling of those feelings deemed socially appropriate for a particular gender or sex.

- *Gendering play* is the determining of activities, games, and toys to be considered culturally suitable for children assigned as "girls" or "boys."

- *Gender performing* are behaviors enacted to demonstrate identification with one gender or the other.

- *Gender pronouns* are ones that refer to who we are, and they are sometimes not associated with assigned gender: she, he, zhe, ner (pronounced "nare"), they/their.

- *Gendering sports* occurs when physical games or activities (sports) are segregated by gender or believed to be suitable for only one gender.

- *Other gendered behaviors* include ways we are culturally expected to use our bodies through gesture, postures, or mannerisms in alignment with a female or male gender.

The demands on any child to conform may be considered restrictive when they are exploring or needing to affirm their gender identity or expression. All these *gendered* attributes, except for identity, are public communications—both conscious and unconscious—endowed with particular meaning. These dimensions may reflect an authentic gender identity or one adopted to appease others. Additionally, gendering attributes or expressions can have a limiting effect, confining the range of possibilities to either feminine or masculine, thereby suppressing language flexibility. In response, many individuals devise their own terms or refuse to engage with gender-laden language (Bockting, 2008; Boswell, 1997; Doan, 2010; Riley et al., 2013).

Challenges for Parents

There are as many differences in parental attitudes and reactions to their child's gender differences, needs, and/or dysphoria as there are families. These responses emerge as a function of the child's disposition and the individual family dynamics, "cultural beliefs . . . power and privilege" (Gray, Carter, & Levitt, 2012, p. 15). When parents have had little or no experience dealing with issues of gender identity, there may be little assistance they can offer (Hill & Menvielle, 2009). They may be concerned about whether their child has a mental illness, have questions about how to respond, or be confused about what nonconforming gender identity and expression mean (Hegedus, 2009; Vanderburgh, 2008). Accessing helpful information and knowing what to do can be challenging when resources are scarce and parents feel alone. One parent offered the following explanation: "We were worried, concerned and confused about what to do. Should we have allowed her to transition at five [years old] or waited to see what her adult choice would be? I was always hoping for it to be a stage or for her to be just a young lesbian. I wanted to do the right thing but could not find support or education. There was little information about girls and gender differences" (Riley, 2012b).

Later, when they recognize and appreciate their child's gender needs, parents may self-blame or feel guilty about having pressured their child to conform or for not having sought help sooner (Hill & Menvielle, 2009; Pearlman, 2006; Riley, Sitharthan, Clemson, & Diamond, 2011a). In one study, parents came to recognize, through developing an understanding of their child's unhappiness, that their attempts to control their child's behavior and expression had been destructive (Hill & Menvielle, 2009). Developing empathy may also challenge parents' own feelings, beliefs, and biases, promoting changes in values and behavior. Wren (2002) found that parents "give up expecting to fully understand or control their child's predicament" (p. 390) and over time, through personal growth, come to accept their child's gender and identity.

Research reveals that the younger the child is when they begin to exhibit gender nonconformity, the less of a surprise it is for the parents when the child later requests support (Hegedus, 2009; Hill, Menvielle, Sica, & Johnson, 2010; Riley et al., 2011a; Wren, 2002). Initial observations of difference may arise when the child verbalizes confusion or is disturbed about incongruent body parts. One parent described it in the following way: "We went looking for causes, did some research and eventually concluded that this was something nobody controls. . . . We needed to learn to manage our anxiety, learn to live with uncertainty and ambiguity as his or her identity emerged over time . . . [and] keep him safe while keeping any stigma externalized" (Riley et al., 2011a, p. 187).

Parents may initially hope their child's behaviors or concerns will be a passing phase. One father explained: "For me it was a kind of shock. I didn't know what to do. I didn't want to accept that. I mean I thought it was a sort of a phase or something" (Hill & Menvielle, 2009, p. 255). A number of authors refer to this initial shock, which may trigger a crisis for the family (Brill & Pepper, 2008; Hegedus, 2009). Pearlman (2006) interviewed mothers of adolescents and adult children experiencing gender dysphoria and found that changes brought on by puberty (for example, adolescent hormonal changes, increased desires for independence, emerging exploration of identity) may also add to the destabilization brought about by the exposure of the child's gender variance. Pearlman quoted this mother's initial response to her child's disclosure: "At age 15, she told me she wanted to be a boy and have a sex change. I was so angry. I said, 'Well, yeah, well you do that, but right now you're a girl so get over it.' I made it clear that I didn't want to discuss it" (p. 103). Another reported: "He tried to explain it to me. I didn't have a clue. I never heard of it. 'You're what! You're not really a she. You're a he? How could that happen?' I was in horror" (p. 102). Some parents described grief about the loss of their hopes and dreams for their child's future (Hill & Menvielle, 2009) and how their own "world fell apart" (Pearlman 2006, p. 102). There were, however, parents whose reactions were more positive. One said, "He was always my son, we just didn't know it" (p. 105).

Finding competent help can be challenging since the majority of health-care professionals have little or no training in this area (Riley, Sitharthan, Clemson, & Diamond, 2011b; Tishelman et al., 2015). Differing views on the best course of management are based partly on whether the practitioner considers it a mental disorder (Simons, Leibowitz, & Hidalgo, 2014; Vanderburgh, 2008). This discord among professionals can leave parents confused about the most suitable approach to their child's situation. Consequently, parents express frustration about having to educate those same professionals, who are supposed to be educating *them*. In spite of the benefits of affirmative therapies (Gray et al., 2012; Hill & Menvielle, 2009; Olson, Durwood, DeMeules, & McLaughlin, 2016) and the damage caused by reparative or conversion therapies (Burke, 1996; Vanderburgh, 2008), coercive and aversive conditioning is still practiced. In addition, significant harm may be done by delaying intervention or not intervening at all (Cohen-Kettenis, Delemarre-van de Wall, & Gooren, 2008). The different treatment protocols require parents somehow to know the most suitable approach for their child, which can be especially difficult since professional communities hold widely divergent opinions.

Parents may also find themselves educating school principals and staff about their child's needs. Managing resistance of school authorities may require parents to provide educational materials, make available a supportive gender professional, or offer referrals to other resources. Facilitating social transition may include promoting the child's right to wear clothes of their choice and use preferred bathroom facilities. Parents may also feel the need to ensure that social marginalization and bullying are handled appropriately (Hill & Menvielle, 2009). This role for parents may be especially difficult when these rights are absent from school policies and when legislation and resources are limited. One parent explained: "If we don't get that support [from the school] we may have to move, and that would be a huge disruption to our child's sense of belonging and protection . . . to then find himself in an unsupportive district" (Riley et al., 2011a, p. 189).

Parents may face hostility or accusations from family, friends, and members of their community, sometimes daily. They may also be subjected to external pressures and the tyranny of stereotyping, and feel blamed or excluded by family members or others outside the family for failing to enforce gender conformity (Wren, 2002). Parents may even be reported to child protective services as the result of others' ignorance, misinformation, or fear. Riley and colleagues (2011a) stated: "They [the parents] had been reported to authorities by another parent who assumed that the child's gender variant behaviour meant the child was being abused at home" (p. 188). Some parents have expressed their sadness, disappointment, and hurt about being misunderstood, feeling rejected by and alienated from people they care most about (Hegedus, 2009). One parent explained: "People believe we are making him gender variant or worsening the situation by buying him girl's stuff. Therefore [they say] it's our fault, that we are irresponsible parents" (Riley et al., 2011a, p. 188).

Parents worry about their child's safety, knowing they cannot always be available to protect them (Di Ceglie & Coates Thummel, 2006; Riley et al., 2011a; Rosenberg, 2002), and specifically whether they will be a target of hostility or violence (Hill & Menvielle, 2009; Riley et al., 2011a). In addition, they may have fears about what physical changes their child may need to make and, if so, what their future will look like with regard to finding meaningful employment and establishing intimate relationships (Di Ceglie & Coates Thummel, 2006; Hegedus, 2009; Rosenberg, 2002).

Also of concern for parents is knowing how and when to set age-appropriate limits (Riley et al., 2011a; Wren, 2002) and to what degree those limits are determined (or not) by their child's gender. For example, is it necessary to control expression and preferences while in public? These issues may highlight parents' concerns regarding safety or judgment versus their children's need for expression (Hegedus, 2009), matters that are heightened when parents feel alone in their decision making. Explaining the importance of connection, one mother said: "What would be extremely helpful is understanding how other parents handled the situation through different stages of school life . . . what they did, what worked, what didn't" (Riley et al., 2011a, p. 187).

Many parents have expressed their discomfort in using pronouns preferred by their child, or they may avoid using them altogether (Brill & Pepper; 2008; Riley et al., 2011a). Doan (2010) wrote: "Many people do not understand the power of these little words and how painful the persistent use of inappropriate pronouns can be" (p. 647). Describing the difficulty with using pronouns, another mother clarified, "It's a habit. Not resistance" (Pearlman, 2006, p. 97). Habits, however, can be changed. Awareness of the ways in which parents' reluctance to use the child's chosen pronouns may affect their child is critical.

Some parents have concerns about how to refer to the past. One parent stated: "What do I do with those memories? How do I talk about my infant [who] was a female to people who only know that I have a son? . . . They're not gonna understand. I don't understand" (Pearlman, 2006, p. 103). Accepting the child's input will help ensure that their view is included and respected. Parents may treasure the memories and photos of their child's history, however, whereas the child may not wish to have on display any evidence of themselves before their transition. If and when tensions such as these arise, negotiation is key.

Other day-to-day issues for parents can include managing the effect of anxiety and/or depression (e.g., refusal to go to school or leave their room), emerging sibling issues, or even simple things like buying birthday cards (Brill & Pepper, 2008; Hegedus, 2009; Riley et al., 2011a). This may also be combined with managing their own anger at having to deal with others' ignorance and reactions (Di Ceglie & Coates Thummel, 2006; Rosenberg, 2002). As a result, family life can become dominated by the child's individualized needs over everyone else's (Pearlman, 2006).

These are just some of the concerns of parents, certainly not a comprehensive list. Indeed, many parents of older children have found that the disclosure offered answers to years of confusion, filled in many gaps, and provided much-needed relief (Pearlman, 2006). Engaging with the information can allow parents to finally pinpoint "the problem," have a name for it, and identify the kind of help they all need (Pearlman, 2006). Supporting professionals should also acknowledge and appreciate that the variations of responses each parent and family have are unlimited and require unique input and solutions.

Parents' Role

Research shows that parents' attitudes to their children have a significant influence on their children's self-esteem, social support, and overall mental health (Ryan, Russell, Huebner, Diaz, & Sanchez, 2010). When parents are affirming of the child's gender identity and willing to provide ongoing support, the child is likely to be more resilient (Grossman et al., 2011; Ryan et al., 2010). Keeping communication channels open, being a good listener, becoming an advocate, and finding helpful professionals are likely to result in fewer behavioral problems than those experienced by children whose parents are more rejecting (Hill et al., 2010). For example, transgender youth with strong parental support have a much reduced risk of attempted suicide (Travers et al., 2012).

We also know that parenting style, attachments, and support are predictive of future adjustment. Parenting styles have been linked to self-esteem (Buri, Louiselle, Misukanis, & Mueller, 1988), happiness (Furnham & Cheng, 2000; Heaven & Ciarrochi, 2008), and coping (Uwe, Hempel, & Miles, 2003) in children. Secure attachments and positive familial experiences in childhood are linked to healthy adult relationships (Feeney, 2008), social competence, civic engagement (Whitley & McKenzie, 2005), and positive outcomes in adulthood (Price-Robertson, Smart, & Bromfield, 2010). For example, children who experience encouragement, love, affection, and appropriate boundaries have been shown to have "higher levels of self-esteem, hope and subjective happiness" (Price-Robertson et al., 2010, p. 7). Additionally, Grossman and colleagues (2011) found that high self-esteem, personal mastery, and perceived social support are predictive of reduced symptoms of trauma, mental illness, and personality problems. Conversely, when families are more rejecting toward their adolescents with differences in gender and sexual orientation, risk behaviors increase significantly (Ryan et al., 2010). When children are pressured to conform to gender expectations, they become vulnerable to a compromised sense of self and more likely to continue behaviors that place them at risk (Carver, Yunger, & Perry, 2003; Yunger, Carver, & Perry, 2004).

Recommendations and Support

Both the research and clinical practice literatures indicate that a supportive family environment is likely to result in the healthy development of all children, including those with differences in gender identity and expression (Durwood, McLaughlin, & Olson, 2016; Gray et al., 2012; Olson et al., 2016). The challenges these parents face may be overlooked by professionals, whose focus may be more on the child, and who may not be aware that parents' compromised capacity to handle the difficulties facing them can have a significant effect on their ability to support their child. Although it is acknowledged that attitudes toward children with gender differences have undergone significant change over the last ten years, recent findings indicate that the majority of parents' reactions remain negative (Grossman et al., 2011; Travers et al., 2012) and that there are still (1) limited support available to parents; (2) a general lack of awareness of gender differences as well as inconsistent management of bullying in schools; and (3) insufficient education available to professionals (Riley, 2012a).

Part of the clinical professional's role is to balance the parents' concerns with the needs of the child. Understanding the challenges that parents encounter allows the practitioner to converse with them in a meaningful and respectful way, even when their attitudes or behaviors are not necessarily supportive (Riley, 2015). By exploring the influence they have, it is hoped that parents will reflect on their child's needs and change when it is in the child's best interests. The aim is to facilitate successful incorporation of the child's gender needs while managing any conflicting feelings or agendas.

Benefits for parents in facing these challenges have been outlined by Hill and Menvielle (2009). They found that parents identified becoming more creative, more understanding, and overall better people. Asking for their advice to other parents, they highlighted three key recommendations (pp. 264–265):

1. *Educate yourself:* read books, take part in studies, and talk and listen to other parents;

2. *It's not your child—it's you:* critically examine your beliefs, make efforts to understand your child, work on yourselves as parents, be mindful of the

fact that it is not your child who needs to change — it is you as the parents. Seek therapy if necessary;

3. ***Accept the child for who they are:*** support your child, create a safe haven for them, and let them be themselves.

A number of health-care professionals have recommended various approaches to help parents meet the challenges of raising a child with differences in gender identity or expression. Hill and Menvielle (2009) urged professionals to consider the child as part of a larger system in which consideration be given to the dynamics of those systems (and people within them) in order to find resolution to problematic behaviors. They acknowledged that creative approaches may be necessary for parents to manage uncertainty and for them to begin to develop more empathy. Lev (2004) described a developmental process model of integration that is inclusive of the whole family. She encouraged clinicians to address the child's emotional discomfort, normalizing their experience, while fostering change in the family and social systems that perpetuate the child's suffering, through education and advocacy. Ryan and her colleagues (2010) recommended that professionals help families promote their child's health and well-being through fostering family communication and advocacy, connecting with role models and supporting organizations, and embracing the child's (LGBT) friends through displays of affection while supporting their identity. Simultaneously, parents' discomfort should be acknowledged and validated as well. They also recommended that the clinician assess the family's reactions to the child's difference, alert parents to the consequences of negative reactions, and provide information about local support, counseling, and educational resources. This approach acknowledges that all parts of a child's life are crucial to their adjustment.

The role of health professionals may also include working with other family members, school staff, neighbors, and any other local community organization in which the child is active in order to facilitate a successful pathway. Likewise, advocacy on an individual basis for a child or through external organizations casts a wider net of support, as well as helping parents thoughtfully monitor the reactions of disapproving family members, other parents, friends, or neighbors.

In summary, the pressures on and decisions faced by parents in raising a gender nonconforming or transgender child are affected by the lack of research and professional knowledge. These children are broadly subjected to various forms of *gender abuse* by individuals and society. Parents may find that they become responsible for educating schools and others around them as they advocate tirelessly while handling negativity and hostility. These pressures combined with the history of professional ignorance not only hinders parents' access to help, but also disrupts their ability to provide the opportunities and protection to which all children are entitled.

REFERENCES

Alanko, K., Santtila, P., Harlaar, N., Witting, K., Varjonen, M., Jern, P., . . . & Sandnabba, N. K. (2008). The association between childhood gender atypical behavior and adult psychiatric symptoms is moderated by parenting style. *Sex Roles, 58,* 837–847.

Blumer, M. L. C., Ansara, Y. G., & Watson, C. (2013). Cisgenderism in family therapy: How everyday clinical practices can delegitimize people's gender self-designations. *Journal of Family Psychotherapy, 24* (4), 267–285. doi:10.1080/08975353.2013.849551. Bockting, W. O. (2008). Psychotherapy and the real-life experience: From gender dichotomy to gender diversity. *Sexologies, 17,* 211–224.

Boswell, H. (1997). The transgender paradigm shift toward free expression. In B. Bullough, V. Bullough, & J. Elias (eds.), *Gender blending* (pp. 53–57). Amherst, N.Y.: Prometheus Books.

Brill, S., & Pepper, R. (2008). *The transgender child: A handbook for families and professionals.* San Fransisco: Cleis Press.

Bullough, B., & Bullough, V. L. (1998). Transsexualism: Historical perspectives, 1952 to present. In D. Denny (ed.), *Current concepts in transgender identity* (pp. 15–34). New York: Garland.

Buri, J. R., Louiselle, P. A., Misukanis, T. M., & Mueller, R. A. (1988). Effects of parental authoritarianism and authoritativeness on self-esteem. *Personality and Social Psychology Bulletin, 14,* 271–282.

Burke, P. (1996). *Gender shock: Exploding the myths of male and female.* New York: Anchor Books/ Doubleday.

Carver, P., Yunger, J., & Perry, D. (2003). Gender identity and adjustment in middle childhood. *Sex Roles, 49,* 95.

Clark, T., Lucassen, M., Bullen, P., Denny, S., Fleming, T., Robinson, E., & Rossen, F. (2014). The health and well-being of transgender high school students: Results from the New Zealand adolescent health survey (Youth '12). *Journal of Adolescent Health, 55* (1), 93–99.

Cohen-Kettenis, P., Delamarre-van de Waal, H., & Gooren, L. (2008). The treatment of adolescent transsexuals: Changing insights. *Journal of Sexual Medicine, 5* (8), 1892–1897. doi:10.1111 /j.1743-6109.2008.00870.x.

Costa, L., & Matzner, A. (2007). *Male bodies, women's souls: Personal narratives of Thailand's transgendered youth.* Binghamton, N.Y.: Haworth Press.

de Vries, A., & Cohen-Kettenis, P. (2012). Clinical management of gender dysphoria in children and adolescents: The Dutch approach. *Journal of Homosexuality, 59* (3), 301–320.

Di Ceglie, D., & Coates Thummel, E. (2006). An experience of group work with parents of children and adolescents with gender identity disorder. *Clinical Child Psychology and Psychiatry, 11* (3), 387–396.

Doan, P. L. (2010). The tyranny of gendered spaces—Reflections from beyond the gender dichotomy. *Gender, Place & Culture, 17* (5), 635–654.

Durwood, L., McLaughlin, K. A., & Olson, K. R. (2016). Mental health and self-worth in socially transitioned transgender youth. *Child & Adolescent Psychiatry, 56* (2), 116–123.

Ehrensaft, D. (2011). *Gender born, gender made: Raising healthy gender-nonconforming children.* New York: Experiment.

Feeney, J. A. (2008). Adult romantic attachment: Developments in the study of couple relationships. In J. Cassidy & P. R. Shaver (eds.), *Handbook of attachment: Theory, research, and clinical applications* (pp. 456–481). New York: Guilford Press.

Furnham, A., & Cheng, H. (2000). Perceived parental behaviour, self-esteem and happiness. *Social Psychiatry and Psychiatric Epidemiology, 35* (10), 463–470.

Gagne, P., & Tewksbury, R. (1998). Conformity pressures and gender resistance among transgendered individuals. *Social Problems, 45* (1), 81–101.

Gray, S., Carter, A. & Levitt, H. (2012). A critical review of assumptions about gender variant children in psychological research. *Journal of Gay & Lesbian Mental Health, 16* (1), 4–30. http://dx.doi.org/10.1080/19359705.2012.634719.

Grossman, A. H., & D'Augelli, A. R. (2007). Transgender youth and life-threatening behaviors. *Suicide and Life-Threatening Behavior, 37* (5), 527–537.

Grossman, A., D'Augelli, A., & Frank, J. (2011). Aspects of psychological resilience among transgender youth. *Journal of LGBT Youth, 8,* 103–115. doi:10.1080/19361653.2011.541347.

Hartley, R. E. (1959). Sex-role pressures and the socialization of the male child. *Psychological Reports, 5* (1), 457–468.

Heaven, P., & Ciarrochi, J. (2008). Parental styles, conscientiousness, and academic performance in high school: A three-wave longitudinal study. *Personality and Social Psychology Bulletin, 34,* 451–461.

Hegedus, J. (2009). When a daughter becomes a son: Parents' acceptance of their transgender children. PhD diss., Alliant International University.

Herdt, G. (1993). *Third sex, third gender: Beyond sexual dimorphism in culture and history.* New York: Zone Books.

Hill, D. B., & Menvielle, E. J. (2009). "You have to give them a place where they feel protected and safe and loved": The views of parents who have gender variant children and adolescents. *Journal of LGBT Youth, 6,* 243–271.

Hill, D. B., Menvielle, E. J., Sica, K. M., & Johnson, A. (2010). An affirmative intervention for families with gender variant children: Parental ratings of child mental health and gender. *Journal of Sex & Marital Therapy, 36* (1), 6–23.

Landolt, M., Bartholomew, K., Saffrey, C., Oram, D., & Perlman, D. (2004). Gender nonconformity, childhood rejection, and adult attachment: A study of gay men. *Archives of Sexual Behavior, 33* (2), 117–128.

Lev, A. (2004). *Transgender emergence: Therapeutic guidelines for working with gender-variant people and their families.* Binghamton, N.Y.: Haworth Press.

Martin, C. (1995). Stereotypes about children with traditional and non-traditional roles. *Sex Roles, 33* (11/12), 727–751.

Meyer, W. (2012). Gender identity disorder: An emerging problem for pediatricians. *Pediatrics, 129* (3), 571–573. doi:10.1542/PEDS.2011-3696.

Olson, K. R., Durwood, L., DeMeules, M., & McLaughlin, K. A. (2016). Mental health of transgender children who are supported in their identities. *Pediatrics, 137* (3), e20153223.

Pearlman, S. F. (2006). Terms of connection: Mother-talk about female-to-male transgender children. In J. Bigner & A. R. Gottlieb (eds.), *Interventions with families of gay, lesbian, bisexual and transgender people: From the inside out* (pp. 93–122). New York: Routledge.

Price-Robertson, R., Smart, D., & Bromfield, L. (2010). Family is for life: Connections between childhood family experiences and wellbeing in early adulthood. *Family Matters, 85*, 7–16.

Pyne, J. (2014). Gender independent kids: A paradigm shift in approaches to gender non-conforming children. *Canadian Journal of Human Sexuality 23* (1), 1–8. doi:10.3138/cjhs.23.1.CO1.

Riley, E. (2012a). The needs of gender-variant children and their parents. PhD thesis, University of Sydney. Retrieved from http://ses.library.usyd.edu.au/bitstream/2123/8749/7/E_Riley_thesis_November2012.pdf.

Riley, E. (2012b). The needs of gender-variant children and their parents. PhD thesis, unpublished raw data, University of Sydney.

Riley, E. A. (2015). Adolescent gender diversity assessment: An in-depth collaborative conversation. *Journal of Child & Adolescent Behaviour, 3*, 241. doi:10.4172/2375-4494.1000241.

Riley, E. (2018). Bullies, blades, and barricades: Practical considerations for working with adolescents expressing concerns regarding gender and identity. *International Journal of Transgenderism, 19* (2), 203–211. doi: 10.1080/15532739.2017.1386150.

Riley, E., Clemson, L., Sitharthan, G., & Diamond, M. (2013). Surviving a gender-variant childhood: The views of transgender adults on the needs of gender-variant children and their parents. *Sex & Marital Therapy Journal, 39* (3), 241–263. doi:10.1080/0092623X.2011.628439.

Riley, E. A., Sitharthan, G., Clemson, L., & Diamond, M. (2011a). The needs of gender-variant children and their parents: A parent survey. *International Journal of Sexual Health, 23* (3), 181–195. doi:10.1080/19317611.2011.593932.

Riley, E., Sitharthan, G., Clemson, L., & Diamond, M. (2011b). The needs of gender-variant children and their parents according to health professionals. *International Journal of Transgenderism, 13* (2), 54–63. doi:10.1080/15532739.2011.622121.

Rosenberg, M. (2002). Children with gender identity issues and their parents in individual and group treatment. *Journal of the American Academy of Child & Adolescent Psychiatry, 41* (5), 619–621.

Ryan, C., Russell, S., Huebner, D., Diaz, R., & Sanchez, J. (2010). Family acceptance in adolescence and the health of GLBT young adults. *Journal of Child and Adolescent Psychiatric Nursing, 23* (4), 205–213.

Simons, L., Leibowitz, S., & Hidalgo, M. (2014). Understanding gender variance in children and adolescents. *Pediatric Annals, 43* (6), e126–e131.

Sycamore, M. B. (2006). Reaching too far: An introduction. In M. B. Sycamore (ed.), *Nobody passes: Rejecting the rules of gender and conformity* (pp. 7–19). Emeryville, Calif.: Seal Press.

Telfer, M., Tollit, M., & Feldman, D. (2015). Transformation of health-care and legal systems for the transgender population: The need for change in Australia. *Journal of Paediatrics and Child Health, 51,* 1051–1053.

Tishelman, A., Kaufman, R., Edwards-Leeper, L., Mandel, F., Shumer, D., & Spack, N. (2015). Serving transgender youth: Challenges, dilemmas, and clinical examples. *Professional Psychology: Research and Practice, 46,* 37–45.

Travers, R., Baur, G., Pyne, J., Bradley, K., Gale, L., & Papadimitriou, M. (2012). *Impacts of strong parental support for trans youth: A report prepared for Children's Aid Society of Toronto and Delisle Youth Services.* Trans PULSE. Retrieved from www.transpulseproject.ca/research /impacts-of-strong-parental-support-for-trans-youth/.

Uwe, W., Hempel, S., & Miles, J. (2003). Perceived parenting styles, depersonalization, anxiety and coping behavior in adolescents. *Personality and Individual Differences, 34,* 521–532.

Vanderburgh, R. (2008). Appropriate therapeutic care for families with pre-pubescent trans-gender/gender-dissonant children. *Child and Adolescent Social Work Journal, 26,* 135–154.

Wallace, R., & Russell, H. (2013). Attachment and shame in gender-nonconforming children and their families: Toward a theoretical framework for evaluating clinical interventions. *International Journal of Transgenderism, 14* (3), 113–126. doi:10.1080/15532739.2013.824845.

Whitley, R., & McKenzie, K. (2005). Social capital and psychiatry: Review of the literature. *Harvard Review of Psychiatry, 13* (2), 71–84.

Wood, H., Sasaki, S., Bradley, S. J., Singh, D., Fantus, S., Owen-Anderson, A., . . . & Zucker, K. (2013). Patterns of referral to a gender identity service for children and adolescents (1976–2011): Age, sex ratio, and sexual orientation [letter to the editor]. *Journal of Sex & Marital Therapy, 39,* 1–6. doi:10.1080/0092623X.2012.675022.

Wren, B. (2002). "I can accept my child is transsexual but if I ever see him in a dress I'll hit him": Dilemmas in parenting a transgendered adolescent. *Clinical Child Psychology and Psychiatry, 7* (3), 377–397.

Yunger, J., Carver, P., & Perry, D. (2004). Does gender identity influence children's psychological well-being? *Developmental Psychology, 40,* 572–582.

19

The Experiences of Parents of Transgender Individuals Who Transition in Adulthood

Katherine Rachlin, PhD

The gender transition of a child is a major event in the life of a parent. As transgender and gender nonconforming people are increasingly visible in the culture at large, those who come out as transgender have more positive, supportive, and even unremarkable responses from their friends, coworkers, and employers. In contrast, many parents will be shaken to their core by the disclosure that their child is transgender, may transition, or is transitioning.

At the first meeting of a support group for parents, we went around the room as people responded to the prompt "Tell us about yourself." One woman said: "Well, I have two sons and a daughter. My oldest son is a teacher and lives in Maryland. He is married and has two girls. My youngest is single and lives in Los Angeles, and my daughter is a writer. She and her husband live near me. They have three children—two boys and a girl." The original question to her was "Tell us about *yourself*." A parent's self-definition is partially constituted by the presence of children and grandchildren, who are, in turn, partially defined by gender. Changes made by one family member inevitably mean changes for the family. More specifically, a person's gender transition is not theirs alone. It is a transition for their parents, siblings, and extended family as well, an emotional journey that requires time and support.

Parents whose children come out as transgender or gender nonconforming in adulthood have unique challenges. Adult children may inform their parents that they are exploring gender, that they have come to a new understanding of their gender, or that they intend to undergo a gender transition; they may have had this wish all their life, or they may have had a recent unexpected awakening; they may desire only a change in name and pronoun or a complete social and medical transition from one expressed gender to another.

As a therapist, I see the full range of positive and negative reactions of parents when their adult children reveal an intention to transition. One of the differences

Lev, Arlene I., Gottlieb, Andrew R., *Families in Transition*
dx.doi.org/10.17312/harringtonparkpress/2019.04.fit.019

between transgender children and transgender adults is the potential for the latter to have hidden their gender identity for decades. Some parents find that the disclosure confirms something they had suspected all along, but it had never been made explicit. For them, the transition has a sense of continuity. Even those who are surprised and troubled early on may be supportive over time after they see how beneficial the transition has been for the person they love. Most parents' primary concerns are that their child be safe, happy, loved, and successful. The proof that this is possible is clear from the large numbers of happy, successful transgender people, many of whom are partnered and parents themselves.

A World without the Internet: Isolation versus Possibility

There is a significant divide between people born before the Internet and those who have never known life without it (Cook-Daniels, 2006). Younger people come of age in a culture in which they are exposed to a world of transgender visibility. This influences their expectations, their life choices, the experience of their identity, their gender expression, and their comfort with discussing gender and sexuality. They may regard gender nonconformity as a viable option and pursue a satisfying life in their true gender from an early age. Older gender non-conforming adults usually experienced isolation during their formative years. They may have developed survival strategies when they learned to please their parents, conform to social norms, and hide their identity, building a life around a *false self* (Ehrensaft, 2011). Many of these adults say that they would have transitioned earlier if they had had the resources available today.

Parents of transgender adults may not believe their child is truly transgender because they were not obviously so in childhood. The increasing visibility of transgender children is a positive cultural shift (Krieger, 2017), but it may also raise unrealistic expectations that are contrary to the experience of transgender adults. People who are visibly transgender in childhood are *not* more authentic or valid or real than those who come out later in life! Some transgender adults were transgender in childhood, some were not; others tried to come out but were shut down by the adults around them. For practical reasons, many adults who were transgender in childhood effectively concealed it.

Those who felt transgender in childhood but kept it hidden as best they could will often share their memories of early transgender feelings when coming out to their parents. They may draw attention to evidence of a cross-gender identity throughout their life—clues they believe the parents "should have" picked up on. They may remind their parents that they hated wearing dresses (if assigned female) or were "caught" wearing dresses (if assigned male). Parents may or may not remember these events and share these observations. Even if they do recall cross-gender expression, they usually did not recognize how monumental it was in the life of their child. They were also living in a time before transgender topics were in the media. They were not informed and educated about transgender possibilities and could not identify that experience in their child.

In contrast, many people challenge gender norms throughout their lives to such an extent that no one is surprised when they come out. It makes intuitive sense to those around them. Nevertheless, it may still be very difficult for parents to adjust. In their minds, a masculine or gender nonconforming daughter is *still* a daughter; a feminine or gender nonconforming son is *still* a son. A transition in which the parent no longer has the son or daughter they knew can be a major crisis for them. Even when a parent can understand the need for their child to transition, it can be emotionally and socially difficult.

The realization that their child has been hiding something significant can be both disorienting and deeply wounding. Hurt that their child did not share the struggle with them, they also fear that the person they love will be lost. The transgender person may experience continuity within themselves in any gender, but the external changes that take place in gender transition may be such that the parents see their child becoming unrecognizable. The familiar aspects of their child's voice, face, hair, silhouette, movement, name may change and become alien.

A Lifetime of Memories

Parents of adults have a long history with their child that parents of younger children could not have. They do not have to wonder what their child will be like as an adult in their assigned gender. They already know. Most parents have troves of photographs of their children. But parents of adults have documented their many years together in ways that a younger family could not: the child's wedding, grandchildren's graduations, the parents' 40th anniversary party. All this may become emotionally fraught. What is to be done with the evidence of this lifetime? And what becomes of the name?

A person's birth name belongs to the parents as much as to the child. Some transgender adults name themselves; others ask their parents to rename them. They may have been told—or may ask—what their name might have been had they been assigned a different gender. The loss of the person who answers to that given name can be deep. Parents frequently say that they feel the child they have known and loved is dying, though, obviously, they realize that the person is still alive (Boss, 2007; Norwood, 2013a). "Parents of a transgender child find themselves asking 'Is my child here, or gone? Are they the same person, or are they a different person?'" (Wahlig, 2015, p. 312). They grieve the loss of the child's gendered embodiment, the gendered relationship—mother-daughter, mother-son, father-son, father-daughter—and the identity they had as that parent.

They've Been through This Before

Some people disclose they are lesbian, gay, or bisexual long before they disclose as transgender, so their parents will have been through an earlier coming out. On the one hand, if it took years for parents to acknowledge and accept their child's sexual orientation, gender identity may seem like another mountain to climb. On the other hand, the earlier experience can be a preparation for the one that follows, inching the family toward acceptance, providing the transgender member with a more welcoming environment.

No matter how a parent reacts to their adult child's gender transition, at some point they will probably share this information with others. They may avoid disclosing to friends because they are in denial, hoping nothing will change; or because they fear being judged, or worry about creating an awkward situation; or because they do not want attention paid to it; or because they cannot anticipate the effect and the outcome of the transition on the friendship. Fortunately, many parents find that, after disclosing, most friends are supportive. But even when friends want to be supportive, they may not know exactly how. They may be upbeat when the parent feels bereft, offer sympathy when the parent doesn't want sympathy, or ask questions that feel invasive. Parents may need to guide their friends and be explicit in communicating what they want them to do or say, whether that means periodically checking in about how they are doing or refraining from mentioning it entirely unless the parent brings it up.

Coming out to friends is different from coming out to family. Parents may fear *their* own parents' reactions much as the transgender adult feared *theirs*.

The opinions of siblings and extended family members—grandparents, aunts, uncles, cousins—may also carry great weight. Fear that negative reactions may be directed toward them and/or their child is common. Parents may come out *for* their adult child—sharing the news with the family. In so doing, they come out as the parent of a transgender person, and, in turn, the relative now becomes the grandparent/aunt/uncle/cousin of a transgender person as well. Older relatives will have known them since infancy; younger relatives will have known them all their lives. Wanting to protect the transgender person and have family members treat that person with respect, the parent may have to serve as an educator and advocate, teaching others what it means to be transgender, what their child's transition entails, and what their needs are in terms of name and pronouns. Those roles can be difficult to navigate, however, particularly if the parents are in conflict about the issue themselves.

Loss can come up in unexpected places. Gender transition may necessitate new ways of handling information about their child's history. Parents may be asked to deny sources of pride in their pre-transitioned child and remain silent about past accomplishments that were achieved in the assigned gender. Military service, athletic awards, degrees from sex-segregated colleges, and membership in sex-segregated associations are some of the possible sources of documentation that can betray a person's original gender status. That the person was a U.S. Navy SEAL, a Girl Scout, or a professional football player is information that the parent might have shared in the past. Now they too have a secret.

Naturally, parents are affected by how much acceptance and understanding the world offers to their child. The ease of appearing as their affirmed gender or their ability to blend genders makes young transgender children more readily acceptable. They also embody the idea that people come into the world with a gender identity. This is particularly true if they are clear and outspoken about their gender very early in life. They and their families may benefit from the natural sympathy toward children.

The transgender adult who has been through puberty in their assigned gender may bear its physical traces, which can never be fully erased. Transgender adults do not elicit the kind of sympathy reserved for children, and their lives are more complicated. They may be a parent and a spouse and a child simultaneously; they may have invested decades in a career and now risk financial instability; they may anticipate loss of safety, privilege, and social status as they become part of a stigmatized minority. Those who have a partner and children are often taken to task for imposing hardship on their family because they disclose later in life. Late-life transition may be viewed more as a choice than as a biological or medical need, and thus they may be more stigmatized (Norwood, 2013b). Conditions that make transition harder for the transitioning adult also make transition more difficult for the parents.

Encountering Transition Later in Life

Sometimes the transition occurs just when parents would naturally be scaling back and simplifying their lives. One father I counseled remarked that he and his wife had anticipated a life of increased relaxation as they headed toward retirement. Instead, they were emotionally absorbed in their child's transition. His wife plunged into a deep depression over losing her daughter—now her son—and the couple was fighting more than at any time in their marriage. Even without a child in transition, retirees often face their own crises, which can involve loss of professional identity, a loss of community, and a loss of income security. It is a time of life that involves facing one's aging body and inevitable mortality and the loss of friends and family members who decline and pass away. Older parents are likely to have peer groups and social circles for whom the concept of gender diversity may be more foreign than it is for those of younger parents. They may experience shame and anticipate negative judgments, social stigma, or ostracism; they may reevaluate and question their success as parents, or blame themselves for the difficulties facing their child. Parents of transgender adults are more likely to be married longer, remarried, widowed, or caring for a disabled partner than their younger counterparts.

Couples will usually approach the transition the same ways they approach other challenges. If they usually fight when stressed, they will fight; if they usually unite, they will unite. It is not unusual for the gender transition of a child to create tension between the parents, each of whom has their own style of reacting to change. Both parents may be equally distressed about the transition. But one may be more willing to be actively supportive; the other may need more time to adjust and be angry if the other parent appears "on board," forcing them to choose sides. A couple who has been married for many years is likely to have weathered difficult times and can rely on that history to survive this as well. Though divorced parents may receive the news separately, they may desire to process this experience together, even if contact has been infrequent in recent years. This may bring them together. In these families there may be stepparents and stepsiblings, which compound the number of important people who may be affected.

Caught in the Middle

How do parents navigate the effects of transition among family members? The transgender person may have siblings who get right on board with their new brother or sister's gender role, who use preferred names and pronouns, and who model acceptance of the new aunt or uncle for their own children. Others resist the transition and try to shield their children, creating a rift within the family. Parents may be caught in the middle between their desire to support the transgender person and the fear of losing other relationships. For example, this might play out by spending Christmas Eve with the transgender child and Christmas day with the other sibling in whose home the transgender person is not welcome. Or if the transgender adult is separated or divorced, parents may be torn between their transgender child, the ex-spouse, and their grandchildren, wanting to maintain a connection with everyone. What is a parent to do?

Having Their Own Lives

Parents of adults are usually independent in ways not feasible for parents of younger children. While emotionally involved with their adult children, those parents will probably have their own separate lives and have the option to take time apart when needed.

Just as parents can exercise independence, so can their adult children. While younger children are dependent on their parents for survival, adults can more easily distance themselves or cease communication entirely. Parents of adults may be confronted with the reality that contact with their child, and possibly contact with grandchildren, may be contingent on actively demonstrating acceptance of their gender identity. If the child feels a lack of acceptance from the parent, they may retreat. In turn, the parent may withdraw because the loss of their child is too painful. Alone in their separate corners, both suffer rejection, anger, and despair. Maintaining contact and keeping a communication channel open is important in the long run.

Parents of adults know their child as an autonomous person who has made many major life decisions. Yet they may question the person's judgment and rationality after being informed about a possible or impending gender transition. This decision, one that the transgender person has come to through years of careful deliberation, may appear to the parent to be impulsive, self-destructive, unrealistic, or ill-advised. Parents may attempt to assert control, reclaiming their role of decision maker, caretaker, and guide. But they now lack the authority that they once had and may be frustrated that the control is no longer in their hands.

Whereas parents of younger children have the stress that accompanies the responsibility of making decisions for and with their child, parents of transgender adults may be stressed about not having a voice at all in those decisions. People over the age of majority can decide for themselves and, if they have the money or resources, can finance their own transition. On the one hand, a relationship with their more independent child may leave parents feeling helpless, and this can lead to panic, anxiety, anger, and depression. On the other hand, not having responsibility can potentially free the parents from the stress of making decisions, so that they can devote their energy to what is happening, rather than what they think *should* be happening.

This dilemma becomes especially salient when parents are asked for financial support for transition. Transgender adults may legally make their own decisions, but they are stymied if they do not have sufficient funds; they may ask parents to contribute to therapy, hormones, surgery, and other transition-related expenses. Not all adult children need this assistance, and not all parents have financial resources to offer, but those who do will be faced with difficult decisions. Parents may enthusiastically do what they can to ameliorate their child's discomfort. Others who are more conflicted may not want to enable the transition. This may change over time as parents go through their own process.

One thing that many parents may be more likely to financially support is the storing of reproductive tissue for their children who are still of reproductive age. Once a person starts hormone treatment, there is the possibility that their fertility could be compromised. Some individuals are certain they will never want to be parents or already know that they want to adopt. Others may appreciate the opportunity to postpone that decision, and the option to store sperm or eggs may be a good investment.

When small children have medical needs, their parents are usually the ones who accompany them to doctors' appointments, pick up prescriptions, give them medication, and oversee their care. When transgender adults have medical needs, they may or may not want mom and dad to come to medical consultations, escort them to surgery, or manage aftercare. Being left out can be terribly painful, yet being involved can be emotionally stressful for everyone. During surgical preparation and recovery, focus must be on the patient, who may prefer the involvement of someone with a little less investment than their parents. In some cases, it may be best for parents to stay involved at a distance through good communication and by providing essential help when the person is recovering at home.

Alternatively, not every parent wants to be involved in medical care. This may be because there may be conflict over transition, distance, expense of travel—or just because they no longer see that as their role. They have no expectation of involvement and no need to be on-site for medical procedures. This reflects the nature of the relationship that they have established as independent adults.

Shifting Roles

One of the many challenges faced by aging parents is the inevitable shift in roles that evolves between them and their children. Later in life, parents may be dependent on their adult children to physically care for them, advocate for them, and/or financially support them. The older the transitioning adult, the more likely it is they will have parents who are physically fragile; the older the parent, the more likely it is they will not have a fully functioning partner, or a partner at all, on whom they can depend. It may be particularly difficult for those parents to access support because they may have limited mobility and independence.

Similarly, the transgender adult may be physically dependent on the parent because of illness or injury, either on a temporary or a longer-term basis. That parent may need to assist with care—for example, bathing, dressing, or being with the adult child in the hospital. These experiences will bring them into contact with their child's transgender body. They must advocate for their child and model kindness and respect in medical settings (Auldridge, SAGE, Tamar-Mattis, Kennedy, Ames, & Tobin, 2012; Witten & Eyler, 2012). If their child is terminally ill, or if the parent loses that child to death, the parent may mourn both the person they knew in their affirmed gender and the person they knew before transition. A parent who outlives their child may also be faced with writing an obituary, holding a funeral or memorial service, and having conversations about their adult child with friends and family—tasks that involve many legal, financial, and emotional decisions and social encounters. Will the parent respect their child's identity and use their preferred name and gender on all things related to their memory? That depends on many factors, including how the parent understands and makes meaning of their child's transition (Norwood, 2013b).

The Last to Know

The desire to avoid hurting or angering parents is one of the most common reasons that people postpone transition. It is not uncommon to hide or downplay their affirmed gender expression when they see the parents—even long into transition. I know transgender women who will refrain from wearing dresses and makeup around their parents out of sensitivity for their comfort, and transgender men who allow their parents to call them by a female name long after they have established lives as men. Parents' difficulty in accepting and accommodating transition will lead children to be creative. Many an adult child has taken steps toward transition before coming out to their parents because they feared the news would "kill them." Some are so avoidant that they begin hormones and even have surgery without any dialogue with their parents. They may even wait until their parents pass away before they come out (Zamboni, 2006). Of course, these children do not want their parents to die. They simply can't imagine living authentically while their parents are alive. One of the goals of gender-affirming therapy is to realistically test the belief that parents are immovable obstacles—a perspective as unfair to the parent as it is to the child.

The death of a parent often initiates major changes in the life of their child. I have known people to go back to school, get married, relocate, and/or begin a gender transition. A parent's death initiates a new phase of life and stands as a reminder that life is short. No wonder so many middle-age clients come to therapy to discuss gender after a period of mourning. Many have spent years caring for aging parents, and once that responsibility is lifted, they seize the opportunity to actualize themselves.

People often fear telling their parents and grandparents about transition because of their own misconceptions about older people. Transgender individuals and their siblings may want to protect their parents from potentially upsetting information because they think that the parents are brittle or fragile. It is not true that seniors are necessarily more conservative, inflexible, or incapable of change. They may have wisdom and experience, often see that life is short, and advise their loved ones to do what makes them happy.

There are many transgender people whose parents are nearing the end of life, and they feel the desire to be fully known and loved by that parent before they die. Depending on their health, the parent may or may not have time to fully process this disclosure. During my many years in practice, I have heard poignant stories of dying parents who affirmed their child's identity by acknowledging them as their son or as their daughter, for example, giving them an affirming compliment or calling them by their chosen name in their last conversation. I have rarely had the opportunity to discuss with the parent what it was like to be given the news as they were leaving this world. One of my patients brought her terminally ill mother to meet with me days after the patient had come out as female. The mother, in her late eighties, quietly told me that she felt sad for her child because she thought it would be a "hard life." She died two weeks later. Though my patient felt somewhat guilty for having burdened her mother, she also felt relieved to have been seen by her mother as female and to be freed from keeping a secret.

Support Groups

Parents of transgender adults may feel out of place in groups for parents who have small children or adolescents. Yet parents of transgender people have issues in common, such as grief, loss, and coming out, and many parents experience great warmth and support from other parents regardless of the age of their children. The lack of contact with other parents who have adult children, however, can make them feel more alienated, especially if their child was not visibly transgender in childhood.

Not all parents find the transition to be a crisis. Some are naturally flexible and their relationship with their child is so solid that they handle the changes with relative ease. They join their child in the pleasure of moving toward their desired goals. Those parents may have a lot to teach others who are struggling. But the traumatized parent who reacts to the transition with grief and anger rarely finds it helpful to know that others are having an easy time. They need to have conversations with people who validate their feelings and understand their suffering, particularly during the initial period after disclosure, a time when many parents *are* in crisis. Parents who struggle in early transition may want to find others who share that struggle. After a period of support, they may be ready to see the light at the end of the tunnel and move toward acceptance.

Research shows that parental support has a profound effect on the health and well-being of transgender youth and adults (Tittsworth, Dykes, & Cabuses, 2008). And family therapists recognize that parents are as much affected by their children as children are affected by their parents (Brill & Pepper, 2008; Ehrensaft, 2011; Giammattei, 2015). Lev's 2004 Family Emergence Model illustrates how transition affects the entire family and how each person can go through a process that may include four stages: Discovery and Disclosure, Turmoil, Negotiation, and Finding Balance (pp. 280–281).

How can we assist parents whose children go through a gender transition later in life? They need services, including support groups, conference programming, and educational material specifically designed for them. Parents can greatly benefit from information and education about transgender people, their community and culture, as well as medical options. Peer support can be transformative when people find compassion, kindness, recognition, and camaraderie. Parents also need *time* to adjust. It may take at least a year or two to *begin* to absorb and accept the changes that occur when someone transitions. For the individual who is transitioning and for the family as a whole, it is an ongoing process.

REFERENCES

Auldridge, A., SAGE, Tamar-Mattis, A., Kennedy, S., Ames, E. L., & Tobin, H. J. (2012). *Improving the lives of transgender older adults: Recommendations for policy and practice.* Washington, D.C.: Services and Advocacy for GLBT Elders and National Center for Transgender Equality.

Boss, P. (2007). Ambiguous loss theory: Challenges for scholars and practitioners. *Family Relations: An Interdisciplinary Journal of Applied Family Studies, 56* (2), 105–111.

Brill, S., & Pepper, R. (2008). *The transgender child: A handbook for families and professionals.* San Fransisco: Cleis Press.

Cook-Daniels, L. (2006). Trans aging. In D. Kimmel, T. Rose, & S. David (eds)., *Lesbian, gay, bisexual, and transgender aging: Research and clinical perspectives* (pp. 21–35). New York: Columbia University Press.

Ehrensaft, D. (2011). *Gender born, gender made: Raising healthy gender-nonconforming children.* New York: Experiment.

Giamattei, S. V. (2015). Beyond the binary: Trans-negotiations in couple and family therapy. *Family Process, 54,* 418–434.

Krieger, I. (2017). *Counseling transgender and non-binary youth.* London: Jessica Kingsley.

Lev, A. I. (2004). *Transgender emergence: Therapeutic guidelines for working with gender-variant people and their families.* Binghamton, N.Y.: Haworth Press.

Norwood, K. (2013a). Grieving gender: Trans-identities, transition, and ambiguous loss. *Communication Monographs, 80* (1), 24–45.

Norwood, K. (2013b). Meaning matters: Framing trans identity in the context of family relationships. *Journal of GLBT Family Studies, 9* (2), 152–178.

Tittsworth, E. S., Dykes, J., & Cabuses, C. (2008). Family relationships and their correlations with transsexual well-being. *Journal of GLBT Family Studies, 4* (4), 419–432.

Wahlig, J. L. (2015). Losing the child they thought they had: Therapeutic suggestions for an ambiguous loss perspective with parents of a transgender child. *Journal of GLBT Family Studies, 11* (4), 305–326.

Witten, T. M., & Eyler, A. E. (2012). Transgender and aging: Beings and becomings. In T. M. Witten & A. E. Eyler (eds), *Gay, lesbian, bisexual, & transgender aging: Challenges in research, practice, & policy* (pp. 187–269). Baltimore: Johns Hopkins University Press.

Zamboni, B. D. (2006). Therapeutic considerations in working with the family, friends, and partners of transgendered individuals. *Family Journal: Counseling and Therapy for Couples and Families, 14* (2), 174–179.

20

Transition in Four Voices

Barbara Rio-Glick, MSW, Shelley Rio-Glick, MSW, Sonya Rio-Glick, AJ Rio-Glick

When coming out as trans, AJ asked that we use the pronouns he, him, and his, as they identified as a boy. After three years, AJ realized they were nonbinary and so we now use they, them, and their, even when discussing their early life. While AJ genuinely identified as a man for a few years, part of their process as a trans person has resulted in identifying more with "butch" as it aligns to womanhood, although AJ does not now identify as a woman. This is all to say that what follows describes our experiences and thoughts on AJ's initial coming out as a trans man.

Barbara Rio-Glick (a.k.a. River)

As a lesbian feminist, I thought I had hit the jackpot when my doctor told me that my twins were both girls. It's not that I hate men. It just seemed that, as a lesbian who had never even had a brother, it would be so much easier to raise girls. My job would be to help them grow into strong, confident women who would care for the world and all its creatures. As a mother of boys, however, my job would have been to teach them to recognize the privilege they are afforded in our society and then to use it only for good. The thought of somehow making this appealing, despite all the cultural dictates regarding what it means to be male, seemed like a huge task. So, believing myself to be the mother of two girls, I set about raising powerful girls and thought I was being fairly successful. But when, almost 16 years later, one of my "girls" told me they were a boy, I felt like my world had shattered. All sorts of illogical reasons why it couldn't be true immediately filled my mind. You know how your mind plays tricks on you when something seems too big to be real? When AJ told me they were a boy, I remember thinking: "That's impossible. They are an identical twin," and "They're too short to be a boy." Never mind that none of that made sense. It brought me comfort at the time.

Mostly I was overcome by a colossal sense of grief that I could at first only verbalize as "losing my little girl." I was filled with sadness, with fear, with worry. My mind was full of disturbing thoughts: "Will my child be killed by some hate-filled, transphobic idiot?" "Will someone love my child, or will it be a sad, lonely

Lev, Arlene I., Gottlieb, Andrew R., *Families in Transition*
dx.doi.org/10.17312/harringtonparkpress/2019.04.fit.020

road for them that, at worst, culminates in suicide?" "How will my friends, family, and the straight world react?" "Will Shelley and I somehow be blamed as lesbian moms?" "Will we be faced with dealing with heterosexist views of the deficiencies of lesbian parenting?" "What if it's a phase and they change their mind, but it's too late, after they've made some irreversible changes to their body that no longer feel right?" After all, it seemed like a trend among young people, especially those in our circles.

As a feminist lesbian, I felt particularly ashamed that I was thinking this was a "phase," as it was so reminiscent of things leveled at me and my community when my generation was coming out. Yet the phase theory made some sense to me as a social worker. There seemed to be at least a few plausible psychological explanations. Maybe they needed to claim a separate identity from their identical twin sister, Sonya, who, with her extroverted personality and more visible disability, tended to command much of the family's attention. Or perhaps it was their way of individuating in an all-female family of women-loving women. The apparent similarity to those early psychological theories—that is, that gayness was rooted in childhood sexual abuse or the result of a having a dominant mother combined with a passive or absent father—was not lost on me.

AJ quickly cut through my initial denial (and the comfort it afforded me) by requesting a binder for their chest. They had been processing and researching online incessantly for months and were ready for this change—NOW! So many feelings gripped me. But I calmly told them that Shelley—their other mom—would have to know before they would be allowed to bind their chest. I think I knew this would buy me some time since I was no more ready for AJ to bind their chest than they were to disclose to Shelley. I shared their nervousness about how Shelley would react while feeling guilty for keeping a secret from her, knowing that keeping secrets was not acceptable in our relationship. As it turned out, it was three long months before AJ finally told her, something they insisted on doing alone, despite my offer to help. Holding this information and processing a myriad of feelings by myself were difficult, including my own fear of Shelley's reaction, which I suspected might be quite explosive.

As time went on, I began to want AJ to tell Shelley, as I was weary of holding all these feelings inside and knew we would eventually have to deal with this as a family. Finally the day came. AJ told Shelley, who angrily refused to talk about it, saying she needed time to process this information before she could discuss anything with me. In turn, I reacted with anger at this perceived abandonment.

Home became a difficult place for all of us. The situation reminded me of when a dear friend's parents divorced after her brother got AIDS because the father could not deal with it. I seriously wondered if that would happen to us.

After a few excruciating weeks, Shelley and I began to talk. It didn't go smoothly at first, but we were eventually able to hear each other's very different perspectives. Fortunately, we live in a community with other parents of trans kids and a world-renowned expert on trans issues, who also is a dear friend. I initially resisted attending the local parent support group and instead chose to speak to my friend, who was very understanding and reassuring, saying things like "Your child is not likely to kill themselves," and "They're not likely to change their mind," and "Someone will love them." Shelley and I went to conferences and spoke to parents outside our community. I was shocked (and embarrassed) to meet straight parents much more accepting than I. How could it be that I, the lesbian, was still entertaining the notion that "maybe this is just a phase"? But those more enlightened straight parents assured me that they had once been where I was. I struggled to believe them.

Shelley and I limped along, trying to make sense of all this. At some point AJ had told Sonya and she, true to her name (Sonya means wisdom), reacted positively. When I finally found my way out of my self-absorbed bubble of pain and thought to ask Sonya how it was for her, she said something like, "I'm fine. I never really thought of AJ as a girl." She supported them completely from the start. Maybe it was that "twin thing," or maybe she really is wiser than the rest of us. Either way, she was quite annoyed that Shelley and I were taking so long to get on board.

Meanwhile, AJ was getting more and more insistent about who they were, what they needed (male pronouns at that time), and how quickly they needed it. They came out as a boy at the Emma Willard School, a private girls' institution, having been led to believe it was safe to do so. They also came out in the community and were hired by the Pride Center to go to local schools and raise awareness. Suddenly the school administration told us that since AJ identified as a boy, the school was no longer the best place for them, and they would have to leave in two weeks. We were incredulous. How dare they? Shelley and I quickly found our better angels, educated ourselves, and supported them unconditionally in a fierce battle to win the right to remain at the school they loved so much. Despite several long, heated meetings with the administration and the help of a lawyer, we eventually came to see that, even if we won the right for AJ to stay, it was now a hostile environment. Even though this was a traumatic experience, which cannot be minimized and from which AJ has still not recovered, the silver lining was that it united us as a family. Shelley and I had become AJ's fiercest advocates, which, as social workers, we do well. It felt good to be a team again.

Over time I came to realize there was more significance to who I thought I was losing. It wasn't just "my little girl." I was also losing my little feminist baby butch, whom I adored. From the time AJ was very young, all my lesbian friends were sure we had a baby dyke on our hands. I was not always so certain this was the case, but I was definitely not unhappy when, after coming out as a lesbian in middle school, that was who they seemed to be. AJ seemed just like all the butches I had known and loved: masculine feminists, who saw their butchness as not only who they were, but also as a political act in a society that relegates femaleness to a narrow definition. I feared that testosterone would change AJ. But one day, during the first year of taking "T," AJ came home from their new school and we had a very deep conversation about life. I knew that AJ, as sensitive as always, gender notwithstanding, would always be AJ. They would look different and the world would see them differently. But underneath, they are who they are. I hadn't lost anyone.

It's now been a little over three years since AJ told me they were a boy. They took testosterone for two years, had top surgery a year ago, and are now happier with their body. More recently, though, they started to identify as nonbinary, changing their pronouns to *they* and *them*. This new identity has brought up new fears for me, and I struggle not to infect their process with those fears. This time around, Shelley and I are able to discuss our feelings and support each other. I can, in my better moments, take a large view and recognize that this is AJ's journey and it is my privilege to be a part of it. I am no longer grieving my little girl, or my baby butch, or any projections of mine on what it means to be a man. The sadness subsided when I realized that, internally, AJ has always fundamentally been the same person. Gender does not define them. As a feminist, I believe that, in part, gender defines us, but it also defines how the world sees us and treats us. Gender is just another one of those arbitrary binaries that tries to neatly divide the world into this or that. AJ is one of an amazing community of brave young people who know this truth deep in their souls. It is now up to us to listen to them.

Shelley Rio-Glick

When I was told by my partner in confidence about AJ's desire for a binder and new identity, it was gut-wrenchingly hard for me to accept as a possibly true and permanent reality. And though we disagree to this day about the timing of River's providing these facts to me, it is clear that I was the last family member to be directly told by AJ. As a result of River's and Sonya's being the chosen confidantes months before I could openly respond and address the issue, I spent nights of interrupted sleep, days of ruminating, rationalizing, denying, and stewing in my uninformed, prejudicial juices.

My being the last to know was not new to our family pattern, nor was my resentment of it. The complexity of maintaining family relationships—those of parent to parent, parent to child, child to parent, child to child—was clearly being strained as we tried to meet this challenge as individuals and as a family. And our family's functional as well as dysfunctional pathways arose in a heart-beat to meet it all.

From being a self-perceived "progressive" household of four multigenera-tional, powerful, perceptive women, headed by two professional, relatively "cool" feminist lesbians with two exceptional daughters to being a household of two older, "what just happened" dykes, one aware, intelligent, and exceptional daugh-ter, and a demanding, self-identified adolescent male clearly was, to say the least, emotionally tumultuous. We were, in fact, in crisis.

If anyone thinks that being gay makes it easier to navigate changes of gen-der identity within the family, they have never known the power of culture, parental fantasy, expectations, self-esteem, denial, and terror. All that is unex-amined, repressed, or mistrusted comes to the surface. For me, and I suspect for my partner, childhood wounds and personal history were deeply triggered, get-ting in the way of my very concerted effort to be the best parent, best partner, and best team we could be—at least at first.

After AJ came out to me, the urgency to understand as well as my tendency to vocally escalate under stress was construed as anger and rejection. And there was, though I hate to admit it, probably truth to that observation. But the deeper and more meaningful truth was my raging terror at the risky life they would con-front as a trans man. This anguish was tethered to whatever related unbidden and unfinished personal conflicts I had.

Before I knew much else about being transgender, I was already very much aware of the violence directed at the trans community as well as the high sui-cide statistics for young trans people. The ever-changing boundary that lies between parent and teen, I'm sure, was instrumental in retriggering so much of the trauma, slights, and hurts associated with my own experience of grow-ing up female and queer in a very harsh world. Emotionally, I felt so fractured. My ability to be discerning was clearly compromised, and AJ's blunt teenage certainty did not help. I really did not want to repeat the devastating and emotionally severing response of my own parents to my misunderstood queer journey. I felt so helpless to keep them safe. I was imploding with a combination of pain, fear, and grief.

I berated myself and felt embarrassed for not seeing it coming in this kid who literally slept on my heart from the time they came home from the hospital. (The truth is I might not have missed it, just misread it.) In my capacity as a clinical social worker treating adolescents, I was aware of their need to be independent and psychologically separate, to find and define themselves. I did my best and tried to patiently respond *as if* they were goth, or wanted to quit school or, G–d forbid, enroll in the Young Republicans! Maybe I could "fake it 'til I could make it." My parental touchstones of success and self-esteem seemed foolishly tied to parental fantasies of who this kid was and would be. I wondered if we had any real relationship. It all seemed to be evaporating right before my eyes. Huge foundational cracks appeared, but then again, I reminded myself: that's how the light gets in.

Within a matter of months, after it was all out in the open, I was fortunate to recognize that the bold decision to act on their feelings as well as the timing of that decision needed to be respected. The pain and terror I was feeling were mine to deal with. I must say that the hurtful, rejecting behaviors I saw AJ receiving from the school administration and summer music program were clearly catalytic in speeding up my much-needed process of transformation. What was absolutely clear to me was that, whether I understood this "transition thing" or not, my job as a parent was to help in any way I could.

With a great deal of intention and introspection, I addressed many deep personal issues related to sexuality and gender. I also read and went to conferences alone and with family to learn about transitioning, living as a trans person, how to *be* supportive, and how to *get* support from others. This was helpful. Things got better within the family. This also prepared and enabled me to make a space for my newly constituted family in the context of our outside daily lives. Coming out to others, often in the most unanticipated, sometimes awkward, spontaneous circumstances, opened my eyes to the unsuspected support of a deeply changing social and political culture. And as such, it emboldened my confidence to clearly confront and manage adversarial conversations.

My resolve to be as fully present and supportive as I could meant coming to terms with my personal history. I was confronted by the need to deeply reexamine my political, social, and spiritual identities as well, even though these were my cherished mainstays of nourishment, connection, and intelligence. I found

AJ's predilection for the gender binary disconcerting and confusing because I thought it socially constraining and politically regressive to feminist ideals.

Additionally, what I was thinking and feeling about feminism was being challenged by AJ's school and camp as they justified their insensitive rejection and dismissal of a self-questioning 16-year-old as ethical, feminist, principled behavior. To me it seemed arbitrary, hypercritical, and unprofessional. My beloved LGBT community was awash with political infighting, as vitriolic speech between trans women and those who identified as radical lesbian feminists played out in our media. Neither side embraced for me the ties that bind a community.

I am a product of the 1970s' nascent Gay Liberation and women's movements. They provided the first real place of belonging for me, and I saw the socially and intellectually evolving communities as my home. To my heartfelt gratitude, they became my tribe. It was that experience that guided my principles of parenting and the creation of my nuclear and extended family. The willingness to explore what I truly valued and to deconstruct and reconstruct what I believed, particularly as those beliefs related to trans issues and maleness, took the courage of a Mama Bear. I surprised myself with revelations of flawed reasoning and assumptions as well as effective, unconscious bias. In particular, I understood that the deconstruction of gender itself was indeed the next step in expanding feminist theory. A rejecting and constricted view of maleness had also pervaded my thinking and unexamined feelings. As a result of this intense, introspective adventure, I evolved, became more inclusive, and felt far less tyrannized by the rigidity of decaying dogma and emotional baggage. I found myself able to hold and appreciate feminist theory as well as the complexity of simply not knowing without anxiety. I came out of this process intact, clearer, with a deeper understanding of *many* things, less certainty about many *other* things, and enamored with the ultimate mystery of *all* things. I still call myself a feminist and a lesbian, and I know my family is still part of a more inclusive tribe, be it called the LGBTQ or queer community.

I see AJ's journey as that of the incredible and remarkable poet they always were, putting together astounding metaphors and observations in the service of beauty and truth, and as the truly spiritual work of an engaged soul seeking to be itself. As a Jew, I think of the Torah and the varied translations and broader understanding of Genesis 5:2: "Male and female created He them."

I have no idea what the poem of AJ's life will look like. In the meantime, I remain the very proud mama of a remarkable kid who is supported by their loving and remarkable family, friends, and community. It's been quite a journey for us all—remarkable, quite remarkable.

Sonya Rio-Glick

I don't remember exactly what they said. Maybe it was something like "I feel more like a man than I do a woman." Depending on who we're with, they often say I was the first to support them. People ask me all the time how I feel about my twin coming out as trans. Not *if* I feel but *how* I feel, as though I'm entitled to feelings about something that isn't mine.

Once I was at a friend's house and she asked inquisitively, "How do you feel about AJ's changes?" as though *changes* was the best word for all they were experiencing. When I said I didn't necessarily "have feelings," a strained look came over my friend's face, and she said insistently, "But you must feel *something*." I wasn't insensitive to what my sibling was experiencing, just happy to let them live their life as they wished, which was in contrast to so many others who felt the need to project their feelings and opinions onto AJ's experience.

My upbringing in the queer community as the daughter of a lesbian couple, combined with my own experience as a queer-identified person, as well as my experience as a person living with disabilities, enabled me to think simply: this is just another part of who my twin is. It is natural to be a little confused, but I didn't understand my family's fear or sadness, and I definitely did not understand the larger world's feelings of entitlement to information, or the open bewilderment regarding the physical transition itself.

Yes, I was happy that AJ was coming into their own. I did not, however, feel a sense of loss that so many others describe. I wasn't actually losing anything. AJ, my sibling, will always be my sibling and is still my twin. They were and still are the person I share all my milestones with; the person I can have an entire conversation with just by looking at; the person I can be uncensored with, dealing with the many trials the world throws at us through laughter; the person who knows why I am upset without an explanation; the person I can giggle with at two in the morning over hot dogs; the person who calls me out when I need to be called out. AJ always has my back, and this was my time to have theirs.

AJ was healthy and happy. Yet, because of the responses of others, I was suddenly some amazing pillar of strength owing to my "lack of selfishness" that was more a lack of astonishment at transgender existence. Selfishness was assumed, as though prioritizing one's own feelings about something entirely separate from oneself is not only allowed, but expected and encouraged.

In my new role as "sister of a trans person," not only was I *supposed* to have my own feelings, but I was also *supposed* to manage the feelings of others, including, at times, my parents. It was as though my own lack of reaction was somehow interpreted as an opening to take on the reactions of others. Once I was in the car with my mom, when suddenly she said, "I just don't understand why this is necessary, do you? I don't know what it feels like to want to be a man, or how you learn to ask for that." My answer was simple: I didn't understand, but I didn't need to. The one who needed to understand was the person who was asking to be called "*he*" (at the time), and we had to trust that AJ understood themselves.

People think I, as their twin sister, feel everything they feel, think everything they think, and understand everything they understand. Though this is sometimes true, it does not extend to the trans experience. I was just as clueless about dysphoria and the ins and outs of what they were feeling as everyone else. While I couldn't anticipate what it was to transition, in moments of pain, when the weight of the world seemed to fall on my brother's shoulders, I felt that weight, too. And when they were so happy to finally see changes and finally feel at their core like themselves, I felt that joy as well.

I had to be present for a certain amount of external navigation, particularly at school, to manage the feelings of peers. The town we lived in was small, so even though we did not go to the same school at the point of their coming out, people at my school found out about their transition before I had any reason to tell anyone there. This made me feel like some sort of public relations specialist in the worst way. I was AJ's only voice in a setting they were not a part of. If I somehow said the wrong thing, or said too much, or said something to the wrong person, I would be misrepresenting them. But if I declined to answer or if my answer was deemed insufficient, then that negatively influenced the opinion the person asking held of me, because I was the one they interacted with every day. I was already struggling socially in high school, and so the news of their transition and whatever judgments came along did not help my social standing. I did not blame this awkwardness on my brother at any point because it wasn't like I was losing friends—it didn't feel as if I had many friends to begin with, the reasons for which were ultimately unrelated. At some point, however, it felt like their transition contributed to my alienation at school. I knew this was out of my control, which is why this was the hardest part of managing my sibling's transition: not the changes they made, but the changes the world made because of AJ's deeply personal, private decision.

For example, at my school the senior class enjoyed a senior lounge, where students went to socialize. The room was filled with couches, tables, and lockers only for our class. Once, when the room was packed, one girl suddenly blurted rather loudly, "So does your brother, like, have a dick now?" The room became quiet, all eyes on me. The seconds seemed to tick by more slowly than usual as my breath caught in my throat and I tried to think of the best answer. I could barely move past how insanely insensitive and transphobic her question was, regardless of whether we were speaking about my family or not. It just so happened that we *were* speaking about my family and we *were* in front of 45 people who didn't really like me. Our eyes were locked and I knew I wasn't getting out of this. I'm not a very religious person, but in that moment I prayed that AJ would be okay with the answer I gave. With a little sass in my voice I said, "It doesn't work like that," then proceeded to get up and leave the room as swiftly as I could. The chatter commenced behind me, and the day continued. To everyone else, it was just one uncomfortable moment that they *could* and *would* forget about. But that single moment epitomized for me the hardest part of the entire transition process, and the actual transgender person was nowhere in the vicinity.

After a while I got used to my role as public relations specialist. I also felt the sting of transphobia so acutely it sometimes surprised me since I am not trans myself. When my twin was expelled from their high school solely for being trans, I was so deeply shocked and angered that it actually took me longer to accept than AJ. I would daydream about seeking some sort of revenge on the institution long after AJ was able to say, "It is what it is," and acknowledge that retaliating would not be constructive. Even after the initial shock of this more blatant instance of discrimination that they endured faded, I didn't think I'd ever be able to completely understand how quickly people were able to thrust judgments on an experience that they had no context for. Like any loving family member, I vehemently disagreed with the mistreatment they received from institutions and organizations.

Two years following this particularly harsh instance of discrimination by the school, I assumed that I was healed from seeing them go through that. I was explaining to a friend what happened pretty casually, as though I were recounting a difficult test I took or a date that went badly. I knew this person well and just anticipated sympathy. And sympathy is what I received—at first. I didn't think much of it, and we went on with our day, having conversations about other things. But then later that evening, we were in the car together when she suddenly told me that she agreed with AJ's being expelled from school for being trans. She argued that, because it was an all-girls' school, AJ had no place there from the moment their identity at all deviated from the female side of the gender binary. She gave little regard to the nuanced complexities of the situation: the fact that they had yet to physically transition in any way at the time of their expulsion; that they had just started attending the school and were thriving there; that the decision was motivated by monetary issues rather than by the safety of them or their peers; and most important, my friend did not prioritize the hard truth that an educational institution did not care at all about the well-being of a student whom it had accepted into its community and had therefore invested in. I was floored, feeling betrayed.

I felt trapped in the seat next to my dearest friend, but at this point the struggle had nothing to do with AJ. Now this was my problem, my deteriorating friendship. And now I *did* have feelings. My friend whom I built a relationship with—not AJ—felt so moved to openly get behind unnecessary trauma that, at that point, both AJ and the rest of my family had not only endured but overcome. As a cisgender person who did not witness this catastrophe, my friend had no way of truly understanding the gravity of the situation in such a way that could ever enable her to rightfully form such an opinion. I cried to her, trying to explain, but still, she stuck by her opinion. When I went home from that visit, I still viewed AJ as my sibling, and I still disagreed with what others burdened them with arbitrarily. My friend's open judgment did not change how AJ saw themselves or how I saw them. But that particular disagreement *did* change how I saw my friend. Some could say that in this regard AJ's transition was a blessing, because as twisted as it seems, had it not been for the transition, I would've gone on unknowingly with this friend, never understanding how different we really were.

Maybe someday I will suddenly start missing some ghost of a sister. Maybe someday the grief that everyone talks about will hit me like a truck. I highly doubt that, however, because it's hard to grieve for someone you get to see every day, whom you get to laugh with every day, whom you get to call *twin* every day. It felt as though the rest of the world tried to grieve for me, inserting a strife that wasn't there. My being completely fine with their bodily changes and using different pronouns, and the complete lack of change in our sibling relationship, seemed, for many people watching, rather curious because transition is thought to be out of the ordinary and deserving a reaction.

For many, gender transition is a unicorn. For me, it is just another horse. If AJ had transitioned and everyone else had used their preferred pronouns, refrained from making them feel unwelcome, and *not* asked for details about their body, then I would have nothing to say about their transition, because it would've just been another day in the life. But instead I write about how difficult other people's reactions were, because that's where the difficulty for me is: in everyone *other than* the person who transitioned. As the whole world ran amuck trying to process something that wasn't theirs to claim, AJ, the one in the middle of it all, found themselves and eventually blossomed. I was just there to soften the blows that continue to come from all sides and run damage control in the face of the insensitive questions, the feelings of entitlement to personal information, and the neglect of the fact that, at the center, was just one then-16-year-old who was and is trying to live with an experience that is complex in ways that neither I nor any other cis person could ever fully conceptualize for ourselves.

AJ Rio-Glick

In late spring of 2013, I reluctantly told my mother River that I wanted a chest binder. I say "reluctantly" only because the binder I needed had to be purchased online, and being 15 years old, I was without a credit card of my own. The only money I had came directly from my parents at the end of each week in the form of an allowance if I did certain chores and behaved well. I would need her credit card to make the purchase. This was not the first time I asked.

Casually, months before, I had asked. Initially, not much hope had been riding on my wish. I tried to see getting a binder as a future event to dissuade myself from being disappointed when my mom inevitably said no. She didn't say no; instead, she tiredly said she wanted to "do research on it" in a way that implied, to me, "Let's not talk about this anymore." I also remember hearing a silent promise behind her words, one that rested in the moment that might come after research had been done. I deliberated over whether it was really there.

Over the months before that, starting in the winter of that year, I had tried to tell my parents I was genderqueer and questioning my gender, but each time they had failed to respond. I felt like my declarations were being totally ignored. I constantly debated whether I was being too timid and needed to be bolder, or if that would rock the boat too much. As much as my sister, my moms, and I might all try to pretend we are not, we are a rather dramatic bunch, and not often the best at direct communication. Thus, I think lurking in my mind was the thought that, in order to get anything across to my family at all, I would have to create some type of standout event of a declaration—a formal, dramatic, unwavering "coming out," if you will.

That spring, I had seen a trans man speak at an event sponsored by my city's Pride Center and the local GLSEN chapter. Having come out as bisexual when I was 13, then gay at 14, and, of course, having a queer family, I volunteered at the center, had been a part of their queer choir when I was 12, and had attended their youth group and many other events over the next several years. By the time I was nearly 16, I thought I had seen pretty much the philosophical extent of what the Pride Center had to offer me, so I was taken aback when I resonated so strongly with the speaker at the event. He was there because he was a prominent presence on YouTube, having documented his transition on the platform for years. I stayed up late for weeks, hiding under my covers after I met him, watching as many of his over 200 videos as I could.

In one of his videos, he suggested making the journey of questioning one's gender and transitioning a family process, mostly so that there would not be a gap between where I stood versus where my parents stood. I thought this made sense. But in June, when I pressed my mother for my binder, my beating heart wracked my thin frame, my eyes danced frantically, and I realized that for all my efforts, I had failed at bringing us together. Inevitably, some dramatic event would have to occur.

Suspecting that my mother River hadn't done her research and wasn't planning on it, I had taken things into my own hands. I went to her with webpage after webpage of trans men talking about proper, healthy ways of binding. I set up the Underworks checkout page with one tri-top chest binder already in the digital cart. I tried to present it as a simple, seamless process—all she'd have to do was hand over her credit card and be done with it. Finally, when it seemed like she couldn't find any more reasons to protest (her most notable admonishment was "I thought you said you weren't a boy!" to which I responded, "I'm not, I just want to try it out"), she hissed that she didn't feel comfortable doing this without telling my other mother, Shelley, a move that struck in her the deepest fear I had ever seen.

I hadn't exactly planned on keeping anything a secret from Shelley, but when I had tried to engage her in the past on issues involving my gender questioning, she had either dismissed it entirely or laughed openly about it. I immediately recognized her as a controlling force for the previous year and a half, after I had accidentally come out to my eighth-grade English class as bisexual and she demanded that I create a list of everyone who might know I was not straight. Although she was clearly very afraid for me, I dismissed these fears, seeing them as outdated and irrelevant to the nuances of my school. I never wrote the list; I assumed that any fears that were surfacing for her came directly from the coming-out experiences of her own youth, which had occurred over a half century before mine.

When I began to transition, I felt that she would be the biggest mountain standing in the way. I had not, at that point, planned on how I would confront her. I didn't see why she needed to be made aware of the finer points of what questioning my gender entailed, especially since she had not shown any effort to engage in it in any meaningful way. I had, however, entered that conversation with River resolute on coming out of it with an e-mail in my inbox confirming shipment of my binder, so when River left to go to Shelley's office (a cabin in our backyard called the Outback), I sat at the dining room table and waited anxiously, somewhat in denial of what was to come. River came back and told me that Shelley was "shocked" to hear that I was questioning my gender, which she had told Shelley upon requesting her presence to discuss the purchase. Although I would later expand on this to Shelley, bringing on a whole host of other feelings, I felt, for a brief moment, nothing other than insulted and offended. For months, I had been telling anyone who would listen that I was questioning being a girl, that I liked being seen as "masculine," that this was confusing me, and that I was hoping to get a chest binder if I could. Had she really been so oblivious?

Of course, the answer was "yes." Shelley has ADD and is notorious for being oblivious in lots of ways. This could be endearing, such as when she has an intelligent conversation with a stranger on spiritual healing while her shirt is buttoned totally incorrectly. But her forgetfulness could be incredibly angering and hurtful, as it was then. Could she really sit at the dinner table and not hear a word of our conversation? Perhaps her obliviousness in this instance came more from a place of fundamental denial rather than stop-and-go functioning. For whatever reason, it felt in line with a pattern of hers. I felt sad and totally defeated for a second, as I realized that all my attempts to follow what little advice I had gleaned from YouTube had been the opposite of successful.

Shelley came back into the house and demanded that the three of us meet in the family room. My anger disappeared immediately and I became afraid again. My parents have always been über-overprotective of my sister and me, and I often lamented to my sister that I felt that if they didn't understand every small point of everything involved in our lives, we would not be able to do anything. Here my mom was even controlling the location of our meeting, moving me from the dining room to the family room. I was all too aware of the power my parents wielded over my transition.

I sat nervously on the couch next to River, facing Shelley as she sat in one of the chairs perpendicular to the couch. I prepared for the big event that I had been so sure was inevitable. As I sat facing her—her arms crossed, frowning angrily, as though she had already been offended—underneath my beating heart and all the fear that came with it, I was still annoyed, annoyed that I felt I had to defend myself after I'd been explaining this for so long. Annoyed that she was taking control of the situation, of my gender, my identity, and demanding justification, as though my gender couldn't exist as it was without her approval.

My parents are lesbian feminists. Everyone in my family is female, including my dog, Kira, and the dog we had before her, and the one before her. My parents raised my sister and me with rather woman-centric values, both consciously and unconsciously. Though at the time I had not yet considered the political implications of my transition, the unspoken reason that it was so shocking for me to transition was perhaps because no one in my family ever really thought about men as primary actors in our lives, and to try so actively to be one would initially be seen as misogynistic.

Later, after I had been on testosterone for about a year, I struggled with the expectation that I should be comfortable with men. I rarely had male friends, and the only men I really *knew* beyond the ones who made fun of me in middle school were my teachers, my uncle Byron, the fathers of River and Shelley, respectively referred to as Grandpa and Dood, and the two sons of my parents' lesbian friends, who are close to me in age, both of whom are queer. Thus, something I would struggle with later on in my transition was not fully understanding what it meant to really live out a male experience and perception in our society, especially as someone who has never really felt comfortable around men or even cared about them—kind of peculiar for someone who would come to defend their male identity so strongly that they would get kicked out of the world's oldest all-girls' high school, the Emma Willard School. Eventually, I would decide to stop injecting testosterone, realizing that my time identifying as male had come to a close. Today I identify as nonbinary, and exploring what it means to be masculine, born female, distinctly not-male, trans, all in one body, is a process I now share relatively easily with my parents.

At the time of my coming out, however, the conversation that followed was difficult, and I stumbled through, trying to explain myself as Shelley's voice grew fraught with tension, the anger on her face spilling through her mouth. A few days earlier, I had anxiously searched the Internet for a concrete definition of *dysphoria*, a word that I knew only as a sort of prerequisite for being trans and which all the trans people online seemed to struggle with endlessly. I wondered: Do I have this? But it was used so abstractly that I could not decide, and the question lingered in the back of my mind as I watched video after video. I eventually would come to define my own dysphoria as the feeling of looking in the mirror and not recognizing the reflection, or not being able to picture myself in my head, or hearing my voice and thinking it was someone else's. Now I understand what my own dysphoria is rather thoroughly, but because dysphoria is a feeling unique to those who are gender nonconforming, it is, in my experience, extremely difficult to explain to a cis person. How can a cis person conceptualize what it is to be trans when it contradicts every tenet of self-identity that cis people so rely on?

So when I flung out the word *dysphoria* in front of my parents, it felt funny and out of place tumbling around inside of my mouth, as though I was urgently claiming something for myself that I needed desperately to serve me but that I wasn't even sure was mine to use. The only reason I clung to it then was that it was the one thing that trans men seemed to agree on: all trans men have dysphoria. I would later come to disagree with this statement, but at the time *dysphoria* as a term was the only thing uniting trans people to me and the only word that I could be sure would pop up in the writing of actual trans people. Thus, I resorted to it as something to bring me legitimacy when everything I was feeling about myself was being challenged.

I tried in vain to describe my dysphoria about my voice to my mom: "When I speak, it just doesn't sound like me. It doesn't sound right." Her face turned red as she gained volume: "What does that mean!? What do you mean, 'It doesn't sound right!?' What do you want to sound like?" I didn't know what to say, and I mostly just wanted to leave.

"I don't know. Like . . . deeper?" All the other trans men wanted their voices to sound deeper, and in theory, I did too. As I often didn't even realize it was me speaking when I spoke, I'd decided that depth of pitch seemed like a good idea and something to aspire to, as deep voices accompanied the bodies that I yearned to emulate. That deepness also represented the opposite of my voice— although I'd always had a lower voice than other girls, I still had an undoubtedly soft, womanly voice, and I couldn't conceptualize what my voice might sound like with the deep timbre of testosterone. I wasn't even sure if this was what I truly wanted, but it was something I could say to give myself credibility and the confidence that comes with knowing that others, somewhere, might support me.

"Why!?" she asked. Her eyes looked wild. I could tell she was totally out of her element, and for her, this was truly coming out of the left field.

"I don't know" was the only answer I had.

What followed was a rather chaotic year that involved, among other events, being forced to leave Emma Willard at the end of the fall semester after coming out as trans and then entering college in the spring—a year and a half earlier than expected. When I left Emma Willard, my family and I hurried to come together, in a sense, as we consulted lawyers, advisers, therapists, and friends in order to fight the administration, at the same time searching urgently for my next school. Any lingering fear and doubt over the specifics of my transition were pushed to the side. My parents felt that their priority was my well-being regardless of my gender identity and that these events reinforced this for them. I also witnessed my parents learn a lot in a short span of time as they argued for trans people and trans rights. Their positions on many issues shifted dramatically between June and December 2013.

Today my moms and I have open lines of communication on issues of gender and sexuality. They ask me candidly about different pronouns, share things they read, and, as I have now decided to take a break from testosterone injections, they ask how I feel about my changed and changing body. We exchange articles and books, not to support our individual viewpoints, but to share wisdom and new perspectives in a way that feels less invasive and more collaborative. I wish I could go back to 2013 and give little me a hug and say that it's going to be all right, and to remind myself that my parents will love me no matter what, even if it takes a while for that to be manifest in the way I wanted.

PART 7

Educational Concerns: How Do Parents Manage and Advocate for Gender Nonconforming Children and Transition-Related Issues in a School Setting?

Wallace Wong and Sabrina Chang address how gender dysphoria might be alleviated by a social transition, offering a practical guide for parents on how best to advocate for the child in the context of the school setting. The cultural divide as it relates to approaching gender dysphoria is further complicated by a lack of research and the shifting perspectives within the mental health communities, which serves to further confuse parents. Social transitioning offers a "test drive" for the child or adolescent (and their families). Changes in appearance, names, and pronouns may be enough for some but are only a step toward medical intervention for others.

Considering *where* to start the transition, *when* to start it, *what* to expect of and request from the school staff, and *how* to use available supports both in the school and in the community are best decided by way of active dialogue and collaboration between parent and parent, parent and child, parent/child and school staff, parent/child and specialists or consultants, which make a successful transition more likely — the authors' central theme. Their case, "Edith and William," demonstrates how to put it all together.

In a companion piece, "Please Stop Calling My Daughter 'He,'" Deborah Coolhart focuses on safety. As the facts show, schools are breeding grounds for harassment, physical assault, and sexual violence, not only by students, but by staff as well, which leaves the transgender student completely vulnerable and affects not only academic potential and performance but physical and mental health and overall psychosocial adjustment later in life. How do we make schools a safer place?

Coolhart recommends an individualized, youth-centered plan that addresses policies and procedures, staff training, the use of correct names and pronouns, public accommodations, dress codes, team sports, and privacy concerns. Depending on the age and capabilities of the child or adolescent, the parents may take an active role, a modified role, or no role at all in formulating the plan. Difficulties arise when parents are conflicted about their child's transgender status. But assisting with this more specific, time-limited task may be quite cathartic for parents, helping them not only to sharpen their advocacy skills, as was the case with Celia's parents, but also to move them in the direction of understanding and acceptance.

21

Social Transitioning for Gender Dysphoric Children: A Practical Guide for Parents

Wallace Wong, PsyD, R Psych, Sabrina C. H. Chang, MA

Raising a child with gender dysphoria often introduces unique challenges to the already difficult task of parenting. At first, parents may overlook the possibility of gender dysphoria, instead perceiving their gender nonconforming child as a "tomboy" or a "sissy boy" because of their cross-gender preferences in clothing, toys, and games. When these children grow older and become better at expressing themselves, they may describe unhappiness about their physical sex characteristics and function, disgust with their genitalia, and/or desire to be the other sex. These feelings can be expressed by a child as young as three years old. It is often at this point that parents realize gender dysphoria may underlie cross-gender behaviors and preferences. So, what can a parent do with this information?

This chapter aims to inform parents and professionals of what we believe to be the best parenting practices to assist gender dysphoric children with social transitioning in a school setting. At the present time, the research on this population is scarce, and there are diverse views on when and how to implement a social transition. In this chapter we will introduce some practical ideas gleaned through our clinical experiences.

Social Transitioning

Social transitioning refers to a change in social gender role aimed at exploring and consolidating an individual's gender identity. Contrary to popular belief, social transitioning does not necessitate gender reassignment surgery or any medical interventions. Rather, for gender dysphoric children, it can involve changing their appearance (e.g., clothing, hairstyle), name, pronouns, and other reversible expressions. For example, an affirmed girl may grow long hair, wear dresses, adopt a new name that is socially constructed as female or androgynous, and ask to be referred to with female pronouns (e.g., she, her). Social transitioning

Lev, Arlene I., Gottlieb, Andrew R., *Families in Transition*
dx.doi.org/10.17312/harringtonparkpress/2019.04.fit.021
© 2019 by Harrington Park Press

gives the child freedom to experiment with gender expression, encourages self-acceptance, and facilitates gender consolidation. Research suggests that a gender-affirmative approach, which includes social transitioning, minimizes the risk of depressive symptoms, poor self-esteem regulation, self-harm, and suicidal ideation, gestures, and attempts (Grossman & D'Augelli, 2007; Hidalgo et al., 2013). While some may want medical or surgical intervention as their eventual goal, many find social transitioning sufficient.

In trying to determine if, when, and how social transitioning should proceed for a gender dysphoric child, open discussion (or dialogue) is key. Before beginning this process, parents and professionals should carefully consider the child's wishes and take their needs seriously (Edwards-Leeper & Spack, 2012; Menvielle, 2012). At times, the child's and the parent's wishes may be different. The professionals will then play a significant role in facilitating their communication, addressing the parents' concerns while providing adequate information so they can best support their child.

Some older children undergo medical treatment during social transitioning. For instance, preteens have the option of taking hormone blockers, such as gonadotropin releasing hormone (GnRH) analogs, which can delay the onset of puberty to give the child more time for gender exploration (Edwards-Leeper & Spack, 2012; Khatchadourian, Amed, & Metzger, 2014; Minter, 2012). These options, however, are not available for younger children since they do not need puberty blockers.

Challenges Parents Frequently Meet

Parents of gender dysphoric children are met with unique challenges. The first is the dearth of information available on how best to parent a child who has distress about their gender. To complicate this, guidelines for health-care professionals for treating these patients are also scarce, and published materials on this topic are often written in general terms. For instance, the WPATH Standards of Care guidelines (Coleman et al., 2012) encourage flexibility when working with gender dysphoric children because of their complexity, variable outcomes, and the lack of research. The guidelines also encourage extreme caution, leaving the clinician with vague directions. Thus, it is often up to the clinicians and parents to decide what may be best. Some adopt a more conservative position, fearing that they may harm the child's future if they condone their behavior; others use shame and guilt, sending the message that certain behaviors are unacceptable, denying children support when they need it most. Therapists with an affirmative approach tend to welcome the process of social transition, seeing this as a learning opportunity to assist parents to help their children further consolidate their identity.

Furthermore, it is not uncommon for parents to experience prejudice and stigma that sometimes comes with having a child with gender dysphoria. Even in the absence of overt discrimination, parents often find themselves having to explain and justify to their loved ones why they made certain choices. This process can be emotionally exhausting and compel some parents to go back into the closet, further isolating them, deterring them from seeking additional resources, and hindering their ability to support other families facing similar challenges. Our suggestion is to avoid going through this alone. We encourage parents to seek out their local LGBTQ communities and resources, where they can get more support and understanding. If parents live in remote areas, connecting with others online can be helpful. We have witnessed many overly stressed parents feeling significantly relieved once they were able to connect, knowing they were not alone, and learning from those who have had similar concerns.

Experienced parents often serve as mentors for those newly coming out, providing them with useful information and tips, which can prevent unnecessary mistakes in the planning stages. Many also find it helpful to join a group, such as PFLAG, in which they can learn how to disclose to family and friends, deal with potential criticism, and process their feelings. We have found that those who are able and willing to share their worries with other parents often feel less overwhelmed and more confident in providing care and support for their gender dysphoric child.

Some Helpful Information to Get Started

Understanding Gender Dysphoria

According to the *Diagnostic Statistical Manual—Fifth Edition, gender dysphoria* is defined as the distress that may accompany the incongruence between experienced or expressed gender and assigned gender (American Psychiatric Association, 2013). Part of the reason for the change from gender identity disorder (GID) in the *DSM-IV-TR* (American Psychiatric Association, 2000) was to help clinicians shift their focus on the distress rather than on rigid gender stereotypical behaviors or expressions (Dresher, Cohen-Kettenis, & Reed, 2016; Lev, 2013).

The *DSM-V* diagnostic criteria for gender dysphoria for children still place significant emphasis on gender nonconforming behaviors, roles, and expressions. This is controversial, as many clinicians contend that gender nonconforming preferences are natural, and that interpreting a child's choice of toys, mannerisms, or clothes or their friends' genders as signs of pathology is inappropriate and can mislead parents and others to further stigmatize these behaviors.

It is important to distinguish between gender nonconforming and gender dysphoric children. Gender nonconforming children may reject stereotypical gender roles and expressions that society assigns them, but they do not necessarily experience significant discomfort with their bodies. Gender dysphoric children exhibit a marked incongruence between their physical bodies and their affirmed gender, which often creates significant distress and interferes with their daily functioning. In other words, *not* all gender nonconforming children are dysphoric. Both gender dysphoric and gender nonconforming children may require support from professionals, but gender nonconforming children who are not gender dysphoric may not require a diagnosis. Parents should be aware that there are special considerations in diagnosing gender dysphoria and that an assessment should be made only by specialists with training and clinical experience.

Several factors can influence the emotional and psychological health of gender dysphoric children (Egan & Perry, 2001). They are often bullied, teased, and pressured at school to behave in a way that is stereotypically consistent with their natal sex. These experiences can have a profound effect on their mental health. Research shows that the pressure to conform places them at a higher risk for anxiety, social withdrawal, and self-deprecation (Carver, Yunger, & Perry, 2003). Harassment at school is related to absenteeism, decreased educational goals, and lower academic performance (Byrne, 2013).

The Gay, Lesbian, and Straight Education Network (GLSEN) did a survey in the United States and found that 90% of transgender youth experienced verbal harassment, more than 50% experienced physical harassment, and more than 25% were physically assaulted (Greytak, Kosciw, & Diaz, 2009). In addition to what these children face at school, their experiences at home are also critical. Research found that gender dysphoric children had poorer psychological health when the following risk factors were present in their home environment: (1) lack of supportive caretakers; (2) differing levels of support between caretakers; and (3) unhealthy communication patterns (Leibowitz & Telingator, 2012). Indeed, how parents approach a child's gender dysphoria has a significant effect on their gender health (Ehrensaft, 2016).

Different Approaches to Gender Dysphoric Children

Children are beginning to disclose gender variance at younger ages (Edwards-Leeper & Spack, 2012; Minter, 2012). Our society remains divided about which approach to take. Parents can encourage their children to be happy with their assigned gender, dissuading social transitioning and gender nonconforming behavior, punishing cross-gender behaviors, and reinforcing gender stereotypical behaviors. While some parents may see this as beneficial, this approach may actually be harmful to gender nonconforming children (Pyne, 2014). Parents risk sending the message that gender nonconforming behavior is "bad." Children then feel ashamed or guilty when they engage in or even have the impulse to engage in these behaviors. Research confirms that repression of gender expression can increase the risk of depression, substance abuse, unprotected sex, and suicidal ideation or gesturing later in life (Minter, 2012). Additional studies also reveal that this approach is often unsuccessful at eliminating gender nonconformity (Bryant, 2006; Coleman et al., 2012; Hidalgo et al., 2013).

Others suggest parents redirect their child to use only neutral expressions of gender while exploring and developing their gender identity on a cognitive level. This happens when they acknowledge their child's gender dysphoria, telling them that it is permissible to think about gender, but discouraging them from acting out their feelings (de Vries & Cohen-Kettenis, 2012). Though this may work for some, we find it relatively ineffective for children with severe dysphoria since it requires they "tone down" or "deny" their authentic self in order to blend in. The underlying message is that being gender nonconforming equates to being undesirable.

Many clinicians endorse a gender-affirmative approach (Leibowitz & Spack, 2011; Leibowitz & Telingator, 2012), one in which parents encourage their children to explore the entire range of gender expression while providing emotional support and implementing measures to ensure safety. Social transitioning is one of the pillars of that approach.

For Parents Contemplating Social Transitioning: Steps to Consider

We understand that some parents are not completely on board with their child's decision to socially transition. While some may fear the potentially negative effects that the social transition may cause, others fear judgment from those who question their decision in supporting their child. For those who are in the contemplating stage, we often advise the following:

1. Parents can become informed by gathering information, either online, through books, or by talking to others.

2. Parents can consult and/or schedule family sessions with a specialist in order to evaluate the pros and cons of proceeding with the child's social transition. Professionals can help them better understand whether social transition is in the best interest of their child. A specialist can also be present at meetings with school officials to facilitate the social transition at school.

3. Parents can attend support groups. This can help them understand how others have made the decision to transition, develop coping skills, and be encouraged by others' successes. Parents who reside in more rural areas where there are no groups can consider participating online. Parents can be mentored by those who have gone through this process successfully so that they can feel more comfortable sharing their fears.

For Parents Starting Social Transitioning: Steps to Consider

Planning for social transitioning is best done by the child, the parents, and professionals in collaboration. Open dialogue should occur throughout, as should monitoring of how the process is unfolding for everyone and brainstorming solutions to any obstacles. Everyone will need support. If feasible, having the child attend some of the school meetings and offering input will help them feel part of the process as well as part of the solution.

Consult with Your Child

Though some parents are receptive to gender nonconforming behaviors, their fears, depression, anxieties, and shame may result in discouraging those behaviors. In our opinion, encouraging the child to share their gender dysphoric feelings sends these messages:

1. As your parents, we want to understand your distress.

2. As your parents, we want to not only validate your feelings, but also take steps to make things better for you.

3. As your parents, we want to know to what extent social transitioning may make you feel better about yourself.

4. As your parents, we want to advocate and develop a support system for you so that you will feel safe to live your authentic self openly and with less fear.

5. As your parents, we want you to know that what you say matters.

6. As your parents, we want you to know that you matter.

Consult with Specialists

To ensure a successful transition, it is critical to consult with a gender-affirmative specialist, perhaps from more than one discipline, during all points in the process. They will assess the child's needs and developmental stage in order to advise parents on the best ways to implement social transitioning while educating them on how to best advocate. After the initial assessment, the specialist(s) will closely monitor the child's desire to continue the process. We also encourage parents to periodically check in with the child to evaluate how they are feeling during this time. Though parents may want to ensure their child is "on the right track," some children object to this, saying, "Why do you keep asking me every day? You don't ask my brother that question." Excessive checking-in, however, may be a sign that the parent is still holding on to the hope that this is "just a phase." In these situations, we often encourage parents to examine their own biases and how those may shape their actions and reactions. The most important part of this is that the child be aware that they can change, modify, or revert to any gender role or expression that fits best without losing their parents' love and support.

Choose a Setting

If parents and child have decided to move forward, then the question is: Where is the best place to start? A social environment has many layers, the one most intimate and close to the center usually being the home, followed by extended family, friends, extracurricular clubs, and school (see figure 21.1). We recommend starting at the center and moving outward, assessing how each step is going for the whole family (Wong, 2011b). One way to proceed is to first allow the child to engage in social transitioning with immediate family members at home on the weekends, then gradually expand this to small family gatherings. Or some children may want to start at the outer circle by living full-time in their affirmed gender across all settings. While that may be fine for some, it may feel premature for others, especially for those who live in small or rural communities, where everyone knows the child. In these cases, a more gradual process may work best, allowing more time to plan. The key is to have the child go through the process in as safe and supportive a way as possible.

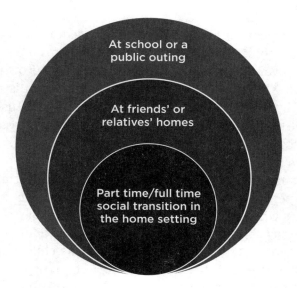

FIGURE 21.1 Embedded System of Social Transitioning Progression

Social Transitioning at School

If your child has lived in their affirmed gender at home and expresses a desire to transition in other areas of life, the next step would be to expand to either the school setting or with selected friends and family members. Our experience has been that many children prefer school be their next step in order to end leading what they feel is a double life, though parents sometimes prefer introducing social transitioning to relatives and family friends *before* involving the school. Both, however, could go on simultaneously.

As parents probably have more control at home, some may face more challenges in the school setting, where there are more parties involved in the decision-making process, some of whom may not be receptive to input from parents. Nonetheless, parents can take steps to minimize complications once their child is ready. Before introducing the child in their affirmed gender, we advise parents to think about what social transitioning will entail and set up meetings with school administrators to talk about what changes to anticipate and what accommodations would be helpful. Ideally, these meetings should occur throughout the transition to maintain an open dialogue between the child's family and school staff.

Timing and Setting

The starting time for a social transition will be unique for each child because of differences in their ages and their social environments. Before beginning the process, it is best to evaluate all factors, including the child's own comfort level. Ideally, the beginning of the school year or the school term is a good time to start since this will allow both the school and the family to use the vacation time to prepare. The transition may also appear less abrupt to classmates. Parents must take into account their child's feelings as well as their own when making decisions about timing. Parents have to gauge whether to keep their child at the same school or, assuming there are other schools in the area, transfer the child to another school, perhaps one that is more supportive. This option may not be available to families who live in small or rural communities.

Some families may choose to keep their child's transitioning private; others may have the child live with close relatives so that the child can attend a new school in a different district. If the child remains at their school, they will have an already existing support system, that is, familiar peers and staff. Parents will also know at least some of the school officials and may be better positioned to advocate. If the child stays in the same school, however, that means that many will know about the child's transition and may use the opportunity to harass or bully. Some children think that having a fresh start is more critical. But this may mean that the child will not seek to disclose, keeping their past a secret, which may provoke shame and anxiety. It is the reason why we always evaluate the benefits and risks so that everyone can make informed decisions. There is no "right way" to do this, and each family has to weigh the pros and cons of the available options. Regardless of their choice, we have observed, in working with hundreds of children, that parents unequivocally report that once social transitioning began, their child became more confident, more outgoing, and more motivated to attend school, and there were fewer power struggles at home, which resulted in time and energy that were freed to build closer relationships.

Name and Clothing

If the child has a preferred name, it is important to ask the school to change its records. For schools that do not allow formal changes, parents should ask to register their child's preferred name on the class roster so that teachers will use it during roll call. If school uniforms are required, a discussion about this will be necessary as well. Parents should advocate for their child's right to wear the uniform or other articles of clothing that align with their affirmed gender. Some schools that require uniforms may be initially reluctant to accommodate this request since they fear it may raise questions and concerns from other students and their parents. It is important, however, for parents to point out the advantages of this practice. For example, wearing gender-affirming clothing can actually help children pass, thus blending in better among their peers and protecting them from being questioned or harassed.

Educating School Staff and Other Parents

Depending on the school staff's level of knowledge, parents may need to educate them on how best to address questions from other parents and children in a way that satisfies their curiosity but remains respectful of the child and their family. Parents will benefit from clearly delineating what can and cannot be disclosed to others. It is often helpful to provide some additional resources and reading material. *When Kathy Is Keith* (Wong, 2011b) and *My Princess Boy* (Kilodavis, 2009) are examples of two good books on gender variance written for children. A useful resource for school officials and educators is *Supporting Transgender and Transsexual Students in K–12 Schools: A Guide for Educators* (Wells, Roberts, & Allan, 2012).

In addition, we recommend parents prepare a letter intended for other parents, disclosing the transition status of their child. It is often best to give the letter to the school staff along with instructions on whom to dispense it to. Including some links so that others can educate themselves is also helpful. Usually we advise parents to instruct school staff to give the letter only to those parents who have raised concerns. If they continue to express anxiety or fear after reading it, we encourage (1) setting up meetings with those particular parents along with specialists and school officials to address any misinformation, and (2) suggesting a referral to the school counselor and/or specialists who may be able to address their concerns about the presence of a gender nonconforming child.

Some of the parents we have worked with have expressed annoyance, even anger, about having to prepare a letter, viewing it as an unfair step to have to take, since parents with cisgender children never have to go through a similar process. We acknowledge that it may feel unfair, but we have also seen the advantages of putting preventive measures in place. The letter is often instrumental in minimizing the chances that another parent will take actions that will ultimately harm the child.

Parents can also encourage the school to hold assemblies aimed at celebrating diversity to increase awareness and acceptance. To provide further education and training for school staff and students, parents should consider connecting them with community LGBTQ educators, such as those affiliated with gay and lesbian centers. Many have the necessary training and experience to offer consultation. Parents could also include these educators in the planning process before implementing social transitioning at school. This would allow more input from supportive professionals.

Bathrooms, Changing Rooms, and Physical Education Classes

Bathroom and changing room use will inevitably be a source of contention. Ideally, children should use the facilities consistent with their affirmed gender. Parents of both cisgender and gender nonconforming children as well as the children themselves may be worried about safety. It is important to understand, however, that for some gender nonconforming children, using bathrooms of the opposite gender can, at times, create even more distress. Accessible or unisex bathrooms are a good option and, if all efforts fail, use of the staff or nurse's bathroom could be considered, even as a temporary solution. Strong advocacy by the parents or a specialist might be necessary to bring about necessary policy changes at the school, the district, the state, or the federal or province level.

As for physical education classes, parents can encourage the school to have less gender segregation. Activities that are organized by gender may create more distress for the gender nonconforming child, who may be made to feel they don't belong to any group. Coed physical activities can be suggested as an alternative. For activities that remain gender segregated, parents can advocate as well, requesting the physical education teachers and coaches monitor their child's safety. More adult supervision not only can provide a buffer against teasing and bullying, which can occur more often during physical activities, but also sends a message of inclusion. If the school is inflexible, an alternative solution might be for the child to fulfill the physical education course requirements through private lessons in a sport of their choosing through local community centers or community sport teams.

Whom and What to Tell

Some children consider their decision to transition as private. Although this option may seem easier in that it circumvents potentially uncomfortable situations, the act of hiding an important part of their identity may deter developing feelings of closeness with their friends and result in opting out of certain social activities, such as play dates or sleepovers, fearing that their "secret" will be uncovered. In contrast, other children disclose openly and are completely transparent, which affords them the opportunity to live more authentically. Though honesty may be best in the end, it carries some risk at times, given the transphobic society in which we live. More beneficial might be a position somewhere in between: selecting to disclose to those who will probably be supportive, a decision that a child has a right to make independently or in discussion with parents.

The Role of Specialists

In our opinion, all gender dysphoric children do not necessarily need therapy; rather, they should have the opportunity to explore their gender in a supportive environment. Thus, we believe a major role of the health professional is to facilitate the child's social transitioning by advising parents on how best to create a safe space. The specialist can (1) monitor the progress of the transition and, if relevant, assess the child's readiness for medical interventions; (2) advocate on behalf of the child and the parents and assist in educating school staff on the child's status; and (3) collaborate with the school counselor to devise the best approach for the child's social transition. Those specialists may include family doctors, psychologists, psychiatrists, family therapists, mental health counselors and social workers.

Parents play an integral role in a child's social transitioning, and we want to highlight the fact that, in our experience, it is not unusual for many parents to experience the complex grief of "losing" their son or daughter, face discrimination and prejudice, and no longer have the support of friends and family members who do not agree with social transitioning as an appropriate course of action. We counsel parents to carve time out of their busy schedules in order to explore their own feelings, engage in introspection, improve self-care, advocate for themselves, and actively expand their support system, perhaps by including other parents who have gone through a similar process. Indeed, a child in transition is an entire family in transition, and everyone should be emotionally fortified during this journey.

Case Example: Edith and William

Edith and William are Euro-Canadians who reside in a suburb of Vancouver. Both work full-time. They report having gay and lesbian friends in their social circles, but they have been exposed to transgender people only through the media, mostly TV shows and the news. They have three children: Steven, age 10, Mary, age eight, and their youngest, Sophia, age seven, an affirmed girl, originally named John. According to Edith and William, Sophia has been experiencing conflict about her gender since the age of three. The parents requested help because of her school refusal, frequent arguments over clothing choices, and asserting she was a girl. They were both relatively open-minded, allowing her to wear dresses and engage in other behaviors considered stereotypically feminine while at home.

At first they thought it was "just a phase," and they tried to explain to Sophia how she was anatomically different from a girl. They encouraged behaviors that were more in alignment with her assigned gender, to which Sophia often responded with sadness and frustration. This persisted until she began kindergarten. Since the school staff was welcoming of gender nonconforming children, Edith and Williams decided to let Sophia fully explore herself, allowing her to use her chosen name along with female pronouns. During that time, both her parents and teachers reported that Sophia was functioning well behaviorally and socially.

When she was about to begin elementary school, however, her parents were aware that stricter rules would apply. After some consideration, they no longer permitted her to present as a girl at school, thinking it would be socially easier for her to live in her assigned gender. This led to constant battles over her attendance and attire. She would insist on wearing dresses to school and, while there, wanted to be treated as a girl. She wet her pants on several occasions because she did not want to share the bathroom with the boys. All of these behaviors affected her socioemotional development in adverse ways. At the same time, her parents observed that Sophia had become more withdrawn and less socially engaged. This prompted them to seek consultation from our office.

During our assessment, it became apparent that Sophia's gender dysphoria was significant and had been consistent since she was three years old. She was convinced she would grow a vagina someday and frequently asked when she would grow breasts. Though Edith was more flexible in relation to gender expression, William hoped he could modify Sophia's presentation so she could attend elementary school as a boy. We discussed the idea of having Sophia socially transition to her affirmed gender in the school setting, about which they expressed fear, not knowing how to initiate this process. Our clinical team, which included a mental health counselor and a psychologist, helped them understand that fear is a common reaction and, subsequently, set up a few counseling sessions focused on working with the couple, sensitizing them to Sophia's struggles and how they might be optimally helpful.

Their main concerns were that Sophia might be bullied by her peers as well as what the other parents' reactions might be to her presence at school and the effect that might have on their own children. Knowing that others have dealt with similar fears, we invited Edith and William to attend our parents' group, hoping it would lessen their anxieties and help them feel less alone.

Parental support is critical to the child's success. Though some may take longer to come around, others are quickly on board after understanding the pros and cons as well as being equipped with a detailed plan for the transition. Both Edith and William appeared to feel less anxious, knowing that we would be actively assisting *and* that we had successfully done this with other families. After giving this considerable thought, they agreed to try it out.

Though they were unsure at first, it became clear that the advantages of transitioning at her current school outweighed the benefits of transferring to another since Sophia was acquainted with her classmates and liked her teachers, and the school was open to the idea when the possibility was brought to the principal's attention. Since her two older siblings were also attending the same school, remaining there would be less disruptive for everyone. Sophia's parents spoke with their other children about this before bringing them in for a few family sessions, at which we discussed the plan and answered their questions, such as (1) what to say to other kids if they ask about Sophia, and (2) what to do if they see her being harassed. We suggested that the siblings, if asked, say that Sophia is a girl and that if they have further questions, they should direct them to teachers and school officials. If they see her being harassed, they should immediately inform any available staff member as well as tell their parents as quickly as they can.

In addition to the parents and our clinicians, the initial meeting included the principal, her primary teacher, as well as a few support staff — for example, the school counselor and the school bus driver. With the parents' and Sophia's permission, we gave the school a copy of her assessment report, which laid out the details of our recommendations, ways to implement the social transition plan, and a diagnosis of gender dysphoria.

At the next meeting, we asked that staff use her chosen name and female pronouns in addressing her while retaining the birth name and natal sex in her registration record until the parents legally implement a name change. We also recommended that Sophia be permitted to use the female bathrooms and discouraged gender-segregated activities during PE classes. The school preferred Sophia use the unisex bathroom and the staff bathroom for the first year while observing her progress, but it agreed to modify this if everything went smoothly.

Since all these changes required planning, we requested the social transition start at the beginning of the next school year, which was only a few months away. Before that, we arranged for an educator to provide some sensitivity training to the staff and the students, all of which was key in setting the stage. The educator gave a similar presentation to Sophia's class to reiterate important points about diversity and accepting those who are different. The primary teacher was asked to closely monitor any teasing or bullying that could occur, since some children were aware of Sophia's assigned gender. A handful of staff members were also informed of Sophia's transition so that she would feel comfortable going to them for additional support should a crisis arise or if she just wanted to talk. We also provided the school library with a list of transgender-related children's books as well as informational books for parents.

We anticipated that parents of some of the other students might be worried about exposure to a gender nonconforming child. In response, Sophia's parents prepared a letter that they gave to the principal, explaining and educating other parents, and also listing some useful resources. Whenever parents expressed concern, the principal shared this letter with them. We recommended that after the transition was initiated, members of the care team should meet regularly to monitor and evaluate her progress. Even though this plan was developed in a relatively detailed way, ongoing adjustment was needed to (1) track Sophia's progress; (2) amend any loopholes that the original plan might have overlooked; (3) problem-solve; and (4) modify the plan when Sophia entered a different developmental stage, particularly parts of the plan that related to her peer relationships.

Our experience is that a successful social transition requires ongoing effort and teamwork. Monitoring Sophia's progress and making adjustments on the basis of her developmental needs are crucial. Specialists are typically more involved in the beginning of the process, especially in initiating the plans. As the parents and the school officials become more skilled and experienced, however, the specialist should phase out and provide consultation on an as-needed basis.

Over the next few months, Sophia's transition at school went relatively smoothly. There was only one child who voiced confusion about Sophia and asked his mother about this. The school responded by immediately providing the letter to the child's mother and explaining the situation using the information they learned from the clinician, educator, and Sophia's parents. The child's mother was satisfied with the letter, as it gave her direction on how to explain things to her child. Shortly after her transition, Sophia attended school more regularly, had fewer arguments with her parents, and overall remained well-adjusted.

We took an active role throughout — assessing, counseling Sophia's parents, and delineating and executing the plans along with the care team. In the beginning, we met once a month with the other professionals to monitor her progress, gradually decreasing this to once every three months. Currently, we meet with Edith and William periodically to address any issues relative to disclosure and to help refine their advocacy skills. We also meet with Sophia individually every six months to monitor her development and address any concerns she has. Thus far, she has been consistent, persistent, and insistent with regard to her gender. Edith and William report that Sophia has become more confident, particularly in socializing with her female peers.

Each social transition plan is unique, depending on the child's development, environment, and the availability of resources. Direct involvement of a specialist is recommended, especially in the early stages. Parents' support, or the lack thereof, will probably determine the outcome. Our experience demonstrates that, if everyone works together, gender dysphoric children not only get a chance at life, but also can thrive and flourish.

REFERENCES

American Psychiatric Association. (2000). *Diagnostic and Statistical Manual of Mental Disorders (DSM-IV-TR)*. Washington, D.C.: American Psychiatric Association Publishing.

American Psychiatric Association. (2013). *Diagnostic and Statistical Manual of Mental Disorders (DSM-V)*. Washington, D.C.: American Psychiatric Association Publishing.

Bryant, K. (2006). Making gender identity disorder of childhood: Historical lessons for contemporary debates. *Sexuality Research & Social Policy*, 3 (3), 23–39. doi:10.1525/srsp.2006.3.3.23.

Byrne, J. (2013). *Transgender health and human rights* [discussion paper]. New York: United Nations Development Programme.

Carver, P. R., Yunger, J. L., & Perry, D. G. (2003). Gender identity and the adjustment in middle childhood. *Sex Roles*, 49, 95–109.

Coleman, E., Bockting, W., Botzer, M., Cohen-Kettenis, P., DeCuypere, G., Feldman, J., . . . & Zucker, K. (2012). Standards of Care for the health of transsexual, transgender, and gender-nonconforming people, Version 7. *International Journal of Transgenderism, 13* (4), 165–232. doi:10.1080/15532739.2011.700873.

de Vries, A. L., & Cohen-Kettenis, P. T. (2012). Clinical management of gender dysphoria in children and adolescents: The Dutch approach. *Journal of Homosexuality, 59* (3), 301–320. doi:10.1080/00918369.2012.653300.

Drescher, J., Cohen-Kettenis, P. T., & Reed, G. M. (2016). Gender incongruence of childhood in the ICD-11: Controversies, proposal, and rationale. *Lancet Psychiatry, 3,* 297–304. doi:10.1016/S2215-0366(15)00586-6.

Edwards-Leeper, L., & Spack, N. P. (2012). Psychological evaluation and medical treatment of transgender youth in an interdisciplinary "gender management service" (GeMS) in a major pediatric center. *Journal of Homosexuality, 59,* 321–336. doi:10.1080/00918369.2012.653302.

Egan, S. K., & Perry, D. G. (2001). Gender identity: A multidimensional analysis with implications for psychosocial adjustment. *Developmental Psychology, 37,* 451–463.

Ehrensaft, D. (2016). *The gender creative child: Pathways for nurturing and supporting children who live outside gender boxes.* New York: Experiment.

Greytak, E. A., Kosciw, J. G., & Diaz, E. M. (2009). *Harsh realities: The experience of transgender youth in our nation's schools.* New York: Gay, Lesbian and Straight Educational Network (GLSEN).

Grossman, A. H., & D'Augelli, A. R. (2007). Transgender youth and life-threatening behaviours. *Suicide and Life Threatening Behaviour, 37* (5), 527–537.

Hidalgo, M. A., Ehrensaft, D., Tishelman, A. C., Clark, L. F., Garofalo, R. O., Rosenthal, S. M., Spack, N. P., & Olson, J. (2013). The gender affirmative model: What we know and what we aim to learn. *Human Development, 56,* 285–290. doi:10.1159/000355235.

Khatchadourian, K., Amed, S., & Metzger, D. (2014). Clinical management of youth with gender dysphoria in Vancouver. *Journal of Paediatrics, 164,* 906–911. doi:10.1016/j.jpeds.2013.10.068.

Kilodavis, C. (2009). *My princess boy: A mom's story about a young boy who loves to dress up.* Seattle: KD Talent.

Leibowitz, S. F., & Spack, N. P. (2011). The development of a gender identity psychosocial clinic: Treatment issues, logistical consideration, interdisciplinary cooperation, and future initiatives. *Child and Adolescent Psychiatric Clinics of North America, 20,* 701–724. doi: 10.1016/j-chc.2011.07.004.

Leibowitz, S. F., & Telingator, C. (2012). Assessing gender identity concerns in children and adolescents: Evaluation, treatments, and outcomes. *Current Psychiatric Reports, 14,* 111–120. doi:10.1007/s11920-012-0259-x.

Lev, A. I. (2013). Gender dysphoria: Two steps forward, one step back. *Clinical Social Work Journal, 41* (3), 288–296. doi:10.1007/s10615-013-0447-0.

Menvielle, E. (2012). A comprehensive program for children with gender variant behaviours and gender identity disorders. *Journal of Homosexuality, 59,* 337–356. doi:10.1080/0091 8369.2012.653305.

Minter, S. P. (2012). Supporting transgender children: New legal, social, and medical approaches. *Journal of Homosexuality, 59,* 422–433. doi:10.1080/00918369.2012.653311.

Pyne, J. (2014). The governance of gender non-conforming children: A dangerous enclosure. *Annual Review of Critical Psychology, 11,* 79–96.

Wells, K., Roberts, G., & Allan, C. (2012). *Supporting transgender and transsexual students in K–12 schools: A guide for educators.* Ottawa, Ont.: Canadian Teachers' Federation.

Wong, W. (2011a). Where do I belong: A case study of two Asian trans-youth in Canada. *International Journal of Arts & Sciences, 4,* 455–464.

Wong, W. (2011b). *When Kathy Is Keith.* Bloomington, Ind.: Xlibris.

22

Please Stop Calling My Daughter "He": Advocating for Teens and Preteens in the School Setting

Deborah Coolhart, PhD, LMFT

About a year ago, the parents of 15-year-old David found out that their child was transgender. During the previous year, his parents have been working hard to understand and accept their child, who is now dressing in a more feminine way and requesting to be referred to as Celia. Recently, Celia's grades have been plummeting and she has been skipping school, asking her parents if she can drop out. Her parents have been frustrated by these changes and feel helpless. She tells them that she just can't deal with going to gym class and being forced to use the boys' locker room. She also says that some of the other kids at school regularly make cruel comments about how she dresses, and it doesn't help that the teachers are still calling her "David." Celia's parents are concerned not only about their child's educational achievement, but also for her physical safety. They want to advocate for Celia at school but don't know where to start.

Parents of gender nonconforming and transgender youth often notice a change in their child's school performance or hear them talk about school as a difficult place to be. Their child may, in reality, be the first "out" transgender student the school has ever had. School personnel are often uninformed and unaware of their unique challenges. Even when they *are* aware, they may not know how to appropriately deal with those challenges or how to create policies that facilitate fair treatment. Additionally, staff may be overtly unsupportive, making the environment unpredictable, even hostile. This chapter provides an overview of gender-related harassment and its consequences and discusses what parents can do to advocate.

Gender-Related Harassment and Its Consequences

Research consistently demonstrates that schools are unfriendly, often unsafe places for gender nonconforming and transgender students. The National Transgender Discrimination Survey, the largest-scale study to date on transgender discrimi-

Lev, Arlene I., Gottlieb, Andrew R., *Families in Transition*
dx.doi.org/10.17312/harringtonparkpress/2019.04.fit.022

nation (6,456 participants), found 78% reported harassment, 35% had been physically assaulted, and 12% experienced sexual violence, all within the school setting. Higher rates of harassment were found for students of color and those from low-income families. Male-to-female participants reported more violence; female-to-male participants reported more harassment and bullying. Not surprisingly, 15% dropped out (Grant et al., 2011). Similarly, GLSEN's Harsh Realities Report found transgender students reported higher rates of discrimination and lower levels of safety compared to lesbian, gay, and bisexual students. Of the transgender participants, 90% heard negative remarks about their gender expression sometimes, often, or frequently. Gender nonconforming kids were targeted as well, even when they were not LGBT-identified (Greytak, Kosciw, & Diaz, 2009).

More disturbing is that transgender students experience mistreatment not only from peers, but also from school faculty and staff. In this same study, 39% reported hearing negative remarks about their gender expression from the adults in charge. The Transgender Discrimination Survey indicated 31% had been harassed by teachers or staff, 5% had been physically assaulted by teachers or staff, 3% had been sexually assaulted by teachers or staff, and 6% had been expelled because of gender identity or expression (Grant et al., 2011). Other times, school staff may not be the direct source of harassment, but they often fail to intervene when harassment occurs. McGuire, Anderson, Toomey, and Russell (2010) explored the academic climate for transgender youth, who perceived their teachers to be mostly indifferent to threats from peers. Harassment has serious consequences for mental and physical health, and these problems may be more severe for transgender youth in comparison to their lesbian, gay, and bisexual counterparts (Espelage & Swearer, 2008). Victimization has been linked to poorer mental health, greater risk for STDs and HIV, negative psychosocial adjustment in young adulthood, decreased life satisfaction, and increased depression for LGBT youth (Russell, Ryan, Toomey, Diaz, & Sanchez, 2011; Toomey, Ryan, Diaz, Card, & Russell, 2010). Bullying often specifically targets gender nonconformity, which may have unique implications for transgender youth (Toomey et al., 2010).

Other studies explore the consequences of school harassment and mistreatment specifically for transgender kids. GLSEN's Harsh Realities Report indicated over half of transgender students are truant on a regular basis, absences increase, grade-point averages decrease, and, perhaps worst of all, future aspirations are compromised, all reactions to the threat of victimization or its actuality, and all affecting educational and vocational achievement (Greytak et al., 2009). In a study of transgender female adults, chronic depression and suicidality were directly linked to verbal and physical abuse or harassment during adolescence, which highlights the reality of long-term consequences (Nuttbrock et al., 2010). The Transgender Discrimination Survey found a link between physical health risks and negative or traumatizing experiences in the school environment, noting higher rates of drug and alcohol abuse, smoking, suicide attempts, sex work, homelessness, and HIV (Grant et al., 2011).

It seems obvious that a supportive school environment will have a positive effect for gender nonconforming and transgender youth, such as helping foster resiliency in navigating the stressors in their lives (Singh, Meng, & Hansen, 2014). In their study of LGB youth, Goodenow, Szalacha, and Westheimer (2006) found that antidiscrimination policies decreased suicide attempts, so the outcomes for transgender students would, no doubt, be similar. Increased teacher intervention in situations involving harassment and a special attachment to a trusted adult were both associated with increased feelings of safety (McGuire et al., 2010).

With chapters nationwide, Gay-Straight Alliances (GSA) offer opportunities to socialize and advocate, and they play an especially important role in creating a supportive environment, facilitating both short- and long-term resilience, a greater sense of connection with the academic experience, decreased depression, greater educational attainment, and an increase in self-esteem (Diaz, Kosciw, & Greytak, 2010). Creating change at policy, administrative, faculty, organizational—that is, systemic—levels has profound, long-range implications for everyone, not just for those who are gender nonconforming and transgender. Where can we begin?

Parent Advocacy in Middle and High School Environments

When a gender nonconforming or transgender student is in need of advocacy, it's likely that parents are also struggling with their own emotional processes in adjusting to their child's gender identity. Some parents may not feel ready or knowledgeable enough to approach school personnel. It is normal for them to go through their own period of adjustment, and if they are feeling conflicted at this stage, it may be in the family's best interest to enlist outside help. Because of the serious mental and physical health consequences that can result from school harassment, it is imperative that advocacy occur sooner rather than later. If parents require help, one option is to seek a trans-affirmative therapist or helping professional who can be an advocate in the school setting alongside the parents and the child (Coolhart & MacKnight, 2015). Similarly, there may be other local trans-affirmative resources, such as LGBTQ centers or youth organizations, where assistance can be found. When local resources are not readily available, parents can use online resources to help equip them with the knowledge and the strategies they'll need (see the appendix to this chapter).

Some parents quickly begin to educate themselves about what it all means, what the challenges are, and how vital it is to support their children. By immersing themselves in the literature and connecting with other transgender people or their parents, they are better able to move to a place of understanding and, eventually, acceptance. These parents may feel ready to advocate for their child on their own but may benefit from the knowledge and experience of others who have "been there."

In the case of Celia, her parents wanted to do what they could to advocate, but at the same time, they were struggling to understand her. Because they were at the beginning of the process, they worried that they might not know how to answer questions posed to them. So it made sense for me, their therapist, to accompany them to a meeting with school personnel. (Note: If parents are not yet ready or willing to advocate, the therapist may approach the school without the parents and/or work clinically to empower the child to advocate for themselves [see the appendix to this chapter].)

The following sections outline common challenges faced by gender nonconforming and transgender youth, suggestions for facing these challenges, and ideas for formulating an individualized plan to help create a sense of safety.

Creating Youth-Centered Plans

When it comes to designing a plan, one size does not fit all. Each school has different challenges (e.g., locations of gender-neutral bathrooms, use of gendered uniforms), and each person has unique preferences about how to navigate them. The student's desires and comfort level should be accurately reflected and each plan should be individualized with attention to safety, particularly if there has been a history or suggestion of violence toward these students.

When formulating a plan, parents should talk to their child about what they are experiencing at school, what situations cause distress, and how they would like these problems handled. If parents plan to meet with school personnel, the child may or may not want to attend but should be given a choice. On the one hand, should a younger child opt out, parents need to have a full understanding of what preferences the child has so they can accurately represent them. On the other hand, an older adolescent may not want their parents to be present and may be capable of advocating for themselves. Ultimately, the goal is to find solutions that work for the school *and* for the student.

Harassment and Safety

If a student has experienced harassment or bullying in the school environment, it is urgent the matter be dealt with quickly. Parents should speak with school personnel about the contexts in which the harassment or bullying is occurring and what the outcomes have been—for example, whether staff witnessed it and intervened. Parents should ask what policies, if any, are currently in place and request that their child be included in developing or refining those policies (Lev & Alie, 2012). Because it is common for staff not to intervene when harassment occurs (Greytak et al., 2009), parents should inquire directly how staff will be trained to increase their sensitivity, how they will be expected to respond when they witness harassment, and what the consequences will be if they do not act in a timely and appropriate manner.

Those experiencing distress at school may benefit from developing a safety plan and being in control of its execution (Coolhart & MacKnight, 2015). This plan is designed to allow a student to quickly exit a high-stress situation. Based on their input about where and when they most commonly experience conflict, a plan can specify where they can go when the situation occurs, whom they can talk to, and how they can find a safe haven. Because connection to a trusted adult in the school environment may aid in feelings of safety (McGuire et al., 2010), the plan should identify who that person—a teacher or counselor—would be and how to locate them during a crisis.

Names and Pronouns

Using names and pronouns that accurately reflect a child's gender identity is key. A great deal of stress can be caused when they are not used or are misused. The literature consistently states that using chosen names and pronouns, ones that match their gender identity, is the most sensitive and appropriate course of action, even when that chosen name is different from their legal name (Brill & Pepper, 2008; Cho, Laub, Wall, Daley, & Joslin, 2004; Coolhart, Baker, Farmer, Melhaney, & Shipman, 2013; Lev & Alie, 2012). Both should be adopted by all school personnel. Using the wrong name or pronoun can also call attention to the student's transgender status, creating the possibility for mistreatment.

Parents should talk to the school administrator about how their child should be properly identified and how that will be communicated to the teachers and school staff. If possible, that name should be permanently changed in the system to avoid future mistakes, such as when substitute teachers take attendance. Also, parents can request that official school forms be updated to include transgender identities, rather than just the standard male and female categories (Brill & Pepper, 2008), so that students have the option of identifying outside the binary system. Again, because some school personnel may not be supportive, parents should ask how they will be trained and what the consequences would be for intentionally misusing names and pronouns.

Bathrooms and Locker Rooms

Public bathroom and locker room use is notoriously stressful for gender nonconforming and transgender kids. In most places, there are two clearly labeled choices—male and female. Since transgender youth often feel uncomfortable in—even barred from—using these facilities, it is important that the school, together with the student, come up with a clear, individualized plan for bathroom and locker room use—safety being paramount (Coolhart & MacKnight, 2015; GLSEN and National Center for Transgender Equality, 2016). In general, a child should be allowed to use the bathroom and locker room that matches their gender identity unless there are significant safety concerns (Coolhart & MacKnight, 2015). For example, a transgender male may desire to use the boys' bathroom because he wants to be like other boys. If the parents or the school feels strongly that this presents a safety risk, it may be necessary to discuss other options, such as using the nurse's or teachers' bathrooms.

Single-user bathrooms, such as that in the nurse's office, may be appropriate if there are concerns about privacy or discomfort on the part of either the transgender student or the other students. The single-user option might then be made available to anyone who feels uncomfortable (GLSEN and National Center for Transgender Equality, 2016). This approach emphasizes inclusion and places the responsibility for managing discomfort on those experiencing the problem, rather than solely on the gender nonconforming or transgender student.

Dress Codes and Sports

In a school where there are different dress codes for boys and girls, being forced to wear clothing that is inconsistent with one's gender identity can cause discomfort and dysphoria. Thus, adherence to the dress code that is consistent with gender identity is optimal (Brill & Pepper, 2008; Coolhart & MacKnight, 2015; GLSEN and National Center for Transgender Equality, 2016). But the same rules should apply to everyone. For example, a transgender female should never be reprimanded for wearing something that is "too feminine" if it is something that other girls would be allowed to wear.

Whether or not a student has medically transitioned, they should be allowed to play sports consistent with their gender identity (GLSEN and National Center for Transgender Equality, 2016; Griffin & Carroll, 2010). In some schools, policies may prohibit that from happening, and parents may need to consider whether they want to advocate for change—of course, in consultation with their child (see the appendix to this chapter).

Other Gender Segregation

Schools often have activities in which students are separated according to gender. It is generally recommended that they reduce or eliminate this practice (GLSEN and National Center for Transgender Equality, 2016), which may be relatively easy to do. For example, instead of dividing the class into girls and boys, split the class down the middle or have students count off by ones and twos.

There may, however, be situations in which gender segregation cannot be easily avoided—for example, in health class. This could be particularly uncomfortable for a transgender student who may not be fully represented in either section. One option would be for the general classes to include a discussion of transgender health, though, understandably, that adolescent may feel singled out. Other options include an individualized lesson for the transgender youth or teaching all genders together.

While some schools provide coed gym class, where all activities are mixed, other schools still include curricula that are clearly segregated. In these situations, again, the student should take an active part in figuring out the most comfortable solution. In general, they should be allowed to participate in activities that are congruent with their gender identity, though this may not always be best for others. In that case, the student's preferences and the administration's creativity should be combined to develop a plan that works for everyone.

Confidentiality and Privacy

All students have the right to privacy and this includes information about their gender (GLSEN and National Center for Transgender Equality, 2016). If someone transitions and remains in the same school, they may not have a need for confidentiality because others probably know. In this situation, that student should be consulted about whether and how they want their identity discussed by staff with students. Any concerns about privacy should be respected. Someone who is living "stealth," their identity unknown to others, may need more support, however. For example, a student may have transferred to a new school in order to socially transition, and so students and some personnel may be unaware of their status. With their child's desires in mind, parents should discuss with the administration who in the school needs to know and who doesn't, how confidentiality can be maintained, and how to respond when their child's identity is being questioned (Coolhart & MacKnight, 2015).

Conclusion

After I attended a meeting at school with Celia, her parents, and school personnel, a plan was developed. One of the most helpful outcomes was the commitment the school made to consistently use Celia's chosen name and female pronouns. Over time, her identity as a young transgender woman became clearer to Celia's peers. While this led to some questions at first, the students eventually began to understand and accept her for who she was. Celia was clear about how to handle any harassment she encountered, and with the support of school personnel, the conflicts greatly decreased.

The second outcome was an agreement about bathroom and locker room use. Celia did not want to walk all the way across the school to use the nurse's bathroom, but she still felt a little uncomfortable in the girls' bathroom when there were others around. The solution was that teachers would readily offer Celia a bathroom pass whenever she asked during class. That way, she was able to use the girls' bathroom when it would probably be vacant. Similarly, the gym teacher agreed to overlook Celia's tardiness so she could change in the girls' locker room after most of the other girls were finished. These changes led to Celia's feeling safer at school, and, as a result, her grades began to improve. Celia's parents felt supported by my attendance and learned more about how to advocate.

For gender nonconforming and transgender youth, school is often a place of conflict. Dealing with this insensitive, often hostile environment makes it difficult not only to achieve academic success, but also to have more basic needs met, such as a sense of safety. Every student deserves to feel safe, and advocacy is often required.

Research indicates that parental support is vital and may reduce the risk of multiple physical and mental health problems, which may lead to homelessness, drug and alcohol abuse, smoking, incarceration, sex work, suicide ideation and attempts, compromised self-esteem, depression, and diminished life satisfaction (Grant et al., 2011; Greytak et al., 2009; Travers et al., 2012). Parents who advocate for their child in the school setting are clearly demonstrating their support, even when they are struggling to fully understand and accept. Working with the school to appropriately manage those challenges can reduce stress and increase the sense of control and mastery. This is imperative for achieving positive mental and physical health outcomes, both present and future, thereby contributing to increased acceptance of transgender people in society at large.

APPENDIX: RESOURCES FOR ASSISTING WITH ADVOCACY

Beyond the Binary: A Tool Kit for Gender Identity Activism in Schools (2004), by Stephanie Cho, Carolyn Laub, Sean Saifa M. Wall, Chris Daley, and Courtney Joslin, includes information parents could present to administrators about creating trans-affirmative policies and training.

The Gender Quest Workbook: A Guide for Teens and Young Adults Exploring Gender Identity (2015), by Ryjan Jay Testa, Deborah Coolhart, and Jayme Peta, includes a chapter designed to help youth navigate the school environment.

Gender Spectrum (www.genderspectrum.org) provides education, training, and support for creating gender-sensitive environments. Links and training programs for schools as well as information on ways to implement programmatic change can also be found on this website.

On the Team: Equal Opportunity for Transgender Student Athletes (2010), by Pat Griffin and Helen J. Carroll, provides useful information about organizing policy change for transgender athletes.

REFERENCES

Brill, S., & Pepper, R. (2008). *The transgender child: A handbook for families and professionals.* San Francisco: Cleiss Press.

Cho, S., Laub, C., Wall, S. S. M., Daley, C., & Joslin, C. (2004). *Beyond the binary: A tool kit for gender identity activism in schools.* Gay-Straight Alliance Network, Transgender Law Center, and National Center for Lesbian Rights. Retrieved from http://gsanetwork.org/files/resources/btbonline.pdf.

Coolhart, D., Baker, A., Farmer, S., Melhaney, M., & Shipman, D. (2013). Therapy with transsexual youth and their families: A clinical tool for assessing youth's readiness for gender transition. *Journal of Marital and Family Therapy, 39* (2), 223–243. doi:10.1111/j.1752-0606.2011.00283.x.

Coolhart, D., & MacKnight, V. (2015). Working with transgender youth and their families: Counselors and therapists as advocates for trans-affirmative school environments. *Journal of Counselor Leadership and Advocacy, 2* (1), 51–64. doi:10.1080/2326716X.2014.981767.

Diaz, E. M., Kosciw, J. G., & Greytak, E. A. (2010). School connectedness for lesbian, gay, bisexual, and transgender youth: In-school victimization and institutional supports. *Prevention Researcher, 17* (3), 15–17.

Espelage, D., & Swearer, S. (2008). Addressing research gaps in the intersection between homophobia and bullying. *School Psychology Review, 37* (2), 155–159.

GLSEN and National Center for Transgender Equality. (2016). Model district policy on transgender and gender nonconforming students: Model language, commentary & resources. Retrieved from https://www.glsen.org/sites/default/files/Trans%20Model%20Policy.pdf.

Goodenow, C., Szalacha, L., & Westheimer, K. (2006). School support groups, other school factors, and safety of sexual minority adolescents. *Psychology in the Schools, 43* (5), 573–589. doi:10.1002/pits.20173.

Grant, J. M., Motett, L. A., Tanis, J., Harrison, J., Herman, J. L., & Keisling, M. (2011). *Injustice at every turn: A report of the national transgender discrimination survey.* Washington, D.C.: National Center for Transgender Equality and National Gay and Lesbian Task Force.

Greytak, E. A., Kosciw, J. G., & Diaz, E. M. (2009). *Harsh realities: The experiences of transgender youth in our nation's schools.* A report from the Gay, Lesbian, and Straight Education Network (GLSEN). Retrieved from https://www.glsen.org/sites/default/files/Harsh%20Realities.pdf.

Griffin, P., & Carroll, H. J. (2010). *On the team: Equal opportunity for transgender student athletes.* National Center for Lesbian Rights, Women's Sports Foundation. Retrieved from http://www.nclrights.org/wp-content/uploads/2013/07/TransgenderStudentAthlete Report.pdf.

Lev, A. I., & Alie, L. (2012). Transgender and gender nonconforming children and youth: Developing culturally competent systems of care. In S. K. Fisher, J. M. Poirier, & G. M. Blau (eds.), *Improving emotional and behavioral outcomes for LGBT youth: A guide for professionals* (pp. 43–66). Baltimore: Brookes.

McGuire, J. K., Anderson, C. R., Toomey, R. B., & Russell, S. T. (2010). School climate for transgender youth: A mixed method investigation of student experiences and school responses. *Journal of Youth and Adolescence, 39,* 1175–1188. doi:10.1007/s10964-010-9540-7.

Nuttbrock, L., Hwahng, S., Bockting, W., Rosenblum, A., Mason, A., Macri, M., & Becker, J. (2010). Psychiatric impact of gender-related abuse across the life course of male-to-female transgender persons. *Journal of Sex Research, 41* (1), 12–23. doi:10.1080/00224490903062258.

Russell, S. T., Ryan, C., Toomey, R. B., Diaz, R. M., & Sanchez, J. (2011). Lesbian, gay, bisexual, and transgender adolescent school victimization: Implications for young adult health and adjustment. *Journal of School Health,* 81 (5), 223–230. doi:10.1111/j.1746-1561.2011.00583.x.

Singh, A. A., Meng, S. E., & Hansen, A. W. (2014). "I am my own gender": Resilience strategies of trans youth. *Journal of Counseling and Development, 92,* 208–218. doi:10.1002/j.1556-6676 .2014.00150.x.

Toomey, R., Ryan, C., Diaz, R., Card, N., & Russell, S. (2010). Gender-nonconforming lesbian, gay, bisexual, and transgender youth: School victimization and young adult psychosocial adjustment. *Developmental Psychology, 46* (6), 1580–1589. doi:10.1037/a0020705.

Travers, R., Bauer, G., Pyne, J., Bradley, K., Gale, L., & Papadimitriou, M. (2012). Impacts of strong parental support for trans youth. A report prepared for Children's Aid Society of Toronto and Delisle Youth Services. Retrieved from http://transpulseproject.ca/wp-content/ uploads/2012/10/Impacts-of-Strong-Parental-Support-for-Trans-Youth-vFINAL.pdf.

PART 8

Support Groups: What Is the Parent's Experience of Available Support Groups and Advocacy Organizations?

The support group exerts a unique therapeutic power all its own, as the following four pieces attest. It is typical for most of my own clients, whom I see individually, to wonder, at some point, if how they feel is typical of the ways others feel in a similar situation. When I normalize their experience, they let out a sigh of relief. Part of the intrinsic value of the group is in seeing one's thoughts, feelings, and actions mirrored in others, which gives one the comfort of not being alone.

Melissa MacNish not only gives us a history of the support group for parents of transgender youth that grew out of Greater Boston PFLAG, but also documents, in their own words, the process parents went through in bravely acknowledging, both publicly and privately, the ways they moved through their vulnerabilities to become capable facilitators, helping others who may be just beginning to find their way. But help goes in both directions. In assisting parents new to the group, those more senior members can see more clearly where they themselves have been *and* afford newer members the opportunity to imagine that their situations can get better. Looking back and looking forward are two sides of the same coin.

Who better than Rex Butt to ask, "What's a parent to do when professional help might be unavailable?" Confronted in 2002 with the reality of having a 23-year-old trans daughter, with virtually no information to go on, he quickly got to work—nose to the grindstone—eventually starting the Kingston, New York, chapter of PFLAG and, with his wife, Karen, becoming their transgender coordinators for a decade. His essay "Peer Support for Parents of Gender Nonconforming Children" highlights the benefits and risks of the types of help that *are* available. Whether it's through larger groups meetings at the local LGBTQ center, church, or synagogue, or through smaller, more intimate gatherings in a member's home, or through e-mail exchanges, phone calls, or listservs, Butt substantiates the fact that quick, reliable, consistent support comes in all forms.

Summer camp is in Nick Teich's blood. It's in his family's blood. So it seems only natural to pay homage to those formative experiences by envisioning a similar setting for gender variant and transgender youth, something Nick wished he had had when he was younger. Out of that vision, Camp Aranu'tiq and its umbrella organization, Harbor Camps, were born. Although the camp was designed primarily for children and adolescents, over the years he and his staff offered a support group for parents on the first day of the season; they then went on to expand the concept to a family camp, one in which groups for parents became an increasingly important programmatic focus, so hungry were parents to make contact with one another. These experiences were, in some cases, the first time parents met others who were also raising gender variant or transgender children, an invaluable experience, the importance of which should not be underestimated.

Lauren P. is learning to reconcile the splits — not only those splits that relate to the obvious ambivalence about how our culture handles difference, or those good-bad, gay-trans, pink boy–trans girl splits that get played out in what are supposed to be safe spaces. I'm talking about the confusion, the fear, the terror, the agony, as well as the joy, the pride, and the sense of wonder that come with raising any child, trusting that the person inevitably unfolding before your very eyes is the person they were meant to be. Lauren captures all that in her story, "Tom-Girl, Trans Girl, Pink Boy: Finding a Support Group for All." As she helps her daughter, Jenny, more fully evolve into her self, Lauren evolves in her own right, embracing all of *her* self, becoming a more complete person in the process.

23

The Experience of Parent Facilitators in a PFLAG Support Group for Parents of Transgender Youth and Young Adults

Melissa MacNish, MA, LMHC

When a youth comes out as transgender, parent support is imperative (Erich, Tittsworth, Dykes, & Cabuses, 2008; Grossman, D'Augelli, Howell, & Hubbard, 2005; Lev, 2004; Lev & Alie, 2012; Malpas, 2011). At the Family Acceptance Project, Ryan, Russell, Huebner, Diaz, and Sanchez (2010) found a direct correlation between mental health outcomes in LGBT youth and family acceptance or rejection. The more supportive the family, the more positive the outcome; the more rejecting the family, the more negative the outcome. Parents of transgender youth often struggle with the difficult balance between supporting their child while simultaneously managing their own complicated feelings about their child's identity.

This chapter explores the evolution of the Greater Boston PFLAG support group for parents of transgender children, drawing from the parents' experience as both group members and facilitators. The material is partially based on a series of individual interviews I conducted in person or on the phone with 10 participants: one married couple and eight mothers, all of whom are white, of European descent, cisgender, heterosexual, and middle to upper middle class. Eight have children who identify on the trans-masculine spectrum and two have children who identify on the trans-feminine spectrum. Eight are parent facilitators and two are original members of the group. The age range of the parents is 48 to 67; the age range of their children is 15 to 32.

These interviews consistently reflect what the research reveals: even supportive parents evidence an ever-changing kaleidoscope of feelings when facing their child's transition. They can be depressed, angry, fearful, disappointed, shameful, guilty, skeptical, and confused—to name just a few emotions—not only immediately after disclosure (Krieger, 2011), but even years later. Clearly, these families are undertaking their own transition as they work to better understand their children (Lev, 2004; Pepper, 2012).

Lev, Arlene I., Gottlieb, Andrew R., *Families in Transition*
dx.doi.org/10.17312/harringtonparkpress/2019.04.fit.023
© 2019 by Harrington Park Press

Before their children came out, most of the parents I interviewed had never met a transgender person. Instead, they imagined the worst, drawing from fragments of news stories, images of transgender people as victims of hate crimes, or sensationalized topics on television talk shows. These images are now starting to shift as we are in the midst of a "burgeoning transgender community, which is battling to de-pathologize gender nonconforming identities" (Lev & Alie, 2012, p. 44), as more and more individuals come out and fight to claim who they are with pride. When our support group first started, however, there were few positive public faces of the movement.

These parents have many fears for their children: harassment, discrimination, and physical harm. But they also worry that when their children are grown, they will not be able to find a partner or will regret having had permanent body modification (Krieger, 2011). In addition to the stigma that exists for those who are transgender, *parents* of a child who is transgender are also stigmatized (Lev, 2004) and fear being blamed for who their child is or having their decisions challenged when a child comes out. There is a history in the psychoanalytic literature of parental causation, that is, pathology, in the etiology of transgender identity (Hill & Menvielle, 2009). Wren (2002) writes, "Dominant psychological theories have leant heavily on psychoanalytic accounts and have seen family dysfunction at the root of the problem" (p. 378). Not only can this stigma lead to isolation, hindering parents from moving forward in their own process, but it can also obstruct access to any support that may be there for them (Menvielle & Tuerk, 2002).

Parents and clinicians might find it helpful to be aware of the stage models of family process that can help normalize their experience. One example is Lev's Family Emergence Model (2004). Her stages include (1) Discovery and Disclosure, (2) Turmoil, (3) Negotiation, and (4) Finding Balance. Emerson (1996) uses Kübler-Ross's (1969) five stages of grief—Denial, Anger, Bargaining, Depression, and Acceptance—to dramatically highlight the loss parents can feel during this process, applying these stages specifically to a family member's experience.

Participation in support groups—whether in person or online—can serve as an important act of self-care, helping guide parents through these stages as they process feelings and, it is hoped, move toward greater understanding and acceptance (Coolhart, Baker, Farmer, Malaney, & Shipman, 2013; Hill & Menvielle, 2009; Lev, 2004; Lev & Alie, 2012; MacNish & Gold-Peifer, 2014).

Getting Started

The Greater Boston PFLAG Parents of Transgender Children Support Group started in the fall of 2008. PFLAG is the nation's foremost family-based organization committed to the civil rights of LGBT people, founded in 1973 (Parents, Families, and Friends of Lesbians and Gays, 1999). I was working at a community health center that served a high percentage of transgender youth and young adults and had been referring parents to Greater Boston PFLAG—the only resource available at the time. I began to receive feedback that they did not feel comfortable at meetings where they were the only parents of transgender children, as their more specialized needs were not being met. One parent reported that someone in the group expressed the sentiment that they were glad their child was "just gay" and "not transgender." Not surprisingly, these parents were coming away from the meetings feeling more isolated than ever. Though they could relate to some of the issues discussed, they had their own unique set of concerns. It was evident that these parents could benefit from a group that consisted *solely* of parents of transgender youth. Historically, support groups have been useful interventions for people with a common source of stress. Schopler and Galinsky (1993) write, "They form social networks that have the potential for bridging gaps in service and for providing emotional support, guidance and information" (p. 196).

I contacted the local PFLAG chapter and asked if we could collaborate and start a group specifically for parents of transgender children and hold these meetings at the clinic where I was working. The executive director at Greater Boston PFLAG was very receptive. Initially, the group met weekly, led either by me or one of our two clinic interns, and regularly had three to six parents. Those original members had young adult children who had already transitioned, those parents being in Lev's (2004) final stage, Finding Balance. Before attending her first group, Alice, whose child had come out a number of years earlier, remembered thinking: "I am so over all this and I am so done with this whole process. I don't need a group. I could have used a group a couple years ago. . . . I thought, 'Oh, okay, I'll go once.'" She followed up by describing how she felt before attending her second meeting: "I remember I went in and said, 'Okay, I'm gonna do this.' I have things I suddenly realized I have to talk about. Like I wanted to know what people did with their family pictures. I had a list of things that I hadn't talked about all these years. I didn't have anybody to talk to."

Mary, another member of the first group, thought that because she was already so far along in her process, she would only casually use the group, mostly for social purposes. But because she found so much comfort being with others going through a shared experience, she made more of a commitment. Lillian echoed that sentiment: "I think it was good to have a place to go. It was good to be with other people."

It took some time for the group to expand. But in the spring of 2009 more parents started attending. Mary reflected, "By the time we had a new member come to the group, [who] just found out [about their child], we were comfortable together and ready to nurture someone else." After forming a trusting, cohesive unit, the original members were now able to use the newly expanded group in a different way, serving as role models or guides for those just beginning. I believe the experience of those initial meetings with Alice, Mary, and Lillian (and sometimes their husbands)—our core group—allowed them to cultivate a safe, nurturing space, or in Winnicottian (1965) terms, a *holding environment,* for newer members.

There were differences in their motivation levels at the time members started attending. Some began immediately after disclosure, so desperate were they to talk to other parents. Alyssa observed: "There was nothing holding me back. It was a big deal [only] because it was an hour away. I was feeling pretty desperate to connect with other people." Other parents took a longer time to find the courage. Susan stated: "It took me about three months to get there. I was really nervous—nervous about who was going to be there. Were there going to be people that I knew? When it's so secretive, you really have to trust that people are going to keep things confidential."

Many of the parents described a lack of both experience with and understanding about gender identity, though they *were* cognizant of the stigma of being transgender. Menvielle and Tuerk (2002) write about *secondary stigmatization,* resulting in isolation and feelings of shame on the part of the parents, clearly a potential obstacle when trying to engage them. Goffman (1963) describes this as *courtesy stigma,* that is, having a close connection to or an affiliation with someone who is stigmatized. He discusses different ways in which people deal with a courtesy stigma: avoid the stigmatized person or terminate the relationship. He also says, "One response to this fate is to embrace it, and to live within the world of one's stigmatized connection" (p. 30).

Alyssa hadn't spoken with anyone outside her family and close friends until she attended the group: "I had shared with a few friends and family, but most people whom I told cried, which wasn't very helpful. I was feeling very isolated. I was really trying to avoid friends because I wasn't ready to talk about it." Alice echoed her: "I talked to my siblings, a few close friends, but we didn't get a very positive response from most of the people. We were kind of in our own little bubble as a family." For some, the group became the only safe place to share their thoughts and feelings.

The stigma connected to transgender identity and the narrative of parental pathology as the root cause seem to create a fear in parents about what kinds of people will be attending these meetings. Ruth's thoughts: "When I walked into [the] group, everybody looked pretty okay. And then as I heard people speak, I thought, oh, these are people just like me. They have families within a typical range, they have concerns within a typical range, they didn't seem to have any major instabilities themselves. So it was like the normal people. It was a sense of relief because then right away I felt like I could share things. And it was very reassuring in that sense because it was like, wow, automatically a lot of my fears were alleviated." After hearing from other group members, she realized that they all had similar worries, wondering what kind of families they would find. Ruth continued: "I had a lot of, I don't know if it was trepidation, somewhere between trepidation and curiosity. Basically I had no idea what to expect. One of the big unknowns for me when my child came out was [wondering] who else was transgender. It's really embarrassing to have to admit. But I was like, are these a bunch of dejected, deeply troubled, marginal people, and my kid will be like the normal one?"

The normalizing process that becomes inherent in the group challenges the stigma the parents once felt. Fields (2001) describes this as *de-stigmatizing identity work* in her study on groups for parents of lesbians and gays.

The First Meeting

The parent facilitators all have very fond memories of their first meeting as members. They experienced a range of feelings—from being initially overwhelmed to being relieved when it ended. Overall, though, it can be powerfully liberating to share stories so personal for the first time (Rosenberg & Jellinek, 2002). In Phyllis's words: "It was a very positive experience, people were very welcoming. Tears, there were tears. When you come to this meeting, you have come to a place of acceptance. As hard as it is, you are here, you are accepting it, you are trying to get on board and support your kid."

Parents find it helpful to hear about other families who are further along and discuss how well their children are doing. Alyssa said: "I felt so tremendously relieved. Most were farther along in their process with their child. It made me feel hopeful. It was enormous to be able to talk with other people who got it. It restored hope that my kid could have a happy life, hearing about stories of [other] people. I didn't know who my child would be and who would love him. I was afraid for him. I felt an enormous sense of connection and relief and like I wasn't alone in the process."

As parents start from a place of fear and lack a frame of reference for a group of people who their child is now claiming as their own, there is tremendous relief in hearing stories from others whose children are doing well. Vanessa recalled: "I was in such shock at that time that I don't remember any details at all. I was afraid about what this will mean for my kid. Will he be happy? Will he be safe? I just remember [that] hearing stories of the other people, whose kids were older and doing well, was so reassuring."

Ruth reflected on the intimacy and safety of these groups, "Talking about their situation and why they were there, people did it in a very revealing way, and that made me feel really comfortable being vulnerable." Susan reiterated the importance of hearing others' experiences: "We felt we were doing good in our bubble, but worried about the world in general. After hearing the stories from parents with older kids doing well, it was a weight off our shoulders."

Functions of the Groups

The group provides a means for members to share similar concerns. It is a safe space in which to voice their sense of loss, increase their understanding of gender, and practice using appropriate pronouns. Parents discuss many topics, including medical and surgical interventions, name change, and disclosure to family and friends.

A major function of the group was facilitating the mourning of their child's identity as a son or a daughter (Broad, 2011; Malpas, 2011; Menvielle & Tuerk, 2002; Wren, 2002), much as parents of lesbian and gay men mourn the loss of who they hoped and imagined their child would be (Gottlieb, 2000). Sharing these experiences of loss can help foster acknowledgment and acceptance of the new reality (Wren, 2002). Phyllis highlighted the importance of having the support group as her own space to do that grief work: "I mourned losing a daughter for quite some time. But I wasn't going to lose my child, and I could set that aside and focus on what my child needed [from me in order to] move forward. Then I would have my private time away from that and be able to mourn." Broad (2011) describes PFLAG groups as providing a space for "a parental coming out in terms of grief in need of support and eventual advocacy that can be done through love" (p. 400).

Another benefit of the group is its psychoeducational function. Clarifying the differences among sex assigned at birth, gender identity, gender expression, and sexual orientation is central to being able to understand their child's experience (Lev, 2004; MacNish & Gold-Peifer, 2014). Alyssa described her confusion: "I knew that from the beginning I wanted to be accepting. I knew I wanted to be as supportive as I could. I didn't understand being transgender. I thought maybe it was a phase or a fad or maybe he would change his mind or we wanted to slow things down. I didn't really understand the difference between identity, expression, and sexual orientation."

Many parents struggled to differentiate gender identity from gender expression. Once they came to a deeper understanding that gender identity is who you feel yourself to be and gender expression is how you demonstrate it, they were able to have a better grasp of their child's experience. They often had the assumption that if you are born male you will be a man, be masculine, and be attracted to women; likewise, if you are born female, you will be a woman, be feminine, and be attracted to men. They quickly learn from the experiences of the group that is not always the case and that identity can develop in a variety of ways.

When a child comes out as transgender they will often request a name and pronoun change. This can be extremely hard for parents and requires them to shift language from son to daughter or vice versa. Phyllis noted: "It was helpful to practice. The first few times we used the new pronouns was during group and nobody flinched. If we stumbled and made a mistake, we could easily correct ourselves without our child being there." Alyssa related:

> The group was helpful for [practicing] pronouns. I might not have been ready to try it out with family or other friends. It has been an evolving process because my child really prefers gender-neutral pronouns. For a long time they allowed me to use male pronouns, but they preferred me to use *they, them,* and *theirs.* It is hard in the regular world. I resisted using *they* because I thought it described my singular child in the plural. I thought that in talking about that with other people, it would be confusing. It really helped me when I heard other parents use it to talk about their children even when I found it confusing, which I did. Other people modeled that in doing it for their children, and that helped me be more willing to use them myself.

Many parents struggle if their child decides to undergo body modification to further their transition. For children who are of age, this is a decision they can make for themselves. But for parents whose children are under 18, it is a decision they must make with their child. The group can provide a tremendous amount of support. Vanessa explained:

> Hearing about people's different experiences with different doctors, getting a legal name change, or their child starting on T [testosterone] was a really big deal for me, especially because my child was a minor and I had to give consent and take responsibility for it. I had to decide what was right for my kid and that was really hard. It felt like a horrible position to be in. The group was helpful in hearing other people's experience of going through that process and how many people's children were so much happier once they were able to obtain medical intervention. It reassured me that it could be a good thing for my kid.

Alyssa articulated how the group supported her during this time: "The group was really wonderful around surgery. They supported me by e-mail and text when he had surgery out of state. I was really alone there most of the time. Just knowing that all these people were there thinking about me and sending positive energy, really supporting me, checking in, asking me how I was and how things went—it really made me feel connected and not alone."

Disclosing a child's new gender identity can be a very arduous undertaking, especially at the beginning, when parents are trying to understand it themselves. Most start by telling close friends and extended family, but the process of disclosure with acquaintances can be a process that unfolds over the years. Alyssa highlighted how the group was helpful for her during more challenging family disclosures: "The group was really supportive in navigating family, particularly my husband's family, who live in the South and are conservative Christians. I got ideas from other people on how they navigated difficult, uncomfortable situations with others. Not only that, when I came back it was really helpful to be able to process what had happened with the group and get support for the experience I had. Nobody else would really understand what that was like, and the support group people really got it!"

Vanessa shared what she refers to as the "supermarket disclosure": "When you are in the produce section and you see someone you haven't seen in a while and they ask how your daughter is, you get to the point where you are able to sum it up, briefly and succinctly, without sobbing or tearing up. You see the other person standing in front of you nodding their head and saying they are happy for him. That is when you realize how much group has helped to bring you to that point. I think the group check-ins helped with this."

Becoming a Parent Facilitator

As the group members became more comfortable, it seemed that many of those more established members began to informally co-facilitate with me. I would start holding back when an intervention needed to be made and inevitably one of the group members would step forward. As a natural response, I began to assume a more secondary role within the groups. I spoke with the executive director of Greater Boston PFLAG about having them move toward a peer-led model similar to that followed by the other general PFLAG groups, which had always been the goal. Around that time, I approached the members to see if they wanted it to be parent-facilitated, full-time—with my support—through training and consultation. They eventually became comfortable with the idea after they realized that some were already informally acting as co-facilitators by using skills modeled by the interns and me. I drafted a proposal that highlighted the importance of having a therapist continue to stay involved in the groups. I then trained a handful of members and held bimonthly consultation groups to support their work.

As a group, the parent facilitators are extremely dedicated and have taken on a commitment that allows for continuity in the group structure and membership. I asked what motivated them to move into that role. Abe explained: "I wanted to give back because I had gotten so much out of the group. It made my 'new normal' feel more normal; it accelerated that process for me. I wanted to be able to reach out to other people." Abe's wife, Phyllis, continued: "At some point we realized we weren't coming for support anymore. We were trying to show support for people who were behind us in the process." Pamela reflected: "I felt that PFLAG had done so much for us. We had such a great experience and I saw we could be there for other parents. There were not a lot of people with young kids and I thought being a parent of a younger kid could add something that wasn't there otherwise."

Alice highlighted the importance of finding common ground: "I think I realized that we were in a really good place as a family and every family's journey is different. But that maybe there was something about our journey that might be helpful to another parent." She went on to talk about the importance of providing hope: "Even [if] to say it's not the first thing I think about every morning [or] the last thing I think about every night, for a long time it was. [But] I probably haven't cried about it in two or three years. So to not just say [to others] it is going to get better but to say, look, it really can happen."

There are many different roles of a parent facilitator, but a major one is to provide a safe space. Ruth eloquently described how she viewed this: "To make people feel welcome, to be a good listener, [and] above all, to make it clear indirectly or directly that I am completely accepting of each person's understanding of their own experience. To me, that is the holy grail of peer support."

Alyssa shared a similar ideal: "Making it possible for providing a safe environment where people can share and feel the same kind of connection and support that I felt in a nonjudgmental way. I also feel my role is to make sure that people who come to the group have an opportunity to be heard and get what they need from the meeting. I guess I also think of it as a way to personally share myself and know that I am available to talk to [them] outside the group."

Susan related that "being a voice of reason or a voice of calm can help while people are [under stress]." Being a facilitator entails giving of their time and of themselves. I asked the parents what it is they get out of the groups now that they are also facilitating. Ruth responded: "Unbelievable relationships. I don't know how it happened that we have such fabulous people, but we do. The people who come to group are wonderful, but the facilitators are a very unique group of people—I think because we have the commitment that we have. I know we all feel that responsibility. That is a real special bond."

When a New Parent Comes to the Group

The parents agreed that it is usually a more emotional experience when a new parent attends for the first time. Phyllis recalled: "I just want to give them a hug. We are here to help. There are times when I will still cry about not having a daughter. They are more infrequent and further apart and I am happy I have a son. But there are still times where my heart chains get tugged." Susan said, "Sometimes when a new parent comes in and breaks down, it brings me back to the very beginning and some really bad feelings and memories." The triggering of these past experiences and feelings allows the facilitators and more seasoned members to connect in an emotionally authentic way with a new parent.

Many of the parents feel a common responsibility to provide a safe, welcoming experience. Ruth observed: "I get a little nervous because that is where my social anxiety comes out. It's like being a hostess and wanting everyone to feel comfortable. I feel very aware—too aware—of making sure they feel comfortable. Because I don't have control over a lot of it, and the group will not be everything to everyone, and it won't be right for some people. But even having said that, I have this idea that my job is to make sure it is useful to the maximum number of people."

Many of these parents talk about how welcoming a new parent reconnects them to their emotional experience at the beginning. Vanessa explained: "It takes me back. I don't always remember much but when they talk, it's like, 'Oh, God, do I remember that!' I can empathize with them and I think we try and provide reassurance. We try and care for them, especially for brand-new people, that they have a positive experience; to try and make sure they feel good about being here because there are not that many groups out there; trying to make sure that they have a good experience and get what they need so they can come back." Pamela felt secure "knowing that our group is out there reaching other people, that there is a need we are fulfilling. What is even better is seeing the new people come back, knowing that we are doing something really good."

Looking Back, Looking Forward

I asked the parent facilitators to reflect on how far they have come. "What would your present self say to your former self—when you first found out?" The responses were heartwarming. Abe advised, "Hang on, it's going to be a bumpy ride." Phyllis added: "Love him through it. It will all be worth it in the end because I really love who he has become, and that would not have been possible without this transition." Alice reflected on something that one of her other children said to her: "He wishes we had been less cautious and more celebratory right from the get-go. I think that that might be easier [for] a young person, but I also take to heart what he said, that maybe we didn't need to worry about stuff so much. Maybe we could have been just more celebratory, not that we weren't on board. We were kind of cautious; there were things I was worried about."

Alyssa reflected on how much she has grown as a person after going through this experience:

> Even though things might be different than I had hoped or expected, they will still be fine. The most surprising thing is how much my life has been enriched by sharing this journey with my child and sharing the journey as a family. Not only within our family, but our whole social group and advocacy group has changed. I can't imagine going back. My world is so much larger. On the whole, even though it's not something I would have chosen or expected, it's been a really wonderful, broadening experience for our family. We have met wonderful people and made amazing friendships. It has opened me up in ways I didn't even think about before.

Currently the Parents of Transgender Children Support Group meets at different locations in the Greater Boston area and hosts seven groups a month, one of which is specifically for parents of MTF children. There are 24 parent facilitators—six fathers and 18 mothers—who rotate co-facilitation. There are over 300 people on the mailing list, and the most well-attended group has been known to have had over 30 members at one meeting. The majority of the parents who attend have children in their mid- to late teens and twenties.

As the group evolved through the years, we were always reevaluating the needs of the parents. To ensure that facilitators would continue to get their needs met as group members, we trained them to work in pairs and rotate their schedules so they could also attend as members. They are encouraged to use consultation with me as well as their peers to process groups that are emotionally intense or groups that are hard to manage. Greater Boston PFLAG holds a yearly training so that the facilitators can enhance their skills and be reminded of the important tenets of leadership: speaking from one's own experience and not giving advice. The group is also supported by an evolving list of guidelines that are read before every meeting. Some of the main points are: "Everyone is welcome here; every story is treated with respect. In telling our stories, we learn acceptance. Each person speaks only for himself or herself. We share experiences rather than opinions, and everything said here is confidential." These agreements serve to hold members to a set of expectations that can be used for reference if needed. The guidelines evolved as the group needs have shifted with the change in size and dynamics. One of those changes was a timed check-in as the groups enlarged. Another was an expansion of the confidentiality rule, which now reads: "Confidentiality is of the utmost importance given the sensitive nature of our children's identities. Parents' and children's names, schools, work places, and topics of groups should not be discussed with anyone who is not in attendance at a particular group."

Ruth, who has been involved in other (non-transgender) support groups, reflected on the uniqueness of these groups and why she felt they have been successful: "The one thing that might be important about our group is that there is a DNA that allows the replication of a pretty good thing, unless someone could convince me otherwise. I think that having a professional [clinician as] part of the group during its beginning, no matter how excellent the initial peer group leaders [are]—and they [are]—clinical check-ins, which allow for a constant pushing of a refresh button of all things important, rotating leadership, that structure lives today—[and works]."

To my final question, "Can you still see yourself leading these groups in 10 years?" the answers were mixed. Alyssa responded: "Probably not, as much as I like doing it. I think 10 years into the future I might be too far from sharing the experience for parents who are new. I see facilitating as a step in the journey, [although] I can see myself continuing to be an advocate and being involved with the LGBT community." Pamela answered: "I do. I like the people who I've met. I feel that I have something to offer other parents. My child should know I am very serious about her journey and that she knows that I am committed."

Future Considerations

As I stated at the outset, since the group's inception, most of our members have been white and middle to upper middle class. I often wondered whether this homogeneity was a strength or a limitation. On the one hand, it may have helped members connect quickly, given their obvious similarities; on the other hand, it may have been a barrier for people of color. How can we effectively reach across difference to foster support and build community so that more can benefit from this model? The Greater Boston PFLAG office has recently partnered with an organization that serves LGBT youth of color to start a support group at their location and is brainstorming different ways to do outreach to try to bridge this gap.

Another dilemma continues to be the predominance of parents of children on the trans-masculine spectrum. Though there are many similarities between them and parents of trans-feminine children, there are also many differences, and this proved to be alienating to the latter. Starting their own separate group proved helpful in increasing the retention of parents with trans-feminine children; however, many of the parents of trans-feminine youth access both support groups. Susan spoke to this: "The way society views and treats MTF is very different than FTM. A lot of the issues are unique, and the parents of FTM don't necessarily understand. The way society views a female turning male is an improvement in your social status. We are more used to female masculinity, whereas there is no getting used to seeing a guy looking like a girl."

As the ratio of mother to father peer facilitators demonstrates, the group has historically been dominated by mothers. Abe reflected: "Shortly after we started coming, me and two other dads had a *broment*. Everything this one dad said resonated with me and vice versa. It was really nice, I found it really helpful, and I felt a little less isolated. Before that, I would be the only guy in the room." Though there have recently been an increasing number of dads who are coming more consistently, Greater Boston PFLAG is still considering a separate group for them. More recently, PFLAG began a support group for siblings and other family members of transgender people.

In the preface to her book *Trans Forming Families: Real Stories about Transgendered Loved Ones*, Mary Boenke (2008) states, "In PFLAG we often say there is one more stage—celebration" (p. viii). After being involved with these support groups for the past ten years and witnessing the commitment of the parent facilitators, I couldn't agree more. I have witnessed time and again parents becoming more open-minded and authentic in their own identities and relationships as the result of having a transgender child. In reference to the parent groups at the Ackerman Institute in New York, Jean Malpas (2011) similarly notes, "As the mantle of isolation and shame falls off, new experiences of confidence and pride emerge" (p. 467). Susan observed, "Just as importantly, the group is also a place where parents empower and celebrate each other's achievements."

Further, celebration often evolves into activism. Brill and Pepper (2008) reference this in their book, *The Transgender Child*: "There is a natural overflow into your daily life when you realize there is nothing wrong with your child. If the problem lies within the system, you work to change a system that discriminates against your child" (p. 59).

For me as a clinician, it was in these groups that I began to gain a clearer understanding of the many nuanced emotions parents experience when their child comes out; they also showed me the necessity and power of community as a source of healing. I was given the privilege to bear witness to their struggles and triumphs, and it has been invaluable in my work, not only with these families but with my other clients as well. Simultaneously, at the time the group was forming, I became a new mother. So this experience highlighted the importance of parenting intentionally. I feel I have a deeper sense of what it means to do whatever it takes to support and love my children unconditionally. By choosing to support their child, making the commitment to attend these groups, and actively shifting their worldview, these parents have been and continue to be an inspiration.

Peer-led support groups offer the unique opportunity for those sharing similar struggles to find a path forward using the power of collective experience. The peer leaders' commitment and passion can be seen through their relationships with each other as well as in caring for other members. Of the 24 parents I have trained as facilitators, all are still actively leading the groups, which continue to have great benefits for peer leaders, current members, and potentially for parents who have yet to attend. Alice summed it up:

How grateful I am for group. I didn't know how much I needed it until I was there. I mean I really didn't know how much of [the] journey I hadn't done. I am very grateful that it was started, that people committed to it. I think I would be in a much different place if I hadn't had the benefit of it. We often say our family is a better, stronger family, not just about this issue, but in general. I feel like I am more understanding and more open and more reflective about things, so my life is in so much of a better place because of it.

REFERENCES

Boenke, M. (ed.). (2008). *Trans forming families: Real stories of transgendered loved ones.* Washington, D.C.: PFLAG Transgender Network.

Brill, S., & Pepper, R. (2008). *The transgender child: A handbook for families and professionals.* San Francisco: Cleis Press.

Broad, K. L. (2011). Coming out for parents, families and friends of lesbians and gays: From support group grieving to love advocacy. *Sexualities, 14* (4), 399–415.

Coolhart, D., Baker, A., Farmer, S., Malaney, M., & Shipman, D. (2013). Therapy with transsexual youth and their families: A clinical tool for assessing youth's readiness for gender transition. *Journal of Marital and Family Therapy, 39* (2), 223–243.

Emerson, S. (1996). Stages of adjustment in family members of transgender individuals. *Journal of Family Psychotherapy, 7* (3), 1–12.

Erich, S., Tittsworth, J., Dykes, J., & Cabuses, C. (2008). Family relationships and their correlations with transsexual well-being. *Journal of GLBT Family Studies, 4* (4), 419–432.

Fields, J. (2001). Normal queers: Straight parents respond to their children's "coming out." *Symbolic Interaction 24* (2), 165–167.

Goffman, E. (1963). *Stigma: Notes on the management of spoiled identity.* Englewood Cliffs, N.J.: Prentice-Hall.

Gottlieb, A. (2000). *Out of the twilight: Fathers of gay men speak.* Binghamton, N.Y.: Haworth Press.

Grossman, A. H., D'Augelli, A. R., Howell, T. J., & Hubbard, S. (2005). Parents' reactions to transgender youths' gender nonconforming expression and identity. *Journal of Gay and Lesbian Social Services, 18* (1), 3–16.

Hill, D. B., & Menvielle, E. (2009). "You have to give them a place where they feel protected and safe and loved": The views of parents who have gender-variant children and adolescents. *Journal of LGBT Youth, 6* (2/3), 243–271.

Krieger, I. (2011). *Helping your transgender teen: A guide for parents.* New Haven, Conn.: Genderwise Press.

Kübler-Ross, E. (1969). *On death and dying.* New York: Macmillan.

Lev, A. I. (2004). *Transgender emergence: Therapeutic guidelines for working with gender-variant people and their families.* Binghamton, N.Y.: Haworth Press.

Lev, A. I., & Alie. L. (2012). Transgender and gender nonconforming children and youth: Developing culturally competent systems of care. In S. K. Fisher, J. M. Poirier, & G. M. Blau (eds.), *Improving emotional and behavioral outcomes for LGBT youth: A guide for professionals* (pp. 43–66). Baltimore: Brookes.

MacNish, M., & Gold-Peifer, M. (2014). Families in transition: Supporting families of transgender youth. In T. Nelson & H. Winawer (eds), *Critical topics in family therapy* (pp. 119–129). New York: Springer.

Malpas, J. (2011). Between pink and blue: A multi-dimensional family approach to gender nonconforming children and their parents. *Family Process, 50,* 453–470.

Menvielle, E., & Tuerk, C. (2002). A support group for parents of gender-nonconforming boys. *Journal of the American Academy of Child & Adolescent Psychiatry, 41* (8), 1010–1013.

Parents, Families, and Friends of Lesbians and Gays. (1999). *Our trans children.* Washington, D.C.: Parents, Families, and Friends of Lesbians and Gays (PFLAG).

Pepper, R. (2012). *Transitions of the heart: Stories of love, struggle, and acceptance by mothers of transgender and gender variant children.* Berkeley, Calif.: Cleis Press.

Rosenberg, M., & Jellinek, M. S. (2002). Children with gender identity issues and their parents in individual and group treatment. *Journal of the American Academy of Child & Adolescent Psychiatry, 41* (5), 619–621.

Ryan, C., Russell, S. T., Huebner, D., Diaz, R., & Sanchez, J. (2010). Family acceptance in adolescence and the health of LGBT young adults. *Journal of Child and Adolescent Psychiatric Nursing, 23* (4), 205–213.

Schopler, J. H., & Galinsky, M. J. (1993). Support groups as open systems: A model for practice and research. *Health & Social Work, 18* (3), 195–207.

Winnicott, D. W. (1965). The theory of the parent-infant relationship. In Winnicot, *Maturational processes and the facilitating environment* (pp. 37–55). New York: International Universities Press.

Wren, B. (2002). "I can accept my child is transsexual but if I ever see him in a dress I'll hit him": Dilemmas in parenting a transgendered adolescent. *Clinical Child Psychology and Psychiatry, 7,* 377–397.

24

Peer Support for Parents of Gender Nonconforming Children: Benefits and Risks

Rex Butt, PhD

Public awareness of the transgender community in the United States has grown exponentially in the past decade. A steady flow of mainstream news reports and entertainment vehicles demonstrates that awareness. Before the turn of this century, the media coverage was minimal and focused primarily on sensationalist exposés of middle-age transsexuals, the most prominent examples being Christine Jorgensen in the 1950s and Renée Richards in the 1970s. Muted exposure continued throughout the end of the twentieth century. More recently, transgender issues have gained the attention of mainstream media: Hilary Swank won the 1999 Oscar for her portrayal of Brandon Teena in *Boys Don't Cry* (Kaplan, Koffler, Sloss, & Peirce, 1999) and repeated the feat in 2004, playing the gender-bending Maggie Fitzgerald in *Million Dollar Baby* (Eastwood, 2004). Even more eventful, in 2013 Laverne Cox became the first transgender actor to play a featured role in a television series, winning an Emmy for her portrayal of Sophia Burset in *Orange Is the New Black* (Kohan, 2013–). A few months later, *TransParent* (Soloway, 2014–2017) emerged with Jeffrey Tambor in the lead role, transitioning from Mort to Maura Pfefferman. Caitlyn Jenner's recent transition has provoked even broader coverage, occupying a prominent portion of ESPN's Espy Awards and spawning a reality series, *I Am Cait* (Bidwell, Jenkins, Jenner, & Metz, 2015–2016). Accompanying this exposure has been a proliferation of documentary films, books, websites, and blogs that provide support for transgender adults, helping them sort out who they are and how they fit in. Despite these examples, coverage of transgender issues remains scarce. Films and television have offered only a few transgender roles that do not reinforce stereotypes and even fewer examples of transgender performers in such roles.

The media expanded their focus beyond adults in 2007 with Barbara Walters's 20/20 episode, "My Secret Self: A Story of Transgender Children" (Arledge & Goodman, 2007). Thanks to subsequent coverage, the nation has become more

Lev, Arlene I., Gottlieb, Andrew R., *Families in Transition*
dx.doi.org/10.17312/harringtonparkpress/2019.04.fit.024
© 2019 by Harrington Park Press

aware that children are refusing at early ages to be constrained by the traditional gender binary. In 2011 the journalist Lisa Ling presented a 45-minute documentary on the lives of five trans people, including one child, and followed up with each of the five three years later (Bucher, Smith, Ling, Burke, & Davie, 2011; 2014).

Jazz Jennings, one of the children interviewed by Walters in 2007, has gained prominence. She was featured in a three-part documentary on the Oprah Winfrey Network (Fordstat et al., 2011), has written a children's book (Herthel & Jennings, 2014), and has her own reality television series (Aenges, Tarantino, O'Neill, Mays, & Miller, 2015–). But as the essays in this volume attest, attention to the needs of the parents of these children has lagged far behind the support for the transgender community, and progressive voices have been calling attention to that gap (Lev, 2004).

Let me speak personally. In 2002 my 23-year-old daughter came out. Her actual words were "I'm not gay; I'm transsexual." Being an academic, I was on the computer within the hour to see what information was available. The answer: pornography—screen after screen of hits that offered crass titillation, but nothing to offer insight into my family's plight or to help me understand how to support my child. Luckily, when we shared the situation with our former pastor, he referred us to friends who were going through the same dilemma. When reconnecting with yet another couple, we found out that they, too, had a trans child.

Shortly thereafter, I attended the Translating Identity Conference at the University of Vermont. After one of the sessions, a student suggested that I contact PFLAG, which surprised me. Knowing that the acronym stood for Parents, Families, and Friends of Lesbians and Gays, I had assumed that the organization did not address gender. Learning otherwise, I became active, helping found New York's Kingston PFLAG Chapter, which serves the Hudson Valley. My wife and I became its transgender coordinators. In that role we have mentored and counseled dozens of families and have presented trainings and workshops at schools and conferences since 2007. I also took a full-year sabbatical to complete research that would allow me write the book that I wish had been available to me when my child came out. That research included interviews with 75 parents who had transgender children across the United States, Canada, and the United Kingdom.

Since the time my daughter came out, younger children have been insisting that they do not accept the gender binary, creating a dilemma for their parents.

These parents, who are still raising their children, have a unique list of concerns that neither I nor others have had to face. When four-year-old Jenny says, "Stop calling me a girl. I'm a boy," parents want to know if this is "just a phase." What is the likely outcome? Will Jenny eventually desist and accept that she is a girl, or will she persist and identify as transgender? Unfortunately, there is not enough research to answer that question (Riley, Sitharthan, Clemson, & Diamond, 2011a). Parents want to know whether it is better to go along with what the child says or, as some prominent voices recommend, ignore or discourage cross-gender behavior (Zucker & Bradley, 1995). They want help figuring out how to deal with all the social implications for their child and their entire family. The answers to those questions are not easy to sort out.

Although almost all the parents I have worked with are open-minded, some are still alarmed at first, as was this mother of a 14-year-old girl:

> My initial reaction was . . . I don't even know if I can describe it. Shock! Shock to the point of an out-of-body sort of feeling. Not because I had any strong feelings about transsexualism or any sort of difference because I don't. But shock. I couldn't take it in at that point. But we talked and she cried and I cried. But I didn't sleep. The thoughts that were going through my head were, "Can this be? People get confused all the time in adolescence about sexuality." That was before I understood about sexuality as being distinct from gender. . . . The next few days were just sort of quiet. I remember saying to her, "We should take our time. People do get confused in puberty," and she was really very patient with me. (Butt, 2015, p. 6)

This mother's mind-set is typical of those I have encountered. She was focused on her daughter's needs rather than her own, but she did not want this to be happening to her child and was hoping that this would not be a burden her family would have to bear.

Having now spent nearly a decade mentoring and counseling, I look back and see that the needs that I was sorting through years ago are mirrored in the sessions that I have facilitated as a PFLAG transgender coordinator. For many families, we are "the only game in town" because, like so many other areas of the nation, New York's mid–Hudson Valley has an inadequate supply of therapists who are trained to work with the transgender population, and it is not unusual for me to receive multiple requests for referrals in a month. Although there are roughly one million residents in the area, I have found only four therapists to whom I can refer, and three of the four are a two-hour drive for most families. The Hudson Valley is not unique. Nationally, the list of therapists who focus on the needs of gender nonconforming children and their parents is still quite short. Yet these parents, hungry for support and guidance, face a unique dilemma. It is not enough for them to merely nurture their child's realization and assertion of their self-concept. Now they must simultaneously help the child determine how to negotiate an emerging sense of self through the maze of accepted social structures (Malpas, 2011), even while they themselves feel outcast since their family's "difference" complicates daily interactions with friends, family, and coworkers. Most parents experience a sense of shame, blaming themselves for somehow having created this "flaw" in their child (APA Task Force on Gender Identity and Gender Variance, 2008; Riley et al., 2011b). They often find it difficult to locate a physician or therapist who is adequately trained to help them (Riley et al., 2011b), which reinforces their sense of isolation and shame and creates greater resistance to getting help (Menvielle & Hill, 2010).

In my experience, it is not at all unusual to spend weeks or even months in private coaching before a parent will hazard the risk of attending a meeting. The key for the coach is to open doors continually. For example, I am currently mentoring a mother of a trans man. Nine months ago she was overwhelmed by the loss of her daughter. It took several one-on-one conversations over a period of three months before she felt ready to speak with anyone else. She finally accepted an invitation to meet with two other families. During that meeting, she said only, "I can't accept that I have lost my daughter. That's really hard for me." After additional one-on-one counseling sessions over a few more months, she came to her first formal meeting and has come regularly since then. She still says almost nothing during meetings but has expressed appreciation privately, saying that she has gained a sense of comfort just from hearing parents share their concerns and feelings. Despite her diffidence, she feels much less alone and embraced by the group. This experience is typical. Once parents take that first step, they invariably find themselves in an unfamiliar, though warmly supportive, environment in which their family's concerns are no longer so oppressive and the worries they harbored privately are shared by others.

Because of the dearth of professional help, parents have relied on one-on-one peer counseling, mentoring, and group meetings, which might happen face to face, by telephone, or through web-based listservs. Each of these settings has the potential to meet parents' needs, but each also has limitations and risks. The most common and generally well known of these is the PFLAG meeting. Three years after the Stonewall riots in 1969, PFLAG began when Jeanne Manford accompanied her son along Fifth Avenue in what would become New York City's annual Pride March. During that event, several gays and lesbians approached her, asking if she would speak to their parents. She agreed, and through her work and that of like-minded parents, the organization grew to national prominence during the ensuing decades ("Our Story," n.d.).

In 1998 a small group of informed and assertive parents convinced PFLAG to become the first national civil rights organization to add the transgender community to its mission. Many of its chapters, like mine, have seasoned transgender coordinators. Families with gender variant children are becoming the new norm. Our Kingston Chapter, for example, has become almost exclusively focused on their needs. It is the unusual meeting that includes a new parent with a gay or lesbian child. While facilitating a training at PFLAG's 2015 national convention, I learned from chapter leaders across the nation that my experience is not unique. There has been a strong influx of families who come for support in sorting out the challenges of raising a gender variant child, and leaders are scrambling to accommodate them.

Managed by individually incorporated chapters across the nation, PFLAG meetings generally take place once each month and last for two or three hours. Parents who attend are encouraged, but not required, to share their stories and concerns. Each chapter, though officially affiliated with the national organization and committed to its mission, is self-governed. One meeting might be carefully structured by a facilitator who enforces boundaries, including no judgments, interruptions, or cross-talk; another might allow for open interaction among the members, which results in a much more free-form discussion. Invariably, these larger, more formal discussions afterward break into individual, informal conversations. Regardless of the meetings' format, PFLAG provides a forum for parents to unburden themselves and share their doubts, fears, worries, frustrations, breakthroughs, triumphs, and celebrations.

The response from first-time attendees is almost universally positive, and they often express relief in finding an open, accepting, and nurturing environment. They report it to be freeing just to spend time in the presence of other parents with a shared experience. "I feel better just being here and knowing that you are here" and "It's great to know that we are not alone" are typical comments. Through the conversation, parents invariably gain insight into additional issues that are likely to arise, strategies to address those issues, and detailed information about resources and research from more experienced members. The diversity of perspectives and experiences of the participants often provides unexpected insights. A new parent might sense a particular connection with another attendee and arrange a separate conversation, which might grow into an ongoing relationship between their families. Finally, some parents find the experience so confirming and compelling that they become deeply involved and may eventually lead meetings and trainings, offer phone support, start new chapters, and become vocal and effective advocates not only for their children but for the entire LGBTQ community.

Although these outcomes are certainly not surprising, other, less expected results are not uncommon. Some parents are happy that the meeting is facilitated by a nonprofessional, their sense being that nobody in the room is there to analyze or evaluate what they have to say. My PFLAG chapter includes transgender adults who share their perspectives, which can help parents gain insight into their child's experience. Their participation can have quite a powerful influence on a parent. When a mother asked for help to understand how her 13-year-old son could possibly know that he is a girl, she listened quite intently while a middle-aged trans woman recounted her thwarted effort to get her parents to accept her and her 40-year battle to fit in and play the mandated male role, only to end up estranged from her entire family, including her only child.

There are also times when a mundane comment creates a powerful response. Years ago, a grandfather who was struggling to comprehend why his 20-year-old MTF grandchild needed "to switch," said, "I don't get it. He has a girlfriend, and I know that they're happy. But he says he's going through with the operation. How can she be okay with this, and what happens after the operation?" My answer was, "I guess that they are just attracted to each other, and they'll figure out plumbing issues as they go along." His response at the time was no more than a quizzical frown, but the following month, he arrived transformed, joyfully reporting that he now "got it." I figured that his progress was thanks to his wife, a bit of a tough cookie, who had done a great deal of research and was insistent that "this is real" and that they owed it to their granddaughter to "get with the program and support her." So I was surprised when he said, "No, it was what you said about plumbing last month. That's what straightened it all out for me. I get it now." To this day, I have not been able to reconstruct how that comment could have created such a result.

There are times, however, when even well-meaning comments can create upset. Despite any coaching that the experienced participants might have received regarding effective participation, they are not trained therapists, and they sometimes ask prying questions or try to assuage fears by offering encouragement that sometimes steps over the line. "It gets better," for example, might seem innocuous, but it once prompted this response: "How can you say that? Look at the suicide rate for these kids! It doesn't always get better." Even worse is the moment when someone might say something such as, "You shouldn't feel that way." Fortunately, such incidents are very rare (occurring twice in all my years of experience), but no amount of coaching or correction from a facilitator can erase the fact that a judgment has contaminated the atmosphere.

Beyond unhelpful or unintentionally provocative comments, there are several issues that can create problems for parents, location being one of them. With over 400 PFLAG chapters across the nation, there is usually one within a reasonable drive for most people, though attending may not be an option for those who live in remote areas. Many gatherings are held in LGBTQ centers or accepting churches and synagogues, and such venues alone keep some parents away. Having found a meeting does not, however, guarantee that help will be available. There may be no other parents of gender nonconforming children present, and not all chapters have a transgender coordinator. So the new parent, having come for support and solace, might listen to the concerns about raising gay and lesbian children and feel an even deeper sense of isolation.

One final problem for the new parent is that PFLAG's mission is to support people who are LGBTQ, their families, and allies, educate members and the public, and advocate for inclusive policies and laws. Even though the meeting may be structured to separate those three elements, it is inevitable that a new attendee, who has arrived in an emotionally fragile state, may become reticent to share fears and doubts after taking note of the attitudes of others present. A few years ago, I attended a session in which a new participant listened to other parents bemoan lack of support in schools, describe efforts to address bullying, and vent anger at a position taken by a local politician, but she heard no misgivings or worries about how to cope with the tensions within their families. When it was her turn to speak, there had been no suggestions that it was acceptable to express doubt or discomfort, so she shared a few minor concerns but made it clear that she was unconditionally supportive of her son. Later, in a private conversation, her son told me that he had received no emotional support from his parents and that his mother had often been verbally abusive. When the son recently returned to a meeting, he reported that his mother had come to accept his transition and was now fully supportive. Although the outcome for this family was positive, the mother's attitudinal shift was certainly not the result of her PFLAG experience.

There are additional options for the parent who cannot or prefers not to attend a formal group. These include e-mail or phone counseling and less formal gatherings that vary from one-on-one conversations to a home meeting with a few selected participants, chosen for their ability to address specific needs. Often these options are offered in combination: an e-mail query, followed by a phone call, then perhaps a small group with one or two other parents or couples. Of course, e-mail and telephone interactions allow for anonymity, and all these options are more intimate and are more easily focused on the needs of the new parent than a full-fledged meeting that might include a score of strangers.

Finally, there is an impressive amount of support available through listservs dedicated to the parents of trans children. At present, there are two of note, both accessed through Yahoo groups: TransFamily, established in 1995 by two PFLAG parents, Karen and Bob Gross, and TYFA Talks, established in 2007 by TransYouth Family Allies, an organization that was also founded by PFLAG parents. Both listservs are managed by volunteers, who dedicate significant time in support of those who subscribe. Both groups carefully vet members through personal interviews and both are moderated for content and tone. Boasting nearly 600 subscribers, TYFA Talks is restricted to parents of children between three and 18 years of age, and TransFamily, with 450 subscribers, serves families regardless of the age of the child. Some people subscribe to both, but once a child turns 19, the parents must leave TYFA Talks.

These listservs provide parents with significant benefits that group meetings, whether formal or informal, cannot match. The following information is based on interviews and e-mails with four dedicated PFLAG parents: Karen and Bob Gross, founders of TransFamily.org, which offers PFLAG meetings in northeastern Ohio and sponsors TransFamily along with five other transgender-based listserv discussion groups; David N. Parker, who has been active with TransFamily since its inception and, along with his wife, Joan, and the Grosses, was instrumental in guiding PFLAG to its support of the trans community; and Shannon Garcia, president and cofounder of TransYouth Family Allies. Beyond the listservs, all these PFLAG veterans have years of experience in traditional meetings as well.

The first benefit is the immediacy of response. Typically, new participants are showered with welcoming, supportive messages from current members, and any post might receive up to a dozen responses within 24 hours (Parker, 2015). Further, it is not unusual for a parent new to the process to be overwhelmed with the abundance of knowledge shared in a first exposure to group discussion, the result being that even a burning question might be forgotten. In contrast to a face-to-face meeting, a follow-up question is easily addressed on the listserv and can be asked at any time (Gross & Gross, 2015). Although the primary focus of the discussions is to support new participants, those more experienced express appreciation that, by writing posts to newer members, they gain further insight into their own process (Parker, 2015). Of course, anyone can opt to exchange e-mails off-list with another member to explore details in private or to search the entire history of posts to check on previous discussions of any topic.

The listservs offer several other significant benefits compared to face-to-face meetings or phone calls. Perhaps the most prominent is that anonymity can be maintained since, after registering, one has the option of masking identity and participating in the discussion under an alias. No topics are off limits, and there are often spirited discussions. Further, parents of younger children benefit from the perspective provided by parents of teens (Garcia, 2015).

Although it is common for an individual's participation to wane once her or his needs are met, several stay on for years. Given the size of the groups, along with the vast experience of many members and the wide geographical spread, very specific and helpful information is often shared—for example, a lead on an endocrinologist who offers a sliding fee scale for hormone blockers (Garcia, 2015). Also, given the level of experience of the participants, nuanced distinctions are sometimes illuminated. For example, a father who struggled mightily when his trans daughter had come out years ago, recently posted a comment that examined his daughter's request to be referred to as "a woman" rather than a "trans woman," since she had *always* identified as a woman. He also shared how he had come to understand that "MTF" might be particularly offensive because the M focuses attention on what his daughter and others see as secondary. Yet he has resolved to continue to refer to her as a trans woman within the context of the listserv, so that those new to the group will understand he is not writing about a cisgender woman. One final benefit is that, more than in any other context, participation in these listservs encourages parents to write more openly and extensively about their experiences, concerns, and frustrations. Even the mere exercise of writing itself can enhance physical health and psychosocial adjustment (Pennebaker, 1990).

As is true of any support structure, listservs have inherent limitations, though problems are rare. Moderators have had to intervene a few times after aggressive or otherwise inappropriate comments were posted. In all but one case, the issue was resolved without the offender's being removed from the group. Of course, this is a tiny fraction of tens of thousands of posts. Given that information is submitted only through print, there have been misunderstandings regarding the tone or intended meaning of some posts, which has caused flare-ups and consternation. In all cases, however, explanations and apologies have put the discussion back on track. The one additional drawback that is part of the Yahoo group structure is that each new post operates under a subject heading and can garner an explosion of responses and responses to responses, all of which remain under that heading unless someone remembers to refine it. The result is that discussions can be hard to track, and second- or third-tier responses may have nothing whatsoever to do with the initial subject. Given the long list of benefits, however, there is much to be said for participation in one or both of the two groups.

In conclusion, given the insufficient number of therapists with adequate training to help families of transgender and gender nonconforming children, parents have tapped into an extensive body of peer support. The primary pillar of that support has been PFLAG, which adopted trans-inclusive policies in 1999, leading the way for other nonprofit organizations. With its affiliated chapters across the nation, PFLAG has provided thousands of families with the guidance and education needed to better understand their children and to work through the myriad issues that confront them. Although not directly affiliated with PFLAG, two significant listservs have been developed to provide quick, informed response. Though not flawless, the peer support provided through these venues has been of high quality and is likely to remain vital, even after there *are* enough therapists to fill this ever-increasing need.

REFERENCES

Aengus, J., Tarantino, J., O'Neill, C., Mays, S., & Miller, C. (executive producers). (2015–). *I am Jazz* (television series). Los Angeles: This Is Just a Test Media.

APA Task Force on Gender Identity and Gender Variance. (2008). *Report of the task force on gender identity and gender variance.* Washington, D.C.: American Psychological Association.

Arledge, R. (producer), & Goodman R. (director). (2007). My secret self: A story of transgender children (television series episode). 20/20. New York: ABC News Productions.

Bidwell, M., Jenkins, J., Jenner, C., & Metz, A. (executive producers). (2015–2016). *I am Cait.* (television series). Los Angeles: Bunim/Murray Productions.

Bucher, A., Smith. D., & Ling, L. (executive producers), Burke, H., & Davie, M. (directors). (2011; 2014). *Our America with Lisa Ling* (television documentary). Brooklyn, N.Y.: Part2 Pictures.

Butt, R. (2015). *Now what? A handbook for families with transgender children.* Oakland, Calif.: Transgress Press.

Eastwood, C. (producer & director). (2004). *Million dollar baby* (motion picture). Warner Bros.

Forstadt, E., Gottwald, M., Hayes, B., Mahon, W., & Streb, K. (executive producers), Stock, J. (director). (2011). *I am Jazz: A family in transition* (television documentary). Carrboro, N.C.: Figure 8 Films.

Garcia, S. (2015, January 8). Personal communication.

Gross, B., & Gross, K. (2015, January 11). Personal communication.

Herthel, J., & Jennings, J. (2014). *I am Jazz.* New York: Dial Books for Young Readers.

Kaplan, C., Koffler P., & Sloss, J. (executive producers), Peirce, K. (director). (1999). *Boys don't cry* (motion picture). Twentieth Century Fox.

Kohan, K. (producer) (2013–). *Orange is the new black* (television series). Santa Monica, Calif.: Lionsgate Entertainment.

Lev, A. I. (2004). *Transgender emergence: Therapeutic guidelines for working with gender-variant people and their families.* Binghamton, N.Y.: Haworth Press.

Malpas, J. (2011). Between pink and blue: A multi-dimensional family approach to gender non-conforming children and their families. *Family Process, 50* (4), 453–470.

Menvielle, E., & Hill, D. B. (2010). An affirmative intervention for families with gender-variant children: A process evaluation. *Journal of Gay & Lesbian Mental Health, 15* (1), 94–123.

"Our Story." (n.d.). PFLAG. "About Us." Retrieved from https://www.pflag.org/our-story.

Parker, D. N. (2015, January 9). Personal communication.

Pennebaker, J. W. (1990). *Opening up: The healing power of expressing emotions.* New York: William Morrow.

Riley, E. A., Sitharthan, G., Clemson, L., & Diamond, M. (2011a). The needs of gender-variant children and their parents: A parent survey. *International Journal of Sexual Health, 23,* 181–195.

Riley, E. A., Sitharthan, G., Clemson, L., & Diamond, M. (2011b). The needs of gender-variant children and their parents according to health professionals. *International Journal of Transgenderism, 13,* 54–63.

Soloway, J. (producer & director) (2014–2017). *Transparent* (television series). Picrow & Amazon Studios.

Zucker, K. J., & Bradley, S. J. (1995). *Gender identity disorder and psychosexual problems in children and adolescents.* New York: Guilford Press.

25

Camp Aranu'tiq: Notes from the First Camp for Transgender and Gender Variant Youth

Nick M. Teich, LCSW, PhD

When I was about five years old, I told my parents I wished to be a boy and to have my hair cut short. They obliged. But because I didn't have access to the knowledge that gender transition from female to male existed, minor modifications like hair and clothes were the best I could do. I had not yet fully realized that my expressed desire to be a boy was "real," or even possible.

Some of the most positive experiences of my life were as a camper from 1993 to 1999, as a counselor from 2000 to 2003, and as a member of the leadership team from 2005 to 2006, all at the same summer camp in Maine. Despite the fact that it was an all-girls' camp, for me this was a place where I could be myself—a far cry from how I felt at school. I looked forward to the late June start, and I even had a calendar on which I counted down the days. I told my parents after that first summer that I wanted to be a camp director. Both of them had attended camps as kids, so it was important to them that their children do the same.

I accepted that society considered me a girl and remember happily shopping for my camp uniform before my first summer: white polo shirts, white T-shirts, and blue shorts. There was nothing particularly feminine about this clothing, which, in hindsight, may have been a factor in my choosing that particular camp. Over time, I was completely accepted for being an "ultra-tomboy." The effect camp had on me was profound, and most others around me shared that feeling. Over 20 years later, the friends I made there are still some of my closest.

When circumstances precluded my returning to the camp in Maine, I began volunteering each year at a weeklong charity camp. Several years later, I realized that I needed to move forward with transition. I had been very depressed and could not figure out why I felt so out of place. I was 24 when I first met another trans man, and a couple of months later I was on the road to transition, knowing full well that *this* was the missing piece of me. When I disclosed my intention to transition to the staff at camp, the initial response was positive. Several board members even told me that they were "happy" for me. But events

Lev, Arlene I., Gottlieb, Andrew R., *Families in Transition*
dx.doi.org/10.17312/harringtonparkpress/2019.04.fit.025

took a sharp turn when, about a month later, the board called me on the phone and, with their lawyer on the other line, told me I could not return, "for the good of the kids." I was profoundly shocked, hurt, and deeply perplexed by their radical change in attitude. It took a couple of months for this to sink in. It made me realize how often blatant discrimination occurs, and that I had been fortunate until that point.

It was this incident that led me to begin thinking about how kids like me could successfully attend overnight camp with all the constraints that our society puts on gender. Some of the parents I initially spoke with assumed their kids would never go to overnight camp because of bunking, bathroom, and safety considerations and because few camps, if any, were sufficiently equipped and willing to take them. (This is becoming less and less the case, as I and others consult and train on how to integrate these kids into mainstream programs.) The wheels were now in motion.

I founded Camp Aranu'tiq, a nonprofit overnight summer camp for transgender and gender variant youth, in 2009, during my final semester in social work school at Boston College. It was a leap of faith. Would enough parents, many of whom struggled with the idea that their children might be transgender, actually enroll them? Would the local regulators requiring overnight camps to separate children by their (assigned) gender flexibly accommodate us? Would we attract enough volunteer counselors?

I began by assembling some friends from different parts of my life who had expertise and interest to serve on our board of directors. At a furious pace, I began learning how to create and run a nonprofit. Over the next 18 months, our board reached out to families at conferences, through e-mail and Facebook, and to doctors and therapists who worked with the transgender community. I found a camp to rent in August 2010, raising enough money to cover all costs, making it tuition-free for everyone. Volunteer requests came pouring in. Parents signed up their children, some after meeting me and speaking to me, and some not. By the first day of camp, we had 41 campers and nearly 20 volunteers. And after a conversation with the state youth camp inspector, it made sense to him that we had all gender-neutral bathrooms.

We knew from the very beginning that it was important to keep our location private because of the sensitive nature of our population. Over the next several years, we rented camps in two states before raising the capital to purchase our own property: a 116-acre lakefront in New Hampshire.

Overnight Summer Camps in the United States

Overnight summer camps originated in the United States in the second half of the nineteenth century (Eels, 1986) and have continued to play an integral part in youth development. One study surveyed parents about what changes, if any, they observed in their children as a result of attending overnight camp. They reported positive outcomes in ten domains, including "identity, making friends, social comfort, independence, [and] peer relationships" (Henderson, Whitaker, Bialeschki, Scanlin, & Thurber, 2007).

The American Camp Association published a study about the benefits of camp, looking at a nationwide cross section, including day and overnight camps, coed and single-sex camps, and nonprofit-independent, agency nonprofit, and for-profit independent camps. Results showed that "the greatest strength . . . was 'Supportive Relationships'—specifically, the quality of [the connection] between youth and adult staff, . . . these . . .[being] stronger at camp than in any other arena outside the family system" (Scanlin, Gambone, Sipe, & Daraio, 2006, p. 1).

Camp Aranu'tiq: Therapeutic, Yes; Therapy, No

Studies show that between 64% and 87% of transgender or gender nonconforming youth report being verbally harassed at school (Grant et al., 2011; Greytak, Kosciw, & Diaz, 2009; Kosciw, Diaz, & Greytak, 2009; Whittle, Turner, & Al-Alami, 2007), as well as bombarded with questions about their gender by helping professionals and parents. From the very beginning, it was important that Camp Aranu'tiq be established as a place where these young people could feel normal: no questions about gender, or how they choose to express themselves; no therapy groups; no gender education or workshops—just plain old camp. I often tell people that the only difference between us and other programs is our population. It's a safe place to meet lots of people who truly understand. It takes a great deal of effort to organize an experience that will "work" properly, but when it does, the therapeutic effect happens organically.

We know this anecdotally as well as from our surveys. In 2015, 93% of campers said that after attending our program, they (1) felt more comfortable with their gender identity; (2) had more confidence; (3) possessed more effective strategies to get through emotionally difficult times; and (4) were more connected to a community of transgender and gender variant people.

Nearly all our campers are in therapy or take part in support groups (or both) throughout the academic year. This is helpful and necessary for many of them. But camp is time away from the pressure to talk, except by choice.

Demographics

Since our inception we have served children from 40 states and five countries. The balance between those female or feminine-identified who were labeled male at birth and those male or masculine-identified who were labeled female at birth was close to 50-50 for our first five summers. In 2015, 185 of our campers identified as male or masculine and were labeled female at birth, whereas 129 of them identified as female or feminine and were labeled male at birth. The remainder had an "other" gender identity or expression. We have always operated on a first-come, first-served basis, so the gender breakdown is always random.

In 2016 we provided $62,000 in financial aid, which ranged from partial help with tuition to full scholarship, including airfare and ground transportation in certain circumstances. Of the parents who are separated or divorced, several have ongoing custody issues relating to their child's gender identity. Each year we have a handful of campers whose guardians are grandparents or other relatives or who are in state custody. Very often their parents are faced with difficult decisions and may not agree on how to raise that child, which can cause conflicts in marriages or partnerships (Teich, 2012). Of course, this is not always the cause for breakups, but it can put an additional strain on those relationships.

Since the vast majority of our kids are under 18, they need permission to attend from parents or guardians. Those who do permit their children to participate fall on a continuum: some are outspoken advocates, some are reluctant to give consent, and some are in between.

Parental Anxiety

For our first-ever summer session, we had 41 campers, ranging in ages from eight to 15, parameters that are in sync with many other overnight camps. The 15-year-olds often return, excited to be back with their friends. We affectionately refer to them as "seniors," and each may opt to carry a few adultlike responsibilities, such as mentoring a selected younger "sibling."

On our application, we ask if new parents have any concerns about sending their child to us. Most often cited are those regarding safety and homesickness. One of our volunteers asked a parent half-jokingly why she trusted us to care for her daughter since that was our first year of operation. The mother thought it would be an opportunity for her child, who had few friends, to connect with others who were going through a common experience, and she had a gut feeling it was going to be positive. I have encountered few, if any, parents who had extreme anxiety about sending their child, probably because of selection bias. Parents who have those worries would probably not send their child to *any* overnight camp. Many times it's the parents who have a more difficult time separating.

Occasionally parents wonder whether their child's gender identity might be influenced by peer pressure. For instance, if a child is gender variant or undecided about where they fall on the gender spectrum and is affiliating with youth who are more confident in their identity and its expression and who may have even begun medical transition, will that child feel as if they too should "pick a side"? My answer is that our camp is a safe place for these kids to be who they truly are. No one has to be someone they're not, either in identity or in expression, and the notion of transition means something different for everyone. Aranu'tiq is a place where kids can try on a new name or pronoun for a day, a week, or several weeks. Some continue to use those names upon their return home and some decide not to. Therein lies the beauty of a place where someone truly feels safe.

We do our best to ensure that all campers understand that anything transition-related must be a family decision. Although our counselors, all of whom are at different points on the gender spectrum, may intervene if they hear conversations between campers that include too much advice giving, at the same time we are in a safe enough space where these kids can discuss those topics. For example, if a counselor hears a camper say to another that they "have to be on hormones" by a certain time in order to transition properly, or they "know that everyone should get surgery," that counselor will step in to say that isn't necessarily true and that being transgender can mean different things to different people. But we cannot, and would not, monitor each and every conversation, as this would restrict their freedom to speak. What one child might see as information gathering another might interpret as pressure.

Parent Meet-up Groups

Even before our first summer session, we recognized the importance of having an optional parent group for those who can make themselves available on opening day. This was initiated by Melissa MacNish and Marissa Peifer, mental health professionals in the Boston area. Both have served as assistant directors at Aranu'tiq since its inception. The parent group we organized during our inaugural summer session, in 2010, was held before many of the other support groups specifically for these parents sprouted up nationally. Many were meeting other parents like themselves for the first time. Emotions ran high. While it was validating, there were many conflicting feelings—happiness that their children would spend a week surrounded by others like them, but difficulty acknowledging the challenge of having a transgender or gender variant child. In *Transgender*

Emergence, Arlene Lev (2004) writes that parents "will need reassurance that their children's sex or gender development is not 'caused' by their parenting, although their children's self-esteem will be impacted by their reactions" (p. 332).

A 2008 qualitative study of 12 parents of transgender young people found that not only had all of them maintained a relationship with their children, but that many of those relationships had improved since their child had come out. These parents sought support outside the family and found that speaking with other parents of transgender youth was especially helpful (Gold, 2008).

Clearly, making a connection to other parents is validating. Though our meetings are held only on the first day of summer session, in some cases those are the only times a parent has the experience of being with others like themselves.

Family Camp

After three summers of successful programming just for youth, we decided to create a family camp. The purpose was to provide a space where families could spend quality time, bonding through activities that encourage teamwork and fun, which was popular, no doubt, because of the lack of connection that sometimes befalls family members as they cope with the stresses of everyday life. Though our first effort was very successful, we made some key observations.

In the mornings we scheduled activities for the kids while simultaneously facilitating a discussion group for the parents. Afternoons and evenings included joint activities, such as relay races, kickball, and down time. While these activities were enjoyable, we hadn't considered that parents might have wanted more time with one another. We observed many parents making plans for their kids to be with other kids so that the parents could have enough time to connect with each other. In our second year we programmed optional moderated parent groups in the afternoon as well as camp counselor supervision of kids for an hour between our evening activity and bedtime. We had a very high level of participation in the afternoon groups and again saw parents convening to talk to one another both in the hour after the evening activity *and* after putting their kids to bed.

Parents who choose to attend a generic family camp often do so because they want to spend quality time with their families in a fun atmosphere where they don't have to think about activity or meal planning. It appears that our families were drawn to us so that they could (a) give their child a chance to spend time with other transgender and gender variant kids, and (b) have time to speak to other parents about their experiences. This makes sense given that we serve a niche population. It was thrilling, however, to see just how much the parents craved connection with one another, given that most had never met before. Even the "veterans" who might have signed up thinking their kids would get more out of it generally spent a lot of time in these discussions. Those more experienced often enjoy the feeling of being able to help others new to the challenges of raising a transgender or gender variant child. Our camp has provided *them* the opportunity to learn as much from others, however.

Siblings

Family camp was also the first time we came into contact with the siblings of our campers, though some we had met casually during drop-offs and pickups. As members of the camp administration, we were interested in observing the dynamics between all the siblings—those transgender or gender variant and those not. We quickly realized that because most of the activities were not segregated, it was often difficult to discern who was transgender or gender variant and who was a sibling. A brother of one camper thought his sister was a "weirdo" because she identified as transgender. After his experience with us, he realized that there are a lot of kids "just like her."

We experimented with a group in which we asked them what it was like to have a transgender or gender variant brother or sister. Although reluctant to talk at first, most of them warmed up and spoke about the challenges of (1) feeling left out by parents, (2) having the burden of protecting their sibling, (3) avoiding getting teased while in school, and (4) struggling with name and pronoun changes. Not intended as a therapy group, this was a way for us to show them support and help them be heard.

Dads' and Moms' Groups

Our first family camp had 26 families in attendance, including 26 transgender or gender variant kids, 23 mothers, 14 fathers, one uncle, and 14 siblings. Our second had 39 families in attendance, including 40 transgender or gender variant kids, 40 mothers, 19 fathers, two aunts, and 24 siblings. That year we experimented with an optional "Dads' group" and "Moms' group." These were the only groups that were closed to those who did not fit the role. Themes centered primarily on ways for them to be involved in their children's lives and ways to demonstrate acceptance. We now have at least two family camp sessions per year in New Hampshire and California.

Conclusion

I have learned many things in my first nine years as director. The overwhelming feeling of acceptance that pervades the camp does not exist in a vacuum. Though we are successful in helping children, our work cannot be done without parents and guardians. Acceptance begins at home, where our campers spend 49 to 51 weeks a year. Without a strong foundation of a loving family or guardian support system, transgender kids would have the deck stacked against them. As Brill and Pepper (2008) write, "Parents' responses to their children's gender variance are far more influential than any other factor in their lives. When parents use effective . . . strategies, they can dramatically counteract the negativity their children experience elsewhere" (p. 76).

More and more parents are learning how critical acceptance of their transgender and gender variant children is, though the challenges are many. Because of them, I believe there will be a brighter future for their children, who, with their support, can live life more authentically.

REFERENCES

Brill, S., & Pepper, R. (2008). *The transgender child*. San Francisco: Cleis Press.

Eells, E. P. (1986). *Eleanor Eells' history of organized camping: The first 100 years*. Martinsville, Ind.: American Camping Association.

Gold (Peifer), M. L. (2008). A qualitative investigation into the process of family adjustment to transgender emergence. PhD diss., Massachusetts School of Professional Psychology.

Grant, J. M., Mottet, L. A., Tanis, J., Harrison, J., Herman, J. L., & Keisling, M. (2011). *Injustice at every turn: A report of the national transgender discrimination survey*. Washington, D.C.: National Center for Transgender Equality and National Gay and Lesbian Task Force.

Greytak, E. A., Kosciw, J. G., & Diaz, E. M. (2009). *Harsh realities: The experience of transgender youth in our nation's schools*. New York: GLSEN.

Henderson, K. A., Whitaker, L. S., Bialeschki, M. D., Scanlin, M. M., & Thurber, C. (2007). Summer camp experiences: Parental perceptions of youth development outcomes. *Journal of Family Issues, 28* (8), 987–1007.

Kosciw, J. G., Diaz, E. M., & Greytak, E. A. (2009). *2007 national school climate survey: The experiences of lesbian, gay, bisexual and transgender youth in our nation's schools*. New York: GLSEN.

Lev, A. I. (2004). *Transgender emergence: Therapeutic guidelines for working with gender-variant people and their families*. Binghamton, N.Y.: Haworth Press.

Scanlin, M., Gambone, M., Sipe, C., & Daraio, S. (2006). *Inspirations: Developmental supports and opportunities of youths' experiences at camp*. Martinsville, Ind.: American Camp Association.

Teich, N. M. (2012). *Transgender 101: A simple guide to a complex issue*. New York: Columbia University Press.

Whittle, S., Turner, L., & Al-Alami, M. (2007, February). Engendered penalties: Transgender and transsexual people's experiences of inequality and discrimination. *UK Equalities Review*, 5–97.

26

Tom-Girl, Trans Girl, Pink Boy: Finding a Support Group for All

Lauren P., PsyD

Our child, originally named John, was assigned male in utero. We still have the 20-week ultrasound picture on which my husband circled the penis pointed out by the technician. That first year, we dressed John in jeans, football jerseys, and baseball hats. From age 18 months on, however, he gravitated to all things "girl"— in clothes and toys. *Dora the Explorer* was a favorite, as was the color pink. He wore towels on his head for long hair and chose girls as his friends. At two and a half, John loved to wear my niece's dress-up clothes. When she gave him her purple sequined princess dress to take home, John was in his glory. That dress was frequently worn in the house as well as outside, including our annual block party. Although his preschool picture shows him wearing a blazer and jeans, after school he would run home to his *Wizard of Oz* dress-up box. At that point, we viewed ourselves as progressive parents of a "sensitive" son. Honestly, we were more worried about his separation anxiety and sensory integration issues, particularly those related to the loud noises that often triggered major meltdowns.

As four-year-old John entered prekindergarten, we increasingly fielded his requests for pink clothes by trying to find those or other brightly colored compromises in the boys' section. No easy feat. For Halloween that year, I selected his costume: Diego, Dora's cousin. Though I thought it was a great choice, John did not. He wore it to school but immediately took it off when he got home, then improvised a witch costume for the evening's trick-or-treating.

During that period, we began to notice that when John drew a picture of himself, it was always as a girl. He became obsessed with choosing his younger sister's outfits each day, as well as dressing up his stuffed animals in her clothes. This was the year the bathing suit wars began. If it had been up to him, John would be in a flowered two-piece. At that point, I drew the line, mainly out of terror that he would be targeted.

My husband and I are both open-minded clinical psychologists who had some experience working with LGB teens and adults and an understanding of child development. Although I had briefly treated one college-age transgender

Lev, Arlene I., Gottlieb, Andrew R., *Families in Transition*
dx.doi.org/10.17312/harringtonparkpress/2019.04.fit.026

client, the challenges of growing up LGBT were definitely not included in our training! As John's gender variance persisted, we were in an ever-growing swirl of confusion, worry, and intense love for our child. We had already begun reading about gender diverse children, but now our instincts told us it was time to consult a specialist.

Luckily, our professional contacts led us to one of the few psychologists who was an expert in the field. We shared our confusion with him: Was this a phase? Did these gender issues relate to John's anxiety and sensory integration issues? Were we seeing a gender variant (GV) boy, one who maintains a male identity, but with a more traditionally feminine gender expression, combined with the likelihood of being gay? Or were we looking at the possibility of a "trans girl," one who is assigned male at birth but who has a female gender identity as well as a feminine gender expression, a child who may socially transition to living as a girl who will probably consider puberty blockers, hormone treatment, and/or surgery?

We also needed guidance on how to parent John while we all figured it out. Balancing self-expression with safety was the suggestion, allowing his identity to naturally emerge while simultaneously running interference with society, explaining to John that other people may have different "rules" for how girls and boys "should" act. Easier said than done. But we did our best—proud of how understanding we appeared to be externally despite how agonizing it was internally.

In the spirit of following John's lead, I was always watching his behavior relating to gender. A very significant moment for me occurred at John's end-of-the-year pre-K picnic. As the teachers spread out a big parachute and suspended it in the air, they told the boys to "go under it." John did not. The teachers then let it fall to the ground and told the girls to "sit on top of it." John scrambled on. I watched as the teachers insisted he come off, and saw him looking very confused and tearful. Somewhere deep down in me, this identification with femaleness registered and fueled thoughts that this was more than "just a phase" or signs of a gay orientation.

That summer, John was unexpectedly given a way to understand his experience. He was talking to two sisters, Katie and Jessica, new to our neighborhood, who had two moms. John told the younger girl, Katie, how much he "loved Disney princesses," to which she replied, "Oh, I like those, too!" Apparently she was just being polite because Jessica exclaimed, "No, you don't. You hate princesses. You are such a tomboy!" John asked what a tomboy was. Jessica answered, "It's a girl who likes boys' stuff." John then wondered, "Well, I'm a *boy* and I like *girl* stuff, so what am I?" Jessica matter-of-factly said, "You're a tom-girl." I will always remember how ecstatic John was, as if the clouds had parted and a golden light illuminated his presence, a chorus of angels singing their hallelujahs in the background. He had suddenly, finally, found the words to describe himself.

As John entered kindergarten and we continued to follow his lead, we allowed him to dress as the Little Mermaid for Halloween, purchased a few neutral girls' clothes, and permitted him to grow out his hair. We felt so alone as parents, trying to do what was right for John while also feeling judged by others. The silent judgments in the form of questioning or uncomfortable looks were the hardest to bear. In the spring of that year, our gender specialist recommended that we join a listserv for parents and caregivers of GV boys in order to develop a support network. We were *so* ready to be connected to other families. We quickly contacted the coordinators and went through their screening, during which a coordinator advised us to "tell John who he is: a boy who likes girls' things." This phrase was encompassed in the term *tom-girl* that John had already embraced.

I felt relief after that one phone call. The next morning, as though he sensed a seismic shift in our own readiness, John came down in his *Sleeping Beauty* nightgown for pajama day at school, and, within a week, he asked to wear girls' clothes full-time. E-mails were sent to family members ahead of our Easter gatherings to inform them that John would be in girls' clothes. We continued to emphasize that other people may have reactions to him that might not feel good, but John was persistent. There was a continual balancing act regarding what limits to set for John's safety, how to give him, as our friend put it, "sovereignty over his own identity," and how to regulate the amount of discomfort and anxiety *we* could tolerate at any time.

We immediately started posting on the parent listserv as we struggled with all this, and we were thrilled to find out that, through the efforts of these parents, a family weekend camp had been created. We attended for the first time in the summer after John finished kindergarten. The camp—an oasis in an otherwise barren world—provided an opportunity for the children to meet others like them, and for parents to get education and support. What a welcome difference it was from the confused and bewildered stares of those around us trying to figure out our child's story. Here our kids could "just be kids" and express themselves freely, and we could relax in the presence of other parents who understood the road we had been traveling.

After an ignorant comment made to my husband by a school aide, who wondered how long we would "allow" John to wear girls' clothes, we requested that the staff be trained in gender variance before John started first grade. Happily, the principal agreed, and everyone had a positive response. In addition, John had a wonderfully supportive first grade teacher, who reduced the activities in which the class was split by gender and effectively managed John's meltdowns.

But as the fall progressed, John bemoaned, "I am the only one like me in the whole school." He began expressing a wish for a "magic wand" and, when pressed, told us, "The wand will turn me into a girl." He started showing signs of depression, stated that he hated his name, wished to be "nobody" or "to be dead," and emphatically declared, "I am not a boy!"

A very upsetting incident occurred after I showed John and his three-year-old sister, Sophia, a children's book on body safety: one page with a girl body and another with a boy body, both in bathing suits. I said to John, "I know you feel like a girl but you have a boy's body, so these are your private parts." John had a complete meltdown, crying, first trying to rip the page out, then throwing the book across the room. I was stunned. (Relatedly, by age four, he consistently sat down to urinate. When he did, John would tuck in his penis so as not to see it and would proudly show me the result. These behaviors suggested body dysphoria, one of the hallmark traits of transgender children.) At that point it was clear that all of us needed more therapy. Our gender specialist was an hour away, so continuing with him for ongoing weekly sessions was just not feasible. Luckily, we found an experienced, more local clinician.

Once in therapy, John seemed more at ease. In any role-playing games with his sister, he began to use the name Jenny, along with female pronouns. We later learned that he had asked his therapist to call him Jenny very early on in their sessions. As the spring progressed, John's preference for Jenny expanded from just role-play games to everyday home life. Sophia jumped on the bandwagon and became Jenny's biggest supporter. Both she and John frequently corrected us when we referred to him as male. It was an overwhelming time. Then, in a family therapy session at the end of first grade, John requested to live fully as Jenny. It was then that she informed us that she had been thinking of this name since pre-K!

While not surprising, this request still sent us into a tailspin. During the next few days we did more research, spoke to our therapists, and did major soul-searching. Jenny was "full steam ahead" and, as luck would have it, the family camp just happened to fall on the weekend following her request. "What a great place to launch Jenny!" we said to each other and to her therapist. It was a safe and accepting space in which to try out public life in her affirmed gender.

The change in Jenny was immediate. This anxious child boldly informed us the first morning of camp that she was going down to breakfast by herself, and when we arrived at the dining hall, she was ensconced at a table with another family. She shocked us by participating in the talent show without telling us beforehand, confidently dancing to Lady Gaga's "Poker Face" with a mostly improvised routine. As the audience shouted and cheered, "Go, Jenny," tears filled my eyes. This was one of those moments, few and far between, when all doubts recede, and I believed we had made the right decision. I was so grateful to my fellow parents and the adult volunteers who had created this space. In that moment, I experienced what I have found to be a beautiful thread running through the pain and confusion of the transition process: the joy of knowing we are seeing and honoring our child's soul.

That year's camp was the boost we needed to return home and face the daunting task of facilitating her transition among family and friends, and preparing the school for her to enter second grade as Jenny. Around that same time, we also joined an additional trans listserv that tended to draw more parents and caregivers of children who had or were moving toward social transition.

After a relatively smooth year, we packed up for our third family camp weekend, eager to see friends we had made there, and hoping to make some new ones. It started out on a positive note. There were fun activities for the kids and informative workshops for parents. The organizers had done a wonderful job. We could not have predicted at the outset that, sadly, the weekend would end with one of the most significant and painful experiences our family had encountered since Jenny's transition began.

Midway through, I began to notice subtle tension in the discussions both in and outside our workshops. Parents were wondering what their child's ultimate outcome would be: a GV boy or a trans girl. Perhaps I was more attuned to these conversations because Jenny was one of only three trans girls among perhaps 20 GV boys. As parents expressed their wishes and fears about what they thought would be their child's "best" and "safest" path, I recall being a bit rattled as I got the impression that transitioning was seen as the less desirable outcome.

One mother of an 11-year-old boy overtly expressed this view, repeatedly stating: "I just want my son to be gay." This family was from a politically conservative state and her child had already been subjected to religious condemnation by peers. In one emotionally intense workshop, a panel of transgender and genderfluid teenagers each shared their story and then responded to questions. This mother practically interrogated several of the MTF (male-to-female) teens, asking: "Exactly *when* did you know?" and "How did you *know* you were not gay?" I could completely empathize with her underlying fear for her son and her drive to understand, but her delivery was bordering on harassment. Her anxious questioning triggered in me older, familiar pangs of doubt: Did we transition too soon? Will Jenny tell us if she begins to think of herself as a boy? Is that even possible? I felt defensive and protective of our child and our affirmation of her female identity, but on the whole, the general sense of community among the parents outweighed these negative feelings—that is, until the last hour.

As I was saying good-bye to some of the other mothers and Jenny was nearby, happily engaged in conversation with a few older kids, I suddenly felt the wind knocked out of me as she ran up, threw her arms around me, and started sobbing. I was shocked. She was in a hysterical state, her words coming out in fits and starts, making it difficult to understand what had happened. As I worked to calm her, Dylan, the 11-year-old son of the anxious mother, approached us, and began apologizing to Jenny, perhaps hoping he could distract her enough that she wouldn't need to tell me what had occurred. Finally, she said that Dylan had asked her if she was on hormones. She told him: "No, but I will be someday." Dylan reportedly implored her, "Don't do it!" and proceeded to offer gross misinformation, saying things such as "You will die early" and "They will put in breast implants that will explode when you are in an airplane at 30,000 feet." I felt so betrayed and shocked that this happened in one of our only safe havens.

I went to Dylan's cabin to speak with his mother. He had already gone back and told her some version of events. She was very apologetic and directed him to apologize to me. He did so in a very submissive but disingenuous way that made me doubt his sincerity *and,* at the same time, feel very sad for him. I realized that someone had fed *him* this misinformation, too, and I wondered if his frightening Jenny was his only way to communicate his own confusion and fear about *his* future. Could it have been a coincidence that this same boy whose mother would rather he "just be gay" was trying to scare our child out of being transgender? If his family had given Dylan this distorted information as a way to influence who he felt himself to be, maybe scaring Jenny was a well-intentioned attempt to protect her. Or perhaps it was an expression of anger and jealousy in the face of having his identity chosen *for* him. As angry as I was about his behavior, I was even more empathic to his imagined suffering.

It was a long, quiet, four-hour drive home. We had several conversations with Jenny to reassure her we would research all the information about hormones before we made any decisions, and we kept reinforcing the fact that Dylan's information was inaccurate. Thankfully, she was pretty easily calmed, but as parents we remained quite shaken. Another mother, not knowing if we knew about the incident, e-mailed me later that day to report that her son had witnessed the conversation and had cried about it on their drive home. His version was even more upsetting than Jenny's.

We decided to write to the whole group about what happened, without mentioning the boy's name, in order to consider what we might learn from the incident to make our future camp experiences safer. We shared our view that this "acting out" may have been an expression of the fears and concerns of early adolescent children facing the onset of puberty, concerns they cannot really articulate, for which the camp had yet to find a forum. We proposed some concrete ideas for the next year.

I think we got a response from only one parent. In all likelihood, this could have been related to the fact that the GV listserv was going through structural changes that affected how we were to post. Given my lack of technical savvy, it may be that our e-mail did not reach a large portion of parents. It also points to one of the limitations of an online support group. You never know if the lack of response means that you are being ignored or disagreed with, or simply that recipients never got the message or have not checked their e-mail. The end result, however, was the same: we felt unheard and unacknowledged. We needed validation that this incident should never have happened in a place created to provide support and safety. As controversial as the presence of gender nonconforming and transgender children is, it is not surprising that societal fears and tendency toward "good-bad" splits would make their way into this safe zone as we grapple with understanding it all. But those in charge of such events need to be ever vigilant in monitoring the destructive expression of those fears. We needed others to see the underlying GV boy–trans girl split and to consider how it might have set the stage for Dylan's behavior.

Ironically, around that time, I observed similar splits across the posts on both listservs. These posts were the first time I came across the term *pink boy,* used to denote a gender variant boy or tom-girl. In this case it was being used by a member of the trans list to direct a new parent to the GV list because her child, as she described him, appeared to be a pink boy. This generated a flurry of tense conversations across the two lists about whether one was really for pink boys while the other was for trans girls. The focus seemed to be on how the two groups were different rather than on how they were similar. The distinction just did not sit right with me. Yes, the trans girl has some unique issues to face that the pink boy may not, such as changing names, monitoring puberty, and accessing puberty blockers. And yes, as a psychologist, I know this need to categorize things is part of a search for order. But feeling that either my child or another child was being relegated to the "other" category created an "us versus them" mentality, a division that left me anxious. We had already been placed outside the mainstream simply because of who our child was. This felt like déjà vu, and I told my husband the title of our life at that time could be "Out of the Mainstream—Twice."

My discomfort raised an ongoing dilemma: Should we stay with these current support networks and help mold them into what we envisioned, or should we keep moving until we found one that was right for us? On the one hand, the loyal moralist in me was inclined to stay because I felt so indebted to both these listservs for all the support we *had* gotten, and I have always been a person who tries to make things better in whatever context before deciding to move on. On the other hand, I wanted and needed forms of support that soothed me rather than agitated me. It just felt so hard during those years immediately before and after Jenny's transition. My husband and I were emotionally raw from dealing with the ever-present fear for Jenny's physical and emotional safety. We felt pressure to explain Jenny and ourselves everywhere we went and were desperate for something that worked for us *now*.

I had also realized that, for me, another downside of online support was binge-reading posts just enough to overwhelm and distract myself. I spent many late nights and lunch hours gripped by heart-wrenching stories of other faceless families' struggles, stories of cruel bullying, schools refusing to change their policies on bathroom use, family court judges equating affirming a child's gender with child abuse, the single mother struggling to pay for blockers or hormones. I was not so good at limiting how much I took in at any one time, and there was often no one present with whom to immediately process my reactions. I was gradually able to see that our family needed a more stable and structured forum, one that provided (1) a face-to-face, regularly occurring group with a relatively stable membership, and (2) a trained leader with an affirming approach, who would be attuned to individual differences, be competent to handle group dynamics, and create safety.

I was delighted when we found a highly respected program in a city an hour from where we live, one that provides monthly caregiver support groups with a concurrent playgroup for transgender and gender creative children. Jay, the director of the program and the leader of our caregiver group, presents a balanced, calming leadership style. Though at first I felt sad for the parents in the group who had pink boys or blue girls amid a majority of transgender children, Jay pulls us all together to better understand the rigid ways in which the world views gender. He has a wonderful capacity to weave together our commonalities while honoring our diversity, fostering an environment in which all realities are validated and all outcomes are valued. The trans girl–pink boy split, both in the group and in my mind, is no longer an issue, instead replaced by a curiosity about our child's path rather than a need to control it or judge it. This is not because the split is absent, but because when it comes up, Jay helps the group address it. And the reality is, uncomfortable things do happen. There have been moments of conflict in the playgroup, and this time around, *my* child was a transgressor in one of those incidents. The difference is that all the leaders pay close attention to the group dynamics as well as the communication among themselves. Problems are addressed quickly and effectively so that learning and growth can happen over time.

I am so grateful for the existence of both listservs, one of which I am still on. They provided an initial, crucial bridge to other families when we really needed it, and they continue to be the source of relief and critical information. At the same time, they could not have given us the same experience of sitting and talking, in person, with fellow parents and caregivers with whom we could build ongoing relationships, which have turned out to be profound and long lasting. Over these five years, we have attended birthday parties, name-change parties, bat mitzvahs, and funerals. We communicate with each other outside the group for problem solving and support.

Most important, Jenny has developed close friendships with many of the kids from her group, which we hope will endure. Her journey will be uniquely challenging in ways most of us cannot understand, but these other children will. No longer does Jenny have to identify as "the only one like me."

Now she is not alone.

APPENDIX: BEST PRACTICES FOR THE CARE OF TRANSGENDER YOUTH

"Principles of Gender Affirmative Care and Support" were developed by a group of mental health, medical, legal, and educational professionals gathered together at the 2014 Gender Spectrum Symposium and Conference in the San Francisco Bay Area and at the Gender Conference East in Maryland. In this work-in-progress, members of multidisciplinary gender clinics as well as individual providers from around the country sought to establish a shared set of values and beliefs, and to codify an approach "committed to ensuring that all young people are affirmed in their efforts to understand, express, and identify their gender in an authentic manner."

Principles of Gender Affirmative Care and Support

As individuals and organizations constituting the Gender Center Consortium, we are committed to ensuring that all young people are affirmed in their efforts to understand, express, and identify their gender in an authentic manner. We start with the assumption that all children and youth have a fundamental right to determine for themselves who they are and what, how, and when to communicate about their gender with others. We understand that, alongside development, a confluence of sociocultural factors—familial, religious, racial, ethnic, social, linguistic, regional, and many more—affect how a young person's gender will be perceived, responded to, and sometimes challenged or repudiated by others. Therefore, we are also committed to providing the adults who love and care for young people with the necessary knowledge, skills, and resources to affirm and assist them in their efforts to support the gender health of all children and teens, defined as a youth's ability to express gender with freedom from restriction, aspersion, or rejection.

As members of this Consortium, we:

1 Recognize gender diversity as a universal aspect of humanity;

2 Advocate for and support the development of the authentic, self-defined gender of all children and teens;

3 Consider any professional's attempt to alter a child's gender identity or gender expression to align with socially stereotypical norms to be inconsistent with current standards of care, unethical, and potentially harmful;

Lev, Arlene I., Gottlieb, Andrew R., *Families in Transition*
dx.doi.org/10.17312/harringtonparkpress/2019.04.fit.00c
© 2019 by Harrington Park Press

4 Promote healthy development by providing integrated, collaborative care and advocacy throughout and across all domains of a young person's life, including familial, educational, legal, medical, mental health, recreational, social, and spiritual;

5 Take responsibility for helping young people and their families access services by advocating with entities (i.e., medical, mental health, insurance, governmental, etc.) that provide the funding or approval necessary for young people to obtain care and support;

6 Commit to ensuring access to all aspects of affirmative care and support for the disproportionate numbers of gender expansive youth who are homeless, in foster care, in group homes, in juvenile detention, and in other out-of-home settings;

7 Conduct, share, and stay informed about research related to gender-affirmative care within and across disciplines;

8 Participate in and initiate policy level advocacy to depathologize gender diversity and ensure gender-affirmative practices occur across all domains of a young person's life;

9 Begin where parents, caregivers, and professionals are in their understanding and support of transgender and other gender expansive young people, and work collaboratively to enhance the child's gender health;

10 Seek to identify and support other professionals committed to doing work in service of greater gender acceptance for all children and teens, and promote the inclusion of gender-diversity issues in all professional preparatory and training programs;

11 Participate in and lead efforts to educate the public about the needs of gender expansive young people to foster acceptance and ensure that necessary resources are available for their care and support

ABOUT THE EDITORS AND CONTRIBUTORS

Editors

Arlene (Ari) I. Lev, LCSW-R, CASAC, CST, is a social worker, family therapist, credentialed addictions counselor, gender specialist, and certified sex therapist. She is the founder and clinical director of Choices Counseling and Consulting (www.choicesconsulting.com) and TIGRIS: The Training Institute for Gender, Relationships, Identity, and Sexuality (www.tigrisinstitute.com) in Albany, New York. In addition to being a part-time lecturer at the School of Social Welfare at the State University of New York at Albany and the project director of the Sexual Orientation and Gender Identity Project (SOGI), she is an adjunct professor at Smith College School for Social Work and Empire College, as well as the board president for Rainbow Access Initiative, Inc., which provides low-cost therapy to LGBTQ individuals. She has authored numerous journal articles and two books: *The Complete Lesbian and Gay Parenting Guide* and *Transgender Emergence: Therapeutic Guidelines for Working with Gender-Variant People and Their Families,* winner of the APA (Division 44) Distinguished Book Award, 2006.

Andrew R. Gottlieb, PhD, LCSW, received his MSW in 1982 from Yeshiva University–Wurzweiler School of Social Work, a post-master's certificate in 1992 from New Hope Guild–Child-Adolescent Therapy Training Program, and a PhD in clinical social work in 1999 from New York University–Ehrenkranz School of Social Work. He is the author of *Out of the Twilight: Fathers of Gay Men Speak* (2000) and its companion, *Sons Talk about Their Gay Fathers: Life Curves* (2003), the editor of *Side by Side: On Having a Gay or Lesbian Sibling* (2005), the coeditor (with Jerry Bigner) of *Interventions with Families of GLBT People: From the Inside Out* (2006), the editor of *On the Meaning of Friendship between Gay Men* (2008), and an editor at the *Journal of GLBT Family Studies*. Dr. Gottlieb maintains a full-time, private psychotherapy practice in Brooklyn, New York, serving mostly LGBTQ adolescents and young adults. Originally trained as a musician, he is currently assisting the famed pianist Sara Davis Buechner on her autobiography, tentatively titled *Lady of the Season's Laughter: A Chronicle of My Life.* Visit his website at www.andrewr-gottlieb.com.

Contributors

Rex Butt, PhD, is an educator, mentor, advocate, and the father of a trans woman. With 32 years' experience in the classroom, he has taught students varying in age from 12 to 70 and subjects varying in scope from literary analysis to interpersonal communication theory. A few years after his daughter came out, he and his wife, Karen, helped found the Kingston, New York, chapter of PFLAG and served as that chapter's transgender coordinators for a decade. Butt has mentored and counseled scores of families with gender nonconforming loved ones and continues to present support and information sessions at conferences. He resides in Burlington, Vermont, and, as of this publication, is serving as the interim executive director of the Pride Center of Vermont. His book, *Now What? A Guidebook for Families with Transgender Children,* is available from Transgress Press.

Davis Chandler, LICSW, earned their master's of social work at Smith College in 2011. Currently, they work for two programs: Windhorse Integrative Mental Health, a small nonprofit serving adults with extreme mind states and major life disruptions; and Translate Gender, Inc., an education, advocacy, and therapy nonprofit serving trans and gender nonconforming individuals, families, and allies, both based in Northampton, Massachusetts. They identify as queer and gender nonconforming and are committed to social justice, antiracism, and antioppression work in every area of life.

Sabrina C. H. Chang, MA, received her master's degree in clinical psychology in 2012 and is currently a PhD candidate at the University of British Columbia and a clinical fellow at Harvard Medical School, where she is completing her psychology residency at the Massachusetts Mental Health Center. Her research interests lie in the intersection of culture, gender identity, and sexual health, and she is passionate about her clinical work with children, adolescents, and adults in the areas of trauma and anxiety. She currently resides in Boston and is a proud native of Taipei, Taiwan.

Deborah Coolhart, PhD, LMFT, is an assistant professor of marriage and family therapy at Syracuse University and, since 1999, has maintained a private therapy practice specializing in working with trans people and their families. Her scholarly work also focuses on trans youth and their families as well as the readiness process for medical gender transition, intersectionality in queer couples, and the experiences of LGBTQ homeless youth.

Diane Ehrensaft, PhD, is a developmental and clinical psychologist, an associate professor of pediatrics at the University of California–San Francisco, and director of Mental Health of the Child and Adolescent Gender Center, UCSF Benioff Children's Hospital. She specializes in research, clinical work, and consultation related to gender expansive children and assisted reproductive technology families. She is the author of *The Gender Creative Child* (2016); *Gender Born, Gender Made* (2011); *Mommies, Daddies, Donors, Surrogates* (2005); *Spoiling Childhood* (1997); *Parenting Together* (1990); and the editor of two texts: *Building a Home Within* (with Toni Heineman) (2005) and *The Gender Affirmative Model: A Clinical Approach to Supporting Transgender and Gender Expansive Children* (2018) (with Colt Keo-Meier). Many years ago, before the current language was in use, she was the proud parent of a gender expansive child. Visit her website at www.dianeehrensaft.com.

Molly Gardner, MA, received her bachelor of science in family studies in 2014 and her master of arts in social work in 2016, both degrees from Miami University. During her time there, she was a research assistant under Dr. Katherine Kuvalanka, a position she thoroughly enjoyed. Currently, Molly works for Butler County Educational Service Center in a public school setting, which serves low-income families, helping them remove noncognitive barriers to learning, which taps into her passion for empowerment through education. She resides with her husband in Germantown, Ohio.

Irwin Krieger, LCSW, provides clinical supervision as well as training for mental health professionals and school personnel. Earlier, he was a psychotherapist for over 30 years, working with the LGBT community and specializing in the treatment of transgender youth and their families. Irwin is the 2017 recipient of the Connecticut NASW's Lifetime Achievement award and the author two books: *Helping Your Transgender Teen: A Guide for Parents*, 2nd edition (2018), and *Counseling Transgender and Non-Binary Youth: The Essential Guide* (2017). Visit his website at www.IKriegerTraining.com.

Katherine A. Kuvalanka, PhD, earned her doctorate in family studies from the University of Maryland, College Park, and joined the Miami University Family Science faculty in 2007, where she is currently an associate professor. Her research focus is on factors ranging from the proximal (e.g., individual, family, school) to the distal (e.g., legal or political climate) that pose challenges to and foster resilience among families with LGBTQ members. She received funding from the Williams Institute at the UCLA School of Law, the Society for the Psychological Study of

Social Issues, and the American Psychological Foundation. She is on the editorial boards of the *Journal of GLBT Family Studies* and the *Journal of Youth & Adolescence,* and she is the principal investigator of the Trans*Kids Project (http://transkids. info/), a longitudinal study of 50 families with transgender and gender nonconforming children.

Lisette Lahana, LCSW, received her master's in social work from Smith College School for Social Work in 1997. A gender specialist since 2002, she maintains a private practice in Oakland, California, offering psychotherapy services and consultation—locally and nationally through videoconferencing—to clinicians working with transgender, nonbinary, intersex, and questioning adolescents and adults. In addition, Lahana is a clinician at Kaiser Permanente's Adult Psychiatry Department in Union City, California, as well as a part of the Kaiser Permanente Gender Therapist Team at the Multi-Specialty Transitions Department based in the Oakland Medical Center. She frequently lectures on becoming a competent mental health care provider for gender diverse clients and their families and loved ones. Lahana identifies as a queer cis woman and is half Ashkenazi and half Sephardi/Mexican Jewish with roots in Los Angeles. Visit her website at www. LisetteLahana.com.

Scott Leibowitz, MD, is a child and adolescent psychiatrist, the medical director of Behavioral Health Services for the THRIVE gender and sex development program at Nationwide Children's Hospital in Columbus, Ohio, and associate professor of psychiatry for the Ohio State University College of Medicine in Columbus. Dr. Leibowitz has been working with gender diverse and transgender youth since 2008 while training at Boston Children's Hospital and Harvard Medical School. He was named chapter lead for the WPATH SOC8 Adolescent Assessment Chapter and is the cochairman of the Sexual Orientation Gender Identity Issues Committee for the American Academy of Child and Adolescent Psychiatry. Having served as an expert witness on two federal cases involving bathroom bills, Dr. Leibowitz considers himself not only a provider and educator, but an advocate for the trans and gender diverse youth community.

Melissa MacNish, MA, LMHC, received her master's in clinical mental health counseling from Lesley College in 2007 and maintains a private practice at the Meeting Point in Jamaica Plain, Massachusetts. She has been working with transgender and nonbinary youth, young adults, and their families for the past 10 years in a variety of clinical and community settings. MacNish recently launched a socially conscious business called Supporting Alternative Youth and Families through Empowerment and Education (SAYFTEE), which offers workshops, groups, and services to gender expansive and LGBTQI youth and families in Massachusetts. She is a consultant for Greater Boston PFLAG, serves on the Board of Directors, is assistant director for Camp Aranu'tiq of Harbor Camps, and provides trainings on working with gender diverse populations for Maebright, Inc.'s Therapist Training Series. Visit her website at www.sayftee.com.

Jean Malpas, LMHC, LMFT, is the founder and director of the Gender & Family Project at the Ackerman Institute for the Family (www.ackerman.org/GFP), their director of International Training, and a psychotherapist in private practice in New York City. He has presented nationally and internationally on issues of gender, sexuality, addiction, and couples and family therapy. His work with lesbian, gay, bisexual, and transgender individuals, couples, and families has been published in numerous books and journals. Media appearances include a TEDx Talk, "The Gift of Gender Authenticity," National Geographic's "Gender Revolution: A Journey with Katie Couric," and PBS *Frontline:* "Growing Up Trans." Malpas's leadership has been recognized by the first Early Career Award and the Social Justice 2018 Award of the American Family Therapy Academy. Visit his website at www.jeanmalpas.com.

Elena Moser, LCSW, received her master's in social work from the University of California at Berkeley in 1982. She maintains a private practice, offering individual and relationship psychotherapy as well as clinical consultation. Additionally, she is on the clinical and teaching faculties of the Women's Therapy Center, the Psychotherapy Institute, and the Supervision Study Program, all Berkeley-based. Moser brings a relational psychodynamic lens to both her clinical work and her teaching, and she is particularly interested in the intersection of culture and families and how those shape our individual psychologies. Visit her website at www.elenamoser.com.

Cat Munroe, PhD, is a postdoctoral fellow in the Clinical Psychology Training Program at the University of California – San Francisco and a doctoral student in clinical psychology at Miami University. Her primary research interests include the personal and relational well-being of individuals who hold a stigmatized identity (e.g., LGBTQ identity, survivor of sexual violence), as well as those relational factors implicated in risk and resilience after trauma. Munroe's clinical interests focus on complex PTSD trauma recovery among LGBTQ individuals.

AndreAs Neumann Mascis, PhD, is a clinical psychologist with specialties that include gender variance, trauma, and physical and psychiatric disabilities. He has worked as a provider, educator, advocate, and activist with complex people in a wide range of settings. Neumann Mascis founded and developed the Meeting Point, a collaboration of independent health-care providers in Jamaica Plain, Massachusetts, which serves the LGBTQ, survivors of trauma, and disability communities. It is founded on the knowledge that social justice heals, and it is growing to meet the unique strengths and needs of people through responsive community activity, personalized approaches, and physical and mental health care. Visit his website at www.themeetingpoint.org.

Margaret Nichols, PhD, is a psychologist, an AASECT-certified sex therapy supervisor, and founder and executive director of the Institute for Personal Growth (www.ipgcounseling.com), a program in New Jersey specializing in sex therapy and other clinical work with the sexually and gender diverse community. Her primary clinical interests are differences in sexual functioning between same- and mixed-sex couples; transgender and gender nonconforming young people; and those who make up the Q in LGBTQ, that is, kinky, polyamorous, and queer people. More recently, she's published papers on LGBTQ therapy, same-sex couples, kink, and a *Psychotherapy Networker* article on transgender youth. Nichols's engagements as an international speaker include a TEDx talk titled "Beyond the Gender Binary," and presentations at the U.S. Professional Association for Transgender Health, the Psychotherapy Networker Symposium, the Philadelphia Trans Health Conference, and the Gender East conference.

Lauren P., PsyD, is the proud mother of a transgender daughter and a cisgender daughter/sibling ally, both in their teens. She is a clinical psychologist, currently in private practice with a specialty in trauma therapy using Eye Movement Desensitization and Reprocessing (EMDR) and sensorimotor psychotherapy within a relational, integrative approach. She provides affirming individual and family therapy and training for schools and psychological associations on transgender and gender expansive youth, and she works toward increasing multidisciplinary services for transgender youth and families in her state.

C.V.R., PhD, received her doctoral degree in foreign language education from a large state university in the South, and she has published a number of articles on linguistics and language acquisition in various professional journals. She is currently a professor at a small Catholic college, where she teaches foreign languages and cultural studies.

Katherine (Kit) Rachlin, PhD, is a clinical psychologist and gender specialist in private practice in New York City. For more than 20 years, she has worked to support the needs of transgender, transsexual, and gender nonconforming people and their families and partners. She currently serves as a member of the Board of Directors of the World Professional Association for Transgender Health (WPATH) and is a coauthor of *The Standards of Care for the Health of Transgender, Transsexual and Gender Nonconforming Individuals* (7th version, 2011). Her published papers address a range of topics, including the flexible use of the Standards of Care, an intake template for genderqueer college students, psychotherapy experiences of transgender and gender nonconforming people, access to health care, and surgical choice and decision making. Visit her website at https://www.transgendertherapyny.com.

Damien Riggs, PhD, FAPS, is an associate professor in social work at Flinders University, an Australian Research Council future fellow, the author of over 200 publications in the areas of gender, family, and mental health, including *Transgender People and Education* (co-authored with Clare Bartholomaeus) (Palgrave, 2018), and a psychotherapist in private practice specializing in working with transgender youth and their families. Visit his website at www.the-rainbow-owl.com.

Elizabeth Anne Riley, PhD, is a Sydney-based clinician who holds a bachelor's degree in science, a graduate diploma and master's in counseling, and a doctorate from the Faculty of Health Sciences at the University of Sydney, her dissertation being titled "The Needs of Gender-Variant Children and Their Parents." She has counseled trans people and their families for over 20 years; provides clinical supervision, academic supervision to PhD students, training in gender diversity for schools, clinicians, and other service providers; and has authored 12 publications in the field. Riley was a founding member of the Australian & New Zealand Professional Associations for Transgender Health (ANZPATH), and is a clinical registrant of the Psychotherapy and Counselling Federation of Australia (PACFA) and a professional clinical member of the World Professional Associations for Transgender Health (WPATH). Visit her website at www.PeopleSmart.net.au.

AJ Rio-Glick recently graduated from Bard College at Simon's Rock with a BA in social action/social change and creative writing. While there, AJ completed a senior thesis on female masculinity in the queer community. Currently, AJ is based in western Massachusetts and is applying for candidacy in various PhD programs in sociology. Over the course of their life, AJ has pursued activism through outreach, organizing, facilitating cultural competency workshops, and writing about their multifaceted experiences as a trans, queer, deaf, white person. In their free time, AJ likes to read, write, giggle, and watch subpar queer comedy on YouTube.

River (aka Barbara) Rio-Glick, LCSW, is a social worker, educator, political activist, and student and practitioner of nondual spirituality and healing. She loves travel, the outdoors, all four-legged creatures, and the never-ending, twisting and turning journey of parenthood.

Shelley Rio-Glick, LCSW, is a retired clinical social worker who currently owns and operates the Roadside Healing Studio (www.roadsidehealingstudio.com), a nondual healing practice. She identifies as queer and lesbian, enjoys music and playing the ukulele, writing, lifelong learning, political activism, and pickleball. She was blessed with her two kids at age 52.

Sonya Rio-Glick has a background in theater and human services, as well as LGBTQ and disability rights activism. Currently, Sonya works as an advocate assistant in the Colorado Fund for People with Disabilities Mission Supports Program, as well as with Phamaly Theatre Company. Sonya is passionate about understanding and educating others on the many intersections of oppression. In the last several years, she has given several workshops and lectures on different facets of marginalization at places such as SUNY Albany, University of Connecticut, and Northeastern University. In 2015 she released a full-length film on disability entitled *The Souls of Our Feet*. To learn more, visit https://thesoulsofourfeet.squarespace.com. Sonya intends to pursue a career in arts administration with the goal of promoting social justice through theater.

Stephanie Sasso, PsyD, received her degree from the Rutgers Graduate School of Applied and Professional Psychology in 2010 and is an AASECT-certified sex therapist. Her private practice, RISE Psychological Services (www.risepsych.com), based in Highland Park, New Jersey, serves as an affirming space for sexually and gender diverse clients, their partners, and families. Sasso's specialties include individual, family, and group treatment of transgender children and adults. She speaks in a variety of settings on gender identity and other LGBTQ issues, provides training and supervision to mental health and medical professionals on the treatment of gender diverse clients, and consults in educational and corporate settings, including cowriting a K–12 transgender student policy.

Shannon L. Sennott, LICSW, CST, is an LGBTQAI family and sex therapist and an adjunct faculty member at Smith College School for Social Work. Having trained at Smith's SSW and the Eastern Group Psychotherapy Society in New York City, Sennott currently resides and practices in Northampton, Massachusetts. While living in New York City, she cofounded the advocacy and education organization Translate Gender, Inc. She uses a transfeminist therapeutic approach in treating LGBTQAI individuals and families; her specialty interests extend to couples, polyamory, kink/BDSM, as well as alternative family structures.

Irene N. Sills, MD, is a board-certified pediatric endocrinologist and emeritus professor of pediatrics at SUNY Upstate Medical University in Syracuse, New York. She has treated youth with gender dysphoria for more than 15 years and has provided education and training to other health-care professionals in this field.

Nick M. Teich, LCSW, PhD, established Camp Aranu'tiq for transgender youth and its umbrella organization, Harbor Camps, in 2009. He holds a master's degree in social work from Boston College and a PhD from Brandeis University, and he authored *Transgender 101: A Simple Guide to a Complex Issue* (Columbia University Press, 2012). Teich lives in the Boston area with his wife, Erika, and their daughter, Rebecca.

Nena Wang, MA, received her master's of arts in clinical psychology at Simon Fraser University in British Columbia, Canada, where she is currently completing her PhD in clinical psychology. She conducts gender dysphoria and hormone-readiness assessments and provides gender-affirming therapy to gender nonbinary and transgender children and youth. Passionate about working with transgender youth and their families, Wang hopes to serve this population in the future. Because she has worked with individuals with schizophrenia and other major mental illnesses in both inpatient and outpatient settings, her other research and clinical interests include understanding and treating psychosis. When she is not reading or writing research papers, Wang can be found searching for the best sushi, hiking one of Vancouver's beautiful mountains, reading anything in the magical realism genre, or planning her next adventure.

Kelley Winters, PhD, is a writer and consultant on issues of gender diversity in medical and public policy. She is the author of *Gender Madness in American Psychiatry: Essays from the Struggle for Dignity* (2008) and a past member of the International Advisory Panel for the World Professional Association for Transgender

Health (WPATH) Standards of Care, the Global Action for Trans* Equality (GATE) Expert Working Group, and the Advisory Board for TransYouth Family Allies (TYFA). Recognized in the 2013 Trans 100 Inaugural List for work supporting the transgender community in the United States, Winters has presented papers and made presentations on gender policy at annual conventions of the American Psychiatric Association, the American Psychological Association, the American Counseling Association, and the Association of Women in Psychology. When not professionally occupied, Winters wanders the highways of America in an old Mazda, ever in search of comfort food. Visit her website at https://gidreform.wordpress.com.

Carolyn Wolf-Gould, MD, attended Hamilton College and Yale University School of Medicine, completing her family practice residency at the University of Rochester. A family practitioner in Oneonta, New York, since 1994, she has been providing health services to transgender and gender nonconforming youth and adults since 2007, and to date her group practice has seen over 600 patients, many of whom travel several hours to access care. In 2016 she and her team of medical, mental health, and surgical providers received a three-year grant from the Robert Wood Johnson Foundation to explore the possibility of creating a rural-based center of excellence in transgender health for upstate New York. She lectures regularly and is committed to helping move transgender health from the margins to the mainstream. For more information, go to https://www.bassett.org/medical/services/transgender-health-services/.

Wallace Wong, PsyD, R Psych, works in British Columbia, specializing in treating transgender clients as well as children and adolescents who present various sexual health issues. Wong is a reviewer for and an editor of *Caring for Transgender Adolescents in BC: Suggested Guidelines* (2006) and *Moving beyond Trans-Sensitivity: Developing Clinical Competence in Transgender Care—Project Summary and Analysis in British Columbia* (2006). He has also published two children's books, *When Kathy Is Keith* (2011) and *It's So Gay and It's Okay* (2014).

ACKNOWLEDGMENTS

Andrew R. Gottlieb

I originally conceived this as purely a storybook, one in which parents, in their own words, would highlight the triumphs and tribulations of raising a gender diverse child. When I ran the idea by Bill Cohen, president and CEO of Harrington Park Press, however, he informed me that he was now exclusively publishing academic texts, and he asked if I could convert it into something for classroom use. I confessed I couldn't do that alone but would need a coeditor, someone who knew the academic literature, someone who had the professional contacts, and someone steeped in that world. Bill immediately suggested Arlene Lev. I knew Arlene as another editorial board member of the *Journal of GLBT Family Studies,* from having edited her beautifully written, compelling review of *Brokeback Mountain,* and having heard wonderful things about her book *Transgender Emergence.* When we finally spoke, Arlene voiced concerns that, in signing on, she feared stretching herself a bit too thin, given all her other professional commitments at the time. But, obviously, she eventually agreed and brought her immense creativity and singular vision to this project. Thank you, Arlene.

I would also like to recognize all our contributors who, having freely given their time, their energy, and their expertise, and from whom I've learned so much, had the patience to sustain the grueling editorial process I put them through. Without them, there would be no book. Thank you, all.

And, of course, to Bill Cohen, a pioneer who, after decades, remains steadfastly committed to publishing important texts on emerging LGBTQ issues. Thank you, Bill.

ACKNOWLEDGMENTS

Arlene I. Lev

When we began this project, I somehow imagined that editing a book would be easier than writing one. Another myth destroyed. The reality is that it has taken much longer and was much more difficult than I had anticipated. But I am grateful to have had a staunch colleague in Andrew Gottlieb, a wise clinician, a detailed and careful editor, and a good friend, whom I have never met, except for our online connection, though we live just three hours apart. He might possibly be one of those secret *lamed vavnikim*—the 36 righteous men of Jewish tradition, who are humble, compassionate, and lift the burdens of those in pain, and whose merit, it is said, is so great that they keep the world from destruction.

In soliciting articles for this book, Andrew and I reached out to amazing researchers and clinicians, scholars who are daily breaking new ground in their work with families, children, and youth. We collected stories from the families themselves, who bravely shared their process. All these writings were authored by clinicians and parents of gender creative children, both trans and cis, as we attempted to make room for a diversity of voices engaged in professional dialogue. I am very proud to be part of this community of colleagues, and I humbly acknowledge their contributions.

I also need to acknowledge the glaring gaps in our work, however. Although we tried hard to solicit more voices of people of color, persons with non-Western perspectives, trans professionals, and those with a less Eurocentric view, our book reflects more white, cisgender, and U.S. and Western perspectives than we would have preferred. In numerous conversations with colleagues, especially those of color and those who are trans, I was made aware of how many are struggling with competing demands on their time and energy while they work to complete PhDs, care for newborn children, and forge professional relationships within a complex and dangerous political climate. I acknowledge their limitations, miss their voices in this book, and recommit to constantly elevating the most marginalized members of those who speak for our professional communities.

I also wanted to highlight the work of colleagues who have lived and worked in the shadow of CAMH (the Centre for Addiction and Mental Health) in Toronto, Canada, so that they, too, could relate their experiences as providers serving children, youth, and families harmed by reparative therapy practices. But litigious institutions can sadly still stifle full freedom of speech. Without those voices, this book is less than it could've been. We invited Dr. Ken Zucker to write for us, offering him a space to present his ideas and perhaps his evolution during the past decade. He agreed to do so, then abruptly ceased to respond to repeated attempts to reach him by e-mail and phone. We are Facebook friends, and I have seen pictures he has posted, sweet, grandfatherly pictures with his grandchild, and I can't help wondering how it would affect him if gender creativity emerged within his own family. He might read that sentence as if I'm putting a pox on him, but the opposite is true. I'm wondering if his heart would soften.

Nearly 15 years ago, Bill Cohen took a risk publishing, *Transgender Emergence,* a 500-page tome by an unknown writer. I am forever grateful to his continued support as our field has grown and matured.

The past few years have been the hardest of my life, and this book has been stalled many times. Andrew, Bill, the contributors, and my family have been endlessly kind to me when I could not write a word for months. I am deeply grateful for their care and patience while I struggled to meet my obligations. Our children take us on wild journeys, many unexpected, and not all with happy endings. Parents are fierce in their need to protect their children, and therapists should never lose sight of the fact that their protectiveness is born of deep love. My own life journey has opened up a well of compassion in me for all parents who do the best they can under challenging circumstances

INDEX

Page references followed by an italicized *fig.* indicate illustrations or material contained in their captions. Page references followed by an italicized *t.* indicate tables.

birth name, 325

bisexuality, 90, 94, 216–217

Blakemore, S., 125, 236

blissful symbiosis, 163

Bloemena, E., 244

blogs, 402

blood clotting, 238–239

Blumer, Markie L. C., 308

body dysphoria, 45, 254, 270, 276, 284, 425

body image, 158

body mass index (BMI), 239, 243

body modification, 392–393

body norms, 254–255

body parts, renegotiating normative meanings of, 254

Boenke, Mary, 399

Boesen, M. J., 263

Bolin, A., 254

bone health, 235–236

books, 271, 402

Bordini, B., 265

"Born This Way" (song; Lady Gaga), 142

Boss, P., 325

Boston Children's Hospital, 143

Bouman, W. P., 113

Bowers, M., 240

Boys Don't Cry (film; 1999), 402

Bradley, Susan J., 61, 74, 89, 93, 164, 165, 166, 167–168, 170, 180, 197, 213, 259, 404

brain, 42, 43; adolescent, 30, 122, 127; developing, and medical interventions, 235, 236; parenting and, 128–130; relationships and, 125, 129–130; self and, 125–128; shame and, 121

brain imaging, 125, 127, 236

Brammer, J. P., 14

breast cancer, 237, 240

breast development, 237

breast malignancies, 238, 243, 244

Brill, S., 41, 68, 102, 114, 312, 314, 332, 378, 379, 399, 421

British Columbia (Canada), 150

Broad, K. L., 391

Bromfield, L., 315

Bronfenbrenner, U., 104, 114

Brown, J., 124

Brown-Smith, N., 104

Bryant, K., 118, 164, 165, 167, 169–170, 172, 360

Bryn Austin, S., 61

Bucher, A., 403

Bullock, P., 171

Bullough, B., 177, 309

Bullough, V., 177, 309

bullying: extent of, 196–197, 214; gender nonconformity extent and, 309; GNC fears of, 273; inconsistent management of, 316; mental health effects of, 214, 359; parental advocacy against, 197, 313, 378; parental fears about, 67–68; reparative therapies and, 170; at school, 316, 374–376, 378, 416; at summer camp, 302. *See also* harassment

Burcombe, R. J., 244

Burgess, C., 272

Buri, J. R., 315

Burke, H., 403

Burke, P., 167, 169, 309, 313

Burne-Goldberg family, 301–303

Burnett, S., 125, 127, 128, 236

Burroway, J., 163, 166, 170

butch lesbians, 208

Butt, Karen, 384

Butt, Rex, 384, 404

Byne, W., 92, 96, 160

Byrne, J., 359

Cabuses, C., 197, 332, 386

Caitlyn, R., 263

California Legislature, 44

Calzo, J. P., 261

Camp Aranu'tiq, 384; acceptance at, 420–421; demographics of, 417; family camp at, 419–420; founding of, 414–415; parent groups at, 418–419; therapy as off-limits at, 416

Campbell, T. L., 258, 260

camps, 271, 384, 414–421

Canada: diverse population of, 150; gender conversion therapies persistence in, 197; gender conversion therapies prohibited for minors in, 44; immigration process in, 151; "invisible college" members in, 162, 164; transgender population in, 150. *See also*

Chinese Canadian families with transgender youth

Canadian National Post, 171

cancer, 237, 240, 241

Card, N. A., xii, 67, 261, 375

cardiovascular disease, 238, 239, 241, 243

care, 143

caregiving roles, 105

Carel, J. C., 234, 235

Carroll, H. J., 380, 382

Carter, A., 311

Carver, P., 316, 359

Case, K., 119

Catalpa, J., 105, 113

Catholicism, 39, 80, 81, 188, 286

celebration, 399

Centre for Addiction and Mental Health (CAMH; Toronto, Canada), 89, 90, 93, 94–95, 99, 164, 167–168, 171–172

Chandler, Davis, 288

change.org, 13

Chee, G., 267

Chen, D., 143

Cheng, H., 315

chest binders, 339–340

child abuse, 24, 313

child/adolescent psychiatrists: affirming treatment and, 140–143; assessments with, 139–140, 145–147; in multidisciplinary team, 143–145; negative connotations of, 136–137; parents as collaborative partners of, 134, 139, 142–143, 147; treatment potentials of, 134, 137–140

Child-Centered Transfeminist Therapy (CCTFT): application of, 298–299, 303; case studies, 294–295, 300–303; language used in, 291; resources for, 302–306; tenets of, 293–297; theoretical foundations of, 288, 291–293

Childhood Gender Identity Service (St. Luke's–Roosevelt Hospital Center, New York), 163

children: cisgender, xii; gay, of gay men, 4–8; minds of, 142; parental gendered expectations of, 308; summer camps and, 416; "wait-and-see" approach to treatment of, 143–144

Children's Gender and Sexual Advocacy and Education Program (Washington, DC), 175

child sex abuse, 4

child therapy, 176

China: collectivist culture in, 150, 151; health professionals in, 156; one-child policy in, 150, 151–152

Chinese Canadian families with transgender youth: acculturation frameworks and, 150, 152–153, 155; case study, 155–158; clinical consultations lacking among, 150–151; clinical guidelines, 153, 156, 158–159; collectivist vs. individualistic worldviews and, 150, 151, 153, 154; first- vs. second-generation, 150, 154; minority status and, 152; one-child policy and, 150, 151–152

Chinese Evangelical Church, 155

Chipkin, S. R., 237

Cho, S., 378, 382

cholestasis, 240

cholesterol: HDL, 243; LDL, 239

Christianity, 13, 18, 109, 170–171, 274, 393

Chung, Y. B., 152

Ciarrochi, J., 315

cisgender, defined, 52

cisgender children, xii, 41–42, 127

cisgender identity, 142

cisgenderism, 252, 254, 257

cisgender parents, xii, 33–34, 128–130. *See also* parents of GNC/transgender youth

cisnormativity, xi, 175, 179

Clark, T., 308

Clarke Institute of Psychiatry (Toronto, Canada), 93, 164. *See also* Centre for Addiction and Mental Health (CAMH; Toronto, Canada)

Clemson, L., 176, 199, 309, 312, 404

clinical practice: affirmative therapy focus for, 174; expansion of, 231; guidelines for, 143; literature dearth for guidance of, 134, 136; for non-Western transgender clients, 156, 158–159; non-Western transgender clients lacking in, 150–151; reparative therapies and, 162

clinicians: as allies, 144; beliefs/attitudes of, 38, 53; CCTFT model and, 297; collaborations with physicians, 262–263, 269, 274–275; family acceptance and, 102–103, 112–114; gender acceptance as goal of, 49–51; gender-affirmation goals of, 26–28; gender

177; gender web and, 38, 43; masculinity/
femininity and, 121; middle age and, 5;
parental acceptance and, 217; political
conflict over, 3; transgender etiology and,
106; treatment success as dependent on
respect for, 134

Curtis, R., 44

cutting behavior, 155, 156

C.V.R., 231

Dahl, R. E., 236

Daley, C., 378

Daraio, S., 416

Darrow, C. N., 6

D'Augelli, A. R., xii, 61, 64, 179, 196, 197, 260,
272, 309, 357, 386

Davey, A., 113

Davie, M., 403

"Death of Leelah Alcorn" (*Wikipedia* article), 13,
20

deaths, 105

de Boer, F., 61, 90–91

de-centering, 38, 49, 51–54, 211

deconstruction, 201, 207–209

DeCrescenzo, T., 272

DeCuypere, G., 72

Defrancisco, D., 122

degendering, 254

DeGeneres, Ellen, 199

de Haan, M., 129

Dekker, J. J., 244

Delemarre-van de Waal, H., 233, 234, 235, 236,
272–273, 313

Deligdisch, L., 244

delinquency, 165

DeMeules, M., xii, 26, 98, 103, 160, 176, 313

demigender, 146

denial, 387

dependent variables, 95

Depo-Provera, 242–243

depression: affirmative therapies and, 357;
clinical assessment/treatment of, 140, 141,
158, 309; as concurrent psychiatric concern, 139; family acceptance and, 23, 61;
family psychopathology and, 165; gender
dysphoria and, 45, 146, 156, 178; as gender

dysphoria symptom, 261, 264–265; as
gender expression repression effect, 56, 68,
360; gender-related violence and, 233; as
grief stage, 387; as harassment effect, 214,
375–376; as hormone treatment side effect,
237; parental management of, 314; parental
support and reduced risk of, 381; rate of,
after coming out, 209; suicidality as result
of, 21

De Roo, C., 271

desistance, 179. *See also* "80% desistance"
dictum

de Slegte, R., 239

de-stigmatizing identity work, 390

De Sutter, P., 271

detransitioners, 28, 31–33

developmental theory, 41

Devor, H., 104, 105, 106, 113

de Vries, A., 44, 61, 72, 96, 119, 175, 179, 180,
232, 233, 272–273, 308, 360

diabetes, 239, 242, 244, 245

diabetes mellitus, 239, 243

*Diagnostic and Statistical Manual of Mental Disor-
ders*, 163, 164, 165

*Diagnostic and Statistical Manual of Mental Disor-
ders* (3rd ed.; APA), 4, 89

*Diagnostic and Statistical Manual of Mental Disor-
ders* (3rd ed., revised; APA), 89, 93

*Diagnostic and Statistical Manual of Mental Disor-
ders* (4th ed.; APA), 89, 90–91, 92–94, 99, 220

*Diagnostic and Statistical Manual of Mental Dis-
orders* (4th ed., text revision; APA), 4, 90–91,
92–93, 94, 358

*Diagnostic and Statistical Manual of Mental Disor-
ders* (5th ed.; APA), 4, 88, 178, 266, 358–359

Dialogic Practice Model, 288, 291, 293, 295

Diamond, M., 42, 74, 120, 123, 168, 176, 199, 309,
312, 404

Diaz, E. M., 359, 376, 416

Díaz, R. M., xii, 19, 45, 61, 67, 102, 176, 197, 214,
261, 315, 375, 386

Di Ceglie, D., 314, 315

difference, recognition of, 288

Dimedio, C., 263

Dimen, M., 42

Dimensions Clinic (San Francisco), 227

disbelief, 201, 202–203

firming treatment of, 140–143; age and, 254; childhood gender identity disorder (GIDC) conflated with, 93–94, 99; clinical guidelines, 158–159; clinician/parent discussions of, 250, 253–255; defined, 88, 358; depathologization of, 359; diagnoses of, 252; DSM-V diagnostic criteria for, 358–359; etiology of, 121, 267–269; family understanding of, 269; genderfluidity and, 178; in gender nonconforming children, 62; health-care training programs lacking in, 265, 312–313, 316, 317–318; mental health effects of, 155, 156; mind/body disjunction with, 138; multi-disciplinary approach to treatment of, 136; parenting challenges of, 356; as "passing phase," xv, 88, 103, 144–145, 179, 199, 256, 284, 288, 312, 337, 362, 368, 392; as pathological, 160; pathology and, 178–179; psychoeducation on, 159; puberty and, 64, 234; "rapid onset," 28, 29, 30; social transition and, 96–97; symptoms of, 261–262, 264–265

gender dysphoric children: bullying/harassment of, 359; differing approaches to, 360; gender nonconforming children vs., 359; home environment of, 359; social transitioning of, 356–357. *See also* social transition at school

gender essentialism, 11, 28–29

gender expansiveness, x, 208

gender exploration, 31, 135, 230, 232–233, 258, 262, 357

gender expression: adolescent exploration with, 31; affirmative therapies and, 173; changeability of, 178; defined, 61, 310 t. 18.1; gender identity conflated with, 93, 99, 392; in gender nonconforming children, 61–62; parental understanding of, 61, 203; pathologization of, 161, 309; psychoeducation on, 159; repression of, 360; social transition and, 356–357; transfeminist approach to, 292

genderfluid, 62, 73, 146, 200

genderfluidity, 178, 225, 292

gender ghosts, 38, 53–54

gender health, 43, 47–49, 57, 173–174, 197, 359

gender identity: adolescent exploration with, 31; affirmative therapies and, 173; changeability of, 61, 178; child-parent communication about, 135; cisgender, 128; core, 41; cultural background and attitudes toward, 153, 154; deaths/funerals and, 330; defined, 61, 310 t. 18.1; discovery of, in traditional developmental theory, 41–42; document changes reflecting, 275; gender expression conflated with, 93, 99, 392; in gender nonconforming children, 61–62; gender-specific assessment for, 158–159; as identity aspect, 140–141, 198; legitimization of, 118–119; medical competencies in, 147; non-birth assigned, 96; parental grief over change of (*see* grief); parental understanding of, 61, 203; pathologization of, 309; peer pressure and, 418; professional evaluation of, 72–73; psychoeducation on, 159; recent science on, 42; research on, 163; sexual orientation conflated with, 173; transfeminist approach to, 292; transgender adult hiding of, 323–324; of transgender youth vs. transgender adults, 322–323

gender identity disorder: childhood (GIDC), 89, 90–91, 92–94, 99; coining of term, 163; DSM-IV diagnoses of, 220; gender dysphoria conflated with, 93–94, 99; pathologization of, 164; renaming of, 358

Gender Identity Project (New York), 24

Gender Identity Research Clinic (UCLA), 163–164, 167

Gender Identity Clinic (CAMH), 94–95, 167–168, 171

gender independence, 308

gendering emotions, 310 t. 18.1

gendering play, 310 t. 18.1

gendering sports, 310 t. 18.1

Gender Management Service (GeMS; Boston), 175

gender nonbinary people, x, 173, 292, 336, 339

gender nonconforming boys, mothers of, 163, 165–167

gender nonconforming children: adult trans community and, 26; affirmative therapy for, 27–28 (*see also* affirmative therapies); bullying/harassment of, 374–376, 416; challenges facing, 10–11, 196–197, 214; clinical care of, 119, 174–175, 179–180, 404–405 (*see also* affirmative therapies; reparative therapies); defined, 61–62; disposition of, 311; family context and, 61–62; gender dysphoric children vs., 359; increased numbers of, 308–309; limited pathways available to, 309; medical care of (*see* family-oriented medical

326; over FTM transitions, 56, 223–225, 336, 339, 405; over loss of hopes for child's future, 312; over MTF transitions, 83–84, 270; parental advocacy and, 204–205; during recovery stage, 211; self-blame and, 203; separation/individuation and, 206; support group assistance with, 391; understanding, 113

Griffin, P., 380, 382

Gross, Bob, 409

Gross, Karen, 409

Grossman, A. H., xii, 61, 64, 179, 196, 197, 200, 260, 261, 272, 309, 315, 316, 357, 386

group therapy, 118, 273, 295

growth stunting, 238, 240, 242

Grzegorek, J. L., 151

guilt, 202–203, 209, 311, 357–358

Haas, A. P., 115, 196

Hage, J. J., 244

Haldeman, D. C., 272

Hammond, R., xii, 23, 150

Hansen, A. W., 376

harassment: extent of, 196–197; gender nonconformity extent and, 309; gender-related, at school, 81, 196–197, 374–376, 378, 416; mental health effects of, 214, 359; negative effects of, 375–376; parental advocacy against, 197, 378; parental fears about, 67–68. *See also* bullying

Harbor Camps, 384

Hardy, J., 239

Hardy, K. V., 123

Harris, A., 41

Harsh Realities Report (GLSEN), 375

Hartzell, M., 120, 121, 122, 125

hate crimes, 283, 387

Hathaway, S., 10

headaches, 261

health care: disparities in, 203. *See also* family-oriented medical care for GNC youth

health insurance, 226, 266, 272, 276

Heaven, P., 315

Hegarty, P., 162, 165, 252

Hegedus, J. K., 199, 201, 202, 203, 209, 211, 311, 312, 313, 314

height, 235

Hellen, M., 209

hematological cancer, 241

Hembree, W., 72, 92, 97, 143, 237

hemoglobin A1c, 245

hemoglobin levels, 243, 244

Hempel, S., 315

Henderson, K. A., 416

Hepworth, J., 260

Herdt, G., 309

Heritage Foundation, 89

Herman, J., 95, 115

Herthel, J., 64, 403

heteronormativity, 175

heterosexism, 105, 174, 175

Hidalgo, M., 41, 62, 68, 74–75, 94, 173–174, 177, 312, 357, 360

Hijra, 42

Hill, D. B., 67, 102, 161, 175, 176–177, 197, 200, 209, 212, 290, 311, 312, 313, 314, 315, 316–317, 387, 405

Hines, S., 106, 113

histrelin implants, 272

HIV infection, 23, 61, 375, 376

Hoffman, T. K., 179

holding environment, 389

homelessness, xii, 376, 381

home schooling, 68

homophobia, 81, 170, 174–175, 198–199, 208

homosexuality, 3, 4, 90, 94; African American mothers and, 227–228; boyhood effeminacy as precursor to, 164, 169, 170; decriminalization of, 172; depathologization of, 165, 170–171, 172, 175; mothers as cause of, 163; pathologization of, 165; reparative therapies and, 162, 163, 172; use of term, 162

horizontal identity, 51–52, 57

hormone receptors, 42–43

hormone therapy: age for beginning, 72, 236; benefits of, 232–233, 246; biopsychosocial approach to, 259; clinician/parent discussions of, 255; educational materials about, 271; family conferences about, 271; feminizing, 236–241; financial support for, 329; informed consent for, 272; longitudinal studies lacking on, 238; masculinizing, 226, 241–245; monitoring, 241, 245; mortality rates, 241, 245; parental decision making

about, 200, 204, 207; reproductive capa-
bilities and, 82–83, 245–246, 271; safety
concerns, 230, 238–241, 243–245; timing for
beginning, 236, 271, 274
hostility, 313–314
House, A. S., 119–120
Howell, T. J., 34, 197, 260, 386
Hsieh, S., 143, 175
Huang, H., 179
Hubbard, S., 197, 260, 386
Hudgins-Mitchell, C., 126, 129
Hudson Valley (NY), 404–405
Huebner, D., 19, 45, 61, 102, 176, 197, 315, 386
Hughes, S. A., 169, 170
Hui, H. C., 151
Huxter, C., 13
hypotheses: ad hoc, 97–98, 99; defined, 98;
validity of, 96, 98
hysterectomies, 244

I Am Cait (TV series), 402
Ibrahim, F. A., 151
ICD-10, 266
idealization, 6–8, 126, 127, 128
identification/internalization, 4–6
identity: during adolescence, 27–28; child/ado-
lescent psychiatrists and understanding of,
137–138; current political conflict over, 3;
gender identity as one aspect of, 140–141; as
multiple, 198; parenting and, 201; vertical
vs. horizontal, xii, 51–52, 57, 198, 200, 202,
215–216. *See also* parental identity transition
illness, 105
Imber-Black, E., 113
immigrants, 150, 154. *See also* Chinese Canadian
families with transgender youth
incarceration, 381
incest, 4
independent variables, 95
India, 42
individualism, 150, 151, 153, 154
individuation, 206
information seeking, 203
informed consent, 272
informed-consent model, 142–143
Institute for Dialogic Practice, 298

Institute for Personal Growth, 203
Institute of Medicine, 178
institutionalized living programs, 263
insulin sensitivity, 239
insurance companies, 266, 272
intake assessment, 265–270
integration, 142
integrationism, 152, 153 *fig.* 8.1
intentionality, 104–105
internalization, 5–6
Internet: coming-out experiences on, 223; family information sources on, 271; gender dysphoria information on, 189, 253–254; gender
reassignment surgery information on, 277;
parental fears about, 154, 202; parental
support on, 213, 403; professional listservs
on, 263; transgender visibility on, 402; youth
and lack of controls on use of, 19
"invisible college," 162–164
Isaac, D. S. M., 126–127
Israel, G. E., 113, 118, 119, 120, 128

Jacklin, C. N., 43
Jacobs, L. A., 214
Jallad, S., 240
James, S., 156
James, S. E., 21, 95, 209
Janssen, A., 179, 214
Jellinek, M. S., 390
Jenkins, J., 402
Jenner, Caitlyn, 199, 402
Jennings, Jazz, 64, 403
Johns Hopkins University, 163
Johnson, A., 161, 312
Johnson, S., 102
Jones, Roy, 14
Jorgensen, Christine, 402
Joslin, C., 378
Journal of Homosexuality, 174
judgmentalism, 203
Jung, Carl G., 5, 29
junk science, 29

Kane, E., 119
Kaplan, C., 402

Riggs, Damien, 230–231
Riley, Elizabeth Anne, 62, 68, 176, 199, 288, 309, 311, 312, 313, 314, 316, 404, 405
Rio-Glick, AJ, 289, 336, 347–352
Rio-Glick, Barbara ("River"), 289, 336–339
Rio-Glick, Shelley, 289, 339–342
Rio-Glick, Sonya, 289, 343–347
risk-taking behavior, 146
Rivers, I., 120, 127
Robert, F., 239
Roberts, A. L., 61, 214, 261
Roberts, J., 113, 196–197
Robichaud, M., 102
Robinson, A., 266
Robinson, Gene, 18, 20
Rodgers, P. L., 115
Rogol, A., 234
Roosevelt, Eleanor, 69
Rosario, M., 61, 196–197, 214, 261
Roscoe, W., 42, 177
Rosenberg, M., 314, 315, 390
Rosenfeld, C., 227
Rosenfield, R. L., 265
Rosenthal, S., 42
Rossi, A. S., 8
Rottnek, M., 172
Roughgarden, J., 177
Rowe, C. E., Jr., 126–127
runaways, 14, 17, 18
rural communities, 362
Russell, H., 173, 177, 309
Russell, S. T., xii, 19, 45, 67, 102, 127, 176, 197, 261, 315, 375, 386
Ruzzi, L., 263
Ryan, Caitlin, xii, 19, 22, 23, 24, 27, 45, 61, 67, 68, 102, 105, 108, 120, 127, 176, 197, 214, 261, 315, 316, 317, 375, 386

safe sex, 276
safe spaces, 47, 48, 367, 389, 391, 394–395
Saffrey, C., 309
SAGE, 330
Saltzburg, N., 109
same-sex couples, 104–105
same-sex parent-child dyads, 209

Samoa, 42
Sanchez, J., xii, 19, 45, 61, 102, 176, 197, 315, 375, 386
San Francisco, 227–228
Sangganjanavanich, V. F., 136, 176
Sansfaçon, A. P., 102, 104, 114
Sasso, Stephanie, 194
Savage, Dan, 13
Savin-Williams, R. C., 21, 261
Scanlin, M. M., 416
Schagen, S. E. E., 233, 272–273
Schechter, L. S., 276
Scheim, A. I., xii, 23, 150
Schiavi, R. C., 162
schizophrenia, 165, 224
Schleifer, D., 254
Schofield, P., 95
school: absenteeism at, 158, 189, 261, 314, 359, 375; antidiscrimination policies at, 376; bio-psychosocial model and, 259, 262; bullying/harassment at, 196–197, 359, 374–376, 378, 416; bullying management at, 316; diversity awareness at, 366; gender awareness lacking in, 316, 374; gender segregation at, 380; gender web and, 43; LGBT visibility at, 282–283; liberal/progressive, 154; parental advocacy at, 197, 313, 317, 374, 376–382; single-sex, 338; transferring, 313, 364, 369, 381; transphobia at, 344–346; unsupportive, 23, 28–29. See also social transition at school
school authorities/personnel, 263, 313, 363, 369–370, 374, 375, 376, 377, 378
Schopler, J. H., 388
scientific method, 96, 98
Seaburn, D. B., 258
Sebastian, C., 125
self: authentic, 151, 360; brain and, 125–128; compromised sense of, and gender conformity, 316; gender affirmation and, 118–120; internal sense of, and pathology, 141; parental sense of, and resilience of, 120; shame and, 121; true, 7, 323. See also gender self
self-actualization, 55
self-blame, 123, 202–203, 204, 311
self-care, 387
self-esteem, 61, 75, 102, 209, 315–316, 357, 359, 381

about, 75–76; medical policies discouraging, 88–89, 97; parental decision making about, 199–200, 204, 360–362, 367; parental fears about, 65–67, 69–71; parental support of, 60, 103, 205; reasons for, 73; religious/cultural opposition to, 80–81; risks from not allowing, 56, 68, 75; setting choice for, 362, 363 *fig.* 21.1; successful, 370; timing for beginning, 271; "wait-and-see" approach to, 179–180, 213

social transition at school, 376; bathroom/locker room issues, 273–274, 366, 379; case studies, 344–346, 367–371; clinical assistance in, 367, 371; clothing for, 364–365, 379–380; confidentiality and, 380–381; disclosure about, 366–367; educating staff/other parents for, 365–366; name change for, 364, 378–379; parental decision making about, 362–363, 363 *fig.* 21.1; parental support of, 313, 356; physical education classes and, 366, 380; resources for, 365; school support needed for, 176; timing/school choice for, 364; transphobia and, 344–346

social workers, 14–15

societal intolerance, 95

society, 259

Society and the Healthy Homosexual (Weinberg), 174

Solomon, Andrew, xii, 3, 19, 20, 51–52, 57, 120, 197–198, 199, 212

Soloway, J., 402

Spack, Norman P., 44, 72, 137, 143, 175, 207, 210, 213, 357, 360

Speer, S. A., 255

sperm banking, 82–83, 245, 329

spironolactone, 237, 238, 240–241

sports, 310 t. 18.1, 380

Standards of Care (SOC7; WPATH), 83, 88, 94, 95, 176, 177, 272, 274

Stanley, J., 263

Starks, M., 61

Statistics Canada, 150

STDs, 375

Steckler, A., 104

Steensma, T. D., 61, 63, 90–91, 92, 96, 97, 119, 179, 213, 232, 233, 272–273

Steever, J., 259, 274

Steinhoff, M., 244

Stepleman, L. M., 119–120

stepparents, 327

stepsiblings, 327

stereotypes, 254, 288, 313

"sticky flypaper" hypothesis, 86, 97–98

stigmatization: affirmative therapies and, 161, 181; dual, 227–228; gender dysphoria and, 44–45; horizontal identity and, 202; of medical care providers, 263–264; mental health effects of, 139–140; minority stress and, 203–204; parental fears of, 84; of parents of GNC, 75, 198, 222, 312–313, 314–315, 358, 387, 389; of parents of transgender adults, 326–327; pathologization and perpetuation of, 309; secondary, 75, 389; of transgender adults, 84, 326–327; of transgender youth, 139–140, 286

St. Luke's–Roosevelt Hospital Center (New York), 163

Stoller, Robert, 163–164, 166

Stonewall riots (1969), 405–406

Stop Trans Pathology movement, 90

stroke, 238

Stuart Little (White), 40

substance abuse, 119–120; family acceptance and, 23, 61, 102; family experiences of, 105, 228; as family secret, 3; as gender dysphoria symptom, 261; as gender expression repression effect, 68, 360; as harassment effect, 376; hormone therapy and, 241; parental support and reduced risk of, 381; among transgender population, 284, 285–286

Sue, D. W., 49–50, 203

suicidal ideation: affirmative therapies and, 357; depression underlying, 21; gender dysphoria as cause of, 146; as gender expression repression effect, 68, 360; parental support and reduced risk of, 381; suicide attempts vs., 21

suicidality, 119–120; clinical assessment of, 158, 179; data analysis on, 21; family acceptance and, 102–103; as harassment effect, 214, 375–376; hospitalization for, 80; plans to address needed, 24; rate of, after coming out, 209; threat of, as used with parents/clinicians, 22–23

suicide: family acceptance and, xii, 61; as family secret, 3; hormone therapy and, 241; pa-